ADMIRAL AMBASSADOR TO RUSSIA

by William H. Standley

Admiral, USN (Ret.)

and

Arthur A. Ageton

Rear Admiral, USN (Ret.)

Chicago · HENRY REGNERY COMPANY · 1955

15065

NATIONS, like people, have a long memory where insult or injury is concerned, a short memory for courtesies offered, for help, aid and assistance rendered in time of need. There is little capacity for gratitude in mankind.

In diplomatic negotiations, look first for self-interest—for your own country in the issues discussed, behind the façade of your opponent's smooth statements or vitriolic charges. You will then base your negotiations upon a foundation of reality. All else is fantasy.

—WILLIAM H. STANDLEY,
Admiral, USN (Ret.),
Former Ambassador to Soviet Russia

ADMIRAL
AMBASSADOR
TO RUSSIA

FOREWORD

THIS is Admiral William H. Standley's behind-the-scenes story of a crucial period in our wartime alliance with Soviet Russia and the critical maneuvers and problems facing the United States of America during his mission to Moscow from April 1942 to October 1943. The views and opinions expressed are those of Admiral Standley as a private citizen. Admiral Ageton collaborated with Admiral Standley for four years in preparing and expanding the narrative into its present form from the notes and diaries which Admiral Standley recorded at the time of the history-making events which his experiences encompassed.

The opinions and attitudes expressed certainly are not to be construed as official or as reflecting the views of the Department of State, the Department of Defense, the Department of the Navy, or the Naval Service. The accounts given are factual and have been as closely related to contemporaneous events of history as the two authors could contrive.

WILLIAM H. STANDLEY
ARTHUR A. AGETON

Washington, D. C.,
March, 1955.

ACKNOWLEDGMENT

PORTIONS of this book have previously appeared in the U. S. Naval Institute *Proceedings* and are here reprinted with permission of the Institute.

We are also indebted to the following publishers for permission to quote: Whittlesey House, *I Was There*, by William Leahy (1950); Alfred A. Knopf, Inc., *Twelve Months That Changed the World*, by Larry LeSueur; Random House, *The Curtain Rises*, by Quentin Reynolds; Harper and Brothers, *Roosevelt and Hopkins*, by Robert Sherwood.

CONTENTS

BOOK ONE

Background for My War with Communism

BOOK TWO

My Tour of Duty in the Soviet Union

CONTENTS

BOOK THREE

End of a Mission

BOOK ONE

Background for My War with Communism

CHAPTER I

The Russians I Knew
Sixty Years Ago

I WAS BORN on the banks of the Russian River of California on December 18, 1872. My acquaintance with the Russians came early in life because it was at Fort Ross near the mouth of this river that the Czarist Russian Government in 1812 established a settlement in a bid to colonize and annex the West Coast of North America.

While still a small boy on visits to my Mother's relatives in the redwood timber country of Mendocino County, I came in close contact with the first and second generation Russian Finns who were our neighbors. I remember them as fundamentally simple, earthy people, absorbed in the lumber industry in the development of which they took a prominent part, yet still very close and devoted to the soil from which they produced much of their living.

Those California Russians were good neighbors, always ready to help you with money or labor if you were in trouble. Their living conditions were incredibly primitive even for my boyhood days of seventy years ago in pioneer California. Of course, they had none of the modern home improvements which we know so well—they cooked in fireplaces or open pits in the yard in crude pots and skillets; there was no running water in the house; and bathroom facilities were an iron-bound wooden tub in the big old kitchen and an outhouse a hundred feet up a path in the woods back of the small house.

They were very proud of their American citizenship and carried out the duties of good citizens not only meticulously but proudly. They insisted that their children learn and speak English and they kept them in school usually through the eighth grade, which was pretty good for those days.

In September 1891, I left California and entered the United

3

States Naval Academy, where I distinguished myself principally by keeping out of trouble with the authorities. I had a wonderful time at the Academy and graduated in 1895 almost exactly in the middle of the class of forty-one. The pay of a passed-midshipman was insignificant and the prospects for advancement were so poor that the best that we could hope for was promotion to lieutenant at 45, to commander or captain at 60 and to the retired list at 64. But I had found Navy life interesting and agreeable to me and so I decided to stay on in the service and see what I could make of myself. The long tall dreams of youth could scarcely have equaled the fascinating events which the next fifty years of my life in and out of the Naval service encompassed.

I was fortunate enough to be assigned to the "Olympia" for my passed-midshipman's cruise—then the most modern and efficient cruiser in the American Navy. When I heard that the "Olympia" had been ordered to duty on the Asiatic Station, my cup was filled. Not only was I to have a wonderful life at sea but I was to be permitted to visit and to know the Orient of which I had heard so many romantic tales when I was a boy.

Not long after we arrived on Station, the "Olympia" was invited to visit Vladivostok as guest of the Russian Government during the celebration of the coronation of Czar Nicholas II. Ignorant of the ways of the fun-loving Russians, we midshipmen looked forward to the week unhappily, imagining an ordeal of tiresome parades and formal balls. The week of May 24–31, 1896 was anything but boring. With ten Russian armored cruisers in port and only one "Olympia," there was scarcely a moment we weren't entertained and hardly any time for work or sleep. Except for the evening when we entertained the Russians on the "Olympia," we midshipmen were guests of Russian Army or Naval officers for every lunch and dinner—and every meal a banquet. Each dinner was followed by a formal ball in the one big ballroom of the town or a very informal dance at one of the many Army camps in the vicinity. The Russians must have had three hundred thousand troops in and around Vladivostok. It was their practice in those days to carry with them their families and many camp followers and entertainers. The Army parties were very gay and festive affairs which lasted far into the night.

To me, this was the introduction to a new way of life. I remember that I was principally impressed with the strength that the Russian Army and Navy maintained at Vladivostok and with the lavish entertainment extended—but I was also confronted by the squalor of the primitive little port city and the utter degradation of the working people of the town and the peasants in the countryside.

But we were young and the tinsel glamor of the society of the local government officials and the officers was very appealing. We were abed late, up early to do a bit of essential work and then the fun began all over again. I recall that we midshipmen soon learned that vodka, the way the Russians drank it, had to be treated with respect. Some of us had considerable difficulty to keep up with our hosts and yet maintain a semblance of decorum. The wiser ones soon learned to take an ounce of olive oil before a party and then could respond to as many Russian toasts of *"Za vasha darovya,"* as were offered. Our hosts tried earnestly to teach us to reply in Russian but we could never quite come by the correct pronunciation—it always came out sounding like "To wash this all over you." But no one seemed to mind.

I retain a particularly vivid memory of the banquet given by the Russian admiral to our Admiral Frederick Valette McNair. A huge U-shaped table was set on the lower floor of the town's big Assembly Hall. On a mezzanine along both sides and across one end of the long room were set smaller tables for the junior Russian and American officers. Both Admirals and their staffs were seated at the head table. Being a staff midshipman, I found my placecard on the inboard side of the U at the extreme right.

When seated, I saw facing me at least a dozen beautiful crystal wine glasses. Not having fortified myself with olive oil, I was very uncertain as to my probable capacity and so I began to turn my glasses upside down on the linen tablecloth.

Lieutenant George Wood Logan, our Flag Secretary, seated himself next to me and whispered, "You mustn't do that, Mr. Standley. It's very discourteous to our hosts."

"But, sir, I'm not accustomed to strong drink," I protested, adding mentally, without a foundation of olive oil. "I'd just rather not take anything to drink."

"Make a show of it, at least," he muttered, as a waiter bent over to fill our glasses.

When the Russian admiral came down with the first of many ringing toasts, I seized the glass nearest my plate which contained what appeared to be a lovely shade of pink lemonade. To my horror, I discovered that it was "tiger" vodka. In an effort to put out the fire, I grabbed a glass of what I thought was water and took a large gulp. It was the infinitely stronger white vodka. I learned about vodka from them.

As the evening progressed through the various toasts and glasses, the stiff formality of the dinner rapidly wilted. Glancing up at the table just above me on the mezzanine, I saw one of the young officers from the "Olympia" beckoning to me. With my classmate, William Christopher Davidson, I left the older officers to their toasts and vodka and climbed up to the mezzanine.

During our stay, the young Russian officers of our acquaintance had become very fond of our American song, *John Brown's Body.* Once again, they urged us to sing it for them. Not in the least unwilling, Chris Davidson and I leaned over the balcony and gave forth at the top of our voices with "John Brown's body lies a-mold'ring in the grave." I can remember yet the sour expression on the face of our Chief of Staff, one Lazarus Lowrey Reamy, who apparently was no lover of vodka-inspired music, however fine it might be. He made it perfectly obvious that neither our conduct nor our singing met with his approval. I had a moment of temporary qualm and Davidson finished the last line, carrying the tenor part by himself. Fortunately, the Russians arose as one man and cheered us to the ceiling. Apparently that ended any consideration of official action against us for our boisterous conduct and outrageously off-key singing.

But it did not end the party. When the more senior officers had taken their leave, the younger Russians insisted that we join them in making a night of it on the lower floor. There was plenty of vodka for it but Chris and I decided that we had about reached our saturation point. As our classmate, David Wooster Todd, climbed up on a table to make a speech of "amity and friendship," we quietly stole out to the cloakroom. We were searching for boat cloaks and caps when several young Russians pounced on us and dragged us back to the party.

Biding our time, we again slipped out. Abandoning our wraps, we ran for the boat landing two blocks away, with three Russians, also without coats or caps, in hot pursuit. We beat them to the pier by a couple of yards, saw the Captain's gig and leaped in under the protection of the American flag. For the Russians chasing us, rank in our own Navy held no terror. Undaunted, the three Russians piled in after us, determined to carry us bodily back to the party.

I have no idea what might have happened—perhaps another unfortunate international incident—had not our Captain just then arrived at the dock. Being an understanding man, he quickly sized up the situation, stepped down into the boat and ordered the cox'n to "shove off and return to the ship."

Chris Davidson, the Russians and I followed the Captain meekly up the ladder, in that order. Happily, several of our messmates were still on deck taking the night air. They took over the Russians and entertained them while Davidson and I laid below for some much needed rest. When I turned out just before noon, the Russians were still sound asleep in three bunks in the steerage.

The Observation Car Incident

An occurrence incident to entertaining us may have resulted in the banishment of a young Russian Navy Lieutenant.

The Admiral took us for a ride on the Trans-Siberian Railroad, which extended about fifty miles from Vladivostok. The higher officials—the Big Brass as it were—were banqueting in one observation car, and in the rear of another car the younger officers were being entertained. The guests were seated on either side of a table extending the full length of the car with our young Lieutenant host seated at the end, his back to the open door. At the appropriate moment our host arose and made a few remarks and then proposed a toast to the President of the United States, and, when his glass was drained, he said in his broken English, "No one can again drink from ze glass," and turning slightly he hove the glass through the open door behind him.

Our Senior officer, Assistant Engineer J. K. Robison, responded, gave a toast to the Czar and then, not to be outdone, said, "No one can again drink from this glass," and anticipating the move, we all turned and hove our glasses, as we thought, through the open windows behind us. Unfortunately, the car windows, of comparatively thin glass, were not open, and our bombardment shattered nearly every window in the car. Our host gasped and turned pale, then, catching himself, he assured us it was *nichevo* (of no import). The trip back to Vladivostok was on a more sober level.

We Dedicate a Cathedral

The ceremonies in celebration of the coronation of the Czar also included some events of a more serious nature. In 1896, Vladivostok was little more than a squalid cluster of huts at the lower end of the harbor, but even then the Russians had visions of the great port city it was to become. Part of this vision was the construction of a great cathedral at the upper end of the bay, about two miles from the village. Four officers from the "Olympia" were invited to attend the laying of the cornerstone. Since the invitation was tantamount to a command appearance, two other midshipmen, our Chief Engineer, Captain Burnap of the Engineer Corps, and I were detailed to attend.

Preliminary religious ceremonies were held in a little church in the village with all the pomp and ceremony of the Russian Orthodox Church. The stiff collar of my "old-fashioned" full dress uniform was wilted long before we left the church.

A procession formed in the street led by three priests in long black robes, white surplices, and bright-colored stoles, swinging incense burners. We four visiting officers found our place in the middle of the ungainly column. As we trudged up the hot and dusty country road toward the site of the new cathedral, a three-seated vehicle something like an old American surrey with a fringe on top drawn by two dispirited Manchurian ponies pulled up alongside. We tried to persuade Captain Burnap to let us hire the *drojski* but he disapproved such action as a deliberate discourtesy to the priests. The *drojski* pulled away and another carrying a young Russian Army officer of our acquaintance took its place. With elaborate gestures, he invited us to join him but we followed the example of our doughty senior and marched along in the blazing sunlight.

The ceremony of laying the cornerstone was even longer and more uncomfortable than the church service. Perspiration ran off my bare cropped head and down across my forehead. With the service in Russian, we could understand nothing that was said. After half an hour, Davidson began to chuckle.

"What's so funny, Chris?" I asked.

"Shhh!" Captain Burnap whispered.

"I was just wondering," Chris said in a low voice, "if they have gotten as high with their blessings as the spire or cross on the steeple."

Captain Burnap snorted down an internal explosion and tried to look severe. When the service was finally ended, he turned to Davidson. "Young man, you were right. They must have said a prayer over every blooming brick and stone of the whole blessed edifice."

To our relief, there was no return procession. We caught a *drojski* and rode back to the boat landing in style.

The "Olympia" Party

We could not hope to reciprocate completely for all of the splendid entertainment which had been extended to us, but on the last afternoon of our stay in Vladivostok, Admiral McNair gave a reception followed by a buffet dinner for certain special guests. It was quite an affair. All of the Russian officers and civilian officials were invited to the reception and they turned out in full force.

In those days, we had a Wine Mess on board, something of a misnomer as its principal stock in trade was Scotch Whiskey and English ale. When entertaining officially, we could charge our chits at the Wine Mess to the official expense account. For this party, the allowances were most liberal. As I recall it, the invitations to the reception said from "4 to 7" but the party went on and on into the night.

After midnight, our boats plied frequently to and from the beach, making alternate trips to the two landings at either end of the bay. With darkness and language difficulties, the Russians were landed at either end rather indiscriminately. I understand that it took a couple of days to sort them out and get them back to their proper ships and Army camps.

On board the "Olympia," we had our troubles, too. The ship was scheduled to get underway in the middle of the morning, but at noon considerable confusion still existed. A head of department noted for an ingrown disposition finally lost patience and reported one of the junior officers for being "under the influence of intoxicating liquor and thereby incapacitated for proper performance of duty." At a later hearing before the Captain, the young officer admitted that he had indulged rather freely of intoxicating liquor during the course of the party but pleaded that he felt quite certain that at no time was he thereby incapacitated for duty. In fact, he felt that he stood up pretty well under his liquor—better than most of the Russian officers that he was entertaining.

The Captain looked across at him with an amused twinkle. "Well, young man, had you remained cold sober during the party yesterday, I would certainly have had you court-martialed for neglect of duty, sir. That will be all, sir. Good morning, sirs."

The "Olympia" eventually got underway that afternoon and set course for Shanghai. Thus ended our memorable participation in the ceremonies celebrating the coronation of Czar Nicholas II.

The Boxer Rebellion

By 1899, I had progressed to the exalted rank of lieutenant (junior grade) and was attached to the old "Yorktown" on the Asiatic Station. When the rebellion of the Boxers broke out into violence, our ship was ordered to Taku Bar, port of entry for Tientsin in North China.

It will be recalled that the Boxer Rebellion was an insurrection against the Emperor of China by a secret society of Chinese which had wide popular support among the working classes and peasants of China. Believing that the Emperor had come too much under the influence of foreigners, the movement had a strong anti-foreign sentiment. When our ship arrived at Taku, the Allied military forces had already engaged the Boxers between Tientsin and Peking with heavy casualties on both sides.

In the anchorage, we found a large assemblage of warships of several nations—Japanese, British, French, German, American, and our old friends, the Russian armored cruisers from Vladivostok. Among this impressive display of foreign naval strength lay one lonely Chinese cruiser. Nominally loyal to the Emperor, there was yet a chance that the crew might go over to the Boxers. To prevent any possibility of trouble, the foreign naval commanders had the firing pins removed from all her guns and stowed in the American flagship, "Newark." Ensign Arthur MacArthur, brother of General Douglas MacArthur, was placed on board with a small naval guard to make certain that the Chinese man-of-war observed strict neutrality.

Shortly after our arrival, we learned that the Seymour Expedition had met strong opposition to its attempt to reach Peking and rescue the personnel of the foreign legations barricaded in the embassy compounds within the big capital city. Our Captain, the first Joseph Taussig, learned that his son, Joe, was in the hospital at Tientsin suffering from a wound in the hip received while he was a member of the naval landing force. Captain Taussig took me along with him up the muddy Pei River to Tientsin to see what could be done for his boy.

Left to my own devices for several days while the Captain

looked out for young Joe, I volunteered for duty in the gunboat "Monocacy." Her skipper gave me command of Li Hung Chang's yacht which he had seized and told me to forage up and down the river for fresh fruit and vegetables for the patients in the hospital, whose diet of regular Army field rations was not conducive to quick recovery. In the course of ranging up the river as far as gunfire permitted and down to the mouth, I ran across quite a number of Russian soldiers and naval landing force.

Incredibly dirty and undisciplined and obviously very disgruntled at the mauling the Seymour Expeditionary Forces had received at the hands of the Boxers, the Russians were unruly and viciously cruel to the Chinese of the city and countryside, many of whom disliked the Boxers as much as the foreigners did. As the Seymour Expedition fell back on Tientsin, I had my first personal experience with the Russian's bent for looting. At the dock at Taku, I saw a particularly ruffianish crew of Russian naval ratings just returned from the front, each with at least one Chinese rifle and some with two or three ornate Chinese swords, while every one of them had a bundle of more valuable loot tied up in his black sailor neckerchief.

From the deck of the "Monacacy," as I watched this rag-tail outfit, I saw a boat containing two Chinese peasant women and several children rowing across the wide stream. As their boat landed on the river bank above the ship, two Russian ratings ran up to them and proceeded to "assist them" out of the boat, literally with the points of their fixed bayonets. Observing this situation, Lieutenant "Mike" McGrann of the "Monacacy" buckled on his pistol belt and went out on the river bank. He had no difficulty persuading the Russians to stop their unprovoked cruelty.

With young Joe Taussig recovering nicely from his wound, the Captain picked me up one morning from the "Monacacy" and we went by steam launch to the anchorage. Imagine our consternation to find that the "Yorktown" was no longer present. Boarding the flagship, we were informed by Admiral Louis Kempff that the "Yorktown" had been sent to the Miaotao Islands to assist the "Oregon" which had run aground enroute to Taku.

Very unhappy, with his finest ship aground and one of his cruisers sailing uncharted waters without her captain, the Admiral was far from affable. "I'd suggest that you return to your command immediately, Captain," he said testily.

Captain Taussig agreed, but how?

"The 'Vladimir Monomak' is sailing in an hour to the relief of the 'Oregon,' " Admiral Kempff told him. "I suggest that you and your young officer take a launch and see if you can't persuade the captain of the 'Monomak' to take you to the Miaotaos."

In contrast to our Admiral, the Captain of the "Monomak" was most affable and pleasant. He installed the Captain and me in his vacant admiral's quarters for the overnight trip and told us that we could have the run of his ship.

Compared to the naval landing force ratings I had seen at Taku, the men of that Russian cruiser were models of smartness and efficiency. I discovered why a few moments later when I stepped out on the quarterdeck to watch the ship get underway. A bearded Russian sailor was climbing the ladder to the after bridge. Saluting smartly, he made some report to the Captain. Evidently what the sailor said displeased the Captain for he gave the sailor a clout on the jaw that sent him flying back down the ladder.

I have one last memory of my dealings with the Russians in the Far East. The food situation in the ships standing by the "Oregon" was deplorable. In those days, we had no mechanical refrigeration in our Navy ships and only a small cold storage space maintained at several degrees above freezing by a severely limited supply of river ice from ashore. With no provision ship for months, the crews were down to canned bully beef, beans and Chinese rice and there was imminent danger of an outbreak of scurvy or beriberi among the men.

In this crisis, our Senior Officer Present Afloat bethought himself of the Russian base at Port Arthur with its excellent storage facilities and decided to send the "Yorktown" to Port Arthur for a load of fresh provisions.

Our navigator had just been detached. Pending report of his relief, I, a mere lieutenant (junior grade)—and a very junior one at that—had assumed the duties of navigator. The Russian Commodore sent us a commissary steward to act as interpreter—a tall handsome man with a long brown beard and laughing blue eyes. I frequently discovered him peering over my shoulder as I worked on the chart during the short run across the Gulf of Chihli, which made me even more nervous than I would have naturally been from inexperience. But I didn't feel like chasing the Russian away. He was our guest and he might be very useful later. So I looked up and smiled at him uneasily from time to time and he smiled back with a peculiar sadness that was even more disconcerting.

Unfortunately, our passage was planned so that we approached the unfamiliar entrance to Port Arthur well after dark. The only light which we could see was a bright white one high on a hill. I was not at all certain that it was a navigational light. My approach to the harbor gave me a very bad time—taking bearings of that one light and running soundings with a lead line, trying to keep the "Yorktown" in the middle of the channel. An experienced navigator, had he been as sure as I was that he didn't know *where* he was, would have promptly advised the Captain to anchor until morning. But I was young and eager and determined not to admit defeat.

The white light on the hill began to blink, rapidly and irregularly. I could read Navy blinker messages but this strange combination of dots and dashes meant nothing to me. Suddenly, the Russian commissary steward pounded up the ladder onto the bridge, his long beard parted by the wind, and cried excitedly, "Stop, Captain, stop! That light—she say, you no stop, she shoot."

To this day, I can recall my intense feeling of relief when Captain Taussig turned to the Executive Officer and quietly said, "Commander, bring the ship to an anchor."

When dawn broke, we discovered that, by good fortune and not good navigating, we had pushed so far into the harbor in the darkness that we hardly needed the services of the pilot who reported aboard. As a penance for my daring navigation, I was sent ashore as "boarding officer" to call upon the local naval commander. He proved to be a short stumpy little Admiral with piercing black eyes and a scraggly black beard. When I presented the Captain's respects, he was quite brusque. "Young man," his interpreter translated his staccato Russian, "it's a good thing you anchored when you did. I was about to tell my shore batteries to open fire on you."

With the misunderstanding cleared up and formal calls between our Captain and the Admiral exchanged, the Russian commissary steward quickly piloted our supply people through the uncharted waters of Russian red tape and we sailed the next day with a large cargo of fresh provisions and so were able to report to Admiral Kempff, "Operation Victual successfully completed, sir."

These early associations with the Russians did not seem remarkable at the time but they stored away in my mind half forgotten memories of certain traits and characteristics of the Russians which were to prove of great value to me forty years later during my Ambassadorship. In my travels through the Russian countryside, in my many visits to collective farms and homes of peasants and workers, I found them to be the same simple, earthy people I had known in my youth, devoted to the soil from which they made much of their living and but little interested in national and international affairs. After all of the propaganda about the wonderful socialistic way of life under the Bolshevik Party of the Soviets, I was frankly amazed to discover that the country people of Russia in 1942 lived under the same primitive conditions that had existed among our neighbors, the Russian Finns, back in Mendocino County sixty years before. And I found that these plain, unaffected people were the same good neighbors I had known as a boy.

Although the Russians I met and knew in Siberia and China were mostly of the aristocracy of civilian officialdom and the Army and Navy, I soon learned that the party officials of the Communist hierarchy in the Russia of 1941–43 had adopted many of the customs and characteristics of their former rulers. They still arose late, lunched long, worked hard during the afternoon and early evening, conferred late into the night and dined at sumptuous banquets at midnight or after. The pageantry, the table finery and appointments, the array of food and the excellent service of a Kremlin official banquet, I was to discover, far exceeded the pomp and circumstance of even the lavish official banquets I had attended in provincial Vladivostok. The new ruling class of Russia also had their same exaggerated enjoyment of play and horseplay. They also liked to try to drink their American guests under the table—apparently not in order to obtain secret information which their victims might reveal under the influence of vodka, I have come to conclude, so much as from a desire to impress upon Americans and other foreigners with whom they competed how much the better men they were. Sometimes they were—and sometimes they weren't.

My limited knowledge of the very difficult Russian language had practically disappeared by the time I arrived in Moscow as Ambassador to the Kremlin, all except one phrase. At my first official banquet, to the toast, "Za vasha darovya," I replied graciously with a warm smile, "To wash this all over you." Pleased smiles of surprise lighted the faces of the Russians about me. "So," the interpreter translated Mr. Stalin's remark, "I didn't know you could speak our language."

"Oh, no indeed I don't," I explained. "I was speaking perfectly good English."

Dour looks succeeded the pleasant smiles. No one understood my little joke, not even the interpreter. And then I remembered, too late, one of the lessons I had learned many years before in the Far East.

What the Russian doesn't understand, the Russian doesn't like.

CHAPTER II

My Early Acquaintance with
Franklin D. Roosevelt

Wʜᴇɴ Woᴏᴅʀᴏᴡ Wɪʟsᴏɴ was inaugurated as President on March 4, 1913, I was serving as Aide to the Commandant of the Navy Yard, Mare Island, California, the ex-naval engineer, Captain F. M. Bennett. It will be recalled that this was toward the end of one of our country's longest periods of peace and an era of industrial expansion and great national prosperity. As was usual for our Republic, despite the warnings of such excellent thinkers and publicists as Rear Admiral Alfred T. Mahan, while our powder was kept dry, we had but few guns to use it and fewer ships to mount the guns.

With reduced Naval appropriations, it became necessary to discharge sixty-two civilian workmen. The Industrial Department selected those men for whom there was no work or whose services could best be spared with least detriment to the performance of the Yard.

At that time, I learned that Secretary Josephus Daniels had selected as his Assistant Secretary a young New York politician with the magic name of Roosevelt, a distant cousin of the great "Teddy" who had vainly opposed Woodrow Wilson in the campaign. I had never heard of Franklin Roosevelt as a national figure before this appointment. We were soon to learn that he was a working politician, wise beyond his years, in all the little tricks of politics which bring in the votes on Election Day.

The principal responsibility of the Assistant Secretary is the administration of the Shore Establishment of the Navy. A week or so after the Inauguration, we received a telegram from the Navy Department inviting our attention to the fact that, of sixty-two men recently discharged at the Mare Island Navy Yard, thirty were Democrats. What was the necessity for this action? The message was signed, Franklin D. Roosevelt.

Captain Bennett got off a letter explaining the reason for the discharges and adding, "The Commandant maintains no record as to the political affiliations of the workmen at this Yard. Furthermore, he wants none, because politics have never entered into the matter of necessary discharges and lay-offs."

A week later, a second telegram from the Assistant Secretary said in effect, "Tut, tut. Action approved, but in the future, *we must look out for our own.*"

In 1915, I was ordered to take command of my old ship, the gunboat "Yorktown," engaged in showing the flag up and down the west coast of Mexico and Central America. In command of the "Cleveland," also engaged in this duty, was my old friend, Commander T. J. Senn. We frequently anchored in the same ports. Unsettled conditions ashore kept us aboard most of the time, and so we visited back and forth, discussing the alarming rumors which came out of Washington.

One of the most serious of these was that Secretary Daniels, despite having married the sister of Ensign Worth Bagley, who died a hero's death during the Spanish-American War, for some reason had acquired a strong prejudice against naval officers, and an intense dislike of the Navy's necessarily undemocratic system of military discipline. By word and deed, he indicated that he intended to eliminate the official and social gap that then separated officers and enlisted men.

I told Tommy Senn of a conversation I had had with Mr. Reuterdahl, the famous marine artist. He told me that when he called upon the new Secretary of the Navy to congratulate him on assuming the direction of such a fine organization the Secretary looked out at the artist sharply under his bushy grey eyebrows, and said, "Reuterdahl, it is my firm intention to break up this gold-lace aristocracy."

We also discussed the rumor that, when Secretary Daniels was being entertained at lunch in the Wardroom of one of our battleships, he grabbed up a handful of fine cigars from a box on the sideboard. Hurrying through a door onto the quarterdeck, he began to pass out the cigars to some enlisted men working on deck.

When the Executive Officer protested, the Secretary turned on him sharply. "Why not? These are fine American boys and the Government should give them just as good as the officers."

"But, Mr. Secretary," the Commander still objected, "the Wardroom officers bought those cigars out of their own money."

Secretary Daniels did not seem to be impressed.

It was one of Secretary Daniels' pet ideas which resulted in my going to the Naval Academy for duty. He had decided that the autocratic system in the Navy stemmed from early training at the Academy. Too much starch and military discipline, he thought. He'd take some of the stiffness out of the curriculum by increasing the civilian staff of instructors and by putting civilian educators in high administrative positions. In line with this program, the Secretary sent Professor C. Alphonso Smith to the Academy as head of the Department of English. He picked out a noted French educator to head the Department of Modern Languages, but the Frenchman opposed the plan violently because he felt it was not in the best interests of either imparting knowledge of languages to the midshipmen or of military discipline in the Regiment. Secretary Daniels was also waiting for an opportunity to put a civilian civil engineer in as head of the department of Buildings and Grounds, to which job Tommy Senn had gone from command of the "Cleveland."

In the Fall of 1918, in line with his idea of bringing younger men to the fore, the Secretary designated Commander Leigh Palmer to be Chief of the Bureau of Navigation with the temporary rank of Rear Admiral. In due course, Palmer selected my friend Senn to be the Assistant Chief. Before detaching Senn from the Naval Academy, though, he had to find a relief for him. Recalling our many gripes together over the new Bureau policy of extending Commander's sea duty to three years, Senn recommended me for the billet.

In San Diego for two weeks leave and recreation, the "Yorktown" had just sailed for Mexican ports when my telegraphic orders were sent. BuNav then tried to get them to me by radio. With radio then in its infancy, for some time we knew that a message concerning me was wandering about in the ether, but it was two weeks before we finally made out its text in full.

When the Secretary heard that Captain Senn was to be detached, he went into action on his plan to put a civilian in the billet. Admiral Palmer explained to him that I had a large family—a wife, five children and a maid—that they had already made preparations to leave for Washington as soon as I arrived in San Diego, and that it would cause me great hardship to countermand my orders as we had to pay for our family transportation out of our own funds in those days. The Secretary was persuaded to delay his action and must have forgotten about it, because it was never thereafter entirely put into effect.

It was during this tour of duty at the Academy that I first became personally acquainted with Franklin Delano Roosevelt. This came about because I was, *ex officio*, head of the Naval Academy Labor Board. It was the duty of the Labor Board and others like it at every Naval District Headquarters to ascertain the prevailing wage rate in various trades and to recommend to the Navy Department a wage scale for each Navy Yard and Naval Station in the District, which would give the labor trades a fair wage rate but would not throw the local wage scale and labor market out of balance. Assistant Secretary Roosevelt had to act on these recommendations for the Navy Department.

Being the head of the Labor Board closest to Washington, when the recommendations were all in, I was ordered to Washington to help the Assistant Secretary take action on them. It was in the course of this duty that I first learned of a character trait which made FDR always prefer appeasement or compromise in a political disagreement to an out-and-out fight.

In those days, Franklin Roosevelt was a big, handsome young man of thirty-four, with a warm and pleasing personality. Athletically inclined from childhood, he loved to play golf and tennis and to sail in competition. In his office in the Navy Department, we would sit down around a long table, FDR and his assistants and I. I remember the big head, the cigarette even in those days cocked at an impudent angle, and his powerful arms and shoulders.

Often there were appeals from the labor trades affected to disapprove the action of a local Labor Board and to raise wages as much as forty-eight cents an hour. Navy wages were increased in those days in increments of eight cents an hour. Almost without exception, FDR wanted to accede to labor's request—thinking no doubt of labor votes at the polls that Fall. Having in mind the purpose of Labor Boards and their difficult position locally if the Navy Department over-ruled them, I always voted for approving their recommendations.

"But, Commander," FDR would say, "don't you think we could give these coppersmiths the raise of forty cents an hour they're asking for?"

"Of course, Mr. Secretary," I would reply, "we can allow the raise, but it is not justified by wage scales in the area, and it would disturb the wage balance in the local governmental establishments. We can't afford to undermine the prestige of the Labor Board."

In the end, there was hardly a protest case that didn't get an increase of at least eight cents an hour.

FDR loved the Naval Academy and the quaint streets and old buildings of Annapolis. On many an occasion, he brought Mrs. Roosevelt down as guest of the Superintendent. There would be a midshipman play or hop or a party at the Superintendent's Quarters. He played an excellent game of golf and always brought along his clubs. After Chapel on many a Sunday, I was happy to make a fourth for a match over the rolling hills of the beautiful little Naval Academy course. In this way, for a time, a friendship both official and personal, was built up that was rather unusual between an obscure commander and a high civil official.

The Years Between

From 1917 until 1932, I doubt that Franklin D. Roosevelt remembered that there was an officer in the Navy by the name of "Bill" Standley. World War I came and went, with convoy escort duties and anti-submarine experience. I moved up to Captain. In 1919, I resumed the humdrum duties of the peacetime Navy, with a stimulating year at the Naval War College sandwiched in between tours at sea.

The post-war sea duty was pleasant—a battleship command and staff duty with Admirals Coontz and Eberle. The Washington Disarmament Conference of 1921 blasted our hopes of having the most powerful Navy in the world with its 5:5:3 ratio in capital ships among Great Britain, the United States and Japan. The United States scrapped a considerable tonnage of effective combatant ships, built and building, while the other signatories mostly gave up obsolete ships or imaginary ships on blueprints. This magnificent gesture also resulted in the Nine-Power Treaty guaranteeing the territorial integrity of China. Japan was one of the signatory powers.

With the gradual eclipse of the modern American Navy, I settled back resignedly into peacetime routine. One of the older men of my class, I could look forward to a few more years on the active list before age-in-grade got me and I passed on to the retired list. With the coming of promotion by selection of a board of Admirals in 1921, the change to retirement for service-in-grade put me on the same footing as my younger classmates but I still felt fairly certain I was so far down the list that I would have to retire before the Selection Board ever reached me.

But it was an exciting period in which we lived. Everywhere, a fear of the rising threat of Communism tended to keep conservatives or dictators in power. In 1922, after the Fascist "March on Rome," Mussolini became dictator of Italy. Kemal Ataturk became president and dictator of the Turkish Republic in April 1923, while in September of that year, Primo de Rivera took over the Government of Spain. In November a little known housepainter and a famous German General staged the Munich beer hall *putsch*.

In July, 1924, I first reported to the Navy Department as senior Navy member of the Joint Planning Committee and Assistant Director of Navy War Plans in the office of the Chief of Naval Operations. My principal responsibility to the Chief of Naval Operations was to promote naval preparedness in an era when every American was enjoying the good things of a post-war boom, had forgotten the war and its lessons, and felt convinced that there would never be another war—and this, although the United States had refused to participate in the noblest attempt at international peace of the centuries, the League of Nations. Unknown to us, we were entering upon a ten year period of international futility when diplomacy failed to forestall aggression, and the Axis powers, growing in strength and boldness, took advantage of confusion and lack of purpose among the democratic powers.

During a tour at sea from July, 1926, to November, 1927, to my astonishment, I came up for consideration by a Selection Board of nine admirals for promotion to rear admiral. There must have been some little cherubim sitting up aloft looking out for poor "Bill."

A Naval officer who later on wrote an article criticizing the workings of the selection system, used my case as an example. Calling me Captain "X," he stated that, as soon as the names of the Admirals serving on the Selection Board were made known, it was generally accepted by officers in the service that I would be one of the Captains selected, and this although I was number 32 on the lineal list of Captains under consideration. He referred to the fact that both Admiral Coontz and Admiral Eberle, on whose staffs I had served through the post-war years, were members of the Board.

The Selection Board reached far down the list and selected me for promotion to Rear Admiral. Although this was very gratifying, as I returned to duty in Washington as Assistant Chief of Naval Operations and Director of Fleet Training in November, 1927, I still could not believe that I had been tapped for greater things.

It was a stimulating and even exciting tour of duty. With the higher rank and closer relationship with the Chief of Naval Operations as one of his principal assistants, I found myself increasingly drawn into plans and maneuvers on the national and international stage, as well as within the naval service.

With the adjournment of the Geneva Naval Parley, under the sponsorship of the League of Nations, where talk, talk, talk, killed all possibility of agreement, we managed to convince President Coolidge that our Naval position was severely compromised. We presented a bill and the President approved the construction of twenty-three ten-thousand-ton cruisers. Yet, in 1928, we continued our unrealistic efforts at international arbitration with the signing of the Kellogg Pact by sixty-two nations renouncing war as an instrument of national policy.

On the eve of the great economic depression which hit the United States and the world, Herbert Hoover became President of the United States, and Ramsey MacDonald headed a Labor Government in England, while a brown-shirted rabble rouser built up the Nazi Party in Germany.

With Mr. Hoover in the White House, there was renewed effort by pacifist organizations and subversive elements not only to reduce the number of cruisers authorized by President Coolidge but also to pursue the will-o'-the-wisp of complete disarmament. Prior to the London Naval Conference of 1931, President Hoover even went so far as to forbid the Navy General Board to discuss or make recommendations as to naval disarmament.

As the head of our delegation of "Naval experts" at the Conference, Mr. Hoover designated his Secretary of State, Henry L. Stimson. Mr. Stimson tried very hard to qualify himself as an expert by extensive discussion with naval officers and conferences with our high naval officials. Naturally, we of the Navy were greatly incensed at the President's action in ignoring the Navy General Board and the Chief of Naval Operations.

Mr. Stimson must have sensed this feeling for he sent for Admiral Hilary P. Jones, who had just retired after being President of the General Board, and requested Admiral Jones to accompany him to London as his principal adviser on Naval matters.

"Of course, Mr. Secretary," Admiral Jones told me later that he said to Mr. Stimson. "I will be quite willing to go, provided the policy followed at the Conference is one which I can conscientiously support."

Mr. Stimson blew up. He knew that no naval officer of any strength or character could possibly approve of the program planned by the President. "Very well, then, Admiral," Mr. Stimson said testily, "I will get the President to order you to go."

"Ah, but you forget, Mr. Secretary," Admiral Jones reminded him, "a retired Naval officer can only be recalled to active duty in time of peace with his consent."

When this impasse became known to some of us younger assistants in Naval Operations, we were very upset. We figured it would be much better for Mr. Stimson to have along an adviser who *knew* about things Naval rather than to have to depend upon his own *guesses* on important issues. While discussing it with Rear Admiral Hutch I. Cone, who was Chairman of the Shipping Board, at his suite in the Chevy Chase Club one evening, an excellent plan was evolved. He would invite General Williams, the Chief of Army Ordnance, my friend, Joe Cotton, the Under-Secretary of State, and myself, to an early breakfast and nine holes of golf before office hours. At this breakfast in his room at the club, the four of us hatched a scheme.

"Joe," said Hutch, "you're to get Stimson to ask the President to add two members to our delegation. One of these must be Secretary Adams. Bill, you're to get Charlie Adams to make a personal appeal to Hilary to go along as Naval Adviser."

"Magnificent!" I cried, "Admiral Jones has the same high regard for Secretary Adams that all of us have. If the Secretary asks him, he'll go."

We all did our spade work. Admiral Jones did attend the Conference as Naval Adviser but he became seriously ill before it had covered much of its agenda and had to return home. Not that it made much difference. Complete disarmament proved to be an impractically idealistic goal. About all the Conference accomplished were some very minor reductions but, what was most unfortunate, Japan demanded and got a raise in her ratio, and the famous "escalator" clause that permitted her to build above her ratio in certain categories, if other smaller nations did. She was clearing the decks for her attack on Manchuria the following year. Our own Administration used the London Conference as an excuse to reduce the number of Treaty Cruisers authorized by President Coolidge in 1927 to eighteen instead of twenty-three, and thus "relieve some of the crushing burden of armament."

During my almost continuous service of six years in Naval Operations, I had often thought about and discussed with other officers the difficult problem of selecting properly qualified officers for the big commands in the Navy—Chief of Naval Operations; Commander-in-Chief, United States Fleet; Commander-in-Chief, Asiatic Fleet; Commander, Battle Fleet; Commander, Scouting Fleet; and others carrying with them the higher temporary rank of admiral or vice admiral. In talking this over with Rear Admiral J. O. Richardson, who was then Assistant Chief of the Bureau of Navigation, which had the responsibility for the detail and orders of officers, we hit upon what we thought would be a better plan. The Bureau of Navigation would arrange for certain flag officers to be assigned such duties from the time of their selection that several of them would be qualified for a certain job to which it was expected they would be assigned, culminating in the top job as Chief of Naval Operations. When this plan was explained to Admiral Charles F. Hughes, then CNO, he heartily approved and Joe Richardson set about putting the plan into effect.

In this connection, I had an opportunity to do a good turn for an officer, a former shipmate, for whose professional accomplishments I had the highest regard. I was in Admiral Hughes' office one day when he said, "Standley, I'm in a quandary. I don't know whom to nominate as Admiral Leigh's successor as Chief of the Bureau of Navigation. Any suggestions?"

I thought for a moment. "Admiral, let me tell you a little story," I said. "My son, Bill, is an ensign in the Junior Officers' Mess on the 'Tennessee.' One evening, not so long ago, all the officers not on watch were over on the beach at an official reception of some kind. When they came down to the landing, there was only one boat—the Captain's gig. Presently Captain Brooks Upham, their skipper, came down to the dock, with his boat cloak on but no cap. 'Get in, young men,' he said, 'I'll take you out to the ship.'

"As he settled back in the sternsheets, Captain Upham explained to his young shipmates that someone at the party had walked off with his cap, apparently by mistake.

"When the boat made the starboard gangway, the Officer-of-the-Deck was startled to see the Skipper climb out of the boat followed by a number of young ensigns, all of them bareheaded.

"Admiral," I went on, "a Captain who inspires that sort of

loyalty from his young officers, if otherwise qualified, would certainly make a first-class Chief of the Bureau of Navigation."

Admiral Hughes agreed, and the nomination of Brooks Upham was soon on the way up to the Secretary.

In spite of the failure of his plan for complete disarmament, President Hoover had ways of accomplishing "disarmament by example." The depression of 1929 had created a very serious economic situation both at home and abroad. The President's solution was stringent economy. Both military services were hard hit. "Payless furloughs" of thirty days each year, cutting officers and enlisted men's pay, were ordered. Building programs were stopped or slowed down. Allowances of enlisted men were sharply reduced to provide savings in Army and Navy budgets.

Although generally agreeable to the President's proposals, in 1932, the Chief of Naval Operations, then Admiral William Veasey Pratt, made a deal with the President's Budget Bureau, whereby the Navy would give up construction of several destroyers if the President would approve five thousand additional enlisted men for the Navy over current budget estimates. The Budget Bureau agreed but somewhere along the line the Navy lost both the destroyer construction and the five thousand men it had bargained for.

As a result of this and other "economies," by the Fall of 1932, the Navy was very short of men. Admiral Pratt hit upon an economy plan which suited President Hoover admirably—something called "Rotating Reserve." In this plan, about half of the destroyers in the Fleet were laid up with skeleton crews in various Navy Yards while the other half were operated with a full peacetime complement of men and officers. After six months, the destroyers exchanged places and some of their men, and the inactive ships went to sea for training. I was at sea at the time and couldn't understand what the plan accomplished or why. It meant that half of the little ships were ready for action and the other half were not even properly maintained, and this at a cost of a not inconsiderable number of officers and men and definite loss of overall naval efficiency.

In accordance with the plan for selecting flag officers and qualifying them for high command, Admiral J. R. P. Pringle had been ordered to sea in 1931 as Commander, Battleship Divisions, U. S. Fleet, with the intention that he would succeed Admiral Pratt as Chief of Naval Operations when he retired in March, 1933, having reached the retirement age of 64. I was then at sea in command of the Cruisers, Scouting Force, with the rank of Vice-Admiral, happily looking forward to being Commandant of the Twelfth Naval District in my native California for a couple of years and then retirement.

Unfortunately, Admiral Pringle developed cancer and died very suddenly. I was told later that, with this sudden crisis, in looking over the flag officers to replace Joel Pringle, I seemed to have had the most experience in the Office of the Chief of Naval Operations. Although not actively opposing my appointment, Admiral Pratt had his own candidate, Admiral Arthur J. Hepburn. Now, my friendly sponsorship of Brooks Upham as Chief of Bureau of Navigation brought forward a strong champion of my cause. While I was waiting to relieve him, Admiral Pratt told me that he had realized that I was the popular choice of the service. Accordingly, he threw his support to me.

Thus it came about, early in 1933, that I received a letter telling me that I would become the next Chief of Naval Operations. A sad combination of circumstances had brought about the happy chance which led me to the top billet in the Navy, when once I had thought I would be most content to retire after thirty years' service as a captain.

There were still some odd formalities to be completed. While not essential, it had become customary for the officer succeeding as Chief of Naval Operations first to fleet up to a sea command carrying the rank of Admiral. I was only a Vice Admiral.

Through the "disarmament by example" program of the Hoover Administration, we had watched our Navy emasculated and reduced by budget economies to a second-rate Navy. Those of us who knew FDR recalled that he was a serious student of Admiral Mahan's writings, a believer in a strong Navy as our "first line of defense," a man with unbounded faith in the value of sea power, and that he had acquired considerable naval knowledge and experience as Assistant Secretary of the Navy. We were happy to have such a man elected to the great office of President of the United States. We felt that soon we would have a President in the White House who would restore our Navy to the position it must have in the challenging international situation we faced, with Hitler's Nazi party dominant in the Reichstag and the Communists of Russia bent upon spreading their subversive doctrine and economic system throughout the world. We were happy to welcome him as our new Commander-in-Chief.

As I have said, Admiral Pratt ordinarily would have retired on

March 1, 1933. Had I relieved him on that date, three days before President Roosevelt's first Inauguration, General Douglas Mac-Arthur, then Army Chief of Staff, would have been senior to me, and the Army would have had the position of honor at the Inauguration. Sentiment, which occupied such an important place in the character of the incoming President, prevented this from happening. FDR discovered that because Pratt was full Admiral, he didn't have to retire on reaching the age of sixty-four, as lower ranking admirals did. Accordingly, he arranged for Admiral Pratt to be held over, even though it stopped the orderly change of command all through the fleet and the shore establishment.

To qualify me as CNO on May 8, 1933, I was ordered to duty as Commander, Battle Force, with the rank of Admiral. Thus was my "prestige" enhanced enough so that, two weeks later, I received dispatch orders to proceed to Washington, D. C., and report to the Chief of Naval Operations as his relief.

A few days before reporting to the Secretary of the Navy for duty, I was invited to lunch with the President in his office at the White House. As I balanced a tray on my knee, we talked of naval affairs and the state of the nation.

"Mr. President," I said, "I think there's something that you ought to know before I take office as Chief of Naval Operations. While I'm certainly not in sympathy with Admiral Pratt's rotating reserve for destroyers, the situation in those ships is merely an example of a condition which exists throughout the entire United States Fleet."

I went on to tell him that I had recently turned over Command of the Cruisers of the United States Fleet and that, from personal knowledge, not one of those ships could steam or operate as an effective unit in combat. Lack of personnel was so acute that ships could not maintain full power for much more than four hours and it was impossible for any of the ships to man all of their battle stations.

"Mr. President," I said very emphatically, "to operate our Fleet on this basis is unfair to the American people. They think that they have a fleet-in-being. In reality, it is a phantom fleet."

I told him of a recent experience while on leave before coming to Washington. On Flag Day, the Fleet was scheduled to stage an enormous Fleet Parade. Curiosity impelled me to go to Point Fermin, a point of land just west of Los Angeles Harbor with cliffs rising sheer from the Pacific Ocean for over a hundred feet, from which vantage point large numbers of persons were expected to watch the parade. The plans had been prepared in my flagship prior to my detachment and so I knew that the Fleet was supposed to steam to the westward from the harbor entrance, make a right angle approach to the shoreline and then head easterly paralleling the rocky promontory of Point Fermin. But for an unheralded fog, which is fairly prevalent in that area, it would have been a magnificent spectacle for the observers on Point Fermin.

But a dense fog screened the off-shore movements of the ships until they turned to the eastward to pass along the Point Fermin shoreline. I recalled the thrill with which the spectators greeted the sight of those glistening gray ships coming out of the white fog, first as spectral forms and gradually taking shape as cruisers, battleships, carriers and train with the little destroyers occupying positions of plane guard and simulated anti-submarine patrol. It was a most impressive sight, a demonstration of America's apparent naval might.

"Mr. President," I said, with all the sincerity in my voice that I could muster, "that demonstration was a gross deception of the American people. I then and there resolved that I would be no party to any further duplicity of that sort."

The President cocked himself back in his chair, rolled his eyes up to the ceiling, and took a drag at his cigarette. Then he took the long holder out of his mouth and pointed it at me, looking directly into my eyes, "Well, Admiral, what do *you* propose to do about it?"

"The Fleet is short some thirty-thousand enlisted men, Mr. President," I told him. "This is what I propose to do. I will ask for an increase in naval personnel immediately. If we don't get it, I am going to recommend that we lay up enough ships so that the ones we do operate will be effective fighting units of a smaller Fleet *ready for action on a moment's notice.*"

The President nodded in apparent approval and the talk turned to other subjects.

On July 1, 1933, in a simple ceremony in Secretary of the Navy Claude Swanson's office, I relieved Admiral William Veasey Pratt as Chief of Naval Operations. Present, as my old friend Orin Murfin, the Judge Advocate General of the Navy, swore me in, were the ailing Secretary; Brooks Upham, the Chief of the Bureau of Navigation; and Admiral Pratt. A peculiar chain of circumstances had combined to bring me to the highest naval command within the gift of my country. My naval career had been successful far beyond the tall, tall dreams of that California country lad of forty-five years ago.

Chief of Naval Operations

Although we worked together closely, I was never an intimate of FDR as were his secretaries, Marvin McIntyre, Steve Early, and "Missy" LeHand, personal friends of long standing. While the President apparently valued my abilities as a naval officer and my advice as Chief of Naval Operations, I never became a member of his inner circle or official family, or a White House hanger-on. Although I was frequently entertained at the White House, it was always because of my official position.

Before I assumed my duties as Chief of Naval Operations, Secretary Swanson had already suffered a severe stroke and he continued to be virtually an invalid during the period that I was CNO. For the entire year of 1936, he was confined to the Naval Hospital.

When Assistant Secretary of Navy Harry Roosevelt died early in 1936, the President appointed no successor, seeming well satisfied for me to continue to be Acting Secretary of the Navy as well as CNO for the rest of my term in office.

Many have doubtless wondered why the President retained Secretary Swanson in office when he was in such poor physical condition. It seems to me this is an apt illustration of two of FDR's character traits—his intense loyalty and his inability to fire anyone he really liked. The President knew that Swanson had absolutely no resources aside from his salary and FDR wanted to help him and his family. Furthermore, the President had an inflated opinion of his own knowledge of naval strategy and tactics and he much preferred to be his own Secretary of the Navy. With no Assistant Secretary of the Navy and Swanson so ill, FDR could run the Navy just about as he pleased.

And so, when he kept Secretary Swanson on, I became increasingly involved in the national and international affairs of the country. Until my retirement, I sat in as a full-fledged member of the New Deal Cabinet. The President and I developed a very successful working arrangement because we both wanted the same thing —an effective, sea-going Navy, fully-manned and built up to full treaty strength.

One of my earliest problems as CNO was to prepare data for

the Navy Budget for the fiscal year 1935. Before we could really get going on our planning, we had to know just how big an increase in enlisted men would be "in accord with the President's fiscal policy." I had told the President we needed thirty thousand enlisted men to bring our ships up to peacetime complement, but the Hoover economy program had closed all but two of our naval training stations. As a result, we could train during the coming year only ten thousand additional men.

I requested an appointment with the President, where I came quickly to the point. The Navy wanted an increase of ten thousand Navy enlisted men and two thousand Marines.

"Why two thousand for the Marine Corps?" the President demanded.

"We have a working agreement with the Marines, Mr. President," I explained. "For every increase of five men in the Navy, we ask for an increase of one Marine."

I didn't think it was desirable to explain at that point that this arrangement was to prevent arguments between Navy and Marine Corps representatives when they went up to hearings "on The Hill."

The President sat back and thought about it only a moment. "Okay, Bill," he said, and that was what he always called me thereafter. "You can have your ten thousand Navy men, but no Marines. Tell the Bureau of the Budget, I say it's all right."

Compromise, compromise, I thought as I walked out of the White House office building. This was not the first time I had run into this penchant of the President's. On the way back to the Navy building, I stopped by the Bureau of the Budget in the old State-War-Navy building just across from the White House. Mr. Henry N. Wiseman, an ex-Army sergeant whom I had known for some years, was the Bureau's Chief Budget Examiner, who handled our Navy budget matters. I went to his office and passed on the President's message.

"Did you get it in writing?" he asked.

His question rather annoyed me. "No," I said shortly. "This is a direct order from the President, Mr. Wiseman."

"Next time, Admiral," Wiseman said, smiling pleasantly, "I'd advise you to get it in writing."

Wiseman was as wise as his name. In the final budget estimates, as they left the White House approved by the President, we were authorized to ask for 5,000 additional Navy enlisted men and 1,000 Marines.

This incident brought me early knowledge of FDR's practice of giving encouragement to everyone, of saying "Yes, yes, yes," whether he was for or against a program. It was important for me to learn this, for few decisions were taken in those early days of the New Deal independent of the President, and, as I was later to learn, the last man in to see him before the decision was taken usually got his way.

Early in the New Deal, before I became CNO, the President had allocated some $238 million of Public Works funds to the Navy, cynically remarking to the Secretary, "Well, Claude, building up the Navy is certainly building worthwhile Public Works."

My next contact with the President was on a visit to Hyde Park to present to him our plan for expending this unexpected windfall. Prohibited from building battleships by treaty, we had prepared plans calling for construction of cruisers, destroyers and submarines.

Taking with me Jerry Land, Chief of the Bureau of Construction and Repair, and Sam Robinson, Chief of the Bureau of Engineering, I flew up to Hyde Park. Having in mind previous experiences with the President, enroute we explored the possibilities and direction of compromise.

I don't know why, when I visited him in his office at the White House, I had never observed it; perhaps it was because he was always behind his big, gadget-cluttered desk, sitting up there with his cigarette at a jaunty angle and his arms and shoulders so husky looking. Somehow, when we were shown into FDR's study at Hyde Park I had in mind a mental picture of the athletic young man I had known and played golf with seventeen years before. When I saw him seated at his desk in the tiny study, I was profoundly shocked.

As well as his powerful upper torso, I could now see how shrunken he was below the waist. His steel leg braces stood alongside the clever wheel chair on which he got around the house without assistance, but he was unable to rise, stand or walk. What remarkable personal courage the man had! Only a shell of the young man I had known but he carried a load of ceremony and official duties which would have broken a healthier and stronger man.

On that occasion we had no reason to look for compromise. The President enthusiastically agreed to our plans and sent us hurrying back to Washington very happy, for we had in our pocket the approval of a naval building program, the first of any importance in long years, the initial step in building our Navy to treaty strength.

Later, in connection with this allocation to the Navy of Public Works funds, I heard the President say, jokingly, to Secretary Swanson, "Claude, you and I sure got away with murder on that Public Works money deal."

Our efforts to obtain authorization and appropriation for a shipbuilding program were always loudly and volubly opposed by a strange combination of pacifist influences—representatives of organizations with such high-sounding names as the National Council for the Prevention of War, the International Council for the Prevention of War, the International Conference for the Preservation of Peace, the Society for the Cause and Cure of Wars, and others, which, either deliberately or unwittingly, supported the subversive, undercover efforts of the Reds or Nazis. Also, there were sincere but misguided organizations such as the Federal Council of Christ's Churches in America, whose Washington representatives carried on an active anti-war and anti-preparedness campaign.

Our efforts to provide for the expansion of the Navy in the light of the challenging events of that era were doubly handicapped by the fact that we always, as it were, had to take two bites at the cherry. We first had to get a bill through the Congress *authorizing* the building of Navy ships and then we had to get appropriations to build the ships through the Bureau of the Budget and the Appropriations Committees of both houses of Congress. Thus, the pacifists had two opportunities to kill or emasculate our programs.

For myself, I could see no reasons in either law or diplomatic protocol why, as long as our authorized naval strength was specified in detail in our various ratified treaties, we should have to go through this double rigamarole every time we wanted to build a ship. It seemed to me that all that should be required was to decide upon the increase, get the money appropriated and go ahead and build the ships.

I put my staff to work preparing the draft of a bill, which, if we could get Congress to enact it into law, would authorize us to have a Navy of treaty strength; would authorize us to build the necessary ships of various categories to bring the Navy up to treaty strength; and would provide an orderly replacement program to keep it at treaty strength.

It did not take the professional and legal staff long to write such a measure but the allocation of tonnage to provide replacements for overage ships was not simple. In commission and laid up "in reserve," we had an enormous number of old World War I "four-piper" destroyers, all of which were both overage and obsolete. In order to prevent all of the new ones from becoming overage at the same time again, we decided to work up a plan for building several destroyers each year over a period of ten or more years.

While these plans were still in the making, I received a phone call one morning from Congressman Carl Vinson of Georgia, Chairman of the House Naval Affairs Committee, whom we later came to call, affectionately, "Mr. Navy," and "The Admiral," one of our greatest friends in Congress in those lean days for the Navy.

Mr. Vinson said, "Oh, ah, naow, Admiral, I understand that you are preparing some kind of bill in your office to, ah, authorize the Navy Department to build up the Fleet to treaty strength."

"Yes, Mr. Vinson," I replied, "we are. I hope to have it finished in a few days."

"Ah. . . . I wonder if you would kindly let me have a copy of your bill, Admiral. Doesn't have to be typed up fancy—just as it stands."

Thinking he wanted a copy to study for his own information, I sent it to him. The next morning, Jerry Land came into my office carrying a copy of the Congressional Record. "You see this, Admiral?" he asked.

There in the Congressional Record was my bill word for word, introduced as the "Vinson Bill" to build up the Navy to treaty strength.

"Oh, oh, Jerry!" I exclaimed. "What's Senator Trammel going to think about this?"

Admiral Land grinned his cheerful grin. "He's going to think we double-crossed him."

I had my secretary get Senator Trammel, Chairman of the Senate Naval Affairs Committee, on the phone. "Senator," I said, "something came up that you're not going to like very much. I sent a copy of a bill to build a Treaty Navy, that we've been preparing here in my office, down to Carl Vinson to look over and he introduced it in the House yesterday as the Vinson Bill. Trying to steal the show from you, I guess."

"That so?" came the noncommital remark in the receiver.

"Yes, sir. But I tell you what I've done. A copy of that bill is on the way to your office by special messenger right now. If you act fast, you ought to be able to get it in the hopper before the Senate meets today and have your name on it, too."

That was how our Navy Department Bill to establish, build and

maintain the Navy at treaty strength became the Vinson-Trammel
Act, which was approved by President Roosevelt on March 27,
1934.

The period of my duty as CNO was a fascinating yet terrible
time to be high in the councils of my country—fascinating because
so many interesting problems rose to be met; terrible, because unlike Americans today who recognize and are ready to meet the
Red Menace, the America of 1933–37 was indifferent or apathetic
to the rise of totalitarianism in the world.

Already in 1933, von Hindenburg had named Adolf Hitler
Chancellor of Germany and he had begun the elimination of all
opposition parties in Germany. That fall, Nazi Germany withdrew
from the League of Nations and the World Disarmament Conference adjourned without agreement.

And 1934 was also a challenging year. In June, Hitler's vicious
purge of dissident elements in the Nazi Party profoundly shocked
the civilized world. Chancellor Dolfuss of Austria was assassinated
by Austrian Nazis in July. The following month, President von
Hindenburg died and Hitler became *Führer and Reichskanzler* of
Germany. Frightened, France, Russia, Turkey, England, Czechoslovakia and Italy joined in an anti-Nazi coalition. Across the
world, Japan assumed exclusive responsibility for peace in Asia
and denounced the Washington Naval Treaty.

Early in 1935, in a plebiscite, the people of the Saar voted to
rejoin Germany. In violation of the Versailles Treaty, Hitler ordered conscription and began to build up his Army, Navy and Air
Force. As appeasement of Nazi Germany commenced in Europe,
the American Congress passed a Neutrality Act that provided that
no American ship might enter a war zone.

The war would come sooner than anyone in America imagined.
In March of 1936, Hitler made his greatest bluff—20,000 Nazi
troops marched into the demilitarized Rhineland. A firm stand by
France and England at that time might have stopped the Nazi
dictator, for he was not then ready for war, certainly not a match
for the Western Democracies *and* he had, then, reached no agreement with Stalin. But the appeasement continued. The first Socialist Government in history took office in France under Premier
Léon Blum. In the Spanish Civil War, Soviet Russia on the Loyal-
ist side and the Nazis and Fascists on Franco's side tested out
their weapons and tactics for World War II. The Rome-Berlin
Axis was formed and an Anti-Comintern Pact was signed by Ger-

many and Italy. In Russia, consolidating his position of power, Stalin directed the notorious treason trials and blood purge which eliminated Old Bolsheviks Kamanev, Zinoviev and sixteen others. That November, Franklin D. Roosevelt was elected for a second term in a landslide victory over Governor Alf Landon of Kansas.

While most of my activities as CNO are not pertinent to this narrative, certain incidents of those dramatic years stand out in my memory.

In November of 1933, Commissar of Foreign Affairs Maxim Litvinov came to Washington and succeeded in negotiating with President Roosevelt the recognition of the Stalin regime in Soviet Russia. When normal diplomatic relations were resumed, FDR's friend, William C. Bullitt, was named Ambassador to Russia.

Apparently, this recognition of Russia was unexpected, for the State Department had no money to outfit the American Embassy in Moscow. When I went to Moscow in 1942, I found towels, bed linen, blankets, table and kitchenware all marked with the symbol of the U. S. Navy. At a dinner with Ambassador Stuart in the Embassy at Nanking six years later, I learned from my fellow dinner guest, ex-Ambassador Bill Bullitt, that the President had directed the Navy Department to equip the Embassy at Moscow as if it were a battleship being commissioned.

As a sequel to the recognition of Russia in April, 1934, two Russians, Paul Yurevitch Oras and Alexander M. Yakimchev, arrived in Washington to be Naval Attaché and Assistant Naval Attaché to the Russian Embassy. No doubt due to the Communist philosophy of that era, both "comrades" reported as "Mister," but Mr. Oras with the rank of Admiral and Mr. Yakimchev with the rank of Vice-Admiral.

Following the usual procedure, the State Department asked the Navy Department if there were any reason why the two "Mister Admirals" should not be accepted as Russian naval attachés. After some hurried consultations, we replied that the Navy Department had absolutely no objection to Messrs. Oras and Yakimchev as individuals but that their high ranks were wholly inappropriate to the positions and we gave about a dozen good reasons why.

A week or ten days passed before the Russian Embassy received the official attitude of the Kremlin. In effect, the Russian Government said, "Oh, their rank, is that all the trouble? Very well, we'll reduce them in rank."

Forthwith Mr. Oras acquired the rank of Captain and Mr. Yakimchev became a Commander and everyone involved was happy.

At the time of Assistant Secretary Harry Roosevelt's death in 1936, I was co-delegate with Norman Davis and William Phillips at the London Disarmament Conference of 1935–36. The other nations represented at the Conference were England, France, Italy and Japan, but Italy was at war with Ethiopia and thus being at odds with the League of Nations was present but not voting.

On January 1, 1936, the Japanese Government made good a previous threat and bolted the Conference. As a result, no agreement could be reached with regard to the tonnage or speed and armament of battleships or size of cruisers. Because he wanted to keep the framework of a Limitation of Armament Treaty in being, President Roosevelt directed our delegation to continue our futile and exasperating negotiations. We did reach agreement on a few unimportant issues, but Great Britain would not negotiate seriously for limitation of naval armament with both Germany and Japan boycotting the Conference.

For a month, the rest of our delegations marked time while Great Britain conducted separate negotiations with Germany which resulted in an agreement that Germany might rebuild her navy to an equality with France and Italy. With this unfortunate accomplishment behind us, the Conference adjourned.

It was during this period that remarks attributed to me made headlines in all the papers of the United States. In order to appear to be still negotiating, Mr. Norman Davis wanted me to have a technical conference with the Japanese representative, Admiral Yamamoto (who later ordered the air attack on Pearl Harbor, promised to dictate peace in Washington, and was later shot down by American fliers in the vicinity of Guadalcanal). I had already exhausted every possible channel for a meeting of minds with Admiral Yamamoto and I told Norman Davis that any further discussion with the Admiral might lead to false conclusions.

However, Mr. Davis arranged for a meeting with Ambassador Matsudaira, during which I was cleverly maneuvered into a technical discussion with Admiral Yamamoto in which the Admiral contended that the Japanese desires for changing the ratios in the naval treaty was based on the fact that changing weapons and changes in the United States Fleet made it essential that the Japanese get a higher ratio in order that they might be secure in their own area, which, after all, was the purpose and intent of the Washington Treaty.

I was suffering from a terrific London cold and during the discussion I had almost lost my voice; when the meeting was over I

attempted to take my immediate departure but Ambassador Matsudaira said, "Now wait a minute for I have something which is
very good for a cold." While waiting for the libation, the Japanese
Admiral again approached me and reiterated statements previously made. I answered, "Well, Admiral, you take the American
Fleet and give me the Japanese Fleet and you will have a sorry
time getting across the Pacific."

Apparently, this conversation was immediately reported to Tokyo and came back to London through the *Paris Herald* in a statement as follows: "The American representative, Admiral Standley,
offers to exchange fleets with the Japanese Admiral and still lick
him."

I can recall so clearly the first Cabinet meeting I attended after
my return from the London Conference. When the Cabinet members had all taken their allotted seats in accordance with seniority
and precedence, the President came in in his wheel chair and took
his place at the head of the table with his customary, "Good morning, gentlemen."

Using first names as was his custom, he opened the business of
the meeting, "Well, Cordell, what have you this morning?"

"Henry, do you have anything for us today?"

This continued around the table until he came to the Navy
niche. "Well, Bill," FDR said, very affably, "we're glad to have
you back from London, but you didn't bring much back with you,
did you?"

"No, sir, not much," I agreed. "But at least we maintained the
treaty structure and brought back a minimum agreement signed
by three of the great powers. Those were your instructions, sir."

The President gave me his famous grin. "Well, Bill, what have
you this morning?"

I looked across the table at Madame Perkins and then around
at Secretary Henry Wallace and Vice-President Garner. I cleared
my throat and faced the President. "You will recall, Mr. President,
that, preceding the Conference, when Japan threatened to bolt,
you told me that, if she did so, for every ship she laid down,
the United States would lay down three. Now, Japan has bolted.
While we have, as yet, been able to get no specific information,
we feel morally certain that Japan has already inaugurated a battleship building program with at least two battleships laid down.
Great Britain has announced that she is proceeding to lay down
two battleships immediately. We now have two battleships—the

'New York' and 'Texas'—overage according to treaty. Every single one of our battleships will be overage before we could possibly replace one of them. And so, Mr. President, I strongly recommend that we proceed at once with plans to build at least one battleship."

The expected pacifist reaction was instantaneous. Madame Perkins exploded with, "Ah, horrible thought."

Secretary Wallace chimed in, "A tragic decision for world peace."

And Vice-President Garner, "Mr. President, the very mention of building battleships will cause an explosion on The Hill."

I looked around at my opponents with a smile. "Mr. President, during the past four months, while I have been at the Conference in London, I have made it my business to keep my finger on the pulse of American opinion by reading the editorials of the country newspapers from all over the United States. I am certain that I can assure you that every explosion on The Hill over battleships will mean votes for the Democratic Party."

I knew that the President was personally in sympathy with my desire to commence making plans for new battleships. About a week after this Cabinet meeting, he sent for me. "I'm all for your battleship program, Bill, but I'm apprehensive over the political reaction. An enormous amount of work has to be done before the keel of a battleship can be laid. Why can't we change the wording in the Navy Budget somewhere so that you can get to work on the battleship plans without specifically mentioning battleships in the bill?"

I went back to my office and consulted with Jerry Land and my legal experts. A few days later, I informed the President that we saw no reason why we couldn't carry out his suggestion. FDR told me to see Congressman Buchanan of the Naval Appropriations Sub-Committee and tell him that the President would like to have such a change made in the bill which was then under consideration by his Committee.

I went up on The Hill and told the Congressman what the President wanted.

"Did the President ask you to tell me this?" he asked.

"Yes, sir," I replied.

Congressman Buchanan reached for his telephone. "Give me the White House," he said. And in a moment, "Mr. President, this is Congressman Buchanan. Admiral Standley is in my office now. He has just given me your message about changing the Navy Appropriation Bill so that the Navy can make plans for battleships without mentioning battleships in the Bill."

He was silent for a moment, listening, and then, "Well, Mr. President, to make such a change will result in questions which will disclose the intent of the changes. Congress won't like such a subterfuge."

He listened again for a moment. "Mr. President, if you want to build battleships, let's call 'em battleships. Any other way is sure to cause trouble."

The next Sunday morning, while this discussion was still at its height, I was waiting on the first tee with my regular foursome ready to tee off, when Commander Bogart from my office came across the lawn toward me. He drew me aside. "Admiral, I have a foursome here, including Senator James F. Byrnes and Congressman McMillan. Our fourth failed to show up. I think it would be a swell idea for you to join us."

I explained to Ike Yates and Henry Sutphen of my regular foursome that Senator Byrnes was Chairman of the powerful Senate Appropriations Committee and Congressman McMillan was a member of the House Naval Affairs Committee. Ike and Henry readily agreed that I better not fail to seize this opportunity.

Well, I've played a good game of golf for many years. When our foursome came into the locker room, Ike and Henry were waiting for me. "How'd you make out, Admiral?" Henry whispered.

"Fine," I whispered, "I won us a battleship."

As a matter of fact, the outcome of this pleasant round of golf was the building of two great battleships which served with such distinction in surface actions and in carrier task forces all through the Pacific War—the "Washington" and "North Carolina."

I also had my troubles with the Russians while I was CNO. They were the most avid seekers after information that I have ever seen—even more earnest and zealous than the Japanese, whom, many thought before the War, topped all other races in the collection of both useful and useless information. The Russian attachés, military, naval and commercial, picked up everything— copies of all technical and trade magazines and military and naval professional magazines, blueprints of everything from nuts and bolts to washing machines, tractors and combine harvesters. They haunted the Patent Office, studying our descriptive patents and their sketches and buying copies. That they made good use of this sort of information, I have no doubt, as I saw plenty of evidence of it during my stay in Russia. But what they were particularly eager to obtain was information as to mechanical processes and industrial methods.

The Russian Naval Attachés were always and forever asking to put inspectors in various factories and technicians in plants to learn either the whole production line or assembly line technique or a part of it. They had a habit of placing a small order for some machine or device in which they were interested and then not reordering. Later, hundreds and even thousands of them could be seen in use in the Soviet Union. Having no patent or copyright treaty with Russia, the Western democracies had no protection against such commercial vandalism.

I recall one incident which was particularly irritating to the Navy. We had given the Russians special permission to put some thirty technicians in an American factory which was building machinery for the Navy. Some months later, the Soviet Government, through their Naval Attaché, asked to double this number. We were astounded at the request and decided to look into the matter a bit before granting permission. To our chagrin, we discovered that the Russians, without getting permission from anyone, had been replacing these thirty technicians every three months and thus getting four times as many trained men in one year. Needless to say, they were not permitted to double the number in that factory.

As must be the case in a land where freedom of speech is guaranteed, it was not long until the Russians discovered that we were making plans to build new super-battleships. Much to my surprise, even before money had been appropriated for the "Washington" and "North Carolina," the Director of Naval Intelligence came to me one day with a Russian request for the plans of our latest battleships. Under considerable pressure, we finally told the Russian Naval Attaché that we would be able to give them some of the plans of the "West Virginia," the latest battleship we had in operation, *circa* 1923. As soon as he had time to communicate with Moscow, he was back protesting that the "West Virginia" plans would not do at all. They must have the plans of our latest and fastest battleships now on the drawing boards. And if we didn't mind too much, it would be very nice to have the plans for their fire control installation and detailed information as to how we manufactured our sixteen-inch turret guns.

Of course, we refused and, at the time, I thought we were successful in keeping these plans from the Russians. In the light of recent disclosures, I am inclined to believe that the Russians, by devious maneuvers, actually did get everything they were asking for officially back in 1936. But they didn't get it from me!

On only one occasion during my tour of duty as CNO do I recall that the President took action in the Navy contrary to my wishes. While I was preparing to go to London for the Disarmament Conference, the question of a successor for the Commander-in-Chief, U. S. Fleet, came up. I asked Secretary Swanson to hold the decision in abeyance until I returned.

When my return was delayed, the President became impatient. Although he was told that his action would not be in accordance with my recommendations, he re-appointed the Admiral who then had the Fleet. When I returned, Secretary Swanson informed me that he had told FDR that his action was contrary to my wishes and that I had what I considered especially good reasons for my recommendation.

"But I told the President," the Secretary added, "that if he and I made the appointment, Admiral Standley would accept it."

I looked at the poor, sick old man and I didn't have the heart to argue with him. "Mr. Secretary," I said, "you leave me no other recourse but to resign and I don't feel that it would be to the best interests of the Navy to offer my resignation just now."

The year of 1936 was difficult, a hard, grueling grind. Although I was still *persona grata* with the President, I had decided in September that I did not want to continue as CNO beyond the date on which I would normally retire in the ordinary course of events. On my sixty-fourth birthday, December 18, 1936, I would reach the statutory age for retirement. If I were a Rear Admiral, the current law would require that I retire on January 1, 1937.

Accordingly, I made up a slate of names of the officers I considered to be qualified and eligible to be my relief and recommendations as to the other necessary changes in high command in the Fleet. I asked for an appointment with the President.

After we had exchanged our usual pleasant greetings, I asked for his permission to retire on January first and recommended Admiral William D. Leahy as my successor.

"What's the hurry, Bill?" he asked. "You don't have to retire, you know. You're a full Admiral and can stay on as long as you like. Why don't you just continue on, at least until the end of your term?"

I looked at him sharply. Franklin D. Roosevelt was a persuasive individual but I had made up my mind and I did not intend to be persuaded. "I'll tell you why, Mr. President. It's my responsibility to provide for orderly changes of command in the Fleet and shore billets. As you know, many of these changes in assignment depend on who is ordered to relieve CNO and when his relief takes place. If I didn't hold the rank of Admiral, I would have to retire for age on the first of January."

I smiled at him to take away the sting. "Mr. President, we've had a very pleasant relationship and I've enjoyed working with you and for you. But I remember that you kept Admiral Pratt on after he was due for retirement and, then later on, you had to kick him out when you wanted to get rid of him. I wouldn't relish being kicked out. Therefore, I am going to submit my request for voluntary retirement on January first after forty years of active service."

Under the law, such a request has to be approved. It was the first rift in the lute. FDR did not seem to be at all pleased because I didn't want to stay on as CNO. In fact, he seemed to take it as a personal affront that any naval officer would not jump at the chance to continue on active duty as his Chief of Naval Operations.

My last meeting with the President before my retirement came about over the question of my employment in civilian life after January 1, 1937. I had been offered two positions. The first was as Director of Foreign Participation of the New York World's Fair of 1939 at a very nice salary. The other was an offer from the Shipbuilders' Association to become their Washington representative— or paid lobbyist—at about three times the salary offered by the World's Fair. I took the occasion to ask the President's advice as to which of these two positions he thought I should accept.

"Why, Bill, take the shipbuilders' job, of course," he said, without any hesitation.

"But, Mr. President," I protested. "Think of the inferences which might be drawn, some of them of possible detriment to your Administration. For almost seventeen years, I have been extremely active, persistent and to some extent effective in persuading the Congress to build up the Navy. If I accept a high salaried position with the Shipbuilders' Association, my patriotic motives will be impugned and there could be a lot of valid criticism leveled at both of us. On the other hand, my long service and large family haven't left me in a very good financial condition. I've got to find some kind of civilian employment for a few years after I retire."

The President leaned back and considered for a few moments,

blowing smoke rings at the ceiling. "Bill, of course you're right," he said presently. "You can't take the shipbuilders' lobbying job. You better go with Grover Whalen at the World's Fair."

So it came about that, on the first of January, 1937, after forty-five years of continuous active duty in the Navy, in my own office I stood by and watched my life-long friend, Bill Leahy, sworn in as my relief as Chief of Naval Operations and as Acting Secretary of the Navy. I had sailed a long and interesting course. Now, I looked forward to a few more years of useful public service in civilian life and eventual complete retirement to my native California.

CHAPTER III

I Try to Withdraw from
Public Life

As I RETIRED from the post of Chief of Naval Operations and from the Navy, I was very tired, with a weariness that seemed to have sunk into the very marrow of my bones. For four years, I had been carrying on my own very active job and for much of that period the heavy duties of ceremony and performance of both Secretary and Assistant Secretary of the Navy had been mine. My family had already preceded me to California. I decided that a sea cruise through the Canal to San Diego was just what I needed. It also seemed more fitting for a sea-going Navy man with forty-five years of service behind him to *go ashore* for retirement. How could you "swallow the anchor" if you had no anchor to swallow?

Accordingly, I arranged to take passage on the old battleship "Wyoming" which was proceeding to the West Coast on an amphibious training cruise with some elements of the Fleet Marine Force.

I shall never forget our first night out of Hampton Roads. I had reported on board very tired and so I was early in the bunk and was soon rocked fast asleep by the soothing motion of a ship in the seaway. A few hours later, I was startled out of a sound sleep by the first blast of a fog whistle which seemed to be blowing right in my stateroom. Alarmed and annoyed because I hadn't been informed of the fog, still half asleep, I climbed out of my bunk and was pulling on my clothes to dash up to the bridge, when suddenly I awakened enough to remember that I was retired, only a passenger, and no longer responsible for the safety of ship or formation. What a joy it was to pull off my trousers, climb back into the bunk and roll over with my face to the bulkhead. I was still chuckling happily to myself as I went back to sleep.

I had planned to spend some time in California, resting and enjoying the company of my family, of whom I had seen all too little during the past four years, but on my arrival at San Diego, a telegram awaited me. "Urgent that you report for duty with the World's Fair by February fifth," I read. I handed it to my wife with a sigh.

"Well, it's you, yourself, Hal, that's always getting yourself into these fixes," she said, and that's all the sympathy I got from her.

I arrived in New York on February 4, 1937. The next morning, I reported to Grover Whalen in his temporary office in the Empire State Building and immediately went to work as Director of Foreign Participation of the New York World's Fair, 1939, Incorporated.

The Administration Building at Flushing Meadows had not been completed and so I was assigned offices on the 82nd floor of the Empire State Building. My assistant turned out to be Ed Roosevelt, another one of FDR's innumerable cousins, who had spent most of his life in France and didn't have much experience at doing anything. He was a pleasant individual to have around and I understand that he had the original idea of leasing the Flushing Meadows dump as the Fair site, which left New York with another very lovely park.

I soon realized that I should have been on the job earlier. Much hard work had to be done before we could even approach any foreign country and ask them to participate.

Becoming weary of the frequent importunings of other countries to take part in a World's Fair so extravagantly wonderful that it would outclass all previous World's Fairs or Expositions, the European countries had formed a World's Exposition Bureau with an agreement that no member of the Bureau would consider an invitation to participate in a Fair until the Bureau had passed on the regulations of the Fair at one of its regular meetings in Paris.

Furthermore, protocol decreed that all invitations to foreign countries to participate in our Fair must be issued by the State Department, which required a Joint Resolution by both houses of Congress. And so, Ed and I turned to preparing *Regulations for the New York World's Fair, 1939, Incorporated,* which we hoped would get by the Exposition Bureau and yet not hamper us too much in the administration of the Fair.

Original plans for the Fair contemplated zoning Flushing Meadows—commercial exhibit zones, international zones, state zones, city zones, etc. Ten of the zones were set aside for exhibits by the various departments of our Federal Government. We also wanted the Government to build a huge display building at the center of the Foreign Government Zone to house a general United States exhibit. Our Federal Government was, of course, expected to defray the cost of constructing the Federal buildings. In addition, the World's Exposition Bureau required that a Fair furnish free to each country a substantial covered area in the Foreign Zone. We hoped to obtain funds for constructing these exhibit areas also from the Congress. In all, it was estimated that our United States Treasury would have to contribute about $5 million—an immense sum of money in those pre-war days. But, after all, this was New York, the home state of our President, and the Fair would make work, an important objective of the New Deal. Grover Whalen told me that the President had promised to approve the appropriation bill if the Congress would pass it. I found myself making frequent trips to Washington to help lobby these two measures through Congress.

Eventually our regulations were completed, covering the commitments indicated above and special requirements as to size and height of buildings for foreign government exhibits, free space available, and areas on which foreign governments could build. The Joint Resolution passed and was approved. The appropriation bill for the $5 million seemed to have a fair breeze on its way through Congress.

And so, Grover Whalen and I and a large party of Fair officials set off in the French liner Normandy on a junket to Paris and London, ostensibly to present our regulations and get the approval of the World's Exposition Bureau, but we timed our sailing so as to be in Paris for the scheduled opening of the Paris World's Exposition of 1937 on May eleventh and in London for the Coronation of King George VI in June.

Our meeting with the Bureau was highly successful. Our regulations were found to be "in due form and technically correct" and participation of member countries was approved. Unfortunately, the opening of the Paris Exposition was delayed but we gained useful information from a pre-opening tour of the grounds. We had a delightful time at the Coronation in London but bad news clouded our pleasant social occasions. Word came to us that FDR had vetoed the $5 million appropriation, giving as a reason that the amount was too great and that he thought we could very well get along on half that amount. When we got back to New York, we discovered that San Francisco had rocked the boat. Observing how easy it had been for New York to get a $5 million appropriation through the Congress, San Francisco had asked for the same amount to help finance her exposition, also to be held in 1939.

To ensure that the Fair buildings would be constructed and stocked with exhibits by the date scheduled for opening, Grover Whalen had set a deadline for the submission of plans of all buildings to be erected by private firms and foreign governments. Since I had negotiated contracts with all of the governments, it was up to me to get these plans in and approved. Evidently having had more experience with the Russians at International Expositions than I, the British insisted on having inserted in their contract an agreement to the effect that, if any other nation was granted more space than the British, then they must be given additional space to make up the difference. As other contracts were drawn up, the various governments insisted on this "most-favored-nation" clause.

I had no trouble at all with anyone but the Russians. In spite of all my pleas and urging, they just wouldn't get in their plans. Whenever I approached their Fair representatives, they always called in Russian Ambassador Oumansky. Ably assisted by that expert in delaying tactics, the Russians waited until the last day before the deadline and brought in plans for a building much too large for the plot assigned to them, with a spire on it topped by a Red Star which was considerably above the height limit set.

On the recommendation of General Denis Nolan, Director of States' Participation in the Fair, and myself, the Design Board disapproved the Russian plans. They must have heard the Red wail all the way to the Kremlin. Oumansky appealed to Grover Whalen. Being an expert in personal publicity, Grover Whalen made headlines by reversing the decision of the Design Board, even though this action resulted in giving the Russian exhibit 8,000 feet more display space than assigned them in their contract, required moving the Rumanian Building, the Czechoslovakian Building, the Japanese area, a road leading to a bridge already constructed, and the entire New England plot, as well as a number of partially constructed buildings.

Immediately, I began to receive angry complaints from the British and other nations, which demanded additional space under their "most-favored-nation" clauses. All I could do was explain that the Russians had forced this situation upon us, that there just wasn't any more space and that I was "so sorry."

The New York Press somehow picked up the news on the prospective situation of the "Red Star over all," including the American colors on the Federal Building, and made a newsman's holiday of it. To appease the Press, Grover Whalen had the "Parachute Jump" moved from the amusement area to the Foreign Government Zone and had a flagpole erected on the top of it which hoisted Old Glory a few feet higher than Soviet Russia's Red Star.

Ridiculous as it may appear from the distance of seventeen years, as a result of this episode I soon found myself in a very embarrassing position with the foreign representatives with whom I had worked so closely for some months. When the situation became no longer tolerable, I took the only course open to me—I submitted my resignation. Grover Whalen refused to accept it. I went on leave of absence from my job at the Fair and represented the New York Fair at the opening of the Golden Gate International Exhibition, February 18, 1939, a very pleasant occasion in my old home town of San Francisco.

At Grover Whalen's urgent solicitation, I returned for the Grand Opening of the New York World's Fair on April 30th. Shortly thereafter, my resignation was accepted. Thus ended my only excursion into Show Business—one of the greatest propaganda extravaganzas of our interlude between wars.

My Brief Excursion into Private Business

For some time, infinitely more serious events had been occupying my thoughts. During the two and a half years since my retirement, I had watched the march of world events with increasing concern. In 1937, the Moscow Treason Trials and second blood purge of Old Bolsheviks had established Stalin in firm control of Soviet Russia. Hitler denied all German guilt for World War I. The Japanese invaded China and quickly captured Peiping, Tientsin and Shanghai. Japanese bombers deliberately sank the U. S. S. "Panay" on the Yangtse River. In December, 1937, Italy quit the League of Nations.

In January of 1938, the first session of the U.S.S.R.'s "Red Parliament," the Supreme Soviet, convened in the Great Palace of the Kremlin, with Joseph Stalin as one of its delegates. On March 11, Hitler marched at the head of his troops across the Austrian frontier and joined that country to the German Reich in "indissoluble union."

Later that year, Czechoslovakia bowed to Nazi threats after being abandoned by her Western Allies at Munich. And much to my amazement, on December 6, 1938, France and Germany signed a pact for "pacific and good neighborly relations." Thus encouraged, early in 1939, Hitler took Memel and Mussolini, with considerable effort, occupied Albania.

During this "war of nerves," Joseph Stalin and his submissive Politburo watched anxiously from the Kremlin. Since most of this new German territory was close to the Russian frontier, the Kremlin regarded Hitler's maneuvers with growing fear and an increasing feeling of insecurity. There, despite Neville Chamberlain's announcement of "peace in our time," patent for all to see were the growing tensions which would lead to war. Yet, somehow, even at that late hour, my fellow-countrymen seemed to think that we could be spared a part in the coming world conflagration.

Prior to separating my connection with the World's Fair, I became associated with the Electric Boat Company of New London, Connecticut. Upon being released by the Fair, I accepted a job with the company as a consultant. A shipbuilding firm principally experienced in construction of submarines, they had gotten a contract for building some PT (motor torpedo) boats and they wanted the benefit of my experience in their development. It was a type of naval combat craft new to our Navy but one about which I had some personal knowledge due to our research in the Navy Department and my contacts abroad.

We soon found that, not only was no suitable engine being manufactured in the United States but also no American engine firm was geared up to produce one in much less than a couple of years. The PT type of craft was peculiarly adapted to short range work. They could be based in the small secluded harbors along the coast, dart out at high speed, deliver their attack and get away almost before they could be discovered. In other words, they were peculiarly fitted for close-in defense work around the British Isles. With the approach of hostilities in the Pacific area, the Navy Department considered that these boats would be of special value in the Philippine area.

Our Navy Department had word that the Scott-Payne Company, a British concern, had developed one of these PT boats to a high state of effectiveness, and Henry Sutphen was authorized to proceed to London and enter into a contract for the purchase of one of these boats. While it was not generally known, I saw the letter of instruction that Secretary Edison issued to Mr. Sutphen, and this letter gave specific authorization and instructions to purchase a PT boat from the Scott-Payne Company. The contract with the Scott-Payne Company called for three British Rolls-Royce engines as power plants for the speedy torpedo craft; however, before the completion of the contract, the British Air Minister took over the Rolls-Royce plants. It was only through my influence and personal acquaintance with Lord Chatfield, my British vis-a-vis at the Disarmament Conference in 1934–1936, then Minister of Defense, that the Air Ministry was persuaded to release to the Scott-Payne Company for completion of the contract three of the Rolls-Royce engines. Looking back on it, I somehow feel that my salary was well earned. But for me, perhaps, MacArthur would have had no Bulkeley with his MTB Squadron in the Philippines on Pearl Harbor Day.

My association with the Electric Boat Company brought me into close contact with many prominent New York industrialists, through whom I learned of the activities of the Russian agency, Amtorg. Widely publicized as a purely commercial organization for the promotion of export and import trade between the United States and Soviet Russia, Amtorg was reported at that time to have on deposit with two New York banks a sum of $100 million to finance their purchases in the United States. Of course, we now know that they were financing many other less open and proper activities as well. Not satisfied with the plans for the old battleship "West Virginia" which we had offered the Russian Government, agents of Amtorg were very active in 1939 trying to get the plans the Navy Department was then completing for our latest battleships. I felt quite sure in 1939, as previously stated, that the Russians didn't get the plans, legitimately. Now, I am not so sure that they did not manage to get them, in one way or another.

Much of the luncheon conversation in those days was about Amtorg and its tremendous purchasing fund. All the New York industrialists wanted a piece of their business. As far as I know now, the only order they placed publicly was for six small diesel engines which they bought from the Electric Boat Company.

My sojourn in private life was very brief. For one who had long been identified with government, the march of events of late 1939 and 1940 made it inevitable that I should again become involved in public affairs.

While British and French military missions were conferring in Moscow with opposite numbers in the military hierarchy of their Russian partner in the anti-Nazi coalition, the Soviet Government announced on August 21, 1939, that a trade agreement between the German Reich and the Soviets had been concluded and would be followed by a mutual non-aggression pact, which was signed in Moscow on August 24th. With tacit Russian agreement to keep hands off, on September first, Hitler unleashed his terrible blitz-krieg. To the amazement of the Western World, Poland, a nation of 35 million people, was defeated in a month. Cynically, Russia invaded Poland from the east on September 27th, and that poor country was again partitioned. England declared war on Germany and France soon followed suit. World War II had fallen with frightening impact upon our troubled world. Hampered by the Neutrality Act, our Administration, while obviously eager to help Great Britain, declared our neutrality.

President Roosevelt had not yet announced his decision to ig-nore the example of George Washington and seek a third term as President. He knew that the isolation sentiment in our Great Mid-dle West was very strong. Such organizations as the William Allen White Committee "to give all aid to England short of war" and the America-First Committee formed very strong political blocs for which the President had considerable respect. For these and other reasons, the President no doubt felt that he couldn't get the Congress and the country to go along with him on an outright declaration of war to aid Great Britain.

Regardless of how isolationist the country might be, there was no doubt where the President's sympathies lay. In his urgent desire to aid England and France, he instigated policies which directly violated our neutrality. We were committing acts of forthright bel-ligerency in the name of neutrality every day. These unneutral acts of our administration were accomplished by "executive agree-ments without the advice and consent of the Senate." Such was our agreement to exchange for British bases in the Western Hemi-sphere "not through private media" fifty overage but still very serviceable destroyers, an unneutral act in direct violation of in-ternational law.

I was completely in sympathy with the Administration's efforts to help the Allies, but I did not approve of the President's meth-ods. I thought we ought to take our place on the firing line. To me, war appeared inevitable. I was for an all-out war effort against the Nazis at a time of our own choosing—but soon.

While this "destroyer for bases" agreement was under violent discussion on the radio and in the press, I was invited by Mr. Francis Pickens Miller, a prominent citizen of Pickens Hill, Fair-fax, Virginia, to have dinner with a group of his friends who were discussing an important matter on which they would value my advice. I accepted and we gathered for cocktails and dinner one evening in June of 1940 at the Columbia Club in New York. The party consisted of about 20 members, a cosmopolitan and interesting group of influential men from many fields of civilian life. The individuals were all members of the *Special Committee* under the *National Policy Committee* on the *Purpose of the Armed Forces.* In addition to Mr. Francis P. Miller, among the group were such men as Richard F. Cleveland of Baltimore, Maryland; Herbert Agar of the *Courier Journal,* Louisville, Kentucky; Mr. Hanson Baldwin of the *New York Times;* Mr. Raymond Leslie Buell, publisher of *Fortune,* Time and Life Building, New York; Mr. W. L. Clayton of Houston, Texas; Mr. Henry Sloan Coffin of New York City; Mr. Lewis W. Douglas of New York City; Mr. Henry Hobson of Cincinnati, Ohio; Mr. Ernest M. Hopkins, President of Dartmouth College; Mr. Henry R. Luce, publisher of *Time* and *Life;* Mr. Whitney H. Shepardson of New York City; Mr. Henry P. van Dusen, New York City; Major George Fielding Eliot of Brooklyn, New York; and newspaper columnists Robert Allen and Joseph Alsop. Mr. Cleveland was chairman of the National Policy Committee and Mr. Francis P. Miller was vice-chairman of this Committee. Mr. Miller acted as spokesman for the group and after the amenities and a good dinner, it developed that the matter on which they wished my opinion was this: owing to differences in such equipment as guns, torpedoes and machinery, would those fifty overage destroyers be of any material use to the British Navy?

I looked at the distinguished group, considering for a moment, "Of course, gentlemen," I replied. "The British badly need destroyers for escort work. Assuredly, those old destroyers will be of the greatest value to the British Navy. An experienced destroyer crew can adjust itself to the unfamiliar equipment in no time at all. As long as proper munitions, spare parts and supplies are forthcoming, they will be just as effective as their own old destroyers."

The gentlemen about the table nodded in agreement. But they had other things on their minds. "Admiral," one of them said, "we thought you would agree with us on that issue. But now, we have a more serious problem. Considerable unfavorable public reaction has developed. We have been discussing ways and means of bringing the thinking public around to our way of looking at the deal."

The discussion became general. After some argument, the group agreed that the most effective way to get their viewpoint across was with a radio broadcast by a nationally known and respected figure. One of them turned to me, "How about you, Admiral?"

I was considerably taken aback at this suggestion. Not that I objected to going on the air to advocate their viewpoint, because I had had extensive experience in public speaking and radio broadcasting and I believed in their cause. "No, sir," I objected. "Nobody remembers Bill Standley any more. I haven't the prestige and national standing to undertake the job. General Pershing's your man. He's about the only one I know of who can do a first class job for you."

Considerable argument followed, with one and another urging me to undertake the task for them. Finally, it was agreed that General Pershing was their man. They decided to send Messrs. Hugh Douglas and Herbert Agar to Arizona to urge General Pershing to go on the air to support the views of the group on the destroyer deal.

The dinner broke up in pleasant agreement and I thought that my part in the matter was ended. Douglas and Agar returned with General Pershing's promise to broadcast for them but their report of their mission was not reassuring. They had found the great General in a pathetic state of infirmity. At first, he had flatly refused their request. The last time he had broadcast, he told them, it left him a nervous wreck. He had vowed that he would never go on the air again.

Douglas and Agar pleaded with him, pointing out the tremendous importance of awakening America to its peril and making Americans realize on which side their sympathies and their interests lay. "General, we wouldn't try to persuade you further," Agar told him, "but you are the only man who has the national prestige as a military man and a statesman to do the job."

Reluctantly, Pershing undertook the task. I listened to the broadcast. You could tell he was a sick man but he made a noble effort. I thought he gave a very effective presentation of the issues and the need for all-out aid to the Allies.

His broadcast had one very startling effect—it stirred the Isolationist Press to reams of frenzied criticism.

"What does an old General know about destroyers in modern war?"

"Who stirred up our respected national hero to war-mongering?"

"Why did the Anglophiles pick on a retired General to spur Congress to help their British friends?"

Some of the articles were personally critical of General Pershing and his advanced age in an outspoken and vituperative fashion.

Finally, one arch-isolationist paper in the Middle West asked, "If this destroyers for bases deal is such a fine plan, why doesn't one of our distinguished Admirals come out in support of it?"

That question got me right back in the middle. I attended another meeting with the group and was finally persuaded to make a broadcast. "But I have my conditions, gentlemen," I said. I felt it was only fair to warn them, since they would put up the money for the air time on a national hook-up. "I am not in full accord with this idea of turning over unmanned destroyers to the British. We are already in the war, declared or undeclared. We're committing acts of belligerency every day. Turning over these destroyers on the flimsy excuse of a swap for bases is another outright violation of neutrality. I believe that the time has come to take our place on the firing line. Send them destroyers, yes, but send them *all* we have available, fully-manned and ready for action on convoy duty or anywhere else the British Navy wants to use them. If the President and the Secretary of the Navy do not disapprove, that is the kind of broadcast I will make to the country."

Emissaries from the group went to Washington and returned with the assurance that I needed. As I played golf frequently with Frank Knox, the new Republican Secretary of the Navy, I also sounded him out. At 10:15 P.M. on August 10, 1940, from a studio of the Columbia Broadcasting System in New York, I went on the air. Here are some of the things I said:

> On June tenth, with some thirty other American citizens, I signed a statement urging this country to declare immediately that a state of war exists between this country and Nazi Germany. We gave as our reasons that we believed that Nazi Germany is the mortal enemy of our ideals, our institutions, and our way of life; that in the Nazi view the American defense program means that the United States has already joined Great Britain and France in opposing the Nazi drive for world dominion; that if the British Navy be destroyed or captured, if the French Army be defeated, we shall have to face alone our job of defending the Americas from triumphant and power hungry aggressors, operating against us from across both oceans; that what we have, what we are, and what we hope to be can most effectively be defended on the line now held in France by General Weygand.* Therefore, all disposable air, naval, military and material resources of the United

---

* By June of 1940, the Nazis had unleashed their *blitzkrieg* through the Low Countries against France. By June 4, King Leopold had surrendered the Belgian armies and the remnants of British and French armies had been rescued from Dunkirk. General Weygand defended a shaky line across France north of Paris.

States should be made available at once to help maintain our common front. Nationwide endorsement of the defense program shows that the American people have ceased to be neutral in any sense. For that reason alone and irrespective of specific uses of our resources thereafter, the United States should immediately give official recognition to this fact and to the logic of our situation—by declaring that a state of war exists between this country and Germany.

Since June, the situation for our country has become far more serious. Germany has conquered and overrun France and is now literally hammering at the gates of England. Today, the only force that stands between us and German military power is the British fleet.

We are told if the Axis powers are victorious, we are in no danger from a direct attack. The truth is, our trade freedom depends entirely upon British and American sea power. With British sea power in the Nazi hands, let us see what would happen if the dictators decided to wage a war of strangulation, instead of a war of land, sea and air movement, against us.

In the first place, we should soon find that our goods would be driven from the markets of the world. Our trade would diminish. Our standards of living would decline beneath anything we have ever known. The welfare and happiness of every man, woman and child in this country would suffer. If we consented to live under this form of economic tyranny, we would find that the least effort on our part to live in any degree of political or religious liberty would bring down on us the dire specter of starvation or the threat of direct attack upon our weakened country.

In the narrow waters between England and the continent of Europe, large warships cannot operate safely in the face of attack from the air, from underseas, from land batteries on the continent and from speedy torpedo boats. Over that same channel, where passed the rescued from doomed Dunkirk, the invader plans to come. Large ships probably cannot be fought in those waters. The British must depend in a large measure upon destroyers to break up that amphibious assault and to convoy through dangerous submarine waters the merchant ships upon whose cargoes the very life of the British people depends. Their enemy knows this only too well. Bomb and torpedo take a daily toll of British shipping in the Channel.

There may not be enough British destroyers to do this work. And so, the British have asked us for some of ours—only for our old World War I craft, surplusage for our purposes. We are now using some of them in our declared "limited emergency." What emergency can be greater than the one which now calls upon them to engage in active service against this vile enemy of the human race?

And so I say, we should send ships to help the British, to prevent, if possible, the loss of the British Isles and their whole fleet, while we prepare, as best and as fast as we can, to protect ourselves and our friends in our own hemisphere from the attack that we know must come if our friends, the British, cannot hold out. Where then would be the protection of our "splendid isolation" of 3000 miles of the Atlantic Ocean of which our isolationists prate? This is a protection to us only so long as the control of those ocean spaces remains with us or our friends. When that control passes to an enemy, at that moment this ocean becomes a broad highway by which our enemy can approach to throttle and destroy us.

These little ships—and indeed, our American fleet—were built and maintained in readiness to keep the enemy from our shores. In the nature of the emergency which faces us today, I would abort that menace; I would use those ships for the purpose for which they were built.

But, say our critics, the British may need more help, and still more and more. Then, give it to them. All the help we can, without stint or limit. And if the British homelands be lost, open our ports to the ships of their fleet and continue the battle from this side of the Atlantic until final victory is won.

You cannot appease Hitler. You cannot buy security. Who will cash our billion dollar checks? We must have men to operate the machines of war we hope to build; peace-minded as twenty years without war have made us, let us pull ourselves together and call into existence a truly national register of our entire American manhood and throw into the face of any would-be enslaver of mankind the defiance of forty-five million American men, each willing to serve in army, navy, air force or industry, wherever he can best contribute to the salvation of his country and the cause of freedom for all on this earth.

Let us drop all pretensions and subterfuge. Let us stop talking in terms of "limited emergency" when we are really in a state of war.

Let us openly and courageously declare that a state of national emergency exists and give the President full powers to take all necessary measures for the total defense of America, including the mobilization of our entire national strength and whatever disposition may be required of our land, naval and air forces.

Let us have total defense and have it now!

What a magnificent gesture that will be to give pause to these devil men, new hope to our friends who still stand proudly erect before the common enemy, and to those equally our friends who wait with longing hearts for the deliverance for which, under the Providence of God, they shall not wait in vain.

As I read over again this old speech, I think how parallel is the situation we face in the world of today. We went on, in 1940, to a state of national emergency. Our destroyers engaged in running duels with Nazi submarines protecting convoys as far as Iceland in our un-neutral and undeclared war with the Axis. Our ships were hit and sunk, our sailors were killed by our enemy and still we were not at war. In the year and two months that followed that speech, we made frenzied efforts to prepare for the war that appeared ever more and more inevitable—but, when it came on December 7, 1941, we were not ready. Our growing forces at no time constituted a sufficient threat to the Nazis to cause them to turn aside from their avowed purpose of world domination.

Now we are faced with a similar but more menacing threat to our free world and our principles of individual and national freedom. I am glad to see that we have learned something from history. In consort with the other nations united in the United Nations Organization, we have not hesitated to meet aggressive action with military action. We are even now extending the helping hand to our friends in Western Europe and Great Britain as we never did before World War II. And we have made our position crystal clear for all in the world to see what we will do if our friends should again be attacked.

A final incident in this destroyer deal. I was playing golf one Sunday with Secretary Knox. The swap of bases for destroyers had been approved. "Bill, there's one thing in this destroyer transfer that disturbs me," he told me, as we waited on the fourth tee at the Burning Tree Golf Club. "We've made arrangements to deliver the destroyers to the British in Halifax and give the British crews a brief trial run before we turn them over. But how are we going to get the crews home without violating Canadian territory in a very unneutral fashion."

I could see that he was being somewhat facetious but he was half serious, too. "That's easy," I said. "Send 'em up in pairs, one to be turned over, the other to come home with both crews on board."

That was what the Navy finally did. Before long, renamed for cities and towns which had names common to England and America, those fifty little old "four stackers" were performing outstanding duty on convoy escort with the British Fleet.

I Retire Again (Briefly)

These and similar activities presently brought me into difficulties with my associates in the Electric Boat Company. As a burnt child dreads the heat of fire, Henry J. Carse, President of the

Company, feared association with such "war-mongers" as the Miller Group and I. Having once been dubbed a "merchant of death" by the infamous Nye Committee of Congress, he was afraid that my activities might again subject officials of the Company to the same opprobrium. While sympathetic to his position, I felt that a new condition faced the world and that I had to proceed along the course I had taken according to my own conscience and following my own lights. Accordingly, I decided to relieve the Company of its embarrassment, terminate all my civilian activities, and retire to private life—completely, this time.

In anticipation of this move, my wife and I returned to San Diego, California, to the home which my wife had built when I was away at sea back in 1909, when we had a family of four children. With our children now all married and several of them with families of their own, this house was much too large for just us two. We looked about San Diego County and arranged to trade it in on the *Villa Zee Zaw,* situated on an avocado and citrus fruit ranch at La Mesa, a few miles back of San Diego. I had the firmest intentions of spending my remaining active years on our rancho, raising avocados, oranges and grapefruit for the market, a dream that many a Navy man carries with him all through his years of active service.

After my wife and I had moved our possessions into our new home and were well-settled, I returned to New York alone to liquidate my business connections and return to *Zee Zaw* to make a lot of improvements in the property which we had in mind. On February 11, 1941, as I waited in the office of the Electric Boat Company at 40 Wall Street for the scheduled meeting of the Board of Directors, I was somewhat uneasy for I knew that about half the members of the Board did not see eye to eye with President Carse as to my recent activities. I anticipated a rather stormy session.

The others one by one arrived. As we were moving into the Board Room, the chief clerk came up to me. "Admiral, you're wanted on the phone. Long distance from Washington." I excused myself and went to a phone in a private office. It was "Chips" Carpenter, Assistant to the Chief of the Bureau of Navigation, which, at that time, managed the affairs of naval personnel, their procurement, commissioning, orders to sea and shore duty, and so forth. Upon proclamation of the "Limited Emergency" I had volunteered for any duty which the Navy Department might consider appropriate for me.

I was not at all surprised to hear "Chips" Carpenter ask, "Admiral, would you be willing to come down to Washington for active duty as a member of the Planning Board of the Office of Production Management?"

"Why, certainly, 'Chips,' " I replied. "If they need me and want me, they can always have me."

"Can you report to Secretary Knox tomorrow morning at ten?"

"Can do," I said, and with the usual amenities, we both hung up.

As I returned to the Board Room, the Board was already seated about the long table awaiting my return. "Mr. President," I said, standing behind my high-backed chair. "I have information important to this meeting. I have just been recalled to active duty by the Navy and report tomorrow. Of course, I will, with regret, have to resign from the Board."

It was wonderful to see the tension relax with my announcement. As I left the office, I thought, "This must set some kind of a record for a brief retirement to private life."

The Office of Production Management

I was never happy in my association with the Planning Board of that hydra-headed monster set up by the President to manage our Defense Production, with its dual executive, Knudsen-Hillman. At first, the Board was under one of the subordinate departments of the office. After a stiff fight, we managed to get it transferred to the head office of OPM, where it belonged.

Our Board was made up of men who had made a name for themselves in their particular fields of industry, men who had good ideas as to what should be done to get ready for war. But the very name of our organization—the Planning Board—was a misnomer. We should have been making plans for speeding up production to be approved by the head of OPM. We made the plans but the Board's recommendations got nowhere. The head seemed unable to think, let alone to make decisions. How could it, when it was a two-headed monstrosity—Knudsen-Hillman—both men of firm opinions and vigorous ways of expressing them, and they did not get along well at all personally. Time and again, our Planning Board recommended that OPM be reorganized with a single executive director, who would have the necessary authority to make the required decision. But again, FDR compromised. Labor must have its full share in production management in the rearmament program, even if it meant that the program bogged down in a slough of administrative indecision. How could anyone seriously expect prompt and cogent decisions from such a monstrous two-headed executive?

Accustomed as I was to prompt decision and action in the Navy, I felt so strongly on this subject that I made a very critical report to the Chairman of the Planning Board, Mr. Robert E. Doherty of Carnegie Tech. Of course, it got nowhere with our dual-head, but, perhaps, it had something to do with the later reorganization into an effective office with one director, Mr. Donald Nelson.

One day during the Summer of 1941, a copy of a letter written to the Secretary of the Navy by Congressman Carl Vinson, Chairman of the House Naval Affairs Committee, came to my desk in OPM. The Secretary was asked for a report on the activities of all retired officers, any reports they had made, any articles they had written, and what salaries they had received. This request was passed on to me to supply information as to my activities.

Together with my letter answering specific questions, I enclosed a copy of my stinging report on the organization of OPM. In this report, I cited specific instances where lack of decision by OPM as to use of critical materials had seriously hampered industry in its defense production efforts. I forwarded my letter to Secretary Knox through my Board Chairman and the double-headed executive at the top of OPM. Every effort of persuasion and intimidation was made to have me withdraw the report as an enclosure to my letter but I stood pat. My position was: my letter had been written at the request of the Secretary of the Navy, who was my boss; it was his letter and what he did with it was none of my business; the report on OPM had been prepared by me; and the matter was now out of my hands.

Later on, I checked up. My letter with the enclosed report did go to Congressman Vinson and eventually appeared before the Truman Investigating Committee. I feel very sure that report, pigeonholed by the hydra-head of OPM, caused the removal of Knudsen and Hillman and the appointment of Don Nelson as the Director of that Organization.

CHAPTER IV

The Beaverbrook-Harriman Mission
to Moscow

DURING my eight months with OPM, I frequently played golf with Secretary of the Navy Knox and Assistant Secretary John Sullivan. They were well aware of my unhappy situation in OPM. Early in September, 1941, Admiral Stark, Chief of Naval Operations, called me on the phone. "Bill," he said, "How'd you like to go to Moscow for a short visit?"

I had heard rumors about the Beaverbrook-Harriman Mission to Moscow in connection with Lend-Lease to the Soviets. "In what capacity?" I asked.

"American Naval Representative with the Beaverbrook-Harriman Mission."

"Fine with me," I replied. "On one condition. Get me out of this mess in OPM—permanently."

He chuckled and agreed. A few days later, I received orders from the Secretary of the Navy informing me that I had been "appointed by the President a member of a Special Mission to the U.S.S.R., with the personal rank of Minister," and that I was "hereby detached from my present duties and would proceed and carry out such orders in connection with this mission as may be directed by the President of the United States." Such shore duty beyond the seas, I was informed, was required by the public interest.

Two incidents will illustrate the devious workings of the Russian mind. A Navy flying boat, the flag plane of one of our Naval Air Commanders, had been put at the disposal of the Mission for the trip to London. It was so beautifully equipped for our purposes that I immediately conceived of the idea of using it for the rest of the trip from London to Moscow. This, of course, required

61

clearance with the Soviet Government and a lake of sufficient depth and obstacle-free run to land the plane somewhere in the vicinity of Moscow.

In order to confirm information shown on maps which the Navy had, I made an appointment with Russian Ambassador Ouman-sky, who was planning to accompany us on the trip to Moscow. Oumansky assured me that a lake shown on our map on the out-skirts of Moscow actually existed and had ample depth of water and area for landing the big flying boat. Fortunately, we decided not to take the Navy plane on to Moscow. During my stay there as Ambassador, I frequently rode all over that "lake area"—in an automobile. It never had been a lake.

Some time later, a friend of mine asked Maxim Litvinov, who was then Russian Ambassador to Washington, "What about golf? Admiral Standley's quite a golf enthusiast. Will he be able to play in Moscow?"

The word came back to me that Mr. Litvinov said, without any hesitation, "Oh, yes, there are many golf courses in the vicinity of Moscow."

Mr. Litvinov must have known that there was not and never had been a golf course anywhere near Moscow.

We proceeded in the Navy flying boat via our new naval base at Argentia, Newfoundland, and the British base at Stranraer, Scotland, to London. Enroute, I discovered that I was a member of the Mission only because Mr. Averell Harriman, who was then Expediter of Lend-Lease to Great Britain in London with the rank of Minister, had insisted that I be relieved of other duty and sent along. I have him to thank for getting me out of OPM, a tre-mendous debt, which I am happy to acknowledge.

The other members of the American Mission who traveled with me and in two Army B-24's were Mr. Averell Harriman, Mr. Wil-liam L. Batt of OPM, Major General James H. Burns, Harry Hop-kins' Executive Officer in the Lend-Lease Administration, and Colonel Phillip R. Faymonville, who acted as Secretary of the Joint Mission. In London, we were joined by Major General James E. Chaney, then the ranking American Army Air Corps officer in London. We also met our British opposite numbers: Lord Beaver-brook, Minister of Production, Mr. Harold Balfour, Under Secre-tary of State for Air, Sir Archibald Rowlands, Sir Charles Wilson, General Sir Hastings Ismay, Chief of the Imperial General Staff, and General G. N. Macready, his Assistant.

For several days, the members of the Mission gathered around the conference table for discussion and preparation. Our discussions left no doubt as to our Mission. We were to do everything within the power of our two nations to keep the Russians fighting until Spring, when, rather optimistically, we hoped the Allied potential power could be applied in sufficient strength to draw off some of the pressure on the Soviets. In Mr. Harriman's words, "Give and give and give, with no expectation of any return, with no thought of a *quid pro quo*."

I was rather uneasy about the trip via cruiser to Archangel, an uneasiness that was shared by the senior members of the Mission, for none of us could forget that, in World War I, Lord Kitchener was killed when a German U-boat torpedoed a British cruiser enroute to Archangel. Had I been a free agent, I would have much preferred to travel with the junior members of the Mission directly across areas controlled by the Luftwaffe in two Air Corps bombers piloted by Major A. L. Harvey and Lieutenant L. T. Reichers, who made a truly remarkable flight at very high altitudes all the way to Moscow. But I would have missed considerable excitement and not a few thrills.

We embarked in the British heavy cruiser HMS "London" at Scapa Flow, both British and American members being assigned to the Admiral's suite. On the seven-day trip, we got to know our opposite numbers quite well. The weather was so foul that we saw but little of the coastlines we followed. Not a few of the civilians were desperately seasick. Finally, the weather cleared. On the morning of September 27th, I turned out on deck to see the rocky, inhospitable shore of Arctic Russia, the low hills already topped with crests of snow. We anchored behind the bar at Archangel at a few minutes before ten.

A very smart-looking Russian destroyer, expertly handled, came alongside the "London," and Russian Rear Admiral Delinen came on board, paid his respects to the Captain and then to the heads of the Mission. His interpreter informed us that he came to extend the greetings of the Soviet Government and to put the destroyer at our service for the long trip to the inner harbor.

About 2 P.M., we boarded the destroyer. The crew was smartly paraded at Quarters. At Admiral Delinen's request, Lord Beaverbrook and Mr. Harriman inspected the crew. After this inspection, representatives of the Commissars of Foreign Affairs, and of the Army and Navy paid their respects to the chairmen of the Mission.

Inside, the destroyer didn't look so very smart. It had been raining but this did not account for greasy decks, dirty paintwork and other standards of cleanliness far below those of our Navy. Built at Leningrad, she carried no multiple-barreled anti-aircraft machine guns such as our 40-millimeter. I judged her to be about on a par with our World War I four-stackers.

After an hour's trip up the river past Archangel, we transferred to a flat-bottomed, paddle-wheel ferry boat, where we were given the first of a number of Russian meals, each as lavish as a banquet. Food and drink in the greatest variety and profusion was heaped on the tables. Some delicious fruit and wine had been sent all the way from the Caucasus especially for this meal.

Some of us spent the night on the Admiral's yacht, which was specially equipped for such duty, and the rest on the ferry boat, moored to a wharf adjacent to the Archangel airport. After a hearty breakfast, much photographing and lots of palaver through interpreters, the Russian Admiral and his covey of aides took us to the airport. One of the interpreters was a very striking-looking woman wearing the uniform of a Navy junior grade lieutenant. All of the interpreters spoke good English with the heavy accent of the Russian. It was obvious to all of us that a special effort was being made to make us feel welcome in the Soviet Union just at that time.

In those days, little factual information leaked out about the fighting in Russia. The Germans made extravagant claims. The Russians said almost nothing for outside distribution. As we flew from Archangel to Moscow in four rather ancient-looking Russian-built transports of the Douglas DC-3 type, we had no idea what to expect in the way of German air opposition. For a while, I watched uneasily as four Russian two-engined fighters led the way, skimming low over the trees which covered the flat countryside.

The transport flew just under a heavy overcast not more than a few feet above the treetops, it seemed to me. Apparently this was common practice, for the Russians with us seemed to think nothing of it. I guessed that they followed such a flight plan because in Russia they do not have air communication facilities, radio beacons, and control towers and procedures at all comparable to ours. While skillful in handling their planes the pilots are negligent of the usual safety measures, never stopping at the head of the runway to make final checks or rev-up the engines. They seemed very careless as to position; on two occasions, we wandered into forbidden zones and ground anti-aircraft guns opened up on us. Most of their fields are narrow strips constructed to take advantage of average wind conditions. The pilots must consider it cowardly to circle the field; they dive for the nearest end of the field; landing up-wind or down-wind made little difference to them. And any sort of regular maintenance routine is obviously foreign to the Russian character; they fly 'em till they crack-up!

We cruised at altitudes between 350 and 500 feet over wide areas of dense green forests, with occasional clearings, lumber camps, and logging roads. This forest gradually gave way to open country where a few small herds of cattle grazed and some cultivation was noted. All along the way, there was evidence of considerable construction of new waterways, with much industrial activity and extensive housing developments as we neared Moscow. After a little more than four hours, we circled slowly above an immense airfield from which position we could see in the distance the crenelated spires and bulbous domes of Moscow. I looked at my watch as our wheels touched the paved runway—1:10 P.M., September 28, 1941.

All of the Russian Mission, with whom we were to confer, turned out on the cold, wind-swept airfield to meet us. I recognized Foreign Minister Molotov and Mr. Oumansky. There were many other Russian dignitaries and both British and American Ambassadors and their staffs. Press representatives and news photographers were out in full force.

At a flag staff topped with three separate prongs flew, at the same height, the flags of our three nations, the Red Star of Russia in the center with the British on the right and Old Glory, looking strangely lonely under the circumstances, on the left.

A snappy band and guard paraded. The band played the three national airs. After a short salutation in Russian, which was not translated, the Guard presented arms. As the heads of our Missions approached, the Commander of the Guard made a speech of welcome and the members of the Guard indicated approval of his speech with one word uttered in unison—"*Da.*" I was later told that this was the first time since the October Revolution, within the memory of anyone present, that such honors had been accorded a visiting foreign delegation. My, but they were out to please and impress us. And we had orders to "give and give and give!"

Our arrival ushered in the first snowfall of that terrible Russian Winter of 1941–42. We were driven to our quarters in Moscow.

On the evening of Sunday, September 28th, Mr. Harriman and Lord Beaverbrook met Stalin in the Kremlin. At 1 P.M. on the 29th, we went to our first plenary session; committees on Army, Navy, Air Force, raw materials, transportation, and medical supplies were formed; we attended another sumptuous luncheon-banquet; committees met, organized, and planned procedure, but we accomplished no real work.

On the morning of the 29th, meeting Mr. Harriman in Spaso House (the American Embassy), I asked him how the meeting with Mr. Stalin had gone. He was enthusiastic. "Beaverbrook and I considered the meeting extremely friendly," he told me. "We were more than pleased with our reception. The meeting lasted over three hours."

It was not for ten years that I learned what went on at those Kremlin meetings. Mr. Stalin was very cordial as he opened the meeting by giving them an extremely frank discussion of the Russian military situation. Germany had a superiority in the air of 3–2, in tanks 4–1, in infantry divisions 320–280. The Russian dictator went into detail as to supplies required, listing them in order of priority as tanks, anti-tank guns, bombers, anti-aircraft guns, armor plate, fighter and reconnaissance planes, and barbed wire.

Even at this early meeting, Mr. Stalin brought up the question of drawing off Nazi power from the Russian Front by opening up a Second Front in Europe. He asked the British to send forces to help the Russians fight the Germans in the Ukraine.

Mr. Harriman took up the matter of delivering American combat aircraft via the Alaskan-Siberian air route, a subject which was to cause me considerable difficulty later. At first, Mr. Stalin seemed to regard the project favorably, but when Mr. Harriman suggested delivering the planes with American crews, Mr. Stalin decided that the route was too hazardous. Mr. Harriman also brought up President Roosevelt's concern about religion in Russia, mentioning the adverse effect on American public opinion of the anti-religious attitude which was attributed to the Russian Communist Party. Mr. Stalin brushed his question aside, brusquely remarking, "American public opinion doesn't concern me so very much."

The heads of Mission parted from Mr. Stalin in an atmosphere of good will and cordiality which left them jubilant. They told me that afternoon of the 29th that, if our Mission had been ready with the staff work, they believed that Stalin would have signed an agreement—any agreement—then and there.

What with banquets, late hours, and early rising to work all day with our committees, we on the working level were having our troubles, too. One of my colleagues described our committee meetings as exercises in frustration. Certaintly, the Naval Committee, which I headed for the American delegation, could get nowhere at all. We made various proposals for a program of naval supplies but Admiral Nikolai Kuznetsov, Commissar for the Navy and my opposite number in the Russian delegation, wouldn't even comment. I never felt that this indicated a lack of desire to cooperate as much as a lack of information and indecision. If we had had specific weapons and supplies to offer, the Russians *might* have told us where they were to go. Admiral Kuznetsov had the further disadvantage that he was also charged with defense of the Coastal Area and he probably just couldn't say where the items intended for shore stations would be used.

Such were my views, then. Now, I'm not at all certain that the Russian Navy men weren't just evading the issue. As usual in Soviet Russia, nothing of real importance could be decided below the highest level of government. Certainly, we gave away a vast amount of naval supplies in those three days. But we had been instructed to ask for no *quid pro quo*. The only exchange of information we received was due to the personal influence of Admiral Kuznetsov; we took home with us Russian Hydrographic Codes which our Naval Attachés had been vainly trying to obtain for months.

By the morning of the 30th, our heads of Mission were in what might best be described as a mood of indigo blue. Mr. Stalin had not been at all cordial. The Russian Premier was restless the night before, pacing the Kremlin conference room continuously, smoking one cigarette after another, and giving other evidence of severe strain. When Lord Beaverbrook and Mr. Harriman presented letters from Mr. Churchill and President Roosevelt, he glanced at them and tossed them on the table.

During the long presentation of items of arms, munitions, raw materials, and other supplies available, he expressed the strongest dissatisfaction with what we had to give, showing enthusiasm only once when Mr. Harriman offered 5000 jeeps.

Lord Beaverbrook and Mr. Harriman left this middle-of-the-night conference very depressed. On the evening of the 30th, Nazi propagandists filled the air lanes with the news that the conference in Moscow had broken down, that the American and British delegations could never reach a working arrangement with the

Bolsheviks. To us, it seemed as if for once Herr Goebbels might be telling the truth.

The meeting in the Kremlin the night of the 30th was vastly different. Stalin said, "It is up to the three of us to prove Goebbels a liar." When Lord Beaverbrook presented his memorandum listing everything that the Russians had asked for and stating those items which could be delivered immediately and in full and giving also those items which could not be delivered or on which delivery would have to be delayed, Mr. Stalin received the memorandum with enthusiasm.

During this meeting, Stalin again stressed his need for transport, for American jeeps and trucks. "Winning this war depends on the gasoline engine," he said. "The country which can produce the greatest number of gasoline engines will be the victor." He brought up again the matter of postwar aims and wanted to discuss politics, but Lord Beaverbrook again put him off.

Mr. Harriman tried again and again to bring the discussion around to Pacific affairs in order to obtain Stalin's view on the situation in the Far East, but without success. It was at this conference that Mr. Harriman urged Mr. Stalin to communicate directly with President Roosevelt, an arrangement that was to cause me untold trouble.

As the two hours of the meeting passed, the conference reflected the highest degree of satisfaction and pleasure on both sides. The conversation became more and more friendly and even intimate. When the Russian Premier had tea and food brought in, the conference took on the atmosphere of a love feast. Mr. Stalin parted with the heads of Mission that evening by inviting them to have dinner with him the next evening.

The following morning, Mr. Harriman called the American delegation together and informed us that an agreement had been reached with Premier Stalin. I was astonished when he said, "Get busy and turn in your reports at once. You will have only three or four more days." At that point in our low-level negotiations, none of our committees had more than scratched the surface of the possibilities of extending Lend-Lease aid.

Of this last meeting, Mr. Harriman wrote in his report:

> The meeting broke up in the most friendly fashion possible. Stalin made no effort to conceal his enthusiasm. It was my impression that he was completely satisfied that Great Britain and America meant

business. In spite of my lack of knowledge of the language he had indicated by his manner throughout the three nights of conferences (totaling about nine hours) very clearly his reactions to everything we said, either favorable or unfavorable or that he was not interested.

I left feeling that he had been frank with us and if we came through as had been promised and if personal relations were retained with Stalin, the suspicion that has existed between the Soviet Government and our two governments might well be eradicated.

There can be no doubt that Stalin is the only man to deal with in foreign affairs. Dealing with others without previous instruction from Stalin about matters under discussion was a waste of time.

In the midst of a losing war, needing aid of any and all kinds, the Russians seemed very anxious to close up the Conference and get rid of us. I couldn't understand it. There wasn't much evidence of the war in Moscow. Every night, we heard considerable gunfire, but we never heard or felt a bomb explode. I found myself wondering—was this gunfire employed to impress us, or, like the Chinese, to make a big noise to bolster the Russian courage? When I asked about the gunfire, the Russians explained the absence of German bombers and bombs falling on Moscow by the efficiency of this anti-aircraft defense.

At 3 P.M. October first, we attended our second plenary session, Mr. Molotov presiding. He arose and announced a full agreement among our three delegations. The First Confidential Protocol between the United States and Great Britain and the Soviet Union was signed and sealed by Mr. Harriman, Lord Beaverbrook, and Mr. Molotov.

The Protocol included more than seventy main items and eighty medical items—everything from planes, tanks and destroyers to army boots and socks and paint products. The final agreement a few weeks later, which made the "lease" in Lend-Lease look like it meant what it said, specified that, in this First Protocol, shipments up to the value of one billion dollars would be financed under Lend-Lease, that no interest would be charged on this indebtedness, and that payments on this principal would begin five years after the war and continue for ten years. President Roosevelt, in one of his person-to-person cables, also asked Mr. Stalin to make special efforts to facilitate the *purchase* in the Soviet Union of such raw materials and commodities available as the United States urgently needed.

The signing of the Protocol ended the business of the meeting.

Attendants broke out champagne and toasts were drunk and extravagantly laudatory speeches were made.

At every opportunity, I took occasion to look about the big old city. It was obvious that extensive construction work was underway. Several lines of the subway had been completed. Although the Germans were approaching Moscow, these projects were still active. Streets were being widened; houses moved or rebuilt; huge apartment houses and public buildings were going up along the main thoroughfares; concrete seawalls were being constructed along the Moscow River. It was difficult to slip unobserved into the back streets of Moscow, but I did. There, I found a great difference—all the filth and squalor of the slums of any great city.

For such large squares and wide streets, there were very few people in Moscow. Perhaps, they had already evacuated some of the working population to plants in the Urals. The people that I saw seemed to be strangely out of place in the capital city of a great country. They were dressed warmly enough but in plain clothing such as laborers wear in America. Most of them had overcoats and gloves. Many women wore two pairs of cheap cotton stockings. These people we saw on the streets were clearly of the laboring class which the Bolsheviks call the Proletariat. With a generally blank expression on their faces, they reminded me of the dumb cattle on my grandfather's farm back in California—intent on living but not understanding why. They would duck out of the way of our honking official Soviet limousine, barely miss being run down, and look around at the uniformed driver without the slightest expression of rancor. With the streets dark except for a few shaded traffic lights, pedestrians reminded me of frightened rabbits hopping across a road to keep from being run down. Even the traffic policemen had to jump to dodge a speeding government car.

These people I saw in the streets were poles apart from the government officials we met in our daily conferences and at the endless banquets and parties. In fact, I immediately sensed a wide gulf between the two classes in that "classless society." It is a gap which is filled in America by our great middle class to which there is no counterpart in Russia. I seemed to sense, in the absence of a middle class, an answer for many of the strange actions of the "upper class" of government and Party officials. Perhaps they are uncertain and suspicious because they do not have the support and stabilizing influence of a middle class. And perhaps, eventually, there will emerge from the present Russian proletariat an effective middle class of petty officials, foremen and white-collar workers. I think this will be certain to come, eventually, in Russia, but it will take time—much time.

One afternoon, I was taken by Admiral Kuznetsov for a visit to Moscow Aircraft Factory No. 1. The thousands of employees I saw at work there left me with the distinct impression that here was the beginning of the New Russia. Raw materials of every kind flowed into the shop and came out as complete and effective fighter aircraft. Boys and girls, some as young as 15, worked as apprentices. Young men and women turned out finished parts on lathes with efficiency and dispatch. The foremen were vigorous, active young men who seemed quite capable of handling their jobs. While it was actively engaged in accelerated, top-priority war production, this factory was at the same time taking in green hands (raw material) and turning out competent mechanics and technicians.

I saw no old men in the factory and only a few elderly women. By our standards, the shops were crowded and badly lighted but only one workman wore glasses. The laborers worked in three shifts, 24 hours a day, six days a week. They had Sunday off, but many of them came back to the shop on Sunday to work without pay. They had a slogan—*Every tap of the hammer means more planes for the men at the front.* From the detailed work I saw in the shops, the raw materials waiting in cars on the sidings, and planes in all stages of completion on the assembly lines, I felt quite certain that this was not a "show factory" to impress us, but a war production plant engaged in the serious business of making aircraft for the Red Air Force.

The workmen I saw in this plant had a different appearance from people on the streets of Moscow. Better housed and fed, they had the confident air of competent craftsmen everywhere. They knew what they were doing and they could see the results of their labor. They seemed interested in their work and intent on increasing production to help the men fighting at the front.

Toward the end of our visit, I inquired of a bright looking young man, "What would they do with this factory, if Moscow fell?"

"Moscow will not fall," he replied.

When I pressed the question, he said, "Plans are already made to move this factory, with its lathes, machine tools, workmen, material, housing and provisions, back into the interior."

There was every evidence around Moscow that, emulating the

Chinese, some factories had already been transferred to the interior. The reply of the foreman convinced me of his truthfulness.

In all our contacts with government and Party officials, they tried to impress us with a show of splendor and grandeur as fabulous as pre-Communist Russia, rather than with the advantages of life of the common man under the Dictatorship of the Proletariat and a socialistic economic system. During our stay in Russia, every event, even the inspection of the factory, was the occasion for an elaborate spread of food and drink. For those who managed the State, there was an abundance of everything—sugar, butter, meat, game, caviar, fish of all kinds, both smoked and raw, delicious fresh fruit, cucumbers which they ate raw like an apple; bread, cake and all sorts of sweets were spread upon the groaning boards with the utmost profusion. Even at the opera! Between acts, we were expected to indulge freely in food and drink as part of our official government entertainment. This show of Communist pomp and ceremony reminded me of similar lavish spreads in Vladivostok and aboard the Russian flagship in Vladivostok Harbor under the last of the Czars. If we could judge by the lavish staging of the opera, the splendor of the ballet and the enthusiasm of the audience, especially in the stalls, the Russian people of both classes still loved the magnificence of an earlier day.

Upon completion of the labors of any mission or conference, diplomatic custom calls for an audience with the ruling potentate and a banquet in honor of the visiting dignitaries. We were not to be disappointed by the Communist ruler of Soviet Russia.

The banquet which Mr. Stalin gave in the Kremlin was the high point of our visit to Moscow. Dinner was "laid on," as our British colleagues would have it, for 6 P.M. A special convoy of cars, in close column and distinctively marked, took us through the heavily guarded gates of the Kremlin. Persons embarked in each car were identified by the chauffeur—a member of the secret police. Through the gathering dusk, we could see but little of the richness of the old palace, for the parks and grounds and even some of the smaller buildings, I suspect, were covered with camouflage canvas, painted to represent buildings similar to those in the neighborhood outside the Kremlin walls.

Servants—called "Special Attendants" in Soviet gobble-de-gook —ushered us through the Entrance Hall and the Hall of Deputies into the reception rooms, where we were to await the presence of Marshal Stalin. The interior of the palace was well preserved and certainly as elaborately furnished as in the days of the Czars. The guests included all members of the Politburo, high ranking officers of the Russian Army and Navy, and other principal Soviet officials; the Ambassador of Great Britain, our Ambassador Laurence Steinhardt, and members of their staffs; members of our Mission, Ambassador Oumansky, who acted as our interpreter in our talk with Stalin, a few foreign and Russian newspaper men, two American bomber pilots who had flown some members of our Mission from London to Moscow, and several British and American residents of Moscow. After all guests had assembled, Stalin came into the room through huge doors at one end and moved around the room, shaking hands with each guest and welcoming him.*

Marshal Joseph Stalin seemed to me to be a pleasant and simple man, short and slightly stooped, and even then beginning to show his age. While he lacked color in his cheeks, he appeared to be in excellent health and spirits. He was dressed in an extremely simple uniform, which looked a good bit like an ordinary Russian laborer's costume, but was made of excellent material and was expertly tailored to fit him well. He had a slight squint, which gave him a sleepy look, but behind his sleepy appearance, during the evening, I discovered a discerning and piercing eye.

After Stalin had greeted his guests, we moved into the banquet hall—the magnificent Catherine-the-Great Room—about thirty feet wide and a hundred feet long, finished in white marble. Three large columns down the center of the room and panels in the corners of the room were decorated with vertical strips that looked like green jade. Immense chandeliers of clouded glass and gold hung from the ceiling at the center of each end of the hall. Around the walls, clusters of lights with shades of clouded glass and gold contributed a note of splendor.

At a table on a raised dais along one side of the room, Stalin sat with the chairmen of the Mission, the Ambassadors, and other members of the Mission on his right and left. Other tables seating twelve each were laid perpendicular to the table on the dais on the opposite side of the room.

Marshal Stalin made a speech of welcome which an interpreter translated as he paused. It was a magnificent banquet, served by "Special Attendants" in a very efficient manner, but we jumped

* I understand that this custom came down from court procedure in Czarist days.

up so often in response to a toast to someone or other that I did but poor justice to the repast. I counted a total of 31 toasts during the evening. Late in the dinner, Stalin had our two bomber pilots brought to the center of the room before him and he proposed a special toast to them. Then, Stalin arose and personally extended them his felicitations.

After dinner, Stalin withdrew for a few moments and then rejoined us in an ante-room for coffee and liqueurs. He moved among his guests, conversing first with one and then another, discussing with them various problems of our Mission and of the war with the Nazis. He seemed to be extremely well informed on the affairs of our countries, particularly of Great Britain. He was very free and frank in the advice he gave to Lord Beaverbrook. "If the British Empire is to survive," he said, "it must become a land power as well as a sea power."

When we finished our coffee, we were conducted to a projection room where we were shown a Russian propaganda film glorifying Russian military might, which we were told had been made three years before, but which I had seen in Washington in 1935. Then, we saw a Russian musical film, which was quite good and which I enjoyed, despite the language difficulty. Silent attendants, moving expertly through the dark room, kept our champagne glasses full.

In the ante-room after the movies, Lord Beaverbrook and Mr. Harriman took their leave of Stalin. The Marshal then moved about the room, telling us all good-bye, and retired. As I walked down the long Kremlin corridors with the Counselor of our Embassy, he told me that this was the first time such an elaborate ceremony had been staged in the Kremlin since the Bolshevik Revolution.

It was three A.M. when I turned in at Spaso House, and I was up all too early for my last meeting with Admiral Kuznetsov at which we managed to give him a few thousand more items. That morning, Mr. Harriman received a cable from President Roosevelt.

I want to express to you and your associates the great satisfaction I have with the successful culmination of your mission in Moscow. I think that you all did a magnificent job.

The afternoon of October 2nd was spent in making diplomatic calls and visits of farewell. It was that afternoon that I ran into Colonel Faymonville, our Mission Secretary and one of Harry

Hopkins' Lend-Lease boys, in Spaso House. "When are we leaving?" I asked.

"The rest of you are leaving the fifth," he replied. "But I am staying on."

That was how the news was broken to me that Faymonville would remain as our Government's direct representative in Moscow for Lend-Lease aid. I expressed some polite word of congratulation and hurried back to my work. I understand that Faymonville was left in Moscow at Harry Hopkins' urgent request. Spot-promoted to brigadier general, he was still in Moscow in that capacity when I returned to the Russian capital.

On October third, we worked on our reports. Some Mission members went on sight-seeing trips. That evening at the American Embassy, Ambassador Laurence Steinhardt gave a dinner to return the hospitality which had been extended to us. This dinner and the ensuing party lasted far into the morning of October 4th. And we were scheduled for takeoff from the Moscow airport at nine! I had hardly turned over to compose myself to sleep before an orderly came for my baggage.

As I drove to the airport with our acting Naval Attaché, Commander "Ronnie" Allen, I took the opportunity to ask him how he liked duty in Moscow.

"It's very interesting, Admiral," he replied, diplomatically.

"Come, now," I said. "Of course, it's interesting. But is it fun?"

He shook his head slowly. "Not much. Our families all had to be evacuated. It's worth the life of a Russian to get chummy with foreign embassy personnel; so we do the best we can in our tight little circle of foreign diplomatic and press representatives. Not even any outdoor sports to which we are accustomed. If you go hunting, you're as apt to bag an OGPU agent as a deer. It's pretty lonesome and dull."

Five months later, I was to recall this conversation, word for word.

At the airport, we stepped out into a 60-knot wind howling across the runways from the northwest. I wondered why we were going to take off in such vile flying weather. It seemed unnecessarily hazardous. Three Russian transports taxied up. The same honors and ceremonies piped us aboard and we took off into the teeth of the gale, leaving the ground after a run that was not more than a hundred yards. The air was incredibly rough, the plane falling off on one wing, righting, and taking sickening drops in down drafts. Everyone was violently airsick for the whole passage to Archangel. Later, we learned that on October 2nd, the Nazi armies had started their "last drive" to capture Moscow. Doubtless considering a hasty evacuation of Moscow, Mr. Stalin didn't want our Mission captured in Moscow or shot down on the way out.

We arrived at Archangel about 2:30 P.M., much battered in body and depressed in spirit, a condition that was not improved by the icy blasts which met us as we disembarked from the planes. Back aboard the Admiral's yacht and the ferry boat, another sumptuous meal was spread before us, for which we had little appetite.

We embarked in the Admiral's barge and rode out to the mine sweeper "Harrier," which took us on to the "London." Admiral Delinen and his staff and the personal representatives of the Commissars of Foreign Affairs, War and Navy stayed with us, courteous and attentive to the very last. Despite high winds and tumultuous seas we safely boarded the "London." At 9:30 P.M., Saturday, October 4th, we passed out of the territorial waters of the U.S.S.R. I felt an unaccountable lifting of spirits, which was certainly not brought about by the peculiar "rolling and pitching we care about, and the foam on the crest of the wave," in which the beautiful old "London" was embroiled. No, I was quite simply and fervently thankful that I was a free American, a citizen of a free country, where the proper consideration is given to the rights and privileges of the individual man.

In London, we went into a huddle with our British co-delegates to examine our commitments in the light of the agreements reached at Moscow. We went to Moscow, not knowing what we had to give that they might want, and ended by promising them everything they asked. Now, we had to make an effort to coordinate the giving between the British and ourselves. It was a problem that, so far as I know, was never solved to the complete satisfaction of any country or individual concerned—but Uncle Sam gave—and gave and gave—oh, how he gave!

We returned to the United States in a Navy flying boat, stopping at Horta, Fayal, the Azores and New York. When we arrived at the Washington National Airport about noon, October 18, 1941, the Beaverbrook-Harriman Mission passed into history. We had started the flow of supplies, which would become a flood of Lend-Lease aid to Russia, the extent and effects of which would be most surprising, and, in the end, would extend into fields and would continue in time far beyond the expectation of those original negotiators. We had been ordered to "give and give" and we had carried out those orders with efficiency and despatch, but little did we know, in those Fall days of 1941, that a few years later we would also be "taken" by the Russians without even a "Thank you" by way of return.

For that, from all the government officials, civil and military, up and down the line, we received the Navy's traditional message of congratulation after accomplishment—"Well done."

CHAPTER V

The Pearl Harbor Débacle

As the end of the year 1941 came to our troubled planet, I was serving on active duty in the Navy Department Office of Public Relations, with the interesting but rather exhausting job of presenting Navy "E" (for efficiency) pennants to industrial plants which had done a good job in producing war materials for our rearmament and for the supply of our undeclared allies in the fight against Nazi tyranny. I was run-down, half-sick, and over-fatigued and I had been long away from my family and so I asked for and was granted a month's leave over the Christmas Holidays. I returned to my home and family early in December.

On December 6th, as the guest of my old friend, Mahlon Vail, I went up to Temecula Rancho, in Riverside County near Temecula, for some quail shooting. I remember sitting around the open fire in the big stone fireplace of the ranch house that evening, discussing ways and means of getting to certain choice hunting grounds the next morning. The shortest route led through some marshes but would take an hour less than the longer road over higher ground. The young cowboys of the ranch argued in favor of the high ground. "That marsh area is too soft this time of year, Mr. Vail," they told the Boss.

Mahlon pooh-poohed their contentions. "I know the way through those marshes, young fellow. I'll take us through." As usual, the Boss won.

We were up and had breakfast before daylight the morning of December 7th. Dawn was just breaking over the eastern mountains as we set out in caravan the short way, Mahlon leading in his light car. We could hear him singing loudly and quite off key as he drove gayly along the twin paths across the pastureland which made a very bumpy road. His song was short and not sweet. I saw his car plunge into the reeds at the edge of the marsh area.

Almost immediately, it was hopelessly mired—the wheels at the edge of the marsh area spinning in the soft mud without any traction whatsoever.

The other car in the party was mine—a "U-Drive-It" I had hired in San Diego. Neither car had shovels or tow wire. Mahlon said, "Let me take your car, Admiral. I'll go back to the house for a truck. You hunters will have to walk. On your way, then and good hunting."

We shouldered our shotguns and game bags and slopped through the marsh on foot. The shooting was the kind you dream about. In due course, we had our limits and started back. As we rounded a low hill, we saw the mired car in the marsh but no relief expedition. When we reached Mahlon's car, we saw the ranch truck and my hired car coming up the road.

Before they ever reached us, I seemed to feel something unusual in the air. When the car and truck reached us, Mahlon and five cow hands silently climbed down. No word of greeting—just silence. I sensed a tragedy of some sort. Still without a sound, they surrounded me and began a weird war dance, with Indian war-whoops and capers. Still, I was mystified, wondering if they had suddenly taken to loco weed.

After a couple of minutes, they stopped their foolishness and Mahlon, with appropriate solemnity, told us that the Japs had struck the Pacific Fleet at Pearl Harbor in a sneak attack without a declaration of war. Thus was the news broken to me, almost twenty-four years after our entry into World War I, that our country was at last embarked in a truly world-wide war, not the war to contain Nazi aggression for which I had been pressing. I shall never forget the clutching at my throat and heart and the momentary fear I felt, for I knew how desperately unready we were for any kind of a war in the Pacific.

"The Fleet!" I cried. "Did they catch the Fleet in Pearl Harbor?"

Mahlon nodded slowly. "I don't know how bad it is, Admiral. The radio said the attack was continuing. The ships and docks are a mass of wreckage and a pall of smoke hundreds of feet high hangs over Pearl Harbor."

Back home, I sent a telegram to the Navy Department, stating that I was ready for any kind of active duty anywhere. For ten days, we stayed glued to the radio, tensely reading the scant war news in the papers, while the Japanese bombed Manila, Baguio and Cavite Navy Yard, landed in Malaysia, shelled the California coast from a submarine, invested Wake Island and sank the "Prince of Wales" and "Repulse" north of Singapore. It was an agonizing period of frustrating inaction.

At ten A.M. on December 17th, I received a telegram from the Navy Department to "proceed immediately" priority one, and report to the Secretary of the Navy at ten A.M. the next morning in Washington, D. C. I caught the eleven P.M. plane out of Lindberg Field, transferred at Pittsburgh, springing priority to "bump" another passenger, whom I have recently learned was a Mr. Jesse Hough, at present Manager of the San Diego Transportation Company, and reported to Secretary Frank Knox as ordered.

"Well, Admiral," he said, "we're in a mess and, as always, we need your help."

He told me briefly about the Presidential Commission headed by Associate Justice Owen J. Roberts, about which I had, until then, seen nothing in the Press. "That's your first job, Admiral. Go over to the Munitions Building and report to Justice Roberts as a member of the Commission."

When I arrived at the Board Room in the Munitions Building, the other four members of the Commission were already in session. Justice Roberts sat at the head of the table, Rear Admiral Joseph M. Reeves, a former Commander-in-Chief of the U. S. Fleet on his right; Major General Frank McCoy, an able retired Army officer was then president of the Foreign Policy Association; and across from him I was amazed to see Joseph T. McNarney, a Brigadier General in the Army Air Corps, member of the Army General Staff and sort of Rear Admiral Kelly Turner's opposite in the War Department as Major General Leonard T. Gerow's assistant in War Plans Division. Yet, there at the other end of the table as a witness and, as I was soon to realize, a defendant, sat Kelly Turner supporting the testimony of his boss, Admiral Harold R. Stark, Chief of Naval Operations, who was then testifying before the Commission.

Somewhere along the line, Admiral Stark had acquired a peculiar nickname. "Hello, Betty," I said to him, and shook hands. I was presented to Justice Roberts and spoke to the others at the table. They made room for me and proceeded with the questioning of Kelly Turner and Admiral Stark. I had not been seated there very long before I realized that either McNarney ought to be sitting beside Turner as a defendant or Turner ought to be in ... s a member. The latter alternative would have suited me ... tter, for, of all the difficult and onerous duties in a long career of public service, my membership on that Presidential Commission was beyond comparison the most unpleasant.

When the Judge Advocate had finished with Admiral Stark and Kelly Turner, I tried to satisfy my curiosity as to just what I had gotten into. What was the nature of this Commission—was it an Army or Navy board, a joint commission or what? What rules governed its procedure: Army, Navy or civil? Had we power to summon witnesses and enforce their attendance and to administer oaths and take testimony thereunder? The answers I got were not at all reassuring.

It was a "mixed"—and a very mixed up—Presidential Commission with civilian, naval and military members, for which there was no precedent in law, custom or jurisprudence. Mr. Walter Bruce Howe, a civilian lawyer with little or no military court-martial experience, was Judge Advocate. Justice Robert's private secretary (I cannot recall his name now) was temporarily put on the Federal payroll and made secretary to the Commission. Colonel Lee H. Brown of the Marine Corps had been detailed as Provost Marshal to the Commission. Our two court reporters, one a young lad just out of business college, not only had no court experience but also were not even fast and accurate stenographers. Witnesses were being examined on their own conscience, that is, without swearing.

To express it in an extremely kindly fashion, the make-up of the Commission and the conduct of its proceedings were most unusual. I personally knew of many Army, Navy and Marine Corps officers with wide legal experience as judge advocates of service courts and boards who would have been much more logical selections as judge advocate than a lawyer with no such experience and no knowledge of naval and military matters, terms and phraseology. If it were a means of avoiding prejudice, then how could one account for the appointment of General McNarney as a member? If this appointment was because of his knowledge of current activities in the Army General Staff, then Kelly Turner or his principal assistant should have been a member instead of either Admiral Reeves or myself, both of whom had been retired and out of touch with naval affairs for some four or five years. We could not possibly be expected to be as familiar with events leading up to the Japanese attack on Pearl Harbor as Joseph McNarney or Kelly Turner.

As to personal prejudice, from my long experience in the Office

of Naval Operations, which had the responsibility for all operations of the Fleet and for the readiness of plans for its use in war,
and from my continuous effort while CNO with but moderate
success to build up the Fleet and to improve the war readiness of
our outlying naval bases, I could not help but be prejudiced in
my views as to the over-all responsibility for the success achieved
in the unprovoked attack which the Japanese naval air forces made
upon the Territory of Hawaii. I knew from first-hand experience
the shortcomings of our base at Pearl Harbor, for which Short and
Kimmel were in no way responsible. From the beginning of our
investigation, I held a firm belief that the real responsibility for
the disaster at Pearl Harbor was lodged thousands of miles from
the Territory of Hawaii.

As I have said, I was shocked at the irregularity of the procedure of the Commission and at the reliance placed upon un-
sworn testimony. As a result of my protest, a joint resolution was
rushed through Congress in a few hours authorizing us to sub-
poena witnesses and to administer oaths. We were now somewhat
better equipped to do our job.

After the first sense of shock at the Japanese sneak attack on
that "day of infamy" was succeeded by a feeling of outrage, a rising tide of indignation in the country reflected in both Houses of
Congress nearly brought on a joint Congressional investigation
there and then. In my opinion, our Presidential Commission was
hurriedly ordered by the President on December 16 to forestall
just such a Congressional investigation at that time. In support of
this view, it is interesting to note the following chronological se-
quence of events leading up to the President's action on December 16.

At eight A.M. December 9th, Secretary of the Navy Frank Knox
left Washington in his own plane, "conscious of his share in the
blame for the surprise attack at Pearl Harbor."* Almost the first
thing he asked Admiral Kimmel, Commander-in-Chief of the Pacific Fleet, at Pearl Harbor was, "Did you receive our dispatch the
night before the attack?" Kimmel told the Secretary that he had
not, to which Knox replied, "Well, we sent you one—I'm sure we
sent one to the Commander of the Asiatic Fleet." Admiral Kimmel
later testified that he had checked the files and found no record
` `ny such dispatch from the Secretary, in which his Chief of
` `iral W. W. Smith, bore him out. Subsequent investiga-

and Lindley, *How War Came* (New York: Simon and Schuster,

tion in Washington failed to reveal that any such dispatch had been sent.

Secretary Knox returned to Washington on December 15, and hurried to the White House. Although it would not be known for another four years that Knox, in his private report to the President, did not place exclusive or specific blame on Admiral Kimmel and his opposite number in the Army, Major General Walter C. Short, I think that he was very sensitive of the failure of the Navy Department and of himself properly to alert the Commander-in-Chief in Pearl Harbor. Secretary Knox returned from the White House to issue orders for the removal of Admiral Kimmel as Commander-in-Chief of the United States Fleet. Then, he called the press to his office and announced that a total of 2,897 Army and Navy personnel had been killed, 879 wounded and 26 were missing in the Pearl Harbor disaster. Thus, two days before our Commission met, the decision had been made and the commanders relieved of their posts, although the announcements were held up for two more days. Thus, in the eyes of citizens of the Republic, without a thorough investigation and with no opportunity to defend themselves, Kimmel and Short were held responsible for the débacle at Pearl Harbor.

The activities of our Commission were long and frenzied. It first met in Washington on December 17. I sat in on December 18. We took 2,173 printed pages of evidence and exhibits, including that taken in the three days before we left Washington for Pearl Harbor. The entire Commission and staff flew to Pearl Harbor, arriving there on December 21st, where we convened and took more testimony. We made our report to the President on January 24th. By then the peril to our country was so evident and the pressure of other events was so absorbing that I felt quite sure that nothing would be done to correct any inequities in punishment already administered or withheld.

Because of inadequate reporters and inaccurate reporting, much of the recorded testimony was badly garbled, which led to much dissatisfaction and to feelings of unfair treatment at the hands of the Commission by a number of interested parties. Especially was this true of Admiral Kimmel, who later protested that, although he had been treated as if he were a defendant before the Commission, he had not been informed that he was on trial or that he was an interested party in the investigation. In contrast to General Short, who retained the services of his staff to help him make up his complete and detailed report to the Commission, Admiral Kimmel's staff immediately put to sea with his temporary successor, Vice Admiral William S. Pye. As a result, he had no one but an aide to help him with his report nor any Fleet records to consult in preparing it. That was why he had to make his report to the Commission orally and as factually as he could, answering freely and frankly and from memory such questions as we wished to ask.

The contrast between the testimony of the two commanders created a very unfavorable reaction toward Admiral Kimmel in the minds of some members of the Commission. There was even opposition when Admiral Kimmel asked permission to have an officer, his aide, present to assist him in his appearance before the Commission. Of course, he was permitted no counsel and had no right to ask questions or to cross-examine witnesses as he would have had if he had been made a defendant. Thus to both Short and Kimmel were denied all of the usual rights accorded to American citizens appearing before judicial proceedings as interested parties.

In spite of the known inefficiency of the Commission's reporters, when Admiral Kimmel asked permission to correct his testimony, in which he had found so many errors that it took him two days to go over it, the Commission voted to keep the record as originally made, although the answers recorded to many questions were obviously incorrect and many of them were even absurd. At my urgent insistence, the Commission did finally authorize Admiral Kimmel's corrected testimony to be attached to the record as an addendum.

Even we naval members did not see eye to eye as to the facts adduced. At the beginning, Admiral Reeves indicated quite openly his opinion that Admiral Kimmel and General Short were entirely at fault. I could not subscribe to this view. I felt that, with all of the information available to them in Washington, Admiral Stark and General Marshall were equally culpable and should share with Short and Kimmel the blame for faulty judgment and for incorrect interpretation of information available to them. Otherwise, they should have issued positive instructions for an all-out alert against a seaborne attack on the base and the Fleet, which they knew was assembled at the moorings and anchorages in Pearl Harbor that fatal Sunday morning.

␣␣␣␣General Marshall and Admiral Stark knew that three times ␣␣␣␣the Japanese had commenced war operations with a ␣␣␣␣ck on their prospective enemies. On the night of December, 41, not only all of the information which they had passed on to General Short and Admiral Kimmel was in their possession, but also they had considerable other recent intelligence, obtained by reading the coded despatches of the Japanese, which indicated that Japanese military action was imminent. They also knew, or should have known, the state of unreadiness which existed on the island of Oahu. With information that came in during the night of December 6–7, both General Marshall and Admiral Stark should have recognized that war was imminent and that an attack was on the way toward some American base. It was their responsibility so to inform General Short and Admiral Kimmel, as well as the Far Eastern military commanders.

Even with Admiral Stark at the theater the evening of December 6th and General Marshall out for a canter in the park for two and a half hours on Sunday morning, December 7th, positive indication of the impending attack on Pearl Harbor was available to them when they reached their offices that morning. Stark had an opportunity to warn Kimmel any time after he read the intelligence despatches in his office at nine A.M. (3:30 A.M. Pearl Harbor time). When Marshall received the same information at 11:25 A.M., there was still about two hours to go before the attack. A telephone with a scrambler attachment stood on his desk over which the War Department had on previous occasions talked directly with General Short.

Admiral Stark felt that he had to confer with General Marshall after his ride and so he did nothing, although the Navy had direct radio communication with the Commander-in-Chief in Pearl Harbor. Nor did General Marshall pick up his telephone and call General Short. Later, the Chief of Staff gave as his reasons the danger of a breach of security if the message were given over the telephone and fear of precipitating an overt act against the Japanese. Yet, a few hours later, General Marshall talked by telephone with General Short.

General Marshall finally chose to alert General Short against the expected attack by radio. Through some misadventure, his message was classified "Routine" instead of "Priority" or "Extra Urgent." Army radio communications with Hawaii had not been working well for some days and so the warning of impending hostilities was encoded and sent to General Short by commercial radio. A strange delay ensued. A messenger boy was on his way to Fort Shafter with the message when the Japanese struck. The message was finally decoded and delivered to General Short at 3 P.M., December 7th.

On the civil side of government, the President, Secretary of State, and Harry Hopkins were equally well-informed as to the trend of events and the critical current international situation. They had been notified that the Japanese Fleet was "lost" from the radio air lanes. Yet no action was taken by high civil authorities to ensure adequate readiness in our Fleet and at our overseas bases. The ugly terms "air attack" and "war" appear nowhere in the ineffective messages of warning despatched under the close coordination and with the full knowledge of these high civil officials during the weeks before December 7th.

An Army Board of generals convened to investigate Pearl Harbor criticized General Marshall severely for the mishandling of his last message of warning to General Short:

> It is important to observe that only one means of communication was selected by Washington. That decision violated all rules requiring the use of multiple means of communication in emergency. In addition to the War Department telephone, there also existed the FBI radio, which was assigned a special frequency between Washington and Hawaii or vice versa. . . . We find no justification for a failure to send this message by multiple secret means either through the Navy radio or FBI radio or scrambler telephone or all three.[*]

On June 17, 1940, when conditions were much less menacing than in December 1941, Naval Intelligence lost radio track of the Japanese Fleet for a few days. General Marshall sent General Herron, General Short's predecessor, a message which directed, "Immediately alert complete defensive organization to deal with possible trans-Pacific raid."

How much such a warning would have meant to General Short and Admiral Kimmel at any time during November and the first week in December, 1941! How much even two hours warning would have meant to the 2,897[†] officers and men who were killed in the Pearl Harbor raid, if such a message had been given by scrambler phone in code or in the clear to either General Short or Admiral Kimmel that morning of December 7th!

It was my conviction, confirmed in our investigation, that Pearl Harbor resulted because of a lack of military readiness. If we had ⏋ sufficient naval patrol planes, we would have been operating

⏋ of Army Pearl Harbor Board as printed in the *United States News,*
945, p. 32.
⏋ty figures cited were those obtained by the Roberts Commis-
⏋gures put losses at 3,303 Army and Navy personnel killed.

a complete off-shore air patrol in accordance with approved plans, and the approach of the Japanese planes and the position of the Japanese carriers would have been discovered; if we had been in a proper state of military readiness, the fast carrier forces, cruisers and destroyers would not have been on detached service supplying outlying bases, and only one division of battleships and their escorts would have been found in Pearl Harbor that Sunday morning. How little we have learned! If we had been in a proper state of military readiness in June, 1950, the North Korean Communists would never have dared to attack.

As it does now, the responsibility for this state of affairs rested upon the Great American Public operating through their elected representatives in the Congress. Beginning Armistice Day 1919 at the end of World War I, a wave of pacifism engulfed our land. The Washington Treaty scrapped the 1916 naval building program which would have given the United States the most powerful fleet in the world. In subsequent years, this pacifistic attitude resulted in mistaken economies which brought our country up to Pearl Harbor almost totally unprepared for the sort of attack which came on December 7, 1941, either militarily or mentally.

Holding these views, which I felt that our investigation had confirmed, I could not in good conscience agree with the Commission's findings that Admiral Kimmel and General Short were solely responsible for the Pearl Harbor disaster. However, I alone of the members of the Commission held this view. My attempts to have this attitude reflected in our findings resulted in a number of acrimonious arguments.

On one occasion, when I persisted in objecting to one of the "findings of fact," Justice Roberts said, rather impatiently, "Well, if Admiral Standley won't agree to this finding, he can always submit a minority report!"

"I am well aware of my rights in this premise, Justice Roberts," I replied. "If I do have to make a minority report on this matter, I shall state that the report you are making is false. The evidence we have taken will certainly bear me out."

This particular difference of opinion was eventually adjusted to my satisfaction. While in the end, I did sign the completed report, I felt and I still feel that it did not present the whole, true picture. The findings as to sins of commission presented true enough statements, but the many sins of omission in the picture were omitted from our findings because the President, in his Executive Order setting up the Commission, had specifically limited its jurisdiction by directing us to determine "whether any dereliction of duty or error in judgment on the part of the *United States Army or Navy personnel* contributed to such successes as were achieved" in "the attack made by Japanese armed forces upon the Territory of Hawaii on December 7, 1941."

Such instructions precluded any investigation into the activities of high civilian officials in Washington before the Japanese were committed to the attack and when it was known to be imminent, as to information available to these civilian officials and such decisions and actions as they may have taken to inform the Hawaiian commanders as to their immediate danger or to order them to assume an adequate state of alertness. Evidence as to the performance of duty of these officials came to us only through testimony given before the Commission by Army and Naval officers. The high civilian officials, including President Roosevelt, could not be summoned to testify before our Commission under the terms of the Executive Order establishing it.

Upon my return from Pearl Harbor, I reported to Secretary of the Navy Knox. "Mr. Secretary," I told him, "our investigation certainly confirms your statement that neither the Army nor the Navy were properly alerted for an air attack on Sunday morning, December seventh."

Mr. Knox then asked me what I thought of the command set-up in Hawaii.

"Mr. Secretary," I replied, "under the circumstances, Admiral Kimmel and General Short had to be relieved of their commands. Yet I can't help regretting that Admiral Kimmel had to go. I have never seen the Fleet in a higher state of efficiency than was evidenced by my observations during the course of our investigations at Pearl Harbor."

Many years have passed since that troubled time. Since the War, I have read everything I could get hold of on the subject of Pearl Harbor. I have reviewed as much of the transcript of our record as I could find, which is another curious situation. The report of our Commission, as made up in Washington after our return from Pearl Harbor, consisted of three parts; the full minutes of the proceedings and of all testimony taken; a brief transcript of important testimony taken; and a digest of the record which served as our report to the President. When I was looking for these records in Washington after the War, only the digest and the report could be found in any of the government files.

In my personal files, I recently came across a letter from Justice

Roberts addressed to me on January 26, 1942, in which he stated:

I have today signed the original copy of the very full minutes of our proceedings and am enclosing a correct copy of the minutes in the sealed packages being deposited with the War and Navy Departments. According to the resolution of our Commission, I shall retain in safe custody the original minutes which will at all times be at the disposal of any member of the Commission.

In addition to the investigation by the Roberts Commission, the following Pearl Harbor investigations were made:

A preliminary and hasty investigation by Secretary Knox prior to the investigation by the Roberts Commission.

An examination of witnesses by Admiral Thomas C. Hart, USN, under a precept dated February 12, 1944.

A Naval Court of Inquiry headed by Admiral Orin G. Murfin, U. S. Navy (Retired).

An investigation by Rear Admiral H. Kent Hewitt ordered by the Secretary of Navy on May 2, 1945.

An investigation by the Army Pearl Harbor Board headed by General George Grunert, U. S. Army, President.

An investigation by the Joint Congressional Committee in 1945.

The investigation by the Roberts Commission was the first complete investigation. It was made directly after the event at the place of the attack when events and circumstances were fresh in the minds of the various witnesses. In its report, the Commission stated:

The Commission examined 127 witnesses and received a large number of documents. All members of the military and naval establishments and civil officers and citizens who were thought to have knowledge of facts pertinent to the inquiry were summoned and examined under oath. All persons in the island of Oahu, who believed they had knowledge of such facts, were publicly requested to appear, and a number responded to the invitation and gave evidence.

Various rumors and hearsay statements have been communicated to the Commission. The Commission has sought to find and examine witnesses who might be expected to have knowledge respecting them. We believe that our findings of fact sufficiently dispose of most of them.

Some of the findings of these various investigations and boards were at variance with the findings of the Roberts Commission. In view of the foregoing statement, I am convinced that the facts reported in the Roberts Commission findings, bearing in mind the limitations imposed upon us, are more accurate, more authentic and more thorough than any of the investigations made from three to four years later.

Had our Commission *not been limited in its jurisdiction,* my subsequent study of the case has led me to believe that we would have arrived at much the same conclusions as those expressed in the minority report of the Joint Committee of Congress, which read as follows:

> The messages sent to General Short and Adm. Kimmel by high authorities in Washington during November were couched in such conflicting and imprecise language that they failed to convey to the commanders definite information on the state of diplomatic relations with Japan and on Japanese war designs and positive orders respecting the particular actions to be taken—orders that were beyond all reasonable doubts as to the need for an all-out alert. In this regard the said high authorities failed to discharge their full duty.

This report then concluded:

> Having examined the whole record made before the Joint Committee and having analyzed the same in the foregoing conclusions of fact and responsibility, we find the evidence supports the following final and ultimate conclusion:
> The failure at Pearl Harbor to be fully alerted and prepared for defense rested upon the proper discharge of two sets of interdependent responsibilities: (1) the responsibilities of high authorities in Washington; and (2) the responsibilities of the commanders in the field in charge of the fleet and of the naval base.
> The evidence clearly shows that these two areas of responsibilities were inseparably essential to each other in the defense of Hawaii. The commanders in the field could not have prepared or been ready successfully to meet hostile attack at Hawaii without indispensable information, material, trained manpower and clear orders from Washington. Washington could not be certain that Hawaii was in readiness without the alert and active cooperation of the commanders on the spot.
> The failure to perform the responsibilities indispensably essential to the defense of Pearl Harbor rests upon the following civil and military authorities:
> FRANKLIN D. ROOSEVELT—President of the United States and Commander-in-Chief of the Army and Navy

HENRY L. STIMSON—Secretary of War

FRANK KNOX—Secretary of Navy

GEORGE C. MARSHALL—General, Chief of Staff of the Army

HAROLD R. STARK—Admiral, Chief of Naval Operations

LEONARD T. GEROW—Major General, Assistant Chief of Staff of War Plans Division

The failure to perform the responsibilities of Hawaii rests upon the military commanders:

WALTER P. SHORT—Major General, Commanding General, Hawaiian Department

HUSBAND E. KIMMEL—Rear Admiral, Commander-in-Chief of the Pacific Fleet

Both in Washington and Hawaii there were numerous and serious failures of men in the lower civil and military echelons to perform their duties and discharge their responsibilities. These are too numerous to be treated in detail and individually named.

As far as Short and Kimmel are concerned, the tragedy of Pearl Harbor was the fact that they were, and had to be, removed from command without a hearing and that war conditions prevented bringing them to trial by general court-martial before the end of the War. Thus, these two officers were martyred, as it were; for in my opinion, if they had been brought to trial, both would have been cleared of the charge of neglect of duty. The long delay in public investigation of Pearl Harbor served to identify them thoroughly in the public mind as jointly responsible for the disaster, while other Army and Naval officers and high civilian officials, equally or more culpable, went on to serve their country in that War and to win promotion and distinction. I feel now, as I have always felt, that General Short and Admiral Kimmel would have rendered equally distinguished service in that great War, had they only been given the chance.

In time, history will register the fact that the United States committed a much more overt act than use of the scrambler phone which General Marshall feared so greatly. Admiral Kimmel had established a "training sector" about the Hawaiian Islands—had proclaimed and publicized it in the Honolulu Press (where the very efficient Japanese espionage agents certainly noted and reported it), with a statement that "any submarine found within the training area would be summarily sunk." Between 0633 and 0645 Sunday morning, December 7th, a submarine was discovered submerged within that training sector, was attacked by the

United States destroyer "Ward," and was sunk. Although the Japanese attack planes were already on their way to their sneak attack, they did not commit the first act of the war.

The Commanding Officer of the "Ward" immediately reported by radio his action against the submarine but, because of previous false alarms, the Chief of Staff requested confirmation. Before an answer was received from the "Ward," Japanese bombs began to rain down upon the unalerted Pacific Fleet and Pearl Harbor Naval Base.

The "incident" which certain high officials in Washington had sought so assiduously in order to condition the American public for war with the Axis Powers, had been found. The cost, 3,303 Army and Navy men killed and excessive damage and virtual immobilization of our Fleet for months to come, was too high a price to pay for a war that was inevitable in any case.

Surprise Orders

We completed our report on the Pearl Harbor investigation in a month and a week. I was once again assigned to duty with Navy Public Relations presenting Navy "E's" to war industries in the Middle West. When I returned from a trip in February, my secretary told me that Mr. Averell Harriman had phoned several times and wished to see me the instant I returned to Washington. I put on my cap and walked over to his office.

"Hello, Admiral," he said as we shook hands. "Have a seat. Are you going to Russia?"

Needless to say, I was startled. I knew that Ambassador Laurence Steinhardt had recently returned from Moscow "for consultation."

"I thought I'd finished my duty with the Mission," I replied cautiously, trying to figure out what was in the wind. "I don't have any reason to go to Russia. Something wrong with Lend-Lease over there?"

"Plenty," he said shortly. "That's not it. The President wants you to go to Moscow as his Ambassador. He was going to ask you, himself, but he decided to leave it up to Secretary Hull so that you can decline with honor,. if you wish. I'm sure that Secretary Hull will let you know the President's wishes, soon."

We visited briefly and I went back to my office to clean up the backlog of paperwork that had accumulated. FDR had probably asked Averell to go to Moscow as Ambassador; Averell didn't want to go, and so he suggested that I be sent, instead.

I didn't care for the job. All American families had been evacuated from the Soviet Union; no one would be allowed to return for the duration of the War. I had had a brief but rather mild sample of the rigors of Russian Winter and of the poverty of diplomatic social life in Moscow. Well, I thought as I went to work on my papers, he hasn't asked me yet. Maybe if I stop thinking about it, the whole thing will simply go away.

It didn't. A few days later, Secretary Hull asked me to come to his office in the State Department. I had known Mr. Hull well enough to be on a "Bill" and "Cordell" basis and I was fond of him; we sat in on the same Cabinet meetings for months. There was no informality, now; he called me "Admiral" and otherwise treated me with courteous but distant official politeness. Tersely, he informed me of the President's wish that I go to Moscow as American Ambassador.

I sat there beside his big desk, silent for a moment. "I'd like to think it over, Mr. Secretary," I said, just as formally as he. "I'm going up to Boston to visit my son for a few days. When I return, I'll give you my answer."

The more I considered the position, the less I liked it and I about decided to beg off because of "waning years and infirmity." My wife and I went up to Boston by train that weekend. Still, our country is at war, I thought, as the car wheels clicked over the rail joints. You don't refuse duty, however onerous, in wartime. I certainly could be more useful in Moscow than presenting Navy "E's" for the rest of the War, a job that was becoming decidedly boring.

We held a family conference in Boston that weekend; I decided to go. Upon my return to Washington, I so informed Mr. Hull, quite formally. "I'll have to go home to California, first."

We were at our *Villa Zee Zaw* on February 23, 1942, when I received the telegram from the State Department:

> Sir, I have the honor to inform you that your commission as Ambassador to the Union of Soviet Socialist Republics of Russia has been approved and signed. It is requested that you report to the State Department to receive appropriate instructions before commencing your mission.

A few days later, the Navy Department informed me that the assignment was in accordance with their wishes and that I would be returned to my former status on the retired list so that I could accept the appointment—my third retirement! Thus, in the quaint formality of Government officialese, I commenced my "steward-ship of American interests" in the Soviet Union.

Having, as it were, burned my dock behind me, it was incumbent upon me to prepare to take up my new duties. My first concern was the welfare of my wife while I was gone and therefore I had to arrange for the management of our home and seven acres of avacadoes in La Mesa, California, the *Villa Zee Zaw*. The responsibility for the care of this property would fall upon Evelyn, which had certainly not been the plan when we bought it. The manager who had been with the place ever since I bought it had agreed to stay on; but the moment he heard that I was going to Russia, he decided that he must go into war work—at a higher rate of pay. Faced with this dilemma, I sought out my good friend, Father O'Donohue, of La Mesa; with his assistance, I engaged a Mexican, Eduardo Valdez, who appeared to be a loyal and efficient worker, to manage our ranch.

My family was scattered across the face of the Western Hemisphere—my daughter, Vivien Wincote, was in San Diego; Marie Herron was in San Francisco; and Evelyn was in Foreign Service in Chile; my son, Captain W. H. Standley, Jr., was in Boston; my two Byrne grandsons, sons of my daughter, Helen, and Commander James Byrne, were in Washington.

My wife and I left San Diego on February 26th. On arrival in San Francisco the next morning, we visited my daughter, Marie, and her husband, Eddie Herron, and phoned Mrs. Standley's eight brothers and sisters in the vicinity of San Francisco and my two sisters in Ukiah. Late that afternoon, we had a family reunion at the St. Francis Hotel; at 8:30 that evening, we took the Overland Limited for Washington, where we arrived on Monday, March second.

Upon reporting to the State Department, I was assigned office space and three secretaries with Loy Henderson, then Chief of the State Department's Division of Eastern European Affairs. I took up the work of briefing and indoctrination preparatory to assuming my duties in Moscow.

After the passage of so much time, it would be impossible to record every detail involved in my indoctrination, but it will be interesting to note the contacts I made with certain individuals, nearly all of whom had some Russian axe to sharpen or a message for a friend in Russia. After every one of these visits, it was necessary to discuss the matter with State Department officials to obtain a full background on the questions involved.

I was astounded to learn the number of our citizens who had some interest in our relations with Soviet Russia. As soon as my appointment was announced, I was beset on every hand. Some of this interest in Russia involved bad debts of previous regimes in Russia and worthless bonds of Czarist governments. By far the most persistent and touching were the relatives of the missing Polish officers who were taken prisoner when the Russians marched into Poland in 1939. Wouldn't I, please, try to get *some* information about their loved ones?

I recall a Mrs. Divines, a middle-aged Polish woman, who came to see me in my temporary office. Her husband was a doctor with the Polish Army. She pressed a letter into my hand. "When you see him in Russia," she said hoarsely, in her broken English, "give it to him. They try to tell me he is dead, but I do not believe them. You will find him. Give him this letter, please, and God will go with you all your days."

As I looked into her broad, sorrow-lined face, I couldn't help but experience some of her shining faith. By an odd coincidence, I was able to help that one poor woman. Two years later, a Polish military surgeon walked into my office in Kuibyshev. He had first been transferred from Kozielsk to a prison camp in Siberia to care for his fellow Poles. Later, released from all captivity, he made his way on foot and by rail from Siberia to Kuibyshev. When he told me his name was Divines, I handed him the letter his wife had given me in Washington. His expression of surprise and delight was ample reward for all the effort I expended in behalf of the Poles during my tour of duty in Russia.

My first contact in the State Department was with Mr. Ray Atherton, who had been Chargé d'Affaires when I was in London as delegate to the Disarmament Conference, 1935–36. My old friend, Henry Sutphen, of the Electric Boat Company, came to Washington and we had many talks; Henry was very worried about my health and assured me a number of times that he would always be at my call in case I needed anything while I was in Russia.

I had my first interview with the President on Thursday, March 5th; after lunch on the corner of his desk, we covered the whole wide scope of international affairs and problems.

That same evening, the Homer Cummings-Pinehurst Golf Tournament crowd gave a dinner in my honor at Burning Tree Golf

Club; at its conclusion, they presented me with a Hamilton gold watch and a safety razor.

Among other things which demanded attention was my wardrobe, a subject which deserved careful consideration. I consulted Russian Ambassador Oumansky as to the climate in Moscow; he told me that Moscow was comparable to Washington. I would need the same kind of clothing I used there. I took with me everything from the airiest kind of clothing for extremely hot weather to the heaviest clothing for extreme cold. I certainly needed all my heavy clothing and had to buy more but I had on a Palm Beach suit only once while I was in the Soviet Union.

The California Society of Washington gave me a testimonial luncheon on Sunday, March eighth. The next day, Mrs. Standley and I were guests of Lord and Lady Halifax at the British Embassy on Massachusetts Avenue. That afternoon, I attended the funeral of Mrs. Davis, the wife of Ambassador Norman Davis, with whom I had been associated for many years, my co-delegate at the Disarmament Conference, 1935–36.

I was in constant touch with various governmental authorities, not only in the State Department but also in the Navy Department, the War Department, and the White House. Secretary Hull, Under-Secretary Welles, Mr. Ray Atherton, Mr. Loy Henderson, Mr. Breckinridge, and anyone else who had knowledge or advice to give me about Russia were interviewed.

Mr. Willis Booth, who was head of the Russian Chamber of Commerce in New York, gave me valuable information about the Russians. The Polish Ambassador came to see me several times about the missing Polish officers.

I visited the Navy General Board and heard Admiral Thomas Hart, just back from the Philippines and Java, where he had commanded the Asiatic Fleet, give a talk about the situation in the Far East. I discussed the foreign situation with Mr. Jesse Jones of the RFC and the question of aid to Russia with Bill Batt, who was a member of the Beaverbrook-Harriman Mission; he gave me a lot of good advice with regard to the Lend-Lease situation. "You'll have trouble with that, Admiral," he said, prophetically.

I lunched with T. V. Soong, who represented Chiang Kai-shek unofficially in Washington.

On March 14, I had my final interview with President Roosevelt, at which time we had a very intimate and detailed discussion of my duties in Moscow and the more pressing problems. That afternoon, I conferred with Mr. Loy Henderson, Mr. Ray Atherton, and Mr. Jimmy Dunn, to whom I revealed the subject matter of my conversations with the President, so that the State Department wouldn't feel left out.

The following day, a Sunday, I took my two Byrne grandsons to Annapolis and we decorated the grave of their mother and my daughter, Helen Standley Byrne, in the Naval Academy Cemetery, situated on a pleasant green knoll above the Severn River.

On Monday, March 16th, I had my final contacts: with T. V. Soong for lunch, a visit with Mr. John Winant about the British situation, an informational conference with Mr. Willis Booth, of the Russian Chamber of Commerce. My interview with General George Marshall was cut short when aides brought him the news that General MacArthur had escaped by PT-boat from Corregidor; the War Department was worried about the Press release and public reaction to MacArthur leaving his command. At 3:00 P.M., I paid my last call on Sumner Welles, Under Secretary of State.

During this briefing period, I had been in almost daily touch with Mr. Loy Henderson, who would be my immediate boss in the Department, and with Mr. Welles. At my several luncheon conferences with FDR, the last on the Saturday before I left Washington, *I was given complete and detailed information and instructions as to questions I was expected to take up in my first meeting with Mr. Stalin, and the official United States Government position on each of these issues.*

I had no illusions as to my qualifications to be a diplomat. I knew that I was just an ordinary, run-of-the-mine Naval officer as far as diplomatic experience went. My long service in the boiling cauldron of Official Washington would be helpful. I had never swallowed the phony philosophy of the Kellogg Pact that "we renounce war as an instrument of national policy." I was realist enough to know that, when diplomacy and policy fail, war comes to take its place. With Clausewitz, I believed that war is a continuation of diplomatic effort by force of arms. In accepting my post, I was actuated by the belief that my military experience would carry me through my duties for as long as the war continued. I had no desire to serve longer.

Perhaps Franklin D. Roosevelt, who was an omnivorous reader, had information about past missions to the Russian capital denied to me. It would have been a great comfort to me if I could, at that time, have read the following despatch from the American Minister to Russia, Mr. Neill S. Brown, dated at St. Petersburg on January 27, 1853:

... I am of the opinion that a Minister from the United States, particularly at this time, ought to be a military man. I mean a man that has seen actual service, and who would be able to maintain his pretensions. This is not suggested for the mere vain show of wearing a uniform, but because the government of Russia is a military government. The military is the predominant taste of all, from the Emperor to the peasant; and this capital during the greater part of the year abounds with officers, whose education and accomplishments render them an interesting society, and whose acquaintance would be valuable.

There is no question but that a minister of respectable military attainments and reputation would have much more might than a mere civilian. The ordinary reasons for such an appointment are, in my judgment, enhanced by the present position and prospects of Russia. Its influence over the rest of Europe is irresistible, particularly with the German states. Its vast military power and military spirit are the secrets of this ascendancy, aided by a system of diplomacy which has perhaps no equal.

On the morning of March 19, 1942, as I stood with my wife at the great windows of the terminal building at the Washington Airport, waiting for an Army transport to take me away on the first leg of my long flight to Moscow, I felt that I was facing the most challenging duty that my country had ever asked me to undertake. I had no misgivings. I was almost seventy. My naval career was behind me. I need not have accepted any other responsibility, but my country had called to me in wartime and I felt I had to answer that call—to assume important responsibilities at an advanced age in a new field. I made up my mind I would approach them with the same spirit of loyalty, devotion, and determination which had brought me to the top in my chosen naval profession, with but one question foremost in mind at all times—is this for the best interest of my country?

I was determined to look out ahead at the future—not back over the long years since I lived as a boy on the banks of the Russian River. Again I recalled a favorite quotation from *The Keys of the Kingdom:* "How can we reconcile the life we have lived with its beginning?"

CHAPTER VI

Flight to Moscow

THE great four-engined transport climbed easily into the sky and pointed its nose southward. I couldn't help but feel an exhilarating lift of spirits. After so many weeks of preparation, I was off on the great adventure.

Yet, as I looked down at the rolling, green-clad hills of Virginia flowing away behind us, I felt a certain sadness. This was *my* country, my *own* country, which I was leaving on a perilous mission and which I was seeing, perhaps for the last time.

I looked around at the rest of my party—Captain Jack Duncan, going along as my Naval Attaché; Commander Frederick Lang of the Navy Medical Corps, the embassy doctor; and Eddie Page, a young State Department official, who had been with us on the Beaverbrook-Harriman Mission, as Embassy Secretary. Jack Duncan had been my aide and flag lieutenant both in cruisers and when I was CNO. Doctor Lang is one of those good, all-around internal medicine men you sometimes find in the Navy Medical Corps and a fine dry-land shipmate. As for Eddie Page, I never ceased to rejoice that I had not ventured forth on this mission without that splendid guide, philosopher and friend.

I slept for a while. When I awakened the turpentine pines and peach orchards of Georgia were beneath us. By early afternoon, we were flying above the tangled sub-tropical foliage of the Everglades to land at three at West Palm Beach.

Our schedule called for take-off at eleven. We went to a hotel in Palm Beach to freshen up and then out to Joe Davies' palatial estate for dinner. In view of my subsequent experiences with Joe Davies, I want to record here my exact impressions of this visit as I entered them in my log of the flight:

Joe Davies invited all of my party to dinner, *en famille,* just the Davies family and us. You never saw such grandeur as on the enor-

99

mous Davies' estate—a palace of a house with beautifully kept grounds and gardens, an eighteen-hole golf course and a large swimming pool. The inside of the house reeked of richness—beautiful furniture, costly rugs, rare paintings, many of them collected during his sojourn in Moscow as our Ambassador. We seated ourselves to gold dinner service and solid flat silver. I noticed with amusement that his colored valet took keen delight in addressing Mr. Davies as "Mr. Ambassador."

Well, we enjoyed ourselves despite the riches. Joe Davies is a member of the Homer Cummings-Pinehurst Golf Tournament crowd to which I belong and so I knew him fairly well. When he couldn't be present at the dinner they gave me at the Burning Tree Country Club before I left Washington, he sent me a copy of his book, *Mission to Moscow*, which was autographed by him and by every man at the dinner. Now, he gave an autographed copy of his book to each member of my party. He sent us to the airport in a limousine equipped to operate everything by electricity with buttons in the back seat—a grand arrangement for a "back seat driver." The Davies certainly treated us royally. Joe is a grand fellow.

Presently, with final good-byes said, we boarded our plane, the engines revved-up for testing at the head of the runway, the gigantic wheels of the C-54 rolled down the wide path of concrete, the plane slid smoothly into the air and circled for altitude.

Below us, the white lights of Palm Beach winked and glittered, etched in lines of color drawn by neon tubes. It would be many a day before I would see another city alive and glowing with night lights. We passed the coast, the breakers falling lazily one over another on the white sand beach. I looked back astern; the lights of the city had faded; now we belonged to the sea and the sky. The big transport purred soothingly through the black night.

Our plane had been stripped of all the conveniences which once made it a "plush-job," and extra gas tanks had been installed in the cabin. While it was fast and smooth-riding, there were few comforts. The crew was made up of Air Corps Captains on their way to combat duty in the Middle East. They didn't realize that bunks had been installed for the comfort of my party and so we spent a most uncomfortable first night. There was no water for washing and barely enough to drink. Finally I dozed off and then slept soundly. When I awoke, it was full daylight with a fiery sun shining out of a clear blue sky.

We made a landfall, swooped low over an evil-looking jungle land, and came down in a huge clearing surrounded by Quonset

huts painted a dark brown. It was Trinidad, building up to an
important air and naval base. After inspecting the base we dined
with General Conger Pratt and took off at midnight for Natal,
Brazil, the jumping-off place for the Atlantic crossing. The next
day, we flew across the delta of the Amazon. There is an awful lot
of river there, with islands in between. Sometimes over the river,
we could see no land ahead or astern. The swamps and low lying
islands were alive with water buffalo, cattle, sacred ox, goats,
sheep, pigs and many wild animals I could not identify. Flocks of
birds of all colors filled the air, the most conspicuous being red
flamingo.

We touched down at Belem at 10:13 A.M. and the pilots decided to spend the night. The ghost town of the Brazilian rubber
industry, Belem was a sad city of decadence, with once impressive
buildings now in an advanced state of deterioration.

Since we had a long flight ahead of us, we turned in early
and were airborne before eight. The flight to Natal was over flat
wooded country with considerable land under cultivation, the center of cotton growing in Brazil. A wild ride into town in a jeep
got us a combination lunch and dinner. We were back at the airport for a six P.M. take-off for Roberts Field in Liberia, where we
arrived too late for breakfast but just in time for "brunch" with
the contractor's superintendent directing the work on the airfield.

On the way across the waist of Africa, we stopped at Accra on
the Gold Coast, Kano, Nigeria, and Khartoum on the Nile. All the
fields we visited were being improved by contractors under the
supervision of Pan-American Airways, of which I was a director.
I was mighty proud of "my company" on that trip. Three seasoned
Pan-American pilots, Henry Kristofferson, George Kraigher, and
John Yeomans, all later to become Colonels in the Army Air Force,
pioneered the route. The Army Air Transport Command took over
and absorbed the PanAm organization. Now, I saw them working
together with wonderful harmony, the Army discipline controlling
and directing the PanAm civil-air efficiency.

Supervised by PanAm engineers, the civilian contractors had
commandeered existing airports and cleared the jungle for new
bases. The Army moved in, bringing sanitation and American living conditions to equatorial Africa, where ordinary living constituted a challenge to a white man to survive. The jungle didn't give
up easily; yet, as I went through, I saw thousands of young Americans living comfortably and healthfully, eating and sleeping as
well as at home. There were always movies and radio programs.

USO troupes enroute to the Middle East frequently stopped off and gave a show at these isolated outposts.

In sharp contrast were the squalid conditions in such "mud-hut" native cities as Kano. Situated in the middle of Africa, the desert heat was almost insufferable. Dirt and disease were everywhere. Naked children, sheep, goats, donkeys, camels, and dogs all mixed and milled together indiscriminately on dusty streets, which became mudholes in the heavy rains. Buzzards swooped down from their perches, catching in mid-air scraps of meat thrown from the fly-infested meat markets and abattoirs. Fresh water from hydrants installed by the British were not regarded with favor because they were not understood. The natives much preferred a stagnant pond in the middle of the village which had served as a water reservoir for generations. Extermination of the race apparently was prevented only by an obviously high birth rate.

The natives were extremely superstitious. I saw one young woman lying in the street, who was said to be possessed by an evil spirit. In her contorted writhings, she had worn a depression into the dirt of the street. No one would go near her for fear of being similarly possessed. I was moved to wonder who provided this pitiful creature with the food and water which kept her alive in her torment.

Black native troops, recruited and trained by the British, served as guards at the airfields. They had instructions to challenge anyone who approached the field or the planes and to shoot, if a satisfactory reply was not immediately forthcoming, an injunction which they took all too literally. As a result, the first word that you learned on reaching Africa was "Abokina," which means, "I am your friend."

So it was, as we proceeded across the whole width of Africa. We came in for a landing one morning at six at Khartoum, where we had our first view of the storied Nile. We were off again at eight and flew all the way down the Blue Nile above a narrow strip of richly fertile irrigated farmland with the endless sands of the desert on either side.

We circled lazily over Cairo, looking down on the Pyramids. I was surprised to see that there were several groups of three pyramids, with the largest and most famous close to Cairo. Apparently every King or Emperor built unto himself a massive shrine so that he would be remembered by his subjects, particularly those who labored to haul the great stone blocks to the top.

Cairo was a most welcome change. Our party put up at Shepheard's, the famed hostelry where it is reputed that you will some day see anyone you ever knew if you wait long enough in the bar or lounge. We had two large suites opened up into one. It was delightful to strip off our dirt and sand encrusted khakis and luxuriate in a soaking bath. Yet, for days afterward I felt soiled from the grit and dirt of equatorial and desert Africa.

I was now on my own as far as transportation was concerned, for our Army plane dropped us here. Since our American Minister, Mr. Kirk, was unable to suggest any air transportation, my first act after my bath was to call up Mr. Frank Gledhill, a traveling vice-president of Pan American, who was in Cairo with a DC-3 transport, making a survey of air routes to the Middle and Far East. His plane was equipped with de-icers and all the other modern flying and navigational equipment. Best of all, he had as pilot, George Kraigher, whom I have mentioned earlier, a Serb who knew the terrain of the Middle East thoroughly from long acquaintance with it in airplanes and who understood and spoke Russian fairly well.

When I got in touch with Frank Gledhill, I discovered that he had been vainly trying for some weeks to get a visa to enter Russia. He was delighted when I suggested that he deliver my party to Kuibyshev, to which temporary capital the American Embassy had moved during the siege of Moscow. His plane seemed a Heaven-sent deliverance out of our difficulty.

There was yet the problem of getting permission for him to fly me into Russia. I wired the Embassy at Kuibyshev with a date line at Cairo of March 27th, "Leaving for Kuibyshev in my private plane via Teheran, where I will arrive on March 31. Please get clearance for my plane and crew and arrange for Russian co-pilot and radioman to meet me in Teheran."

"Well, Eddie," I said as I gave the message to Page, "that will get us permission to take Gledhill's plane in or make certain that the Russians have one meet us at Teheran."

If I had had more experience with the Russians, I doubt that I would have had the temerity to suggest such a thing. Possibly, it was just such rashness that resulted in the Soviet Government granting permission for my private plane to deliver me to Kuibyshev. They also provided a Russian plane at Teheran, which I didn't use.

We were delayed for two days in Cairo, during which time we followed the usual tourist trails—the pyramids, the sphynx, rode camels, lunched at Mena House and dined with the American

Minister at his country place. When I saw the Mena House golf course, I decided that I must have one last game of golf before resigning myself to a golfless Russia. We had no golf clothes, clubs or shoes, but we managed to borrow clubs and played seven holes in our everyday linens. At last, I could say that I had played golf in the shadow of the great pyramids.

We took off from the Cairo airport at eight A.M. on Sunday, the 29th of March, crossed the Suez Canal between Great Bitter Lake and Mount Sinai, passed up the Mediterranean coast over Gaza and Judea to Jaffa, where we circled for a look at this Jewish city; then landed for gas at Lydda.

After a brief fueling stop we were off again. It seemed to me that I was traveling back along the years to ancient history, as we flew over such Biblical place names as Jerusalem, David's Tomb, Bethlehem, the River Jordan, Jericho, the Dead Sea, the Sea of Galilee, to Baghdad, storied city of the *Arabian Nights,* where we stopped for gas. It was arid, mountainous country dotted with what from the air looked like black rugs—the portable tent homes of the nomadic shepherds who have watched their flocks on those hills since the dawn of time.

From Baghdad, we flew across the desert in bumpy air through a continuing storm that sent sand spiraling in dirty clouds thousands of feet into the air. At 4 P.M., we landed at Basra, the great port city of Iraq, located on the *Shatt al Abra* formed by the junction of the Euphrates and the Tigris Rivers. Basra is also the terminus of the railroad up through Iran into Turkey. I had been told of the great difficulties our troops had been having to get our ships unloaded, so we arranged to stay over for a day at the comfortable, modern airport hotel, so that I could see what needed to be done to improve transportation and increase the flow of supplies to Russia.

The next morning, we left the airfield in a fast motor boat and spent the day inspecting waterfront facilities. The equipment for unloading was most inadequate for the job to be done. They had particular trouble unloading railroad iron, great quantities of which were arriving daily for use of our troops in laying a railroad north to the Caucasus. The American soldiers were doing the best they could, but there just weren't enough cranes at dockside or enough piers. The Army had to import stevedores as the Iranians had no stomach for such hard labor. Sometimes ships, after a long wait, would be diverted across to Karachi in India. Many ships had to wait two or three weeks to be unloaded; with world shipping so short, such delay simply could not be tolerated. I decided that the main trouble was lack of power machinery for handling heavy lifts and took occasion to make strong recommendations, which were adopted.

The Army was also having trouble delivering planes. They came to Basra knocked down in crates. The Air Corps had established a very efficient assembly plant, where they assembled the planes and tested them; then parked them at the airport to await Russian pilots. I saw hundreds of P-40 fighters and Aircobras sitting there in the shifting winds, sanding up. By the time the Russians got around to taking delivery on a plane, its engine was full of grit. They complained bitterly of improper assembly and testing. I took occasion to clear up that point, when I got to Moscow.

Late in the afternoon, we visited the English oil refinery on Abadan Island, a veritable paradise compared to Basra.

We had a beautifully clear day for the flight north to Teheran. We had to climb to fifteen thousand feet to get over the mountain passes and, even then, mountain peaks towered above us on either hand. Dressed in summer clothes for the desert, we went almost immediately to below zero weather, but our Pan-American plane was heated and comfortable all the way. We followed winding railroad tracks through the mountains. At 10:50 we slid in over the snow-capped peaks which surround Teheran and landed in the heat of Iran's capital city. From the air, Teheran was whitely beautiful, but, like any city in the Near East, its beauty doesn't stand up under closer inspection.

Doctor Lang and I were put up at the American Embassy by American Minister Dreyfus, while Eddie Page and Captain Duncan were sent to a hotel high on a neighboring mountain. We found clearance for the plane waiting for us and expected to get away Friday morning. However, a Persian sand storm blew up and we had to lie over until Saturday.

Teheran is a curious city. My first impression was of filth, disease and poverty surrounding shabby magnificence. The old Shah, Reza Pahlevi, wanted to modernize and streamline his capital city and so he had made everyone build large three-story houses whether they could use all the space or not. Now, the new architecture is peculiarly sandwiched in with the old.

There are few shops. Fridays and Saturdays were holidays, and everyone turned out into the streets. Beggars dressed in ragged, quilted clothing pleaded for *baksheesh*. The gutters were wide and deep and filled with a slowly moving discolored water. I was told that this was Teheran's fresh water system. Perhaps up in the mountains, it had been sweet and clear, but not in Teheran. Along one block, I saw a naked boy bathing, a woman washing clothes, and a beggar drinking from a rusty can, all from the same sluggish discolored stream.

In spite of such unsanitary conditions, an enormous number of Iranians somehow manage to survive. Nearly every Westerner catches almost immediately a case of the Teheran Trots, the Iranian version of dysentery. Vegetables and fresh fruit looked inviting in the market stalls but the Westerner ate them raw at his peril. The Army frequently inspected abattoirs and meat shops and just as regularly banned their products from our troop messes. Military personnel lived on C-rations composed principally of American canned goods.

Teheran had a difficult "Polish problem." 28,000 soldiers had been released by Russia and sent to Teheran, many bringing with them their families and hundreds of orphaned children. These were some of the Polish troops which later fought under General Anders in Italy with such courage and distinction.

I visited their camp on the outskirts of the capital. It was heartrending to see the orphan children wandering about the camp, with no parent or relative to care for them, but the Polish soldiers had refused to leave them behind. Sickness was rife among them. They had little clothing because most of what they wore into Iran was burned to destroy vermin. Many of the children were under-nourished, as you could tell from the distended belly of near starvation.

I knew that millions of human beings all over the world were starving and homeless, but this was the first DP camp that I had seen. Starvation has a very different meaning when you meet it face to face. Yet, unwilling or unable to return to Communist Poland after the war, many of these poor people still wander the face of the earth, homeless and hungry.

I was entertained by Minister Dreyfus at luncheon, by the British Ambassador at dinner, and by the Russians at another dinner. The Russians laid on one of their enormous banquets—eight courses beside the *hors d'oeuvres*—with three meat courses in addition to fish—beef filet, chicken and partridge. We rose from the table, wined and vodka-ed, as logily uncomfortable as a waterlogged ship.

An American military mission to Russia under Major General John N. Greely, U. S. Army, had been waiting for months in Teheran for visas to admit them to the Soviet Union. I met General Greely at dinner at the Embassy. A more discouraged and unhappy man, I have seldom met. His mission was to observe and represent the American Army in assisting the Russian war effort. It seems that the Russians felt it unnecessary to have such a large mission and wouldn't let any of them in.

General Greely asked me to take with us into Russia himself and as many of his mission as my Pan-American plane would carry. I felt it would be most unwise to enter upon my new duties by introducing into the Soviet Union a mission to which they objected, and so I had to refuse. As I recall it, General Greely never did get into the Soviet Union. After waiting for more than a year for visas, General Greely was relieved by General John R. Deane, who, in October 1943, took a much larger American Military Mission to Moscow without any difficulty about visas whatsoever.

But such is not at all unusual in Russian diplomatic relations. I recall that our Minister to the Russian Court, Mr. Neill S. Brown, reported to the State Department in 1852:

> The policy of Russia seems not to be based, at present, any more than it was at former periods, on settled principles or to be guided by any fixed landmarks. Expediency is the great test. And what may be expedient today under a given state of facts, may be inexpedient tomorrow under the same state of facts.

After waiting out a sand storm, we finally got away from Teheran in our Pan-American plane at eleven A.M. on Saturday, the fourth of April, for Baku, a Russian oil port on the Caspian Sea.

Since I had refused to take any passengers, we had on board only my own party as previously described; the five-man crew of the plane; Frank Gledhill; Russian co-pilot and radioman; and my Russian escort, a Major of the secret police (NKVD) who had been sent to Teheran especially to "protect" me. They gave our plane call letters "USASA," which the Russian pilot told me meant "United States, Admiral Standley Airplane."

The Russian Ambassador was at the airport to see us off, as were our Minister and some of his staff and General Greely and officers of his mission, looking very wistful. In order to clear the snow-capped Elzbourg Mountains, we had to climb rapidly to 16,500 feet, which left me feeling dizzy and light in the head. There were clouds and a sort of milky mist high in the air; presently the visibility grew worse. After we crossed the mountains, we had to come down and run under the clouds at a very low altitude. We reached the shore of the Caspian Sea at the mouth of the Snizel Uzen River, a coffee-colored stream which dirtied the blue Caspian for miles out from the shore. We circled the town of Rischt at its mouth and headed along the coast at 900 feet for Baku, where we planned to spend the night. We circled over Baku and the surrounding oil fields several times before we touched down on a muddy airfield at 10:30 A.M.

Baku is a very old city of some 850,000 people. It reminded me of the oil fields on Signal Hill at Long Beach—oil derricks by the thousand and a greasy film over everything. The odor of crude oil hung heavy on the air.

At the airfield, we were met by a representative from the People's Commissariat for Foreign Affairs, who took us off to the Intourist Hotel, where we had what was no doubt once the Royal Suite. It was lavishly furnished and decorated, even to a baby grand piano, but, as I was to find in most hotels in Russia, little attention was paid to the details of cleanliness. However, we were comfortable.

That evening, we were entertained at a Turkish opera. Of course, we couldn't understand what was said. The singing was most unusual; it sounded something like the bleating of a kid for its mother. The lovers sang their parts all through the opera in this queer nasal chant. It was a very interesting experience—if you only see and hear it once.

Weather reports were so slow coming in that we did not get away for Kuibyshev until 10:50 A.M. We headed up the Caspian shoreline until we were half way to Astrakhan, then pointed the nose of the plane directly for Stalingrad, which in Czarist days was known at Tsaritsin. Although it was lovely spring at home, this countryside was still covered with ice and snow. Outside, it was bitter, below zero weather, but in our heated plane we were warm and comfortable. I gave thanks that I had not taken the unheated, uninsulated transport the Russians had sent to Teheran for me.

We circled Stalingrad for a good look at the town. This was before the city had fallen under the siege to the Germans and it was still, from the air, an impressive sight. We landed on a snow-covered field, expecting to gas up, get weather reports, and go on to Kuibyshev. It was after four with only a couple of hours flying time left before dark. Having had experience with Russian flying conditions, I had no desire for after-dark flying. A low-pressure storm center was coming down out of the north and the weather man was not at all sure just when it would reach us. After considering all factors, pilot Kraigher and the Russian co-pilot decided to spend the night in Stalingrad. Since this was unexpected, it threw the officialdom of Stalingrad into a tailspin. By dint of much shouting and gesticulating in Russian, they made their decision stick.

We were taken to the officer's mess at the air school, where they had somehow contrived the usual Russian spread—smoked fish, caviar, cucumbers, pickles, ham, chicken, and several vegetables, plus plenty of vodka; when we finished dinner, I began to wonder how much of my stomach I had left to give for my country. There certainly was no shortage of food.

After dinner, we were taken in a battered limousine that rattled and wheezed, old and feeble enough once to have carried the Czar, over a bumpy, slushy road into the city. The Intourist Hotel, so they said, had been converted into a military hospital and was filled with wounded soldiers from the front. Our lodging for the night had, in Czarist days, apparently been a schoolhouse. When I visited Stalingrad after the siege and German defeat, all that remained of that building after the terrible bombardment was one end wall.

All the other members of my party and the crew were quartered in a large dormitory. In keeping with my diplomatic position, I was given a private room—formerly the school slop room. We had one broken down toilet and washstand for all hands. But the beds, Army cots, were comfortable and we slept under some of the finest woolen blankets I have ever seen, manufactured in a factory in Stalingrad, I was told.

In a large room of the schoolhouse, our hosts kept spread at all times a fair simulation of a Kremlin banquet. A coterie of official servants met our every need. Despite our unusual accommodations, we were quite comfortable.

During our stay, the Mayor of the city, a Communist Party representative, and the local head of the NKVD were always with us. Together with my NKVD Major, they saw me to my door when I turned in and they were patiently waiting outside when I came out in the morning. After dinner, our hosts took us to a movie house, which was more than half underground. I was told that it was so constructed for protection from the bitter cold of winter. However, Field Marshall Von Paulus found it gave him good protection from Russian artillery shells, for it was from the entrance of this same underground theater that Von Paulus emerged to surrender the remnants of his shattered army to the Red Army Commander.

The Russian film depicted the defense of Stalingrad during another war, the civil war of 1918–1919. J. Stalin was the hero of the play. Because of his successful defense of the city, the city was renamed Stalingrad. Of course, the play showed him to the best advantage as a Hero of the Revolution.

When I arose the next morning, the old snow was covered with a new white blanket eight inches deep. With a heavy snowfall continuing and with bad flying weather reported all the way to Kuibyshev, we decided to stay on in our schoolhouse for yet another night. Our Russian hosts were even more attentive. The banquet spread was more lavish and liquid refreshment, particularly vodka, flowed with greater freedom. Having some regard for my health, I excused myself and retired early. Some of my party stayed on to compete with the Russians in their favorite indoor sport.

When we left the plane, the Russians had insisted that all of our effects which were portable must be taken from the plane to the schoolhouse. Apparently pilfering was not uncommon and the local NKVD didn't want to be held responsible for loss of the new American Ambassador's kit enroute to his station. Among the effects delivered to the schoolhouse was a case of Scotch whiskey belonging to Gledhill.

Not to be outdone by Russian hospitality, toward the shank of the evening, Frank asked if he couldn't be permitted to supply the liquor for the remaining toasts. The Russians happily agreed. Not accustomed to Scotch, they poured it out like vodka, half a water glass of liquor neat, which they tossed off in a couple of gulps. After the second round of Scotch, our Russian hosts slid quietly under the table and were heard from no more until morning.

We took off from Stalingrad early on Tuesday, April 7th, and flew up the wide valley of the Volga River. The countryside wore a white coverlet of new snow. We landed at a military airfield about eighteen miles from Kuibyshev. The Counselor of our Embassy and Chargé d'Affaires, Mr. Walter Thurston, and several other members of the Embassy staff met the plane. The Russians had provided ancient limousines which took us over terrible roads, rutted and oozy with sticky clay from the melting snow. So ended my flight into Russia, 14,000 miles in eleven days, with 95¼ hours in the air. After two days rest and relaxation at our *residentia*,

Frank Gledhill and his crew took off for Teheran and Cairo to resume their aerial survey.

I Report for Duty

The Russian governmental situation was very complicated. When the fall of Moscow seemed imminent in the fall of 1941, the official seat of the Soviet Government and all members of the Diplomatic Corps were evacuated to Kuibyshev, once known in earlier days as Samara. However, the President of the Presidium of the Supreme Soviet, the venerable old Bolshevik, Mr. Mikhail Ivanovich Kalinin, and Marshal Stalin never left Moscow. Mr. Molotov, the Commissar of Foreign Affairs, remained in Kuibyshev only a few days when he too returned to Moscow. The branch office of the Commissariat in Kuibyshev was directed by Mr. A. Y. Vishinsky, famed as the prosecutor of the blood purge trials in the thirties, and Mr. I. E. Lozovsky. As a result, I found myself in an anomalous position. Mr. Thurston had to continue as Chargé d'Affaires until such time as I could present my credentials to Mr. Kalinin, for he, not Marshal Stalin, was the titular Chief of State of Soviet Russia.

Since I could not afford to remain in Kuibyshev, I immediately asked for a Russian plane to take me to Moscow. At 8:37 A.M. Saturday, 11 April, my same companions plus Mr. Thurston, and I took off for Moscow. As our plane circled the huge, empty Moscow airport, I was what our Navy lads during the war used to call an "eager beaver." I was full of confidence tempered by hope that I could do much to help coordinate the war effort of the Western Allies with the action on the Russian front. My instructions before I left Washington had given me authority to approach Molotov and Stalin in a frank and open manner, lay the cards on the table, and, as it were, "talk turkey" in plain sailorman language. These men with whom I was to deal, I told myself, were only men, human beings born of woman. With my long experience in handling men from every walk of life, surely I would have no trouble with these.

As we flew low over the city, I saw the bulbous domes of the Kremlin, darkened by camouflage paint to an unusual drabness, in contrast to the glittering water of the Moscow River which split the city, Red Square, the mighty spire of St. Basil's church. As we let down for our landing, I saw a little group of dignitaries waiting on the snowy field in the bitter cold. Behind them, the bayonets on the rifles of the guard of honor glistened in the bright noonday sunlight. I looked at my watch as we touched down. It was 12:43.

I took a deep breath, trying to deny the excitement which possessed me. "Moscow," I said, paraphrasing General Pershing in World War I, "we are here."

Except that a minor official of the Foreign Office, not Molotov, met me, the greeting was almost identical to the one previously described for the Beaverbrook-Harriman Mission. Welcoming smiles gave an artificial brightness to the dark Russian faces. Greetings were exchanged in English and Russian without interpreting. Then, my Russian escorts led me down to the Guard for the usual courtesy of inspection. We stopped while an excellent military band played the *Internationale,* followed by a sprightly rendition of the *Star Spangled Banner.* The Guard was a fine-looking platoon of strapping six-footers, handsomely turned out in the best tailored uniforms I saw in Russia.

Our Embassy cars took us away. During the five mile drive to Spaso House, we saw factories teeming with workers. Since it was the noon hour, workers went in droves in and out of the gates. Many of the factories were surrounded by high board fences—war industries, an Embassy aide told me. The buildings along the streets seemed even more dilapidated than in September. The winter cold had spalded off more stucco. Repairs and painting were needed everywhere.

New construction had been halted leaving many buildings in a half-finished condition. Beside the Moscow River, the stubby steel girders of what was one day intended to be the Palace of the Soviets rose exposed to the corroding elements. I saw block after block of stores, closed and boarded up. With every effort being expended on the war effort, there just weren't any consumer goods for the people.

I was full of curiosity and not a little annoyed because Walter Thurston could give me so little information as to what went on behind those Moscow walls or within the buildings. I found it hard to believe that a person could live in Moscow for three years and not know *something* about the government buildings and walled-off spaces of the capital city. After I had been in Moscow for a year and a half, I knew but little more about them than I found out on that first day on my ride through the city with Mr. Thurston. Therein lies the difficulty our American people find in obtaining an understanding of the USSR and the Russian people. Even when you reside in that country, it is impossible for you to see much of its cities and rural areas or to get to know at all well any of its people. Living as we do in a free country, our people simply cannot comprehend the conditions under which the ordinary citizens of the Soviet Union exist.

Most of the young and middle-aged men and women wore some sort of uniform, usually of rough material and ill-fitting. Such civilians as we passed, usually the very young or the very old, while warmly clad, wore the cheapest and most unbecoming clothing. Most had on overcoats and warm woolen gloves. Women wore two pairs of baggy cotton stockings, over which they pulled the usual cloth and skin Russian boot, which those fortunate enough to have boots wear in Russia during the winter. Malnutrition was evident among the children and the old people. Workers and men and women in uniform, while spare and wirey-looking, seemed to be vigorous and healthy. Able-bodied women did much of the heavy work of the city—sweeping streets, clearing off snow, driving cars and trucks, digging ditches, and such little building repair work as I saw in progress.

At Spaso House, I quickly unpacked my personal gear, impatient to get on with my new job. At that moment, I sincerely believed that Stalin and other Russian governmental officials eagerly awaited my arrival so that we could get on with settling some outstanding problems, too long neglected. How naive of me!

Nothing could be accomplished over the weekend. On Monday, I requested an interview with Mr. Vyacheslav Molotov, then both a member of the Politburo and Commissar of Foreign Affairs. That afternoon, Molotov received me in his office in the Kremlin. I was never able to figure out the arrangement of offices in the Kremlin. This outer office of Mr. Molotov's was pretty much like all of the rest that I visited—a few shiny chairs, conventional office furniture, no papers on top of the desk, no filing cabinets, a heavy, rich rug on the floor, heavy drapes drawn so that the room must always be lighted by electricity even at mid-day.

Mr. Molotov was seated behind the desk at the far end of the room, a square chunk of a man, with a wide face, sharp eyes, and a completely impassive expression. He rose on stumpy legs to greet me and indicated a seat across the desk from him. Seemingly, he intended to be open and expansive, apparently trying to create just the right atmosphere of cordial cooperation and friendliness.

Of course, there is always a language difficulty in these meetings with Soviet officials. When I reflected on our conversations later, I could not help but realize the many advantages which the Russians had. With Molotov and to a lesser degree with Stalin, I always felt that they understood a lot more of what we said in English than I ever did of their Russian. Here is how we compared.

Mr. Molotov had been out of the Soviet Union but once in his life—a visit to Berlin before the war—while my acquaintance with foreign countries was quite extensive. He had, through his officers in various countries, and a most efficient system of espionage, a working knowledge of conditions in foreign countries, while I knew almost nothing of conditions in the Soviet Union. He spoke no English. His interpreter, Mr. Pavlov, had a complete command of both Russian and English and several other languages. I understood almost no Russian at all and therefore had to depend completely upon Mr. Pavlov's translation or upon Eddie Page, who had a good command of Russian and usually went with me to these interviews. Mr. Molotov spoke and understood French readily while my knowledge of French was inadequate.

When you have to sit back and wait for an interpreter to translate your remarks, you never get a feeling of achieving a full mental contact with the Russian official across the table. First, you had to listen to a stream of rapid Russian from the official. Mr. Pavlov scribbled notes in shorthand and then read the translation in his faultless English. I couldn't check up on his translation with Eddie until we left the meeting. Somehow, you always had a feeling that the interpreter wasn't playing exactly fair, although that, of course, was ridiculous. Mr. Pavlov would not have long survived in the Kremlin had he trifled with the original script and Mr. Pavlov has been around for a long, long while.

This situation at interviews gave promise of many interesting experiences. I soon discovered that negotiating through an interpreter is like kissing through a cheesecloth—little satisfaction can be gotten from either.

Mr. Molotov's delivery of his remarks in Russian was sharp and incisive. I didn't find him the cold individual that some observers have reported. His fine brown eyes are bright and clear. He smiles from time to time, lighting up his heavy countenance. In months to come, I felt that I got as close to him as any foreigner could ever get to a Soviet Russian official, but I didn't delude myself that we ever became really friendly. We just didn't have an opportunity to achieve such a relationship. But I never felt that Mr. Molotov operated with any personal animosity toward me.

Our conversation began with the usual amenities through Mr. Pavlov. Molotov inquired as to my trip to Moscow, about my family and of the health of President Roosevelt. I expressed my appreciation of his kindness in letting me fly to Kuibyshev in my private plane. We both expressed hope that we would have a pleasant and effective association in bringing our countries closer together in the war effort against our common enemy.

I requested an appointment with President Kalinin in order to present my credentials. Mr. Molotov was silent for a moment. Presently Mr. Pavlov interpreted his next remark. "Mr. Kalinin will be happy to receive you at two P.M. tomorrow."

I then asked for an appointment to see Marshal Stalin at an early date as there were certain urgent matters for discussion between our governments which had been entrusted to me for presentation to Mr. Stalin. Molotov said something sharply in Russian, which Pavlov translated, "Mr. Molotov will have to consult Marshal Stalin before he can make an appointment for you."

I was beginning to learn. Every question, of even the most minor importance, eventually passed up to Stalin for decision.

Even when you have an appointment, an official visit to the Kremlin is not a casual affair. First, you must be invited. It is well not to be late but it is apt to cause you considerable embarrassment if you are early. Taking my entire staff with me, we went from Spaso House in three dilapidated automobiles, which seemed to be the best that our State Department could provide for their Embassy in Moscow. We were followed closely by my Russian NKVD "protectors" in their little car. A platoon of Red soldiers stood guard at the gate. After questioning my chauffeur, their officer assigned a soldier to ride the running board of each of our cars. My bodyguards remained outside, feeling, no doubt, that I was perfectly safe in the sanctuary of the Kremlin. The chimes struck two as we entered the massive arched doorway of the Great Palace.

We went down the same long corridor which I had followed the day before and into either the same outer office or another very much like it. Waiting for me was Mr. Maxim Litvinov, with several uniformed officers of the Foreign Office, the Chief of Protocol, his assistants and the interpreter. As we waited, a contingent of news and motion picture photographers filed silently into the room.

There was none of the boisterousness our own newsmen exhibit. They stood in a corner of the office near the door and waited. Presently, a diplomatic aide ushered us through the far doorway into a long board room, with a large, highly polished table down its center at which twenty people could be seated. My staff followed and lined up behind me as I went down the long room to meet President Kalinin, who was standing in front of a door with his *alter ego,* the interpreter.

The interpreter said something to Mr. Kalinin, which must have been my presentation, for the President bowed slightly and held out his hand. After I had been presented, I handed him my letter of credence, written in the quaint formal phraseology following the diplomatic protocol of an earlier day. I, a distinguished citizen of my country, the letter said, would "reside near the government" of his Excellency. It paid me the compliment of mentioning my high character and ability and ended, rather oddly I thought when addressed to a Communist of pronounced anti-religious sentiments, with the hope that God would have his Excellency in his wise keeping.

Mr. Kalinin glanced at the document and handed it to the interpreter with a remark in Russian directed at me. "We welcome you to the Soviet Union," the interpreter said.

As we chatted about the world situation (if one can be said to chat through an interpreter), I took the opportunity to size up Mr. Kalinin. Even then, he was a very old man, with snow-white hair closely clipped to his head, no moustache, a pointed grey beard. I observed a cast in one of his eyes and thought he might have a glass eye. He wore a plain blue suit with a sort of string tie. An Old Bolshevik, he was one of Stalin's staunchest supporters and most trusted associates. While as President of the Presidium, he possessed little actual power, as a member of the Politburo, he no doubt exercised considerable influence with Stalin.

"I am pleased to be sent to Russia as Ambassador from my country, Mr. President," I said pleasantly. "I am here primarily to do everything I can to help your country get on with the war. President Roosevelt told me to extend to you his warmest greetings and to express the hope that you continue in good health."

I then presented each member of my staff, which completed the ceremony. I made my adieus and headed for the door, followed by my staff.

While we were in the conference room, a battery of still and movie cameras had moved into position in the outer office. When

I went through the door, I was met by a rapid fire clicking and grinding of cameras. When I tried to hurry through the photographers, I discovered that was not the plan. President Kalinin had followed me to the door. I was to be photographed with him. I went back and we posed until the boys had enough, very much like a similar experience at home, except that, in Russia, it was, "One more please. Just one picture more, Comrade President."

With this ordeal by camera over, we left the Kremlin. I was now United States Ambassador Extraordinary and Minister Plenipotentiary to the Soviet Union.

As I have noted, I had thought that Marshal Stalin would be eager to see the new United States Ambassador, if only to persuade him to expedite the delivery and increase the quantity and variety of Lend-Lease material. Not at all! Days went by, a week and then ten days, a not unusual treatment of a new foreign representative in the Russian capital.

While waiting, more or less on tenterhooks, I received a coded despatch from the State Department, which went something like this:

> It is suggested for your consideration that, under no circumstances, should you take up with Marshal Stalin or Mr. Molotov any of the matters discussed with you prior to your departure from Washington. If either of them bring up those subjects, act as if you have no knowledge of them.

I sat looking at the despatch. "What goes on here?" I asked Eddie Page, handing him the message. He read it and shook his head. "Beyond me, Admiral."

"We can't get anywhere on such a basis," I burst out. "It's ridiculous on the face of it."

The matters to which the message referred apparently covered the whole scope of my briefing in Washington—such important unsettled questions as the release of the Polish officers captured by the Red Army when Germany and Russia partitioned Poland in 1939; permission to fly planes across Siberia to deliver them to the Red Air Force; coordinating Red intelligence activities with those of the other allies; establishment of better radio communications between America and Russia; release of American aviators interned in Russia if they made forced landings in Siberia after raids on Japan; and a better exchange of information on technical and tactical matters. Still in the discussion stage was the matter of

weather codes and weather data, a subject which the British had
been negotiating with the Russians since before the Beaverbrook-
Harriman Mission.

I sat down at my desk and wrote out a message to the Department, which went as follows:

> Replying to your recent message, to act as you suggest would un-
> dermine my prestige and influence with Marshal Stalin even before
> I present my credentials to him. How can I pretend to know nothing
> about important matters at issue between our governments, when
> Mr. Stalin and Mr. Molotov know that I must have full knowledge
> of them or I would not be here as diplomatic representative of our
> government?

Since I never received an answer to this despatch, I decided to
ignore the Department's "suggestion."

In searching the records recently, I came across a telegram
dated April 11, 1942, the day that I arrived in Moscow, from President Roosevelt to Premier Stalin, which reads as follows:

> It is unfortunate that geographical distance makes it practically
> impossible for you and me to meet at this time. Such a meeting of
> minds in personal conversation would be greatly useful to the con-
> duct of the war against Hitlerism. Perhaps if things go as well as we
> hope, you and I could spend a few days together next summer near
> our common border off Alaska. But in the meantime, I regard it as of
> the utmost military importance that we have the nearest possible ap-
> proach to an exchange of views.
>
> I have in mind a very important military proposal involving uti-
> lization of our armed forces in a manner to relieve your critical west-
> ern front. This objective carries great weight with me.
>
> Therefore, I wish you would consider sending Mr. Molotov and a
> general upon whom you rely to Washington in the immediate future.
> Time is of the essence if we are to help in an important way. We will
> furnish them with a good transport plane so that they should be able
> to make the round trip in two weeks.
>
> I do not want by such a trip to go over my friend, Mr. Litvinov, in
> any way, as he will understand, but we can gain time by the visit I
> propose.
>
> I suggest this procedure not only because of the secrecy, which is
> so essential, but because I need your advice before we can determine
> with finality the strategic course of our common military action.
>
> I have sent Hopkins to London relative to this proposal.
>
> The American people are thrilled by the magnificent fighting of

your armed forces and we want to help you in the destruction of Hitler's armies and material more than we are now doing.

I send you my sincere regards.

In looking back on the events in Moscow during my regime as Ambassador, it is interesting to note the lack of information furnished me with regard to matters being discussed by Great Britain and the United States. For example, with one despatch, President Roosevelt had by-passed not only me, his Ambassador to Moscow, but also the Russian Ambassador in Washington. Although I had an interview with Mr. Molotov on April 13, and Mr. Stalin and Mr. Molotov on April 23, and again with Mr. Molotov on April 25, in none of these interviews was mention made of Mr. Molotov's plan to visit London and Washington.

I am quite certain that British Ambassador Sir Archibald Clark-Kerr knew of Molotov's impending visit to London, but he did not inform me until May 28, when he invited me to the British Embassy to read the agreement with the British which Mr. Molotov had signed in London on May 26th. It was then that I also learned that Mr. Molotov had left Moscow for London and the United States the same afternoon that I had last visited him.

The record also shows that the subject of the second front and the question as to whether the landings should be made across the English Channel or from the south through Europe's "soft underbelly" was being discussed even before I arrived in Moscow. As a matter of fact, BBC announced at the time of Sir Stafford Cripps' earlier trip to Moscow that he had promised a second front in Europe when the situation justified it.

This was an early exemplification of a pulling and hauling in different directions by our State Department and other agencies of our government, notably the Lend-Lease Administration, which were to plague me during the whole course of my mission to Moscow. As I waited for Stalin to make up his mind that it was time to see me, I could see that I was in for a bad time in the land of the Soviets. But like any good sailor, I resolved to square my hat, carry out my orders, and do the best I could. Thus was my ship of state launched. I was underway on the sea of diplomacy with the rocks and shoals along my course but indifferently charted.

BOOK TWO

My Tour of Duty in the Soviet Union

CHAPTER VII

The Life of a Diplomat Among the Soviets

WHILE I waited for Marshal Stalin to receive me, I tried to get settled down in Spaso House, an impressive-looking mansion, which took its name from unpronounceable Spa-sopeskovskaya Square.

Spaso House can best be described by referring to four rough sketches I made. View No. 1 shows the front elevation. Behind its impressive façade is considerable shoddiness. The banister railings and columns, while having the appearance of marble from a distance, are actually constructed of metal plastered over with cheap cement. The stucco had spalded off the walls in irregular patches.

View No. 2 shows the plan of the house and gardens. The establishment was ideal for regal entertaining but the house and grounds could not be kept up properly during those war years. The bombings of 1941 had broken many window panes. Wind blew in around the beaver board, which we used to replace broken panes; in the winter you could occupy some of those dark and gloomy rooms only if dressed in heavy fur clothing.

The lawns were not cut or rolled. Trees and shrubs had died from neglect. An improvised air raid shelter made an ugly hump in the middle of the rear garden. The heating plant in the basement was well-constructed and doubtless had once had ample capacity, but, like everything else in Moscow, it was in a low state of repair. To keep from freezing, we installed oil stoves in a number of rooms, with smokepipes projecting through the windows.

View No. 3 shows the ground floor plan of the Embassy. Visitors to Spaso House step into an imposing entrance hallway done in natural mahogany with six black and white (imitation) Italian marble columns down its length, climb some "marble" stairs a half-deck up, as it were, into a broad hallway. To the right, he sees a matching "marble" stairway leading up to the second floor. In the area to the right, are an automatic elevator which accommodates four persons but is rarely operative, a small bedroom, downstairs lavatories and toilet, a telephone booth and switchboard. In the other corner in what was once a small sitting room, we had an office.

This large hallway and the two-story high Great Hall are decorated in a white "marble and gold" effect, with large white columns spaced throughout the two halls as indicated. In the center of the Great Hall ceiling hung the pride of our Embassy, a magnificent chandelier, heavily gold plated and festooned with hundreds of beautiful crystals. At the rear of Great Hall is an oval "State Dining Room," with wall lights hung with clusters of crystal. Once handsome plaster cornices and frescoes were flaking off. Wall coverings of once exquisite satin were dirty and torn; some of them hung down the walls in tattered strips.

The opposite end of Great Hall is partially partitioned off by columns and "stub walls," which give it the air of a separate room. Large French doors open out onto a lower veranda overlooking the front garden, which I could imagine lighted by strings of colored lights or Japanese lanterns and peopled by elaborately costumed ladies and uniformed gentlemen of the Czar's court society. On the second floor, alcoves open out on Great Hall from all sides, from which guests could look down upon the stately measures of a grand march.

Between "marble" columns, the visitor entered yet another hallway leading to the smoking room on the left and the service pantry on the right. Beyond this hallway in what once had been a large library, we had our movie room. The two projectors were located in a booth in the smoking room.

Beyond the movie room was an enormous banquet hall constructed by Bill Bullitt when he was our first Ambassador to the Soviet Union. In my time, it was filled with furniture and other gear evacuated from our embassies in the Baltic States.

View No. 4 is a partial second floor plan. On the side shown in considerable detail, the elevator and the riser from the front stairway are indicated, as is the arrangement of the suite I occupied at the rear of the house.

View No. 5 shows our Chancery, called *Mokhovaya* (Mŏck-hō-vă-yā), on Mokhovaya Ulitsa next door to the National Hotel. From its upper floors, you could look down on the Kremlin gardens. From front windows, you looked across Red Square at Lenin's small but impressive tomb.

Before the War, Mokhovaya was the office building of our Embassy, with apartments not needed as offices used by personnel of the Embassy as living quarters. Each floor contained six apartments, two large ones on each side of the center arch and a smaller apartment at the center, front and rear. In the rear was an enclosed "garden," half of which was devoted to a tennis court.

With the early bombings all of the windows were broken. Ambassador Steinhardt moved the Embassy offices to Spaso House, which was somewhat more habitable. When I arrived in Moscow, Mokhovaya was used to house the offices of such "stray" agencies as Lend-Lease, Military and Naval Attachés, and the Red Cross. Gradually, as we made order out of the chaos, we moved the Embassy offices back into Mokhovaya, where we had a "window on the Kremlin."

View No. 6 shows the layout of the house and 20 acres of ground at our *dacha*, situated on the bank of a small river, with a high board fence surrounding the three other sides to shut out the prying eyes of the proletariat. The boat landing in the river served as a mooring for a small Embassy launch, the engine of which was generally inoperative. We made a vegetable garden to supplement our scanty allowances of fresh vegetables and greens. When properly kept up, the grounds must have been lovely, but the greenhouse, the bathhouse, and other outbuildings were badly run down and I was never able to get the Russians to repair them.

View No. 7 shows the floor, front and side elevation plans of the *dacha*, two stories high in front and one story in the rear. The upper floor had three bedrooms, bath and large hallway. With a cool breeze off the river, we found our *dacha* a refreshing retreat from the sweltering humidity of Moscow in Summer.

Like all property in the Soviet Union, these buildings belonged to the Soviet Government, from whom our State Department rented them at an exorbitant rental.

My Staff

When the seat of Soviet Government was officially shifted to Kuibyshev in the Fall of 1941, Ambassador Laurence Steinhardt skeletonized his staff. Some twenty clerks and all American female citizens, both wives and clerks, were sent home. The rest of the staff was divided between Moscow and Kuibyshev.

When Ambassador Steinhardt was called home in November, 1941, Mr. Walter R. Thurston, Counselor of the Embassy since April 14, 1939, was promoted to Minister Counselor of the Embassy and *chargé d'affaires,* and so continued until I presented my credentials to President Kalinin on April 14, 1942.

With Mr. Thurston's long experience in the Foreign Service, I always felt that he was much better qualified to represent the interests of the United States in Moscow than a retired admiral of the U. S. Navy. However, the decision was not his or mine to make. If Walter Thurston harbored any feeling of resentment or disappointment, he never indicated it in any way. A warm friendly character, I found him a tower of strength to lean upon in the early weeks of my mission. He continued to serve faithfully and loyally until he was detached and left for home in September, 1942.

I recall talking to him about his nearly four years of continuous residence in Moscow and Kuibyshev. "Time I was going home, Admiral," he said. "The Russian girls are beginning to look good to me."

I soon discovered that I had inherited an excellent staff. Among the State Department career men were Mr. Charles E. Dickerson, our First Secretary, Mr. G. Frederick Reinhardt, Third Secretary, and Mr. Llewellyn Thompson, who took charge of the Moscow Embassy and Chancery when the rest of us went to Kuibyshev. Among the Military Attachés were Major Joseph (Mike) Michella, Captain Richard Park, Jr., Captain James O. Boswell, Captain Robert E. McCabe, First Lieutenant John R. Allison and First Lieutenant Hubert Zemke. Lieutenant Commander Ronald H. Allen was holding forth as Acting Naval Attaché. He had as assistants, Lieutenant Samuel B. Franckel and Lieutenant George D. Roullard. As I have previously noted, I brought with me Captain Jack Duncan, who assumed the office of Naval Attaché; Eddie Page; and Doctor Lang of the Navy Medical Corps. In Vladivostok, Mr. Angus Ward was our Consul General. Mr. Scovell headed the Moscow office of the American Red Cross. We had several civilian clerks and a number of enlisted men of all services, as communications personnel and stenographers. While they cannot each be mentioned here by name, all were loyal, hard-working men, living under extremely difficult conditions in a country whose people were far from cordial.

In addition to the official members of my staff, also present in Moscow were the personnel of other official and semi-official agencies for which the Ambassador had a certain responsibility. Among these was Brigadier General Phillip Faymonville, U. S. Army, our Lend-Lease representative in the Soviet Union. On many occasions, he proved to be a most valued aide, but, since he did not come directly under my authority, I found his activities an almost constant source of difficulty and embarrassment.

Beside these American members of my entourage, certain Russian and other foreign assistants played a not inconsiderable role in my daily life. With an Embassy and a residence both in Moscow and Kuibyshev, certain individual messengers and chauffeurs accompanied me on each change of headquarters. We maintained a staff of cooks and servants at each house.

In Spaso House, beside the usual Russian cooks, housemaids, chauffeurs, telephone operators, we had engineers to keep operating our antiquated heating plant of two oil and one coal furnaces. We also had two Chinese houseboys, Chin Po Fan and Tung Yu Lin, who had been evacuated from one of the Baltic States to our Moscow Embassy. Although outnumbered, like all good Chinese servants Chin Po and Tung Yu ruled the Spaso roost.

The most trusted Russian employee was Phillip O. Bender, who had been with the Embassy since recognition of the Soviet Government in 1933. While rated on our books as messenger and telephone operator, Bender spoke many languages fluently and was often called upon to interpret for us. I found him a reliable and loyal worker, which was probably the reason that he was later thrown into prison by the secret police. This brings me to one of the most interesting and, to freeborn Americans, *the* most puzzling aspect of Russian life under the Communist dictatorship.

The Soviet Secret Police

Under Czars, there was always a secret police organization.

On January 27, 1853, Mr. Neill S. Brown, our American Minister to Russia, reported:

> Nothing is more striking to an American, on his first arrival here, than the rigor of the police. It would seem that the capital was in a state of siege. And among all the astringents put into requisition for the preservation of peace and order, none is so abhorrent as the censorial power. As a proof of the extent to which it is carried, I may mention that the late message of the President of the United States was not regarded in all its parts as a safe document for Russian read-

ers, and came to their hands scathed with the censor's knife. . . . It is
difficult in many instances to see the reasons of the application of this
power; and no doubt it is often capricious.

Just before the October Revolution, OKRANA was the hated in-
stitution of repression. Destruction of the OKRANA was a fighting
slogan of the Bolshevik Party. OKRANA was destroyed by the
Kerensky Provisional Government, but, almost immediately after
the Bolsheviks seized power under Lenin, the Communist Government established a police commission, which became known to
the Russian people and the world as the dread CHEKA, from the
initials of the Russian words which made up its full name. At the
time I was in Russia, the secret police was called NKVD. It was
administered by Beria, often considered the Politburo member
closest to Stalin. Before that, under Chief of Police Yagoda and
Beria the secret police was called GPU (Gay Pay Ooo), and OGPU;
since then it has been succeeded by twin organizations, MVD and
MGB.

In the Russian police state, the secret police serve many useful
functions.

> It is the instrument of Terror.
>
> It suppresses the resistance of the bourgeoisie.
>
> It guards the Soviet people against enemy agents, foreign and
> domestic.
>
> It is a counter to the "aggressive, frankly expansionist course of
> American imperialism," (which is the present party line).

Whatever the Bolshevik polemics, the naked fact is that the Communist Party could not long remain in power, without the Terror
which the various names of the secret police inspire in the vast majority of Russians, who are not Communist Party members at all.
Among things which an NKVD (or MVD and MGB) accomplishes
for the Communist regime are:

> It provides the penal labor and virtual slave labor which have
> made possible the exploitation and development of industries and
> areas where no other inducement could attract labor exercising
> free will.
>
> It keeps less regimented labor working, despite limited incentive
> in the way of desirable consumer goods.
>
> It administers both the slave labor and "free" labor forces of the
> nation for the dictatorship, operating its own vast complex of indus-
> trial establishments and providing labor for other industries.

It operates the concentration camps.

It recruits, trains, administers and assigns the so-called "Free Labor Force" of young men and women to provide a source of labor for both agriculture and industry. About a million young men and women per year are "recruited" for assignment to four years of labor *wherever assigned* after completion of a training period.

It exercises political control and eliminates opposition to the regime, not only among the general public but also within the party and on the highest governmental levels. As witness the elimination of Chief of Police Yagoda in the Blood Purge when he joined up with Stalin's enemies.

I have mentioned that an NKVD major joined our party in Teheran. I never knew his name but I took to calling him Mike. He accompanied me as far as Moscow but, as soon as I presented my credentials and my safety became of more importance to the government, Mike was relieved by a detail of NKVD operatives, which maintained a squad of three with me wherever I went, except when I was in our own compound or in Soviet Government buildings. Only the British Ambassador and I were so "honored," although all members of the Diplomatic Corps were doubtless under continuous scrutiny. When I took a constitutional or, on a fine day, walked down to Mokhovaya, one of my NKVD boys would take station fifteen paces ahead of me, one directly behind me, and one fifteen paces to the rear. When I went in a car, it was always followed, day or night, by an NKVD car with three of my boys as passengers. If I went out for a day's jaunt, another squad was sent out to "relieve for lunch." When I went to the opera or theater, seats on my left and right and immediately behind me were reserved for my boys. Occasionally, I would decide to take in a show on the spur of the moment, obtaining my tickets from one of the staff who had put in for them through official channels in his own name. This always caused consternation among the boys but they were equal to the occasion. Occupants of seats on my right, left and behind me were summarily dispossessed to make way for my protectors.

I tried to look upon the services of these NKVD men in the spirit in which I was told they were offered—for my protection and safety. A small shack was set up alongside our gate to facilitate the performance of their duties. I soon found out that they wouldn't accept food or drink, but they were eager for American cigarettes, and I kept the boys supplied. If I lost them on a drive into the country, I always turned back until I found them. When my ancient car broke down, the boys gave me a lift home.

The mere mechanics of living in Russia are very complicated. Coal and oil for our heating plant were rationed and obtainable only after extensive negotiations in each case with Burobin, the literal translation of the longer Russian name for which it stands being, "The Administration for Service to the Diplomatic Corps." On one occasion in Moscow when we were running short of fuel, I was informed that I could get the oil requested if I would take a tank load. After filling all of our tanks, we found that the oil was of a very inferior quality, usable for heating only with great difficulty. On another occasion at Kuibyshev, when our coal bunkers were almost empty, I was informed that I could obtain the coal requested only if I would furnish the labor and transportation. I borrowed some trucks from Lend-Lease and put my entire staff, both men and women, to work. Everyone shoveled coal until our bunkers were full.

Food rationing was severe and rigid. While probably no worse for us than for the Russians, the resulting diet seemed fantastically inadequate to Americans accustomed to hearty eating. For example, the ration of eggs varied from five to ten per month per person, depending upon the importance of the person, and eggs frequently were unavailable at the fixed-price store operated for the use of foreigners. If you went into the "open market," where peasants were permitted to sell their excess produce, you would pay for chicken and beef $3.50 to $7.00 per kilogram (2.2 pounds), ham $8.50 to $10.00 a kilo, cabbage $1.00 a kilo, carrots 75¢ to $1.00 a kilo, apples $2.25 a kilo, and so on. Even at those prices, food was in such short supply that you could never depend upon getting what you wanted.

Therefore, we ran a commissary in the Embassy, importing canned goods and other staples. Every American plane that came into Moscow brought as heavy a load of foodstuffs and other essentials (many of which the Russians classified as luxuries) as we could arrange for on short notice. We also kept chickens for their egg production and as a welcome supplement to our meat diet when we butchered those which did not produce satisfactorily—although we felt with each hen killed somewhat like the boy who killed the goose that laid the golden egg. The supplement to our diet of fresh vegetables and salad greens from our gardens at the *dacha* outside of Moscow and in the Embassy residence grounds at Kuibyshev, I am sure, kept us from becoming completely anemic. By such means, we fed the personnel of our various missions and sometimes kept the cost within the allowance made by our government.

Like other Americans, who go to Russia full of good will for its people, I looked forward to better understanding between our countries if only we could come to know each other better. I had high hopes of contributing my small part toward such understanding by exhibiting always an open friendliness toward the Russians I might meet and by making firm friends of at least a few. How dashed were my hopes after a few weeks in Moscow!

I soon learned what every representative of our country has to know—we were almost completely isolated from the Russian people by propaganda, by fear of punishment and by activities of the secret police. With three NKVD boys accompanying me everywhere, few Muscovites cared to stop and chat with me, no matter how friendly I might appear.

As a result, we of the foreign colony lived together in a tight little city within a city. We saw each other daily, both on business and socially. On limited food supplies, entertainment budgets and in the midst of a war, we couldn't entertain frequently, but when we did, we entertained each other. Soon we knew each one's favorite story and when to get up and excuse ourselves if we didn't want to hear a tale again. We saw the same operas, ballets, and stage shows over and over again. We grew to know each other almost too well. We got to know the Russians not at all.

Not that we didn't invite the Russians to our parties and religiously go to theirs when they entertained officially, but the men in the Kremlin had no intention of letting any Russian become in the least bit friendly with a foreigner. Many a member of the pre-Communist intelligentsia and other dissident Russians were re-educated in Siberian labor camps for no worse offense than being seen too often in the company of foreigners.

Officially, we met with top-drawer officials of the Foreign Office and the Soviet Government on business fairly often, but months went by before I saw Mr. Kalinin again and sometimes weeks passed before an appointment could be made to see Mr. Stalin. Only Mr. Molotov and his assistants at Kuibyshev, Mr. Vishinsky and Mr. Lozovsky, made themselves readily available to me. At social gatherings, we saw the higher officials only when the Russians entertained, and then under the handicap of the formality of a Kremlin banquet or at a state occasion such as the opening of the Union Congress or a reception to some visiting dignitary from the West.

On the occasions when I entertained in the Embassy, I always made it a point to invite all of the higher officials of the Ministry of Foreign Affairs, and of the other Ministries of the government, as well as members of the Politburo whom I had met, and all of the high ranking military and naval officers I knew. We also invited prominent writers, artists, actors, opera singers, and ballet dancers. Of course, all of the Diplomatic Corps and the gentlemen and ladies of the Foreign and Russian Press received invitations to our parties. Only a few of the Russians ever showed up, usually a minor official of the Foreign Office, a general or an admiral, some junior officers and an occasional artist. Except for a few individuals, they received our welcome stiffly, took no more than two drinks, remained coldly aloof, and left early, as if afraid to be long exposed to the corroding influence of the foreign "Capitalist-Imperialists."

One exception to this aloofness was the Naval Commissar, Admiral Nikolai Kuznetsov. He seemed to feel that common bond of sympathy which exists between men who go down to the sea in ships. Frequently I was asked to visit him in his office where we discussed freely every phase of naval tactics and particularly the strength of the Japanese Navy and their Merchant Marine. However, we always met in his office. If he had a wife, I never met her. Occasionally, it was whispered that the reason Admiral Kuznetsov was different was because he was a former White Russian, the only one holding the position of a commissar.

All invitations had to be issued through the Foreign Office. We put R.S.V.P. on our invitations, but no one ever acknowledged or accepted. You never knew how many Russians would show up. Of two or three hundred Russians invited to our Fourth of July reception, the response might be three and it might be thirty. I often suspected that the Foreign Office delivered only those few invitations which it wanted accepted—probably, as one of my staff put it, with a postscript that said, "Go, but don't drink much, don't talk at all, don't stay long, and don't have any fun."

As to detail, I recall one cocktail party and buffet supper I gave for the Chiefs of Mission, their first secretaries and military attachés, and their ladies. The Greek Ambassador was the only Chief of Mission who was absent.

For plain, wholesome food, our Embassy cooks were the best in Moscow. We served four cold-storage turkeys sent in by plane from

Army supplies in Iran; the cooks had roasted them to a turn; the butler had served them up on silver platters at both ends and on each side of our long dining table, with three crocks of baked beans spaced around the table, an ample supply of caviar, and various types of rolls and bread.

For drinks, we served a vodka punch (which I avoided assiduously), a delicious Russian white wine, French champagne, and a limited selection from our slender store of canned fruit juices.

Eight ladies came to our party—the Yugoslav Minister's wife and two daughters, the Czechoslovakian Ambassador's and First Secretary's wives, the Iranian Minister's daughter and the wife of the Iranian Counselor, and the wife of a Swedish Embassy secretary. Since my French is bad and my Russian non-existent, my social chit-chat with the ladies was severely limited.

We placed the large victrola in an alcove off the Reception hall; a careful selection of soft music furnished a low background for the conversation during the evening. The new Chiefs of Mission had an opportunity to meet the other members of the Diplomatic set. As our guests departed, all of them, and especially the ladies, told me (through an interpreter, when necessary) that they had had a marvelous time.

I recall being in Mr. Molotov's office one day discussing Lend-Lease deliveries, when he made a surprising statement, "Even the man in the street knows we are getting Lend-Lease supplies from our Allies."

"That may be so, Mr. Molotov," I replied. "But we have no contact with the man in the street. In fact, foreigners have no contact with the Russian people at all. The man in the street does not dare to talk to us. If we should happen to make a friendly contact, our Russian acquaintance will inevitably ask us *not* to see him again as it would endanger his liberty, his freedom and quite possibly his life."

Mr. Molotov protested that this was not so. Immediately thereafter, the Russians set up in Moscow under the management of a Mr. and Mrs. Alexandrov a private club for the specific purpose of entertaining foreign diplomats in Moscow.

When invited to a party at this club, we were usually asked to furnish the foodstuffs, while the management supplied the drinks, the music and the Russian guests, usually such public figures as Mr. Tolstoy, the writer, Mr. Ilya Ehrenburg, the newspaper correspondent, and stars or lesser performers of the ballet, opera, screen and stage.

As for Russian official entertainment, of which there was considerable during my tour because of the many visiting "very important personages," I was always invited and so were a number of my staff. We always went, were cordially received, and were handsomely wined (or vodka-ed) and dined. For the middle of a grim war for survival, these official entertainments were excessively lavish, the food was over-rich, and there was always more than enough to drink.

Elsewhere, I have described in detail the several official banquets which I attended in the Kremlin. In addition, on three occasions, Mr. Molotov entertained the representatives of his principal Western allies. All three of these formal luncheons had remarkable similarities. Each was held in Spiridonov House, each menu was nearly identical to those in a Kremlin banquet, and the caterers and "special attendants" were the same as those who had served us in the Kremlin. There was also the usual "battle of the vodka," with eight or ten different kinds of vodka and wine at each place. The toasts ran on for hours. With attendants hovering over you, you had little opportunity to skip a course without seeming deliberately rude.

At the first of these luncheons on June 26, 1942, given as a welcoming party for Sir Archibald Clark-Kerr and myself, twenty-four places were set, including the Ambassadors, the heads of divisions in the two Embassies, and a number of senior officials of the Commissariat for Foreign Affairs.

This unusual spirit of good will and the vodka covered the several hours of the entertainment with a rosy glow. We had an opportunity to discuss some of our problems informally. This luncheon probably served its purpose for I left Spiridonov House feeling that we had laid the foundation for further discussion and cooperation with the Russians.

I have elsewhere described the second of these luncheons, given on May 26, 1943, to celebrate the anniversary of the signing of the Anglo-Soviet Agreement. That another luncheon was given in Spiridonov House by Mr. Molotov on June 11, 1943, has always seemed to indicate to me that the Foreign Office was "caught in a bight." They had given a sumptuous official luncheon to the British Ambassador to celebrate this Anglo-Soviet Pact, an agreement that it was already obvious consisted principally of vague promises for an indefinite future, while the Master Russian Lend-Lease Agreement negotiated by Mr. Molotov in Washington a year earlier had nearly gone unremembered. At any rate, our invitations gave us only one-day notice that Mr. Molotov would entertain and that I would be the honored guest.

In a letter to my wife, I described it as follows:

It was most evident that it was an American party. At the table were some thirty guests, with Sir Archibald on Mr. Molotov's left and I in the place of honor on his right, and Mr. Pavlov, our favorite interpreter, on my right. Mikoyan, Commissar for Foreign Trade, was again co-host in the hostess' place across the table from Molotov. On Mikoyan's right was Martel, Chief of the British Supply Mission [newly promoted to Field Marshal], and on his left was our Mike Michella, the first time he had been recognized as representing our Military. Apparently without significance, Mr. Litvinov, who [as Ambassador] had signed the treaty [in Washington] and who was in Moscow at the time, was absent "because of illness."

I was toasted almost as soon as we were seated at the table; in fact, as in most official Russian banquets, the toasting went on during the entire meal. Sir Archie followed me, and the speeches went through all of the military and the representatives of the two Supply Missions to the Red Cross, to which our Mr. Hubbel responded pleasantly.

I had prepared a speech which was brief and to the point; it went about like this:

Mr. Molotov, etc., etc., it gives me great pleasure to represent the United States Government here, today. In order to make secure those things which men set store by—in short, freedom of speech, freedom of worship, freedom from want, freedom from fear, freedom of opportunity—we have joined in a grand alliance among the United Nations to combat a ghastly tyranny. But we must be sure that, in defeating that tyranny, we do not set up another tyranny to govern men's lives, to try men's souls.

But I hit a happy chord at the end, something along the line that we all, British, Russian and American, had the same human needs, the identical human aims.

To which, Mr. Molotov responded amiably. All in all, it was a most gratifying experience.

Yes, indeed most gratifying. As I recall Mr. Molotov's "amiable response," he said something along the line that this agreement

and this congenial meeting "gave promise for further cooperation
and collaboration, not only during the war but also in the post-war
readjustment period and the years of peace to come."

In Moscow, when I was there, we had an unusually able and
personable corps of foreign correspondents. United Press had
Henry Shapiro and Meyer Handler; Associated Press Henry Cas-
sidy, Eddy Gilmore and Bill McGaffin; the New York *Times* Cyrus
Sulzberger and Ralph Parker; Edgar Snow, the authority on the
Chinese Communist movement, came in to write some articles
for *Saturday Evening Post;* and Bill Downs of *Newsweek,* David
Nichol of the Chicago *Daily News,* Robert Magidoff of NBC, Janet
Weaver of the *Daily Worker,* Irina (Skariatina) Blakeslee and
Quentin Reynolds for *Colliers.*

Most of them lived in the huge, decrepit old Hotel Metropole
on the "Square of the Revolution." Almost as isolated from the Russians as the rest of us, they joined in our limited round of social
events and contributed immensely to the enjoyment of our simple
amusements by their ready wit and fresh viewpoints.

And then there was always the theater, the opera, and the ballet, and to a lesser extent, the sport show. I have mentioned that
you couldn't simply walk up to the box office and buy a couple of
tickets for the night's performance. Diplomats obtained tickets for
specific performances by applying to the Foreign Office several
days in advance.

The Kremlin has abandoned its effort to disassociate the Russian people from all of the cultural values of their forefathers.
After almost a generation of proscription, Leo Tolstoy was again
the most widely read author in the Soviet Union. While the theater
presented many propaganda dramas, apparently constructed to
specifications by "state artists," we also saw revivals of the classics,
The Cherry Orchard, Anna Karenina, The Marriage of Figaro, and
The Three Sisters. Although propaganda in many vehicles was so
exaggerated as to be ridiculous, much of the acting was magnificent.

The Russian Ballet is still probably the finest in the world, with
the old routines always the best loved and best performed. The
Ballet seldom introduces more than one new spectacle in the course
of a season. I was informed that there was a factory whose sole
product was costumes for the theater guild. The Ballet and the
Opera were always available should we care to go. Pageants such
as *Swan Lake, Eugene Onegin, The Nut Cracker Suite,* and *Barber*

of Seville, to mention only a few, rotated in almost regular succession at a small theater in Moscow, the only playhouse available, since the enormous Bolshoi Theater was under repair for damages sustained when the Germans bombed Moscow.

The main floor of the theater was similar in arrangement to any theater in the United States, i.e., a foyer or main entrance, a main floor sloping from rear to front with two wide aisles separating three blocks each containing about four hundred seats. A cross aisle and a rail about three feet high separated the front orchestra seats and the lesser dignitaries of officialdom from the proletariat in the main orchestra. Before the raised stage was the pit for an orchestra of up to a hundred pieces. Above the orchestra around the theater were plush-lined boxes for very important dignitaries. Those with little influence sat in two galleries at the rear of the theater.

Beneath the foyer was a large room called the Bull Pen, circular in shape with large columns at the center, which the patrons of the theater used as a promenade during intermissions. Scenery for the Ballet was shifted during intermissions, which came two or three to a performance, each of them just about as long as the act preceding it. Since "No Smoking" signs were prominently displayed in theater and foyer, nearly everyone descended to the Bull Pen, where smoking was permitted. The Bull Pen was an excellent place to see the great and near-great on parade. Actresses, artists, presidium members, and gold-braided and be-medaled admirals and generals promenaded about the great circular room. Here was an excellent spot to meet and talk to Russians we could never meet elsewhere.

The Moscow theater is still one of the most colorful in the world. When the curtain fell at the end of an act, the star and her supporting actor came through the curtains to the front of the stage. A cheering section of teenagers and the Russian equivalent of bobby-soxers bore down to the orchestra rail and shouted their approval of their favorites. I can hear them, now, this crowd of youngsters, crying to the beams of the great vaulting hall, "Golubin, Golubin, GOL-LUBIN!" Sometimes they would persist in this claque for ten minutes, with the stars returning again and again.

After some months, one became bored with the same spectacle over and over. I must have seen *Swan Lake* eight or ten times. Toward the end of my sojourn, we took to attending one act of a show each evening, taking as much as a week to see one ballet or play, and thus avoiding the long and tiresome intermissions.

Life at Kuibyshev

For centuries past, at the juncture of caravan trails from China and India, where the Samara River enters the storied Volga, stood the old trading town of Samara. Although a thousand miles from the sea, it was a port city, with the Volga and Volga boatmen providing the transportation. The greatest city of the Volga region, the old town had a colorful and storied past. Like so many Russian cities, when the Bolsheviks came to power, they changed the name of Samara—to Kuibyshev in honor of Old Bolshevik Kuibyshev, member of the Politburo from 1927 to 1934.

We returned to Kuibyshev as winter broke and spring came to the Valley of the Volga. The warm weather had broken up the ice in the rivers and melted the snow in the hills. Ice jams in the sharp bends of the river had backed up flood water until it reached the second stories of houses across the river. I was told that these same houses always flooded in the spring, the residents moved out until the water subsided, then came back and cleaned up the debris, with a great good humor that was amazing to the Western mind.

As provisional capital of Russia, Kuibyshev was a melting pot—peasants, factory workers from further west in Russia, foreign correspondents and diplomats from many Western nations, the Far East and the Autonomous Republics of the Soviet Union. Factories moved into its outskirts, swamping its housing facilities, creating serious food and sanitary problems. Sheepskin-coated peasants, workers in serviceable heavy clothing, intellectuals and officials in European business suits crowded the cracked sidewalks.

A small town suddenly required to house half a million refugees, Kuibyshev faced frantic demands for housing, water mains, expanded sewage service. At the same time it had a food shortage replete with long breadlines outside the few bakeries, and great difficulty providing fuel for the bake ovens and flour and salt for the bread.

Most of the Westerners and other foreigners lived at the Grand Hotel, a misnomer despite its fifty-five rooms: for over a hundred years, it had had no inside bath or toilet facilities. When they were finally installed in 1942, the hot water boiler blew up after a few weeks' service, and a replacement was long in coming. At the public washroom up the street, bath and lavatory accommodations were decidedly primitive.

For most of the correspondents and diplomats quartered at the

Grand, life was deadly dull. A militiaman posted at the door encouraged the natural reluctance of Russians to enter a hotel catering chiefly to foreigners. The guests were a cosmopolitan group—Soviet officials, younger attachés of foreign embassies, American and British correspondents, three Japanese correspondents, and Polish officers. Members of the Mongolian People's Republic Military Mission were most colorful in native costumes of long blue kimonos fancily embroidered, with a swarm of sturdy black-eyed children, just about the noisiest bunch I've ever heard.

At a table in the dining room, you would often see a mixed crowd of attachés, correspondents, Russian officers, and an occasional young Russian woman, who somehow dared to slip by the sentry to dance with the foreigners after dinner. Far too small for all the bounce and noise of its patrons and, sealed up like an Egyptian tomb, you needed radar to guide you through the smoke fog. When vodka loosened the tongues, you could hear comments on almost any subject.

A large three-story building called Chancery on the main street housed our offices, my apartment, and accommodated most of my aides, attachés and clerks. For servants, we had several Russians employed in various capacities, three German women, and our Russian messenger boy, Morris, who looked out for Eddie Page and the other officers. The Russian and German servants, with chauffeurs and various other employees, lived together in a state of amiable, multilingual confusion and disorder in the basement of the Chancery building.

Although Chancery was in a bad state of repair—flushing water not available above the first floor, heating equipment sadly insufficient—we were fairly comfortable the first few weeks of Spring, 1942. However, the approach to my apartment and office was made through other apartments and utility rooms, which was embarrassing when receiving foreign representatives and entirely incompatible with the dignity of an Ambassador. On May 9th, Jack Duncan, Freddy Lang and I moved into a small house called Sadovia at the center of town, a ten-minute walk from the Chancery, which my predecessor had leased from the Russian Government at an enormous rental.

Once the ornate and gingerbready town house of a rich merchant, Sadovia was also in a bad state of repair. With seeds brought from the States, we planted flower beds along the sides of the house and a vegetable garden in the rear, where we raised excellent lettuce, lima beans, peas, squash, tomatoes, cucumbers, beets, carrots, green corn from transplants, and other garden truck to supplement our monotonous diet. The rear fence provided a convenient backstop for golf balls when I practiced chip shots to keep my hand in.

With the advance of Spring and warm weather, we were infested with the age-old scourge of flies and other insects, which swarmed through unscreened windows. Several of us came down with "Jippy-tummy," which Irina (Skariatina) Blakeslee called Kuibyshev cholera. With both the Samara and the Volga used as sewers, it was small wonder. I requested the local office of Burobin to install screening which we had imported from the United States. They replied that there were no carpenters available. When we could stand the flies no longer, Eddie Page, Morris, and I turned to, and in one day screened the entire building, in a fashion no American carpenter would approve, but our screens did keep out the insects.

During the summer months, Sadovia provided pleasant and comfortable quarters, with plenty of light and a cool breeze off the river. When winter came, we had the usual difficulties with the Russian wall heating system. Small fireplaces were located in the walls of the building. Fires were lighted in these small furnaces early in the morning to heat the walls, which were supposed to remain warm all through the day. However, with extreme cold, heat generated in the walls was insufficient to satisfy the needs of men accustomed to effective heating plants in American buildings. In the heating plant at Chancery, dirt, corrosion, and years of neglect had taken their toll. We fought a continuing battle for enough coal to keep the radiators in remote rooms from freezing. As usual, Burobin had neither spare parts nor engineering talent to make repairs. Fortunately, some of the Navy men on our staff had engineering experience and we made our own repairs. By building a fire early in the morning and stoking the furnace furiously all day, we managed to survive the Russian winter.

My contacts with the Foreign Office in Kuibyshev were made with that same Mr. Andrei Vishinsky who later climbed to eminence in the Soviet governmental hierarchy. Of medium height and full figure, Mr. Vishinsky had auburn hair and a florid complexion. He gave me the impression of being extremely shy, for his face flushed a brilliant red upon the slightest provocation, and he had but little to say, two traits quite in contrast to the nature of the white-haired, bitter, vitriolic Soviet "statesman" we saw in action on the international scene after the War.

His assistant, Mr. Lozovsky, considerably older than Mr. Vishinsky, with greying hair, pointed moustache, and Van Dyke beard, knew English well but was gruff, blunt, and plainspoken. A clever operator, Lozovsky had a real facility for turning a sharp question back on you so that you were the person stabbed. I found both of them interesting and usually agreeable, but, during the whole of my service in Kuibyshev, I never got a direct answer to any question from either of them. Any problems we had were fed into the Soviet bureaucratic machine at Kuibyshev, but the answers came from Mr. Molotov or Mr. Stalin in Moscow. It became routine to divide my time between Kuibyshev and Moscow.

Most of the representatives of other foreign countries also maintained offices in Kuibyshev. Our relations with representatives of friendly states were most cordial and enjoyable, but circumstances were such that I became more intimate with some ambassadors and ministers than with others.

Common purpose and common language brought me into almost daily contact with the British Ambassador, Sir Archibald Clark-Kerr, later, as Lord Inverchapel, accredited to our government in Washington. A Scotsman and proud of it, Sir Archibald had spent much of his foreign service in the United States and had married a Chilean beauty. Ruddy, handsome, impeccably dressed, more cosmopolitan than most officers of the British Diplomatic Corps, he was almost entirely lacking in those British character traits which Americans find irritating. During my stay in Russia, Sir Archie was most cooperative. There was never even the slightest rift in our personal or official relations. He has since passed to the great beyond, but I still cherish the memory of his warm friendship.

Sultan Akhmed Khan, Dean of the Diplomatic Corps and Ambassador from Afghanistan, was a tall, dignified man with a distinguished beard. In spite of his long residence in Soviet Russia and his familiarity with Russian bureaucracy, he lived in a continual state of alarm because, for hundreds of miles along the northern border of Afghanistan, all that divides that helpless country from the Communist colossus is the muddy Oxus River.

The Chinese Ambassador, tiny Mr. Foo Ping-Sheung, had a round, unlined face and looked so young that you might have thought him a boy. His principal concern was the Chinese province of Sinkiang. Some years earlier, the Russians had insisted upon assuming responsibility for maintenance of peace in the province, in exchange for which they demanded trade preference, raw materials, and other advantages. Under pressure of war, the Russians pulled their police out of Sinkiang and left the Chinese citizens at the mercy of local bandits. Like the Afghan Ambassador, Mr. Foo persisted in trying to get me to present his case to our government and to use our good offices with the Soviet Government. He remained in Moscow until 1948, when he returned home to become Nationalist Chinese Foreign Minister. I heard a rumor that he has since committed suicide.

We could not be completely open and frank with all of our colleagues. The Ambassador from Czechoslovakia, Mr. Zdenek Fierlinger, a handsome Slav, spoke English fluently and had a lovely French wife, but he was Communist in his sympathies. After the War, he returned to Czechoslovakia and became first Communist Prime Minister.

Mr. Stanoje Simich, the Yugoslav representative, was a fluent linguist. Because of German occupation of his country, he had his family of wife and two pretty daughters with him. During my stay in Russia, the United States was supporting Mihailovich, while Mr. Simich was a Tito supporter.

A long-haired, starry-eyed individual was Ambassador Luis Quintanilla from Mexico; he had an American wife and owned a farm in Pennsylvania. Possessed of an affable charm, intelligence, and a disarming candor, he soon became one of the most popular diplomats in our Corps. He arrived in Kuibyshev with nothing but papers accrediting him to the Soviet Union. Since he was practically a neighbor back home, we gave him office space, a typewriter, and stenographic service, help, and advice, until he became oriented.

It didn't take long! He came away from his first conference with Marshal Stalin full of praise for the man in the Kremlin. "I knew he was a great leader," he was quoted as saying, "but I never knew that he was a clever statesman as well. He has an extensive knowledge of the world, even of Mexico and Central America."

He had found Stalin smiling and utterly charming. "I wish Henry Wallace could come over and meet Stalin," Quent Reynolds quoted him after his meeting with the Russian dictator. "I can imagine Henry Wallace sitting down with Stalin and talking crops and arguing about when seeds should be planted. In his broad outlook on life, Stalin reminds me of Henry Wallace. Like Wallace, Stalin is intensely patriotic and, like him, he has a great love for the land."

Gradually Quintanilla began to get the distant treatment which

Soviet officialdom accorded to all foreign representatives, whatever the color of their politics. He got around more in Russian society and saw much more of the country and the people than the rest of us could for a while. He was still in Russia when I left, but no longer such an ardent partisan of the Russian form of Communism.

Mr. William Slater, the Australian Minister, came to Moscow expressing outspoken admiration for Communist ideology yet eloquently affirming that he recognized the defects of its manifestation in Soviet Russia. He intended to devote his efforts to help make the Russian experiment in Marxism become a more perfect approximation of a socialist heaven-on-earth.

In the power-hungry ranks of Soviet officialdom, his efforts were not appreciated. Within six months of his arrival, I sent him to Teheran in one of our planes under the care of a medical attendant, a completely disillusioned partisan, who insisted that his weakened mental condition was due to the frustration of his attempts to help the Soviets solve their many problems.

The Swedish Minister, Mr. Wilhelm Gustav Assarson, was supposed to be neutral like his country, but, with Sweden profiting from trade with Germany throughout the War, Sir Archibald and I felt that any information we gave him would pass right through to the Nazis.

Iranian Ambassador Mahomed Saed and his wife were delightful persons, but he was soon called home to become Iranian Prime Minister.

One of the most delightful members of the Corps was Dr. Stanislaw Kot, the representative of the Polish-Government-in-Exile. Immediately after matters of protocol were disposed between us, Dr. Kot entertained me at dinner. He spoke English fluently and was a delightful conversationalist. In order to make me feel more at ease, a member of his staff, Mlle. Aszkanazy (whom some of the younger members of our staff impertinently called The Ashcan) was placed on my right. Speaking many languages, she kept me abreast of the multilingual conversation. Since both Dr. Kot and Mlle. Aszkanazy were ardent bridge players, we saw a great deal of them at Sadovia. As a result, there was an almost daily discussion of the very complicated Polish situation.

In addition to representatives of friendly powers, accredited to the USSR were Ambassadors from Japan and Bulgaria, countries with which the United States and Great Britain were at war. I tried to avoid them but was not always successful. At Kuibyshev, each legation was assigned a day on which its staff could use one of the two tennis courts in town. On one occasion, with three members of our staff, I was playing tennis when, despite the precautions of the Foreign Office, four Japanese began to play on the adjacent court. When their tennis ball wandered into our court, the Japanese would thank us with excessive politeness in perfect English when we returned their ball. We thanked them just as effusively for similar courtesies, but not in Japanese. In diplomacy, *la politesse, toujours la politesse,* even with your enemies.

Josef (Djugashvili) Stalin

As I waited to report to Premier Stalin that month of April, 1942, I began to give serious consideration to the many problems I faced. In a Communist police state, I reasoned, there will inevitably be a dictatorship. Negotiating with a dictator will always be difficult for a "diplomat" reared in the democratic tradition. Stalin was the dictator with whom I had to deal. Some personal observations of Marshal Stalin and his associates gathered during the months of my sojourn in the Soviet Union may be illuminating to those who may have to negotiate with another Communist dictator.

Josef Stalin's family name was Djugashvili; Stalin, meaning steel, was an alias adopted during the years of his underground work in the Russian revolutionary movement. Born a Georgian, he had all of the good and bad characteristics of that heritage. He was courageous but liked to move with caution; a thorough realist with no sentiment in his makeup; suspicious and vengeful; capable of cogent and quick decision; observing traditional Georgian standards of morality, he was deceptive when it served his purpose, and believed whole-heartedly in the doctrine that words are meant to conceal your real thoughts—it is actions that count.

It has often been said that Stalin had no friends. He cleverly acquired Lenin's prestige after his death and always contrived to bolster his current party line by quotation from Lenin's writings. Of the original seven members of the Politburo, who inherited power from Lenin, four were executed as Fascist spies or counter-revolutionists, one was exiled and assassinated, and one committed suicide on the eve of trial. The survivor, Josef Stalin, entrenched himself in complete and unchallenged control of Party and government of the Soviet Union and effective control of International Communism and several satellite nations.

Little is known of Stalin's private and family life. So far as I know, none of his family lived regularly in the Kremlin, even during the War. The only way the world knew that he had more than one wife was through the announcement of the death of his second wife in 1932. He is said to have married a third time soon after the war. His new wife was never seen in public with him. Of his known sons, Major Jacob Djugashvili of the Red Army was captured at the defense of Smolensk. Another son worked up to a generalcy in the Red Air Force and was unfavorably known about Moscow as a playboy.

Stalin disliked pomp and ceremony. His apartment in the Kremlin was simply decorated and of modest proportions. He had a *dacha* on the Minsk road to which he retired late in the evening after his working day.

Stalin trusted no one. He was reported to have a super-secret police, responsible only to him, whose duty it was to check up on the NKVD and his official bodyguard. All of those I know who have conferred with Stalin agree that he was highly intelligent and well-informed on Russian and international affairs.

With the exception of short visits on party business, to London and Berlin in 1907 and to Krakow, Poland and Vienna, Austria in 1913, Stalin had seen little of the outside world prior to the Teheran and Yalta conferences, and therefore, from his own personal experiences, could know but little of what was going on therein.

Under a veneer of doctrinal Communism laid over the prejudices of the Georgian, Stalin embraced the nationalism of the Czars. Internally, this caused little trouble because nationalist expansion of Soviet territory generated the power to establish Communist regimes in surrounding countries where local Communists were not strong enough to accomplish a revolution themselves. In International Communism, Russian nationalism served to cause confusion between competing nationalisms of satellite countries.

A cocky, healthy-looking individual, with swarthy complexion and an Oriental cast of countenance, his short pompadour and moustache were jet black. He usually dressed in a cheap-looking khaki tunic, snapped close about the throat, with high Russian boots outside the legs of his trousers.

Seated, with only his husky torso in view, he appeared to be of average height. When he stood, he was much shorter than I. I scarcely noticed the marks of smallpox about which I have read so often. His eyes were dark brown, large, and very alive and penetrating. He had an infirmity which I have never seen mentioned—a withered left arm and a clubfoot. He was adept at covering up the infirmity of his arm and you didn't see him walking enough to attribute the sailor-like roll of his gait to a clubfoot.

Mr. Stalin spoke no English and I'm not sure whether or not he understood much. During my many interviews, he always doodled until the Russian translation commenced, when he devoted his full attention to the interpreter. While he was speaking to me in Russian, he frequently took up doodling again, looking up occasionally to meet my eyes.

In conference, Mr. Stalin's manner was ordinarily calm and pleasant and, because of long years of subservient acquiescence to his views, quite self-possessed. When he was angry, his eyes could look at you "as cold as steel," as some writers have expressed it. There is no doubt that he could be calculatingly rude and abrupt when aroused or irritated.

Stalin's closest associates were all either Old Bolsheviks or military men. Vyacheslav Molotov and Anastas Mikoyan were his constant advisers on their specialties, foreign relations and foreign trade. General Fillip Golikov in 1943 became Stalin's aide-de-camp, a bald, husky Red Army man, who knew the West from duty in several countries and a mission to the United States and Great Britain in 1941. He had commanded troops at the front.

Marshal Klimenti Voroshilov was a long-time associate of Stalin but wielded more political than military influence. The real military genius in Stalin's entourage was Marshal Georgi Zhukov, brain of the General Staff, who, as Deputy Commander-in-Chief, was Marshal Stalin's link with the armies at the front.

Georgi Malenkov, once Stalin's private secretary, later an important member of the Party Secretariat, and Andrei Andreyev were said to be in training to take over Stalin's job as General Secretary of the Party. Reminiscent of the *Troika*, which took over on Lenin's death, of which Stalin was a member, a rumored triumvirate in 1943 included these two and Andrei Zhdanov, former secretary of the Leningrad Party, President of the Russian Republic, and Major General in the Red Army. With consummate skill, Zhdanov directed the defense of Leningrad as Chairman of the Leningrad Military Council. Stalin's favorite, he was number one alternate for running the Party. At the time I was in Russia, Zhdanov seemed to be headed for the top spot in the Kremlin.

His sudden death under peculiar circumstances after the War, removed him from the Russian political scene, and Malenkov's star began to rise.

Shrewd, intelligent and very smooth-talking, Andrei Vishinsky was one of my principal contacts in the Foreign Office. Nikolai Shvernik, head of Soviet trade unions, was in training to replace the venerable Old Bolshevik, Mikhail Kalinin, as President of the Supreme Soviet and its Presidium and titular head of the government.

At the top of the heap, as sometime General Secretary of the Party, member of the Orgburo and the Politburo, Supreme Commander of the Armed Forces, and Chairman (Premier) of the Council of Ministers, stood Josef Stalin, undisputed boss of the Party and Dictator of the USSR. This was the man, an absolute ruler in the classical sense, upon whose pleasure I waited.

I began to follow a sort of routine. I turned out at seven, bathed and shaved. At 7:30, Chin Po served breakfast in my bedroom. Immediately after breakfast, I sat down at the desk in my sitting room, brought my diary up to date, and expanded on the daily events in a letter to my wife, which I kept running from day to day until an opportunity came to mail it.

If the day were fine, I walked to my office in Mokhovaya or the Chancery in Kuibyshev. We took up the business of the day— telegrams and communications from the Department and other agencies, conferences with members of my staff, interviews or visits from other diplomats or the Press. At 12:30, I returned to the residence for lunch, took a nap, followed by a long walk to observe the Russian people and their habits or a drive into the country. In Moscow, I could go anywhere I chose, *except* where sentries barred the way (and there were hundreds of them) into government buildings or factories, unless specially invited, or into a theater without advance arrangements. I couldn't buy a ticket on a train or ride in a Russian airplane without permission of the Foreign Office.

Upon my return about four P.M., I called at the office, then moved on to Spaso or Sadovia for cocktails and dinner. Evenings, I went to the Ballet, theater, or a special musical, played bridge or billiards with some of the staff, or gin rummy for low stakes with Eddie Page and Jack Duncan. When possible, we tuned in the BBC news at eleven. And then to bed.

On occasion, I felt that I was doing some good for my country and helping the United Nations get on with the war. Very often, I labored under a feeling of complete frustration, without conviction of accomplishment, sustained only by that "hope that springs eternal."

During that month of April, 1942, the confidence of the Allies of the United Nations was shaken by several world-shattering events, which doubtless occupied the time, thought, and energy of the Russian dictator. Often, with an uneasy feeling of distress, I wondered if the military disasters would ever end.

In the Pacific, with Allied armed forces reeling under Japanese blows on Pearl Harbor, Manila, and Malaysia, General MacArthur had been ordered to Australia and General Jonathan Wainwright had surrendered Bataan, withdrawing 3,500 Navy and Philippine Scout personnel to Corregidor. Singapore and Java had fallen.

On May 5th, General Wainwright would surrender Corregidor to General Tomayuki Tamashita. Already established in New Guinea and the Admiralties, the Japanese were headed down the ladder of the Solomons for Australia. On April 18, General Doolittle's sixteen B-25's from the carrier "Hornet" hit Tokyo, Nagoya, and Kobe.

In North Africa, the battle for the southern coast of the Mediterranean was going badly. Rommel's drive into Egypt cut off a garrison of 25,000 British Empire troops in Tobruk and swept within seventy miles of Cairo before it outran its supply.

In Russia, initially welcomed by the peasantry of the Ukraine and White Russia as deliverers, the German armies had swept across the Don, besieged Leningrad, and penetrated into the Caucasus. Minsk, Smolensk, Kiev, Kursk, Orel were tremendous Nazi victories, with huge bags of Russian prisoners.

But during that terrible Winter of 1941–42, the Red Army came back strong. Marshal Stalin had knowledge denied to the rest of us by a thoroughly effective censorship. In February, 1942, the threat to Moscow and Leningrad was beaten off. By April, the Russians were driving down the six-lane military highway toward Vyazma, the same route by which Napoleon advanced upon Moscow and along which he made his tragic retreat.

Although General Von Paulus advanced on Stalingrad with an army of 300,000, the tide of German conquest in Russia had begun to ebb. With Tolstoy, we could agree that, for the Nazis as well as for the French, "Victories are not always an invariable sign of conquest. . . . Just as water flowing over dry land is absorbed by the dry land, so did Russia absorb the French Army."

With the help of planes, arms, munitions, and supplies from American and British Lend-Lease, and by the bombing of lines of communication by the Allied planes, even so did the Russian land mass absorb the Nazi Legions.

I busied myself with routine duties. I attended the theater, Ballet, and opera. Frankly, I was terribly bored, but I could do nothing but wait as patiently as possible for my "audience" with Premier Stalin.

I took long walks, frequently marching. around the Kremlin walls, convoyed by my escort of NKVD boys. Unlike Jericho, the walls of the Kremlin remained firmly rooted in the centuries and the Russian soil, protecting, as they had a long line of Muscovite kings, this new dynasty of Russian power, privilege, and glory, to whom the most powerful of Soviet Russia's allies among the great Western democracies and its new Ambassador were as mendicants coming cap in hand in supplication to a feudal lord.

CHAPTER VIII

Early Experiments in Diplomacy

I WAS BORED. My routine duties, the walks around the Kremlin wall, the short drives into the country, all these combined to make me realize how unpleasant the position of an American official in a foreign capital can be made by removing just one thing to which he has been accustomed since birth—freedom of action, freedom to come and go when, where, and as he pleases.

I had imagined that my job would be a very busy one—Ambassador in the capital of an important ally in the middle of a great war—I expected to be engaged in a furious round of conferences, negotiations, "making representations," delivering notes from my government, presenting *aide memoire*—yet here I had nothing. Even gin rummy, cribbage, and billiards palled.

"Take it easy, Admiral," Walter Thurston counseled. "Enjoy these lulls when they come. There'll be times when you'll be so pushed and rushed, you'll long for a few moments just to sit—and not think."

Had I but known it, this situation was nothing new in the capital of all the Russias. Ninety years before, Mr. Neill S. Brown, American Minister at the "seat of government" of the Czar, reported to the State Department:

> The position of a minister here is far from being pleasant. The opinion prevails that no communication, at least of a public nature, is safe in the Post-Office, but is opened and inspected as a matter of course. Hence those Legations that can afford it, maintain regular couriers and never send anything by mail. The opinion also prevails that ministers are constantly subjected to a system of espionage, and that even their servants are made to disclose what passed in their households, their conversations, associations, etc. Of all this I have no positive evidence, but I believe there is some foundation for such charges. To be made to apprehend such a state of things is exceed-

ingly annoying. If therefore I do not write as often as may be desired, this is my apology.

And if I do not furnish matter of more interest, it must be attributed in part, at least, to the great difficulty in obtaining correct information. No courtesy or liberality whatever is shown in this respect by the Government. But I do not believe I have any grievances on this subject but what are common to other Legations. Secrecy, and mystery, characterize everything. Nothing is made public that is worth knowing. You will find no two individuals agreeing in the strength of the army and navy, in the amount of the public debt, or the annual revenue. In my opinion it is not intended by the Government that these things should be known. . . .

This is a hard climate, and an American finds many things to try his patience, and but few that are capable of winning his affections. One of the most disagreeable features he has to encounter is the secrecy with which everything is done. He can rarely obtain accurate information, until events have transpired; and he may rely upon it, that his own movements are closely observed by eyes that he never sees.

The Russian mind seems naturally distrustful; and this is especially so with the Government officials. Everything is surrounded with ceremony, and nothing is attainable but after the most provoking delays.

In addition to all of the difficulties that Minister Brown recorded, I had another serious complaint—I was being ignored.

I Report to Premier Stalin

After so long a wait, I became uneasy and wrote a letter to Mr. Molotov, asking if, by chance, his office had inadvertently overlooked my request for an appointment with Mr. Stalin to discuss some urgent matters. I had an answer from Mr. Molotov that same afternoon. No, he had not forgotten me. Marshal Stalin had been so busy with matters at the front that he had been unable to make time available for a conference with me.

Finally the word came. Mr. Molotov informed me that I could see Premier Stalin on Thursday, April 23rd, at four P.M., twelve days after my arrival in Moscow. I was to learn that this was just about par for the course.

At five minutes before four, my ancient limousine drew up at the Kremlin gate and I was escorted as usual to the door of the palace and down the long corridors. I had been carefully briefed and had with me notes for my statement. Mr. Molotov awaited me in the outer office and we were immediately ushered into an adjoining conference room.

Like almost every other Soviet conference room I visited, along one wall it had a long, highly-polished conference table with one end covered by a green-baize cloth and straight-backed chairs arranged about it; in an opposite corner were a group of deep leather chairs about a low table, a flat-topped desk in the other corner, and close to the conference table a small stand for a pitcher of water and some glasses. The floors were almost as highly polished as the tables; a few small rugs offered a hazard for the unwary on that slick floor. The whole atmosphere was utility, not swank or comfort.

Premier Stalin stood with Mr. Pavlov, his interpreter, at the far end of the room. I moved down the long room and exchanged greetings. "I'm glad to return to Moscow and to renew the many pleasant friendships I made while I was here for the Conference in October," I tactfully commenced my career in diplomatic negotiation.

Mr. Stalin nodded and motioned me to a seat on his left. Mr. Molotov and Pavlov sat across the table on Stalin's right. Since I had come alone, Pavlov did the interpreting. Stalin picked up a pencil and began to doodle, looking up at me in a moment as if to say, "Well, what have you got on your mind?"

I took a deep breath. "I am the bearer of special greetings of friendship from President Roosevelt, Marshal Stalin," I began. "The President wishes me to express to you his admiration for the magnificent courage, fortitude, and resourcefulness shown by the Red Army and the Russian people in meeting the Nazi attack and turning it back, an admiration shared not only by the American people but by all liberty-loving people of the world."

When I paused to let Mr. Pavlov translate my remarks, Mr. Stalin stopped doodling and listened attentively. I waited, thinking that he might wish to comment on each subject as I brought it up, but he motioned me to proceed.

"The President also asked me to tell you that there was good reason for the traditional friendship between our two peoples," I went on, "even before America became a nation. This reason is found in the character of the two peoples. We both realize that the misunderstandings which sometimes arise are due to the great distances which separate us and the lack of rapid communications. The President told me that he was sure that if the two of you could sit down together and talk matters over, there would never be any lack of understanding between our countries. To this end, and as may be entirely practicable, President Roosevelt wishes me to urge you to meet with him somewhere in Alaskan or Siberian waters during the next summer to discuss the entire problem of world affairs."

After this passage was translated, Mr. Stalin broke his silence. "I am grateful to President Roosevelt for his greetings and kind message. The question of a meeting between us has been the subject of an exchange of notes. I still have hopes that it can be brought about."

I thanked him and went on, "The President regrets the delays which have occurred in the delivery of Lend-Lease supplies and fully hopes and believes that the United States will be able to live up to the established schedules by the end of this month. He realizes the vital necessity of the united effort of all the United Nations and he is determined, and has issued instructions, that the highest priority be given to the production of supplies for Russia. Any obstacles in the way of the flow of these supplies for Russia must be removed. As Ambassador to the Union of Soviet Socialist Republics, it will be my purpose not only to sustain but also to foster the traditional friendly relations existing between our two countries and to further in every way possible this policy of President Roosevelt. To the best of my ability, I will continually seek out and remove obstacles to the free flow of supplies to your country."

Mr. Stalin looked up at me with his alert brown eyes. "I appreciate the sentiments which you have expressed," he said slowly. "I, too, will help in every way that I can to eliminate such obstacles."

I told him that I was glad to hear him agree with our policy. "In furtherance of this purpose, Marshal Stalin, I would like to discuss with you certain obstacles which I believe could and should be removed."

I then brought up the question of communications. "There is an air-ferry service from the United States across Africa to Basra, Mr. Stalin. If only we had a shuttle line from Basra to Moscow or Kuibyshev, communications between Russia and America could be greatly speeded up."

As an example, I mentioned the delay in obtaining from Russia spare parts and replacements for thirty-five bombers immobilized at Basra. Waiting for the supplies from America held up their delivery for several weeks. "Then, look at the time it takes to transmit specifications and books of instructions required to expedite production and delivery of material to you. These things must now go by ships under convoy, which, of course, sometimes never arrive. This delay would be almost completely removed if we could establish a regular and efficient air service between our countries."

I then invited his attention to another and shorter route—from the United States through Alaska and Siberia. "There is no reason in the world why both routes shouldn't be established and a schedule of frequent flights maintained."

When Mr. Pavlov reached this point in his translation, Stalin broke in. "Has your Government investigated the practicability of an air route from Canada via Greenland and Iceland to Murmansk and thence to Moscow? This route is much shorter than the Basra route. The Alaskan-Siberian route is not only much longer but for many months of the year would be entirely unusable because of weather."

"I feel sure that my government has investigated the route you recommend," I replied. "I assume that they consider it impracticable on account of the weather. I have been told that the Alaskan-Siberian route can be used in all except the worst of weather. As for military airplanes, we already have airfields which make delivery of planes as far as Nome, Alaska, a simple matter. If similar facilities exist in Siberia, bombing planes could be delivered on the Russo-German fighting front ready for immediate action. While fighters probably could not make the long flight across Siberia on an economical basis, American fighters could be employed in Siberia, thus relieving you of the necessity of sending Russian fighters to the Siberian air bases over your already overloaded railway."

Again I assured Mr. Stalin that my suggestions were only in the interest of furthering and expediting the flow and delivery of war supplies and combat aircraft, hoping that such assurance would convince him that we had no ulterior motive in pressing for the Alaskan-Siberian route.

Mr. Stalin's jaw set stubbornly and his expression was far from benign as he answered, "I'm sure that the Canada-Greenland-Iceland route is the most practicable but I'll have the Alaskan-Siberian route studied. We will also look into the matter of expediting communications." He paused for a moment and came as close to smiling as I ever saw. "I'm afraid our *friends,* the Japanese, won't like the Alaskan-Siberian route, but that is no insurmountable obstacle."

Thinking to ease the tension a bit, I thanked Mr. Stalin for permitting my private plane to fly me to Kuibyshev. "I'm also very grateful for the transport which you sent to Teheran for us. Of course, I knew nothing about it until I reached Teheran."

At this little sprig from an olive branch, Mr. Stalin only stared at me owlishly for a moment and resumed his doodling, making what looked like lopsided hearts of all sizes and positions. I then brought up the matter of the Russian technicians who had been sent to America. "They are very able men, Mr. Stalin, in every way comparable to our own technicians, but we wish that you would give them more authority. If you would, we believe that considerable delay could be avoided. These two things—better and faster communications and greater authority for your technicians, permitting them to make decisions on the spot, would really help us to avoid delay."

As he replied, Mr. Stalin's eyes might be described as—some correspondents have said—gentle and expressive, and his voice had a queer humorous quirk to it. "If our technicians were given greater authority, we would receive only about half as many useful supplies from America as we now get. Your American contractors are such super-salesmen they can sell our technicians on the idea of accepting materials not up to specifications. You know, we had been warned against one of your light machine guns, but our *experts* there accepted it. We got delivery on a lot of them and none of them worked."

I hadn't been briefed on that incident and so I went on to discuss a large quantity of low-viscosity powder which the Russians had requested.

"Such a big order is far beyond the capacity of our production," I explained. "We would have to build an entirely new factory to make it. I understand that you already have such powder under production. If you would furnish us the plans and design for your factory, we could expedite the production and delivery of this powder immensely."

Again I tried to make plain that we wanted these plans only in order to expedite, not just to obtain the plans for our own selfish uses.

Mr. Stalin continued doodling. "The powder we asked for is a very simple powder which can be produced in most any powder factory in any country."

"That's not the information that was given me," I objected. "I was told that it is a very special kind of powder requiring special apparatus. We understand that you are now producing this powder in Russia. For us to produce the quantity that you have requested will require a new, very large factory."

Mr. Stalin looked up at me quizzically. "I think you're mistaken. I believe that our order was for an ordinary powder, but I'll have the matter looked into. If we have such a complicated powder and if we have plans for such a factory, we will make them available to you."

Again, I pointed out how improved air communications would expedite the delivery of these plans to America. Then I took up the matter of raw materials. "What we need very badly, Mr. Stalin, are chrome, manganese, platinum, and asbestos. Thus far, we have received only very small quantities from the Soviet Union. These materials are urgently needed for our war effort and to manufacture things ordered by Russia. I hope the quantity delivered to us on reverse Lend-Lease will be considerably increased."

"We have already substantially increased our shipment of raw materials to the United States," Mr. Stalin protested. "But the ships into which we loaded them were sunk by Nazi submarines."

"There are two reasons for obstacles and delay in delivery of Lend-Lease materials," he went on. "First of all, your contractors don't want to accept Russian orders. The manufacturers are much more agreeable in England. In America, however, we have come to feel that the contractors just don't want Russian orders. The second cause is the lack of shipping and heavy loss of ships because ships from America are not convoyed. The British convoy their ships and protect them much better than the Americans do. That is why the flow of supplies from Great Britain is much better than from America."

Being a Navy man, I was considerably annoyed at this criticism of our convoy system when we had been in the War only a little over four months, but I tried not to let my words or voice show it. "In America, we have investigated every suggestion which would help us protect ships at sea and safeguard their cargoes," I replied, a bit stiffly, I am afraid.

"I want to ask you a question," Mr. Stalin broke in. "Why don't you build cargo submarines? Cargo submarines could cross the ocean without interference from Nazi submarines and could deliver their supplies directly to our own ports without danger of being sunk."

"I'm sure that the question of building cargo submarines has received careful consideration in my country," I replied. "If their use is practicable and desirable, my country will certainly not fail to build them."

"Well, I'm having the question of cargo submarines investigated over here."

The interview had already become overlong. Wishing to break it off, I expressed my appreciation to Mr. Stalin for receiving me. "If I discover any other obstacles to delivery of Lend-Lease supplies," I said, "I'll ask to see you again."

"By all means," he replied, apparently with hearty good-will. "That will always be arranged."

When Mr. Stalin made no move to rise, I knew that he must have something else on his mind. To break the rather long silence, I asked him if he had any information about the projected Spring activities on the Eastern Front which might be of interest to our President.

Mr. Stalin looked up at me. "Please tell President Roosevelt that large reinforcements are being brought up on both sides of our front. I do not know when or where the attack will be made. There will be many difficulties for us and no successes at first. We have stopped our ground offensives for the moment but our attack aviation is breaking up German troop concentrations and attacking their supply lines with some success."

"How about the Far East?" I asked.

"So far as I can see, there is no disposition on the part of Japan to create a crisis out there. Of course, the Japanese are increasing their forces along the borders of Manchuria and on Saghalien Island, but then, so are we."

"We musn't forget Port Arthur and Pearl Harbor," I put in.

"The Soviet Union is not going to be tricked," he replied, sharply. "We remember Port Arthur very well and we often think of Pearl Harbor. We do not trust the Japanese. We are ready for them."

"We remembered Port Arthur and we mistrusted the Japanese, too," I said drily. "But still we were surprised at Pearl Harbor."

Mr. Stalin then came around to the subject which was on his mind. "One of your American bombers landed in Siberia the other day. Its crew is safe and will be well cared for, but of course, we will have to intern them. I regret that, but it is necessary in order not to have trouble with our Japanese friends."

"I understand that all the other planes landed in China," I offered. "That one must have been unable to reach Chinese territory."

Said Mr. Stalin, coldly, "The pilot told our officers that he had orders to land in Siberia."

"I have no information about this incident but I am certain they had no such orders, except in dire emergency."

Mr. Stalin rose from the table and pushed back his chair. I got to my feet and we shook hands. "If I can be of any help to remove obstacles to good American-Soviet relations," he said in parting, "call upon me at any time."

"Thank you Mr. Stalin," I replied. "If I can be of any help to you in killing Germans, please let me know."

He had half turned away from me, but now he turned back. There was a gloomy look in his deep brown eyes. "The Russians are killing many, many Germans at the front." He shook his head sadly. "The poor Germans have orders that they must not retreat, must not give way to us a single inch. The result is that we are killing them like pigs. There is just nothing else to do with Germans but kill them."

And so ended my first interview with Mr. Stalin.

On Malaya Lubianka not far from the center of Moscow stands St. Louis de Francis, an old French Catholic church designed by the same architect who produced the marvelous Bolshoi Theatre. At the time I was in Moscow, its priest was Father Leopold Braun, an Augustinian monk from New Bedford, Massachusetts, who was educated at the Assumption College in Worcester, was ordained, and then did post-graduate work at the Augustinian Monastery in Louvain, France. Just after the Litvinov-Roosevelt agreement in 1933, which provided for American recognition of Soviet Russia, Father Braun came to Moscow with Ambassador Bullitt to be assistant to Bishop Eugéne Neven, a French cleric of his Order, who was at that time Admirative Apostolic to Russia.

When the Bishop returned to France for a brief holiday and the Russian Foreign Office refused him reentry, the young priest from New Bedford became Apostolic Delegate and pastor of St. Louis.

It was indeed a challenge. The church was in a horrible state of disrepair. The vows of his Order rendered him penniless, dependent upon the charity of his parishioners. Unwilling to lock his church against chance visitors seeking its sanctuary, it was five times robbed. Vandals once stole the silver chalices from the altar. He had a church and a home, but he was dependent upon the caprices of Soviet bureaucracy for fuel to heat them and means to repair them. He had a small wreck of a car, but had to beg gasoline, as the Government would issue him no gas ration card.

By streetcar, subway, and on foot, it took Father Braun half an hour to forty-five minutes from his lodgings to St. Louis for a daily seven o'clock Mass. He often held ten services in a single day, commuting back and forth by the unwieldy Moscow transportation system. Many times, he shivered through the interval between services in his frigid study in the church, rather than face the bitter cold of the Moscow winter.

On the positive side, he had 25,000 parishioners in and around Moscow, but thousands of them were afraid to show their faces in his church. But for the pitiful offerings of black bread, root vegetables, infrequently a chunk of meat, dry beans for Russian bean soup, and an occasional bottle of Caucasian wine, which members of his congregation left on the offering table at night, and gifts from members of the Embassy staff and our commissary, Father Braun might have starved.

Having in the Roosevelt-Litvinov agreement guaranteed religious freedom to American citizens in Russia, the Soviet Government did not actually oppose the young priest, but they passively obstructed him at every turn. Many times, our Ambassadors interceded for him with Russian officials, lent him money and gave him encouragement. At the time I arrived in Moscow, his food ration had been cut so low that, even with the help of the parishioners, he was hard put to keep up strength enough to carry on his heavy duties, and Chargé d'Affaires, Walter Thurston, had written a number of letters to Burobin without any helpful action.

Although I am not a Catholic, I regarded Father Braun as our American Chaplain in Russia. Still, we could not give him diplomatic status and let him buy at our commissary without unpleasant repercussions. Being usually penniless, he could not afford to buy food in the open market.

On numerous occasions, I gave him food from my own mess and also furnished him with firewood. I wrote a letter to Burobin asking that he be issued ration tickets for gasoline. Although Eddie Page and Mr. Thurston had warned me, I was surprised and soon annoyed at the slow response and inaction of Burobin bureaucracy.

It didn't take long to become exasperated with mail delivery to the Russian capital. All our mail, both official and personal, had to go by courier in State Department pouches. Just for fun, I mailed a letter to Mrs. Standley in the Moscow Post Office. Sadly tattered and obviously having been opened frequently for inspection, it reached her three months later. Despite excellent cooperation from the Army Air Transport Service, a letter despatched from Moscow and answered immediately in Washington often took six weeks for the round-trip. Such long delay not only interfered seriously with the conduct of official business but it was also personally obnoxious to me. I had long been in the habit of exchanging daily letters with my wife, and I missed the comfort of this correspondence.

With these and other issues confronting me, I sought an interview with Mr. Molotov. At 3 P.M., April 25th, we again met in Mr. Molotov's office in the Ministry of Foreign Affairs. I took Eddie Page with me. As before, we sat at the long, highly-polished table, Molotov's heavy figure at the end with Mr. Pavlov, the interpreter, on his right. I sat opposite Pavlov with Eddie on my right. Mr. Molotov looked at me with a bland expression on his wide face.

After the usual exchange of polite phrases, I began the conference. "My Military Attaché, Colonel Michella, has received a dispatch from General George Marshall, Chief of Staff of our Army, asking that I express to your government our appreciation and gratitude for the courtesies extended to the crew of our American bomber which landed in Siberia. We were particularly grateful to learn their names, as that lets us put their families at ease as to their fate. General Marshall also wishes me to assure you that the landing was made on Russian soil only because of an extreme emergency and was not in the least intentional."

Mr. Molotov listened impassively while the translation was made. "Thank you, Mr. Ambassador," he said smiling at me as he spoke in Russian. "Please convey to your government our request that steps be taken to prevent any such landings in the future as they are extremely embarrassing to my government in our dealings with the Japanese."

"I'm sure that such instructions were issued before this mission, Mr. Molotov," I retorted. "However, one cannot always avoid such an incident. Anyway," I went on, speaking lightly, "it was much better for them to land on Russian territory than to be taken by the Japanese."

Mr. Molotov's face was cold and impassive as he said, "Please convey my request to your government."

"Of course," I agreed readily enough. I went on to remind him of the many questions which I had discussed with Mr. Stalin. "Some of them will probably require future discussion with Mr. Stalin or yourself, Mr. Molotov, and things will be constantly coming up which require discussion with the Commissar of Foreign Affairs. I am planning to return to Kuibyshev, but if you expect to remain in Moscow, I am sure I will find it necessary to come to Moscow frequently, if conditions permit."

Mr. Molotov smiled affably. "Certainly, that is perfectly understandable and agreeable. Just let Mr. Vishinsky or Mr. Lozovsky in Kuibyshev or myself know and transportation will be arranged."

The discussions were proceeding so pleasantly, and on such a friendly basis that I ventured to throw in some less pleasant matters. "There is one question I discussed with Mr. Stalin which is causing great concern. Here we are, the United States of America and the Union of Soviet Socialist Republics, allies in a great war. We are both striving in every way to help each other. Of the utmost importance is rapid and regular air-mail service between Moscow and Washington. We will soon take the matter up formally, but I want to leave this thought with you because it is highly important."

His pleasant expression vanished into that vast impassiveness of which he was so readily capable. When he didn't answer me for some time, I went on to take up the matter of my Naval Attaché. "I brought Captain Duncan, an officer distinguished by long and excellent service in our Navy, to be my Naval Attaché. Captain Duncan has already opened up a number of subjects for discussion with Admiral Nikolai Kuznetsov, Commissar for the Navy. He is discussing these matters now with a Captain Zaitsev of Admiral Kuznetsov's office. Since these important discussions are not yet completed, I would like to leave Captain Duncan here in Moscow when I return to Kuibyshev."

"That is a matter wholly within your discretion," Mr. Molotov said coldly.

I then referred to the case of Father Braun. "To promote cordial relations between our two countries, may I ask that you interest yourself in this matter, Mr. Molotov. You will recall that your Government guaranteed to American residents in the Soviet Union freedom of conscience and religion. Father Braun, unofficially, but in a very real way, is our American chaplain in Moscow. He's here with the concurrence of your government to carry on his Roman Catholic religious work among his parishioners, but the poor fel-

low has been placed in such a low category that his food ration
will barely keep him alive. We have already written several letters
to Burobin without result. They have not even answered our last
note."

"Many of our people, who are engaged in work not essential to
the war effort, are living on an even more restricted ration, one
which provides them a bare subsistence level of nutrition," Mr.
Molotov put in.

I wanted to say that Russians could live on less than an American, even a poor priest sworn by his vows to poverty, but instead,
I protested, "But surely the People's Commissar for Foreign Affairs will want to avoid an unfortunate situation which might be
misconstrued by the American people to be persecution of the
only Western representative of Christian religion in the Soviet
Union. I do hope that you will find it possible to take a personal
interest in this case."

Mr. Molotov looked at me quizzically for a moment. "*Nyet, nyet,*"
he burst out and he went on with a long and angry-sounding tirade
in Russian, his heavy face darkening into a scowl. "The Commissar says that he will be happy to take this matter up in due course,"
Mr. Pavlov translated calmly. Mr. Pavlov is a very astute interpreter.

As he spoke, Mr. Molotov's face fell into its habitual impassiveness. He had the edge on me in this exchange. From his service
abroad, he could understand English, and I could understand
little more in Russian than "Yes," "No," and "Let's have a drink."
For this reason I always took along with me Eddie Page or someone else who spoke Russian like a Russian.

At this point, Mr. Pavlov informed me that Mr. Molotov had
a question to take up. "A letter was received from the Kuibyshev
American Embassy last month, which requested permission for a
United States Army officer to be detailed as liaison officer with
the Free Poland army forces in Russia. I don't want to take this
matter up officially, but we have difficulty understanding why you
need such an official. Why can't the Polish and American Military
Attachés in Kuibyshev arrange all such business between them?
We would have to have further information before we could grant
this request."

I thought I had been pretty thoroughly briefed for this interview, but I hadn't heard about this issue. All I could do was admit
my ignorance and promise to advise him further when I had consulted the files.

"What is the news from the Front?" I changed the subject.

I received the usual off-hand reply. There was "very little information," fighting here and there with some gains in some places and losses in others, but generally, "It was a period of inactivity with both sides apparently getting ready for an offensive." In spite of the great battles fought, and won and lost, on the Russian front, as far as I was concerned officially, there always seemed to be this "period of inactivity," the lull before a storm which I learned about second or third hand via the news broadcast from BBC.

"I heard in Kuibyshev that the Japanese have demanded that you move your troops back from the Siberian frontier and dismantle some batteries which they seem to find offensive," I tried another tack. "I was told that your government told the Japanese that you would be glad to comply if the Japanese moved back their troops and batteries first."

For the first time, Mr. Molotov looked a bit startled. "There's nothing to that rumor," he said firmly. "The Japanese have never even suggested such a course of action."

I sat silent with my arms resting on the table for a couple of minutes, waiting to see if he had anything further to offer. When the silence began to grow awkward, I pushed back my chair and rose to go.

In taking our leave, we mouthed the usual polite phrases—Mr. Molotov had been most kindly and courteous; he assured me that he wanted to help us to clarify any obscure situation and remove obstacles, while I offered to be of service to him in such endeavors at any time. We parted on a most harmonious note that "he would always be at my service and ever ready to see me at a moment's notice." And indeed, during the months of my service in Russia, except for certain lapses noted, he was invariably agreeable and cooperative.

As we rode home, I harked back to the period when I was preparing for my mission to Moscow, and recalled how I planned a new and more personalized diplomacy. I would meet the Russian officials man-to-man, get to know them, their likes and dislikes, their hobbies and avocations, and thus establish a sound basis for firm personal friendships. I was beginning to realize how naive I had been. A few of the scales had dropped from my bemused eyes.

Back in Spaso House, I held a brief staff conference in my second floor sitting room, with Mr. Thurston, Mr. Dickerson, Eddie Page, Jack Duncan, Colonel Michella, Ronnie Allen (Duncan's assistant), and Doctor Lang present.

"You certainly hit him on a tender spot with that Father Braun plea," Eddie said while we waited for the group to assemble.

"They're still awfully sensitive about religion," Mr. Thurston put in.

"Yes, your older Russian peasant still clings to his Orthodox religion with grim determination," Dickerson put in. "And there's a lot of soul-searching among the proletariat, even among the Party members, despite the avowed agnosticism and downright atheism of the Party leaders."

We went over my interview, as we were to go over many another in the months to come, looking for a trend, searching for an attitude that was always hard to find. I brought up again the matter of where it was best for me to locate our permanent embassy.

"Mr. Steinhardt always felt that his post of duty was at Kuibyshev," Thurston put in. "He only came to Moscow when he had to settle important business and he couldn't get action in Kuibyshev."

"Which was just about every item on the agenda," Ronnie Allen put in.

"I'm inclined to agree with Mr. Steinhardt," I said. "My post of duty is in Kuibyshev. I will return just as soon as you can get me transportation, Eddie. We'll leave Mr. Dickerson and Mr. Thompson here, and you'll have to stay until you clean up your business with Admiral Kuznetsov, Jack. How soon can you get us a plane ride, Eddie?"

"Couple of weeks, sir."

"Too long," I said. "I want to leave within a week."

I saw Thurston and Dickerson exchange glances and Ronnie Allen shook his head. "Within a week," I reiterated.

As usual, there was delay and procrastination. In the interval, I managed to keep busy. A week or so earlier, I had called on the Commissar for Trade and Transportation, Mr. Anastas Mikoyan, with whom I had made friendly contacts during the Beaverbrook-Harriman Mission. In his official capacity, he was also administrator of our Lend-Lease program, and therefore a man whom I felt I ought to know. I was still laboring under the delusion that I could make friends with these Russians and thus improve our relations with the Soviets and expedite the progress of the war.

Commissar Mikoyan was a short, dark, carefully tailored man, an Armenian, with dark eyes, a pinched face and a huge Semitic nose. He looked like the movie version of a big banker or executive or a high-pressure sales manager.

I knew that Mr. Mikoyan gave elaborate luncheons for visiting foreign dignitaries, particularly any of those who had anything at all to do with supplying Russia with war or industrial commodities. I had heard these visitors propose toasts to his ability at "horse-swapping" at such luncheons, and I had faced the reality of his sharp practices across the conference table. And so I thought I was ready for him—still, I didn't see why we couldn't be friends.

I was not alone in such naïveté. About this time, Quentin Reynolds wrote:*

> "Zhit stalo luche, Tovarishchi, zhit stalo veselye," Stalin cried. "Life is better, comrades, life is gayer." It was too. They were, they felt, on their way somewhere. That is all they want now—to go back and pick up where the war forced them to lay off. All of this is not only my opinion but is the opinion without exception of every British, American and French correspondent in Moscow. We have as much to fear from Soviet Russia as we have to fear from the Eskimos. And, as a threat to our liberty and our established way of living, the Dies Committee offers a far greater danger.

So I tried to be friendly with Mr. Mikoyan. Since I was supposed to have considerable to do with Lend-Lease, at least potentially, I was not surprised to receive an invitation to dine with him on April 26th. The dinner was given at the Government Guest House, an old mansion of the Czarist era called Spiridonov House. The table was set for twelve in the fine old dining room, with crested silver, gleaming silver candlesticks and all the trappings of a first class official Russian banquet. Among the other guests were his Vice Commissar, A. D. Krutikov, and Major General I. F. Semischastnov. We had a sherry cocktail before dinner, two kinds of vodka at each place, several kinds of wine including champagne and three cordials and a brandy after dinner. Pre-dinner appetizers included two kinds of caviar, preserved breads with scads of butter (very scarce in Russia just then, something like three dollars a pound on the free market), smoked fish, and raw cucumbers.

The entrées consisted of two kinds of chicken, partridge and jellied pork, with which they served potato salad, three kinds of vegetables, and beets in sour cream, while dessert was chocolate ice cream with cake and fruit, both fresh and candied.

Seated between Mr. Mikoyan and General Semischastnov, I found the conversation rather hard going even though both could speak English fluently, until I happened to touch upon the excellence of the wines.

* Quentin Reynolds, *The Curtain Rises* (New York: Random House, 1944).

"Ah, yes," Mr. Mikoyan agreed. "You know, I spent a year in your United States and at every opportunity I studied your methods of winemaking. You have some wonderful wineries in California and New York State. I made notes and took some of your wine-making recipes back home to Russia. Since then, we have been able to produce some really excellent wines and champagne."

Sipping the glass of champagne at my place, I had to agree—it was as delicious as any French champagne I could recall.

Mr. Mikoyan chuckled. "I also did something else for Russia—for our children. I introduced your Eskimo Pie into our country."

Much to my surprise, the subject of Lend-Lease did not come up during the evening.

The next morning at breakfast, Eddie Page brought me word that arrangements had finally been made for our trip to Kuibyshev. At 9:20 A.M. on April 29th, we took off from the Moscow Airport in a battered old Russian version of the cargo C-47. Flying at tree-top height, with a Russian pilot who must have thought he was a stunt man in a flying circus, after an eternity of emergency air situations which would have baffled and confounded an advanced student at Corpus Christi, we finally touched down at Kuibyshev airfield at 2:30 P.M. I have never been as relieved to climb down out of a plane onto the good earth. I told Eddie Page that no sort of crisis would ever again induce me to take passage in a Russian transport plane. Of course, I was wrong. It was not many days until I was again risking life and limb in pursuit of my official duties to my country.

CHAPTER IX

Country Life Among the Soviets

O NE of my earliest resolutions was to take advantage of every opportunity to meet and know the Russian people and the conditions under which they lived. In view of the restrictions imposed upon Western diplomats, this was extremely difficult.

In Kuibyshev, as in Moscow, we were "confined to limits," just like soldiers in the Army. During the rainy spring, "limits" were the paved road north along the east bank of the Volga to the Mare's Milk Tuberculosis Sanitarium. How far it was paved beyond the sanitarium, I never discovered, because of a Red Army sentry. There was no paved road south across the Samara River. In summer, a pontoon bridge spanned the Samara and you could cross to the west bank of the Volga on a primitive ferry. In winter, we crossed both rivers over the ice.

With but little work to do after my official calls, and social activity curtailed because of a current crisis in supply of food and drink, time hung heavily on my hands. One winter day, I decided to see how the Russians used the Volga as a highway. With Eddie Page, Dr. Lang, and ever-faithful Morris, our Embassy messenger in Kuibyshev, we drove to the river's edge along roads banked high with snow on either side. We left our car at the ferry landing and walked out along a well-packed road. What was in summer a ferry route was now a broad highway—sleds of all types and sizes hauling grain, wood, ice, hay and household effects, pulled by oxen, horses, men, women and children; the ever-present Lend-Lease Studebaker truck bringing grain, wood, and ice from across the river; and the patient peasants in a strange assortment of overcoats, jackets, fur stoles, blankets and wool shawls plodding along on feet wrapped in straw covered with burlap.

We met several hundred men, women and children guarded by troops with fixed bayonets. At the rear of this long column of hu-

man misery were two fierce dogs on leashes led by a man and a
woman guard, ready to track down any prisoner who might try to
escape. Whether refugees or evacueés, I never learned, but those
poor people were certainly prisoners of the NKVD.

Behind her on a child's sled, one poor old woman hauled a three
month old pig. I had Morris call to her, "Will you sell me your
pig."

"Yes, yes," she cried eagerly. "Eight thousand rubles."

A quick mental calculation translated this into American money
—$750.

I Try to Meet the Russian People

In summer, we were encouraged to go to the swimming beaches
across the Volga. Apparently the Russians considered the roads so
terrible that not even an American would be crazy enough to try
them. Once the dirt roads on the east bank dried to dusty hard-
ness, no restrictions were imposed, other than the physical discomfort of ruts and chuckholes.

While with OPM, I had become interested in the rubber shortage. We had heard in Washington of the Soviet Union's success
in obtaining rubber from guayule and other rubber-producing
plants. Kuibyshev had been mentioned as the center of research
in the growth of these plants.

Upon my arrival, discreet inquiry developed that rubber experimentation was actually being conducted in botanical gardens outside of town. Early in May, I drove out to the "Gardens."

Having in mind some of our own botanical gardens in formal-
ized patterns and immaculately kept, I experienced a rude shock.
The Kuibyshev Botanical Gardens looked very much like an ordinary cow pasture at home. Stone walls were tumbled down, gates
hung open and half off their hinges. While in some of the enclosures there may have been valuable plants and experimental
vegetables, the garden beds were so overgrown with weeds and
brush that cultivated plants could hardly be recognized.

An old man, who looked to be seventy-five but probably was
nearer sixty, came to meet me. Through Morris, I learned that his
name was Terekov and that with his somewhat younger wife and
three other ancients, he was attempting to operate the gardens as
a collective farm. He took me through a gap in the back wall into
another walled-in enclosure where his wife was hoeing weeds be-

tween rows of cabbages, potatoes, cucumbers, carrots, tomatoes, onions, and other young plants.

"All for the Government," he said, waving toward Kuibyshev. This was the private garden of Kremlin officials exiled to this temporary capital.

Shifting to halting English, Mr. Terekov explained that he had studied our language in his early school days. "Please show me your rubber plants," I said.

We went into another enclosure, with Mr. Terekov apologizing for the condition of the gardens. "It is the War. All the young men at the front. Once I had twenty helpers."

Among the brush and weeds, I discovered seven different types of rubber plants, which were later identified for me as of the *Kaug Saugyz* and *Taug Saugyz* families.

"Where are your new rubber plants?" I asked.

Mr. Terekov shrugged his shoulders. "It is all—these from seeds, I raise."

Like many other things in Russia, the startling developments in rubber plant experimentation had been grossly exaggerated. However, some good came from my acquaintance with Mr. Terekov. I learned that plant life in Southern Russia was very similar to that in the northern United States. Because of my early upbringing on a farm, I could talk plant life with this old man, which pleased him very much and also facilitated making contacts with other collective farms.

The following September, when I was preparing to leave for home for consultation, I dropped in to thank Mr. Terekov for his kindness to me. "Is there anything that you would like me to bring you from my country?"

Without a second's hesitation, he said, "Yes, thank you. Please bring me a copy of Bailey's *Botanical Dictionary*."

An Orphans' Home

Because of my membership in the Russian Relief Society and my acquaintance with Mrs. Stanoje Simich, wife of the Yugoslav Ambassador, its Kuibyshev President, I had the rare privilege of visiting an orphans' home near Kuibyshev. They came by for me at the Residentia one morning at eleven, a whole carload—Ambassador and Mrs. Simich and their daughter, Mr. Kataravados, a

young secretary of the Greek Legation and his wife, and Mrs.
Zdenek Fierlinger, wife of the Czechoslovakian Minister.

Because of the snow and the thaw, the going was pretty rough.
Our car got stuck and we had to walk the last mile. When we
reached the buildings of the orphanage, we were met by several
small children between four and six years of age. One of them
took each of us by the hand and led us to the main building, where
we were met by the matron in charge. More children swarmed
out of the building and each one presented a welcome to a member of our party with excellent manners.

In front of the dormitory, a spruce tree had been set up in a
square of frozen snow, fully decorated as if for Christmas. Before
the tree were a number of figures modeled in snow—a two-stack
battleship full-dressed with tiny paper flags, a large Army fort, and
a snow mountain with guns emplaced up its slopes. The matron
told us that these had been in better condition until the recent
thaw.

We went into the dormitory and there met the Kuibyshev inspector of orphan relief, a husky red-faced woman in her mid-
thirties, and the General Inspector of Children's Welfare from
Moscow, a man in his late forties, as well as a reporter from a
Moscow newspaper, several minor local officials, and members of
the orphanage staff.

The dormitory was equipped like a doll house—miniature iron
bedsteads with boards instead of springs and thin mattresses, a
small rug in front of each bed, tables and chairs in small scale
to match the children, and small towels and clothing in lockers
built for small people.

In the children's workroom, I saw exhibits of their work—crude
cardboard folders with cut-outs from magazines pasted in, a collection of pressed flowers, a folder of military equipment including
aircraft, ships, tanks, forts, and guns. On shelves were exhibits of
modeling in clay, woodwork, and models of tanks, ships, guns, and
steam engines, all quite cleverly executed to scale.

The children rose at six, did calisthenics, washed and dressed,
had breakfast, took exercise in the open air if the weather were
favorable, after which they worked at kindergarten classes or on
their projects. At eleven, they were permitted to play for half an
hour, either out of doors or in the playroom. On a small rug in the
playroom, I saw a meager assortment of toys, mostly models of
war machines, soldiers, sailors and airmen, all in excellent condition. The matron told me that the children were required to play

on the rug so that they wouldn't catch cold. "We'd like to have a larger rug," she said wistfully. "But . . ." She shrugged her shoulders expressively.

After this brief play period, they cleaned up and had lunch, followed by naps, more schooling or work, another longer play time, evening exercise, supper and bed by eight o'clock. It must have been a good regimen for they were certainly a ruddy-cheeked, healthy-looking lot.

We had been invited to the orphanage to witness an entertainment intended for Army Day in January, which had to be postponed because of bad weather. The program was scheduled for noon but typical Russian inefficiency delayed it until one-thirty. The entertainment was held in a large room, at one end of which was a large clay model of a fort with guns peeping out of gunports. To one side of the fort was the clay model of a submarine, rather lopsided, and a spruce tree elaborately decorated with Christmas tree lights. We guests had seats at the end of the room opposite the fort.

First we witnessed a march, led by the matron and a group of boys dressed in white sailor blouses, blue bell-bottomed trousers, each carrying a white life buoy with blue lettering, "Leningrad" and "Rostov." Following the sailors were fourteen boy soldiers in full Red Army uniform. After the Army came boy cavalry in blue, each boy carrying the model of the head and neck of a horse and handling the reins as if he were astride a horse. Next came a group of twenty boys in civil costumes representing various occupations and a group of girl *kolkhozes* in full uniform. Last came another group of girls in costumes representing various women's activities in the Soviet Union.

The long column of children came in singing a Russian marching song with great verve and marched clear around the room. A Red Army enlisted man made them a little speech bringing the greetings of the Red Army. One of the smaller boys replied on behalf of the children, sending a message of praise to the Red Army. It was interesting to watch the faces of the children. During the Army man's speech, they were attentive and courteous but I had a feeling that they understood nothing that he said. When the little boy spoke, they leaned forward in their chairs and seemed to take in every word, clapping enthusiastically when he finished.

The sailors put on a stunt with life buoys, marching in formation. The soldiers went through a military drill, deploying, firing their toy guns standing, kneeling, and prone, then assembled and did a snappy manual-at-arms. The cavalry next conducted field maneuvers, riding up and down the room. The girls sang; two sailors declaimed speeches, followed by a soldier, a cavalry boy, and one of the smaller *kolkhoz* girls.

Next came the dances. One might have thought he was witnessing *Don Quixote* or Russian folk dances by members of the Ballet. After each of the various groups danced for us, the whole troupe danced a medley, folk dances, Red Army dance ensembles, waltzing in couples, and individual specialty numbers. Some of the boys came up to the ladies in our group and asked them to dance and the *kolkhoz* girls approached the men. In a moment, you might have seen the American Ambassador, the Yugoslav Ambassador, the General Inspector, the local inspector, the Greek Attaché and their wives paired off with orphan children, gaily dancing a waltz.

The orchestra struck a chord. We adults returned to our seats. The children took their partners and executed a waltz rhythm in perfect time. It was one of the most astonishing performances by small children that I have ever seen anywhere.

After the entertainment, we had tea with the Superintendent, her mother and the matrons. I asked the Superintendent as to the significance of the large Christmas tree at the entrance to her living room.

"Oh, that is not a Christmas tree." She laughed gaily. "At New Year, we have a big celebration and decorate evergreen trees."

I pointed at the figure of an old Santa Claus in a tiny sleigh with his pack full of toys on his back, with a large grasshopper pulling the sleigh instead of a team of reindeer. "Who is that?"

"The Frost Man. He's the one who brings presents to the children."

In one corner of the room was a rectangular cardboard replica of the Kremlin, with its walls, towers and bulbous spires, which had apparently been used as a decoration around the base of the tree. Father Stalin, I thought. The Frost Man. All the presents, toys, and good things come from the Kremlin.

"This is a wonderful work you are doing," I changed the subject. "If there is anything you need to help you with your work, just let me know. I can probably get it for you from the United States in our relief supplies."

"Thank you," she said, smiling warmly.

As we walked down the road toward the gate, I looked back. The little children stood on the porch of the larger dormitory, waving good-bye to us, as children wave to those they love the world over. A lump came into my throat and I began to make plans to help them. But the opportunity never came. I never received any request from the Superintendent.

I Attempt to Visit a Collective Farm

In my effort to get to know the country people better, I decided at lunch one day that I would try to explore the countryside across the Samara. At banquets at the Kremlin, we had been served delicious slices of chilled watermelon. I had been told that the melons came from collective farms just south of Samara.

Some despatches delayed me. And as we turned south down the main street of Kuibyshev, it was late afternoon. With Mr. Loy Henderson, who was visiting me at the time, our messenger, Morris, and my ever-present NKVD boys, we proceeded toward the Samara pontoon bridge.

As we approached the bridge, the branch road from the right leading from the markets and business section of the city was filled with a continuous flow of traffic, country people returning home after disposing of their "free produce." Big Russian wagons drawn by short-necked Siberian ponies under high arched hames, or *duga*, high wheeled-carts pulled by yoked oxen or camels hitched two by two, once fancy carriages pulled by heavy draft horses or donkeys, an occasional wreck of a truck, all driven by old men, young boys or women, crawled along nose to tail, like an enormous snake.

Our driver stopped at the intersection, hoping that ordinary politeness would halt the traffic long enough for us to fall into line. After a considerable wait, with no evidence that anyone intended to let us join the procession, I would have been happy to turn back. One of our NKVD boys jumped out of his car and went ahead to try to persuade a driver to stop long enough to let us into line.

Having no success with persuasion, he grabbed a horse by its nose and bridle. The driver of the two-wheeled cart, an elderly woman, became so enraged that she not only blessed him out roundly in Russian, but also applied her whip vigorously to the horse's rump. The result was a ludicrous wrestling match between the skinny old horse and my bodyguard, the horse trying to get away from the old woman's ugly lashing and being held back by the man at its head, a spectacle that reminded me of a passage from Dostoyevsky. The unequal struggle did hold up the cart long enough for our cars to swing into line, and we crawled along behind a carry-all loaded down with a dozen or more young people, singing stirring Russian songs, chattering gaily and laughing widely when one or another of the boys fell out of the carriage as it braked to a stop.

As we reached the pontoon bridge, we discovered why no limit had been placed to travel across the Samara. The bridge was one-way, with a long wait each time southern traffic was held up so that a few northbound carts could cross. This was the one crossing for country people from the south into Kuibyshev, their only market town. From the southern end of the bridge, a fan of dirt roads let off in many directions, each one of them filled with a milling mass of carts, wagons, carriages, an occasional truck and hundreds of peasants on foot. It was the worst traffic jam that I have ever seen. With no police direction except at the bridge, I began to doubt that we would ever get back to Kuibyshev. The swirling dust, the smell of animals, the stench of sewers emptying into the Samara along both banks, created a situation into which no American would knowingly project himself.

Yet, there was no turning back. I selected a road at random and we rolled slowly along for a couple of miles before we reached a crossroad and could reverse course toward the bridge. With darkness, the mass of humanity had miraculously cleared away from the bridge approaches. We made our crossing and went back into Kuibyshev without stopping once.

I Attempt to Visit the Sanitarium

I have previously mentioned the Mare's Milk Tuberculosis Sanitarium situated high on the bluffs overlooking the Volga bend. The very name of the place intrigued me. Having always been stopped by a sentry on the paved highway just south of the Sanitarium, I asked Mr. Lozovsky to arrange to extend my limits further north so that I could enjoy a longer constitutional ride on a smooth road in the afternoon before dinner.

"Why of course, Mr. Ambassador," he assured me. "I will be happy to see to that for you. But there is really no limit—you can go anywhere you please. The sentries will be instructed to let the Ambassador and his caravan pass. I would advise, though, not to go more than twenty-five kilometers north of town. It soon becomes a wild and desolate country."

I had recently flown over that stretch of Russian countryside and I couldn't recall that it looked any more desolate than other environs of Kuibyshev, but I ignored his remark. If he would arrange for the Red Army sentries to let me pass, I'd use my own discretion where to turn back.

At that time, I had as guests at Sadovia, Mr. Loy Henderson of the State Department, General Follett Bradley of our Army Air Force, who was on a mission to the Soviet Government to see if he could expedite delivery of planes to Russia and persuade the Russians to open up an Alaska-Siberian air route, and Mrs. Irina (Skariatina) Blakeslee, wife of Commander Vic Blakeslee, who had come to Russia to write some articles for *Collier's* magazine. Coupled with my curiosity to see the Sanitarium was a desire to entertain my guests. I bundled them into the Embassy car and, with our NKVD guard following in their battered open car, we set out north along the paved road, hoping that the sentries had been properly instructed.

We were doomed to disappointment. The sentries held their guns at port arms, the worldwide soldier's gesture, "Thou shalt not pass."

With Irina acting as interpreter, I told the senior sentry, "The Foreign Office promised to have orders issued to let the American Ambassador and his caravan pass. Please let us by. We only want to take a short drive up the highway." I pointed dramatically at my ambassador's flag flying from a staff at the front of the car.

The sentry shook his head. "I have no instructions. You cannot pass."

"Please call up your commanding officer. There must be a mistake."

At first, he refused. Irina pleaded with him. Finally, he consented to call his barracks. Irina talked to his CO, but the answer was a resounding, *"Nyet!"*

The sentry leaned his rifle against the sentry box and beat his chest, made a motion of cutting his throat and then picked up his rifle and pretended to shoot the other sentry, who stood by, trying not to laugh at the boss sentry's antics. "He says that, even if it were a matter of life and death," Irina reported, "he could not let us pass."

Somehow I managed to keep a straight face. "Very well," I said. "Tell him I commend him upon his soldierly bearing, his intelligence, and his obedience to orders."

Both sentries sprang to rifle salute, which I returned with a snappy hand salute to my black homburg, and climbed back into my car. On our way back to Kuibyshev, I had the driver cut off the paved highway along some country roads through a residential section called the Polyana Fruenzi. As we returned to the highway considerably shaken up on the rough roads, Irina exclaimed, "I see that conditions haven't improved since I was a little girl in Russia."

We returned to the Embassy, still curious about the Mare's Milk Tuberculosis Sanitarium, but with a better knowledge of the countryside than previously. I tried again many times to get past that sentry box but the answer was always, "*Nyet*." I had been long enough in the country to know that this was the way of the Russian bureaucrat—promise anything but give only what the highest echelon of command tells you to give, and give that only when the *quid pro quo* is much more valuable than what you are asked to give.

I would still like to know—*why* the *Mare's Milk* Tuberculosis Sanitarium?

We Visit the Zhiguli Hills

I had been across the Volga to the bathing beaches a number of times and always looked with longing at the Zhiguli Hills, which, in more ancient days, provided hide-outs for Volga bandits who preyed on the rich caravans passing through Samara. Legend said that these fierce bandits often slit the throats of their merchant prisoners, hung them up by their heels on a raft, and sent the raft down the Volga to warn members of any would-be posse of the dangers of attempting to liquidate the bandits.

Since no geographical limits had been placed on our travel west of the Volga, perhaps, from the eminence of a high hill across from the Sanitarium, with powerful field glasses, I might be able to observe conditions in and around that establishment. After some difficulty, I arranged with the Foreign Office for a motor trip across the Volga with no particular destination prescribed.

In my party, I included Loy Henderson and two Russian linguists, a young secretary from my staff and a lad from the British delegation. We planned to rise early and cross on the seven o'clock ferry. Since the ferries were always late, we felt no apprehension when we approached the ferry house a few minutes after the hour. Probably because the American Ambassador and his party planned to take that ferry, it shoved off promptly at seven for the only time in my experience, taking with it my NKVD boys and their ancient touring car. I was still well protected. When we arrived early for the eight o'clock ferry, my other detail of NKVD men was waiting in a modern Zis limousine.

This ferry consisted of two large, flat-bottomed barges, one moored to each bank of the river as landings, with a third barge as the moving element. Ferry houses had been constructed on the moored barges. The moving barge was jammed so full that there was scarcely standing room for pedestrians—big trucks loaded with steel shovels, potatoes in bulk, an oil tank-truck, passenger cars in a generally more shattered condition than those you see in State-side auto graveyards, wagons, oxcarts, carriages, saddle horses, loads of baled hay, pedestrian cows, goats and pigs, and nearly a thousand men, women and children, all in a holiday mood because it was Sunday. Some trucks and cars were jammed full of picnick-ers with colorful tablecloths and huge lunch baskets, and factory workers going to work their truck gardens.

As a very special privilege (and, I suspect, to keep us from talk-ing to citizens on the barge), my party was ushered on board the towboat, while our caravan of three cars maneuvered onto the stationary barge and across onto the ferry barge. The towboat dropped down alongside the ferry barge, put out lines, and, with many shrill toots, maneuvered the barge across the river. With considerable skill, bucking a swift current, the towboat captain placed the ferry barge gently alongside the moored barge on the West bank, then dropped down and moored outboard to await the return trip.

Once across the river, foot passengers and their ambulant ani-mals disembarked; then, the trucks followed. Each truck had to back and fill into position, to the accompaniment of excited and noisy instructions from the barge master, pull across a heavy gang-plank to the moored barge, and across a second gangplank to a barely discernible road up the sandy river bank. As the first truck left the shoreside gangplank, it made a sharp turn left, rared back as if for a deep breath, and hit the sandy road full throttle. Being lightly loaded, it made the grade, but the second truck stalled its wheezy engine half way up the bank. Men and women in the large crowd watching us disembark rushed down the slope, and, with good-natured shouting, pushed the truck to the top of the bank.

Our caravan of four cars presently assembled on the road above the river. We had ten Russian men in our party—my NKVD boys, their drivers and a CP man from the West bank Oblast—an extravagant waste of able-bodied workers in a land suffering from a serious shortage of farm man-and-womanpower. We drove twenty miles along the Volga to its upper bend, over a road full of ruts and chuckholes and covered with a layer of dust six inches deep. We came to a new paved road leading to the north past a prison camp in an abandoned quarry, barbed-wire enclosed, with towers manned by armed sentries at each corner and at the middle of each side. The paved road looked inviting, but a sentry stood with gun at port arms to bar the way.

We turned back five miles and took a dusty country road into the Zhiguli Hills, passing between fields of golden wheat and fields of stubble, with cut grain already bound and shocked ready for thrashing. At a turn in the road, I saw a group of thirty people standing or sitting around a high stack of grain about 200 yards off the road. "Pull over, Morris," I told my messenger. As we got out of the cars, some ten of our party, young and husky-looking, I discovered that the workers were all women dressed in worn and patched worker's denim. A woman, who looked to be middle-aged but might have been much younger, came to meet us. When we had exchanged greetings, and told her who we were, she said, with evident disappointment, "Oh, we thought you were workers sent to help us harvest our crop."

"Where are your men?" I asked.

"*Nichevo*," she said and shrugged her shoulders. "Off to the wars."

What had once been a prosperous collective farm with over two hundred men, women and children was now being operated by 32 women, trying to maintain a pre-war level of production. Their thrashing machine and nearly every other piece of farm machinery had broken down for lack of proper lubricating oil. Requests for repairs had not been answered. They had no spare parts; no worker knew enough about machines to repair them if they had. Now, they were doing all their work by hand, even beating the grain out with club and flail in the age-old fashion of primitive people. It was a pitiful sight. I wondered if the young Russian men with us might not feel ashamed, but, if so, they showed no sign of it, for this was Communist Russia, where women have equal opportunity with men, equal right to perform even the hardest kind of physical labor.

When we started down the west side of the range we passed onto a typical corduroy logging road and there was no turning back. As we exited from this road we entered a beautiful valley between hills covered with a replant growth of timber. Immediately on our right was an area enclosed by a high board fence with armed guards in towers at all corners and sides—evidently a prison compound of some sort. On the range of hills on the opposite side was an active limestone mine of considerable extent.

As we passed down the ever widening valley following the stream which emptied into the Volga, we passed small fields of ripening grain and fertile gardens growing every conceivable variety of vegetable.

We also passed a number of so-called small villages—"occupied points," the Germans called them in their communiques, when they captured them—ten to fifteen log huts, homes of the limestone miners, banked with dirt as protection against the bitter cold of Winter, huddled together at the base of a forested hill. Some of the roofs were thatched with straw like a peasant's cottage in Provence. Swirls of smoke climbed from their stone chimneys. We ate our lunch on a wide grassy flat along the river bank and looked out across the muddy Volga.

We took a different route homeward—an excellent road up another wide valley through a forest, much like the woods country of Canada or of our own Northwestern states, with much hazelwood, but no nuts or acorns and few berries. I saw little wild life, no squirrels, a few hawks, a couple of cawing crows, but no other birds. Wood for the winter fires had been cut and neatly ricked up in cords. Replanting, following the cuttings, was in evidence in every area.

As we descended from the hills, we came out into another wide valley with many fields of garden truck. Among the women workers, we now saw a few old men and one or two younger men, who must have been overseers. They had picked green tomatoes and piled them in hummocks three feet high and twenty feet long, waiting for trucks to come and take them away. Pumpkins, melons, and Irish potatoes were there in abundance.

I pulled up at a field where a group of women and two men were harvesting large, striped watermelons. With Morris, I went across to one of the men. "Will you sell us some of your melons?" Morris asked.

The old man pulled a red kerchief off his head and wiped his face and neck. "Who are you?" he asked suspiciously.

Morris told him.

"We can't sell them," he said shortly. "They all belong to the government." He turned away, throwing back over his shoulder, "But you're welcome to all you can eat here."

We sat in the dusty field holding long slices of luscious red watermelon, eating them as I had eaten California melon long years ago when, as boys, we raided a neighbor's melon patch in the dark of the summer moon. A group of women workers began to sing a low, sad melody that somehow seemed wonderfully appropriate to the difficulties of their situation.

On another occasion I was invited to take part in the opening of the strawberry season and quite a ceremony was made of the event. The *agronom* in charge insisted that I make a thorough inspection of the 40 acre patch. Accompanying us on this inspection were some 40 strawberry pickers. During the inspection these pickers competed with each other to find the largest and most luscious strawberry, and the winner was not satisfied until I had eaten the one he had found. This attitude was pleasing, because it evidenced the friendly feeling of these Russian country people toward the American Ambassador and things American. But to say the least, I had, on one occasion, more than enough strawberries, especially without the accompanying trimmings in the way of cream and sugar. And while the inspection evidenced that there were plenty of strawberries in the vicinity, none of these strawberries were ever available to my stewards or me in the market in which we were permitted to buy vegetables.

These trips had in a measure satisfied my curiosity. However I still wanted to find the collective farm across the Samara. In September, 1942, with Angus Ward, our Consul at Vladivostok, who was visiting me briefly, and Morris, I again ventured across the Samara on a voyage of exploration. This time, I was better armed with information and had little difficulty finding the farm.

Naturally, there had been no advance notice of my visit. I drove through the little village at the *kolkhoz* and, after some inquiry, found the *agronom*, a very personable young woman, with a pretty young woman visitor and the manager chatting together in a storehouse at the far end of the farm. While obviously surprised to see us, they extended a very warm welcome.

The manager told me that his *kolkhoz* had 3,000 acres of land under cultivation and that their principal produce was garden truck. But they also had a thousand head of cattle, including a fine dairy herd, and raised hogs, chickens and turkeys. This farm furnished most of the vegetables and fresh milk for Kuibyshev.

In reply to my question about melons, the manager took us to a large field, where quantities of watermelon, cantaloupe, muskmelon and honeydew melon were just ripening. The manager graciously said, "Help yourself, sir. They ripen so fast and all at once that we can't possibly harvest them all."

Morris and Angus Ward filled the back end of our car. Meanwhile, I observed that my NKVD boys had become very interested in the young *agronom* and her friend. For the first and only time, my bodyguards deserted me and went with the *agronom* to another field, where they filled their car.

We returned to the storehouse, where the manager gave us all the fresh vegetables that we could carry. He was very pleasant and cordial on parting. "Come again, Tovarich," he said, smiling widely. "Any time you can visit the farm, I'll be glad to give you all the fresh vegetables you want."

The next day, I sent Morris with the Embassy truck and he brought home a full load of vegetables for use of the Embassy personnel. But that was the end of our fresh vegetable spree. A few days later, I received word from the Foreign Office that our visits to the collective farm had not been properly authorized. Future visits would not be made without express permission in advance.

CHAPTER X

The Opiate of the People

To ME, one of the most fascinating facets of Russian life was the conflict between State and Church. From reading Soviet propaganda before the War, I had concluded that Russia was just about one hundred percent atheistic. I knew that, after the October Revolution, Church was completely separated from State and that most of the leaders of the Orthodox Church had been glad to escape to the comparative safety of the Balkan States and Turkey. Many church buildings had been destroyed and others, which had been taken over by the State, were deconsecrated by the remaining clergy, had their steeples pulled down, and were turned into museums. In school, on the stage, in the daily Press, and in special magazines, the Party waged unrelenting warfare against religion. Of the hundreds of churches in the Moscow area, only a few remained open for their parishioners to worship.

When Maxim Litvinov negotiated recognition of the Soviet Government by the United States, one of the principal concerns of President Roosevelt was religious freedom in the Soviet Union. Unable to obtain a guarantee of complete religious freedom, President Roosevelt settled for a promise that all Americans resident in the Soviet Union would have the right to worship as they pleased, in accordance with the dictates of their own conscience. When the "Stalin Constitution" was adopted in 1936, the Western world was happy to see that one of its articles provided in clear and unmistakable language for religious freedom. Still, the anti-religious propaganda and actions continued; the beliefs and attitudes of the men controlling the Party were fundamentally atheistic. The same article provides for "freedom of anti-religious propaganda" without providing for religious propaganda which had been prohibited in 1929. This seriously impeded religious indoctrination.

In America, belief in the complete dominance of atheism in Russia was so widespread that, when we went to Russia with the Beaverbrook-Harriman Mission in 1941, Mr. Harriman was instructed by President Roosevelt to inform Premier Stalin as to this viewpoint and to tell him that the American Press was attacking the Soviet Government because of its hostility to religion. If the Soviet Government would make some concession toward religious freedom, the American public would be much easier to sell on Lend-Lease to Russia. Recognizing the bargaining value of such a gesture, the Communist Party dropped its anti-religious propaganda in the schools and on the stage and suspended publication of the official paper of the Society of the Godless, *Bozholnik*, ostensibly because of paper shortage.

President Roosevelt found these moves very helpful in putting across to Christian Americans his program of Lend-Lease aid to a government which plastered the walls of former churches with the Marxian slogan, "Religion is the opiate of the people." But many Americans insisted that these concessions on the part of the Soviet Government were made solely to impress foreigners.

Such critics were only partly right. When Hitler moved into the Ukraine, he brought with him exiled Orthodox priests, vestments, ikons, and church ceremonial vessels and his conquering armies opened up the churches and invited all to come freely to worship. News of this move spread quickly throughout the Soviet Union. Not only old men and *babushkas* flocked to the churches, but also many young people joined the church in the Ukraine.

I had not been in Russia long before I recognized a major paradox, which I believe will prove to be of profound importance to the future of Russia and of the entire world: First, religion is vigorously opposed by the ruling minority; second, it is widely practiced by the Russian people, even by large numbers of Komsomols and Party members.

Examples of official resistance to the church: Electric current costs a church thirty-five times as much as a government store; coal rations were so severely limited that churches could not be comfortably heated in Winter; Sundays were filled with schedules of movies, sport contests, games and other interesting activities to draw off attendance of the young at church. Too active display of religious zeal damaged a Party member's chance for advancement.

While I was still in Russia, the Russian Orthodox Church made its peace with Stalin and the Church received representation on the Council of Peoples Commissars.

Premier Stalin stated that these concessions to the church were given as the result of whole-hearted support of the Red Army and the war effort.

The first intimation I had of this change of attitude was during a visit from the Patriarch Sergei, Metropolitan of Moscow, on September 18, 1942, at which time he presented me with ten copies of a book which, he told me, presented the disastrous effects of Nazism on the Russian Church and gave the history of the Russian Church and the status of religion in Russia at that time. This was a special edition of only fifty copies prepared for propaganda purposes among the Axis powers. I sent copies to Father Walsh at Georgetown University and Father O'Donohue in San Diego.

I was surprised that such a book could be published in Russia at that time. Subsequent articles in *Pravda* indicated why. Church authorities had promised liberal financial support to the Red Army and the war effort. I have heard that the Patriarch Alexei donated 500,000 rubles for a tank column to be named after Dimitri Donsky, and Alexander Ivanovitch Vyendensky, Primate of the Russian Orthodox Church, donated a precious breast ikon valued at 500,000 rubles.

The loyalty of the church to the war effort is indicated by a typical letter from the Metropolitan Sergei:

Moscow—The Kremlin
To: Joseph Stalin.
   On the day of the 25th anniversary of the Soviet Republic, in the name of our clergy and of all the faithful of the Russian Orthodox Church, I sincerely and prayerfully salute in your person the God-chosen [sic] leader of our military and cultural strength leading us on to victory over the barbarous invasion of our country's peaceful prosperity and the bright future of its peoples. May God [sic] crown your mighty exploits with success and glory.
                   Guardian of the Patriarchal Throne
                   /s/ Sergei
        Metropolitan of Moscow and Kolomenskoy

Similar letters were written by Nicholas, the Metropolitan of Kiev and Galicia, Alexander, Head of the *Reformed* Russian Orthodox Church, Tchobroutsky, President of the Moscow Jewish Community, Kalistrat, the Catholicos Patriarch of All-Georgia, Doctor H. Johnson, Pastor of the Canterbury Cathedral and President of the United Committee for Help to Soviet Russia, and Alexei, Metropolitan of Leningrad.

Later, the Patriarch Alexei was recognized as the Head of the

Russian Orthodox Church. He and his priests loyally supported the "Great Patriotic War of the Soviet Union" and worked earnestly to improve the morale of the people. It was commonly reported around Moscow that Alexei once addressed Stalin as "Our Dear Leader, whom God has sent us."

As I moved in my limited orbits about Russia, all through the countryside and even in the center of Moscow, I found churches operating openly and priests actively practicing and preaching their faith. In my Sunday drives in the back country around Moscow, I frequently visited deconsecrated churches and invariably found small groups of peasants, with or without a priest, engaged in some form of religious worship, quite often the funeral of a member of the community. In one country church, I happened on a funeral service for an old man and found the bodies of another old man and a child waiting in an anteroom for services. Not all of the congregations were *babushkas* and old men, although they predominated because most of the young men were away at war. A few younger women and some children were usually present. On one occasion, Sir Archibald Clark-Kerr accompanied me. We had our picture taken examining the church bells which the Bolsheviks had taken down from the tower to prevent calling the faithful to service.

There were no chaplains with the troops. It was explained to me that the Party Commissars took care of all the spiritual needs of soldiers and airmen, and gave them help and guidance. Our God was only a faith, they said. The Communists also had their faith, in the Party and in Father Stalin—not to cheat, lie, kill or steal, always to try to live correctly with one another. With such faith, what more could one wish?

Even the most ardent atheist in the Party stoutly maintained that anyone who wished to do so could attend service in the synagogue or church, although most of them admitted it would be difficult for a Russian to be a good member of both Church and Party.

I experienced much difficulty in getting to talk to the "man-on-the-street," both because of language barrier and the Russian individual's fear of consequences if he became friendly with a foreigner. I recall one visit I had with a young lad which was most interesting. I met him on one of my early morning walks about Kuibyshev, a tall, slender boy of perhaps fifteen, dressed in what appeared to be a Red Army uniform. He had his tan trousers stuffed into high black boots. His face was thin, unwhiskered, and ruddy, and his military cap perched on his closely clipped head at a jaunty angle. He was sitting on the steps in front of the theater, as I came up to him, with Morris trotting along at my heels.

I stopped and said "Good morning," in Russian. Through Morris, I discovered that he really was a Red Army man, even though so young. "My name is Standley," I told him and I held out my hand. "I am an American."

"Andrei Rossokov," he said, taking my hand with a smile. "We like the Americans. I have ridden your fine Studebaker."

He was speaking of the trucks we had Lend-Leased to Russia in such large numbers. We chatted for a while through Morris, my NKVD boys standing respectfully behind me but close enough to hear all that was said.

"What will you do after the war, Andrei?"

"Go to school. Then, I'd like to take flying."

I lowered my voice. "Do you believe in God?"

He looked puzzled. "*Nichevo*. I don't know."

"Did you ever go to church?"

"*Nyet*. Not ever, but my *bubushka* goes."

He suddenly stood up, very straight and military in his neat uniform. I looked around to see one of my NKVD boys finishing an imperative gesture. "Wouldn't you like to go to church just once—to see what it's like?" I asked hurriedly.

"I must go now," Andrei said nervously. "Goodbye, sir."

"What about church?" I called after him.

I doubt that he understood me, but he said something and ran up the steps into the theater. "He said he likes the Sunday movies best," Morris told me.

I set off up the street at a fast clip. My NKVD boys fell in at their respectful six paces to the rear.

At the end of the street below our American office in Kuibyshev, stood a huge old stone church, which held many services every Sunday. To help satisfy my curiosity with regard to the practice of religion in Russia, I decided to attend that church. I made discreet inquiries and was assured that such a visit was permissable. On a Sunday in May, taking Eddie Page and Morris with me, and protected as usual by my three NKVD boys, I started for church.

As we were leaving the house, Morris asked, "Have you small change with you, Mr. Ambassador?"

I felt in my pockets and shook my head. "Why?" I asked curiously.

"There will be many beggars in front of the church."

I pulled out my wallet and showed Morris my small bills, Russian paper notes for a hundred rubles. "Oh, that will be all right, sir. I'll get change at the church."

A semi-circular driveway led up to the front entrance to the old church. As we approached the driveway, I saw that it was lined on either side by women, incredibly dirty of body and dressed in filthy rags. "The beggars," Morris said in a low tone of voice.

As we approached the first wrinkled old hag, Morris gave her my 100-ruble note and said something to her. She dove into her ragged clothes and came out with a large bag of jingling coins from which she gave Morris change. As we walked up the driveway, Morris dropped a coin into each outstretched hand, crossing himself each time because the Russians believe that such gifts have been touched by the hand of God.

We were met at the door by an usher who welcomed us warmly and conducted us inside. The air was heavy with the odor of incense and the smell of candle smoke. We stood for a few moments at the rear of the church casting a horoscope, as it were, over the situation.

The large Orthodox churches in Russia have no pews. The congregation stand patiently and stolidly during the service, bowing their heads and crossing themselves in unison at proper places in the ritual. The church was crowded that morning; high in his ornately carved pulpit, a priest was delivering a sermon; ushers kept open an aisle from the big doorway to the pulpit through which worshipers came and went. A narrow aisle to the left led up the left side of the church to the altar. Half way up this side aisle stood a table with many short candles burning on it and piles of candles waiting to be lighted. Also on the table were gifts of food and money with notes attached requesting a prayer for some dear one sick, departed this life, or in serious danger.

Along this aisle moved a stream of old women carrying babies in their arms. Morris whispered that their young mothers were either engaged in the war effort or afraid to attend church. As a hostage to the future, they sent the *babushkas* to have their babies christened.

Presently, our usher suggested that we proceed up the left aisle toward the pulpit. As we followed him through the congregation, Morris whispered, "That old lady at the offering table is praying for two boys in the Red Army. 'Take care of them, God,' I just heard her say. 'They're really good boys.'"

As we passed the offering table, we saw many poor Russians making their humble offerings, lighting a candle, leaving a note asking for prayers.

Our usher asked, "Would you like to go on up the aisle behind the pulpit?"

Feeling that this was a rare opportunity to observe religious rites in Russia, I nodded. My party including the NKVD men followed him through the altar entrance at the rear of the pulpit. Behind the altar, three priests and a number of boy acolytes, dressed in the finest of gold-brocaded robes and bearing communion vessels which appeared to be solid gold, were giving communion. The attitude of everyone behind the altar was one of devout religious fervor. We stood among the others with our heads bowed until there came a break in the ritual. I glanced up at the back of the altar. It was covered with ikons, large and small, ornately decorated with rubies and emeralds so large that they looked like colored glass. A crown of the richest silk brocaded in gold, shaped like a bulbous onion, occupied a niche in one corner of the altar.

After some moments of silent prayer, the boy acolytes passed among the communicants with gold collection plates. After making my donation, I indicated to our usher that I wished to withdraw, expecting to leave by the same side entrance. Such was not his plan. He insisted that we pass out over the pulpit just to the right of a priest still preaching a sermon and parade down the center aisle. Thus, the whole congregation knew that the American Ambassador and his squad of NKVD men had attended their church.

As we went down the driveway, Morris continued to press alms into the hands of the beggars.

When we were in Moscow, knowing my interest in religion in Russia, our faithful Embassy messenger, Phillip Bender, often suggested historic spots to visit. One day late in the Fall, Bender took us to visit a former Orthodox Church convent, the Novodevichi Convent. Before the Revolution, this convent had been the center of a large and active parish, housing hundreds of nuns. After the Revolution, the steeple of its church was torn down and its bells removed; for a time, it was a Communist Party museum.

Workers were again preparing the church to be a Red museum.

Every sort of church equipment was stored in the nave and transept of the old church, in a state of the utmost disorder. A workman told Bender that it would be opened as a museum in two
weeks, but that was obviously an overly-optimistic statement.

Here I saw some Doric columns, which once had graced the
front of the church, lying on wooden timbers on the church floor.
In a huge mound at the center of the transept, crated material
brought back from the New York World's Fair, with the familiar
emblem of pylon and perisphere on it, was haphazardly piled.
Ikons and rich vestments in every stage of deterioration were
stacked in piles on the damp floor. Beautiful primitive religious
paintings were stacked up like so much cordwood. Huge murals
and intricate designs on inlay work decorated the walls and domes
of the church.

As we went out into bright sunlight through another doorway,
I saw that the church and the convent buildings were located in a
walled enclosure, much like the Kremlin; on the thick walls, I saw
the ruins of old fortifications. Bender told me that, in ancient days,
whenever the parish was threatened by an invader, the peasants
brought their cattle and goods into the convent walls for refuge;
the convent was always fiercely defended.

We drove along a very rough road to another walled enclosure,
a monastery which once had housed several hundred monks. Construction of its church began in 1524 and was completed twelve
years later; it was in much better condition than the convent
church. A young woman came up and offered, in good English, to
show us around. We were indeed fortunate to have her for a
guide as she was, at heart, an orator, knew the history, and talked
to us about the monastery as long as we cared to listen.

Fabulous ikons and rich vestments were carefully preserved in
cases with glass doors. Walls were covered by fine murals. On one
wall, an excellent artist had painted the crucifixion scene in life-
size; all around this mural, a sculptor had carved in marble miniature scenes depicting events in the Life of Christ. A nearby mural
represented hell, with sinners burning in Dantesque realism, while
across the nave was a mural depicting the delights of heaven with
St. Peter and the angels.

In large niches in three tiers were beautiful life-sized ikons
framed in precious metal set with a fortune in jewels. Apparently,
the government was preparing to restore the building, for patches
of paint had been removed in various places to rediscover the four
styles of interior decoration used in as many restorations. Soviet

architects and artists were copying the designs with camera and brush and palette.

We went out through another doorway into a huge cemetery, the burial ground of the nobility in Czarist days; there were large crypts along the walls of the church with marble-lined vaults, and costly and elaborately carved monuments memorialized the once great men lying there. Since the Red Revolution, this cemetery has been used to bury distinguished members of the Party and the Red armed forces.

Our guide took us to see the grave of Stalin's second wife; the plot was in a bed of beautiful flowers, marked by a large rectangular marble stone topped by a beautiful carving of the death mask and head of the Russian Dictator's wife. Its simple lines and austerity gave the memorial stone a striking beauty.

In the next grave, I was told, lay the body of a young man who, being in love with Ambassador Oumansky's daughter, was so despondent over the fact that the Oumanskys were leaving for Mexico the next morning that he shot his sweetheart and then committed suicide.

On another side of the high-walled cemetery stood urns of Red airmen lost in battle. Our guide told us that only the most distinguished Red Army men are brought here for burial; the rest lie where they fall in battle.

One of the most interesting former monasteries was Kolomenskoye, which I visited in company with Sir Archibald Clark-Kerr and his secretary, John Reed, together with Hamilton, Page, Jack Duncan, and Ronnie Allen. We found an excellent guide awaiting us, although we had not informed anyone that we intended to visit Kolomenskoye that day. She was well versed in the history and tradition of the monastery, which made our two-hour visit extremely interesting.

Kolomenskoye was once the site of the Summer Palace of the czars. Each czar, as he came to the throne, would tear down the previous czar's palace and build himself a new and more elaborate one. Some of the czars didn't like the chapels they inherited, and so they built a new one, which accounts for the three churches within the huge enclosure. The last czar apparently had his father's palace torn down but didn't get around to building a new one.

The three remaining church buildings were constructed in the 15th, 16th, and 17th Centuries. As we entered the 17th Century church, religious services were in progress, with more than fifty men and women participating. In an alcove near the door, we saw the bodies of an old woman, almost mummified, an old man, and a child about two years of age, all awaiting burial services. We respected the services and didn't go through the church, but, from the arched doorway, we could see, in the rear of the church, many of the original tapestries and vestments, ikons and altar ornaments, in all their richness. The belfry and onion-shaped domes were still intact; in the belfry we could see the bells and presently heard the chimes playing. Our guide couldn't discover anyone who could tell us why this church had been left intact and still consecrated for holy service.

Next, we went through the 15th Century church, which was a museum; we saw a model of the last palace and many beautiful religious vestments and tapestries, chalices and paintings, well-displayed; as well as such instruments and implements as carpenter's tools, large wooden food bowls, and ornate drinking cups of the time of Peter the Great.

In the courtyard, our guide showed us a small stone house, which belonged to Peter the Great. On the balcony of another small palace, she said, Ivan the Terrible sat in a stone chair looking out across the valley of the Moscow River and watched his warriors jousting and engaging in gladiatorial combat for his amusement, while he kept his wife safely confined in a nearby brick dungeon. A tall tower pointed out to us, she said, was once part of a huge gate on the Karelian peninsula; Peter the Great had it moved to this site because he liked its graceful lines. Suspended from a heavy steel I-beam supported on two tripods, I saw seven bells, which we were told were cast in the 16th Century and had been removed from nearby church buildings. Under an elaborate canvas cover in the small palace, we saw Ivan the Terrible's simple wooden throne chair.

This was all that remained in this historical place of the glory, pomp, and ceremony of the Romanoffs and the Russian Orthodox Church.

My most interesting religious experience in Russia came at Eastertide. I knew that, in the old days, every Russian, particularly devout or not, took Easter very seriously. Even though there were, in those days, over 200 churches in Moscow, they were always packed with crowds spilling over into the streets in front of the churches.

But officially, Easter was ignored. No mention was made of it in the Moscow newspapers or on the radio. The attendance at church on Ash Wednesday and Good Friday was not spectacular.

On Easter Eve, I decided to give Father Braun, the little Catholic priest from New Bedford, Massachusetts, who was our unofficial American chaplain, some further support in his conflict with Soviet bureaucracy. Although I am a Protestant, I passed out word to my staff that, on Easter morning, I would attend Mass at St. Louis de Francis and that my aides could consider it an official visit.

It was quite a procession that we made. Nearly the whole staff turned out in full dress, the civilians in our diplomatic morning attire, the military aides immaculate in their best uniforms and Commander John Young wearing gold aiguillettes which glittered in the bright Easter sunlight.

It seemed to me that the people we passed were better dressed than commonly, as if they had put on their best clothes for Easter service, just as we dress up at home for the Easter parade. Father Braun's church was crowded when we arrived at the huge front doors a few moments before the ten o'clock service. St. Louis is like a church at home, with vaulting ceilings, a wide center aisle with pews on either side, and a once lovely stained glass window above the altar. An usher and my NKVD boys made way for us down the aisle to the front pews. As at the opera or ballet, my NKVD boys cleared out some worshipers from the pew directly behind me and sat there looking stiff and uncomfortable, as they tried to follow our movements when we stood up to chant or knelt to pray.

I stole a glance behind me. The aisles and the spaces in back of the pews were crowded with worshipers. When the call to communion came, hundreds of men and women trudged up the aisle to the chancel rail to receive the sacrament, a sober, devout procession of "common people" who, in their hearts, prayed for peace in the world just as did their Christian brethren in America.

When communion was over, ushers cleared the center aisle and we marched in a short column down to the arched front doorway. As at Kuibyshev, ragged old women lined up on the steps with their hands outstretched in the ancient gesture of the beggar. I gave each of them a few coins and passed on down the steps into the crowded square.

They call the Soviet Union, "Godless Russia." It is true enough that most of the higher hierarchy of the Communist Party and the Soviet Government are atheistic or agnostic; that Party members are discouraged from joining or attending church; that an Army or Naval officer's career is almost certain to be blighted if he even appears in a church; that religious education is not only discouraged in the churches but is forbidden in the educational program of children throughout Russia.

Yet the parents, the *babushkas,* of the "common people" kept on trying to implant in the hearts of their children the faith of their fathers in the Russian Orthodox Church. Somehow or other, the surviving priests still manage to train young men for the clergy in their own churches and the message that Christ brought to the world nearly two thousand years ago marches on, even in "Godless" Soviet Russia.

CHAPTER XI

Special Representatives and Very Very Important Personages

Thus far in my story, I have attempted to follow a strictly chronological order. But in organizing the material for telling about the rest of my remarkable sojourn in Soviet Russia, I have found that there are so many special events and visits of Special Representatives and Very VIP's that run over a period of some weeks or months that I have decided to tell each one of these incidents, together with necessary background material, as I come to them. I am hoping that this will assist me in showing how difficult it is to do business with the Kremlin, particularly when you have a Chief of State at home and another one in the capital of the state to which you are accredited, who believes in personal diplomacy, either directly or through his own "personal foreign office."

I soon discovered that an ambassador of a powerful state could not approach the master (or masters) of the Kremlin in a spirit of Christian humility with hat in hand as if humbly seeking favors. If you did, you generally came away with only a small piece of the tail of your diplomatic shirt.

Stalin had all of the aces and the jokers in the pack in our games of diplomatic poker, because he knew that we had to play the game with him on his terms. I don't think he ever had any intention of picking up his chips and quitting the game—although our State Department boys and the Boss and Harry Hopkins worried about that possibility a lot. I am quite certain that Mr. Stalin and the other members of the Politburo knew that we had to have Soviet Russia on our team to hold the Nazis while we got ready to hit them on their armored snout and slit their "soft underbelly." I know that the Kremlin "took us for all the traffic would bear" while I was in Moscow, and even more so after I left, when winning the war was certain in 1944 and 1945 and the only questions were when, and who would rake in the blue chips.

I don't claim any special prescience for my actions in those days. But I did soon learn that I got nowhere in my negotiations with the Soviet diplomats if I approached them timidly like a veritable Casper Milquetoast humbly asking for favors and praying that they would have the goodness and graciousness to kindly permit me to give them on behalf of the United States Government fifty of our latest tanks or a hundred B-26 bombers or two hundred Aircobras or anything else under the sun that the Soviet Government might want, including whole powder and tire factories, plane assembly lines, and machine tools by the shipload, some of which I am sure have never been set up and used in Russia to this day. If an Ambassador or a Special Representative approached Mr. Stalin or Mr. Molotov or any one of a dozen other Soviet officials, including Commissar for Foreign Trade Mikoyan, in a friendly, apologetic, or vacillating manner, the Russian didn't regard the visiting negotiator as commonly polite and friendly—he decided that his adversary was weak and afraid of him and he therefore despised and took advantage of him.

Perhaps you recall the "get tough with Russia" policy which our Secretary of State James F. Byrnes finally advocated for dealing with the Kremlin in 1946. That was nothing new; that was the "Standley technique" in Moscow in 1942 and 1943—although I have always felt that publicizing that name for it was unfortunate. In my dealings with the Russians, I came to believe in standing up to them, in being forceful and demanding, in making what promises I was told to make and trying my best to keep them, but also in insisting that they keep their promises to us—and we had a mighty good "or else" in those days, although I had very little success in persuading our government to use it. I had no hesitancy in speaking in a blunt, pointed and salty sailorman fashion. In not a few instances, I had occasion to pound my fist on the table and say, "That we will not take. That we will not do!" The Russian understands that kind of diplomacy and knows how to take it.

For long months, I saw Special Representative after Big Dignitary come to Russia, leapfrog over my top-hatted head, and follow out the Rooseveltian policy—do not antagonize the Russians, give them everything they want, for, after all, they are killing Germans, they are fighting our battles for us. I also watched the situation deteriorate, as I will attempt to show by the special incidents and the parade of Special Representatives with which I will fill many of the remaining pages of this book.

But most of us have to learn by doing. For example—

In 1942, the British and American Governments became properly concerned over the losses sustained by convoys from the North of Scotland and Iceland around the North Cape to Murmansk and Archangel, one of our main supply routes to Soviet Russia. In an effort to afford better protection to the ships of these convoys, the British asked permission of the Russians to establish a squadron of planes at Murmansk, quarters for the 500 officers and men to be provided by the Soviet Government.

When the squadron and its planes arrived in Murmansk, the Russians claimed that there were a total of 700 officers and men and that, therefore, the British had broken their agreement. The Soviet Government accordingly felt compelled to cancel permission for the squadron to operate out of Murmansk.

I had been surprised that they had ever granted such permission, as it would involve considerable flying over Soviet territory by foreign military pilots, and *this* the Russians have never favored. When the Soviet Government suggested that the British turn over the planes to Russian pilots and go home, the Russian reasoning process became crystal clear. To this, the British would never agree, contending that forces protecting the convoys must operate under one command or confusion or misadventure would result. When the Russians were obdurate (or pig-headed, whichever word you like best), the British Government proposed to the American Government that the Murmansk-Archangel convoy route be abandoned in favor of the Persian Gulf-Persian railway and truck route. When this proposal was offered as a power play to the Russians, they took violent exception. The planes and British personnel sat idle in Murmansk for many months while the issue was argued in Moscow, London and Washington. The Russians finally got the planes, which was doubtless what they wanted in the first place.

Perhaps in some areas of human endeavor "a soft answer turneth away wrath," but not in Moscow in those days. Probably as a sop to British pride, certain Russian awards were made to members of the crews of combatant British and American ships protecting the Murmansk convoys and to a number of the merchant crewmen.

When Captain Jack Duncan and Colonel "Mike" Michella heard of this, they conceived the friendly plan of reciprocating this courtesy. I approved of the idea, feeling that, if I could present medals to representative officers and enlisted men of the Red Army, Navy and Air Forces, the word of our American friendliness might spread far and wide through Soviet Russia.

The British Embassy must have concocted a similar plan at the same time, for about the time that we received approval from our Government and 60 assorted medals from the Congressional Medal of Honor down, I learned from a Russian source that the British Ambassador had personally presented a number of British awards to Russian Red Army, Navy, Air Force, and Merchant Marine personnel. I had told Sir Archibald Clark-Kerr of our plan, but this was the first I had heard of the British program, one of a very few occasions when Sir Archibald failed to keep me fully informed.

Mr. Molotov presently sent word to me that his Government approved of our project. Assuming that I would be accorded the privilege of personally pinning the medal on the individual recipient, my Attachés consulted Admiral Kuznetsov, Commissar for the Navy, and Marshal Golichov, Commissar for the Army, in an endeavor to obtain the names of the individuals whom we were to honor in the name of the President of the United States. In the meantime considerable argument arose as to how the ceremonies should be conducted. That was when I should have pounded the shiny table under Mr. Molotov's nose and told him, "No personal presentation by the Ambassador, no medals." But I was new and it was Be-Kind-to-Russia month. In the end, I meekly agreed that I would deliver the medals to Mr. Molotov, who would see that they were awarded to the various individuals by their Commanding Officers, a much less effective propaganda procedure from our point of view.

The ceremony eventually took place on June 22, 1943, in the office of the Commissar for Foreign Affairs in the Kremlin. Present on the Russian side were Mr. Molotov and his Assistant Commissars for Foreign Affairs Lozovsky and Litvinov, Marshal Golichov and Admiral Kuznetsov, and a number of minor officials. I had some visiting Big Dignitaries and Special Representatives, including Mr. Arthur Sulzberger of the *New York Times;* his secretary, Jimmy Reston; Mr. Scovell of the American Red Cross; Captain Eddie Rickenbacker and his physician, Dr. Dahl; my Military and Naval Attachés and other members of my staff. I was determined

to do as good a propaganda job as possible under the circumstances, and so I addressed the group about as follows:

> Gentlemen, as the representative of the President of the United
> States of America in the Soviet Union, it gives me great pleasure,
> through the presentation of these awards and decorations, to honor
> and pay tribute not only to the individuals who will eventually re-
> ceive them but also to all of the Armed Forces of Russia and to the
> Russian civil populace, whose steadfast courage has contributed to
> much to the success of the Red Army, Navy, and Air Forces.
>
> I trust that these awards will be accepted in the spirit in which
> they have been presented—to show the great admiration and grati-
> tude the American people have for the Russian people, to stress the
> need for the same cooperation in peace as exists in the present strug-
> gle against a common enemy, and to offset the efforts of the Axis
> propaganda machine, which tends to forget that we two peoples have
> much in common beside a hated enemy and always tries to empha-
> size the differences between our two peoples which arise chiefly
> from method, not from fundamentals of right thinking, right living,
> and common good will.

After I symbolically handed over the medals to Mr. Molotov,
he replied very briefly and not particularly graciously to the effect
that he was sure that the Soviet Government and the individuals
to whom these awards were presented would be grateful to the
United States Government for its thoughtfulness.

We both uttered many complimentary phrases; official and press
photographers took many pictures; both Russian and foreign reporters scribbled down reams of notes; champagne was served all
around. This presentation had a wonderful press in the United
States. Our Embassy Press Section never discovered any mention
of the presentation whatsoever in Soviet Press or Radio.

In contrast is another occasion when I sought an interview
with Mr. Lozovsky at the Foreign Office in Kuibyshev, which was
granted on August 25, 1942. I had been instructed by the State
Department to take up the matter of the withdrawal of convoys
from the Murmansk-Archangel route. I presented an *aide memoire*
which informed him that the losses on the Murmansk run had become unacceptable—32 out of 38 ships on a recent convoy. Unless
the Soviet Government was prepared to provide better air protection than now afforded, the American Government would have to
consult with the British Government with a view to discontinuing

Murmansk convoys. The *memoire* also referred to the present unacceptable method of supplying rubles* to the crews of American vessels operating in Northern Russian ports and the payment of gratuities to merchant seamen of such vessels.

Mr. Lozovsky glanced at the *aide memoire* and, ignoring the more serious issue of the discontinuance of the convoys, he said, in a most unpleasant tone of voice, "Mr. Mikoyan tells me that every member of the crews of these vessels, from Captain to lowest oiler, has received the full amount of the gratuity in *dollars*, either in Murmansk or Archangel or in the United States. If they were killed on the trip, their families received their bonus. Would the American Government prefer," he asked sarcastically, "that this bonus be paid in rubles in Archangel or Murmansk?"

It was his manner as much as his words which annoyed me, but I controlled my temper while I invited his attention to the reasons stated in the *aide memoire*—that the sailors couldn't spend dollars in Northern Russian ports, that they either got robbed of the very desirable American greenbacks or else had to exchange them for three or four rubles to one dollar, when the official rate was five to one and the diplomatic rate twelve to one. What the United States had repeatedly requested was that the payment of the gratuity in dollars be discontinued and that instead thereof the Soviet Government make available to each crew member a bonus in rubles of an equivalent amount at the diplomatic rate of exchange.

"That would cost my government a lot of money," he protested.

"I consider it only fair considering the dangerous conditions under which those boys operate," I insisted with some heat. "Besides, it will save you your dollars."

"Dollars!" he exclaimed sarcastically.

I jumped to my feet and said, "My Government expects serious consideration of the issues which I have presented to you." I pounded the table with my clenched fist to emphasize my remarks.

---

* The crew members obtained money from the Russians in two ways. Crews of both Navy and merchant ships were permitted to exchange dollars for rubles at the official rate of exchange, but an opportunity was often not afforded them to do so, necessitating that they change their money at disadvantageous rates in waterfront dives. By agreement with the Soviet Government, the crews of all merchant vessels were paid a substantial bonus by the Russians because of the extreme hazard of the Murmansk run. For some reason, which never seemed rational to me, the Russians insisted on paying this bonus in dollars in the Northern Russian ports or in the United States, when the sailors needed Russian rubles to spend in Murmansk and Archangel.

"Good day, sir. Come, Mr. Page." I turned and marched out of the conference room.

As I have previously indicated, the seat of decision rested in Moscow, not in Kuibyshev. A couple of weeks later, at the end of a conference with Mr. Molotov on other subjects, he said, very pleasantly, "By the way, Mr. Ambassador, you will be happy to report to your Government that from the first of next month we will pay our bonus to your crew members in the Northern ports in rubles."

"At what rate of exchange?" I demanded.

"At the diplomatic rate," he said, with a nice smile.

So went my negotiations on these minor and on some major issues. But of the greatest interest were the special events, and the visits to the Soviet Union of Special Representatives and Very VIP's. Perhaps, in my gallery of Special Representatives who visited the Soviet Capital during my tour of duty, it will be best to start off with the most distinguished and important personage of all.

CHAPTER XII

Mr. Winston Churchill and the Second Front

Tнe invasion of the continent of Europe somewhere in Northern France, which later came to be known as establishing the Second Front, was first demanded as early as the
Beaverbrook-Harriman Mission to Moscow in October 1941. But
with every effort of the British Empire expended to plug holes in
the vast perimeter it guarded, the inability of the British to mount
such an operation with any prospect of success was pitifully evident.

With the entry of the United States into the war, the Russian
demands for a Second Front became more frequent and more vigorous, coupled with poorly concealed threats to make a separate
peace with Hitler. Strong supporters of an immediate assault upon
Fortress Europe early in 1942 were plentiful in England and America, among whom was the influential Lord Beaverbrook. Faced by
disaster on every fighting front, wiser counsel prevailed. It was not
until March 1942, that the Army War Plans Division under General Eisenhower began serious planning for a cross-channel invasion of Northern France (ROUNDUP) together with a preliminary buildup of American strength in the British Isles (BOLERO).
A limited operation (SLEDGEHAMMER), was considered justified only in case the situation on the Russian Front became desperate, or the German Army in Western Europe became significantly
weaker. The plan contemplated seizure of a bridgehead, probably
on the Cotentin Peninsula to include the Port of Cherbourg, and
to hold it, if possible, although evacuation and probable loss of
most of the troops involved was a calculated risk.

The plans were approved by President Roosevelt on April 1,
1942. Harry Hopkins and General Marshall were sent to London

on April 4 to sell the proposed plans to the British Government, where Prime Minister Winston Churchill gave their "momentous proposal" his cordial and unhesitant acceptance. This enthusiastic support for a Second Front was somewhat tempered by reservations about the serious situation in the Far East, and the fact that a substantial portion of the resources of both the United States and Britain in men and material had to be earmarked for other more urgent operations.

In the light of subsequent events in Moscow, it is significant to note that BOLERO-ROUNDUP was tentatively planned for the spring of 1943, and the very "iffy" SLEDGEHAMMER for late September 1942.

Also during the period that Hopkins and Marshall were in London, on April 11, President Roosevelt sent a cable to Marshal Stalin asking him to send "Mr. Molotov and a general upon whom you rely to Washington in the immediate future."

It will be recalled that, during this period, I was enroute to Moscow; I had not been previously briefed on these projected activities—it not being considered that it was necessary for the American Ambassador to know—and I was not subsequently advised for reasons which will become presently apparent. Ironically, President Roosevelt included in his cable the phrase, "I do not want by such a trip to go over the head of my friend, Mr. Litvinov, in any way." I wish someone had informed me then that this was the way FDR felt. Or perhaps it would have been even more valuable for me to know that, during the Beaverbrook-Harriman Mission, Mr. Harriman said to Premier Stalin, "I hope you will feel free to cable President Roosevelt directly on any matters that you consider of importance. President Roosevelt would welcome such messages."

To which Mr. Stalin replied, "I am glad to hear this. I have felt that I should not presume to address the President directly."

So was laid the groundwork for the personal negotiations from President to Dictator and vice-versa that was to cause me so much difficulty during my mission to the Soviets.

When Mr. Molotov left on his visit to London and Washington early in May 1942, I was in Kuibyshev and therefore somewhat out of touch. I was informed after he left Moscow that the purpose of his trip was to complete negotiations for the Second Protocol for Lend-Lease aid to Russia, but of utmost moment and yet unknown to me were his negotiations for a Second Front.

In London, I have subsequently discovered, Mr. Molotov's pressure for a Second Front had a cold reception. Although the grand plans for BOLERO-ROUNDUP and SLEDGEHAMMER were thoroughly discussed, Mr. Churchill refused to make any commitment about a Second Front in 1942. In fact, in cabled discussions with Washington at this time, the British mentioned several diversionary operations, shunned the frontal attack across the Channel, and again favored the North African Operation (GYMNAST), which had first been proposed in December 1941, and subsequently abandoned because of lack of shipping and landing craft.

In Washington, Mr. Molotov had a more sympathetic reception. He asked that the Western Allies undertake an operation in Europe in 1942 of such magnitude that forty German divisions would be engaged and thus relieve the pressure on the Red Army on the Eastern Front. He presented very completely and graphically the desperate situation of the Red Army, and asked most directly, "What is the President's answer on the Second Front?"

General Marshall assured him that "we are preparing a Second Front."

The President told him, "You may inform Mr. Stalin that we expect the formation of a Second Front this year."

In Moscow on June 12, 1942, I was astonished to receive the news via a BBC radio newscast that a communiqué issued simultaneously in London and Washington that day contained the following statement: "In the due course of the conversations full understanding was reached with regard to the urgent tasks of creating a Second Front in Europe in 1942."

This brief account of events, completely beyond my knowledge at the time, will help to give an appreciation of the extent to which I, as American Ambassador in Moscow, was behind an opaque curtain of lack of information. It also serves to illustrate how frequently and how completely both Ambassador Litvinov in Washington, and I, in Moscow, were by-passed by the direct personal diplomacy of our Chiefs of State and their Special Representatives.

My first interview with Mr. Molotov after his return took place on June 19th. He was openly jubilant and placed great emphasis on the statement in the communiqué as to the Second Front, and the good effect it would have on the Russian Front. "This *could* mean winning the war in 1942, certainly in 1943."

In a short while, it was evident from articles in the Russian Press and statements over the Moscow radio that the Russian people were being led to believe that the communiqué meant just what it said—there would be a landing in Northern France and an effec-

tive Second Front would be established in Europe in 1942. With
the assurances that Mr. Molotov had been given, how could any
other interpretation be made? But I felt virtually certain that a
successful cross-channel operation in 1942 was impossible. Knowing President Roosevelt as I did, I suspected some kind of double
talk.

As soon as I became convinced of the Russian attitude, I sent a
message to the State Department:

> For the President. Russian people becoming convinced that you in-
> tend a landing and a real Second Front in Europe in 1942. If this con-
> struction on Molotov communiqué June 12 is a false one, strongly
> advise steps be taken immediately to correct this impression, other-
> wise our relations with Russian people will be seriously damaged
> when real intent becomes known.

I received no acknowledgement or reply.

I was in Moscow at the time. A little later, Sir Archibald Clark-
Kerr came to Spaso House to call, and I brought up the subject of
the Second Front. "Why, no, Mr. Ambassador," he said. "I have no
such misgivings, nor have I noticed anything unusual in the Russian Press or among the Russian people."

As a result of our conversation, he must have begun to take
notice. As time passed, it became obvious to the Russians and to
both of us, that there would be no landing in Europe in 1942. Sir
Archibald sent a message to the British Foreign Office, urging that
immediate action be taken to counteract the rising tide of resentment among the Russian people over our failure to establish a Second Front.

At 3:30 P.M. August 7th, Sir Archibald called again at Spaso
House to inform me that distinguished visitors would arrive in
Moscow August 9th. The reason for their visit was Premier Stalin's
displeasure at our British-American suggestions that, because of
the heavy loss of shipping and inadequate protection on the Murmansk convoy route, future shipments would be sent via the Persian Gulf; and, also, Mr. Stalin's disappointment that we had not
established a Second Front in Europe in 1942.

I understood that Prime Minister Churchill was coming to Moscow on a special mission purely British, and it was not until later
that I heard that Averell Harriman was accompanying him. Years
later I also learned that, when Mr. Churchill had left London for
the Middle East and Moscow, eager to get on with the solution

of the problem of explaining to Mr. Stalin that there would be no "Second Front" in France in 1942, Mr. Harriman, who was in London, decided that he should go along. President Roosevelt cabled authority for Harriman to go, but gave him no instructions. Harriman caught up with Churchill at Teheran. Mr. Harriman's presence at the meetings of Churchill and Stalin was taken as tacit approval by the United States of any agreements reached.

Meanwhile, unknown to me, on July 16th, President Roosevelt sent General Marshall, Admiral King, and Hon. Harry L. Hopkins to London to urge the execution of SLEDGEHAMMER in 1942, a SLEDGEHAMMER that would contemplate a firmly established and maintained beachhead on the Cotentin Peninsula. Marshall and King pressed the British War Cabinet and Chiefs of Staff hard, but finally, on July 26, in obedience to President Roosevelt's written instructions to determine upon another place for U.S. troops to fight in 1942, and his cabled decision, they settled for GYMNAST, the North-African Operation, with a target date of October 30. It is really amazing that three months and thirteen days after this firm decision was taken, an operation, which General T. T. Handy has called "unquestionably the most complex operation in military history," GYMNAST, renamed TORCH for security, could be mounted in overwhelming strength.

On August 9th, I was informed by the Foreign Office that Mr. Churchill would be quartered in the elaborate *dacha* of President of the Presidium A. I. Kalinin, five miles out the main highway from the center of Moscow, and that the Soviet Government was making available a new "guest house" for Mr. Harriman, which would be available for inspection as to suitability at 1:00 P.M. the next afternoon.

The property of a wealthy and titled aristocrat before the Revolution, the new guest house was an imposing mansion at No. 8 Ostrovsky and Myortgev Street, which we presently came to call Number Eight. The entrance led into a street level areaway from which steps on either side led up about three feet to the reception hallway on the main floor. Across the front of this hallway was a brass rail, behind it a desk occupied by a tall, husky Russian doorman, splendidly uniformed, who spoke excellent English. On the left of the hallway was a reception room, a library and a small study. Directly to the rear of the reception hall was a large dining room, kitchen, serving pantry and servants' quarters. Off the reception hall to the right was an enormous master bedroom, two double and one single bedrooms, and several tiled and chrome plated bathrooms. The whole establishment was furnished in the elaborate manner of the late Russian Empire period, much more lavishly equipped and decorated than Spaso House. A full staff of servants was in evidence. The establishment was certainly adequate for Mr. Harriman. During his sojourn the dining table was always ready with the choicest foods, fruit and drink available.

As we drove home, I reflected that Mr. Molotov had been put up in Blair House across Pennsylvania Avenue from the White House during his stay in Washington. "Not to be outdone in gallantry," I muttered to Jack Duncan.

A small cottage near the Kalinin *dacha*—two bedrooms with kitchen but no bath—was also offered. We quickly decided on the town mansion, which became the U.S. guest house for the accommodation of representatives of our President during the rest of the war.

With the planes scheduled to stop first at Kuibyshev, and no positive information because of engine failures as to the number of planes arriving, there was considerable uncertainty as to the size and membership of the party and their day and time of arrival. During the morning of August 12, we received final word that the Churchill aerocade of four planes would arrive that afternoon at 3:30 P.M.

A formidable array of diplomats, military personages, photographers and press correspondents turned out well ahead of that hour on the hot and dusty plain of the Moscow airport. The Russian delegation was headed by Mr. Molotov, with Mr. Moloschov, Mr. Sobalov, Mr. Pavlov, the interpreter, a number of Foreign Office secretaries in their fancy diplomatic uniforms, and the largest and highest ranking group of Red Army and Navy dignitaries I had yet seen in a welcoming committee. All the foreign diplomats turned out with members of their staffs, Sir Archibald with his full staff and his military mission resplendent in their best uniforms, and finally myself with all of my staff including General Phillip Faymonville of Lend-Lease. During the hour that we waited, I had an interesting conversation with Mr. Molotov about the military situation in Russia and political affairs in general.

A bit after four, the three planes of the aerocade circled the field, escorted by about twenty Red Air Force fighters. The first plane landed at 4:35 P.M. Prime Minister Churchill disembarked immediately, followed by Mr. Harriman. Churchill paused dramatically at the head of the ramp and made his famous "V" for Victory salute, which was immediately interpreted excitedly by the Russians as a two finger symbol meaning Second Front. In the bustle of welcome, the landing of the other two planes was completely ignored.

The arrangements for the distinguished visitors' reception was much the same as for the Beaverbrook-Harriman Mission—a fine Army Band, the snappy honor guard with white gloves and glittering steel helmets, the flags of the three countries, this time on three poles, each flag at exactly the same height as the other. The Russian officials greeted Churchill and Harriman first, then each Chief of Diplomatic Mission was presented. As Harriman and I shook hands, I gave him a wink and said, "Hi, Averell, surprise?" We gave the photographers five minutes to snap and grind their cameras.

The band struck up the first of the three National Anthems, *God Save the King,* and we stood at salute or bareheaded with our hats over our hearts until the last note of the Soviet Anthem sounded. The distinguished visitors trooped the guard; the guard commander made his welcoming speech. Churchill and Harriman made graceful little speeches into a "mike" conveniently placed at the end of the guard, and then more photographers. Eddie Page, Mr. Sobalov, and I carried Averell Harriman off to his quarters at Number Eight, to which he gave extravagant praise until Eddie and I took him to President Kalinin's *dacha* to call on the Prime Minister.

I have no notes on this *dacha;* I remember only that it was large and low—one story I believe—and sumptuously furnished. What apparently impressed me at the time was the air raid shelter, which I described in detail in a letter to my wife:

A marvelous outlay—almost vulgar in its extravagance—passage walls and stairways of marble, rich carpets, rugs, and stair runners wherever appropriate, complete kitchen and dining room furnishings and equipment, fully furnished suites with an electric refrigerator in each bedroom well stocked with food and wine, air-conditioned throughout, the most modern electrical machinery, including large elevators. In fact, [it is] a large three story building built downward from the surface instead of up. The two small square entrance buildings of thick concrete painted green seem to merge with the trees in which they are located.

We discovered that Mr. Churchill had been scheduled to meet Mr. Stalin in the Kremlin at 7:00 P.M., so Eddie and I took Mr.

Harriman back to Number Eight, from which he left almost immediately to join Mr. Churchill.

Perhaps this is as good a place as any to explain and stress that, owing to the status of Mr. Harriman as an innocent bystander as it were, I was left almost completely out of the picture in the frenzied four days of conferences during the Churchill-Harriman visit and knew next to nothing at the time as to what was taking place, acting as a sort of Chief of Protocol, Liaison Officer, Aide, and general factotum for the two VIP's, particularly for Mr. Harriman, who, I felt, now appeared to be a much more important and unapproachable person than he had been in Beaverbrook-Harriman Mission days. So doth power corrupt—and it doesn't take much!

But if this story is to have any relevance, what was accomplished during those four momentous days must be told. *In the narrative which follows, only on those occasions when I was present, or say I heard or saw something, is this an eyewitness account.* The rest of the tale comes from rumor and information I gathered from the sidelines at the time, confirmed and bolstered by some very extensive and arduous research.

Upon our return to Spaso House, I met Mr. Loy Henderson, Chief of the Division of Far Eastern Affairs in the State Department, who, in addition to assisting Mr. Harriman, had come to Moscow to inspect the administration of the Embassy. Only then did I learn from him of the size and importance of the supporting staff.

In Prime Minister Churchill's party were Sir Arthur Cadogan, member of the British War Cabinet, Sir Charles Wilson, whom I knew from the Beaverbrook-Harriman Mission, Colonel Eie Jacob, Officer of the Ministry of Defense, General Sir Allen Brooke, Chief of the Imperial General Staff, and his aide, Colonel G. Dumphie, Air Chief Marshal, Sir Arthur Tedder, General Sir Archibald Wavell, Commander-in-Chief India, and his Aide, Major Coots, Commander C. R. Wilson, RN, Naval Assistant, and the Prime Minister's personal staff, his private secretary, Mr. Rowan, his clerk, Mr. P. Kinia, and his valet, Mr. Sawyer.

I don't know how he accomplished it on such short notice, but Averell Harriman had also collected quite a staff. Besides Loy Henderson there were General Russell L. Maxwell, from the Cairo Command, General Sidney P. Spaulding, of our Lend-Lease Administration, with whom I would later have long arguments in Washington, a Colonel Kremer, a Lieutenant Gerard, Aide, and

Mr. Francis Stevens, a State Department Secretary. In addition, there were 14 members of the crews of the planes.

After a brief chat with Loy Henderson, Eddie Page and I returned to Number Eight for the best dinner I had had in Moscow for some time, with Generals Maxwell, Spaulding, Faymonville and Follett Bradley.

Meanwhile, the Prime Minister, without rest from his long and tiring trip, had plunged into his work at the Kremlin with characteristic energy. Present at the conference were Mr. Molotov, Marshal K. E. Voroshilov, Sir Archibald Clark-Kerr, Premier Stalin, Churchill, Harriman, and the usual interpreters.

It should be noted that the British Ambassador was present in the Kremlin and was thoroughly cognizant of all that took place at this important diplomatic meeting, while the American Ambassador sat vacuously and pleasantly at dinner at Number Eight listening to the service chatter of four American Army Generals.

In the conference room of the Kremlin, Mr. Churchill set out to explain most directly the reason for postponement of SLEDGEHAMMER, and told of the plans for ROUNDUP in 1943 with full details and proposed strength for this major cross-channel operation. Much of the eloquence and forcefulness of his discussion was lost in the stop-and-go of talking through interpreters. The sometimes long delays while the interpreters argued out shades of meaning brought flashes of the Churchillian impatience and temper, which seemed to please and amuse Mr. Stalin.

To every statement, Mr. Stalin took exception with undiplomatic bluntness that was almost insulting. He told Mr. Churchill that wars cannot be won if you are afraid of the enemy. Mr. Churchill maintained an uncharacteristic calm. Mr. Stalin cut short his explanations by saying, "I do not agree with your arguments, but I cannot force you into action you do not want to take."

Mr. Churchill turned to discussion of the strategic bombing campaign against Germany in which the U. S. Air Force was just beginning to participate. He told Mr. Stalin that he hoped it would produce a substantial increase in beneficial results as it mounted in fury. For the first time, Mr. Stalin and Mr. Churchill agreed. *With perhaps fatal import for the future, Mr. Stalin said enthusiastically, "Yes, and homes as well as factories should be destroyed."* This discussion marked an easing of the tension in the conference room.

When Mr. Churchill explained the decision and the tactics of TORCH Operation, Mr. Stalin showed an immediate and excited interest. They discussed rapidly and animatedly the date of the landing; the political implications; whether Vichy and Spain would come in on the side of Nazi Germany; the chance for success in the landings without serious opposition by the Vichy French.

It was at this meeting, I believe, that Mr. Churchill first coined a famous phrase. He took Mr. Stalin's doodling pad and drew on it an excellent likeness of a crocodile, explaining that the snout and armored head and shoulders were Northern France and Western Europe. "It would be much easier," he said, "to strike at the soft underbelly."

According to Mr. Harriman, Mr. Stalin suddenly exclaimed, "Excellent, may God help this enterprise to succeed."

His calling upon God was not at all unusual for he was, in his youth, trained for the priesthood.

Stalin went on to expound upon the obvious military advantages of TORCH—taking the enemy in the rear, causing Hitler to send substantial reinforcements into Tunisia, bringing French troops into action against the Germans, keeping Spain out of the war, and perhaps eventually knocking Italy out of action.

This meeting lasted almost four hours. I returned to Spaso House about 11:30 P.M. very weary, to find a telephone message that they were all at dinner at the Kalinin *dacha*. Wouldn't I come over?

I had already had two evening meals; it was after the Moscow curfew hour, and the Moscow streets would be as dark as a pile of black cats; I had been to the *dacha* only once and in daylight; I wanted nothing so much as a few hours sleep; but in the diplomatic life, it's always *noblesse oblige*, especially with very VIP's, so I broke out Tommy Thompson to be my Navigator and took off for the *dacha*.

At the table in the dining room, I found Churchill, Harriman, Sir Archibald, Counselor Dalton of the British Embassy, and Commander Wilson, RN. I ordered caviar and vodka and sat back to listen to the excited conversation. I gathered that Churchill and Harriman were elated at the cordiality of the conversations. Both seemed to be impressed at Stalin's intelligence and immediate grasp of the strategic implications of TORCH.

I was weary to the bone and unhappy. For *this*, I had been hauled away from my bed into the stygian blackness of a Moscow night. "Tomorrow comes the freeze," I said sourly, out of the depths of my own experience with the Russians.

Harriman looked up at me sharply. "Oh, not at all, Admiral, not this time."

The Prime Minister was very tired. Small wonder! He was only two years younger than I and he had been through a very rigorous regime. His head nodded and a couple of times he closed his eyes and dozed briefly, looking like an immense sleeping Buddha at the end of the table. He left us at 1:00 A.M. to turn in. I excused myself and Thompson and I went home to bed.

I imagine we all felt pretty sluggish the next day. I spent the morning over telegrams with Averell Harriman, and helped him despatch a report to the State Department of happenings to date. The messages were so jealously guarded and peculiarly handled that no copy or notes about them are present in my papers, nor do I recall much that they contained. The big dignitaries attended a performance of *Don Quixote* during the afternoon, and I joined them for the second act. Loy Henderson and I returned to Spaso House for a hot dog and sauerkraut dinner. Afterward, we went over to Number Eight and found Eddie Page and the boys of the Press enjoying a sumptuous dinner. Averell had held a press conference, but had to leave to join the Prime Minister at the Kremlin. As always, we had an interesting and informative evening with the correspondents and went home to bed about midnight.

That same morning, Mr. Churchill had made his official call on Mr. Molotov in the Foreign Office. The second day freeze was on. To Molotov, the TORCH Operation was "ambiguous." In injured tones, he reminded Mr. Churchill of the firm commitments made to him in Washington and London, and the communiqué of June 12 which promised "creating a Second Front in Europe in 1942." Apparently he indicated most firmly that TORCH could not be considered a Second Front in Europe even if it took place in 1942.

The second conference met in the Kremlin at 11:00 P.M., a working schedule to which the Russians were accustomed, but one designed to exhaust the most rugged Western diplomat. Present were Stalin, Molotov, Churchill, Harriman, Sir Arthur Cadogan, General Wavell, General Brooke, Air Chief Marshal Tedder, and the usual interpreters, one of whom Churchill brought. Mr. Stalin handed to the Prime Minister and Harriman an *aide memoire* of which I was able to obtain this copy:

As a result of exchange of views in Moscow which took place on the 12th August of this year, I ascertained that the Prime Minister of

Great Britain, Mr. Churchill, considered that the organization of the Second Front in Europe in 1942 to be impossible.

As is well known, the organization of a Second Front in Europe in 1942 was pre-decided during the sojourn of Molotov in London, and it found expression in the agreed Anglo-Soviet communiqué published on the 12th June last.

It is also known that the organization of a Second Front in Europe had as its object the withdrawal of German Forces from the Eastern Front to the West, and the creation in the West of a serious base of resistance to the German-Fascist forces on the Soviet-German front in 1942.

It will be easily understood that the Soviet command built their plan of summer and autumn operations calculating on the creation of a Second Front in Europe in 1942.

It is easy to grasp that the refusal of the Government of Great Britain to create a Second Front in 1942 in Europe inflicts a mortal blow to the whole of the Soviet public opinion, which calculates on the creation of a Second Front, and that it complicates the situation of the Red Army at the front and prejudices the plan of the Soviet Command.

I am not referring to the fact that the difficulties arising for the Red Army as the result of the refusal to create a Second Front in 1942 will undoubtedly have to deteriorate the military situation of England and all the remaining Allies.

It appears to me and my colleagues that the most favorable conditions exist in 1942 for the creation of a Second Front in Europe, inasmuch as almost all the forces of the German Army, and the best forces to boot, have been withdrawn to the Eastern Front, leaving in Europe an inconsiderable amount of forces and those of inferior quality. It is unknown whether the year of 1943 will offer conditions for the creation of a Second Front as favourable as 1942. We are of the opinion, therefore, that it is particularly in 1942 that the creation of a Second Front in Europe is possible and should be effected. I was, however, unfortunately unsuccessful in convincing Mr. Prime Minister of Great Britain hereof, while Mr. Harriman, the representative of the President of the United States, fully supported Mr. Prime Minister in the negotiations held in Moscow.

J. STALIN

The pleasant atmosphere of the previous evening had disappeared. Mr. Stalin spoke some plain facts positively and bluntly. The Kremlin didn't like TORCH. The Western Allies had failed miserably to deliver Lend-Lease aid promised. Meanwhile, the Russians were taking the whole weight of the German Army with terrific casualties. Sarcastically, he said that he didn't believe it was too much to ask of the Western Allies to land six or eight divisions near Cherbourg and take some pressure off the Eastern Front.

When Churchill tried to defend his position, stressing the dangers and difficulties of the cross-channel operation, the discussion became heated and acrimonious. Finally Stalin said, "If the British infantry would only fight the Germans as the Russians fight them—indeed, as the RAF has fought them in the air—they would not be so frightened of them."

Churchill's anger flared up. "It is only because of the importance of the business at hand that I choose to ignore the charges you have just made." Churchill then became so eloquent and talked so long and rapidly that his interpreter wasn't able to translate. When he rebuked him firmly, Stalin laughed and the tension eased, but the conference never regained the friendly, cooperative spirit of the previous evening.

Someone told me that Mr. Harriman, at this meeting, was like a moth fluttering around the sparks and flame of the interchange between Stalin and Churchill. When finally he could get into the fire, he asked Mr. Stalin about the plans for ferrying aircraft from Alaska across Siberia. "Plans!" Mr. Stalin snorted. "Wars can't be won with plans."

We spent August 14th taking account of the situation and advising the State Department as to the progress of negotiations to date. Averell saw Mr. Churchill's lengthy reply to Mr. Stalin's *aide memoire*, but I did not. I helped Averell with his reply, an innocuous little memorandum concurring in Churchill's reply, and taking the odd position that "no promise has been broken regarding the Second Front." In the light of the above recorded events, it is difficult to see how President Roosevelt ever reached the conclusion he once expressed to Mr. Churchill "that the Russians do not use speech for the same purpose we do."

We had lunch with Mr. Churchill at the Kalinin *dacha* and afterward we engaged in serious conversation about the turn of events. Averell advanced the theory that the amazing reversal of opinion and attitude by Marshal Stalin was not due to Stalin at all. He recalled that the same alternation of hot, freeze, thaw occurred during the Eden visit the previous year. I didn't know about that, but I agreed with him that we had certainly experienced the same treatment during the Beaverbrook-Harriman Mission.

"I think I know what it is," Harriman said pontifically. "Whenever Stalin gets tough with us, it's the Politburo attitude he's expressing, not his own views on the major subject at issue."

I'd been doing a lot of thinking about that myself. "I can't agree with you, Averell," I said. "From my experience, I believe it's a Soviet technique for negotiation—first day, all smiles, enthusiasm, visitors on top of the world; second day, the big freeze, nothing right, insults, visitors in depths of gloom, got to give Stalin something to make him happy again; third day, with or without concession, a big thaw, sunny skies, everything fine with the world. Today you had the freeze, tomorrow, the thaw."

"Interesting," said Mr. Churchill, but I don't think he believed me. He had just had bad news about the Murmansk run. Of 38 ships in the last convoy, only 6 got through.

But don't worry, I thought as I drove back to Spaso House for a rest before the banquet. If we don't give now, they'll still keep on working for whatever it is they're after, no matter how agreeable they may appear.

We picked up Mr. Harriman and took him to the Kremlin. Mr. Molotov received the guests in the Reception Hall. When all were present, Mr. Stalin came in with Mr. Mikoyan, Commissar for Foreign Trade. As usual, Mr. Stalin made the rounds of our circle, shaking hands with each guest. Then, he took Mr. Churchill by the arm and led the way into the Catherine the Great Room.

In addition to Stalin and Molotov, Mr. Mikoyan and several other members of the Politburo, all members of the Soviet General Staff, and the Defense Committee were present. Among the British guests were the more distinguished of the officers and civilians who accompanied Mr. Churchill, the British Ambassador and some of his staff, and the British Military Mission. The Americans included Loy Henderson, General Bradley and his aide, Eddie Page, General Faymonville, Colonel Michella, Captain Jack Duncan, and several other members of our Embassy Staff.

As usual, we were seated at a long table on a raised dais with four smaller tables seating about ten persons each arranged on a lower level.

The menu was typical of the Kremlin—caviar, bountifully loaded plates of *hors d'oeuvres*, several fish courses, several kinds of game birds, wonderfully roasted, a main meat course, the appropriate wines, and several kinds of vodka.

Almost as soon as we were seated, the toasts began. Mr. Molotov was toastmaster. I thought that Mr. Stalin looked worn and tired, but he soon perked up and was jovial and cordial to all. By contrast, Mr. Churchill was glum, probably still annoyed at the rough treatment he had received at Stalin's hands the previous night.

Contrary to the usual procedure, Mr. Stalin presently took over the role of toastmaster and insisted on touching glasses with each person toasted. He was in rare form. Perhaps if Mr. Churchill had come out of his indigo cloud of gloom, it might have been just another pleasant, uneventful dinner, but he continued to stare about the table with his heavy eyebrows pulled down like awnings housed against a storm.

Only two of the toasts were unusual or significant. General Sir Archibald Wavell was a colorful character who had lost an eye in the service of King and Empire, and an old campaigner in Russia. The unique feature of his speech was that he delivered it in Russian. Afterward, Eddie Page told me he covered his previous service in the USSR, with many a graceful tribute to the Russian people, and that his Russian was almost perfect, a truly remarkable accomplishment for a busy military leader.

The other significant toast was led up to in this way. Mr. Molotov toasted the British Navy and its Admiral Miles, who did not respond. Then Mr. Molotov toasted the American Navy and its Captain Jack Duncan, but passed on so quickly to the next toast that Jack had no opportunity to respond. I looked around at Jack and I could see he was slowly burning under the collar. I shook my head at him and he grinned back.

Later in the evening, Marshal Stalin rose to speak. As best I can remember, his words went like this:

> Gentlemen, I would like to impress upon you the vital importance, in wartime, of accurate intelligence of the armed forces of the enemy; battles, campaigns, and wars can be won or lost depending upon the possession or lack of this information.
>
> I should like to point out in support of this statement a classic example of the effect of lack of information in the first World War. I refer to the British campaign at Gibraltar [which he quickly corrected to the Dardanelles]. The British had conducted a long and expensive operation. The Turks had been thoroughly defeated, and had issued orders to withdraw from the area on a certain day. However, the British, due to a lack of an effective spy service and proper information, were unaware of how badly the Turks were hurt and of their intention to withdraw. So it came about that, early in the morning of the very day the Turks planned to withdraw, the British evacuated their troops, weighed anchor, and abandoned the area to the defeated and thoroughly amazed Turks.

Here we see most vividly the effect of poor military intelligence. For, if the British had had an adequate spy system, they would have remained at the Dardanelles as victors. And if they had remained, the first World War would have been considerably shortened and countless lives and untold treasure saved.

So, again I would like to stress the importance of accurate military information in wartime, and to point out that the most valuable of all people in a country are the spies who carry on the hazardous work of providing this information.

Now, as you know, when we propose a toast in the USSR, it is customary that the one, or ones, toasted respond. But as there is no one present of those whom I now toast, naturally there will be no response. Gentlemen, I would like to have you rise and drink to those of the most valuable and most hazardous service of all—to the spies who provide us with accurate information of our enemies!

I heard Winston Churchill mutter, "If I had the authority then I have now, we'd have advanced, not withdrawn!"

I wondered what had brought forth this outburst; then I recalled that one of the reasons Mr. Churchill had given Mr. Stalin for the decision to abandon a Second Front in Europe in 1942 was the information the British had that certain crack Nazi divisions were in Western Europe, while Soviet Intelligence located these same divisions fighting against the Red Army in Russia, and held that the coast of France was defended by second-rate divisions. I don't know whether Mr. Stalin realized his guest had been Britain's First Lord of the Admiralty, who initiated the Dardanelles Campaign against severe opposition in the British Cabinet, but, in any case, the man who had deliberately insulted the British infantry to Churchill's face the day before was fully capable of this gratuitous insult to the former First Lord of the Admiralty, the British Navy, and the British Army.

Strangely, it was not one of the British—who take a long view in such situations—but my own Naval Attaché who rose to Mr. Stalin's challenge. Jack Duncan was seated at one of the smaller tables, and beside him was one of the Foreign Office secretaries. "Tell Mr. Molotov I want to respond to that toast," Jack said to the young Russian.

The Secretary tried to put him off but, when Jack insisted, he spoke to Mr. Molotov. The Commissar for Foreign Affairs turned and looked at Jack with a sneer on his lips and said, sarcastically, "The next speaker will be the American Naval Attaché, Captain Duncan."

When this was translated, I knew a momentary alarm, but it was too late to do anything about it, as Jack had risen from his seat and, walking up between the tables, he took a position at the rear of Molotov facing Marshal Stalin.

I would like to respond to the toast Mr. Stalin has just proposed, but first I must correct an impression that Mr. Stalin has made that no spy is present. I am a member of the Naval Intelligence Service of the United States—a spy, if you will.

I should like to say to Mr. Stalin that we in the United States are just as well aware as the Russians of the vital importance of accurate information of the enemy. I should also like to say, as an ally, I provide our Russian Ally with all the information that I or my service obtains of our common enemy, the Nazis. I have been in the Soviet Union for more than six months, but so far I have been unable to obtain any information whatever from our Russian Allies about this common enemy.

Mr. Stalin, in his speech, said, "Untold treasure and countless lives would have been saved and the first World War would have been greatly shortened had the British had accurate information of their enemy at the Dardanelles." Would Mr. Stalin like to shorten World War II, save untold treasure and countless lives? If so, then I appeal to him—see that his Allies are provided such information as the Russians obtain of our common enemy, the same sort of information that we are giving them. Certainly, such action would go a long way toward the shortening of *this* World War.

Mr. Stalin rose and said, "Now, that is the kind of talk I understand, the most straightforward, honest words spoken here tonight. I want to assure Captain Duncan he will get the kind of information he wants about our common enemy. I, personally, will be his agent* to see that he does get what he wants. And," he added, "I want to join you in drinking with Captain Duncan because he has spoken out as he did."

Jack stood fast behind Mr. Molotov's chair where he had made his speech, as if to say, "Well, come on and drink with me then."

Mr. Stalin made his way deliberately around the end of the table, glass in hand, and put his arm around Jack's shoulders. We all stood and bottoms-upped our drinks.

The dinner broke up soon after, and I saw Stalin hook his arm through Jack's and walk the length of the room into the salon where coffee and brandy were to be served. Later, Jack told me

* One meaning of the Russian word could be translated "spy," but I have here chosen the less spectacular word.

he took this opportunity to thank Mr. Stalin for promising to be his intelligence agent. "But Marshal Stalin," he went on, "I know how terribly busy you are. You can save yourself a lot of trouble by telling the Commissar for the Navy to do the job for you."

"I'll do that," Mr. Stalin said.

"All right," Jack said, "Why not now?"

He steered the Russian dictator toward Admiral Kuznetsov, who stood near by. Stalin gave him the desired instructions.

At 1:30 A.M. Mr. Churchill excused himself, pleading the fatigue of his long trip into Russia and late hours the two previous nights, thus avoiding a long and poor Russian combat film, which kept some of us up until 3:30. Mr. Stalin left his other guests and walked with him the long distance through the Kremlin corridors to the carriage entrance, where the two oddly contrasting chiefs of state parted with a warm handshake.

As he returned, he met Jack in the corridor. He turned and accompanied Jack to the door, as he had Mr. Churchill.

The Prime Minister had his last conference with Mr. Stalin at 7:00 P.M., August 15th. Mr. Harriman was not present at this meeting. We have been unable to obtain accurate information as to what transpired, but I heard enough to understand that Mr. Churchill had pretty rough going.

Mr. Churchill kept his diplomatic temper, argued persuasively through a new British interpreter from his Embassy, and by the end of the conference the tide of Stalin and Soviet Government enthusiasm for TORCH was again in full flood. Stalin professed to believe that the benefits to the Red Army on the Eastern Front would be significant. The party ended on a note of high cordiality. Mr. Stalin asked, "Won't you come over to my apartment for some drinks?"

Although his plane was scheduled for departure at dawn, Mr. Churchill eagerly accepted. I understand that he had supper with Mr. Stalin and his auburn-haired daughter, Svetlana, and then talked for hours. He returned to the Kalinin *dacha* at 3:30 A.M., wrote a long cable to President Roosevelt, and left for the airport.

We were out at the wind-swept airport before daybreak, Loy Henderson, General Bradley and I. We had arranged for General Bradley's specially equipped VIP bomber to replace the missing British plane for the trip to Teheran. The *bon voyage* committee was somewhat thinner than the welcoming committee due to the hour, but Mr. Molotov and his Russian "big dignitaries" were on hand. Much the same procedure was followed as for the reception, only in reverse. I thought the Prime Minister looked very tired and careworn as he stood at the head of the ramp, but he took the cigar from his mouth, smiled warmly, and held up his "V" for Victory, before he ducked into the plane.

Ten Lend-Lease Aircobra fighters took off as his escort, smothering us in a cloud of dust. General Bradley led off in his plane followed by the three British transports. They circled the field once, and headed south on the ten hour flight to Teheran.

I was told that a "communiqué" would be issued on August 17 for publication on the 18th. The press boys and I watched for it but we never saw it. The diplomatic battle of the Second Front had been fought out on the highest governmental level. It is hard to say to whom went the victory; I am doubtful that there was a clear cut "win or lose." The Russians accepted a Western Allied decision which they didn't like, but were powerless to change. The Second Front in Northern Europe was not established in 1942, but the Soviet Government and the Russian people continued a loud clamor for the Second Front long after Mr. Churchill took off from the Moscow airport that early August morning.

A curious incident resulted from Jack Duncan's interchange with Mr. Stalin at the Churchill banquet. That afternoon after the Churchill-Harriman party took off, I attended my ump-teenth performance of the ballet, *Swan Lake*. At the beginning of the second act, I noticed that the Russian civilian, who had been sitting on my right, had been displaced by Captain Zeitsev, who was Chief of Staff to Admiral Kuznetsov, Commissar for the Russian Navy. We exchanged greetings. In the intermission between acts, Captain Zeitsev asked if I would like to see the Commissar.

I had known and liked Admiral Kuznetsov from the time I first met him during the Beaverbrook-Harriman Mission, and had had no difficulty at all arranging meetings with him, but I sensed some purpose behind Captain Zeitsev's rendezvous, so I told Zeitsev that I would be very glad to have an appointment with Admiral Kuznetsov.

The next day, I received word that the Commissar would be glad to see me at two P.M. on the 18th, and that he wished I would bring my Naval Attaché and Assistant Naval Attaché with me.

At the appointed hour, we met in Admiral Kuznetsov's plush office in the Navy Ministry. Captain Zeitsev was present, but Ronnie Allen did the interpreting. We discussed amicably a wide range of naval subjects from the rank of naval officers to current naval strategy. At the end of an hour, I rose to leave.

Admiral Kuznetsov also rose behind his glass-covered mahogany desk. "Before you go, Admiral," he said, "I want you to know that I have instructed my officers that Captain Duncan is to get all the information that he wants which is not controlled by other departments of the government."

Jack did get to make visits to a number of Russian naval installations and ships which had previously been closed to our Naval Attachés. But as for information, I recall that Jack said about the Stalin incident that he felt, as he shook hands with the Russian Generalissimo, "Here the love feast ends." For, as Jack put it, "Joe turned out to be a lousy intelligence agent."

CHAPTER XIII

The Tokyo Bomber Crew

JIMMIE DOOLITTLE, graduate of West Point, once a regular Army officer, called back to active duty as a reservist, conceived the idea after Pearl Harbor, sold it to the Army Air Corps, and early in the New Year of 1942, began to assemble his planes at Eglin Field in northwest Florida.

Admiral King said in his first war report, "As a carrier operation, this raid was unique in naval history in that, for the first time, medium land bombers were transported across an ocean and launched off enemy shores." The planes could not land on the carriers and their limited range of operation required that the carrier task force had to approach perilously close to Japan. But the situation was desperate. Our high command accepted the probable loss of some B-25's as a calculated risk, but it could not willingly risk the loss of one of our too few carriers.

Late in March 1942, the planes and crews embarked on the "Hornet" at Alameda, California. With "Enterprise" carrying search planes and protecting fighters, the two carriers, escorted by destroyers, on April 18th, when still several hundred miles from the planned launching position, were discovered by a small Japanese patrol craft. The ship was quickly sunk by escort vessels, but the Task Force Commander could not be certain that contact had not been reported. The bombers were launched immediately.

In one of those medium bombers was a crew of five fine American young men—Major Edward J. York and Lieutenant Robert G. Emmens, pilots, Lieutenant Nolan A. Herndon, navigator, and Sergeants Theodore H. Laban and David H. Pohl, engineer and gunner. Herndon found his target expertly. Probably because the red circle in the United States insignia on the plane was so similar to the "Rising Sun" on Japanese planes, anti-aircraft guns didn't open fire on them, and there was no fighter resistance. They made two careful approaches, and accurately dropped their bombs from

1500 feet on the factory designated as their target. After a final look to make sure they had done a good job, Herndon headed the plane across the backbone of Japan toward the China Sea. Their gas supply was now so low that York decided he must land in Siberia. With gas down to the emergency tank, Major York set the B-25 down at a Red Air Force base near Vladivostok.

For a time they had a wildly optimistic hope that the Russians would give them gas and permit them to take off for their designated Chinese base. On April 19th, they were taken before General Stern, Commanding General of the Far Eastern Red Army, who told them bluntly, "An agreement has been reached between our two governments. You will be interned in the Soviet Union until further decisions are made in your case."

In far-off Moscow, we first heard of this "adventurous shot" at our Japanese enemy's homeland on an English language broadcast by Radio Tokyo during the evening of April 18th. The newscaster reported in excited Japanese-English that both Tokyo and Yokohama had been raided for three hours; that Kobe and Nagoya, homes of the Kawanishi and Mitsubishi aircraft factories, had been raided for two hours. The announcer became so emotional during the recital of these dastardly deeds of the fiendish Americans that I could picture the tears rolling down his cheeks.

The next morning, all Moscow papers carried the official Japanese version of the raid under banner headlines. Later press and radio accounts from Japan reacted more normally, stressing that schools, hospitals, and shrines had been damaged and "horrors heaped upon the heads of our little school children."

I was at that time in Moscow waiting to report to Premier Stalin for my first "audience." *I had no official notification of the landing of the American bomber on Soviet territory until April 21st,* when the Soviet Foreign Office sent me word that the crew would be interned near Khabarovsk. I consulted Colonel Michella, my Military Attaché. For a while, we had high hopes that the officers and men of the crew might be permitted to show up in the American Embassy as assistants to the Military Attaché.

On April 23rd, when I reported to Premier Stalin, he spoke of this bomber landing and told me that the crew was safe. "Of course, Mr. Ambassador, they should not have landed on Soviet territory. We'll have to intern them in accordance with International Law."

The next day, during a press conference held by Mr. Lozovsky in Kuibyshev, one of the American correspondents asked, "What would happen if an American plane was forced to land on Soviet territory after bombing Japan?"

With Japanese correspondents present, Mr. Lozovsky was obviously disturbed. He fumbled for words. "There's no use talking about something which may never happen," he said harshly.

The next morning, Soviet newspapers carried an item that "an American war plane had landed in the Soviet Maritime Province on April 18. In accordance with International Law, it has been interned, with its crew." The crew was quoted as saying that they had lost their way after bombing Japan.

Naturally, I was terribly embarrassed at this turn of events. We received roundabout rumors that the Foreign Office believed that we had leaked the news to our correspondents. The boys of the Press came to see me for a statement. "Look, fellows," I said. "I've really nothing for you. The Soviet Government acted in the only way they could, once the news was out."

It was my job to see that these and other American airmen who would be interned in Russia were well treated, and to try to get them released without reservation as to their future employment. At a conference with Mr. Molotov on April 25th, he complained about our bomber landing on Soviet soil, and requested that our Government take steps to prevent any such landings in the future, as they were extremely embarrassing to the Soviet Government in its dealings with the Japanese.

About the middle of May, the Foreign Office in Kuibyshev informed us that Major York and his crew had been moved to Penza, a small town about half way between Kuibyshev and Moscow. I was so busy that I couldn't get away, but, early in June, I sent Colonel Mike Michella and Embassy Secretary Eddie Page to visit them. When they returned, I received a full report as to the crew's situation.

They lived in what might be called a *dacha* in the small village of Okhuna near Penza.

To protect and care for this bomber crew of five, the thoughtful Soviet officials had assigned Red Army Major Mihaiel Constantinovich Schmaring, whom the boys called Mike and whom they appeared cordially to detest, three Red Army soldiers as guards, a woman cook, three maids, and three waitresses. Michella reported that living conditions were not bad, food was fair, Mike had a good supply of Russian cigarettes, vodka was plentiful, but existence was exceedingly dull. Major York told Michella that their train trip from Khobarovsk to Penza had taken them twenty-one days. When I learned that they had been locked in their car on a Kuibyshev railroad siding all day two weeks earlier, and had particularly asked to see someone from the Embassy, I was furious but not particularly surprised.

About two days before Michella and Page reached their *"dacha,"* the General in command at Penza inspected the place and seemed well-satisfied with conditions until he learned that the boys had been kept inside the walled yard. He ordered them released to go swimming and walk around the village. This same General showed Page and Michella about the grounds with every evidence of pride before he permitted them to talk privately to the members of the bomber crew.

Their principal complaint was the dull routine and boredom. They had received no mail, but Page delivered to Emmens a telegram announcing a small red-headed son and informing him that mother and son were doing well. They were anxious for news of the other crews of the Tokyo raid, but we had none to give. The Russians tried to relieve the boredom. They had a volley ball court, a pool table, and several times Mike had brought in Soviet movies and a projector. They studied Russian and learned to play chess. But above everything, they wanted to get out of Russia and back to the war.

Michella explained the situation—the Russians were worried about provoking a war in the East. They couldn't afford to risk an international incident by releasing the crew. But the Ambassador was working on it. He hoped to get them released and send them out of Russia in the not too distant future.

Michella and Page took them some cigarettes, several shirts, some socks, soap, and seven old American magazines. Michella left with them a small English-Russian dictionary that he always carried with him. They had a good meal with the boys, plenty of pickled fish, caviar, and vodka. Their final toast was "to victory of the great nations, the USSR and the United States of America, over the Nazi bandits."

With letters the bomber boys had written, and promises to send mail, medical supplies, and magazines, Michella and Page returned to Kuibyshev.

In August, with the German Army advancing on Stalingrad, the military position of Penza became insecure. Presently, the Foreign Office in Kuibyshev sent word that the bomber crew had been moved to Okhansk on the Kama River, much closer to Kuibyshev than Penza.

I had been talking for several days to the boys in the Embassy about making a trip to visit the bomber crew, but I had not gotten as far as making a request for permission, when Mr. Vishinsky sent for Eddie Page to come to the Foreign Office. They had hardly exchanged greetings when he said, "Mr. Page, can we send NKVD men with the Ambassador?"

"Where is the Ambassador going?" Eddie countered.

"Why, don't you know?"

Eddie shook his head.

"He's flying to Molotov with General Bradley to visit your bomber crew."

It can be confusing, but that's the way things happen in the Soviet wonderland.

Apparently General Follett Bradley, who was in Russia on a mission for our Army Air Corps, had also been informed of his intentions by the Foreign Office in Moscow. He phoned from Moscow, asking me to forgive him for being delayed. He would arrive the next day at 12:30.

General Bradley's plane was an hour late. When I arrived at the airport with Page and Michella, the Red Army Major, who was acting as our guide (guard), took violent exception to Page going, probably because he wasn't listed in the Russians' secret plan. But when I insisted that Page come along, the Major went away and presently came back and said "*Da*" several times, nodding at Eddie.

It was originally planned that we should use General Bradley's plane for the flight, but the Russians decided for various reasons that this would be impossible. The plane provided was a twin-engined Douglas transport built in Russia with another harum-scarum Russian crew. The passenger compartment had two rows of bucket seats outboard. On the starboard side of the compartment, all but two seats had been removed and two large locked boxes secured firmly to the deck. I tried to find out the purpose of the boxes, but no one in the plane seemed to know, which is characteristic of the Russian people—in their work, they know, and they want to know, absolutely nothing about anything for which they have no responsibility; yet about other things, they are intensely curious.

We flew a direct courseline from Kuibyshev to Molotov at very low altitude over beautiful country—much like our Rogue River Valley—passing the flat prairies of the Steppes, open country heavily cultivated, through which the winding Kama River flowed. The low hills along the river were covered with beautiful forests of pine, maple, and silver birch, the leaves just turning to Autumn colors lovely to see.

We arrived at the Molotov airport late in the afternoon, to be met by the Mayor of Molotov, who was also Governor of the Molotov Oblast (Province), the Russian doctor who, as the head of the Medical Institutes of Molotov, controlled the many hospitals located there and was also Oblast health officer, a delegation of Red Air Force officers, airport officials, a Red Army Colonel, and a Health Department nurse. Swollen by evacuation of industry from Western Russia, Molotov had a population of over a million; the mushroom growth of barracks to house evacuated labor was in evidence everywhere in the outskirts.

From Molotov, the Governor informed us, we would be taken by auto to Okhansk to see the bomber crew, return to Molotov for the night and fly back to Kuibyshev the next morning.

But nothing ever seems to run according to plan in the Soviet Union. Like Alice, we found life in Wonderland topsy-turvy and many a Mad Hatter mad, but there wasn't much that we could do about it.

After a considerable delay, we were driven in two cars to a boat landing beside the river, where the Governor's yacht, a small side-wheeler river boat, was moored. About a hundred feet long, 30-foot beam, 9-foot draft, its pilot house was on the upper deck. Forward of the pilot house on the main deck was a promenade deck, also used for dancing. On the deck below was a dining salon which comfortably seated twelve persons. Forward of this salon was an observation salon completely glassed in, which seated five persons.

I was assigned to a sumptuous cabin in the stern, which could accommodate two persons comfortably. Forward of my cabin on each side of the ship were three smaller cabins, a washroom and a toilet. The galley and crew spaces were located abaft the dining salon.

In our company for the trip down river to Okhansk, we had the Mayor and the Doctor who had met us; a pretty hostess, nicely dressed in a modern-styled wool suit, silk stockings, high-heeled silver sandals, her hair freshly done in a pompadour; a caterer with a full retinue of cooks and waitresses; three local policemen in uniform; the local Communist Party leaders; and, of course, my four NKVD boys. In addition, there were the Captain, a naval reserve commander of the River Service, and the crew of the boat.

One can see why I was reluctant to make trips as guest of the Soviets—it was simply impossible to do it informally.

With a few tentative toots, the little steamer backed out into the stream and we headed down river with a current of three knots helping to push us along at thirteen knots. It was the same winding river over which we had flown, its turnings and twistings seeming even more tortuous now that we were navigating them at such speed. The countryside was even more beautiful from the steamer than it had been from the air, the foothills of the Ural mountains rising gently from the river, forested with deciduous trees flaming with the gorgeous colors of Autumn. Turbulent mountain streams tumbled down the hills, so crystal clear and beautiful that I longed for a chance to wet a fly in one of them.

Dinner was served at six-thirty, a slavish duplication of a Kremlin banquet, except that fresh fruit from the Caucasus was missing. Later, when breakfast came, the menu was the same as for dinner. It is difficult to commence the day on caviar, vodka, and cucumbers, but we found that we could if we were hungry enough.

After dinner, I sat in the observation salon until full dark. Then, pleading my age, I went aft to my fancy stateroom and turned in, while some of my younger companions carried on with the Russians far into the night.

When I awoke the following morning and stepped out on deck, I found the steamer secured to a landing. After breakfast, we got underway and stood down the river to Okhansk, and moored to a floating barge secured to tall piles designed to meet the varying conditions of flood water in the river.

As we disembarked, I saw a little group of men in American khaki uniforms at the top of the bluff. They waved excitedly and we waved back. The younger men in our party hiked up the steep path, but the Mayor of Molotov, a number of older Russian officials, General Bradley and I chose to go the long way around, up gullies and through chuck holes, in ancient cars. With broken rear springs, cushions with springs sticking out of the fabric, and no padding, every time we hit a bump, it felt as if we had come down hard on the rear axle.

The bomber crew were billeted in a log cabin, much more primitive than the *dacha* at Okhuna. As we got out of the car, the bomber boys met us in a sort of military formation, with York standing nearest to us. When introductions had been completed, I walked toward the rear entrance of the house with Major York. "Wonderful country," I said, to make conversation.

"Yes, sir, except when you're stuck with it."

I laughed appreciatively. Behind me, I heard Page say, "We stopped up the river last night or we could have gotten in here yesterday. I wish we had. They staged another one of those Russian drinking bouts. You know how those fellows are—won't let you refuse."

We went through the kitchen and sat down around the dining room table, the boys of the bomber crew, Michella, Bradley and I. A Soviet three-star General plopped himself down at one side of the table with a rather homely woman interpreter beside him. I looked around. "Not exactly like home," I said.

The boys seemed diffident. Their first question was about the progress of the war, then the fate of their companions on the Tokyo raid. Bradley promised to try to get them some information.

A Russian enlisted man carried in the box of supplies we had brought with us—some shirts, toothpaste, an English-Russian grammar, and some magazines. "It's not much," said Michella, "but we thought you could use them."

"Gee, that's wonderful," they said in chorus.

They wanted clothing and other supplies, so we had each of them make out a list. Mike Schmaring came into the room and said something to a Major standing behind the General, who passed the word along in a whisper to the General. "Have you been well-treated here?" he asked through the woman interpreter.

York replied that they had. He went on to ask Schmaring to let us talk alone for a few moments. The Russians stomped out. The boys seemed to be very disappointed when I told them we must leave that afternoon. Finally York asked me if I had noticed the food in the kitchen. I had—zakuska, *hors d'oeuvres,* plates of canned fish, scads of red caviar, several kinds of cheese, hard-boiled eggs, boiled beef, and real butter.

"Yes, indeed. It looked good. They been feeding you well?"

"No, sir!" York said firmly. "We've been living on rice and cabbage, tea and black bread for weeks. They brought that stuff in yesterday to give you a party."

They wanted to know if the messages they gave Mike Schmaring had been delivered and thanked us for the package of letters they had received two weeks earlier. "It's so difficult to get messages through the Russians that we didn't try to answer them," I explained.

"Say, York," Michella put in. "Congratulations. You're a Colonel now."

Then they got down to the problem that was closest to their hearts—when would we get them out of there. I had to explain to them that all I could do was try. The Russians were hard people to do business with.

"Well, then, Mr. Ambassador," York continued. "It gets awful cold up here, Mike tells us. If you can't get us released, at least try to get us sent to a town in Southern Russia where it's warmer. We'd be willing to work—we'll do anything they ask. This inactivity is killing us."

"Jeez, yes, sir," one of the sergeants put in. "Mike and the servants are kind to us, but studying Russian and playing volley ball and chess all day and every evening gets pretty damned monotonous, sir. Please get us out."

"I can't promise a thing," I replied. "But you can be sure I'll take it up with the Foreign Office when I get back."

"Our shots are running out," young Emmens put in. "And this is a typhus and malaria area. We're all out of quinine. Don't you have an American doctor? I've had some treatment by these Russian doctors and they're lousy."

I turned to Michella. "We could send Lang up, couldn't we?"

"I don't see why not," he answered. "If you authorize the trip, we ought to be able to get permission from the Russians."

I felt terribly sorry for the boys, but, after all, like the rest of us, they were caught up in the maw of a vast war which might go on for years. I wanted to help them and to establish a procedure for all the others who would land in Russian territory as the home islands of the Japanese came within the bomber line of our advancing forces.

General Bradley broke out a carton of American cigarettes from his brief case and passed it across the table. "Boy!" exclaimed one of the sergeants. "Real cigarettes. We'll have to ration those, Major."

The Russians, who had left the bomber crew alone with us for a little while, pushed back into the dining room. Some remarks in Russian passed back and forth. "The General feels that we should go to the dock now," said Mike Schmaring. "But won't you have some dinner first?"

Remembering the boys' diet of rice and cabbage, I said, "No, thank you, Major. They have enough food and drink on that boat to sink it."

The bomber boys gave Michella messages, letters home, and lists of food and supplies they wanted. As we got up from the table, one of the bomber crew said, "Now, I know what makes prisoners go stir-crazy."

"Oh, it's really not that bad," York broke in. "We're pretty much allowed the freedom of the town, go to the movies whenever Mike reports there's a good one, if we can stand the smell. When it warms up next summer, the swimming will be nice."

"Next summer!" one of the sergeants cried. "Good God!"

"*A Hundred Men and a Girl*," the other one said sourly. "We must have seen it twenty times."

The Russians became importunate. Please hurry? The automobiles would be at the landing any minute now. We must get back before dark. Bradley, a couple of Russian Generals, and I jolted down to the dock in the same car, where we joined the boys of the bomber crew, apparently anxious to hold on as long as possible to this tenuous tie with home. The Molotov automobiles had not arrived.

The senior Russian officials went into one of their wildest arm-waving, shouting conferences. Evidently, they had really intended to return to Molotov by car. Finally, the Major, who had accompanied us all the way from Kuibyshev, told us that we would have to go by boat to the ferry crossing, where the cars from Molotov would be waiting. I invited the bomber crew to come along for the ride.

As I expected, the cars weren't at the ferry. We moored to one of the floats. As I stood on the promenade deck saying "Goodbye" to Major York, I knew how the men felt. I tried to cheer the boys up as best I could without arousing false hope. They were still standing on the ferry barge looking after us and waving, as the little yacht rounded the first bend in the Kama River.

On the occasion of my next visit to Mr. Molotov, I requested that the bomber crew be moved to a warmer climate in some locality where they could be usefully employed in the war effort at work along the line of their specialty. Mr. Molotov was as evasive as ever.

That was September 21st. I told Freddy Lang that I wanted him to make an extended visit to the bomber crew, take some medicine with him, give them any medical care they needed, and see if he could cheer them up. Colonel Michella commenced negotiations with Russian military authorities to arrange the trip. Both Fred Lang and Major Robert E. McCabe from Michella's office were looking forward to the trip like a couple of children on their way to a carnival.

Whenever I could, I pressed the Foreign Office for two things: To let Dr. Lang and Major McCabe visit the bomber crew; to transfer the boys to the south where it was warmer and put them to work.

Unexpectedly, I was called home for consultation, being absent from the Soviet Union from October 10th to January 6th. While I was gone, permission came through for Dr. Lang and McCabe to visit the boys at Okhansk.

Late in November, they went by train, from Moscow to Molotov, where they were snowed in for two days. From Molotov, they went to Nitva and on down to Okhansk by jerk-water trains which stopped more hours than they ran. With one wood-burning heater at the end of every other car they almost froze.

Arriving late in the afternoon, the automobiles assigned to them stalled in the snow. They finally arrived in a horse-drawn sleigh. One of the bomber men grabbed the horses' reins; the rest gathered around the sleigh. After introductions, Major McCabe pulled a large carton and a battered suitcase from under some hay in the back of the sleigh. They proceeded down a path shoveled through snow piled high on either side to the kitchen door. They put the box on the dining room table and opened it. The Embassy Staff had sent the boys some shirts, a stack of old magazines and late books, and some cigarettes. But of chief interest were three bottles of American whisky.

"By God, it's cocktail hour," Emmens said.

By then, the bomber boys weren't used to American liquor. Fred told me that they hadn't had vodka for months. What followed was quite a party. They had a fine dinner, their first since I had visited them in September. After dinner, they plugged in Radio Moscow. Mike and the women "special attendants" performed some Russian dances to folk songs. Mike Schmaring and a couple of the women imbibed too much whisky and were put early to bed.

Dr. Lang examined the officers and men of the bomber crew thoroughly. They were all in pretty good shape, he told me, but there were indications of pellagra and scurvy in all of them. He gave them some aspirin, quinine, sterile gauze, and adhesive tape.

Lang and McCabe stayed with the boys for several days, enjoying a change from the constant surveillance and closely circumscribed life of Moscow, and trying to cheer up the lonely airmen. They consumed all the whisky they had brought and all the vodka that the General had given Mike to entertain them. I imagine that the pilots and their crewmen had a fine time while my two staff men were with them but, as they stood in front of the house waving good-bye to Dr. Lang and Major McCabe, and the sleigh disappeared behind the snow banks which flanked the road, they must have had a very sinking sensation. For they never got the clothes they ordered; they did not receive the package of medicine we sent; they never saw another American in the Soviet Union.

Shortly after I returned to Moscow in January, 1943, on my first visit to Mr. Molotov, I took occasion to ask the whereabouts of our bomber crew and their condition. He put me off, but the next time I saw him, he told me that they were still in Okhansk and were in good health.

I continued to press him for permission to visit the bomber crew and for information about them, until, early in April, he informed me that they had been transferred to Ashkhabad, capital city of Turkmenistan, a town on the Chinese Eastern Railway just across the border from Meshed in Iran.

I recall that, on that occasion, I spoke to him earnestly as follows: "Mr. Molotov, those airmen have now been the prisoners or internees of the Soviet Government for almost a year. That should be time enough to let the Japanese Government forget about them. And beside, what could the Japanese do about it if those men escaped to Iran? It is indeed unfortunate for our great countries to be fighting a common enemy and yet have one of our fine bomber crews held prisoner by an ally and kept from fighting that enemy."

Mr. Molotov looked pretty sour as he answered, "To escape from the Soviet Union is impossible."

It took me many years to learn the end of this story.* On January 8th, Major York conceived the idea of writing a letter to Marshal Stalin. Emmens and he composed it that night and the next day, with Mike's help, translated it into Russian. Putting both the English and Russian versions into an envelope and addressing it to the Russian Premier at the Kremlin, they gave it to Mike to mail, never expecting that it would get further than the second snow drift.

On March 25th, a Red Army Major and a Captain from the Moscow garrison came to their log house in Okhansk. York's letter had been routed to the Red Army High Command for action. The

---

* I am indebted to *Guests of the Kremlin*, by Robert G. Emmens, for the facts on which much of the rest of this story is based.

Major was there to tell them that their first request, to be released from internment, could not be granted. But he came to take them to a city in the south of Russia where they would be given employment. They left for Molotov that afternoon.

On the eight day train ride from Chkolov to Ashkhabad, the Red Army Major permitted Major York and Lieutenant Emmens to strike up an acquaintance with a man called "Kolya," an official of the Foreign Trade Ministry, who was assigned to the same compartment as York. By the time they reached Ashkhabad, Kolya had become very friendly.

At Ashkhabad, the bomber crew lived under the worst conditions of their internment, in a small house made entirely of mud, with two rooms, five iron cots, a table, and five wooden chairs. An old man was detailed to cook and care for them.

They went to work as day laborers in a small overhaul shop for two-wing training planes. York and Emmens dismantled fuselages; Herndon and Pohl worked on instruments; Laban helped with engine overhaul.

Kolya came to see them the evening of the second day after their arrival. For almost six weeks, he provided them with entertainment, advice and sympathy. Finally he agreed to help them escape. He arranged a rendezvous with a Persian "smuggler" in the main square in Ashkhabad. In a fantastic encounter with the Persian, York made a deal for his crew to be smuggled across the border. After some haggling, the agreed price was $250, just about all the American money the boys had with them.

If the Russians didn't provide the contact with Kolya, the "smuggler," the "guide," the sloppy border guards, and the stupid highway guards in Iran, the tale the bomber boys can tell of their "escape" across the border to Meshed is one of high adventure.

Briefly, about midnight, six weeks after the boys arrived in Ashkhabad, a big truck pulled up in front of their house. Kolya was there to see them off. They lay down in the bed of the truck and covered up with a tarpaulin. York passed to the smuggler $100 as part payment. After some frightening delay due to motor trouble and emergency repairs, the truck took off and wound through the darkened streets of Ashkhabad until it came out on the broad military highway leading to Teheran.

After a couple of hours riding in the truck, the smuggler had them get out. A "guide" led them a circuitous and exhausting climb over shale rock, up steep slopes, around precipitous shoulders, through scattered boulders, at a terrific pace up and up toward the border of Iran on top of the mountains which divide ancient Persia and Turkmenistan. At the end of their climb, they came out over a low retaining wall into a ditch beside the highway they had just left. Now, they were in Iran. The "guide" disappeared and presently returned with the "smuggler" and the same truck.

Again, they lay on their backs under the tarpaulin while the truck rolled down the highway through Russian-occupied Northern Iran toward Meshed. Several times, they stopped for examination at Russian roadblocks, without the guards discovering them. Just before noon, the truck stopped again. The "smuggler" motioned them out of the truck. As they stood in the road, the "smuggler" pointed out to them, about four miles away, the spires and bulbous domes of a town. "Meshed!" he said.

They paid him off. After hiding in a bomb crater beside the road, sneaking by the guards on the bridge approaching Meshed, skulking through the city streets, York and Emmens came to the British consulate. The British Vice-Consul, by strange coincidence, recognized their names because he had recently come from duty at the British Embassy in Moscow. He sent a Consulate truck for the other three, which slipped them by the bridge guards handily. Soon reunited, the five of them sat down to a British luncheon, the finest meal they had had in thirteen long months.

For York and Emmens and other members of the bomber crew, it was unquestionably high adventure, with disaster waiting just around every outcropping, over every rise. I have no wish to minimize the derring-do of their "escape," the courage it took to put it through. I know, even with their youth and bodily vigor, I would never want to make that perilous and exhausting climb across the Soviet-Iranian border. I salute them. I do not think a similar passage would be possible today.

In due course, I tried again to obtain permission from the Foreign Office to make a visit to the bomber crew in Ashkhabad. Mr. Molotov was extremely reluctant to discuss the matter, would give me no information as to their whereabouts or the state of their health. About this time, I received, in a roundabout way, an underground report that they had checked in one morning early in May at the British Consulate in Meshed.

From that moment, the Tokyo bomber crew was never mentioned again in any conversation I had with the officials of the Soviet Government. As General John R. Deane put it, "In that land of contradictions, everything is difficult to understand."

CHAPTER XIV

Lend-Lease and Philip Faymonville

L END-LEASE aid to the friendly democracies fighting our battles for us against Nazi tyranny was conceived in the fertile mind of President Franklin D. Roosevelt in December 1940, during one of his fishing cruises. He first called his program Aid-for-the-Democracies. He set Lend-Lease on its course in a press conference he held immediately after his return from the Caribbean and he helped to sell it to the country in his most effective "arsenal of democracy" Fireside Chat on December 29, 1940.

In the very bitter fight which ensued, strong, well-financed groups chose up sides against Lend-Lease and fought it vigorously, trying to capture public opinion from the President, particularly when the bill was under consideration in the Senate. Even Prime Minister Churchill entered the fray with his "Give us the tools and we'll finish the job" speech on February 9, 1941, in the course of which he said:

> It seems now certain that Government and people of the United States intend to supply us with all that is necessary for victory. In the last war the United States sent two million men across the Atlantic. But this is not a war of vast armies, firing immense masses of shells at one another. We do not need the gallant armies which are forming throughout the American Union. We do not need them this year, nor next year; nor any year that I can foresee.

The Lend-Lease Administration went through some rather peculiar growing pains. For several months, it was called Division of Defense Aid Reports of the Office of Emergency Management. FDR designated Mr. Harry Hopkins to advise and assist him on Lend-Lease, but Hopkins' health was so poor that he was never given the title of Administrator. While not actually on the payroll of Lend-Lease, Hopkins ran it for the President and became, in fact, in this large area of authority, FDR's Deputy President. The first Lend-Lease appropriation was $7 billion. By V-J Day, over $69 billion had been appropriated for this purpose.

Mr. Hopkins arranged for his close friend and associate, Major General James H. Burns, then procurement adviser on the Staff of Under-Secretary of War Patterson, to be appointed Executive Officer. Mr. Oscar Cox and Mr. Philip Young were brought into the agency from the Treasury Department. Major Generals Sid Spaulding and George Spaulding were drafted for Production Division and Storage and Shipping.

Since this whole organization cut across the regular lines of authority of the government in a most haphazard fashion, it quickly inspired the enmity of most of the heads of department and agency directors, particularly of the State Department, because chiefs of foreign missions came more and more to conduct their business directly with Mr. Hopkins, thus by-passing the State Department. Salt upon this wound was the appointment of Averell Harriman as Expediter of Lend-Lease in London, with the rank of Minister. With Harry Hopkins conducting correspondence and negotiations for President Roosevelt with Mr. Churchill and Mr. Stalin, and Mr. Harriman having direct and intimate dealings with No. 10 Downing Street, the State Department and Ambassador Winant in London came to know less and less about the progress of negotiations and the conduct of foreign affairs.

As well as weapons and ammunition of warfare, Lend-Lease included merchant shipping, vehicles, fuel, food, industrial equipment, raw materials, and various services. Into the hands of the man who established policy and directed this huge, sprawling agency for the President passed much power for good and evil.

The original reason for Lend-Lease was to give aid and war supplies to Great Britain and embattled Greece. Before the first shipment to Greece arrived, the Nazis had overrun that poor country. For some months, the only receiver of Lend-Lease was Britain. Then, in June, 1941, Hitler began his drive eastward. Winston Churchill immediately promised the Soviets the full support of Great Britain. Extension of American Lend-Lease aid to Russia was clearly indicated, although it was obvious that this course of action would be extremely unpopular with a large segment of the Christian American public, who regarded everything Communistic and Soviet Russian as atheist and anti-Christ, if not the direct machinations of a cloven-hooved, forked-tailed devil.

I had my first personal experience with Lend-Lease aid to Russia while a member of the Beaverbrook-Harriman Mission to Moscow. It was as fellow members of that mission that I came to know Harry Hopkins' right-hand man, General James H. Burns, and Colonel Philip Faymonville, Secretary to the Mission. In the first Protocol signed in Moscow on October 1, 1941, our Mission gave or promised to the Soviet Government everything they asked and more. *Later, Premier Stalin, in effect, signed a promissory note for $1 billion at no interest, repayment of principal to commence five years after the War's end and to continue for ten years.* This loan, as well as a second billion dollar loan, was superseded and rendered inoperative by the Master Lend-Lease Agreement of June 11, 1942, which provided that a settlement for Lend-Lease aid received should be deferred "until the extent of the defense aid is known and until the progress of events makes clearer the final terms and conditions and benefits which will be in the mutual interest of the United States of America and the Union of Soviet Socialist Republics and will promote the establishment and maintenance of world peace." Today, almost ten years after V-J Day, the Soviet Government has still not settled its Lend-Lease account.

One of the unfortunate by-products of this Mission was that Philip Faymonville, spot-promoted to Brigadier General at Harry Hopkins' request, was left in Moscow as Lend-Lease Representative, later head of the U. S. Supply Mission to the U.S.S.R. The protests against the appointment of Faymonville to this post were already vociferous by the time I returned to Washington from the Beaverbrook-Harriman Mission. Ex-Ambassador to Russia Bill Bullitt, under whom Faymonville served as Military Attaché in Moscow, and Mr. Loy Henderson were quoted as feeling that Faymonville was too sympathetic to the Russians.

I was thoroughly briefed as to this situation before I left Washington to be Ambassador to Russia and was given to understand that my authority over American representatives in the Soviet Union did not extend to Philip Faymonville and the Supply Mission.

Due to failing health in the Autumn of 1941, Harry Hopkins decided that he had to reduce his activities. Accordingly, he selected his close friend, Mr. Edward R. Stettinius, Jr., to be Lend-Lease Administrator. Although abandoning titular responsibilities, Harry knew that Lend-Lease policy would still be decided in the White House, and that, under the guidance of the President, most of the decisions made would be his.

Such was the situation when I reported to Moscow as American Ambassador in April 1942. I found General Faymonville well and favorably established with the Russian authorities. The policy of the Beaverbrook-Harriman Mission to "give and give and give without *quid pro quo*" had been extended to cover every wish of the Russians under the contention that it was a Lend-Lease matter. Under General Faymonville's administration and the Hopkins' Lend-Lease policy, the Russians were obtaining not only material covered by the Protocol, but much American and British military information, which could never under any circumstance be considered Lend-Lease material.

Under ordinary conditions, the dissemination or trading of military information is handled by an Embassy's Military and Naval Attachés. In diplomatic protocol, for every bit of information furnished, delivery of some item of information is expected in return. If my Military Attaché, Colonel Mike Michella, had handled this information for our government, he would have obtained much information about German equipment and the Red Army and Air Force which our War Department urgently desired. But Colonel Michella had been evacuated to the temporary Russian capital at Kuibyshev in October where he remained, while Faymonville stayed on in Moscow.

I would like to make clear that, personally, I found Philip Faymonville a pleasant, agreeable fellow, with a warm personality. He had a good presence and was properly deferential.

Upon graduating from West Point in the Class of 1912, he was assigned to the Coast Artillery Corps and all during his career was considered an ordnance expert. But the nature of his service during and after World War I tends to confirm the attitudes expressed above.

In August 1918, he went to Siberia as Chief Ordnance Officer, American Forces in Siberia, where he also served as a member of the Inter-Allied War Materials Committee. After a tour of duty in the States, in January 1922, he was sent to Chita, Trans-Baikal, Far Eastern Republic, as a Military Observer. In the course of these assignments, he became a fluent Russian linguist. When the United States recognized the Soviet Government, he went to Moscow with Ambassador Bullitt in July 1934 and remained there as Military Attaché for nearly five years. With his excellent command of Russian and pleasant personality, he soon put himself on friendly, if not intimate terms with many of the younger officials with whom he was to deal as Lend-Lease Representative several years later.

One of these good friends was Commissar for Foreign Trade Miko-yan, who was his principal contact among Soviet Russian officials.

When Germany invaded Russia, it was freely predicted that Russia would collapse within two weeks, but General Faymon-ville, because of his previous Russian service, was one of the very few who insisted that the Russians would not surrender and would fight to the bitter end; as a result, he has been frequently spoken of as the "General who called the turn."

Upon my arrival in Kuibyshev in March 1942, Colonel Michella immediately reported to me officially his situation with respect to Faymonville, and his difficulties in obtaining information from the Russians. As soon as I reached Moscow, I undertook to correct this unfortunate situation. I discussed the matter with General Faymonville a number of times. I must say, he was always affable, agreeable, and scrupulously polite, but he seemed to be unable to resist the continued demands for information from his Russian contacts. Since both Faymonville and his Supply Mission were specifically exempted from my control and guidance, it was im-possible for me to apply corrective measures or to take disciplinary action, but I did report the situation in several despatches.

In the meanwhile, I attempted to build up the prestige of my Military and Naval Attachés. In August, 1942, I asked for an ap-pointment to see Mr. Stalin, telling Mr. Molotov that I had some military matters to discuss with him. Accordingly, I intended to bring my Military Attaché to Moscow for the conference. This incident is discussed elsewhere, but I did contrive by this action to return Colonel Michella to the "seat of decision" in Moscow.

The day following our conference with Premier Stalin, Michella came to me. Colonel Evtsigneev of the Red Army, Michella's liai-son officer, had asked Mike to call at his office. "He hardly let me sit down, sir," Mike said. "We didn't even exchange polite phrases of greeting before he asked me, 'When are you returning to Kuiby-shev?'"

"That's the same as telling you that he expects you to leave Moscow, pronto, Mike."

Michella nodded. "What shall I do, Admiral?"

"You tell your Liaison Officer this from me: You will return to Kuibyshev when your Ambassador tells you to do so, and not before."

Colonel Michella remained in Moscow. But even though Mike was there in body, he might just as well have returned to Kuiby-shev. Colonel Evtsigneev, the Red Army and Air Force authorities, and Commissar for Foreign Trade Mikoyan continued to ignore him, requesting any information they wanted from General Faymonville.

My difficulties with Faymonville were more or less of a personal and semi-official nature. Meanwhile, Lend-Lease to Russia was experiencing its own more serious troubles. Since I left Moscow in October 1941, limited shipping, difficulty in scheduling convoys, and ship sinkings due to enemy action had made deliveries of Lend-Lease material disappointingly small. While I was still being briefed in Washington, impatient at the lack of progress, in March 1942, FDR directed all U.S. war agencies to release for shipment and ship all material promised to the Soviet Union on the First Protocol, regardless of the effect that this action might have on other phases of the war program.

Perhaps this order was needed to get action at the time it was issued, but it initiated a policy of appeasement of the Soviets from which we have been a long time recovering. The President's directive gave the Soviet Union preferential treatment over our other Allies and our own Armed Forces. As each new Protocol was signed, the officials responsible for Russian Lend-Lease aid need only to refer to the President's directive to obtain everything the Russians requested, subject only to the limitations of production by our industrial establishment and shipping available.

Back in the United States, the President's Protocol Committee had been established, with Harry Hopkins as Chairman and General James H. Burns as its Executive Officer. These two also occupied the same positions in the Munitions Assignment Board. They approached their duties with respect to Russian aid with a zeal that was commendable in the early days of the program when Russia was bearing the whole weight of the Nazi war machine almost unsupported by other fighting forces in the field, but this fanatic desire to help the Russians continued long after the Red Army and Red Air Force were moving triumphantly westward toward Berlin. The Soviet leaders became more and more demanding, and we continued to give and give.

When I arrived in Moscow in April 1942, the Russians were beginning to worry about the expiration of the First Protocol in October. It was obvious that much more than the original $1 billion agreed upon in that Protocol would be required. Furthermore, unknown to me, the "Battle of the Second Front" was being fought out in London and Washington. The serious reduction in Lend-Lease deliveries to northern Russian ports was partly caused by excessive losses of shipping on the Murmansk run, but, also, it was due to withdrawals of shipping for use in preparing for American-British operations about which I knew nothing. Nor did I learn until several days after he left Moscow for London that Mr. Molotov had departed on a mission to Great Britain and the United States and then I was given the information with a blast about the inadequacy of American Lend-Lease aid to Russia and the urgent need for immediate approval of the Second Protocol.

The Molotov negotiations, which were conducted in Washington between May 29 and June 4, 1942, were seriously complicated by the conflicting demands of Lend-Lease aid to Russia and the Soviet demand for a Second Front in Europe in 1942. On May 30th, after a luncheon meeting with the President, Mr. Harry Hopkins, and other government and Congressional figures, the President told Mr. Molotov that, while the United States could produce eight million tons of Lend-Lease goods in the fiscal year commencing July 1st, we could ship only 4,100,000 tons of it to the Soviet Union.

The following day, a Sunday, President Roosevelt conferred with General Marshall and Admiral King. As a result of the plan to conduct a major Atlantic operation that Fall and the critical shipping situation, it was decided that only 2,500,000 tons of Lend-Lease aid could be delivered to Russia during the coming Fiscal Year.

This bad news was broken to Mr. Molotov at a Monday morning meeting by the President. "Yesterday, Mr. Molotov, I discussed questions of tonnage and shipping with the Chiefs of Staff," he said. "Every week, we are trying to build up troop and plane concentrations in Great Britain in order to get at the Germans across the Channel just as soon as possible.

"We are also sending landing craft to England. But the time element involved depends on shipping available. We hope and expect to open a Second Front in 1942, but we could progress more rapidly only if we had more ships. The Chiefs of Staff suggested that, in order to speed up initiating the Second Front, your Government, with this situation in mind, reconsider the Lend-Lease list which you have submitted, remembering that, of the 4,100,000 tons which we planned to ship during the year commencing July first, only 1,800,000 tons consist of material immediately ready for use for military purposes on the Russian Front this summer. The rest is mostly raw materials and other items for production of material which would not be ready for use until next year. In fact,

2,300,000 tons are items that would not be used for fighting at all.

"I therefore propose that your Government consider reducing its Lend-Lease requirements from 4,100,000 tons to 2,500,000 tons. Such a reduction will release a large number of ships for use on the run to Great Britain and thus speed up establishment of the Second Front."

"There will be no cut in the number of tanks or amount of ammunition shipped," Mr. Hopkins put in. "Everything that the Red Army can use in actual fighting will still go forward."

"I will report this suggestion to my Government," Mr. Molotov said. "But I do hope that such non-military supplies as metals and railroad equipment, which have a direct bearing on the solidity of the present front, will not be cut too much. They also are essential. In checking over our Lend-Lease list, my Government will have to reckon with the degree to which any reduction on non-military items would impose restrictions on the Russian rear—on electric plants, railroads, and war production. After all, such things are vital. I hope that they will not be lost from view."

I understand that the President then told him that we expected to establish a Second Front in 1942 and that every ship we could shift to the English run meant that the Second Front could be established earlier. "After all, Mr. Molotov," he said, "ships cannot be in two places at once. Every ton we can save out of the total of 4,100,000 tons will be that much to the good."

Mr. Molotov was not mollified. "*If* the first front still stands fast," he said dramatically, "the Second Front will be so much the stronger."

The next day at a luncheon at the Soviet Embassy, Mr. Molotov pressed General Burns for a convoy a month direct from U. S. Atlantic ports to Archangel, escorted by the U. S. Navy, more B-25 and Boston-3 bombers, and delivery of 3000 trucks a month at Basra or Teheran. When this was presented to Harry Hopkins for decision, he turned down all requests but the trucks, which he promised to deliver.

Mr. Molotov left Washington with a firm understanding as to the new Protocol, but the agreement had not been signed. He professed to be happy, sending word to the President that he was deeply grateful for the help offered. The President could rest assured that all supplies delivered to the Soviet Union would be put to work against the Nazis promptly and effectively and that Russia would continue the war until victory was won.

In a letter to Ambassador Winant in London, Harry Hopkins wrote:*

> Molotov's visit went extremely well. He and the President got along famously and I am sure that bridged at least one gap between ourselves and Russia.
>
> There is still a long ways to go but it must be done if there is ever to be any real peace in the world. We simply cannot organize the world between the British and ourselves without bringing the Russians in as equal partners.

Upon his return to Moscow, Mr. Molotov must have been laboring under two misapprehensions—that there would be a Second Front in Europe in 1942 and that he had completed negotiations for the Second Protocol for Lend-Lease aid to Russia. Yet it was almost exactly two years to the day before the Second Front was opened in Northern France. And, as July and August, 1942, passed, with no signed Protocol from Great Britain and the United States, the complaints about Lend-Lease aid in the Russian capital became more and more bitter and sarcastic. Isolated as I was from information about the above events and from the management of Lend-Lease in the Soviet Union, I yet heard plenty of complaints in my periodic conferences with Mr. Vishinsky or Mr. Lozovsky in Kuibyshev and with Mr. Molotov when I was in Moscow. General Faymonville must have been receiving real pressure.

Faymonville came into my office to see me one morning during the Fall. In the course of our conversation, I brought up one phase of the Lend-Lease situation which troubled me greatly. "General," I said, "we're delivering quite a lot of Lend-Lease material to the Red Army and Red Air Force right now, aren't we?"

"Yes, sir."

"This Protocol business doesn't seem to be slowing it up any, does it?"

"I don't believe so, sir."

"Something bothers me, General. Do we ever get any credit for it?"

Faymonville looked at me with a puzzled expression about his eyes. "Why, yes, Mr. Ambassador. Daily—yes, practically every day—some one of my Russian associates expresses his appreciation to me."

* Robert E. Sherwood, *Roosevelt and Hopkins* (New York: Harper & Bros., 1948), p. 577.

"To you, yes. But not to me. Our Press Section watches the Russian papers very carefully. We haven't found a single item about the tremendous assistance we are giving Russia—the propaganda is all about 'how wonderful we Russians are to stand alone and unaided against the might of the German military machine.'"

"The Red soldier at the front knows about it, sir," Faymonville said rather warmly.

"How do we know he does?" I asked rather bitterly. "The closest our Military Attachés ever get to the front is the ground the Red Army fought over a week before."

"How about the Red Air Force? Their pilots must know they are flying American and British planes."

"True," I ended the discussion, "but the Russian people don't know it. And neither do I. We just can't get any information to speak of about the Russian Armed Forces."

I had my own troubles in this field. From the moment that I decided to go to Russia, my every thought, my utmost energy were given to furthering the Allied war effort. Like everyone who had no previous experience in the Soviet Union, the reported attitude of the Communist rulers toward foreign attempts to alleviate the conditions of the common people seemed incredible. Surely the men in the Kremlin would welcome my friendly efforts to help them establish better standards of living for their people, a standard I now knew from personal observation to be very low. But first, the Russian people must learn about America and Americans, about our ideals, our standards, the way we think, the way we live, our wants and needs in this modern world.

Through all of the disappointments and reversals of the early months of my sojourn in Soviet Russia, this goal remained steadfastly in the forefront of my mind. But how was I to show the Russian people what kind of people the Americans are, when we Americans were permitted to have almost no contact with the Russian people?

I recall that, as this question was running through my mind for the hundredth time, Jack Duncan came into my study. "Are you going to the movies this afternoon, Admiral?"

"What's on?"

"Donald Duck and some British feature, I understand. Sir Archibald is coming over."

"One I haven't seen? Good, I'll be down."

The officials of the Soviet Motion Picture Trust (VOKS) always showed great interest in our American pictures, particularly the technical details of such feature films as *The Great Dictator, Fantasia,* and *Bambi.* Whenever we were showing a new feature, we always invited Mr. Kamenev, Director of VOKS. I saw and spoke to him as I went into our large, downstairs library, which we had turned into a projection room seating a hundred persons. I seated myself beside Sir Archibald, the lights went out, and a Donald Duck short I had seen a dozen times came on. The feature was *Lambeth Walk,* which had been lent to us by the British Military Mission. As it neared its end, Sir Archie turned to me, "Admiral, wouldn't that picture make a wonderful medium for propaganda among the Russian people?"

Something clicked in my mind—the answer for which my mind had been continuously seeking. Right here in Spaso House we had the facilities for initiating an effective propaganda campaign which might have far-reaching effects among the Russian people as well as furnishing much needed entertainment for Americans and other foreigners isolated in the Russian capital.

The next day I sent a telegram to the State Department proposing an educational program for the Russian people through the medium of American motion pictures. By judicious handling of good American pictures, the Russian people would become aware of the possibility of having American motion pictures in their movie houses. Within a short time, the Russian people would be clamoring to see our films. I recommended that Douglas Fairbanks, Jr., then a lieutenant (junior grade) in the naval reserve, be designated as Assistant Naval Attaché for public relations in our Embassy.

I had visions of regular exchange of motion pictures with Russia via weekly plane service to Teheran, which I had just heard that the Russian civil air ministry would shortly institute. Douglas Fairbanks was just the man to establish such a service into Russia, a sort of Lend-Lease of information about our American way of life.

During July and August, Colonel Michella continued to have trouble collecting military information about the German Army because Faymonville was giving the Russians all the information that they wanted. A week or ten days would pass without Michella even seeing his liaison officer, Colonel Evtsigneev. This situation and Mike Michella's reports about it finally became so disturbing to the War Department that General Marshall asked the State Department to have me take the matter up with the Russian Foreign Office.

Being in Kuibyshev, I immediately sought an appointment with Mr. Vishinsky. He was very pleasant. "Why, of course, Mr. Ambassador, I will express your government's views to the proper authorities at once."

For a change, he must have done something about it, for the next time I went to Moscow, Mr. Molotov brought up the subject and assured me that the "properly constituted channels" for military information would be employed henceforth. But Mr. Mikoyan and the Red Army and Air Force Officers were not so foolish as to pay for information with information through Michella when they could get it for nothing from Faymonville.

I asked the General to come in to see me. When he was seated in a chair across the desk, I told him about my instructions from the State Department. "Please try to help us out, General," I said. "Colonel Michella is doing his best, but we can't get anywhere without your help."

General Faymonville seemed to be genuinely concerned and anxious to correct the situation. "Of course, Mr. Ambassador," he said. "I've been trying to do just what you ask. But you see, sir, as Head of the Supply Mission, and representative of Lend-Lease, I'm only a communication agent. If the Russian authorities request information, either military or commercial, I have to pass their request on to the Lend-Lease Administration. If they obtain the information and send it back to me to deliver to the Russians, I have just got to deliver it." He looked at me brightly. "I have it. Why not ask Washington to send all military information through Colonel Michella or Captain Duncan?"

We'd already thought of that, but Harry Hopkins didn't like to play ball that way. He was the President's "own personal Foreign Office" and he preferred the direct approach.

As September came, we began to hear accusations that the British had stolen Lend-Lease material intended for Russia. I tried to find out what was going on. Faymonville wasn't much help, and neither was the State Department. What was causing the trouble was a combination of the prohibitive cost of pushing convoys through to Murmansk at that time and the urgent need of shipping for the North African operation. A number of ships were diverted from Iceland to Scotland, where their cargoes were unloaded so that the ships could be used for other purposes. A cargo of Aircobras intended for Russian use were turned over to the American Air Force for employment in the TORCH operation.

With approval of the Second Protocol by the British and American Governments delayed for months and Lend-Lease delivery decreasing from a flood to a trickle, the Russians quite naturally were unhappy and became suspicious. Even the 3000 trucks per month, which Mr. Molotov had been promised in Washington, failed to show up in Teheran. President Roosevelt and Mr. Churchill argued at length by cable about canceling another convoy to Murmansk. At first President Roosevelt agreed with Mr. Churchill; then, he changed his mind. The Western Allies simply had to find a way to keep sending supplies to Russia. In addition, FDR brought up again his project for committing an air force to the Caucasus to help the Red Army with air support.

If I had been informed of all these conflicting requirements, I *might* have been able to be of some help in Moscow. Such explanation as was made to Marshal Stalin, who already knew about the North African Operation and its approximate date, went to him direct from FDR and Mr. Churchill. I doubt that even General Faymonville knew what was going on, for he became worried and asked me to take up the matter of the Second Protocol with the State Department.

During much of September, I had Mr. Wendell Willkie on my hands. His blasts about the Second Front and Lend-Lease didn't improve my situation in Moscow in the least. Nor was Philip Faymonville of any assistance when I appealed again to him to stop by-passing my Military and Naval Attachés and play ball with us. Again he was pleasant, smooth, and agreeable, but after all he was responsible for Lend-Lease and I was not.

I remember looking across my small office at him one afternoon, standing militarily erect with his hand on the door knob and I thought, "If I were a captain of a ship or admiral of a division again and you were one of my officers, I'd know what to do. I'd say, 'Damn it all, Faymonville, do what you're told or else.'"

But this wasn't the Navy; he wasn't under my command or control; there just wasn't any "or else."

It gave me an idea, though. There was no reason why he shouldn't be under my control. Wasn't I called the Chief of the United States Mission to the Soviet Union? Every American representative in the Soviet Union ought to come under my command. It was a wonderful idea, and I got to work on it immediately.

CHAPTER XV

General Follett Bradley and the ALSIB Air Route to Russia

I HAVE previously told about my interview with Mr. Stalin, during the course of which I took up with him the suggestion that the United States develop an air route for delivery of military planes to Russia through Alaska and Siberia. I did not learn until many years later that this matter had been brought up during the Molotov visit to Washington later that same year. On June 9th, Ambassador Litvinov told Harry Hopkins in Washington that the Russian Government "agreed in principle" to our plan to fly bombers to Russia via Alaska and Siberia. General H. H. Arnold, Air Corps member of the Joint Chiefs of Staff, was asked to get in touch with Ambassador Litvinov to work out the detailed plans for the route.

Late in June, I received a message from the State Department to the effect that "General Arnold feels that the matter of the air shuttle route across Alaska and Siberia should again be taken up with Mr. Stalin." Through the Kuibyshev Foreign Office, I delivered to Mr. Stalin a despatch from President Roosevelt, which made much the same suggestions that I had presented at my first interview. When I received Mr. Stalin's reply to forward to the President, I could see that we were poles apart in our viewpoints. I went to see Mr. Vishinsky.

"I feel that I must have an interview with Mr. Stalin," I told him. "The subject I wish to discuss is a military matter. I would like to take my Military Attaché with me."

This was an effort to get Colonel Michella out of political quarantine in Kuibyshev, to which city the Foreign Office had consigned him some months before. An appointment was granted. We flew to Moscow. At six P.M., July 2nd, Colonel Michella, Eddie

Page, and I presented ourselves at Mr. Stalin's office in the Kremlin. Mr. Molotov and Mr. Pavlov were also present.

After preliminary greetings and pleasantries, I said, "Mr. Stalin, I have three questions which I wish to discuss with you. They all concern the air ferry route across Alaska and Siberia. The first point concerns President Roosevelt's message which I delivered to you a few days ago, and your answer."

Mr. Stalin began a long, rambling discourse about the situation in the Pacific, ending up with the fearful prospect that the Japanese might attempt a surprise attack on Soviet Russia in Siberia. Since we had just won a very decisive naval victory at Midway and the Japanese were quiescent while they built up strength to meet us wherever we might strike, I had little faith in this thesis that they might begin an offensive and I told him so.

"But Soviet Russia must be especially careful to maintain our neutrality in the Pacific area," he explained. "We don't want a war on two fronts, not even against the Japanese. The Germans will find out how terrible a situation that is whenever the British and you decide to open your Second Front."

Tactfully, I again referred to President Roosevelt's note. "I can understand the reasons for your difference of opinion, Mr. Stalin. With your permission, I'd like to discuss a few of them."

Mr. Stalin nodded. "Go ahead."

"I have noted that you failed to refer to our President's suggestion that such bulky goods as fuel and machinery needed for the landing fields be shipped into Siberia via the northern rivers flowing into the Arctic Ocean. Is it correct to assume that you do not need fuel and machinery for this purpose?"

Mr. Stalin bent his head toward Mr. Molotov and conferred with him briefly in a whisper. "In the first place," he replied, "it would be impossible to bring in supplies via those rivers; there is only one more month of open weather fit for navigation. Furthermore, those air fields have already been constructed, equipped, and supplied and are ready for use for your ferry project."

I nodded in satisfaction. "President Roosevelt also asked that an American plane be permitted to make a survey flight to Lake Baikal, taking along Russian pilots. You replied that you wanted this flight to be made in a Russian plane. Will American pilots be permitted to participate in these survey flights?"

Mr. Stalin took the crooked stemmed pipe from his mouth and nodded vigorously. "Yes, there is no question about that."

"Then there is the question of arranging liaison on the staff level to work out details of this project. Mr. Roosevelt suggested that representatives of the Soviet and United States Army, Navy, and Air Forces with authority to make decisions be named by President Roosevelt and yourself to serve both in Moscow and Washington. I believe that you agreed in principle that there must be staff discussions but you felt that these military representatives should hold their meetings in Moscow rather than Washington. At present, we have no air attaché in Moscow; I'll have to ask our State Department to send an air officer from Washington. Would you consider designating one of your air officers now in Washington as your representative to consult with our air representative there? Then, both of them could come to Moscow and work out the details here?"

Mr. Stalin looked up at me briefly and carefully drew three wolves on his doodling pad. "I don't see why much conversation is necessary," he said gruffly. "Already too much talk. Our air fields are ready to receive planes. All I want to know is how many per month and when. As to designating an air officer in Washington, I can see no necessity for any more talk in Washington."

Mr. Stalin pushed back his chair and went to a large wall chart, which included all of European and Asiatic Russia, Alaska, part of China, and Japan. "Here is your route." He pointed to Fairbanks, then Semchan, Yakutsk, Kirensk, and Krasnoyarsk. "Let's have your planes."

As a result of this interview, I sent a despatch to the State Department for the President recommending that an air officer be ordered to Moscow to assist on the staff level in working out the details of an agreement just reached to establish an air ferry route via Alaska and Siberia; as other members of the committee, I recommended my Military Attaché, Colonel Michella, and my Naval Attaché, Captain Duncan. A few days later, I received information that a Major General Follett Bradley of the Air Corps, U. S. Army, had been designated. Toward the end of July, I received a copy of his orders. The contents were somewhat surprising.

The orders are too long to quote here. Suffice to say that my recommendations had been accepted—Mike Michella and Jack Duncan were members of his committee. His mission was to "arrange for the delivery via Alaska of War-Aid airplanes to Siberia and Russia; arrange for United States survey flights to obtain detailed information pertaining to existing establishments in the Siberian areas; furnish to the Soviet Government information concerning the availability of aircraft in accordance with the Russian protocols and contemplated deliveries via the Siberian route."

His orders also designated him to "command all U. S. Army personnel and forces in the USSR," but Faymonville's Supply Mission and my Military Attaché were specifically excepted; he was directed to "seek the cooperation of Brigadier General P. R. Faymonville . . . and coordinate activities in which you both have an interest." He was directed to "cooperate with the American Ambassador and keep him informed of such matters of national interest arising in and resulting from your activities as you may consider appropriate," certainly a weak and evasive statement. Although his orders required him to cooperate with me only as much as pleased him, I gave General Bradley quarters in Spaso House and treated him as a member of my staff, which he accepted with good grace.

Faymonville went out to meet Bradley in Teheran and flew back with him; Bradley's B-24 converted bomber stopped overnight in Kuibyshev and landed at the Moscow airport at 3:30 P.M. on August 6, 1942.

General Bradley was a tall, sandy-haired, thin-faced officer, of medium build, ramrod-like carriage, with a rather retiring personality. A pioneer airman, he took his first flights in an early model of the Wright Brothers' biplane at Fort Riley as an observer for experimental air control of artillery fire; during the course of these experiments, he achieved the distinction of being the first man to despatch successfully a radio message from an airplane in flight. He learned to fly at Mineola in 1916, and received the rating of Junior Military Aviator while engaging in air combat with the Germans in France.

He rose through the ladder of command in the Army Air Corps between wars, flying continuously and having important assignments along the way, being promoted to Major General on February 25, 1942. In July, 1942, he had command of the First Air Force at Mitchell Field, New York, when he was detached suddenly and ordered to Russia on "a mission for the President of the United States."

I took a ready liking to General Bradley; while somewhat diffident, I found him unfailingly good-natured, an interesting conversationalist, and good company. I also felt that he approached his difficult task in a serious and efficient fashion. He held a meeting of his committee the day after his arrival in Moscow and arranged prompt liaison with Red Army and Navy leaders through

Michella and Duncan. Three weeks after Bradley arrived, his survey plane with the designated pilots aboard flew into Moscow. As far as I could tell at the time, his mission was progressing satisfactorily; early in October, I received information that planes were coming in over the Alaskan-Siberian Air Route.

It will be recalled that I planned to have General Bradley take me in his plane to visit our Tokyo bomber crew interned at Okhansk but the Russians provided a plane and insisted we use it. We also set up a fine flight to Krasnoyarsk to meet Colonel Harvey of Bradley's staff and his survey crew, which would have considerably expedited the opening of the Al-Sib Air Route, but the Russians told Bradley on August 26th that this flight would have to be "indefinitely postponed," which was a great pity as that trip would have considerably extended my acquaintance with Soviet Russia.

The Russians did permit me to use General Bradley's plane for several flights on which he accompanied me, an agreeable and entertaining traveling companion. I did not know that the establishment of the air route was not progressing satisfactorily until Mr. Willkie asked me, at our reception for him in Spaso House, if it would be desirable for him to take up the question of the Alaskan-Siberian Air Route with Mr. Stalin when he saw him. I also ran across some of General Bradley's trouble in the matter of visas for the Russian pilots, which I will tell about presently.

But all the while, the General was in "air lanes of trouble" with no prospect of "by opposing, end them." It was only from a copy of his report obtained long after the events that I, the American Ambassador in Moscow, learned of his difficulties and the many frustrations he experienced in his dealings with the Russians. I stress this point because it illustrates and exemplifies the situation in which an Ambassador, supposedly the sole—or at least, the principal—representative of his country in a foreign capital, is placed by a succession of Special Representatives, each independent of the Ambassador and of each other, some with instructions not to show the Ambassador anything, not to tell him about the nature or progress of negotiations. A modern youth might say, "But you can't do that to me!" A successful American businessman would say, "But you can't do business on that basis." They did do that to me and we did conduct our diplomatic business that way—occasionally with some success.

Here in brief is General Bradley's story of his Russian trials and tribulations.

On August 8th, he attended his first meeting with the Soviet delegation assembled to negotiate with him and met his opposite number, General Korolendo. Since General Bradley felt that his mission was important and was designed to help the Russian war effort, he asked the Russian delegation to push development of the air route with all possible speed. The Russians seemed to agree with this view, but their acts belied their words, for General Bradley was informed that the airfields, which Marshal Stalin had told me were constructed, equipped, and ready for use would not be operational until September 1, 1943, more than a year from the day of their first meeting. About all they accomplished was to agree to call the project ALSIB.

At the next meeting, a few days later, the Soviet delegation requested 50 transport planes for transportation of Russian crews to Fairbanks to pick up American combat planes. After consultation by despatch with the War Department, General Bradley told the Russians that this transport job could easily be accomplished with ten transports. When the Russians discovered that the United States would not give them more than ten transports, they threatened to call off the whole project. General Bradley suggested that they undertake the entire project with their own facilities. The Soviet delegation retired to seek advice from higher authority.

While Russian transport crews could operate DC-3's without additional training, it was obvious that Russian ferry crews for combat planes would have to have technical training in the operation of the more complicated new equipment. After weeks of delay, procrastination, and adjournment of meetings to consult higher authority, a plan was evolved for giving Soviet crews the necessary training.

When the War Department was informed of Mr. Stalin's ready agreement to permit an American group to participate in the aerial survey, a survey party of eight Army pilots under Colonel Harvey was organized. A few weeks later, the War Department received information that the Soviet Government would grant visas for only three members. After much protest and negotiation, an 8-man party was accepted. Later, the Russian consular authorities refused to grant visas to Lieutenant Colonel Craiger and Lieutenant Page, then relented; finally the original 8-man party made the survey.

In furtherance of the transport plan dispute, on August 25th, General Korolendo told Bradley that, since neither the United

States nor Russia could furnish sufficient transports to operate the ALSIB air route successfully, utilization of the route would have to be indefinitely postponed. This was the same day that General Bradley was told that he could not go meet his survey group at Krasnoyarsk.

On August 26th, the Soviet Delegation told General Bradley that their government had changed its mind—they would attempt to operate over the ALSIB route on a reduced scale with only the ten American transports.

It was about this time that I was called late one night by a Foreign Office minion and asked to arrange for visas for 110 Russian pilots to proceed early the next morning by air to fly out the backlog of combat planes which had banked up on our Army airfield at Fairbanks, waiting for Russian pilots. I had forseen this difficulty and, at one of my interviews with Mr. Stalin, I brought up the question of pilot visas, suggesting that he ask for an allowance of visas for this purpose so that an individual visa would not be necessary for each pilot on each specific flight.

"That won't be necessary," Mr. Stalin replied. "We will make arrangements for visas well in advance."

But his minor officials had procrastinated again. They had a lot of combat planes in Fairbanks which they needed badly and no pilots there to take over. Of course, I couldn't arrange for 110 visas on such short notice. "Give me the names of your pilots," I told the man on the other end of the phone. "You should make application at least ten days ahead of time, but, to get on with the war, you may send the pilots along and I'll take the matter up with my Government."

I sent a despatch to the State Department stating that I had authorized these pilots to take off, and urged them to make arrangements for their entry at Fairbanks. I never received the list of pilots, but our friendly and agreeable government had a State Department consular officer on hand to meet the pilots in Fairbanks so that the planes could be flown out promptly. I can't imagine the Soviet Government ever being so kind to 110 of our citizens.

On September 19, General Bradley asked that his survey party be permitted to make a detailed inspection of facilities at the fields along the route east to Yakutsk. "*Nyet*," he was told. "Such an inspection is without purpose."

On September 21, General Bradley received a despatch from the War Department which read as follows:

General Belyaev, Head of Russian Supply Mission to U.S., states that Soviet Government will accept airplanes now at Fairbanks for delivery to Russia. After those planes flown out, ALSIB route will be closed to further ferry operations. Request confirmation.

The War Department stopped all planes then enroute Fairbanks wherever they happened to be. Bradley's opposite number on the Soviet delegation professed complete ignorance as to the source of General Belyaev's statement and requested time to consult higher authority.

On October 4, the Soviet delegation told General Bradley that their Government had decided to keep the ALSIB air route open and would continue to take delivery on as many Lend-Lease combat planes as the ten transports the Americans had furnished could deliver crews to Fairbanks.

On October 6, General Bradley received a message from our disgusted War Department that it now considered that ALSIB air route definitely and finally closed. When General Bradley passed this information on to his Soviet colleagues, the news produced a violent commotion. At their urging, he strongly recommended that the War Department reconsider its decision.

On October 8, General Bradley received a despatch advising him that the War Department had reversed its decision.

On October 6, I was in Moscow preparing for my return home for consultation. I took General Bradley with me to the Kremlin for my farewell visit to Marshal Stalin and on October 8, I left Moscow for home. The General did not have an opportunity to tell me of the reversal of decision which the War Department made.

On October 24, the Soviet delegation told General Bradley that, since ALSIB matters were progressing so satisfactorily, their government felt that there was no further need to continue discussions; they had been ordered to dissolve the mission. Future arrangements would be made with the Soviet Mission in Fairbanks, with General Belyaev in Washington, or with General Faymonville in Moscow. The members of the Soviet Delegation had been ordered to other duties. Here again, we note the determination of Soviet officials to handle all purely military matters through General Faymonville, rather than through our Military Attaché.

On November 11, General Bradley had his last conference with General Korolendo; immediately thereafter, he left in his B-24 bomber for Washington, via the ALSIB air route.

Of interest is the citation for the Distinguished Flying Cross which General Bradley received in February 1943 in Washington. After mentioning his participation in an aerial flight from Washington to Yakutsk, "with no thought of personal hardship," the citation goes on to describe flying conditions in the Soviet Union "made hazardous by extremely adverse weather conditions, the proximity of enemy aircraft . . . inaccurate maps, inadequate communications and maintenance facilities, and dangerous overload conditions," and commends him for his "courage and initiative and good judgment in the performance of his duties as leader of the mission. General Bradley successfully concluded an assignment of great importance to his government. . . ."

I think that General Bradley would probably agree with me—flying was the least onerous of his duties. Through his efforts, the ALSIB air route was opened and kept open; hundreds of Lend-Lease combat aircraft were flown to Russia for use on the Eastern Front, when the Russians badly needed all the help they could get. Certainly, General Bradley deserved well of his country for action on a peculiar kind of front for which I have found no precedent among all the Grand Alliances of recorded history.

CHAPTER XVI

The Polish Question

To UNDERSTAND the extremely complex relations between the Soviet Union and the Polish Government-in-Exile-in-London during World War II, we must recall that, when the Nazis and the Russians divided Poland in 1939, the Russians took prisoner more than 180,000 Polish soldiers, of whom about 10,000 were officers. Upward of a million civilian men, women and children fled from the advancing German hordes to a doubtful sanctuary in Western Russia and were evacuated to refugee and work camps as far to the east as Siberia.

The more distinguished generals and civilian leaders of Poland were carried off to Moscow's Lubianka Prison. The rest of the officers were confined in three prison camps near the old Polish border. Of 5,131 regular army officers and 4,096 reserves known to have been captured by the Russians, about 400 reported to General Anders' Free Poland Army in Russia, when he began to organize and train it with Soviet consent after the Nazi attack on Russia in June 1941 made Poland and Russia allies against the Axis powers. The swift drive of the Nazi Legions across the flat plains of Western Russia astonished the world. By July 15, the German Army had captured Smolensk.

At first, General Anders was not concerned that so few of his officers had reported in. Some, he reasoned, had probably been transferred to distant Arctic or Far Eastern labor camps. But by November, when thousands of enlisted men had reported in and not one additional officer, he went to see the Polish Ambassador, Dr. Stanislaw Kot.

While I was in Moscow with the Beaverbrook-Harriman Mission in 1941, Dr. Kot finally obtained an interview with Mr. Stalin. When he asked why the Polish officers had not been released in accordance with the agreement with the Polish-Government-in-Exile in London, Mr. Stalin appeared to be astonished. "They have not been released yet?" he cried, and in Dr. Kot's presence, he called up the NKVD. "What about the Polish prisoners who were in those camps at Starobielsk, Kozielsk, and Ostaszkov?" he demanded harshly. He listened for a moment. "The amnesty applies to *all* Poles. They must be released at once!"

A month later, after collecting from the survivors 4,500 names of brother officers, who had been confined in the three camps, General Sikorsky came on from London and, with General Anders, went to see Mr. Stalin. This time, the Russian Dictator expressed no surprise or indignation. To their questions he gave a very weak answer. "Perhaps," he suggested, "those officers have returned to German-occupied Poland or maybe they escaped from Siberian prison camps into Manchuria."

Knowing what good check the NKVD keeps on all travel in Russia and particularly on foreigners, this explanation was hard to accept. General Anders suggested that perhaps the NKVD, being short of men, was still holding them in some distant Siberian labor camp.

Mr. Stalin smote the table with his clenched fist. "If they haven't released every one of them, someone is going to be sad," he cried. "We will see immediately."

Again, he called up the NKVD headquarters and told them to release all Poles who had ever been in those three camps.

By the time I reached Moscow in April 1942, I realized that the Polish Question was sort of a "burr under the saddle blanket" to the Russians. That was why I avoided any reference to the Poles in my first interviews with Mr. Molotov and Premier Stalin.

In Kuibyshev that Spring, I continued to see a great deal of Dr. Kot. At official meetings in my office or his own and even over the bridge table, his thin face grew longer and more solemn as the months went by and there was no prospect of settlement of any of the important Polish issues.

One of the thorniest problems was that of citizenship of Poles resident in the Soviet Union. Premier Stalin was willing to let some of the Polish war prisoners, organized into combat divisions under the Free Poland Army in Russia, leave Russia to help the British in the Middle East, but he insisted on regarding all Polish Jews as Soviet citizens. He categorically refused to let any of the Polish Jews leave the Soviet Union under any circumstance, a position to which Dr. Kot's Polish Government in London objected passionately.

Dr. Kot's principal concern was to find the lost Polish officers.

But his difficulties over Polish citizenship, evacuation of Polish women and children from Russia, post-war boundaries of Poland, and Polish refugees soon became my worries, too.

I first took up the Polish Question with the Soviet Government on May 27, 1942, when I obtained an appointment with Mr. Vishinsky. I took along Eddie Page. Mr. Vishinsky had a Foreign Office interpreter whose name I have forgotten. Even in Kuibyshev, we sat at a long, polished table. After formal greetings, I opened the discussion by saying, "My government has informed me that the Soviet Government has delayed giving effect to certain clauses of the Polish-Soviet Agreement, particularly in regard to recruiting for the Polish Army among Polish refugees in the Soviet Union, the release of civilians evacuated from Eastern Poland, the release of Polish prisoners of war to join the Free Poland armed forces, and continuing the evacuation of Free Poland Army divisions and civilians to Iran. My Government hopes that the Soviet Government will make liberal interpretation of the agreement. We have no desire to interfere in Polish-Soviet relations but it is the conviction of my Government that a generous attitude on the part of the Soviet Government would further our joint war efforts by promoting a spirit of confidence between Poland and Russia, the two most important of the United Nations in Eastern Europe."

Mr. Vishinsky was silent for a long while, looking down at his hands folded on the table before him, the color flooding into his thin face. Finally, he looked around at me. "I will present your views to my government."

I tried to discuss the Polish Question further but he showed no interest. Finally, I broke off the unsatisfactory interview.

I was new to the diplomatic game as it was played in Russia. Getting no satisfaction from Mr. Vishinsky and Mr. Lozovsky on any issues raised, as soon as transportation could be arranged, back we went to the Russian capital.

Once settled in Spaso House, I again sought an interview with Mr. Molotov. At his office in the Kremlin, I told him that my Government had been asked to assist in evacuating about ten thousand Polish children and their mothers from Russia to Iran and thence to some other country, probably South Africa, where they could be better cared for than in wartime Russia. President Roosevelt, himself, was interested in the project. Before we could carry out this humanitarian plan, we had to obtain permission from the Soviet Government to evacuate these Polish women and children from Russia. "My Government therefore earnestly requests that the Soviet authorities permit this group to leave the Soviet Union."

Mr. Molotov's reply was very long. Mr. Pavlov scribbled furiously to keep up with him. I record his reply in full because it indicates so well the Soviet attitude toward the entire Polish Question.

"I will, of course, report the views expressed by the Ambassador to my Government," Mr. Pavlov interpreted. "However, I would like to give the Ambassador the following resumé of our position in regard to the Polish situation.

"This is not a simple question of evacuation, which would be a small matter, but a fundamental problem affecting our basic relations with the Poles. If this group had been evacuated along with the first group* of thirty or forty thousand, the question might have been satisfactorily settled, although this is doubtful as there is always trouble where Poles are concerned.

"My Government does not wish to start a second evacuation, having just finished the first, since such a move might well cause instability not only among the Polish population in the Soviet Union, but hostile comment among Poles in German-occupied Poland. Poles in that area might think that conditions are so bad in the Soviet Union that my Government is unable to care for and feed the Poles resident here, and that was why my Government had to send them to Africa.

"As was explained to Sikorsky during my recent visit to London, it would appear more advisable to endeavor to improve the situation of the Poles in the Soviet Union than to evacuate such a small group. The entire Soviet population is suffering from the War and the Poles are likewise suffering. However, the Polish Government can feed them. We do not believe that much would be gained by evacuating ten thousand out of a total of a million and a half Poles."

We went on to other matters but the Poles came up again when I told Mr. Molotov that we had cancelled our request to assign one of our Army officers as liaison with the Free Poland Army units in Russia and that the orders of Colonel Henry Zymanski to such duty had been revoked. Mr. Molotov's heavy face darkened and he spoke forcefully, even angrily.

"Whenever Polish questions are brought up, there is always trouble. There are good Polish elements in this country, who have subordinated themselves to our laws, and our relations with these people are friendly. But there are bad elements, who refuse to

* The Polish Army unit, their families, and the orphans I saw in Teheran.

reconcile their views with those of their London Government and who are also hostile to the Soviet Union. Vigorous measures must be taken against those who continue to work against our laws. It seems to me that there are entirely too many people interesting themselves in Polish politics."

My impression as I left Mr. Molotov was that the Soviet Government had a purely political view of the whole Polish question; it was not influenced by considerations of humanity; Foreign Office officials were always displeased and irritated whenever the representatives of another power took an interest in Soviet-Polish relations.

In the succeeding months of 1942, my notes show that the situation of Polish military units and civilians still in Russia steadily deteriorated. When the Nazis and Italians stabbed into Egypt that Fall almost to Alexandria, threatening the whole Middle East position, the Russian Government did agree to let three divisions of Poles and some twenty thousand members of their families leave Russia for the Middle East.

On other issues, however, the tension between the Polish-Government-in-Exile and the Soviet Government continually increased. Polish military authorities trying to obtain the release of the ten thousand officers whom they needed so badly were repeatedly put off. No reason or excuses were given. General Anders and Dr. Kot were not informed whether or not the Germans had captured the prison camps before the Poles could be evacuated, or whether they had been transferred to other camps, or, indeed, anything at all. As far as the Polish authorities could learn, these officers had suddenly and completely disappeared from the face of the earth.

The Poles also had almost continuous trouble with distribution of Polish Relief to which the generous-hearted people of America and other countries of the West were contributing in great quantities. Our Assistant Naval Attaché in Murmansk kept us informed as to the situation in the northern Russian ports. Most of the Polish Relief supplies came in by ship over the northern convoy route. The Poles had stationed two of their officers, Captain Gruya and Captain Loga, at Murmansk to receive and forward relief and military supplies. They had no auto or boat transportation; no gasoline or fuel oil; and but little help from the Russians. One percent of their supplies was damaged in handling at the ports by indifferent prisoners of war working as stevedores; two to five percent were lost by pilfering in the port area; over half of the remaining supplies disappeared between Archangel and Murmansk and the Polish Army camps and refugee areas.

Although these Polish officers had been granted diplomatic status as Polish consuls in the two ports, Captain Gruya was arrested on a train going from Archangel to Murmansk and was taken to the NKVD prison in Archangel, where he was "third-degree-ed." His diplomatic credentials were taken from him and torn up before his eyes. Both Captain Gruya and Captain Loga were run out of the northern ports by the NKVD and eventually made their way south to report in to their Military Attaché in Kuibyshev, leaving the British to attempt to look after their interests.

There was little that either the British or our naval representatives could do for the Poles. The Soviet bureaus, INFLOT and "The Port," took charge of unloading Polish Relief cargoes and military supplies. Our representatives saw their goods piled high on the docks, in warehouses, and loaded onto trains—to disappear into the vastness of Russia. Meanwhile, we received frequent complaints from Dr. Kot and Polish military authorities as to the care of Polish civilians resident in Russia and lack of military supplies for the Polish troops.

Careful examination of the Polish officers who had survived the Nazi invasion of Russia now began to show results. Polish military authorities gradually reconstructed this picture of events: between April and June of 1940, the missing officers were sent down the rail lines from Starobielsk, Kozielsk, and Ostaszkov toward Smolensk. One officer reported a message chalked on the wall of the boxcar which evacuated him, "Second stop after Smolensk, we are being loaded into trucks." The message was left by a Colonel Kubya who had disappeared.

Goat Hill in Katyn Forest is seventeen kilometers from Smolensk!

Dr. Kot visited me frequently. Upon instructions from our Governments, both British Ambassador Sir Archibald Clark-Kerr and I tried our best to help the Polish Ambassador. He brought reports of the arrest of his representatives in Vladivostok for espionage and seizure of relief cargoes in Murmansk and Archangel. In July 1942, Dr. Kot came to me complaining of poor health and told me that he had asked for relief from his position as Ambassador to Moscow.

In that Summer of 1942, Soviet Russia's military fortunes were at low ebb. Sevastapol had surrendered to the Nazi legions and General Von Paulus had laid seige to Stalingrad.

About this time, our Assistant Naval Attaché in Murmansk reported:

It is quite impossible for British or American representatives to look after Polish material since they have enough trouble with their own supplies and with the inefficient way in which most things are handled around the docks by the stevedores and loading crews. I am quite certain that little, if any, of the material consigned to the Polish Embassy [in Kuibyshev] is reaching its destination. I feel quite confident in making this statement, since numerous instances have occurred where ammunition, gasoline, and food consigned to the British Mission have been shipped south and disappeared. Although the British have protested violently, they have not recovered any of it. Soviet officials here state that they are helpless to remedy the situation.

In August 1942, I received a despatch from our State Department which concluded as follows:

In due course, therefore, and in your discretion you may bring up the question of Polish-Soviet relations with the Soviet authorities, pointing out that, while the United States Government has no desire to intervene in this matter, which it realizes involves extremely complicated problems, the solution of which can only be effected by direct negotiations between two governments, it nevertheless hopes that the existing spirit of collaboration shown in connection with the transfer of additional Polish divisions to the Middle East may be furthered to the maximum and that mutual beneficial solutions may be found for the various problems under discussion.

I sought an interview with Mr. Lozovsky, which was not granted until September 9, 1942. After I had explained my mission, I said, "Of course, my government doesn't wish to interfere in Soviet-Polish relations."

Mr. Lozovsky looked at me, rather sourly. "That would be the best thing for the American Government to do."

Taken somewhat aback, I still pressed the question as to the present status of Polish Relief. He told me that 180 of the 370 Polish Relief delegates had been arrested, and went on, bluntly, "This work can be carried on by the remaining delegates in a perfectly satisfactory manner. There were too many of them in the first place. We can't have a number of hostile Poles running all over the Soviet Union unsupervised."

"Well, Mr. Lozovsky," I said, "I just want to express the hope of my Government that the same spirit of collaboration already shown in connection with the transfer of Polish divisions to the Middle East may be continued and that a mutually beneficial solution to the various problems under discussion may be found."

Mr. Lozovsky looked at me coldly. "Polish questions are very difficult to deal with to the satisfaction of everyone concerned."

I pushed back my chair and stood up abruptly to end the discussion and to indicate that I was not pleased. I knew how futile it was. It was like hitting tennis balls against a backstop. No matter how good the stroke, the ball always came back to you. Mr. Lozovsky would never be permitted to return the volley. It was sort of a game; you could never win; but it was awfully good practice. Practice is said to make perfect, but with too much practice you go stale. I'd had more than enough. For quite a while, I gave it up.

I had a more serious problem to face. Another VIP was coming our way, the most important of all the American VIP's who had yet visited Russia during my sojourn. I was probably one of the last ones who needed to know to be told about the projected visit.

CHAPTER XVII

Mr. Wendell Willkie and the
Second Front

I N JULY of 1940 at the Republican National Convention in Philadelphia, apparently in response to a genuine demand of the American people, the Republican Party "drafted"
Wendell Willkie to be their candidate for the Presidency of the
United States. In the General Election that Fall, Willkie polled
22,304,755 votes to the President's 27,243,466. While this was a
comfortable Democratic majority, Mr. Willkie received almost six
million more votes than Mr. Landon had four years earlier, while
FDR received several hundred thousand less. Although not nearly
as dynamic a personality as the President and infinitely less effective as a speaker on campaign tour, Mr. Willkie's earnest liberalism
had caught the fancy of millions of his fellow Americans. If he
were nominated again in 1944, he might defeat the incumbent.
But he must plan his campaign cleverly and keep himself always
in the forefront of his countrymen's consciousness.

In the great game of American politics, potential candidates
for the presidency begin their maneuvers for position early, often
two years or more before the nominating convention. Some such
thought ran through my mind when I received the following telegram from President Roosevelt for delivery to Premier Stalin, with
a dateline in Washington, August 9, 1942:

> Your frank opinion on the following plan, which I think may be
> useful, would be very much appreciated.
> For the primary purpose of explaining to the Governments of Iran,
> Iraq, Turkey, Syria, Saudi Arabia and Egypt the danger they run in
> a German victory and that their greatest hope for the future lies in
> the defeat of Nazi domination of the Near East and the Middle East,

I am sending Mr. Wendell Willkie to visit the Governments of these countries.

For a wholly different purpose Mr. Willkie would like very much to visit the Soviet Union. In addition to seeing for himself the undying unity of thought in repelling the Invader and the great sacrifices which you are all making, he wants to know more about the wonderful progress made by the Russian people.

As you know, Mr. Willkie was my opponent in the 1940 election and he is today the head of the minority party. He is heart and soul with my administration in our foreign policy of opposition to Nazism and real friendship with your government, and he is greatly helping in the war work. For the sake of the present and future I personally think that a visit to the Soviet Union by Mr. Willkie would be a good thing. He would proceed to the Soviet Union by air during the first two weeks of September.

I should be grateful if you would confidentially and frankly inform me whether you would welcome a very short visit by him.

A few days later, Mr. Andrei Vishinsky, Vice Commissar of Foreign Affairs, called me to the Foreign Office in Kuibyshev and handed me the following message from Premier Stalin to President Roosevelt:

I have received your message dated August 9. I may state that the Soviet Government is agreeable to the visit to the USSR of Mr. Wendell Willkie and will show him the sincerest hospitality.

Over a week later, August 24th, the State Department decided further to illuminate my condition of darkness. A telegram informed me that Mr. Wendell Willkie, Special Representative of the President, was leaving Washington August 25th by military transport plane for the Soviet Union via Cairo and Teheran. Mr. Willkie would be accompanied by Mr. Gardner (Mike) Cowles, Jr., publisher of the *Des Moines Register and Tribune, Look Magazine,* and head of the *Register* and *Tribune* Syndicate, and Mr. Joseph Barnes, former foreign editor of the *New York Herald Tribune,* both of whom were serving on "duration-of-the-war" duty in the Office of War Information. Would the Ambassador kindly assist Mr. Willkie and his party to obtain entry visas for his plane and crew? By now, I was so used to Special Representatives and Very Very Important Personages, that I thought I could take them in my stride. The Ambassador would be happy to comply.

On August 26, I received another telegram informing me that Mr. Willkie was being sent on a special mission from the President to the Soviet Union and the Republic of China; that the Soviet Government has been advised of his visit through Ambassador Litvinov in Washington; that Mr. Willkie would carry letters from the President addressed to Marshal Stalin and Generalissimo Chiang Kai-shek; that it was desired that Mr. Willkie's plane stop at Kuibyshev en route to Moscow from Teheran; that the President wanted Mr. Willkie to be permitted to proceed to China by such route as would not pass through India and to continue to the United States via the Siberian-Alaskan air route. Would I ascertain from the Soviet Government whether or not such a flight could be permitted? If so, please make the necessary arrangements. And please inform the Soviet authorities that Mr. Willkie wished to put himself completely at their disposal while he was in the Soviet Union.

We got right to work "making necessary arrangements." The Foreign Office in Kuibyshev was given full information about the proposed flights and was requested to expedite action as Mr. Willkie had already left the United States. Since the question of air routes would come under the cognizance of Soviet military and air authorities, copies of the pertinent State Department telegrams were forwarded to the Moscow Embassy for action by Colonel Michella, our Military Attaché, and General Follett Bradley of the Army Air Corps.

On August 26th, I sent a telegram to Mr. Willkie, care of our Embassy in Ankara, Turkey, advising him of our arrangements for the Kuibyshev stopover. If he planned to make any changes in his itinerary, I said, please let us know immediately. This turned out to be a diplomatic blunder of some importance.

Working closely with local Soviet authorities, we went ahead with plans for Mr. Willkie's visit. The Russians wanted to give him a comprehensive view of the important industrial and agricultural area around Kuibyshev. Plans were made for a visit to a local aircraft factory (always item number one on a Russian list of entertainment for VIP's), a trip up the Volga by steamer, an official dinner to be given by Mr. Vishinsky (Oh, my aching stomach, another series of Russian banquets!), followed by a special performance of *Swan Lake*.

These endeavors were going along nicely, when, on September 5th, Mr. Willkie advised us from Ankara that, unless the Ambassador felt strongly that a visit to Kuibyshev was necessary, he preferred to fly from Teheran to Moscow, leaving Teheran on September 17th.

Ten days of hard work gone to nothing! But what was infinitely worse, the Russians would be furious. With several delicate negotiations hanging, as I thought, in the balance, this was no time to rock the diplomatic boat.

"Why the devil do they bother to keep an Ambassador here?" I blew up to Eddie Page, my secretary.

"To make necessary arrangements," Eddie laughed. "Don't lose your sense of humor, Admiral."

Eddie and I sat down and composed a series of telegrams to Mr. Willkie. We informed him that, since Kuibyshev was, at present, the official seat of the Soviet Government, the courteous and proper thing to do was to make his initial contacts with Soviet officials in the Volga city. Furthermore, the State Department had advised us that he would first visit Kuibyshev and we had arranged with the Russians accordingly. We also told him in detail about plans for his reception and entertainment. I concluded by saying that, unless Mr. Willkie had instructions with regard to his visit to Russia other than the ones stated in President Roosevelt's message, I insisted that he follow the itinerary planned.

We presently received an answer—Mr. Willkie would visit Kuibyshev, arriving on September 17th; he wished to proceed to Moscow as expeditiously as possible; he did not wish to hold a press conference in Kuibyshev. This last provision must have delighted his old crony, Eddie Gilmore of the AP, who otherwise would have been scooped by his rival, Henry Shapiro of the UP, the only correspondent who had come down to Kuibyshev.

On the ninth of September, I received another despatch from the State Department which was dated four days previously.

> Mr. Willkie was requested by the President to consult with you and Mr. Loy Henderson [who was visiting me in Kuibyshev at the time] and then express to Stalin the American Government's hope that all efforts be made to effect an improvement in Polish-Soviet relations. The Polish Ambassador today asked whether there had been any representations for release of 3,400 Polish officers who are reportedly still held by the Soviet authorities in Arctic areas. You may make these representations together with Mr. Willkie or separately.

I could see trouble ahead. Mr. Willkie was not a trained diplomat. Neither was I, but I did have the benefit of five months' experience in negotiating with Soviet officials. In obedience to instructions, I had always gone with my hat in my hand in an apologetic manner, "not desiring to interfere, but. . . ." Whether it was Molotov, Vishinsky or Lozovsky, I always found the Russians unhappy about the Polish question and irritated that I had brought it up.

Having had this experience, Eddie Page and I prepared a despatch to the State Department refreshing their memory on the above events. Then I went on to recommend:

> It is my judgment that Mr. Willkie or other representatives should approach the Premier in a firm and frank manner and as a party in interest and not apologetically. The attitude might be expressed that the friction which had developed between officials of the two Governments, that is, Polish and Soviet, in the Soviet Union is distressing our Government and that friction of this kind between allies will be detrimental to our cause and will profit Hitler; that the President therefore wants it frankly stated that our Government hopes both parties will make every effort to resolve their problems generously and in a friendly manner, realizing that knowledge of the dispute in the hands of the Axis will be a valuable weapon; that a review by both of the parties of the problems can, the President is confident, lead to an understanding, provided there is present a spirit of good will and mutual confidence.

Mr. Willkie was at that time somewhere between Ankara and Teheran. Whether he ever received such instructions from the President or not, I never learned.

While we awaited the great day, we were having considerable difficulty arranging the Moscow-Chungking and Chungking-Siberian-Alaskan itineraries for Mr. Willkie's plane. Daily inquiries at the Kuibyshev branch of the Foreign Office brought no results. The Foreign Office in Moscow batted the ball back and forth with Soviet military authorities. On orders from General "Hap" Arnold, General Bradley got into the act in Moscow, only to be told by Soviet Air authorities that it was strictly up to the Foreign Office. Inquiry at the Foreign Office in Moscow brought forth the response that the matter was in the hands of the military authorities.

There the matter gravitated as the morning of September 17th dawned, as clear and sunnily beautiful as an American Indian Summer day. A little after three P.M., the specially equipped Army B-24 bomber *Gulliver* rolled to a stop at the military airport near Kuibyshev. The welcoming committee could have appeared impressive only to one unaccustomed to Soviet Protocol—the Chinese Ambassador and a dozen of his staff, the British Counselor (Sir Archibald Clark-Kerr being in Moscow), and the American Ambassador and over a dozen of his staff, including Colonel Michella, General Faymonville, and General Follett Bradley, all of whom I had summoned from Moscow for the event. But on the Russian part, the representation for a Very VIP was decidedly on the short side—only Mr. Lozovsky, number two deputy in the local Foreign Office, a couple of his minor assistants, and the Mayor of Kuibyshev and a few of his staff. Mr. Vishinsky was notable by his absence. Apparently, the leader of President Roosevelt's "loyal opposition" didn't rate very high. In Russia, there is no opposition.

I had never met the Republican candidate for President, but, from the newsreels, I recognized the shambling, bear-like figure and shaggy head, as Wendell Willkie climbed wearily down the ladder from the bomber. His blue eyes looked tired. The brief ceremony over, we took him off to a *dacha* made available to him by the Soviet Government where we were served *chi*, the first of too many, too elaborate banquets, whether they were called lunch, dinner or *chi*.

I felt that our President's Special Representative had been slighted, and that the next move was up to the Russians. Not so! At his insistence, after he had rested, I took Mr. Willkie to call on Vice-Commissar Vishinsky and Mr. Lozovsky at the Foreign Office. The two diplomats were affable and cordial enough, but reserved, and I somehow received the impression that Mr. Willkie had his mind on something else.

That evening, Mr. Vishinsky entertained Mr. Willkie at an official guest house with a small dinner, together with Foreign Office and local Government officials, the chiefs of all the foreign missions present in Kuibyshev, and Mr. Willkie's traveling companions, whom I had discovered included his brother-in-law, Commander Paul E. Pihl, as a sort of naval aide. In addition to myself, American guests included several of my staff and Generals Bradley and Faymonville.

The dinner was over-elaborate. In the semi-darkness of an adjacent room, I thought I recognized the familiar face of a caterer often seen at official dinners in Moscow, the same one who officiated at the banquet given for the Beaverbrook-Harriman Mission in Archangel in September 1941.

At ten A.M. the next morning, we were taken to the military airport to inspect an aircraft factory, which was engaged in building IL-2 attack bombers for the Red Air Force. As I had never before been permitted to visit this factory, I was surprised to discover that it was my old friend, Aircraft Factory No. 1, which I had visited in Moscow the previous Fall during the Beaverbrook-Harriman Mission. It had been moved to Kuibyshev a short time after we visited it, machines, raw materials, workers and their families, in a number of freight trains. There it had been set up and was operating again in record time. The manager I had known was gone, promoted or liquidated. The plant had gained by the move, with much improvement in the machine shop and assembly buildings. In many respects, I considered it a modern plant with up-to-date equipment. The new manager told us that the engines were manufactured elsewhere, but that every other part in the plane was made and assembled in his plant.

I recognized some of the faces of the workmen and tried to talk to them, but the foreman gave me no opportunity. Plant officials who spoke English were most guarded in their remarks, evading the questions we asked or ignoring them.

One incident amused me. Mr. Willkie walked up to a man operating a lathe and asked him, "What part is that?"

Quick as a flash, he shot back his own question, in English with a heavy Russian accent, "What about the Second Front?"

Mr. Willkie asked his question again and the lathe operator shot back his. "We'll have it," Mr. Willkie called back as he walked away. "Sooner than you think."

We had lunch in the recreation room of the plant, another official banquet. I began to wonder if I were suffering from induced hallucinations, for again I thought I saw the Moscow caterer, dressed as a factory worker, peering through the recreation room door. I settled the question in my mind; he must be an NKVD man!

That evening, at a reception and dinner at the Chinese Embassy, Ambassador Foo Ping-Sheung entertained almost the same list of guests that Mr. Vishinsky had for dinner the previous evening. Tiny Mr. Foo was very impressive in his ceremonial robes at the head of the table, with Mr. Willkie on his right and Mr. Vishinsky on his left. Next to Mr. Willkie was Afghan Ambassador Akhmed Khan, Dean of the Diplomatic Corps, and a very sensitive old man. Mr. Willkie kept talking to Mr. Foo and across the table to the British Counselor and General Bradley, until poor old

Akhmed approached a state of nervous frustration from neglect. It took repeated efforts on my part to persuade Mr. Willkie to say a few words to the nice old Afghan.

After dinner, we went in a caravan of cars across town to the Bolshoi Theater where the beauteous Tikomirova was dancing *Swan Lake*. We had no sooner settled ourselves in our box seats than a man came through the parted curtains to make an announcement. Eddie Page told me that he informed the audience that "The Honorable Mr. Wendell Willkie, Commissar and Special Representative of the President of the United States, honors you this evening by his presence at our humble performance."

Naturally, this pleased Mr. Willkie. Between acts, instead of promenading in the Bull Ring, we went back stage and Mr. Willkie was presented to the members of the company. As I went up the stairway to our box following Mr. Willkie, I heard his Russian companion say, "But Mr. Willkie, when are Britain and the United States going to open up a Second Front in Western Europe?"

After the final curtain Mr. Willkie made one of those grand gestures for which he was noted. Descending from the box directly onto the stage, he presented Tikomirova with a bouquet of flowers* and caught her up and kissed her soundly. The claque responded enthusiastically with cries of "Tiko-mi-ro-va" and "WEEL-ki."

We left early the next morning, September 19th, a number of my Embassy staff and Mr. Willkie and his party, as guests of the Soviet Government for a trip by steamer up the Volga about fifty miles to Stavropol. Our steamer was large for a river boat and luxuriously equipped, having upper and lower observation decks and a palatial dining room, its tables loaded with the extravagant spread of hot and cold foods and *hors d'ouvres* which characterize the usual Kremlin banquet. Again, I saw my Russian friend with the familiar face, dressed this time as a Volga sailor. Until we left the boat that evening, our trip was one continuous round of food and drink.

Each of the VIPs was assigned an outboard suite consisting of a stateroom, bath and sundeck, elaborately furnished, and with walls veneered in maple polished to a high gloss. A crisp, sunshiny day, we really enjoyed the sundecks.

During the long trip up the river, we were taken on a tour of

---

* You couldn't buy flowers in Kuibyshev. When I told our messenger, Morris, that Mr. Willkie wanted a bouquet, he "requisitioned" the flowers from the garden in front of Soviet Headquarters just down the street.

inspection of the steamer, with a Russian photographer in close attendance. When we came to the wheelhouse, Mr. Willkie pushed aside the helmsman and took the wheel, turning to pose and smile for the photographer. Not minding the course, the ship took a sharp dive toward the east bank of the river. The Captain shoved Mr. Willkie unceremoniously aside, put the rudder hard over and backed full on the engines to keep the steamer off the beach.

At Stavropol, we were taken by automobile to a stock and dairy farm, called a *sovholz* or state farm, where the manager told us about the operation and escorted us to see his granaries, pig styes, some fine horses, and a freshly whitewashed cow barn, the cleanest I've ever seen. When Mr. Willkie commented upon its unusual beauty, the manager said, "Oh, yes, we always clean it up during the summer. The cows are kept in the fields from May to September."

Later, we drove to a pasture five miles away, where two dairymaids tended a herd of fine cows. Instead of driving them to the barn in the evening, the dairymaids milked them by hand in the pasture and a truck brought in the milk. The manager told us that the farm had been supplied with milking machines, but the war prevented installation. Since there was no electricity on the farm, they may still be waiting for a power dam on the Volga to be completed.

Mr. Willkie was repeatedly photographed with farm workers, children, and livestock. He was enthusiastic in his admiration for the beautiful milk cows of the herd, evidencing his friendliness for the Soviet bovines by patting the nearest one available every time his picture was taken, but I noticed that he refused a cup of freshly drawn milk which one of the dairymaids offered him. Instead, he tried to pull her closer to him so that he could have his picture taken with a Russian milkmaid. Apparently, the young girl misunderstood his intentions, for her face flushed a brilliant red and she tried to run away. It took considerable persuasion and some sharp words in Russian from the manager before the young dairymaid consented to pose with our distinguished visitor.

Two dairymaids then brought up the farm's prize bull for inspection. Mr. Willkie approached the bull with the obvious intention of showing the same friendliness that he had shown the cows, but the bull lowered his head and started for Mr. Willkie with a snort. Mr. Willkie might have been seriously injured if one of the dairymaids hadn't seized the bull's nose chain and led him away.

Upon our return to the farmhouse, the manager insisted that

we have *chi* in his "apartment." Already surfeited with vodka and food and with a State Banquet coming up that night, I would have loved to refuse. His apartment turned out to be a comfortable farmhouse. *Chi* was another Kremlin banquet, complete with sturgeon, caviar, vodka, a wide variety of hot dishes, and my Russian friend with the familiar face.

This sumptuous repast was laid out in two rooms, each table seating about twenty-five people. Mr. Willkie and I sat at the main table with the manager at one end and his wife at the other, her eight and ten year old sons on either side of her. In answer to a question, the wife shyly admitted that she had prepared the entire spread with her own hands.

Toward the end of this wholly unnecessary feast, the toasts began to fly. The manager proposed a toast to Mr. Willkie; Mr. Willkie toasted the Russian Communist Party and the Russian people; I toasted Mr. Stalin; Commander Paul Pihl toasted the Military Russians; and I toasted the forgotten woman, our hostess, to which she did not respond. The Commandant of the local Army Garrison leaped to his feet and proposed a toast to "The Second Front in Western Europe."

"Why, of course, to the Second Front," Mr. Willkie acknowledged. "The United States favors a Second Front but Great Britain does not."

Since we had just invaded Guadalcanal during August and our Marines were fighting for their lives, and since there had been some very heated arguments between the British and ourselves over the North African invasion, then but two months away, I could only hope that Mr. Willkie's words would not be quoted to our British friends.

Back in Stavropol Mr. Willkie stopped to talk through an interpreter with the teen-age driver of a horse-drawn vehicle called a *drojski,* when suddenly the young lad shot back, "When are we going to have a Second Front?"

I took advantage of a lull in our strenuous round of entertainment to present to Mr. Willkie the State Department's point of view on the Soviet-Polish problems, and to inform him of the delicate state of negotiations on those issues. It was fortunate that I did, for the Polish Minister-Counselor came to call and asked Mr. Willkie to intercede with Mr. Stalin.

As if we hadn't had a thing to eat or drink all day, at eight P.M., we were seated at another handsomely loaded table in the banquet hall of the Bolshoi Theater; Mr. Vishinsky, the host at the head of the table, Mr. Willkie on his right and I on his left, with an interpreter next to each of us. At the other end of the table sat Mr. Lozovsky, with General Bradley on his right and Mr. Loy Henderson of our State Department on his left. It was the usual Russian menu—first the cold *hors d'oeuvres,* and, when we were completely surfeited, the special attendants brought on hot soup and dinner really began. My Russian friend with the familiar face was there, out in the open, and, resplendent in some sort of uniform, acting as head waiter.

That meal was a gustatory agony. They brought in each dish as a course. To decline made you conspicuous, as the waiter stood patiently behind your chair and would not leave until you had consumed your portion. With some fourteen courses as par, I was in real distress by the time we adjourned to a sitting room for liqueur and coffee.

As at the Chinese Ambassador's dinner, Mr. Willkie talked across the table to General Bradley and myself during much of the meal, ignoring Mr. Vishinsky, until I interceded and drew the Vice-Commissar into the conversation. Whereupon, Mr. Willkie went into a long monologue, pausing now and then to attack the current course with a gusto that he must have retained from his farm boy days in Indiana. As he paused, the interpreter on his right leaned around him and hurriedly translated his remarks. With Mr. Willkie breaking in on the interpreter's Russian to continue his dissertation, his talk was hard to follow, but it went something like this.

"Mr. Vishinsky, I've come to the Soviet Union with the sole purpose of obtaining material which will enable me to give the American people a more favorable picture of the Soviet Union than they now have. Although I have been in the Soviet Union only two days, I know that there is, here, a great reservoir of good will for the American people and I have come to realize how unfairly the Soviet Union has been represented to the American people in the past. False reports have been circulated by certain vested interests which feared that the Soviet Government was trying to spread the Communist system to the United States. For instance, these reports caused many Americans to believe that the Soviet Government prevented freedom of religion in the Soviet Union and persecuted those who practiced religion. I know that these stories are false."

He paused to consume the fish course while the interpreter caught up. "Now, I'm not a man to countenance such duplicity.

The American people have confidence in me. They know that I am a man who will frankly tell them the truth and the whole truth. They know that I can be trusted.

"The American people have also been led to believe that the Soviet Government has abolished private property and hopes to bring about the same situation in the United States. Why, two days in the Soviet Union have convinced me there is nothing to such a view—there's no great difference between the American and Soviet viewpoints. In a few years, the social systems of the two countries will be quite similar."

Mr. Vishinsky looked at him coldly. "I'm not so sure of that, Mr. Willkie," Mr. Lozovsky put in.

Mr. Willkie turned his attention to the other end of the table, gesticulating with one hand in the direction of Mr. Lozovsky. "No? Well, I tell you this, Mr. Lozovsky, give me an opportunity to find the answer to the many questions I will raise and to travel freely and meet the people in the Soviet Union and I guarantee that when I return to the United States I will place the Soviet Union in a much more favorable light before the American people."

"I'm afraid you're over-optimistic," Mr. Vishinsky put in drily. "If you write and speak favorably about the Soviet Union in the United States, hostile persons in your country will say that you have been duped, that you were shown only the most favorable aspects of Soviet life."

"Oh, not at all," Mr. Willkie went on eagerly. "I am convinced that I can do much to bring about a more friendly feeling toward the Soviet Union in the United States. After all, twenty-three million people voted for me for President in the last election. They'll believe what I tell them."

Mr. Vishinsky looked at Mr. Lozovsky quizzically. What kind of control did President Roosevelt have over his citizens if he permitted so many of them to vote for another candidate in the middle of a war?

Mr. Willkie misinterpreted the significance of the exchange of glances. "Just give me full freedom to see things for myself," he continued his monologue. "I assure you that, if I see something which I don't particularly like, or which, if revealed in the United States might create an unfavorable impression, I will keep quiet about it. The greatest desire of my life is to improve Soviet-American relations."

We had, much too late for my comfort, reached the end of the long line of courses. Mr. Vishinsky got up from the table, and we moved into the adjoining room. Once we were seated with black, bitter coffee and liqueur, Mr. Willkie turned to the international field. "Speaking very frankly Mr. Lozovsky," he said to that old Bolshevik next to him, "and this is my personal opinion; only two countries can be depended on to see us through and win the war— the Soviet Union and the United States of America. Without mentioning any other country by name—and I am sure you will know the country to which I refer—I am convinced from my recent travels that Imperialism is dead as the dodo bird."

Mr. Vishinsky and Mr. Lozovsky looked at each other in some astonishment, but offered no comment. A few moments later, Mr. Vishinsky rose and offered a toast. He dwelt at some length on the fact that winning the war would require the best efforts of the *United* Nations. He ended, "To the United States of America, the Soviet Union, *and* Great Britain."

Attendants put up a movie screen and darkened the room and we were presented a long, badly arranged, and poorly photographed military movie. I thought the evening would never end, but finally we were at home in bed at Sadovia. As I composed myself to sleep, I regretted that our distinguished Very VIP guest hadn't shown Mr. Vishinsky more attention, for it seemed to me that a feeling of resentment was indicated at the dinner. It had been a long, tiring but extremely interesting day; yet I couldn't help but feel that Mr. Willkie considered every moment not spent in political effort a waste of his valuable time.

We took off in the "Gulliver" from the Military Airport the next morning, September 20th, at 11 A.M. The turnout was not impressive—the Chinese Ambassador, the British Chargé d'Affaires, some representatives of the Polish Embassy, the Mayor of Kuibyshev—neither Mr. Vishinsky nor Mr. Lozovsky showed up. We flew in clear, cold weather to touch down at the Moscow Airport at 2:15 P.M.

The Diplomatic Corps was well-represented by officials from most of the embassies, including the British Ambassador, and Mr. M. Lunde, the Norwegian Chargé d'Affaires; but the Foreign Office was represented by a minor official named Dekanosov. As I followed Mr. Willkie down the ramp, the small Soviet delegation filed in front of him and he muttered, "I'm delighted to meet you." Then he saw Eddie Gilmore, the Associated Press Correspondent, and shouted to him, "Eddie, God bless you. It's good to see you."

The welcome was something less than spectacular. The Russians seemed to consider President Roosevelt's recent opponent of minor importance, apparently not realizing that Mr. Willkie *might* be the next President of the United States. In Moscow, the party in power took care of its opposition more directly and un-equivocally.

We drove Mr. Willkie and his party to the U. S. Guest House—"Number Eight"—with some of the correspondents trailing along for a story. As I took my leave, he was having his lunch and telling the newspaper boys about his visits to Africa, the Middle East, Turkey and Iran. He had run into heavy British censorship in Cairo and he hadn't liked it. From the press despatches the boys filed during the next few days, I gathered that he spoke to them freely and frankly on every occasion. Through Joe Barnes, Eddie Gilmore and Gardner Cowles, he maintained daily and intimate contact with the foreign correspondents. On September 21st, a brief announcement of the arrival of the Willkie Party appeared in the Soviet Press. That same morning, he received Sir Archibald Clark-Kerr; in the afternoon, I took him to call on Commissar of Foreign Affairs Molotov.

I think he was impressed by the ride across Red Square past the tomb of Lenin, the mummery with the sentries at the Kremlin gate, the NKVD boys riding the runningboards through the Kremlin grounds to the door of the Foreign Office. We sat at the same long, highly polished table in Mr. Molotov's conference room. After the usual pleasantries through Mr. Pavlov, Mr. Willkie began another of his long monologues.

"I certainly enjoyed my stay in Kuibyshev, Mr. Molotov," he said, giving me a smile which I could take for appreciation if I wished. "It gave me a wonderful opportunity to see and judge something of the local situation at first hand. It certainly altered many of my preconceived ideas about the Soviet Union.

"At the present time, I have two main purposes: To go to the front and to travel from Moscow to Chungking via Siberia and then home via Siberia and Alaska. There appears to be some confusion about the arrangements for this flight. Would you be kind enough to arrange for my pilot to be put in touch with the proper Soviet authorities? We'd like to complete as quickly as possible the necessary formalities for the flight."

"That can be done," Mr. Molotov replied.

"It will require your personal attention, Mr. Molotov," I put in. "I happen to know that members of my staff have already been referred back and forth between your office and military authorities. I'm afraid that nothing will be accomplished unless you give specific instructions about the flight yourself."

"I will certainly do that, Mr. Ambassador," he said, slightly smiling.

"If possible, I'd like to inspect some of the factories and hospitals in and around Moscow," Mr. Willkie went on.

"We'll be glad to make every facility available to you," Mr. Molotov agreed. "There are plenty of hospitals, but most of the factories have been evacuated from the Moscow district."

"Well, you see, Mr. Molotov," Mr. Willkie protested, "my main purpose in coming to the Soviet Union is to tell the Russian people what America is thinking and doing during the present war and to take back to the United States a picture of what the Russians are thinking and doing under similar conditions. I feel that this is vitally important because we must have full cooperation between the United States and the Soviet Union, not only during this war but also after the war."

Mr. Molotov looked down at his well-manicured nails. "War necessarily imposes certain restrictions, Mr. Willkie. Some of the factories you might wish to see can not be opened up for your inspection, but I assure you that, so far as possible, you will be shown everything. Now to change the subject, what is your opinion and American opinion in general as to the war situation on the various fronts?"

Mr. Willkie must have been thoroughly briefed for just such a question for he proceeded to give Mr. Molotov estimates, statements, figures, and a comprehensive review of each one of the fronts. In his summary, he drew a very optimistic picture of the prospect for victory in the Pacific and on the North African front.

"The German nation remains strong, Mr. Molotov," he concluded. "Very strong. Yet I am convinced that the Nazis will be defeated, but only by the direct application of military power by ground forces, not by bombings, starvation, or internal collapse."

"The area bombing of cities has had a good effect as far as reducing the German war effort on our front," Mr. Molotov broke in. "I'm sure that it has been of material assistance to the Allied cause."

Somewhat taken aback at this contradiction of his thesis, Mr. Willkie launched into a detailed discussion of aircraft production, in the United States, and gave a very optimistic summary of the merchant shipping situation. When Mr. Molotov had no further comment, Mr. Willkie said, "I have a personal letter from the President of the United States to Premier Stalin. I hope that I may have an opportunity to present this letter to Mr. Stalin in person."

"I will arrange for the visit," Mr. Molotov replied.

Mr. Willkie returned to the matter of the flight across Siberia. "In order for the information I'm gathering here in the Soviet Union to have the greatest effectiveness, it must reach America at the earliest possible moment. I do hope that I will be permitted to proceed to the United States via Siberia and Alaska as I can get home that way a week earlier than by any other route."

Mr. Molotov shook his head doubtfully. "The Siberian route has been explored but never used," he said soberly. "We will have to study the matter. I doubt that the Siberian route will prove practicable."

"The flight to Chungking will present no difficulty," I put in. "That route is in constant use."

Mr. Molotov looked across at me sharply. "I will issue the necessary orders for technical discussions with your pilots to commence immediately."

As in most meetings with Soviet officials, the conversation stopped abruptly. Mr. Molotov sat looking moodily down at his hands clasped on the polished surface of the table. I pushed back my chair and began to rise. Mr. Molotov got quickly to his feet, and Mr. Willkie followed. As we went across the room toward the door, I asked the Foreign Commissar, "Will you kindly try to arrange for Mr. Willkie's visit to Mr. Stalin as soon as may be convenient, as Mr. Willkie's time in the Soviet Union is limited?"

"Of, course, I will arrange it at once."

"How will I get word of my appointment?" Mr. Willkie asked.

"Through the American Embassy," Mr. Molotov replied.

For the next two days, Mr. Willkie was so fully occupied by the Russians that I had an opportunity to catch up on some of my back work. On the evening of the 21st, he attended a performance of Shostakovich's Seventh Symphony by the Moscow Symphony Orchestra; the next afternoon, Mr. Molochkov, Chief of Protocol at the Foreign Office, took Mr. Willkie to visit some Red Army exhibitions, and to a jazz concert that evening. The same afternoon, Mr. Willkie's OWI "aides," Mr. Joseph Barnes, and Mr. Gardner Cowles, Junior, honored me with a courtesy call at the Embassy.

On September 23rd, I had planned to accompany Mr. Willkie on a visit to a munitions plant. After breakfast, I asked Eddie Page

if we had received any word from Mr. Molotov regarding Mr. Willkie's appointment to see Mr. Stalin. He told me, "No."

I mulled the situation over, concerned at the apparent slight to
the President's Special Representative. When it came time to go,
I decided to leave Page behind. "If no word has been received by
noon, Eddie," I told my Secretary as I climbed into the Embassy
car, "get in touch with the Foreign Office and make an appointment for me to see Mr. Molotov this evening."

As we pulled up in front of the impressive mansion where Mr.
Willkie was housed, the sun was shining and I anticipated a pleasant and interesting day. The strapping Russian doorman opened
the car door and escorted me to the entrance of the Guest House.
When I reached the hallway on the main floor, I met Mr. Willkie's
brother-in-law and "naval aide," Commander Paul Pihl. "Time is
getting short, Commander," I said, as we shook hands. "I'm worried about Mr. Willkie's appointment with Mr. Stalin. Has he
heard anything?"

"Why, no, not so far as I know," Pihl replied.

"Oh, yes he has," the English-speaking doorman broke in. "A
message came from the Kremlin this morning. Mr. Willkie is to
see Marshal Stalin at seven-thirty this evening."

Commander Pihl went into the rear of the house and returned
a few moments later. "That's right, Admiral. Seven-thirty this evening."

I quickly telephoned Spaso House and called off Eddie Page's
activities. Mr. Willkie came down the stairs and we got into the
back seat of the Embassy car. With a carload of Soviet officials
leading and my NKVD boys following, we twisted through the
streets of Moscow toward the open country. After an awkward
silence I said, "I understand, Mr. Willkie, you have an appointment to see Mr. Stalin this evening. Is that true?"

To which Mr. Willkie replied, "That is correct."

Whereupon I said, "In view of the fact that Mr. Molotov told
you that you would be informed of your appointment with Mr.
Stalin through the American Embassy, I am curious to know why
he did not keep his word, and why the Embassy received no word
of your appointment with Mr. Stalin." And I continued, "Did you
have anything to do with the arrangement?"

"No, I had nothing to do with it."

"Well, I intend to find out why."

To which Mr. Willkie replied, "Oh, Mr. Ambassador, you musn't do that. I think you are a *big man*. If you do that, it would be the act of a little man."

I did not have to pursue the matter, as I learned that evening that the meeting was arranged by Mr. Barnes through his contacts with Soviet officials he had known when he was a Press representative in Moscow some years earlier.

"In view of the manner in which you were notified," I said stiffly, "I assume that it is not intended I should accompany you to the Kremlin this evening."

"That is my understanding," Mr. Willkie replied. "Of course," he presently broke a rather long and awkward silence, "I'll be glad to inform you as to what takes place at my interview with Mr. Stalin."

I thanked him as politely as I could.

The visit to the munitions plant was a repetition of the visit to the Kuibyshev aircraft factory. Mr. Willkie showed the same keen interest in the workers. A number of women were planted in conspicuous positions in the plant. When Mr. Willkie stopped to converse with these workers, each one of them met him with the question, "When are we going to have a Second Front?"

One of them was quite an elderly woman. After she asked her stock question, Mr. Willkie tried to strike up a conversation through an interpreter. "Please give me some word to take back to the women doing war work in America," he said, with an ingratiating smile, and the old lady's only reply was, "When are we going to have a Second Front?"

Finally, Mr. Willkie planted a kiss on her forehead and walked rapidly away.

From the munitions plant, we drove along rutted dirt roads cross-country to one of the many anti-aircraft batteries defending Moscow. The battery we visited was about thirty miles southeast of Moscow, so cleverly disguised that we passed within a quarter of a mile of it without realizing it was there. Suddenly we swung off the road on twin tracks through meadow grass and I saw four slim barrels pointing at the sky from the top of a low, grass-covered hill. Everything else was underground.

We pulled up and parked. Out of holes in the ground appeared a crew of fifty men and girls. The commander of the battery, a colonel, saluted and welcomed us and led us through a cleverly camouflaged entrance into the underground quarters and command post. The girls lived in two large dugouts lined with logs

and heavy planks, which they had decorated with pictures of Soviet leaders. A big wood-burning heater stood in one corner. Both
barrack rooms were unbelievably clean.

A series of passageways, all plank-lined and floored, led to the
guns, to the visual and radio range finders and computers which
the girls manned, and to the men's quarters. The Colonel explained the working of the guns and the coordination of guns and
range finders.

As it was nearly noon, the Colonel invited us to lunch in the
officer's mess, a long underground room pleasantly lighted and
simply furnished. For once, we didn't have the usual Kremlin banquet. We sat around a long table in rough, homemade chairs, while
Army attendants served us *hors d'oeuvres* of sliced cucumbers, tomatoes, smoked smelt, onions—and vodka. Next came a thick vegetable soup, followed by a fricasseed meat that tasted like veal, and
mashed potatoes. It was a very substantial meal, which the Colonel
told us was served to every man and woman in the battery.

Mr. Willkie was uncommonly silent, apparently still resentful of
my criticism. After lunch came more vodka in heavy tumblers. We
had a series of toasts. Taking advantage of the situation, when we
emptied our tumblers "To the Red Army," Mr. Willkie arose and
called for quiet. "I have an interesting suggestion to offer," he said
loudly. "I'd like to propose a drinking bout between our American
Ambassador, Admiral Standley, and any one of you young Russian
officials or officers. I should think it would be very interesting to
see whether or not a Russian could drink the American Ambassador under the table."

There was an embarrassed silence about the table as the interpreter completed his translation and then everyone began to laugh
and shout at once and some of the Russians gathered around a
young officer, talking excitedly. I got up and called for quiet. "Our
distinguished visitor's proposal is indeed interesting," I said slowly, stopping frequently for the interpreter to translate my words.
"But you see, Mr. Willkie has touted me as a champion, and from
what I have seen, all the young Russians here are quite evidently
amateurs. In America, a champion never risks his title against an
amateur. So, of course, the American Ambassador could never indulge in such a contest."

There was good natured laughter when I finished. I held up my
tumbler and proposed, "To Tovarich and Marshal Stalin, a great
leader." I bottoms-upped my tumbler and slammed it down on

the table. All present followed suit. I turned and moved toward the door of the messroom, stopping to thank the Colonel for our interesting visit and fine lunch. There was an uneasy silence in the Embassy car as we rode back to town.

I was furious. Mr. Willkie's proposal had been completely uncalled for, could only have been caused by resentment, and added up to a silly and awkward attempt to undermine the prestige of the American Ambassador.

But in the Diplomatic Service, protocol rules all. We had planned a reception for Mr. Willkie that afternoon at Spaso House and had invited all of the Diplomatic Corps in Moscow and the gentlemen and ladies of the Press to meet him. As Mr. Willkie had already had a most strenuous day, in spite of his *gauche* behavior, I had my Staff carry out previous arrangements to let him rest in my apartment until our guests had all assembled.

At the proper time, we formed a receiving line in Great Hall and Mr. Willkie came down the long flight of stairs from the mezzanine floor rested and resplendent. In the absence of Ambassador Akhmed Khan of Afghanistan, Sir Archibald Clark-Kerr was Dean of the Diplomatic Corps and first to come through the receiving line. Upon grasping the British Ambassador's hand, Mr. Willkie drew him away to a near corner and engaged him in serious conversation. After a few moments, I went over to them and reminded Mr. Willkie that our other guests waited upon his pleasure. He returned to his position in the line and performed his social duties acceptably until General Follett Bradley came along. Again, he abandoned our guests and seated himself with General Bradley on a sofa some distance from the receiving line. I continued to receive our guests without our distinguished visitor until Commander Pihl came up to me. "Mr. Willkie would like to know if you would be so kind as to join him for a few moments?"

I greeted the few remaining guests, went across the hall, and seated myself beside Mr. Willkie. "Admiral," he said, "do you think I ought to take up with Mr. Stalin tonight the question of General Bradley's shuttle-plane air route from Fairbanks to Siberia?"

I deliberated a moment. "No, Mr. Willkie, I do not. I don't believe that you should take up anything with Mr. Stalin except those matters about which you have received definite instructions from the President. There are certain delicate negotiations underway with which we, in the Embassy, are directly concerned. To discuss them with Mr. Stalin at a meeting at which I am not present would leave me in a most embarrassing position as I would have no knowledge as to what actually took place."

"But, Admiral," he insisted, with General Bradley hearing every word, "coming directly from the President, surely I will have more success than General Bradley or you, you've been so long out of touch."

"Mr. Willkie, I have been very patient," I said, with some heat. "Now, I feel it my duty to remind you that there is only one United States representative in the Soviet Union, and I, the American Ambassador, am that representative."

I returned to my social duties in the receiving line. Mr. Willkie left our reception shortly thereafter and went on to the Kremlin for his interview with Mr. Stalin. Much to my surprise, I learned that Mr. Barnes and Mr. Cowles joined him after his talk and had their pictures taken with Mr. Willkie and the Premier.

We had made arrangements for Mr. Willkie to "visit the front" near Rzhev the next morning, accompanied by General Bradley, Colonel Michella, and General Faymonville. I had also planned to make the trip but, on the advice of Dr. Lang, gave it up at the last minute. Mr. Willkie phoned me about ten P.M.; he had just returned from his interview with Mr. Stalin, he said, and he would be glad to come over to Spaso House and tell me what had taken place.

"But Mr. Willkie, you are leaving for the front at four and need some sleep," I replied. "I'm afraid it's too late tonight. Suppose you come over and tell me about it when you get back."

"All right, Admiral," he said, with apparent relief. "By the way, Mr. Stalin has given me permission to return to the United States via Siberia. Will you put my pilot in touch with the proper Soviet authorities so that he can plan the flight?"

I told him that I would and we took care of it the first thing the next morning.

General Bradley and Colonel Michella returned to the Embassy from the visit to the "front" about 11 A.M., September 25th. As usual, the trip was a disappointment. They were taken to battle areas recently fought over, but which were miles behind the real front. From the point of view of the trained military observer, the trip was valueless.

Mr. Willkie rested that morning and visited some hospitals during the afternoon. About 4 P.M., he called at Spaso House to see me. He, too, had been disappointed in the visit to the "front." To summarize his remarks about the Stalin interview, I quote from a report I made to the State Department at the time:

> Mr. Willkie called at the Embassy . . . and informed the Ambassador that he had taken up the Polish question with Mr. Stalin along the line that had been indicated in the Department's telegram of September 10, pointing out particularly that it was in the common interest of the United Nations that there should be the maximum cooperation and the least possible cause for friction between the different nations fighting against the Axis, that Mr. Stalin had asked specific questions in regard to the Polish complaints, but that he had replied that he did not wish to argue the details of the case.
>
> Mr. Stalin finally said that he would be willing to discuss the Polish question with the Polish officials with a view toward ironing out existing difficulties.

I asked him, "Were any other matters taken up?"

Rather off-handedly, he said, "Oh, yes. The conversation became general, touching mostly on the seriousness of the Russian military situation."

"Have you made any report to the President about your interview?" I asked.

"Oh, no," he replied, "There are other matters so secret that I can't trust them to coded messages or even to the Ambassador."

That statement really rocked me, but he probably didn't notice, because he went on to inform me that Mr. Stalin had said that he wanted to give him a Kremlin dinner, and he wished Mr. Willkie to select the date and submit a list of guests. Mr. Willkie suggested September 26th, and gave him a list, which included his entire party, Generals Bradley and Faymonville, Colonel Michella, Captain Jack Duncan, and myself. This was another peculiar maneuver, as such arrangements normally are made through the Embassy.

The next morning, September 26th, Mr. Pavlov, the Foreign Office interpreter, phoned Eddie Page, and, in a rather casual way, informed him of the Willkie dinner and gave him the list of names which Mr. Willkie had suggested. Were there any other members of the Embassy staff who should be included? Eddie took a supplementary list over to the Foreign Office. Mr. Pavlov then took the position that, since it was Mr. Willkie's party, the Ambassador had better take up the matter of additional guests with Mr. Willkie. I refused to do anything of the sort. Late that afternoon invitations arrived for Eddie and several of the staff. The Foreign Office added the name of Sir Archibald Clark-Kerr.

On the Russian side, the guest list included Marshal Stalin, Admiral Kuznetsov, General Voroshilov, and Messrs. Molotov, Mikoyan, the Foreign Trade Commissar, Beria, Chief of the NKVD, Lozovsky, up from Kuibyshev, Dekanosov and Molochkov of the Foreign Office, Sobolev, Secretary General of the Foreign Office, Sherbakov, Chief of the Soviet Press Bureau, Kozrev, Molotov's Secretary, Oumansky, former Ambassador to Washington, Mr. Pavlov and Mr. Potruback, interpreters—a small affair as Kremlin banquets go.

Mr. Willkie's party was the first to arrive in the reception room where Marshal Stalin was to meet his guests. My staff and I came in immediately behind them. Presently the Russians began to drift in by ones and twos. When all the guests were present, Marshal Stalin came in and went the entire round of the room, shaking hands with each guest.

We moved into the magnificent Catherine-the-Great Room, where the tables were set. Marshal Stalin took the center seat on one side of the table, with Mr. Molotov directly across from him. Mr. Willkie sat on the Premier's right, while I was on his left. Across from us beside Mr. Molotov were General Bradley and Sir Clark-Kerr. The usual overpowering dinner was served. Nothing much of note occurred until it came time for the round of toasts, with Mr. Molotov acting as toastmaster. Mr. Molotov toasted Mr. Willkie; I responded with a toast to Premier Stalin; Mr. Willkie gave a toast to Prime Minister Churchill *in absentia;* Mr. Molotov replied with a toast to the American and British Ambassadors. So it went, until everyone at the table had been saluted.

Only one toast possessed significance. Mr. Stalin arose and proposed, "To airmen of the United Nations," and delivered himself of some remarks, which Mr. Pavlov translated as follows:

"The Soviet Government hesitates to complain about Lend-Lease aid, but it must question why the British and American Governments supply the Soviet Government with inferior war material. The American Government has furnished the Soviets P-40 Fighters, not Aircobras; the British have supplied Hurricanes, not Spitfires. Both of these aircraft are inferior to German fighters which they have to meet in combat.

"Furthermore, 150 Aircobras allocated to the Soviet Union were intercepted by the British Government on their way through Great Britain and used elsewhere. The Russian people know that the

Americans and the British have planes which are equal or superior to the German fighters. They can't see why some of these better planes aren't supplied to the Red Air Force."

When he had seated himself, Sir Archibald rose to his feet. "I have full knowledge of the diversion of the Aircobras which you mention. All I can say at present is that I believe that the disposition made of those planes makes them of far greater value to the Allied cause than if they had been delivered to Russia."

I sat there helpless, wishing that someone would tell me about such matters. Too late to be of any help in the issue, I learned that the planes had been assigned to American fighter pilots in England for use in the North African invasion.

We were all silent for a moment, feeling the strain of such unusual and undiplomatic language on a social occasion, when Mr. Willkie broke the silence by remarking that the Soviet Premier certainly "kept his eye on the ball."

When this was translated, Mr. Stalin didn't understand the American slang. Mr. Willkie drew a laugh when he explained through the interpreter the meaning of the expression in American sport.

"I hope I always keep my eye on the ball," Mr. Stalin said, smiling somewhat grimly.

We left the table about eleven and moved into an adjoining smoking room for coffee and liqueur. About him in one corner of the room, Mr. Stalin gathered Willkie, Pavlov, Molotov, Oumanski, Voroshilov, Sobolev, Sir Clark-Kerr, and myself. Later, Mr. Stalin asked General Bradley to join us. We were seated on a sofa and richly upholstered chairs about a low table. After some light and general conversation, Mr. Stalin looked across the table at me and said, "Why don't you come back to Moscow?"

Somewhat taken aback, I replied, "Mr. Stalin, I ask you the same question—why don't I come back to Moscow? You have established the seat of your Government in Kuibyshev. I supposed that I was complying with my instructions and your desires by maintaining my residence at the seat of Government."

"There's no reason why you shouldn't come back. Are you afraid?"

This question naturally annoyed me, made as it was in front of all those distinguished persons, but I gave a soft answer. "I will be happy to return to Moscow and will do so just as soon as possible. But won't it embarrass you in your relations with the Japanese?"

"Not at all. In two or three months, all of the missions will be back."

To change the subject, I asked Mr. Stalin if he had heard a BBC news report that evening. "The broadcaster quoted a statement made by the newly appointed Japanese Minister for Foreign Affairs that "Japanese-Soviet relations were in the best condition for a long time; that there were no misunderstandings and no difficulties on the Siberian border and no chance of any disturbance there."

Mr. Stalin said he had not heard the broadcast.

"It aroused my curiosity," I went on. "In Kuibyshev, I heard rumors that certain conversations were being conducted between the Japanese Ambassador and the Soviet Foreign Office. It seemed to me that this statement of the Japanese Foreign Minister would indicate that those discussions have terminated harmoniously."

"There have been some discussions," Mr. Stalin admitted. "I was told that the Germans have been demanding that the Japanese attack Siberia. Japan told the Nazis that, if the Germans would supply them with one million tons of steel, five hundred thousand tons of shipping, and aluminum and other alloys and materials which the Japanese economy requires, Japan would consider the German request. The Germans refused, which indicates to me that the Germans have no steel or other raw materials to spare and that Japan must be in a difficult situation as far as raw materials are concerned."

I thanked him for the information, thinking what a difficult job the Nazis would have to deliver the materials requested. To my annoyance, Mr. Stalin again urged me to return to Moscow, reminding me that it was perfectly safe, to which Mr. Molotov nodded his approval.

Joe Barnes and Mike Cowles were seated at another table with several Americans, and their talk was so emphatic that at times I had difficulty trying to follow the conversation around me. Presently, either Mr. Barnes or Mr. Cowles, I did not know which, pointed across the room at Mr. Willkie, and said loudly and enthusiastically, "There sits the next President of the United States."

At midnight, Mr. Stalin had a Russian motion picture, *The Defense of Moscow,* screened in his private projection room for our edification. As a result, we didn't get home until two.

During his brief stay in Moscow, Mr. Willkie had several meetings with Sir Archibald Clark-Kerr, my closest associate and best friend among the members of the Diplomatic Corps. I was not present at many of these meetings, but I was told that, at one of them, Sir Archibald tried to get Mr. Willkie to persuade the American Government to offer some shipments of wheat to the Soviet Union, since the grain shortage in Russia was expected to be severe during the approaching Winter and Spring. As much as I admired Sir Archibald, I was inclined to think that he wanted this offer made in the name of the British *and* American governments in order to reduce the anti-British sentiment which was very strong in the Soviet capital at that time.

At one of these meetings with Sir Archibald, Mr. Willkie and I learned of a Soviet action which caused reverberations throughout the United Nations world. I have recorded how frequently Mr. Willkie was accosted by the question, "What about the Second Front?" That afternoon, Sir Archibald told us of identical Soviet announcements which had been made simultaneously by Russian Ambassadors Maisky and Litvinov in London and Washington. They went about as follows:

> Stalingrad is lost. The Caucasus are as good as lost. When this happens, Hitler will drive up the Volga to the Urals, Moscow and Leningrad will be cut off. Russia will have to surrender.
>
> Molotov's mission* to London and Washington was a colossal blunder, as it led Russians to hope that they would be relieved by a Second Front in Europe in 1942. Stalin promised Churchill that Stalingrad and the Caucasus would be defended; now, they are lost. If Great Britain and the United States had started a Second Front when the Russians first asked for it, the Allies could easily have defeated Hitler. In December 1941, if a Second Front had caused the withdrawal of only twenty divisions from the Russian Front, the success of the Red Army would have been assured. By May of 1942, when Molotov made his visits, it would have been necessary to cause the withdrawal of fifty divisions. To be successful now [September], the Second Front would have to cause the withdrawal of 100 divisions. Now, it is too late.

In the light of later events, it is easy enough to see that this was just another propaganda maneuver to pressure the Western Allies into an early invasion of Western Europe and to keep them out of the Eastern Mediterranean and Eastern Europe. In June

---

* In May–June 1942, Mr. Molotov visited London and Washington to negotiate for a Second Front in Western Europe. A joint communiqué issued by President Roosevelt and Mr. Molotov with the reluctant concurrence of Mr. Churchill led the Russians to expect a Second Front in Europe in 1942.

1942, the Nazis captured Sevastopol. Field Marshal von Paulus continued his investment of Stalingrad. But the attack on Moscow had been beaten off and by October the Red Army had begun to roll down the military highway toward Vyazma.

Mr. Willkie was greatly excited about this news, as, I must admit, was I. But I had recognized the phony nature of the mass appeal for a Second Front from the Russian people to our visiting Special Representative. I don't believe that Mr. Willkie had.

On September 27th, Mr. Willkie breakfasted with Sir Archibald. We arrived at the airport at 10 with about the same representation to see him off.

Mr. Dekanosov did the honors for Mr. Molotov, who was inexplicably absent. As one of the correspondents put it, "Soviet newsreel cameramen were staying away in droves."

Mr. Willkie was his usual exuberant self. He continued to ignore me as much as possible, calling Clark-Kerr to be photographed with him. We took off at 10:15 and arrived in Kuibyshev at 2:15. Mr. Willkie went immediately to his quarters. I saw no more of him, except to do the necessary honors at the airport the next morning. It may have been significant that his plane was delayed for a couple of hours while a doctor was summoned to the airport to treat Mr. Willkie and Mr. Barnes for sore throats.

Many times, I have been asked as to the significance of Mr. Willkie's visit to the Soviet Union. Part of it was, I feel sure, a sincere but misguided effort to help the United States and Russia get on with the war. From the events which I have related above, it was then my opinion that Mr. Willkie was also in Russia principally to enhance his prestige at home and further his political stature in the 1944 Presidential race.

Whether he achieved his ostensible purpose of helping to win the war, I am most doubtful. A successful Second Front in Western Europe was, in 1942 and 1943, beyond the military capabilities of the Western Allies. In this connection, I want to quote from a book, *Twelve Months That Changed the World,* by Larry LeSueur, a foreign correspondent in Russia at that time.

> ... when I arrived ... Willkie was just coming in from a walk.
> "I talk to people every chance I get," he said enthusiastically. "Why, just out here on the corner I talked to two men on the way to work." He paused and added as an afterthought, "One of them spoke English."
> All through breakfast we talked about the Russian situation and its

prospects. "What I want to know," said Willkie, "is whether we should continue sending aid to Russia. Do you think it's too late? Will it fall into German hands?"

We were all surprised to learn that doubt still existed in America whether Russia could continue standing against the Germans. We knew that Stalingrad was not a decisive battle for Russia, but a decisive battle for Germany. If the Germans couldn't secure their eastern flank and grab the Caucasus oil, the prospects of a short war would be much better.

I replied that we might as well send what aid we could because it was being used up so fast that the Germans would never get it.

"What do the Russians want most from their Allies?" Willkie asked.

There was only one answer. "A Second Front," we chorused.

"I must tell that to the American people," said Willkie.

I suggested that the best way to appeal to America was on the basis of "What's in it for us?" Mr. Willkie seemed more of an idealist than that. He shook his shaggy head thoughtfully.

"No," he said. "The American people must be aroused like avenging angels. Avenging angels! That's when they're at their best!" He brushed the vagrant lock of hair out of his eyes. Then he added: "I'm going to give you people a strong statement and see that it gets through the censors."

The next day, the correspondents gave a cocktail party for Mr. Willkie at the Metropole Hotel where most of them stayed. Mr. Joseph Barnes, acting as Mr. Willkie's "press secretary," gave some of the correspondents a typewritten statement from the President's Special Representative, which began—

"I am convinced we can best help Russia by establishing a real Second Front in Europe, with Britain, at the earliest possible moment our military leaders approve. And perhaps some of them will need a little public prodding . . ."

The newspaper correspondents had no trouble getting that statement past the Narkomindel.

As for his other objective, it is still my personal opinion that Mr. Willkie came to Russia more to enhance his political stature than to help the Allies get on with the war—unless he felt that placing his hand at the helm of state in Washington would be the greatest impetus that he could give to the war effort—and he was quite capable of entertaining such an opinion. Nearly everyone has forgotten his dramatic flight home and his barnstorming trip across the country, north, south, east, and west, spreading his belief that he found a "tremendous reser-VWAHR of good will for America all over the world"—and particularly in Soviet Russia. He believed that we could get along with the Russians after the war, that we must look beyond labels and find a working formula for the days of peace.

Robert Sherwood in his book, *Roosevelt and Hopkins,* has recorded that Mr. Willkie's trip "did an enormous amount of good and it also stirred up some trouble." Falling for the Russian propaganda for a Second Front, in his statement from Moscow, as I have noted, he chided the Western Allies for their failure to invade Hitler's Fortress Europe. From Chungking, he upbraided the Western Allies for failure to make an all-out effort to aid China. These two Willkie statements caused President Roosevelt to remark, "You can't have it both ways."

In one of his more dramatic press conferences, this time in Chungking, he was quoted as telling reporters, "When I speak for myself, I am Wendell Willkie, and I say what I damned please." That, I must say, he certainly did, and he had not been briefed well enough to know that commitments already made to other operations even then in course of execution rendered impossible the commitments he favored.

Apparently, President Roosevelt was not greatly put out by the statements that Mr. Willkie gave out on his trip or the speeches he made about the country. But Harry Hopkins was considerably distressed over the rumors circulated on his return about the inadequacy of Lend-Lease aid to Russia and was afraid that Mr. Willkie was doing serious harm to the cause of Allied unity.

Certainly Mr. Willkie caused me plenty of trouble. His activities and maneuvers in the Russian capital had left me in an untenable position; although the only officially accredited American Representative to the Soviet Government, I had been by-passed so frequently, my prestige was so low, that it seemed obvious to everyone in Moscow that I no longer enjoyed the confidence of my own government. Drastic action to reestablish my prestige or withdraw from my mission to Moscow was imperative.

Early in 1944, as the time approached for the Republican National Convention, Wendell Willkie gave an interview to Samuel Grafton, newspaper columnist, who published in the *New York Post* these words of our former Special Representative:

> I tell you that if a man is not, deep in his belly, in favor of the closest possible relations with Britain and Russia, then it does not matter what else he is. Such a man will be anti-labor even if he praises labor twenty-four hours a day. He will be anti-labor because he will

be working for a constricted America, a less prosperous America. For the very same reason the very same man will also be anti-Business, in the deepest sense, even though he may consider himself a servant of Business, even though he falls on his knees before Business. He will be anti-Business because he will be working for a smaller America, a less important America. This is the touchstone to a man's entire position in politics today. Only occasionally does it happen that one issue arises which is so controlling that every other issue is subsidiary to it, and this is it. But it is not enough for a man to repeat the right words about world collaboration. He has to be on fire with it. He has to feel, in his belly, that this is the door which will open outward to an expansion of American activity and prosperity. You can not be wrong on this issue and right on any other.

In looking back on these experiences, it may just be that Mr. Vishinsky was prophetic that night at dinner in Kuibyshev, when he told Mr. Willkie, "Hostile persons in your country will say that you have been duped, that you were shown only the most favorable aspects of Soviet life."

Certainly, in his book and in his speeches, Mr. Willkie told America the favorable aspects of life in Soviet Russia as he had been shown them. Just as certainly, there was, in 1944, no demand for Willkie from the people of America, no clamor of "We want WILLKIE" from the rank and file at the Republican Convention, as there had been in 1940. Thomas E. Dewey of New York was nominated as Republican candidate for President. Three months later, Mr. Willkie entered Doctor's Hospital in New York with a throat infection and passed away after only a brief illness.

CHAPTER XVIII

I Return Home for Consultation

MR. WILLKIE'S visit to the Soviet Union could not help but cause serious complications officially, because his daily and hourly actions had served to by-pass me and undermine the prestige and respect due the American Ambassador. Furthermore, his actions and attitude toward me personally on a number of occasions were openly deprecatory and even hostile.

Immediately after Mr. Willkie took off from the Kuibyshev airfield on September 28th, I called a conference of my closest advisers on the Embassy Staff and Loy Henderson, Chief of Division of Eastern European Affairs, State Department, who was in Russia on a visit of inspection and had been in Kuibyshev and Moscow with me during the whole course of Mr. Willkie's visit. After extensive discussion, we reached the unanimous opinion that Mr. Willkie's activities had been destructive to the prestige and effectiveness of the Ambassador in his mission and decided that I must return to Washington at once, for the following reasons:

1. To indicate to the Russian authorities that I resented such actions as the Soviet Foreign Office had countenanced and facilitated in permitting Mr. Willkie repeatedly to by-pass me and that I did not intend supinely to submit to such treatment.

2. To protest to the President against sending such temporary would-be diplomats to represent him where he was already otherwise represented.

3. To insist that, if I were to return to my post in Moscow, it would have to be with positive evidence of continued confidence in me and increased prestige.

I felt sure that Secretary Hull must have already sensed the unhappy situation created by Mr. Willkie's visit. Since haste was of the utmost importance, on September 29th, I got off a telegram to the Secretary of State, which requested that certain members of my staff and I proceed immediately to Washington for consultation. I recommended that Mr. Loy Henderson be retained in Moscow as Chargé d'Affaires during my absence. Anticipating approval of this request, I had General Bradley's B-24 stand by in Kuibyshev ready for prompt departure on short notice.

Something of a record was established for communication between Moscow and Washington. Three days later, the answer came*—Colonel Michella, Captain Jack Duncan, Eddie Page and I were ordered home for consultation—but the telegram blasted my hope of reaching Washington before Mr. Willkie. Prior to my departure, I was directed to assure both Mr. Molotov and Mr. Stalin that the purpose of my trip home was to expedite our assistance to the Soviet Union. Unfortunately, this necessitated a trip to Moscow.

The telegram also approved my recommendation with respect to Mr. Henderson, which had its ironical aspects. During his visit of more than two months, Mr. Henderson had observed the irritating situation develop as a result of the Willkie tour, but he had also busied himself with a detailed inspection of our routine operations in the Embassy. He realized that, with two embassies to man and all of the female members of our staff removed, we had enough clerical personnel to comply with only the barest minimum of routine requirements.

We had only one male stenographer, who was also code clerk, acting consul, general file clerk, and, in addition, prepared many of the routine reports. The rest of our clerical and secretarial help consisted of Soviet citizens, who could be entrusted with no duties which involved matters of security. In one case, a young Russian female clerk was so badgered by the Soviet authorities to deliver information, which she did not possess, that she married our young American clerk.

Mr. Henderson apparently was not one to make allowances for inflexible conditions. When I sent my telegram asking to go home, Mr. Henderson was busily engaged in writing a voluminous report. He gave me a copy on September 29. It was complete and damning, citing many, many omissions and failures of which

* While Ambassador Standley was enroute from Moscow with the important message which Roosevelt awaited with some apprehension, Hopkins cabled Harriman [then in London] that "None of us knows exactly why Standley is coming home." Robert E. Sherwood, *Roosevelt and Hopkins* (New York: Harper & Bros., 1948), p. 640.

we were fully cognizant. True enough, he gave reasons for failures, but still the report irritated me. With such a small staff, I could see no way to improve our administration. Accordingly, it was with a measure of satisfaction that I received orders to leave Mr. Henderson in charge during my absence.

I sent for Loy and handed him the Embassy copy of his report. "Loy, I hope that you'll be able to correct some of these deficiencies during my absence."

Loy realized that I was annoyed, but he took it in his stride, like the fine gentleman that he is. "Mr. Ambassador, I'll do my best."

We had already prepared a farewell party for Loy, and it was too late to call it off. And so, in effect, I had the odd experience of giving myself my own *bon voyage* that same evening, while the honored guest stayed on.

The interval before my departure was one of those periods when it seemed as if everything happened at once. I called on Mr. Vishinsky in the Foreign Office, told him of my orders, and asked him to arrange an interview with Mr. Molotov and Mr. Stalin in Moscow as soon as possible. The same afternoon, Mr. Henderson called on Mr. Zarubin, officer-in-charge of American affairs in the Ministry, and assumed his status as Chargé d'Affaires. The next day, I called to tell Mr. Lozovsky "Farewell."

On October 3, Mr. Henderson and I went to Moscow in General Bradley's plane. We immediately went into conference with all members of our staff present in Moscow to discuss the general implications of my trip home. During this conference, I learned of one of the most interesting events of my tour of duty in Russia.

At the gate of the Kremlin, the Russians maintained a mailbox into which, from time to time, hopeful correspondents dropped letters to Marshal Stalin and other government officials. These epistles were usually ignored, but, on October 3rd, Henry Cassidy of the Associated Press, dropped a letter into the Kremlin box. At thirty minutes past midnight that same night, he was summoned to the Press Department and delivered the following letter:

Dear Mr. Cassidy:
   Owing to the pressure of work and my consequent inability to grant you an interview, I shall confine myself to a brief written answer to your questions.
   1. What place does the possibility of a Second Front occupy in the Soviet estimates of the current situation?
   ANSWER: A most important place; one might say a place of first-rate importance.

2. To what extent is Allied aid to the Soviet Union proving effective and what could be done to amplify and improve this aid?

ANSWER: As compared to the aid which the Soviet Union is giving to the Allies by drawing upon itself the main force of the German fascist armies, the aid of the Allies to the Soviet Union has so far been little effective. In order to amplify and improve this aid, only one thing is required: that the Allies fulfill their obligations fully and on time.

3. What remains of the Soviet capacity for resistance?

ANSWER: I think that the Soviet capacity of resisting the German brigands is in strength not less, if not greater, than the capacity of fascist Germany or of any other aggressive power to secure for itself world domination.

With respect,

/s/ J. STALIN

October 3, 1942

Of course, we all realized that Mr. Stalin would not have answered this letter of Henry Cassidy's so promptly, or at all, unless Henry had happened to ask some questions on which Mr. Stalin wished to propagandize at the time. Certainly this letter fully confirmed my impression during the Willkie visit that the Second Front agitation he met everywhere was the result of centralized direction.

The other information I received was bad news—General Bradley reported that the Russians had closed the ALSIB air route; his mission was a failure. He, too, had received a secret letter, from President Roosevelt for delivery to Marshal Stalin. Controlling my irritation, for I realized this "by-pass" was none of Bradley's doing, I said, "Fine, General, you shall go with me when I see Mr. Stalin."

Late in the afternoon, October 5th, I took Loy Henderson and Eddie Page and went to Mr. Molotov's office in the Kremlin. After we were seated, I told Mr. Molotov of my projected trip home. "You are no doubt aware of the interruption in the flow of Lend-Lease supplies to Russia. My mission will be to try to remove some of the obstacles to this delivery. As you doubtless realize, some of these obstacles are of a purely military nature. For that reason, I am taking home with me my Military and Naval Attachés and also my Second Secretary. I would like to suggest that it might be very helpful if the Soviet officers who have been the liaison officers with my Attachés could go to Washington with us. While in the United States, they could visit war plants and factories and have an opportunity to see for themselves the extent of our war effort and obtain a better understanding of our problems."

Mr. Molotov looked up from scribbling a note on the pad in front of him. "I'll take up your suggestion, but we have Naval and Military Attachés in Washington. I doubt the necessity for sending liaison officers with you."

I had to smile at this remark. "You made a trip to the United States not so long ago, although you have a Soviet Ambassador in Washington. I believe a visit by the liaison officers actually handling these matters might be helpful."

Mr. Molotov returned my smile. "I took no Naval or Military Attachés with me."

Pleasantly rebuffed, I changed the subject. "I would like very much to see Mr. Stalin before I leave in order to take with me to President Roosevelt any personal message he might like to send. I hope to get away next Thursday, October 8th. I realize that Mr. Stalin is very busy, but, if possible, I would like to see him soon enough to leave that day. I will expedite my work in Washington as much as possible, and I hope to return soon. You know of that stratosphere service being established between London and Moscow? Perhaps I can return that way."

"I hope you will have a quick journey and a safe return," Mr. Molotov observed pleasantly.

"Thank you. I am planning to fly to Teheran in General Bradley's plane. I trust that you will facilitate its departure as much as may be possible."

"There will be no objections or obstacles."

"Thank you, Mr. Molotov, for the cooperation you have given me, and for the many courtesies you have extended. In my absence, I hope that the same courtesies will be extended to Mr. Henderson."

"Of course. I will be glad to see Mr. Henderson at any time."

I had nothing further to discuss, but Mr. Molotov seemed to have something on his mind. To lead him on, I asked about the general situation in the Soviet Union and he gave me an interesting survey of the situation on the Russian front. Although the Nazi troops had smashed into Stalingrad twenty days before, fanatical defenders still held them at bay. He estimated that 200,000 Germans had lost their lives before that city. The Germans in the Caucasus had been stopped in the Valley of the Terek. "They cannot be strong everywhere," he said. "We will hold Stalingrad and drive them out of the Caucasus."

"Have these facts been presented to the officials in London and Washington, who are responsible for dealing with such matters?" I asked.

"Mr. Stalin informed Mr. Willkie as to the situation and he was a Special Representative of your President."

"I see," I said.

"These facts were also discussed with your President in connection with the Protocol for the Second Lend-Lease Agreement for 1942-43. I was given a copy of this Protocol last May, but it has never been signed."

"Who was responsible for the delay?" I asked.

Mr. Molotov shrugged his shoulders. "The fault was not on our side. As you well know, the Beaverbrook-Harriman Mission drew up the first Protocol and signed it in a few days. It expired on June thirtieth. Now, July, August and September have gone by with no Protocol in effect. I understand that the new Protocol is still under consideration by the Americans and the British."

I told him I would do what I could to expedite completion of the agreement.

"What was the effect of Mr. Willkie's visit to the Soviet Union?" he asked.

"Mr. Willkie was highly pleased with his visit, Mr. Molotov, and I feel sure that the President was, too. I know that Washington was most appreciative of the courtesies and hospitality extended to Mr. Willkie. There can be no doubt that his visit will yield helpful results."

With a further exchange of pleasantries and expressions of good will, we took our leave. The next morning, the Foreign Office informed me that I would be received by Mr. Stalin at 7:30 P.M.

I took Eddie Page and General Follett Bradley with me to the Kremlin. Soon, we were seated in the usual room with Mr. Stalin at the end of the long conference table, doodling, and Mr. Pavlov beside him bending an attentive ear to our every word. As the first order of business, General Bradley presented the President's letter to Mr. Stalin; he glanced at it and put it back into the envelope without comment. In the discussion which followed, I learned for the first time some details of the ALSIB air route discussions. After several months of "on-and-off" negotiations the ALSIB air route was "off the track" again; our own War Department, irritated at obstruction and delay, had ordered it closed. The negotiations, which I had initiated in my first interview with Mr. Stalin back in April, had been "approved in principle" but had failed in negotiations on the military level.*

How isolated diplomats are in the Soviet Union! From Larry LeSueur's diary for October 5, 1942, published in his book *Twelve Months that Changed the World*, I discovered that he knew much more about this air route *at the time* than the American Ambassador, as witness:

> October 5 . . . I'm told that numbers of bombers are now being flown into Russia across the narrow Bering Strait between Alaska and Siberia, where the nearest Russian and American islands are only a mile apart. Scores of planes are also coming in across the Caucasus Mountains from Teheran after flying across a series of South American and African air bases all the way from Miami. The Soviet Union is continually expanding its tremendous Red Air Force to supply pilots for the front and to fly the machines in from Alaska and Persia. Some women are being used as aerial navigators on the ferry flights. It's clear that after the war the Russians will possess one of the largest corps of trained pilots among the United Nations.

After this discussion, I said to Mr. Stalin, "I have been called home for consultation to further the United States' efforts to help the Soviet Union carry on the war."

I went on to give him generally the same information that I had given Mr. Molotov. "How long are you going to stay?" was his comment.

"Only long enough to give the President my views and come back. On my return, I'll shift my base to Moscow instead of Kuibyshev."

"Pray God you may."

He was silent for some moments, looking down at his doodling. I noticed that there were streaks of grey in the once jet black hair and lines in his face that the dim lights of the Willkie banquet had hidden from me. Joseph Stalin, like any man with many cares, was growing old. But I could feel no compassion for him. So was I.

"Have you any message for President Roosevelt or any suggestions as to how conditions can be improved?" I asked presently.

He looked up at me challengingly. "I gave those figures to Mr. Willkie. Didn't he tell you?"

"Mr. Willkie neither gave me any figures nor told me what took place at his interview with you," I said hotly. "On the contrary,

* See Chapter XV for the full story.

he said that the information was so secret that he could not reveal it even to the American Ambassador."

Mr. Stalin returned to his doodling. Having in mind my own unenviable situation in Moscow, I asked Mr. Stalin, "Has the information you gave to Mr. Willkie been made known to the Russian Ambassador in Washington? If your Ambassador does not know the contents of the message Mr. Willkie is taking to President Roosevelt, it may lead to confusion in handling the Protocol in Washington."

"Of course, Litvinov hasn't been told about it," Mr. Stalin put in bluntly. "I gave it to Mr. Willkie to take to the President. Such matters can best be handled separately and directly between President Roosevelt and myself."

My conversation with Stalin had been on such a friendly basis that I said, "I am planning to leave for home day after tomorrow. I wonder if you would like me to bring you a souvenir from the United States."

"But I have everything I want here in Russia," Mr. Stalin said, apparently surprised. "I do not need a souvenir from the United States."

"I note that you are an inveterate smoker. Would you like me to buy you some good American pipe tobacco?"

"We have plenty of good tobacco in Russia." Mr. Stalin pushed back his chair and stood up. "I will give you a letter for President Roosevelt," he said, by way of dismissal.

We rose early on the morning of October 8th, breakfasted, and packed the last few items. Most of the house staff were waiting at the door to see me off. As we drove to the airport, I wondered if I would ever be coming this way again. It was hard to guess. I had to tell Franklin Roosevelt some unpleasant facts and he didn't take kindly to such.

We took off in General Bradley's bomber at nine, Loy Henderson, Captain Duncan, Commander Frankel, and I. Back in Kuibyshev, I completed turning over affairs to Mr. Henderson. I also visited my aged friend, Dr. Terekov, at the Botanical Gardens and gave him a present of a package of tea.

I took leave of my other friends in Kuibyshev as if I were leaving for the last time, and made my final call on Mr. Lozovsky at the Foreign Office.

Early morning October 10th was set as our time of departure. On the way to the military airport, we were held up for twenty minutes while a long line of civilian prisoners guarded by soldiers with fixed bayonets trudged by. I was told that they were headed for construction work at the new Kuibyshev airport, just then taking shape on the outskirts of the city.

I shook hands with each of my NKVD boys and told him "Goodbye." With Captain Jack Duncan, Colonel Mike Michella, Commander Frankel, and Second Secretary Eddie Page, I took off in General Bradley's bomber at 7:21 A.M. for Teheran and home. Our route was the usual one—from Teheran via Baghdad, Jerusalem, Bethlehem, the Red Sea, down the Mediterranean coast to Cairo, then to Khartoum, across the waist of Africa and up the coast to Liberia, across the Atlantic to Natal and north to Miami. In general, the trip was uninteresting except for a few incidents of pleasure and color.

In Teheran, Jack Duncan and I were put up at the American Embassy, with Ambassador and Mrs. Dreyfus as hospitable and courteous hosts. I have always considered them one of the most charming and efficient couples in our Foreign Service. They gave us a nice dinner, attended by the Russian and Chinese Ambassadors and the Iranian Prime Minister. With such delightful hosts, I have never understood why President Roosevelt left his quarters in the American Embassy during the Teheran conference to accept the hospitality of Marshal Stalin in the heavily guarded compound of the Russian Embassy. In retrospect, it seems as though it may have been an early sign of the physical and mental deterioration which eventually led to his death.

In Cairo, Eddie Page and I were put up at Ambassador Kirk's residence. One of the high lights of our stay in Cairo was a long talk I had with Field Marshal Jan Smutts of South Africa, who was tremendously interested in everything I had to tell him about Russia. At a dinner given by Ambassador Kirk on October 11th, I met the British Ambassador, Lord Lamson, and his lady. I visited General Maxwell's Industrial School for training the teen-agers of Cairo in the mechanical trades. I also met Air Marshal Tedder, Chief of the Royal Air Force, and our own Lewis Brereton, Commanding General of the Fifth United States Air Force, which was supporting the British Eighth Army in North Africa. Brereton is a graduate of the Naval Academy.

Our next stop of interest was at Accra on the African Gold Coast. Pat Hurley, President Roosevelt's Republican diplomatic General, was also remaining overnight at Accra. We were entertained by Governor Burns, the British Resident, at his quarters. But the event of our stopover was the long evening I spent briefing General Hurley on Russian affairs in general and Moscow in particular. He, too, was on a special mission for the President, the purpose of which was too secret for me to know. As I turned in much too late that night, I reflected with a chuckle, "That's one Special Representative who will no doubt by-pass the American Ambassador, but Loy Henderson, not me."

At 4 P.M., October 19th, we flew into the Miami airport in an Army C-54. I was met by Captain H. J. Benson, commander of naval activities in the Miami area. I'll never forget the exhilaration I felt at being, after so long in Russia, once again in an American city—the theater marqueés, the winking neon signs, the brightly-lighted windows of the shops we passed, even in those war days displaying customer goods so beautiful and varied that they were not even a dream of the "common people" of Russia, the friendly crowd as Captain Benson conducted us along the street to a "Grand Hotel," the like of which was not even on the planning boards in the Soviet Capital!

I found myself looking ahead and behind me for my NKVD boys. But this was America; nobody followed me. The crowds along the street and in the hotel were liberally sprinkled with khaki uniforms of Army, Navy and Marine Corps. Something new had been added—service women in their trim blue and khaki uniforms, any one of them looking ever so much more *chic* than any women in uniform I saw in the Soviet Union.

"This is wonderful," I said to Benson as we went across the plush lobby of the big hotel toward the dining room. "This is marvelous. This is an experience that every American, who thinks there is something to this Communist business, ought to have."

As we took off from the magnificent Miami airport at 11 P.M. in an Eastern Air Line transport, I contrasted it mentally with the large but primitive airport in Moscow. We arrived at the Washington Airport at 4:50 A.M. after sitting up all night. I was terribly tired from the trip, but I was buoyed up by excitement. A phone call to my son-in-law, Commander Jim Byrne, brought me a car and the news that my wife would arrive at Union Station at 7:30 A.M.

I will not soon forget the sight of the Washington Monument through the haze of dawn as we drove across the Potomac, and the dome of the Capitol shining in the early morning sunlight. It was good to be back in America where a man came and went as he pleased and thought and talked and did what he pleased, without constant supervision of seeing and unseen eyes.

My wife's train was late. It was nine-thirty before I saw Evelyn coming up the platform between the tracks and swept her up into my arms. "Oh, Hal, it's been so long," she said. "It seems like an age, much longer than any other separation we ever had."

It had seemed terribly long to me, too, but now it was over and I was home again, where so often I had longed to be.

After checking in at the Mayflower Hotel and a brief rest, I took Mrs. Standley to lunch at the Army and Navy Club. There I chanced to meet General James H. Burns, who will be remembered as a member of the Beaverbrook-Harriman Mission, and Harry Hopkins, Executive Director of Lend-Lease. He had with him General Charles M. Wesson, who represented the War Department in the Lend-Lease Administration.

They shook hands cordially and seemed glad to see me. General Burns asked about Lend-Lease to Russia. "What about the new Protocol?" I asked. "The Russians are really exercised about it. And you'll have to do something about Faymonville. If I return to Moscow as Ambassador, you'll have to put him under my control. I can't have him running wild around Moscow the way he has been."

They excused themselves hurriedly and walked away.

I reported to Secretary Cordell Hull the next morning, little more than a formal "check-in," as he was so occupied, but I took advantage of the opportunity to tell him how detrimental to the smooth conduct of diplomatic affairs was such a junket as Mr. Willkie made.

I was assigned the office and secretariat of Secretary Hull's Special Assistant, Jimmy Dunn, who was on leave. Late that afternoon, my new secretary brought me news that I was to have lunch with the President in his office the next day.

My next step was to inform the Chief Clerk that I wanted him to obtain a copy of Bailey's *Botanical Dictionary*.

I began a round of calls and conferences with various heads of divisions and sections of the State Department, which was to continue for several weeks, briefing them as to present conditions in Russia, the war situation on the Russian front, the purpose of my trip. I took occasion to tell all and sundry about the many headaches caused by the Willkie junket and to urge that each one of them use his influence to prevent similar future visits by Special Representatives, unless they were instructed to work closely with and through the Ambassador. They listened with comforting sympathy but I knew that, as in Moscow with Premier Stalin and his bureaucrats, the decision rested higher up—with the Boss.

I had my own pet project to foster—my plan to educate the Russian people about America by use of selected American motion pictures. In an extensive selling campaign, I had many hours of conference with the Cultural Relations Division of the State Department. I also obtained appointments with other interested officials—the Chief of Naval Operations, the Chief of Staff of the Army, Mr. Robert Sherwood of the Office of War Information (OWI), and President Roosevelt. No one seemed very enthusiastic, but I finally convinced the State Department that my plan was "feasible and acceptable."

Unable to obtain the services of young Doug Fairbanks, I searched my mind for a substitute and hit upon John Young, with whom I had been associated when he handled overseas publicity for the New York World's Fair. With John's contacts in the radio and motion picture industries, I felt sure that he would make an ideal assistant to put my plan into operation.

I persuaded the Chief of Naval Personnel to commission John a lieutenant commander in the Naval Reserve.

Full of enthusiasm, John wanted to begin immediately to obtain a portfolio of motion pictures, but, for the success of the program, I felt that he needed an understanding of the problem which only a short tour in the Soviet Union would give. In the few days available in Washington, he did obtain an unedited copy of the combat films of the North African invasion.

I arrived at the East Wing entrance to the White House at 12:30 P.M. the next day. Ten minutes later, I was ushered into the President's private office. I thought that FDR looked remarkably well, his ruddy complexion and husky upper body a striking contrast to the sallow face and wasted body of Harry Hopkins, who lay back in a big armchair in the corner beyond the Chief's desk. "Hello, Bill," the President said. "What brings you home?"

"Trouble, Chief," I said. "Plenty of trouble."

I went around the gadget littered desk. The President was seated on his wheel chair and didn't have on his leg braces. He shook hands with me cordially. I exchanged greetings with Harry Hopkins and took the chair offered.

"I believe you have a letter for me," he said.

I pulled the Stalin letter from an inner pocket and handed it to him.

He tore open the two envelopes in which it was sealed, glanced

at its two pages and threw it into a basket. "Nothing new! Same information we had from Willkie and Stalin's recent despatch."*
I thought that he sounded relieved.

I never saw a copy of that letter. It was ten years before I learned the contents of the October 7 despatch, which can be paraphrased as follows:

> Difficulties in the deliveries come from shortage of tonnage. To relieve tonnage situation, Soviet Government is willing to agree to certain curtailment of deliveries of American war material to Soviet Union. We are willing to discard for present all deliveries of tanks, artillery, munitions, pistols, etc. But at the same time we are in great need of increase in deliveries of pursuit planes of modern type (such as "Aircobra") and of securing under all conditions certain other supplies. "Kittyhawk" planes do not stand the fight against present German pursuits.

The despatch then went on to enumerate specific numbers of planes, trucks, explosives, aluminum, grain, etc., which Marshal Stalin considered essential. He noted that he had already talked these matters over with Mr. Willkie. The despatch concluded:

> As to the situation at the front, you certainly know that during the recent months our situation in the South and especially in the region of Stalingrad has worsened because we are short of planes, most important of all, pursuit planes. The Germans prove to have a great reserve of planes. They have in the South at least a two-to-one superiority in the air which prevents us from covering our troops. . . . The experience of the war has indicated that the bravest armies become helpless if they are not protected from blows from the air.

I also learned recently that negotiations were then going forward to station British and American air forces in the Caucasus. Who conducted them, I don't know, for the matter never came to my attention. The Russians did not agree to this project until the Teheran Conference.

* The message carried by Standley, however, proved to be substantially the same as the message dated October 7 quoted above. Roosevelt then cabled Stalin that he had received from the Ambassador a full report on the "fighting qualities and strength of your Army and the urgency of your need for supplies." Stalin's brief acknowledgement of this message was delivered by Litvinov to Hopkins for the President. Hopkins was now more than ever "President Roosevelt's own personal Foreign Office." Robert E. Sherwood, *Roosevelt and Hopkins* (New York: Harper & Bros., 1948), p. 640.

One of the White House staff brought in our plate luncheons. I ate off a leaf pulled out of the President's desk; Harry Hopkins from his lap, relaxed against the cushions as if deathly tired. While we ate our luncheon, I made my report to the President as to the general situation in Russia, my estimate that the Russians would hold the Germans about where they were for the Winter, would drive them out of the Caucasus and defeat them at Stalingrad. I told him about the clamor in Moscow for a Second Front in Europe in 1942 and expressed my uncertainty as to what course of action Stalin would take if the war continued into the next summer without tangible help from the Western Allies.

President Roosevelt seemed to be more interested in Marshal Stalin, the man. He asked me many questions about him, his attitudes, whims, eccentricities. He questioned me closely as to my opinion of Stalin's intelligence and shrewdness.

As the waiter brought in pie and coffee, I began to tell him about Lend-Lease. For the first time, Harry Hopkins showed an interest. "The Russians are terribly upset over the decreased deliveries of Lend-Lease materials, Mr. President," I told him. "Mr. Molotov stressed the Second Protocol. I told him I'd do what I could to expedite completion of the agreement."

"It's a very complicated matter," Harry Hopkins said. "They keep changing their requests. We're committed right up to the limit of full production."

"What can we do?" the President asked.

"Stop acting like a Santa Claus, Chief," I replied, still annoyed at the impossible situation in Moscow. "And let's get something from Stalin in return. Faymonville agrees to give them everything in the world they ask for, from a darning needle to a tire factory, which they won't have operating ten years after the war. My advice is to treat Stalin like an adult, keep any promises we make to him, but insist that he keep his promises, too. And if he doesn't make good within a reasonable time, hold out on him until he does. The Soviets will take advantage of any other course of action."

The President and Harry Hopkins exchanged glances. "What's the trouble with General Faymonville?" Hopkins put in.

"I'm glad you asked that, Harry. There's nothing wrong with Faymonville. We get along fine, personally. It's the system. As you know, Faymonville is completely independent of me. Military information which should be handled by Colonel Michella is given to the Russians by Faymonville without the exchange of information which would be obtained if my Military Attaché handled it.

I've spoken to Faymonville repeatedly about this, but he maintains that he is unable to resist the demands of the Russians and
still carry on his Lend-Lease job. General Marshall got so exercised over the situation that I was asked to take the question up
with the Russian Foreign Office. General Faymonville seemed to
be agreeable, but by-passing the Embassy and the Ambassador
continued. When I objected again, Faymonville told me that, as
Lend-Lease Representative, he was only a communication agent,
that he had to forward requests received from the Russians to the
Lend-Lease Administration. When the Lend-Lease Administration sends the information back, he is bound to deliver it. But he
doesn't seem to feel at all responsible for keeping me informed. In
practically every case, his negotiations with the Russians are completed and approved through Lend-Lease before I even hear of an
issue. You can't run a successful diplomatic mission in a country
like Russia, Chief, and operate like that. Face counts too much."

"Is that why you asked to come home for consultation?" Harry
Hopkins asked.

"Only part of it. Using Lend-Lease as an excuse was the State
Department's idea. I'd rather have told Mr. Molotov quite frankly
that I was annoyed at their continual by-passing. Such as the Willkie junket," I said to the President. I went on to give him a brief
review of the many ways and times Mr. Willkie went around me
or over my head, his deprecatory remarks before important Russians, and his general disregard and contempt for the office of the
Ambassador. "When I left Moscow, such by-passing by Special
Representatives and other American agencies in Moscow not under the Ambassador's control had proven to be so destructive to
my prestige that I doubt my continued effectiveness in my mission.
It must look to people in Moscow, as if I no longer enjoy the confidence of my Government."

"Of course, you have my confidence, Bill," the President said,
tapping a cigarette on his desk and fitting it into a long holder.
He looked around at Hopkins. "We'll have to do something about
that, Harry." Hopkins said nothing.

"Drastic action must be taken to reestablish my prestige in Moscow or I can't return as Ambassador," I said firmly.

The President lighted his cigarette and leaned back with it tilted
up at a familiar angle. "What do you suggest, Bill?"

"The Russian officials must be given evidence of your complete
confidence in me, Chief."

"What do you want?"

I ticked off on my fingers the conditions which I felt must be satisfied to accomplish this result.

First, my Naval Attaché should be made a Rear Admiral.

Second, my Military Attaché should be made a Brigadier General, to match General Faymonville's rank and prestige.

Third, General Faymonville must be directed to report to me for duty and be under my administrative direction and control.

A long silence descended on the little office. The President looked around at Harry Hopkins, who sat with his head back on the cushion of the armchair, his eyes closed, his face as wax-pale as death. "We'll see what we can do, Bill," the President said, letting the radiance of his smile warm me once again.

I left his office feeling that, although no definite commitment had been made, the President was in general agreement with my suggestions. I felt justified in laying the groundwork for the desired changes which would lead to my return to Moscow.

Admiral Ernie King, Chief of Naval Operations, agreed immediately to spot-promote Jack Duncan to Rear Admiral. General George Marshall, Chief of Staff of the Army, said, "Brigadier General is not the usual rank of an officer who has duty as Military Attaché, but if that is the way you want it, Bill, Michella will be promoted."

I went to see General Burns and Ed Stettinius in Lend-Lease. They seemed as cooperative as the military leaders, but appearance was not translated into action. For weeks, I waited for Faymonville's orders without results.

In the meanwhile, I appeared before the Joint Chiefs of Staff. After I was seated in the "witness chair," Admiral Leahy greeted me and said, "Bill, you know about our failure to deliver thirty Aircobras to the Russians as promised. We still don't feel able to make that delivery. What do you think about giving them thirteen B-17's instead?"

I thought back to Marshal Stalin's vitriolic speech at the Willkie banquet. "No, Bill," I said, "that would be a big mistake."

"Why, Admiral?" General Arnold put in.

"Because they need fighters, not bombers. Let's face the facts. Treat Marshal Stalin like a grown-up, not a child. Keep your promises to him and make him keep his. The Russians'll take advantage of any other course of action."

In the light of subsequent events, this advice would seem to have been prophetic.

In reviewing my diary during the period that I was home for

consultation, I am amazed at the number and wide variety of contacts I made. Since some of these are important to the later story of my mission to Moscow, I will mention them briefly.

For reasons of State Department protocol, I exchanged calls with the British and Russian Ambassadors, Mr. Wilgress, Canadian Minister to the USSR, and Mr. Hershell Johnson, U. S. Minister to Sweden.

I had conferences with:

The Polish Ambassador during which we discussed the Polish Question in all of its ramifications.

Mr. Robert Sherwood, head of the Office of War Information, and Major General William J. Donovan, Director of the Office of Strategic Services, both of whom wanted to establish representatives of their organizations in Moscow, to which I said "No," unless they came to Moscow as attachés of the Embassy under my direct administrative control.

Mr. E. V. Pittman, War Production Board, and later Head of the Rubber Mission to Moscow. I hope that he found more substitute and synthetic rubber know-how in Soviet Russian than I.

Captain C. S. Stephenson, of the Navy Medical Corps, who later headed a Medical Mission to the Middle East.

Dr. Michail, Department of Agriculture, who became agricultural attaché on the Embassy Staff.

Mrs. Laura Puffer Morgan, who wanted to come to Moscow to work for world peace.

Mr. Irsky, member of the Soviet Purchasing Commission in the United States, who was interested in my plan to educate the Russian people through the medium of American motion pictures.

Not the least important, certainly the most enjoyable and of frequent occurrence during the lovely fall weather of 1942 in the Washington and New York areas, was the renewal of my friendship and competition with old golfing companions, including Secretary of the Navy Frank Knox, Assistant Secretary John Sullivan, Captain Frank Beatty, Jay Hopkins, Ellsworth Alford, and Walt Tuckerman at Burning Tree Country Club; Bob Graniss and Henry Sutphen at Garden City; Orie Wightman of Hudson River; and Bill Morgan, Ned Kolbers, and Captain Adolphus Staton at Chevy Chase Country Club. Our pursuit of the old Scotch game helped to while away many a moment which might otherwise have been very dull, while I waited for Harry Hopkins and the Lend-Lease Administration to make up their individual and collective minds about General Faymonville.

I was in frequent conference with Ed Stettinius, General James Burns, and General Charley Wesson, without results. I soon realized that they were dragging their feet, but I didn't know why.*

One of my most pleasant "consultations" took place during the evening of Armistice Day at the home of Dr. Stanley Hornbeck, State Department adviser on Far Eastern Affairs, whom I had known well since my tour of duty as Chief of Naval Operations. Also present were two former Ambassadors to Russia, Joe Davies and Bill Bullitt, Joseph Grew, our last Ambassador to Japan, and Bill Leahy, who succeeded me as Chief of Naval Operations, and was then Chief of Staff to the President.

Bill Bullitt aired his views on how to win the war, which were interesting as always, but the conversation degenerated into a discussion of the causes of the war. Bill Leahy became impatient and said, "I don't care a damn what caused the war. We're in it. What I'm interested in is future prospects. How about it, Bill?"

I gave him my standard prediction of that period—the Red Army would hold out against the Nazis through the winter. I couldn't predict what would happen in Russia if the War continued into the Summer, without marked improvement in the situation. I took the opportunity to tell this "good right arm" of the President that the recent visit of Wendell Willkie to Moscow had been decidedly detrimental to Allied prestige in Moscow, and that Mr. Willkie had made a poor impression on the Russians.

I was not surprised to hear Bill Leahy say, "During the 1940 campaign I thought he made a good Republican candidate for President. But after I met and talked to him at some length, I lost my high opinion of him."

It was during this period of waiting for Lend-Lease to issue Faymonville's orders that the Chief Clerk came to me. "I have gone to all the book stores in Washington, Admiral, and none of them have a copy of Bailey's *Botanical Dictionary*. I will have to order it from the publishers."

I promptly replied, "Get it at any cost."

Growing more and more impatient at the delay, I put in for

---

* No matter how much you are "on the inside track" in Washington, you never know all that's going on behind the scenes. Ten years later, I was unpleasantly surprised to learn that certain influential persons were already after my Ambassadorial scalp. During this period, General Burns wrote a memorandum to his boss, Harry Hopkins, which included the following suggestion: "Send to Russia an Ambassador of top rank as to national standing, vision, ability, and willingness to serve the country first."

leave of absence. In the meantime, I received an invitation from the New York *Herald Tribune* to address their Forum.

The fears and hopes of that period are interesting. The program for a new League of Nations or United Nations Organization had not yet been announced, but we were either allies or enemies of nearly every nation on earth, including the USSR. Some form of international organization for peace was obviously indicated. I concluded my speech as follows:

> When final victory is ours, each one of the United Nations will have contributed at various times and under various circumstances its full share. I am confident that the ties we have forged in battle will be translated into even closer cooperation and unity in peace and in the great task of peaceful reconstruction that will be before us in the future.

How my viewpoint changed during the next few months!

My departure from Washington was postponed by the news that my daughter, Evelyn, had decided to get married. I saw her through her embarkation on the sea of matrimony at the National Cathedral, paid my son, Bill, a visit in Norfolk, and, leaving Eddie Page in the State Department to look out for my interests and keep me informed, my wife and I left for our home in San Diego on November 22nd.

On December 7, I received a telegram from Eddie:

> No evident action toward issuing orders to General Faymonville. Recommend you return to Washington immediately.

I arrived in Washington on December 8th, reported my return from leave to Secretary Hull, and found myself in the center of the most skillfully operated administrative whirligig I have ever experienced in the bureaucratic Washington wonderland. I went to see Bill Leahy on December 9th. Bill told me, "As far as I know, absolutely nothing has been done about ordering the head of the United States Supply Mission in Moscow to report to you for duty. I suggest that you go to see Ed Stettinius."

Ed Stettinius passed me on to Charley Wesson and General Burns. Wesson said he couldn't do anything without Harry Hopkins' okay. I managed to get an appointment with Harry Hopkins for 5 o'clock, December 10th.

I found him in his office-bedroom in the White House, seated behind his card table desk, his bed littered with papers, notes, memorandums and pamphlets.

"Hello, Admiral," he said, waving me to a seat without rising. I've never seen a man look so sick and still keep producing. And yet, I reflected, he has more power in the United States than anyone but the President and probably more influence and real power among the Western Allies than anyone but the President and Winston Churchill.

"How are you, Harry?" I said, as I seated myself.

He ignored the question. "When are you returning to Moscow, Admiral?"

"That depends on you, Harry."

"How's that?"

I grinned ruefully. "The President directed that orders be issued to General Faymonville to report to me for duty. I have been informed by Mr. Stettinius that *you* are the only person in Washington who can issue such orders. When those orders have been issued, I will leave for Moscow."

Harry leaned back and closed his eyes for a moment. "See Jim Burns tomorrow, Admiral. It will be arranged. We need you back in Moscow very badly just now."

I paid another visit to General Burns the next morning and we reached an agreement on the orders, which were issued the next day:

telegram send—plain—December 12, 1942.
To: The Embassy, Moscow
For: Faymonville
From: Stettinius, Lend-Lease
    1. The function of the United States Supply Mission in the USSR is to represent in that country the Office of Lend-Lease Administration. In performance of this function, the United States Supply Mission shall concern itself with the problems of supply to the Soviet Union under the terms of the Lend-Lease Act and under such other related agreements and protocols which have been or are subsequently to be agreed upon by the United States and the Soviet Union.
    2. The Chief of the Diplomatic Mission is the representative of United States Government in the Soviet Union, who is responsible for the general overall coordination and supervision of the activities of all agencies operating in the USSR including the United States Supply Mission.
    3. The Chief of the Supply Mission will be subject to overall coordination and supervision by the Chief of the Diplomatic Mission,

will keep the latter fully informed on all activities, will consult with and be guided by his advice on any proposed action on questions that are political in character or affect established policies, and will ask his assistance when necessary in the solution of any questions of sufficient importance to justify his participation.

4. In conformity with the above policy, the Chief of the Supply Mission will report to the Chief of the Diplomatic Mission, USSR.

HULL

These orders left something to be desired but I felt that they were strong and specific enough to control Faymonville's activities. Once they were issued, Jack Duncan was immediately spot-promoted to Rear Admiral and Michella to Brigadier General. The State Department finally approved my plan to educate the Russian people through the medium of American motion pictures. John Young was inducted into the naval service as a Lieutenant-Commander, spot-promoted to Commander, and assigned to duty as Assistant Naval Attaché for public relations.

Upon return from my leave, I was informed that the Chief Clerk had succeeded in obtaining a Bailey's *Botanical Dictionary*. Instead of being, as I presumed, one small volume, this botanical dictionary consisted of three large volumes, each about the size of a college standard dictionary. I also received a package containing five pounds of Edgewood smoking tobacco and a smoking set, which friends in New York wanted me to present to Marshal Stalin in their name.

The word soon got around that I was returning to Moscow, and again I was besieged by visitors with an axe to grind in Russia. One of the most interesting incidents was a luncheon with Ambassador Litvinov at the Russian Embassy. Mr. Litvinov gave me a package for his wife (an English woman whose maiden name was Ivy Low) and a letter for his daughter, both of whom were in Moscow.

Litvinov and I discussed not only Lend-Lease and Russian-American affairs, but also world affairs in general and the possible cooperation of our two countries in the post-war rehabilitation of war-shattered countries. Our conversation was going along pleasantly and amicably, when Ambassador Litvinov said, abruptly, "I find a great deal of prejudice against Russia among the American people, which I am at a loss to understand. Can you tell me why?"

"Why Mr. Ambassador," I replied, "the reason for such prejudice should not be hard to discover. Since the Russian Revolution and up to the hour that the Nazis invaded the USSR, the American public has been inundated with a flood of Communist propaganda and the theory of Karl Marx that Communism stands for the destruction of all other types of government by violent revolution. The Third Comintern, to which the Communist Party in America pledged its allegiance, openly endorses this policy. It is the understanding and belief of the people of the United States that the Third Comintern is supported financially by your government and is nothing more or less than an agency of your government and the Russian Communist Party.

"Now, we, in America, happen to like our own form of government. We have thrived and developed the agriculture and industry of our country to a high state of efficiency under our Constitution. We have attained the highest standard of living in the world. Our people enjoy more privileges of individual freedom and personal liberty than in any other country in the world. Naturally we resent the efforts of any group or government to change our form of government by any means other than those provided in our Constitution. This is, I am sure, the sole reason for the prejudice against the USSR which you have observed."

Mr. Litvinov launched into a long dissertation intended to prove to me that the Soviet Government had no influence with the Third Comintern. "It's true that the Communist Party of Russia is a member of the Third Comintern, just as the Communist Party of the United States has a membership, but the Russian Communist Party has no more control, responsibility, or authority over the Third Comintern than any other member. You must realize that the Soviet Government is in no way responsible for the actions and propaganda of the Third Comintern."

I listened to him attentively. When he had finished, I looked across at his round, impassive face, speculating at what went on behind that bland mask. "Now, Mr. Ambassador, I believe that you will agree that I am an American of average intelligence. I have had much more experience in international and world affairs than the average American. I have lived in Soviet Russia and I have seen something of the actual working of the Soviet system and I think I have a pretty good understanding of the direct influence of the Russian Communist Party upon the government of Soviet Russia. If you can't convince me that the Soviet Government has no control over the policies and actions of the Third Comintern, you certainly can't convince the average American. And you haven't convinced me."

At 12:45 P.M., December 14th, Admiral Leahy took me into the President's office to make my departure call. We talked about Russian affairs in general. I urged him to expedite the approval of the Second Protocol for Russian Lend-Lease. Then I brought up again the Willkie visit and similar junkets of Very VIP's and Special Representatives, stressing how difficult they made the conduct of diplomatic affairs. He ignored my statement about Willkie and turned to Bill Leahy with some offhand remark. As we rose to go, my last words to the President were, "Chief, you got your fingers burnt once, with Mr. Willkie. Don't do it again."

Bright and early on the morning of December 19th, we assembled in the waiting room at Bolling Field—Rear Admiral Jack Duncan, Brigadier General Mike Michella, Commander Samuel B. Frankel, Commander John Young, Secretary Alonza B. Calder, Secretary Eddie Page, Secretary Thomas P. Dillon, Army Warrant Officer Jaques, Red Cross Representative Mr. Hubbel, a crew of seven men, including the pilot, Captain Walker, and co-pilot, Lieutenant Polhemus.

General H. H. George, Commander of the Army Air Transportation Service, came down to see us off in the converted B-19 bomber, *Kay Bird,* which Mr. Willkie had used on part of his world trip. I saw him count the passengers and crew and shake his head at the mountainous pile of baggage and freight. There to see us off were my daughter, Evelyn, Mrs. Edward Page, and a number of other wives and friends, all with going-away and Christmas presents, which did not lighten the load. As a result, Messrs. Hubbel, Calder, Dillon and their baggage had to be "bumped" to wait for the next flight to the east.

Presently, the rest of us and our baggage were aboard, and the plane's engines were revving up at the end of the runway. We roared down the field and lifted into the air, climbing steadily above the Potomac River into a gloomy grey sky, headed eastward on the reverse course, away from the blessed peacefulness and freedom of our homeland, toward our posts in the storied capital of the Soviet Union, where not a word is uttered, not a deed is done, not a thought is thought that is not observed and noted in the book kept by the NKVD.

CHAPTER XIX

Moscow Is Our Address

$\mathbf{W}$E LANDED in the snow at Kuibyshev military airport at 12:34 P.M., January 8, 1943. We were met by a Red Air Force General, our new Counselor, our Chargé d'Affaires, Loy Henderson, and our messenger, Morris, with the Embassy "limousine." There must have been a thaw and then a freeze, for the snow along the roads was mud-spattered and frozen solid. The streets and buildings we passed in town looked drab and decrepit, as if an evil fairy had cast a film of dirty grey over everything. The pedestrians seemed to lift their feet, heavy with the shapeless cloth boots of winter, with a sort of frustrated weariness; their faces were covered with the same grey film and under it I seemed to read a haggard desperation. I felt a heavy lump slide down in my chest.

"What a contrast!" I said to Mike Michella.

"Sir."

"I was thinking of our flight into Miami."

The car pulled up in front of the Embassy office building; we went down a path between walls of dirty grey snow. As I thought of the long months of bitter winter still ahead and a renewal of my irritating contacts with the Soviet officialdom, I knew a desperate longing for my own country.

While I was at home, I had arranged for the appointment of Mr. Gene Dooman, a career Foreign Service Officer, to replace as Counselor of the Embassy, Walter Thurston, who had gone home on August twelfth. Mr. Dooman had been Counselor of our Embassy in Tokyo and was interned in Japan for long months. I had known Mr. Dooman since 1935, when we were both members of the American Delegation to the London Disarmament Conference. I was delighted to discover that he had arrived at Kuibyshev ahead of me, and, with characteristic vigor and energy, had already embarked upon his duties.

It was well that Dooman was on the job for Loy Henderson

had been laid up for several days with Kuibyshev "tummy"; John Young came down with it the next morning. We sent for a Russian doctor—an old man. As he examined Young he nodded his head emphatically. "Not typhus this time, Ambassador," he told me. "Now, I am only civil doctor in all Kuibyshev."

When I went over the despatches and letters with Dooman and Eddie Page the next morning, I found a rather extensive exchange between Mr. Stalin and the President about the Second Front. The President was also trying to persuade Mr. Stalin to meet with Mr. Winston Churchill and him in North Africa. Mr. Stalin replied, rather churlishly, that he was too busy fighting the war.

Since, in line with Mr. Stalin's expressed wishes, I had decided to spend most of my time in Moscow, I planned to leave for the Russian capital as soon as I could take over from Mr. Henderson. With Loy still sick, the *Kay Bird* could not leave immediately for Teheran. After consulting with Captain Walker, I decided to take the plane to Moscow, but the weather was unfavorable for flying for six long days.

In the meanwhile, I had the pleasure of presenting my ancient friend, Mr. Terekov, with Bailey's *Botanical Dictionary,* three volumes of it, each about three inches thick. He was extravagant in his expression of gratitude.

Before I left Kuibyshev for the last time, I went to see the old man. He had been ill and looked quite feeble. I'll not soon forget the pathos of his last words to me. "You can not realize, honored sir, what a wonderful gift you have made to the Russian people. I am now translating the *Dictionary* into Russian."

I wonder if he lived to complete that monumental job.

During our four days in Kuibyshev, I decided to make a test run on my plan to educate the Russian people. After considerable negotiation, I obtained permission from the local Foreign Office to use their projection room to screen "an American feature film and some raw combat films of the North African invasion," the latter included as bait for permission. The approval was far from hearty; we were directed to "limit your audience to American and Russian Foreign Office officials and their ladies."

At nine P.M. January 10th, twenty members of the Diplomatic Corps and fifteen Russian officials and their wives assembled in the Foreign Office projection room. The feature film was received with the usual Russian enthusiasm but I heard derogatory remarks and covert snickering in the course of screening the raw combat films. After the show, I introduced John Young, who explained why the combat films were unedited.

When John had finished, I walked across to Mr. Lozovsky and Mr. Zarubin. "Here's why I brought Commander Young to Russia with me, gentlemen. The American people and the Russian people need to understand each other. Your people like our American films. They could teach your people a lot about America and Americans. We could learn much about Russians from your films. I hope to see good American films, both feature and educational pictures, screened every week in every movie theater in Soviet Russia."

Mr. Lozovsky waved his hands excitedly. "That would be wonderful, Mr. Ambassador. I wish you all success with your plan. In fact, I publicly challenge you to the fullest cooperation in carrying it out."

"That you shall have."

As we drove back to Sadovia through the cold January night, John Young was jubilant. "We'll plaster the Soviet Union with our movie posters," he cried happily.

"Easy, John," I cautioned. "Things don't come that easily in the Soviet Union. There is only one man in Russia who knows all the answers."

But I *was* greatly encouraged.

I had long talks with Loy Henderson and Dooman, worked at the backlog of official despatches and telegrams, brought my diary up-to-date, and wrote my wife a long letter about my trip to Moscow. The day after I arrived in Kuibyshev, I made a formal visit of "return to post" to Mr. Lozovsky.

Finally, on January 12th, we received clearance for the flight. After a number of aggravating delays due to weather and engines, we took off at 1:31 P.M. for Moscow. We had a good flight, clear and cold, with occasional snow clouds and light flurries of snow. It was beautiful, flying above a snow-covered landscape, passing over occasional villages of mud-walled huts with smoking chimneys rising out of the white blanket.

The long trip became somewhat monotonous. I thought back to my trip across Africa—the incredible green of the steaming jungle, the desert, then Eritrea and down the beautiful Blue Nile, and across the Middle East to Teheran. Pretty much the same as my first flight to Moscow but there were a few incidents of interest.

We detoured from the straight air route to Cairo and landed at

Gura, Eritrea, which the British had recently taken from the Italian Army. At Asmara, the native craftsmen made fine cigarette lighters from damaged propellors. I was presented with two as a gift and bought two. "Fine," I said. "I'll give one of these to Mr. Stalin." All four were handed to me wrapped in tissue paper in small boxes.

Earlier, before I left Moscow, I had made arrangements to return to Kuibyshev via Tashkent, which is important because it is the capital of Uzbekestan, a Soviet Republic having at that time a population of about seven million. Situated on the frontier between Soviet Russia and Afghanistan, its pasturelands for centuries have grazed huge herds of beef cattle. In wartime, it was not its cattle but its huge cotton crop—about sixty per cent of all the cotton grown in the Soviet Union—which made Uzbekestan important.

I had heard that, in Uzbekestan, the Soviets had accomplished a tremendous increase in agriculture due to mechanization and irrigation; the Uzbeks had put aside the hoe and learned to use the tractor and modern farm machinery. Whole industrial plants had been evacuated from European Russia to Uzbekestan; it was reported to have large synthetic rubber production, huge dams for generating electricity and irrigation—a modern industrial economy superimposed upon a primitive agricultural culture. If half I heard were true, the progress in Uzbekestan during the past twenty years, particularly during the war years, was amazing.

The State Department had asked me to expedite the return of Loy Henderson to the United States. I planned to meet him in Teheran, take over the job, and let him be on his way home by the fastest available air transportation. When I learned that he had been delayed by bad flying weather, I tried to change my flight plan and proceed directly to Kuibyshev. But changing the mind of the Russian official, once it has been made up for him, is about as easy as the metaphysical trick of turning lead into gold. The Russians were adamant—I must carry out my original flight plan. Where earlier I had found the Foreign Office Consular Division most difficult to convince, it now insisted that I see Tashkent and Uzbekestan, whether I would or no.

I picked up the letter I had just finished writing to my wife and read it over again:

It was breaking dawn as we took the air in Teheran; Captain Walker laid his course northeast toward Meshed. As the sun rose, it lighted the snow-covered mountains on our left, the Elburz and Gilan Mazan-deran Ranges. The changing lights and shadows of sunrise were spectacular to see. We followed the railroad and the new highway the Americans were building; there were many trucks and camel caravans on the roads crossing the mountains.

At 9:30 A.M., we crossed the Russian border flying above a flat desert area for half an hour before we passed over a beautifully cultivated landscape, with an impressive network of irrigation canals. From the Oxus River to Bokhara and then to Samarkand and Tashkent, the farm lands below were beautifully green, with irrigation canals laid out in cross-hatched regularity on what had once been a desert floor. In and around Samarkand, I saw at least thirty large areas of new construction, which looked like factories with surrounding wooden barrack buildings.

At 12:06 P.M., we landed at the Tashkent airport, on a large, level plain at the foot of snow-capped mountains; some buildings on the far side looked like the hangars of an aircraft factory. Obviously, this was the center of a busy military training area—I saw many combat type planes on the airfield; we passed hundreds of military trucks, tanks and field artillery on our way into the city.

At the airport, cars were waiting for us; a good looking flaxen-haired blonde met us and said that she would be our interpreter and guide. With a very serious expression, not smiling, she said, "Mr. Ambassador, in the name of the Commissariat of Foreign Affairs, I welcome you back to Soviet Russia and to the Soviet Socialist Republic of Uzbekestan."

She presented us to the Mayor of Tashkent, a quiet Uzbek named Sadik Khusainov, a slight, coffee-colored man, with a mouth full of shining gold teeth and a close-clipped head. A Red Army General, an Air General and some minor Foreign Office and local officials made a respectable welcoming party.

We drove for an hour and a half over what had once been a hard-surfaced road, so badly rutted by heavy traffic that we had a very rough ride. The road followed the course of a river fed by snow from the mountains which rushed like a torrent toward the city. We passed along a broad, macadam street lined by tall poplars and weeping willows, between shuttered stucco houses set back from the street in walled enclosures. I was told that the city had 700,000 inhabitants before the war. "More than two million evacuees have passed through Tashkent to the other cities and farms of Uzbekestan," the blonde Foreign Office lady proudly translated for the Mayor.

"I would like to see more of your city," I replied, but my remark got no further than the blonde.

Our car caravan took us immediately to the walled enclosure of the *Narkomindel,* the local branch of the Foreign Office. Evidently there were no proper hotel accommodations for official guests, for cots and emergency lavatory facilities had been installed on the second floor of *Narkomindel* for our benefit. A special commissary had been imported to provide our meals. I could see now why we couldn't be rerouted to Kuibyshev.

When we had cleaned up and rejoined our hosts, I said to the blonde interpreter, "I would like very much to see the city in daylight."

She gave me a handsome smile. "After *chi*," she said. "First, we must have *chi*."

Behind me, I heard one of my party groan.

In due course, we sat down to *chi*, a typical Foreign Office banquet, with caviar, vodka, and all the trimmings, including an endless succession of toasts. After *chi*, they presented a floor show which lasted until nine P.M. One of the entertainers was the same gypsy dancer who entertained us in Moscow during the Beaverbrook-Harriman Mission. Evidently they did not intend I should see Tashkent by daylight.

At dinner, the man next to me, an important party official to whom even the Mayor was most respectful, began to ask our Assistant Naval Attaché, Commander Frankel, a series of questions. "How long is the George Washington Bridge?" "How long is the Whitestone Bridge?" "How long is the Golden Gate Bridge?" Frankel speaks Russian fluently, so I asked him what was going on. He told me, and added, "This character professes to be very surprised that I don't know the answers. Seems to think I'm kinda dumb."

I put my head back and had my first good laugh of the evening. Frankel flushed a violent red. "Don't be embarrassed, Frank," I said. "This afternoon I asked this same character what some bundles of long, thin, stalks on wagons we passed were for and he didn't know. A few moments later, we passed a house under construction. I saw a worker mixing such stalks with mud to make a roof."

Frankel's face cleared and he laughed heartily. The Party big shot looked around, questioningly. Across the table, our blonde interpreter translated for him. It was his turn to flush a sullen red.

The Army cots had thick cotton mattresses which were fairly comfortable. We slept under heavy new blankets, but my pillow was so big and hard that I pushed it off on the floor. Something in that bed must have been old for it was full of bed bugs. When I turned out the next morning, there was an enormous, well-fed one on my pillow.

We were called at four A.M., and had a wonderful breakfast—grapes and apples for the fruit course, scrambled eggs with caviar in them, vodka, local white wine, and, after all the dishes were cleared away, one demitasse of good black coffee, which made me want six more.

The same official group, which had met us, stayed with us for the trip to the airport; I suspect that they sat outside our suite all night to make sure we didn't slip out into the city. We traveled the same route to the airport.

It was a clear, cold morning, with a strong piercing wind. The blonde interpreter and another Russian girl, who had been with us the previous day, both wore heavy fur coats, but under them they had on thin silk dresses; I hope they had on their long woolies!

It took us from 5:30 to 6:24 to unravel red tape and have our passports examined. Presently, the weather report came in—clear and cold, favorable flying weather. Our hosts cordially invited us to return in the summer when fruit and game would be plentiful.

We flew west along the Tashkent-Kuibyshev railroad, down the Bye Duyea River to the Aral Sea, passing over Novokazalinsk at its northern end at nine A.M. Below, the country was bleak and forlorn, a continuous sea of snow and ice. We passed over several large towns —Emba on the Emba River, the oil center of the Emba oil fields, and two other large towns with many new factory buildings and barracks, which were not on our map. At each station, long freight trains heading west waited on sidings for clear tracks. Our air chart indicated that we passed over a small city, Aralsk, on Lake Aralsk at ten A.M.; many of these geographical places didn't even appear on our English Atlas.

I put down the letter, leaned back against the seat, and closed my eyes. "Quite a trip," I thought. "I'll bet I've seen more of Russia than any other foreigner since the Red Revolution and I'm going to see more."

In thinking back over the trip, I was frankly amazed that the Russians had permitted us to fly that route from Teheran to Tashkent, and even more surprised that they had let us see the vast expanse of territory from Tashkent along the railway to Kuibyshev. But why had they kept us so closely hemmed in at Tashkent? Probably because of all the heavy industry they had transferred from European Russia. Some years later, I learned that the Russians interned our fliers at Tashkent; that may have been the reason they kept us cooped up in the *Narkomindel*.

I must have fallen asleep. Someone shook me; Jack Duncan, pointing toward the ground. I sat up and looked out the tiny window. We were flying along the Moscow River above the ancient capital of the Czars and the modern capital of World Communism. Presently, I saw the crenelated pattern of the Kremlin walls and the bulbous spires of its former churches.

At 5:01 P.M., we landed on the snow-covered Moscow airport.

Dekanosov and a couple of minor officials of the Foreign Office, my four NKVD boys, Tommy Thompson, General Faymonville, and all my Moscow Staff, Army, Navy and Lend-Lease, met us.

It was bitter cold; a freezing wind whipped across the airfield. The rooms of Spaso House didn't seem much warmer. We had cocktails before the fire in my sitting room; the cooks had prepared a grand buffet supper to welcome me home. After dinner, I played a game of gin rummy with Eddie Page, and for once I won. I talked with Tommy and Page until eleven-thirty and turned in. As I tried to reaccustom myself to the bed, I thought of all the times someone had said, "Welcome home, Mr. Ambassador."

Soviet Russia, home? No, never! America for me.

> In that land of peace and freedom
> Beyond the ocean bars,
> Where the air is full of sunshine
> And the flag is full of stars.

I turned my face to the wall and composed myself for sleep. I must get some rest; tomorrow, I would need all my strength . . . and tomorrow . . . and tomorrow.

The next morning, I turned out as usual at 7:30 A.M. to begin the old routine of bath, shave and breakfast at eight-thirty. It was a clear, cold day; the trees in the yard were covered with hoar frost, through which a pale wintry sunlight sparkled and glistened. After breakfast, I hugged a big fire in the fireplace to post my diary and bring my current letter to Evelyn up to date. Then I was ready to begin my routine work, going over telegrams and discussing administrative affairs. Eddie Page arranged an appointment with Mr. Molotov; after lunch, we planned my conference with the Foreign Secretary as carefully as I would plan a naval campaign.

In the late afternoon, I took a short nap and dressed; promptly at six, I presented myself, with Eddie Page and Mr. Dooman, at Mr. Molotov's office.

After I had presented my new Counselor, we discussed my return trip to Moscow. I told him about my detour via Eritrea and the interesting things I had seen there. "I want to thank you for sending me in via Tashkent, Mr. Molotov," I went on. "It was a most interesting experience."

"I'm happy we could arrange it."

"Hereafter, I intend to spend most of my time in Moscow, going down to Kuibyshev only when necessary. That way, I'll be here in Moscow in case of need."

"We'll be happy to have you in Moscow, Mr. Ambassador. I'm very glad."

The next two weeks were very busy. Our Rubber Mission was in Moscow; I saw them frequently and arranged for them to visit the proper Soviet officials. I took John Young with me everywhere, as a sort of naval aide, to expose him to as much of Mother Russia as possible. He met Mr. Kamenev and other officials of VOKS. At every opportunity, he visited Soviet movie houses and saw Soviet motion pictures.

I find the following entry in my diary:

> Discussed Father Braun's problems with him. He said he has noted a new trend back to the old regime's attitude toward religion. Government now separating boys and girls in school. Girls in Red Army sent to the front now coming back 50% pregnant. Employing injections to prevent conception—he used the word *gaspidin*.

On January 16th, I had an unpleasant quarter hour with General Faymonville. After the movies, he came up to my sitting room and I discussed with him the order placing him under my administrative control.

"Are you displeased with my performance of duty, Admiral?" he asked angrily.

"No, of course not. I expect the same cooperation and loyalty that I had before."

"You'll get it," he said, sullenly.

"Look, General," I said gently. "There can be only one Ambassador to the Soviet Union and I am *IT*. That is all there is to it."

My diary says that "I finished reading Henry Cassidy's new book. It's interesting but over-enthusiastic and inaccurate in spots." Also during this period, I read Rhys Williams' book, *Russia the Land, the People, Why they Fight,* Beveredge on Russia, Anna Louise Strong's *I Change Worlds,* and Commander Lang's report on his trip to Ufa.

Each night of those two weeks, I listened eagerly to the BBC news broadcasts, hoping for word from the conference in North Africa. Nothing was coming through officially; I knew that Premier Stalin was anxious for information as to the next move the Western Allies would make. If it didn't turn out to be a cross-channel operation into Western France, he was going to be very unhappy.

My new radio was going through a "thawing-out" process; Thompson's radio was inoperative. For several days, we were without even the sketchy news which BBC provided. *Pravda* was making unpleasant remarks about the lethargy of the Western Allies and asking "what has happened to the Second Front?"

My diary for January 26th records:

> Received telegram from Ambassador Winant [in London] saying Zonike message from Roosevelt and Prime Minister Churchill was being sent to my colleague, the British Ambassador, and for me to get in touch with him and arrange to make joint delivery of the note to Stalin before midnight.

Sir Archibald was on leave in Britain. I contacted Counselor Baggaley, the British Chargé d'Affaires. We spent most of the day arranging for delivery of the note, stressing that we must present it before midnight. To be ready for any hour during the evening, I went to dinner with Jack Duncan at five. At eight P.M., we received information that Mr. Stalin would receive us exactly at midnight.

Eddie Page got up out of a sick bed; at 11:50 P.M., with Counselor Baggaley, Page and Dunlap, I went through the Kremlin gates. A few moments before midnight, we were ushered into Stalin's conference room, where Mr. Stalin, Pavlov, and Molotov awaited us. After some preliminary greetings, Page delivered the note to Mr. Stalin. I glanced at my wrist watch; one second before midnight.

I don't have a copy of the note but I recall that it was a lengthy report on the results of the conference in North Africa, giving Mr. Stalin specific details as to future plans. Much emphasis was placed on the importance of opening up the Mediterranean to Allied shipping which would facilitate delivery of supplies to Russia. No mention was made of a Second Front in Europe.

The note was in duplicate, an original in English and a Russian translation which Eddie gave to Mr. Stalin. The contents must have been a great disappointment to him but Mr. Stalin had a good poker face—he looked at Mr. Molotov and handed him the Russian version without comment.

The conference sagged. I began to talk very fast about my trip.

When this produced no reaction, I said, "Marshal Stalin, allow me to congratulate you on your promotion to Commander-in-Chief of the Red Army."

He shrugged his shoulders, grinned amiably, and took his long-stemmed pipe from his mouth as if he were going to say something then put it back in his mouth without speaking. "Do you recall the last time I saw you—I suggested that I bring you some good tobacco from America?"

He nodded.

"They wouldn't let me do it."

"Who wouldn't let you do it?" Stalin asked.

"Your friends in America. They insisted on sending you a five-pound tin of Edgewood tobacco and a smoking set. I'll send them over to you tomorrow."

"I didn't know I had any friends in America."

"Oh, yes," I replied. "You have many friends, not only in America but also in Eritrea. I have a small souvenir from your friends in that country."

I pulled from my pocket and unwrapped for the first time one of the lighters I had gotten in Eritrea. To my surprise, I discovered that it was engraved, *To Premier Joseph Stalin from Ambassador W. H. Standley.* Marshal Stalin looked at the engraving carefully, held it up for Mr. Molotov to see, and put it in his pocket laughing.

Five days later, my diary notes, "Germans in Stalingrad have surrendered." Surrendering were: Von Paulus, just made Field Marshal Second Class, sixteen generals and about 85,000 men, all that remained of the half a million German troops who fought before Stalingrad, one of the great victories of the war. Now, dimly on the distant horizon we could see ultimate victory; the way led down a broad highway, but there would be many booby-traps and detours along the road before we reached the end in the "Unconditional Surrender," which President Roosevelt was publicizing so widely.

On February second, I decided I would have to make a quick trip to Kuibyshev to set up a proper administration there. We flew in a Russian transport, a horrible flight—thick fog, blind flying, propellors icing with pieces of ice flying off to hit the cabin with a crack like a pistol shot. I was glad when we came out into clear weather half way to Kuibyshev.

I found Dickerson in bed and Dooman ill. Dillon, Calder, and Hubbel were stuck in Teheran, no transportation. Everyone in the Embassy had been sick, with only the old Russian doctor to take care of them. I had Lang come down from Moscow; before long, he had them on their feet, all but poor Dooman. On February 9th, Freddy told me that Dooman would have to go home. The transportation situation was so bad that winter that, sick as he was, I couldn't get him out until April 16th. Again, I found myself without the advice of an experienced Counselor, a situation which continued until July 22nd, when Mr. Maxwell McCauhey Hamilton arrived on the first flight into Russia of "the plane for my own personal use." Mr. Hamilton remained with me as Counselor with the personal rank of Minister for the rest of my tour in the Soviet Union.

My "flying trip" to Kuibyshev turned into an endurance contest. For days and days, I waited for a Russian plane to take me to Moscow, where I had promised Mr. Stalin I would thenceforth make my headquarters. Each day we were scheduled to go; each day the flight was cancelled.

Meanwhile, I was trying to make sense out of our American war with the Japanese. While optimistic news of Russian successes in the Caucasus and the Donetz Basin were widely publicized in Moscow, such radio news as we could get about the war elsewhere caused me to make such pessimistic entries in my diary as "American position in Tunisia not good; Tunisia news not so good;" "Chicago," my old Flagship, sunk in the Solomons; don't understand situation in Solomons—Marines left Guadalcanal, where did they go?" With such distortion of the war news, it was small wonder we began to doubt that we would ever reach that broad highway to victory. Would Unconditional Surrender ever come?

My diary is full of entries about requests for plane passage, requests for visas for plane crews, requests to our government to send in one plane, two planes, any old plane. One of the planes in question was *Gulliver No. 11,* a C-87 transport, apparently named after the Willkie plane. I was interested to note among the requested visas the pilot's name, Klotz—the same Major Klotz, Army Air Corps reserve pilot, who had been Mr. Willkie's co-pilot. He was a nice young officer, half-Russian on his father's side.

Meanwhile, General Faymonville sent Colonel Gray of his Mission to Cairo to make some purchases for Lend-Lease; when he was ready to return, Colonel Gray requested the Soviet Embassy in Cairo to grant visas for the crew of yet another plane, a C-47 transport, to bring his cargo to Moscow. This probably fouled up the visa situation—the Russians didn't want two American transports flying across the Soviet Union. To avoid this, the Soviet Government offered the full capacity of their next regular plane into Kuibyshev to lift our passengers and cargo.

On February 17th, we received information from the Foreign Office that all regular transportation, both plane and train, had been discontinued; if we ever got back to Moscow, it would be on the basis of "catch as catch can."

On February 23rd, I received a telegram from General George, Commander of the Army Air Transport Command, telling me that *Gulliver No. 11* had left Miami, would arrive Cairo on the 24th, would pick up our freight and passengers in Cairo and Teheran and bring them to Kuibyshev and Moscow.

Major Klotz and *Gulliver No. 11* arrived Teheran February 26th. It took two interviews with Mr. Molotov after I returned to Moscow to clear him and his passengers and crew for entry; at the end of our second interview, Mr. Molotov said, coldly, "Mr. Ambassador, I hope that there will be no more necessity for American planes to come into the Soviet Union. The Soviet air service from Teheran will be able to take care of all proper American needs."

Poor Major Klotz! For three weeks, he was stuck in Teheran. Each day, he called at the Russian Embassy for his visas; each day, he was put off without any definite information as to why the visas weren't ready. He finally arrived at the Kuibyshev military airport on March 20th. A Russian uniformed guard was assigned to his plane. Thinking that the guard would ensure the security of the plane, its equipment and cargo, as military guards had at other military airports of various nationalities which he had visited, and all through Russia when he was flying Mr. Willkie, Klotz went to Kuibyshev.

When he returned on March 23rd to take off for Moscow, his plane had been looted, his flying suit and emergency rations stolen; the plane showed evidence of having been thoroughly searched. In preparing *Gulliver No. 11* for flight without a heavy flying suit, Major Klotz caught a terrible cold; when he arrived in Moscow that afternoon, he had a high fever. Freddy Lang put him to bed but his cold progressed into lobar pneumonia. It was three weeks before he could return to flying duty.

Meanwhile, incredibly weary of Kuibyshev and the Russian runaround, with telephone calls, telegrams, and radio messages convincing me that I was urgently needed in Moscow, I put in for passage on the first train that would take me to the Communist capital.

CHAPTER XX

The Great Diplomatic Indiscretion

IT WAS the end of February, 1943. I now had been Ambassador to Soviet Russia for almost eleven months. All during this period, one thing had troubled me above all others—the apparent ingratitude of Soviet Government officials for the aid which the United States Government and the American people were extending to Russia to carry on their war against the Nazis.

Three kinds of aid were coming to embattled Russia from my country. First was Lend-Lease aid, in which I was especially interested both officially as Ambassador and also because I had been a member of the Beaverbrook-Harriman Mission which had virtually forced Lend-Lease supplies on a reluctant Soviet Government. Second was Red Cross aid, shiploads of supplies delivered to Russia by the American Red Cross, supposedly for the relief of exiled Poles and needy Russians. Mr. Scovell, and later Mr. Hubbel, who were sent to Russia as representatives of the American Red Cross, both complained to me bitterly that they were not permitted to supervise the distribution of their supplies and had no certain knowledge as to the use to which they were being put. And finally, there were Russian Relief Supplies, gathered and sent to Russia by Russian Relief Societies all over America under direction of the national chairman, Mr. E. C. Carter of the Institute of Pacific Relations. When I was home for consultation, I discovered that my wife had sponsored this society in San Diego County and that two of my daughters were doing secretarial work for the society. This personal relationship to the problem bolstered my very real and sincere interest in helping the 165 million Russian people who needed help of every kind.

Ever since I came into Russia, I had been constantly looking for evidence that these war materials and relief supplies were actually being received into Russia and distributed to the proper

331

organizations and needy people. My efforts met with scant success. Few of the "common people"* I met had ever heard of any help coming from America.

I, myself, had visited orphan's homes, schools, kindergartens, collective farms, factories, military installations. The one place I saw readily apparent evidence of the proper employment of Lend-Lease material or other supplies was in the transplanted aircraft factory at Kuibyshev, where the new machines in this enlarged factory were of American make.

Periodically, the Soviet authorities made possible "visits to the front" for various military and civilian dignitaries making a grand tour of Russia and for some American and other press and magazine representatives; when I questioned those who returned from "the front," in not a single instance did I discover one person who had actually been at a real front where fighting was currently in progress. I believe, from his description of his "visit to the front," that General Hurley must have come the closest to a real battle line, for he mentioned unburied horses and soldiers' bodies of both armies still lying on the battlefield. Whenever one of these visitors returned from a "visit to the front," I made it standard practice to question him closely as to American material or supplies of any description which he had seen or about which Russian officers had commented. Only one person brought me an affirmative answer; he had seen an American jeep wrecked in a ditch beside the military highway to Vyazma. The markings on the jeep made the denial of its origin impossible.

Doctor Lang, who visited many Soviet hospitals and medical laboratories, failed to observe any American Red Cross supplies or material in any of these institutions. In Moscow, it was widely believed that our Red Cross supplies went to the Red Army.

Each day, our clerks translated interesting articles from *Pravda*, *Izvestia*, the Red Army's *Red Star*, and other Soviet newspapers and magazines; it was a rare occasion when any mention was made of American and British Lend-Lease aid to Russia.

Finally, just before I left for home, Mr. Stalin included in his answer to the celebrated Cassidy letter, "As compared to the aid which the Soviet Union is giving to the Allies by drawing upon itself the main force of the German Fascist armies, the aid of the Allies to the Soviet Union has so far been little effective."

This was a cruel blow; I knew the sacrifices that our Armed

---

* I make this distinction to differentiate the "common people" of Russia from the estimated 2.5 million members of the Russian Communist Party, who ruled Soviet Russia and the tremendous population of non-Communists.

Forces and our citizens were making to send war materials and other supplies to Russia; I knew better than most men the terrible toll in ships and seamen that the Murmansk Convoy Route was taking.

From all of the evidence available to me, it became obvious that the Soviet governmental authorities were attempting to conceal from the Russian people the nature and extent of the aid which the British and American people were giving so generously to the Russian Armed Forces and the Russian people.

To support this view, late in February, 1943, Mr. Stalin issued an order of the day in which he said, "On the absence of a Second Front, the Red Army is fighting the war alone." How could we be building up any "reservoir of good will" among the Russian people in the face of such a conspiracy of silence?

I knew that the new Lend-Lease appropriation bill was up before Congress; though generous, our Congress was sensitive—if it believed that the Lend-Lease material being sent to Russia was "going down the drain," the Congress might well refuse to pass that appropriation bill. Without American war material and supplies, the Red Army would quickly fold up. Somehow or other, we had to keep the Red Army fighting.

On January 27th, while still in Moscow, I received a despatch from the State Department, which read about like this:

> The Second Lend-Lease to Russia Protocol is now being considered in committee. The President is anxious to have this protocol passed by Congress with as little opposition as possible. Cassidy-Stalin exchange may have had an adverse effect on American public opinion and on Congress. It would help if you could obtain a statement from responsible Soviet authorities demonstrating the benefits Lend-Lease aid has accorded to the Soviet Union on the battlefield and to Soviet civilians.

Such statements, I felt, should come from the Commissars for the Red Army, the Red Navy, and Foreign Trade, the latter being the official recipient of all Lend-Lease material and supplies. I called in Mike Michella, Jack Duncan, and General Faymonville. "Boys, here's a copy of a despatch we just received from the Department. It's looking bad for the Second Protocol in Congress. I want each one of you to contact your opposite number and ask him to give me a statement as to the benefits derived from American Lend-Lease aid."

Thinking that the Soviet Foreign Office would be just as anxious as the President to get the protocol passed, I immediately contacted Mr. Molotov. I told him about the telegram I had received but I didn't show it to him. "Mr. Molotov," I said, pausing for emphasis. "This publicizing of the material benefits of Lend-Lease and other aid to your armed forces and your citizens, for which we are asking, is of vital importance to the Soviet war effort. If you want the Second Protocol to get through Congress, I suggest you use your influence to expedite the widest publicity in Russia of strong statements as to the value of Lend-Lease aid from America and Great Britain and the gratitude of the Soviet People for the sacrifices our citizens have been making."

Mr. Molotov looked at me a long moment before he answered. "Mr. Ambassador, we well recognize that it is the duty of the Soviet Government to supply such information. The Russian Government *is* grateful for the aid supplied by the United States Government through Lend-Lease. I will endeavor to facilitate furnishing the information in question."

On February 1st, Michella, Duncan and Faymonville came back to report separately but identically, as if their opposite numbers in Soviet officialdom were fourth grade school boys who had learned to make a recitation for Red Army Day. "The United States Lend-Lease authorities have absolute and detailed knowledge of all material which has been furnished the Soviet Government under Lend-Lease. They also have detailed knowledge of all material which has been lost or destroyed in transit. Accordingly, a restatement of this information by the Russian authorities is unnecessary. Any statement as to the material benefits Lend-Lease has accorded to the Soviet Union on the battlefield and in Soviet civilian life must come from the Foreign Office."

Several days went by, and having heard nothing further from Mr. Molotov, I saw Mr. Vishinsky in Kuibyshev on February 5th, and presented an *aide memoire* enclosing a copy of our State Department's telegram. I brought him up to date on my efforts. "May I ask your assistance in obtaining the release of information as to the extent of help received from the American Government through Lend-Lease?"

Mr. Vishinsky was never one to make extravagant promises. "I will look into the question immediately."

A few days later, Mr. Vishinsky went to Moscow. I had my secretaries make frequent inquiry at the Kuibyshev and Moscow Foreign Offices; no information was released. On January 20th, I went to see Mr. Lozovsky.

"Is Mr. Vishinsky still in Moscow?" I asked.

"Yes, Mr. Ambassador, the Vice Commissar is in a hospital very ill with diabetes; I understand that he was taken from the train in Moscow on a stretcher."

Was this some more of the Russian runaround? I thought so; later I learned that Mr. Vishinsky had indeed been desperately ill. "I'm sorry to hear that," I replied. "Please convey to him my sympathy and my hope that he will soon have a complete recovery. Do you have any information for me in regard to the questions I brought up in the *aide memoire* which I presented to Mr. Vishinsky two weeks ago?"

"I'm not completely informed in the matter, Mr. Ambassador; I'll look it up and give you an answer in a day or so."

At that time, we were also trying earnestly to obtain visas for the crews of two Army planes bringing in Lend-Lease material for Faymonville and for my personal plane. When none of our planes were cleared and no passage on a Russian plane seemed probable, I again had inquiry made as to the Lend-Lease question. No answer was available. Irritated, frustrated, and almost desperate, on February 26th, I made an official request to the Foreign Office to proceed by rail from Kuibyshev to Moscow. I hated the thought of the trip but consoled myself by recalling that we would travel over a section of the main line which connects Moscow with the Trans-Siberian Railway; I should collect some new impressions of conditions in the Soviet Union.

As usual, the Foreign Office procrastinated until the last moment, and then arranged for us to hurry up and wait. Early February 28th, we received word that my request was granted. We purchased tickets for Eddie Page, John Young, and myself, providing for a section each on what the Russians call an "International" car; each section contained three berths.

As an interesting sidelight on Soviet officials, I knew that Sir Keith Officer, Chargé d'Affaires of the Australian Legation, wished to go to Moscow. Since three sections would be more than we required, I told Eddie Page to see the Foreign Office and suggest that we would be happy to make room for Sir Keith Officer. Eddie came back chuckling. A Foreign Office minion had sent word to me. "Tell the American Ambassador—if he has more space than he wants, we will take one section away from him, but we will *not* assign it to Sir Keith Officer."

Kuibyshev to Moscow by Rail

We were packed and ready early the morning of March 1st. At breakfast, word came that the train would not leave before one

P.M., probably about two. The time of departure was changed to four and later to five. We arrived at the station at 5:15, to find the trainmen had become rather impatient. The "International" car had to be moved to a siding to wait for the regular train, which was scheduled to depart at one P.M., but the Lord only knew when it would actually hook on to our car.

At 5:30 P.M., we boarded our "International" car. Instead of moving out into the yards, our car stayed alongside the station platform until the through train hooked on about midnight. While we waited, one of my NKVD boys marched up and down on the platform outside the compartment in which I sat while two of them warmed themselves in the corridor.

The car was divided into four sections with three bunks in each section, two athwartships and one fore-and-aft; between each pair of adjoining compartments was a washroom provided with double entrances. Overhead were storage racks for baggage. At each end of the car in a small compartment were a toilet and washstand, so filthy that we used them only when it could no longer be avoided, and then only with elaborate sanitary precautions. Wide double windows in each compartment admitted plenty of daylight but were almost completely frosted over on the inside, so that sightseeing was difficult. The train was blacked out at night; most of the passengers stood up in the passageway and peered out through the clear spots in the windows. No potable water was provided in the car; when our own fresh water ran out after four days, we gathered snow and had our car guard melt and boil it to make "chow water," as in China in the old days. The car was heated by a small wood stove at one end. We spent most of our days rolled up in heavy grey blankets provided with the bunks.

Our fellow passengers were a nondescript lot, but they must have had position or influence to be riding in an "international" car. Of course, my three NKVD boys came along to protect me. There was one well-dressed young Russian woman named Irma, with a cute little daughter; we gave the little girl some of our cookies, and became quite friendly.

We carried our own subsistence—Army mess kits, canned meat, beans, corn, peas, soup, bread, crackers, bouillon cubes, and what we considered an ample supply of Scotch whiskey and vodka. Page brought a collapsible stove heated by solidified alcohol.

I quote from my diary for March 2nd:

Had a good night. Car warm and more comfortable than B&O

sleeper from Washington to New York, with few starting bumps. Bed hard but comfortable, with no bugs. Turned out late, shaved in cold water, dressed. Breakfast with Eddie Page as chef; emergency ration coffee, fruit juice, cookies, sweet butter.

Passing through good-looking country; lattice-work snow-breaks as at home and trees planted as wind-breaks for homes, roads and rail-roads. A prosperous looking farming country, with orchards, berry patches, cattle in the fields. Passed train on a siding headed south, loaded with decrepit-looking farm machinery, evidently being evacu-ated to the east. Passed several troop trains, boxcars with only a small opening at the top for air—we wouldn't transport pigs in such cars. Made friends with woman [Irma] and little girl; after dinner, woman came in and had some drinks with us and stayed and stayed. With vodka highballs, she became talkative. We quizzed her till 1:30, when I turned in for a good night.

The roadbed was good but we were sidetracked so often there was no judging the efficiency of operation. Our train must have had "Z" priority, for we sidetracked for every freight and troop train we met. We spent the last night and the following day on a siding, a junction where we left the busy troop and freight route for the open road to Moscow. When the train was underway, we went so slowly that a vigorous youth could have caught up and passed the train and sat down and rested long enough to run some more.

I have no way of knowing how many of our stops at sidings were caused by engine breakdown nor how many changes of en-gines and crews it took to get us to Moscow. We saw untold num-bers of engines and freight and passenger cars standing on sidings exposed to the weather, rusting rapidly to disintegration, probably broken-down equipment immobilized for lack of spare parts and the labor and know-how to effect repairs.

"Only a matter of time," John Young said to me, as we stared out at an array of rusted and ruined rolling stock. "At home, this railway would be in a state of complete bankruptcy. I don't see how they keep it operating, with such a waste of rolling stock."

I shook my head, sadly. "And in the middle of a war, too, John. Well, you've seen it now for yourself; typical of conditions in the Soviet Union. Believe me; I know."

About noon, March 3rd, our train stopped at a small station; a Russian girl in an unkempt uniform came into our compartment. "We have a diner three cars ahead," she told Page. "If you will come at once, they will serve you before they open the car to any-one else."

Eddie had previous experience with Russian dining cars and took a dim view. Prompted more by curiosity than a desire for a hot lunch, I finally persuaded him to try it with me. The diner was a dingy, filthy old car, on which Ivan-the-Terrible might once have dined. Its four tables were covered with dirty brown oilcloth, greasy to the touch.

Eddie and I were the only customers. The same girl served us, her uniform now covered with a speckled chef's apron, which once had been white. First, she brought on a greasy, grey noodle soup, black bread, and coarse salt. The next course was greasy noodles and fat salt pork; then black *chi*. I made an extreme effort and got down some soup, a few noodles and the tea; poor Eddie, al-ready suffering from a queasy stomach, couldn't eat any of it.

I'm afraid that those poor people couldn't understand our lack of appetite; they gave us of their best and seemingly didn't know there was any better. I felt ashamed of our apparent lack of ap-preciation but that was all that my squeamish stomach could take.

The trip soon became deadly monotonous and extremely boring. We played gin rummy; we talked with Irma and played with her child; we read, napped, and played more gin rummy. There were some compensations. I quote from a letter to my wife, written dur-ing the trip.

> We find it interesting to watch the Russian people along the way. All of the trains we pass are overcrowded. Women with babies in their arms and their meager belongings strapped to their backs plead with train guards to get into our cars. At every station, hundreds are turned away and plod up the snowy roads, crying from the bitter disappointment and the cold. This is a cruel, hard country.
>
> On passing trains, between every car we see several women hang-ing onto the couplings and clinging to the ladders on the sides of the cars. These peasant women act like dumb oxen. At one station, we saw four old women sawing through a steel rail with a large hack-saw. The temperature was below freezing but the old women didn't seem to mind.

Between our visitors and the boredom, our stock of Scotch and vodka, which we had considered ample, ran out the day before we arrived in Moscow.

Faced with a severe crisis, Irma came to the rescue, repaying courtesies in kind—with two liters of vodka. She must have persuaded my NKVD boys to buy it for her. We also ran out of stove alcohol; our meals that last day were "cold plate" right out of the can.

I quote from my diary for March 4th:

> In afternoon, played gin rummy, lost as usual. Had dinner—cold meat, corn, peas, bread and butter. Arrived Ryzan about 5:30 P.M. Heard that Russians have taken Rzhev. Spent evening talking to Irma and her little girl. Arrived Moscow at 12:30 A.M. Met by all the gang—Jack, Mike, Tommy, Faymonville. Rode home in car with Jack, Tommy, Faymonville. My plane still in Teheran, no visas for crew. Heard news of destruction of Jap fleet off New Guinea. Turned in at 1:30, Kuibyshev time, had a good night.

The distance from Kuibyshev to Moscow is 500 miles; the trip took us seventy-two and a half hours.

My diary for March 5th notes that the temperature in my bedroom as I arose that morning was fifty-nine degrees. Michella and Duncan came in to report—result, no publicity or acknowledgement as to the value of Lend-Lease to the Russian war effort.

I was particularly perturbed at Mike Michella's report. The War Department had kept on asking for information concerning captured German war material. In spite of repeated requests to see or be told about new German guns, vehicles, and explosives captured by the Russians, Mike had yet to see or be informed about anything.

"How's Faymonville making out?" I asked.

"I don't know, sir. He hasn't confided in me."

I had Faymonville come in. He had been unable to make any progress with Mikoyan. "How about military information?" I asked. "Are you doing any better? Can you get anything out of them?"

"Under the present set-up, Admiral," he said stiffly, "Washington doesn't ask me for information any more."

"All right, General," I said with a sigh. "Thank you. That will be all."

The newspaper boys were on another "visit to the front" at Kharkov and would not return until the seventh. I was very unhappy. In the words of my diary, "I hardly know what to do—must wait for further information." We desperately needed all the information about the Germans that we could get. The Russians had plenty but they refused to part with it. I wanted to know about German weapons; I wanted our assistant military attachés to live at the Russian front as our observers lived with the British even before we entered the war; I wanted our military experts to see and have an opportunity to study every new piece of equipment the Russians captured. Such information would save a lot of British and American lives when the time came to open the Second Front in Europe which the Russians so avidly desired.

All of this might well have added up to frustration—diplomatic frustration. But I was not a diplomat; I was not interested in the devious processes by which the Soviet Bureaucracy, and even our own diplomats, arrived at a point of view, an attitude, or a position. I tried to think things through in a straightforward manner and arrive at logical conclusions. I preferred action to red tape. And finally, I believed that the welfare of my own country came first.

Sometimes it is a little thing that triggers a big action. During an official visit to Mr. Fierlinger, the Communist Minister to the Soviet Union from Czechoslovakia, a servant offered me a Chesterfield from a package plainly marked, "From the Fellow Workers Party, New York City," a communistic organization well-known to me. The marking had been stamped on a package in every other respect like the untaxed cigarettes we were sending into Russia in Lend-Lease and Red Cross supplies.

"Where did you come by these American cigarettes, Mr. Minister?" I asked.

"One of our officers is spending the weekend with me. He received them as a gift from the Red Army on the Southern Russian front, where his battalion is fighting."

The young officer came in a little later and I asked him about the cigarettes. "They are given to us quite generously."

"Awfully nice of our Government," I offered.

"Oh, not at all," he said, in his clipped British accent. "From our friends, the Communists, in your great city of New York."

The correspondents returned from Kharkov early the morning of March 7th; as usual after a trip to the front, they filed into the Spaso House library at four P.M., March 8th; the meeting was informal—none of the long "prepared statement" and question and answer period of a press conference. We sat around the big book-lined room chatting: About my train trip to Moscow; spring was coming to Moscow early; living conditions seemed to be improving in the Soviet Union; the Stettinius Report on Lend-Lease, which the Soviet Press had unanimously ignored. Finally, I asked the boys, "How was your trip to the front? Any improvement?"

A few shook their heads. "No closer to the real fighting front than before," Quent Reynolds observed.

I saw that none of them were taking notes; even Page had relaxed, leaning back against the leather cushions of his chair.

"Did you see much American stuff?"

"Not much," Henry Shapiro said, drowsily.

Quite casually, Eddie Gilmore asked the status of the Lend-Lease Protocol.

It was obvious that the boys knew of my efforts to obtain statements from the Russian authorities as to the benefits of Lend-Lease.

"The Second Protocol has been reported out of Committee," I replied. "But that doesn't necessarily mean that Congress will pass the bill. You know, boys, ever since I've been here, I've been looking for evidence that the Russians are getting a lot of material help from the British and us—not only Lend-Lease but also Red Cross and Russian Relief—but I've yet to find any evidence of that fact. You know, the American Congress is a big-hearted, generous body of men, who will go to great lengths to help out a friend, if they know that their efforts are really helpful, but"—and I paused for emphasis—"lacking such knowledge, our Congress might very well take the opposite tack. Since my arrival in the Soviet Union, I have also tried to obtain evidence that our military supplies are in use by the Russians. I haven't succeeded. The Russian authorities seem to want to cover up the fact that they are receiving outside help. Apparently they want their people to believe that the Red Army is fighting this war alone."

I looked about the small circle. The boys were grabbing for pencils and paper. "Is that off the record, Mr. Ambassador?" Henry Shapiro asked.

"No, use it," I said. "I'm simply stating facts which are well known to the authorities. It's not fair—the American people are giving millions to help the Russian people and yet the Russian people do not know where the supplies are coming from. The American people are giving generously because of their friendship for the Russian people. The Soviet authorities apparently are trying to create the impression at home and abroad that they are fighting the war alone and with their own resources. I see no reason why you should not use my remarks if you care to."

I was somewhat surprised at the abruptness with which the boys took their departure. I have heard that they ran the two blocks to the nearest subway station, fumed impatiently at the slowness of the train, and sprinted from the station to the Foreign Office press room, where they beat out my remarks on typewriters provided there. Henry Shapiro told me that the censors didn't want to release their despatches. "Look," they said, "this is no ordinary story. This is a direct quote from the United States Ambassador." Apparently, the censor was afraid to suppress my remarks.

I had made the statement as a result of my futile efforts to get information from the Russians as to the help they had received. I expected some repercussions from the Russians, but I did not expect the furore which my remarks created at home. About nine P.M., Henry Shapiro called me on the phone. "I just received a wire from my boss, Mr. Ambassador. Your statement made front page headlines in all U.S. daily papers."

I realized then that my remarks had been given greater importance than I had intended. I quote from my diary for March 9th:

> Seems my statement re Russian Relief has stirred up a mare's nest at home, with efforts to confuse the issue and confound me with false implications. Duncan came in, jubilant. Staff in general expressed approval—don't think Faymonville will agree. At 9:30 P.M., saw Shapiro; he read me telegrams re implications drawn at home from my remarks. I refused to enter into any arguments with the Press or to expand on what I said. They can draw what inferences they like. To try to explain would put me on the defensive and that I refuse.

I immediately began to prepare a despatch to the Department, which I sent on March 9th; in it, I reviewed the facts and events described above and informed the Department as to just what had happened that afternoon in the library of Spaso House.

I quote from my diary for March 10th:

> At 12, saw British Ambassador [Sir Archibald Clark-Kerr] by appointment; he brought a paper for me to read, but I think he really came to talk about the Press release of my statement. Anyway, he told the Press he thought the statement ill-advised, but he told me that it was time someone said it.
>
> At my request, Molotov said he would see me at 6:30 so I spent 6:30 to 8 with him.
>
> Press bulletin carries Welles' remarks on my press statement. Seems the Press boys' release has created considerable of a stir in the States. Soviets have a very effective way of controlling radio—they cut off

the power and our radio goes dead. Mine has just gone dead! God, what a country!

Meanwhile, we had prepared a second message, which read as follows:

Reference to getting [Press] despatches through censor, there was considerable consultation and delay. Censors appeared quite apprehensive and crestfallen and probable that authority of ranking official in the Soviet Government, probably Molotov, was obtained before [Press] despatches were released.

I have informed the Department of my many and frequent endeavors, without success, to obtain information on material benefits of Lend-Lease supplies to Soviet Union. Question has been discussed with Molotov, Vishinsky and Lozovsky, and emphasis placed on the importance of releasing this information and giving it to the United States, probably as an aid in supporting the pending Lend-Lease legislation.

I had no illusions as to my remarks and knew that they might cause displeasure to some of the Soviet authorities and that there may be reverberations. Department may wish to state that I was speaking in a personal capacity and that the Department was not consulted; however, I do not feel that we should remain silent and continue to accept the seeming ungrateful attitude of the Soviet leaders, especially when relief supplies from the American people are concerned. Hope that my remarks may result in clearing the atmosphere and emphasizing to the Russian authorities that the American people are not satisfied with their policy in this respect.

As we had expected, a telegram came from the State Department asking for a report on the circumstances which occasioned my statement on Lend-Lease. That was one message I didn't have to answer.

On March 10th, promptly at 6:30 P.M., Eddie Page and I presented ourselves at Mr. Molotov's office in the Kremlin. I had some routine business to take up. After this was completed, I inquired, "Have you any matter you wish to discuss with me, Mr. Molotov?"

"Why, yes, Mr. Ambassador, I have. I would like to talk to you about your recent Press conference. I do not question your right to make the remarks you did, but, speaking very frankly, I do not agree with you, for the following reasons:

"The Soviet Press has publicized all statements made in America and England as to military aid extended to the Soviet Union;

the Soviet people get first hand information in the form made available by your American leaders as to what aid comes to the Soviet Union from America. Both Mr. Stalin and I, and other Soviet officials, have expressed our gratitude on a number of occasions for the material assistance given to us; both the Soviet Government and the Russian people give full credit to the importance and significance of Allied assistance.

"The Soviet Government did not consider it wise to emphasize in the Press the great extent of the assistance coming from America as that would be apt to come to the attention of the Axis powers and result in a greater effort to destroy the convoys."

I listened attentively as Mr. Pavlov translated, looking around at Eddie Page for his customary nod of confirmation. "First of all, Mr. Molotov," I replied, "I would like to stress that my conversation with the Press the other day was most informal. The general situation as it affects American relief supplies was brought up by one of the correspondents. I remarked in passing that I had been unable to obtain any evidence from the news correspondents and that my aides and I had ourselves seen no mention in the Soviet Press about the receipt and distribution of American relief supplies, either from the American Red Cross or our Russian Relief Society. This has caused me deep concern; when I was home for consultation, I saw at first hand how the American people were digging down in their pockets to furnish relief supplies out of sheer good will and friendship for the Russian people, and yet they are receiving no recognition of this sacrifice. Mind you, I made no assertion that these relief supplies are not being received and distributed—only that the Russian people are not informed as to the source of these supplies and of the good will on the part of the American people."

"But the Russian people are aware of the receipt of Lend-Lease aid," Mr. Molotov protested. "The man in the street knows by heart the number of tanks and planes we have received from America."

"It is unfortunate that my enforced isolation here in Moscow prevents me from having any contact with the man-in-the-street; I am unable to talk to him or to find out what he knows or thinks."

"Do you make a distinction between Lend-Lease aid of approximately two billion dollars and relief supplies amounting to the insignificant sum of ten million dollars?" Mr. Molotov inquired sarcastically.

"Indeed I do," I said warmly. "Lend-Lease is a business trans-

action between our two governments; relief supplies are the chari-
table manifestation of good will and friendship on the part of the
American people. In my estimation, this gives them a considerable
importance all out of proportion to the amount.

"You see, Mr. Molotov, the way we look at things in America,
good will is a two-way street; only one side of it is being used
because the Russian people have been kept from knowing of the
sympathy and help which the American people are trying to extend to the Russian people.

"With regard to Lend-Lease aid, I have attempted for some
weeks now, without success, to obtain from responsible Soviet
officials, including yourself, public acknowledgement of the benefits to Soviet Russia of the Lend-Lease supplies. As far as I know,
the only definite information released on this subject was Mr.
Stalin's reply to Mr. Cassidy's letter last October."

Mr. Molotov stared down at his plump hands clasped together
on the shiny table top. "I doubt the wisdom of accepting the Stalin-
Cassidy letters as our present attitude. I believe that his correspondence has lost the significance it had last fall."

"With nothing else to guide us and the Second Protocol of Russian Lend-Lease now before the American Congress and the American people, I certainly do not believe that the Stalin-Cassidy
correspondence has lost its significance. Furthermore, the American newsmen and General Hurley after their visits to the front
have told me that they saw no evidence of American planes or
tanks in use at the front."

Mr. Molotov looked up at me startled. "I can't understand that.
Perhaps the sector of the front visited by them was not using
American equipment; there is plenty of it in use at the front."

In reading the above, it might appear that we were wrangling.
I wish to correct any such impression; our whole conversation that
day was on a friendly plane with no spirit of asperity, no bickering
or unpleasantness.

After a short pause, Mr. Molotov continued to assert that the
Soviet people were well-advised as to Lend-Lease aid and were
most grateful therefor; not once did he state that there had been
any publicity in the Soviet Union as to relief supplies sent to the
Russian people by the American Red Cross and our Russian Relief Society or any awareness among the Soviet citizens of the
existence or extent of this relief.

"I am personally interested in the question of Red Cross and
Russian Relief supplies," I pointed out. "This is a matter of good

will and friendship between the American and Russian peoples. My remarks to the Press were actuated by that thought alone."

"I'm afraid, then, Mr. Ambassador, that far more importance is being given to your remarks than appears justified. I regret the misinterpretation that has been placed on them and the resulting bad publicity in the United States."

"I hope that my remarks will not have a detrimental effect on Soviet-American relations."

"No, I do not believe so," Mr. Molotov said thoughtfully. "It may even be that they will have a useful effect in America."

I had thought that they might have a "useful effect" upon Russian officials in Moscow. What Mr. Molotov meant, I can only surmise—it may be that he felt that sentiment in America at that time toward the Soviet Union was on too emotional a basis; a dash of cold water might help.

I concluded my report of the above conference to the State Department as follows:

> Efforts to have me amplify or explain or further discuss my statements, except as stated above in my conference with Mr. Molotov, have been unsuccessful, since I have learned of the repercussions caused by my comments; if I had realized the extent of those repercussions, I certainly would not have made my remarks [on aid to Russia] without consulting the Department. Once made, however, and noting the results, I cannot help but be impressed at the conflagration caused by such a small spark; surely with so much inflammable tinder about, it was well to expose it before a serious explosion resulted. For this reason, and from my isolated position [in the Russian capital], I do not believe that my remarks will result in other than good in the long run and they will help in placing our Russian relations on a more realistic basis and thus contribute to closer understanding and good will, both now and in the post-war period.

In his book, *Roosevelt and Hopkins,* page 705, Robert E. Sherwood has given an unfortunate impression as to the reception of my statement in Washington. After noting that "there were more and more questions from Moscow and very few indications of cordiality," he goes on:

> The prevailing tension was not lessened when, on March 8, Ambassador Standley was quoted as informing American newspaper correspondents in Moscow that Russia was getting American supplies in quantity but was keeping the fact from the people and was leading

them to believe that Russia was fighting unaided. In his book, *The Year of Stalingrad*, Alexander Werth has written that the Standley statement "shocked and pained many Russians, who thought it callous and in poor taste." The attitude of the White House toward the statement was somewhat similar, but Harriman reported from London:

Many of my friends here, both British and American, seniors and juniors, are secretly pleased at the way Standley spoke out in Moscow even if this was an indiscretion. The feeling is growing here that we will build trouble for the future if we allow ourselves to be kicked around by the Russians. As an example of this: Maisky has been conducting private talks with American journalists regarding the inadequacy of aid for Russia from the United States in addition to his public statements about the Second Front.

The reception of the news in the White House actually was a bit different. When the news broke at home in the morning paper on March 8th, Mr. Sumner Welles, Under Secretary of State, broke all records in getting from the State, War and Navy Building across to the White House. With great alarm, he announced to President Roosevelt, "Mr. President, our Ambassador in Moscow has committed a great diplomatic blunder; I fear that we must relieve him at once."

With the American Press screaming for my diplomatic head, the President showed great sense, when, as he told me later, he replied, "Sumner, some Admirals talk too much and some don't talk enough. Some are too frank and some are not frank enough. Let's wait and see what happens."

One of the few encouraging notes from the United States was a telegram which read: "Thank God we have one true American in our Foreign Service; signed: Evelyn Walsh McLean." Listening to the radio in San Diego, reading the newspaper headlines, my wife was literally "shivering in her boots" for fear I would be sent to a Soviet concentration camp or shot at sunrise, but she wrote me a letter in which she said, "Go to it, Hal; give it to 'em good."

As usual, in estimating the temper of the American people, the President was almost psychic. Within forty-eight hours, there was a reversal of feeling; the American Press almost as a whole came to my defense and lauded my efforts at "realistic diplomacy." The Communist newspapers in New York and London lit on me with typewriter ribbons soaked in vitriol.

For three days, there was no comment in the Moscow newspapers; then there came a veritable rash of statements about American aid to Russia. The Stettinius Report was published in full. Daily, the papers mentioned American war material issued on this or that sector of the front or praised the generosity of the American people for some gift of Red Cross or Russian Relief supplies. At last, millions of Russians were finding out for the first time of the generosity and genuine friendliness of the American people.

The culmination of this "be kind to America" campaign came in Stalin's unusually friendly May Day proclamation:

> The people of our country meet May First in the stern days of a Patriotic War. . . . Soviet warriors stood up resolutely in defense of the motherland, and now for nearly two years have been defending the honor and independence of the peoples of the Soviet Union. . . .
>
> The winter campaign has demonstrated that the offensive power of the Red Army has grown. Our troops not only hurled the Germans out of the territory the latter had seized in the summer of 1942, but occupied a number of towns and districts which had been in the enemy's hands for about one and a half years. It proved beyond the German's strength to avert the Red Army's offensive. . . .
>
> Simultaneously the victorious troops of our Allies routed the Italo-German troops in the area of Libya and Tripolitania, cleared these areas of enemies and now continue to batter them in the area of Tunisia, while the valiant Anglo-American aviators strike shattering blows at the military and industrial centers of Germany and Italy, foreshadowing the formation of a second front in Europe against the Italo-German fascists.
>
> Thus for the first time since the beginning of the war, the blow dealt at the enemy from the east by the Red Army merged with a blow from the west dealt by troops of our Allies into one joint blow.

At home, members of our Congress, reading and hearing all these emanations from a Soviet propaganda bureau in reverse gear, overwhelmingly approved the legislation authorizing the Second Protocol for Lend-Lease to Russia. What I had set out to do had been accomplished. The plain, hard-working, repressed citizen of Soviet Russia had learned of his friends in America and their generosity and good will. With continued Lend-Lease, Russia would be enabled to fight on.

Perhaps I can be forgiven for quoting something favorable about myself written during those stormy days. In his book, *The Curtain Rises* (page 88), Quentin Reynolds said:

> Stalin knew something which the misguided communists of New York and London didn't know: he knew that William Standley was a

damn good friend of Russia but that Standley, like himself, was a realist and not a fairy godfather, who liked to distribute gifts anonymously. Stalin perhaps knew the whole story of Standley's statement and what was behind it and was probably chuckling, "Good for you, Admiral."

Only perhaps. I was then, and always have been, a true friend of the Russian people. I doubt that Mr. Stalin considered me a good friend of his Communistic regime or cared whether I was or not. Furthermore, I had been in Moscow long enough to know that a stream of propaganda could be turned on and off like water from a hose. This was merely an example of cause and effect—my statement was the cause; continuing Lend-Lease aid to Russia was the effect devoutly to be desired by both the Kremlin and our own government; the pleasant series of complimentary statements to the United States of America and its people was the means chosen to achieve an end.

But the Russians had other, more long reaching aims. One of the means desired most ardently to achieve those aims was a Second Front in Europe in 1943. The Soviet propaganda stream would change force and direction many times before the invasion forces crossed the English Channel on D-Day, but the end in view would always be right out of Marx and Lenin as interpreted by Joseph Stalin.

CHAPTER XXI

General James H. Burns and Russian Lend-Lease

WE WERE about to be inflicted with another deluge of Special Representatives and Very VIP's. The news came in a telegram we received in Moscow on April 8, 1943, which stated that General James H. Burns, Executive Director of the Lend-Lease Administration and liaison officer between the War Department and the Lend-Lease Administrator, was en route to Moscow in an Army C-87 transport expected to reach Teheran on April 15th. I was not previously consulted or informed, so I didn't know why he was coming or what he wanted to do.

General Burns was not unknown to me. A regular Army officer, General Burns graduated from West Point in the Class of 1908. During his long and successful Army career, he specialized in Ordnance, graduated from both the Army War College and the Army Industrial College, and, making Major General in 1940, reached the climax of his Army service as Chief of Army Ordnance.

In 1940, while Chief of Ordnance, General Burns became closely associated with Harry Hopkins. Mr. Hopkins liked him because he was an officer who accomplished results and worked fast. This association was to continue through the frenzied procurement difficulties before the United States entered the War, through Lend-Lease, up to the day of Harry Hopkins' death. In April 1941, General Burns was appointed by President Roosevelt Executive Officer of the Division of Defense Aid Reports of the Office of Emergency Management, which was the first named coined for the Lend-Lease agency. He had no chairman or director over him, which meant that Harry Hopkins ran Lend-Lease for the President through General Burns. At the same time, Burns continued as a member of the staff of Under-Secretary Patterson, who directed procurement in the War Department.

General Burns remained with the Agency when it became the Lend-Lease Administration; when Mr. Edward R. Stettinius, Jr., became Lend-Lease Administrator, General Burns, the Executive Director, had a direct pipeline to the White House through Harry Hopkins. He kept Mr. Hopkins completely informed as to the situation in Lend-Lease.

Both General Burns and I formerly had been members of the American Delegation of the Beaverbrook-Harriman Mission; I have no doubt that he maneuvered the appointment of his friend, Colonel Philip Faymonville, to be Lend-Lease Representative in Moscow.

During Mr. Molotov's mission to Washington, General Burns was very active in behind-the-scenes negotiations with Ambassador Litvinov and Mr. Molotov. I have already mentioned that General Burns was after my Ambassadorial scalp; in the same memorandum dated December 1, 1942, which recommended an Ambassador to Russia "of top rank as to national standing, vision, ability, and willingness to serve the country first," General Burns made some observations about Russia which are interesting today to indicate how far important persons in government were willing to go to placate and appease the Soviets:

> If the Allies are victorious, Russia will be one of the three most powerful countries in the world. For the future peace of the world, we should be real friends so that we can help shape world events in such a way as to provide security and prosperity. Furthermore, Russia's post-war needs for the products of America will be simply overwhelming. She must not only rehabilitate her war losses in homes, industries, raw materials and farms, but she must provide resources for the inevitable advances in her standards of living that will result from the war.
>
> 7. From the above, it seems evident that Soviet relationships are the most important to us of all countries, excepting only the United Kingdom. It seems also evident that we must be so helpful and friendly to her that she will not only battle through to the defeat of Germany and also give vital assistance in the defeat of Japan, but in addition willingly join with us in establishing a sound peace and mutually beneficial relations in the post-war world.

Among his suggestions for improving relationships were:

> (b) Establish a better spirit of "Comrades-in-Arms" by sending General Marshall, Admiral King and General Arnold or other appro-

priate military representatives to confer with corresponding Russian officials in Moscow or some other appropriate location and to discuss freely our plans, our capabilities and our limitations.

(c) Do everything possible in a generous but not lavish way to help Russia by sending supplies to the limit of shipping possibilities and by sending forces to Russia to join with her in the fight against Germany. . . .

(g) Establish the general policy throughout the U.S. departments and agencies that Russia must be considered as a real friend and be treated accordingly and that personnel must be assigned to Russian contacts that are loyal to this concept. . . .

(i) Offer Russia very substantial credits on easy terms to finance her post-war rehabilitation and expansion.

(j) Agree to assist, in every proper and friendly way, to formulate a peace that will meet Russia's legitimate aspirations.*

This was the sort of advice Mr. Hopkins was receiving and passing on to the President in those fateful days.

In Spaso House, we were in a complete state of confusion of mind. We didn't know whether General Burns was coming into the Soviet Union to inspect Lend-Lease Administration or to investigate the differences existing between General Faymonville and my Military Attaché, General Mike Michella, about which both the Lend-Lease Administration and the War Department had been fully informed. As a result, I sent a telegram to General Burns in Teheran in which I invited him to be my guest in Spaso House, to quarter himself with General Faymonville, or to have independent quarters in a Soviet hotel. With Major Klotz recuperating nicely from his bout with pneumonia, I arranged for a Russian pilot and navigator to accompany him in his plane, *Gulliver No. 11*, to Teheran to pick up General Burns if he needed transportation. Several days later, I received a telegram stating that General Burns was on Lend-Lease business and that he would not discuss military matters with the Russians.

Several items of importance requiring my attention in Kuibyshev, on April 15th I went down to our standby embassy in *Gulliver No. 11*, with Major Klotz, now well enough to fly, but still weak and pale from his severe illness. The following morning, I saw him off for Teheran and Cairo. As passengers, he had poor Dooman, my Counselor, who was headed home for hospitalization, and news correspondents Snow, Kerr, and Holt, who had all

* Robert E. Sherwood, *Roosevelt and Hopkins* (New York: Harper & Bros., 1948).

cleared the customs in Moscow. Two new passengers, a Mrs. Winton and son, who boarded the plane in Kuibyshev, had yet to be cleared. Other passengers were Secretary Dickerson, Commander Freddy Lang headed for the Cairo medical conference, Australian Minister Slater and his Secretary, Mr. Duncan, and British General Pette, acting as courier for the British Legation, all of whom enjoyed diplomatic immunity.

Passengers embarked; Klotz began to warm up his engines. Tommy Thompson went into the small shack used as a customs office to complete clearance of the plane. After twenty minutes or so, Major Klotz stopped his engines to conserve gas. I climbed down out of the plane, where I had been visiting with the passengers, and went to the customs office. A Russian official in proper customs uniform, whom I thought was the customs officer, said to me (with Tommy doing the interpreting), "Tell the passengers to bring their baggage here for inspection."

"All the passengers from Moscow cleared customs there. Except for Mrs. Winton and her son, all the Kuibyshev passengers have diplomatic immunity. Their baggage is already loaded in a United States Army plane—I'll have Mrs. Winton's bags brought in, but the rest of it is going to stay right in that plane."

The Russian couldn't seem to understand "diplomatic immunity" and it took some time to put the whole idea across, which would have been impossible without Tommy Thompson and our Embassy messenger, Morris, as the Russians had no interpreter on duty. Finally, the official nodded and said *Da* several times. I had Mrs. Winton bring one small bag for inspection and climbed back up into the plane and told Klotz, "It's all fixed up. You can warm up your engines again."

Again, there was a long delay. I told Klotz to stop his engines, climbed down out of the plane, and went to the customs shack. The customs officer apparently was having difficulty deciphering the Wintons' passports. By this time, I was so enraged that I really read the customs officer off for his stupid performance and the resulting inconvenience to our passengers. He said something to Tommy. "He says he can't read or write, Admiral," Tommy reported. "The regular customs officer is not here."

There was more Russian interchange. "It's all fixed, Admiral. Morris and I will translate the visas for him; he'll give them the proper chops."

I went outside and found Major Klotz standing beside his plane, looking very tired and sick. "I'm sorry, Major," I said. "I know how wretched you feel. This time, I *think* we've got it licked. But don't warm up your engines again until we're sure."

He smiled at me, wanly. "You know, Mr. Ambassador, I'm half Russian. My father escaped from Russia after the Red Revolution. Of course, he told me a lot about the old country when I was a kid. When I was assigned as co-pilot in Mr. Willkie's plane, I had some doubts about going to visit my father's country; but everything worked so smoothly when we flew Mr. Willkie in and out of Russia that I was delighted with Russia. I was also very happy when I was ordered to pilot *Gulliver No. 11* into Russia on this job. But it's all been very different this time. Mr. Willkie's visit was a special deal—everything was done to impress him, to make things appear smooth and easy. From my experience with *Gulliver No. 11* I'll be delighted to get out of my father's country. I hope I never see it again."

We expected General Burns every day, but flying weather out of Teheran was very bad. He arrived on April 21st, which I described in my diary:

> Received word about 3 P.M. that Burns' plane would arrive between 4 and 5; Thompson and I went to the civil airport to meet him. His C-87 finally landed at 5:40 on the brick runway in the middle of a very muddy field. The party consisted of General Burns, Major Mc-Chesney Martin, and Col. Blake; the crew of Captain Corregia and four others. They brought a heavy cargo of freight and mail. Almost the first thing General Burns said to me was, "I want to push on to Moscow, tomorrow." That was agreeable to me and we made plans accordingly.
>
> I took Burns and Martin with me to our Residentia, *Sadovia,* and had the others delivered to the Chancery. We cleaned up and changed hurriedly, for we had been invited for "Chinese chow" at the Chinese Embassy. Present were my guests and myself, the Chinese Ambassador, General Kuo of his staff, and the Chinese Counselor. We had a sumptuous Chinese banquet but had to leave early for early rising.

The next morning we flew to Moscow in General Burns' plane, a rough trip. We went first to Spaso House. General Faymonville took Burns and his party with him to be his guests, which was all right with me.

The next morning, Faymonville came to my office at my request and we discussed having a party for General Burns. Later, Burns and I called on British Ambassador Sir Archibald Clark-Kerr, who was bubbling over with questions:

Was he discussing (Lend-Lease) protocol with the Russians?

Had he observed any lack of cooperation between the British and Americans along the route he traveled?

What route had he come?

At 5:00 P.M., I took General Burns to make a courtesy call on Mr. Molotov in his office in the Commissariat of Foreign Affairs. Although we had no official subjects to discuss, Mr. Molotov was very pleasant, recalling their previous meetings in Washington.

"General Burns would like to go home via either China or Siberia," I suggested.

"I think it can be arranged," Mr. Molotov replied.

"Mr. Stalin might want to discuss Lend-Lease matters with General Burns," I continued, trying to line this very VIP up for a visit with the ruling potentate, as any good Ambassador should.

"I'll convey your suggestion to Mr. Stalin," the Foreign Secretary said, without much enthusiasm.

"If he wishes to see him, the General will await his pleasure."

Easter Sunday came on April 25th; as I had the previous Easter, with a number of my staff, I went to church in the old French Catholic church, St. Louis de Français, in Malaya Lubianka. The church was crowded for the ten A.M. service, with devout Russians standing, heads bent, in all of the aisles. There seemed to be an unusually large number of children present. Father Braun delivered his sermon in Russian but the ushers gave us a transcript in English. Again my NKVD boys were exposed to religion and were blessed several times during the service by Father Braun.

When I returned to Spaso House, I learned that General Burns and his party had also attended church in St. Louis. John Young gave the story to some of the correspondents; they must have been hard up for news for they put out a press release which made a lot of American papers. One headline I saw: "American General Attends Catholic Church in Godless Russia."

Major McChesney Martin was a curiosity to the Russians. Before he joined the Army, he had been President of the New York Stock Exchange, the youngest in history; since the Soviet Government owns all real estate, industry, and most business enterprises in Russia, there is no stock exchange in Moscow. Furthermore, Major Martin was a teetotaler, an attitude difficult for the Russians to comprehend. They simply couldn't believe that a man of McChesney Martin's stature and importance could totally abstain from drinking alcoholic beverages and they used every conceivable device to get Major Martin to take a drink. When they finally realized that he was a sincere and determined teetotaler, they respected his odd viewpoint and let him drink *chi*.

On April 27th, I gave a party for General Burns in Spaso House, which I described in my diary:

> At five, went home for party and dressed. We had everybody in Moscow who had any interest in Lend-Lease—the British Ambassador, British General Martel and all the officers of his Supply Mission, a number of the British Embassy Staff, all our own officers, State, Army, Navy, civilians of the Supply Mission and the Red Cross, and 23 Russians, all connected with Lend-Lease, headed by Commissar for Foreign Trade Mikoyan, the largest turnout of Russians at any party we gave. I tried to have a receiving line so that Burns could meet everybody, but the Russians didn't seem to take to the idea.
>
> The Great Hall never looked better. John Young had put our new electronic phonograph behind curtains on the balcony, its rack loaded with good records. He took his place at the balcony rail and pretended to direct the orchestra in the various pieces. The illusion was so perfect that many people asked me where I got the wonderful orchestra.
>
> We had a fine buffet set up in the State Dining Room. Afterward, we screened some recent news reels and *Sun Valley Serenade*, which had the Russians talking excitedly among themselves.
>
> It was a grand party; the Russians took a few drinks, really loosened up and seemed to have fun. I had complimentary remarks from all sides; but somehow I don't believe that General Burns really enjoyed the party.

As far as I could tell, General Burns was having a very pleasant and successful visit. But I wasn't happy. I had told the President that I didn't want any more special emissaries sent to Russia unless they were told to report to me and work with and under me as the Chief Representative of the United States of America in Soviet Russia. General Burns certainly was not behaving like that. I ran across this passage in a letter I wrote to my wife:

> April 29—Saw Burns for a few minutes. I went to his office. Am waiting to see if he ever takes any note of "The American Ambassador." He has paid no courtesy call, comes to see me only when I send for him.

This seemed to me to be all a part of the old Faymonville trouble. Upon my return to Moscow, General Faymonville had reported to me for "coordination and supervision"; seemingly our Lend-Lease difficulties had been solved, or so I thought. Mike

Michella said he could see no change in the situation—Faymonville still received requests for information and supplies, got the answers through Lend-Lease in Washington, and passed them back to the Russians without letting Michella in on the exchange. For several months, I had no reason to believe that General Faymonville was not acting in good faith. But lately, he had begun to act more independently, although always perfectly correct in his manner and attitude toward me.

After my party for General Burns, he spent most of his time with Faymonville and I saw him only at parties given for him, of which there were an unusual number.

On April 29th, Colonel Gray of Faymonville's Supply Mission gave a party, which I wrote up in my diary:

> We all went down in the station wagon [several of the embassy staff and myself]. Met a number of ballerinas who were there as guests and the boys enjoyed dancing with these young women, who were all attractive and good dancers. General Burns and his staff were guests of honor; the crew of his plane were also there. Plenty to eat and drink. I came home early, alone, turned in and read *A Lost Empire* by Chevigny, an interesting story of Russian activities in the Pacific.

On April 30th, General Martel, head of the British Supply Mission, gave a dinner in honor of General Burns; among the guests were Admiral Fisher, on from London for a visit, Jack Duncan, Page, and myself. The guest of honor failed to show up—he had gone on an inspection trip with Faymonville and didn't get back to Moscow in time.

I had other troubles beside General Burns and Faymonville. This was the period when the Soviet Government was breaking off diplomatic relations with the Polish-Government-in-Exile. But worse still, I had received a telegram from the State Department that former Ambassador Joseph E. Davies was being sent to Moscow as Special Representative of the President with a secret message for Premier Stalin.

With Burns in my hair, Faymonville acting so very independently, this was too much. I had warned the President about sending any more Special Representatives to by-pass and humiliate me. As I wrote my wife about this time:

> Long before you get this, Davies will be in here. I would be glad if he came in to take my place, but guess there is no such luck. Burns

is to await his arrival and, with Faymonville, they should be able to make whatever decision they want; although the Russians know all about Davies' trip and who is with him, my own government has given me no word whatsoever. However, I am not worrying. They can do what they want. The position of Ambassador here is impossible; I have ceased to struggle. I will do the best I can under most annoying circumstances.

The reason was that, on May Day, the big Communist holiday, I had finally made up my mind. I had been by-passed once too often. I had had enough. I sat down and wrote out my letter of resignation to the President, which was dated May 3, 1943, and which included the following paragraphs:

> I wish to inform you of a decision I have reached. . . . I do not wish to spend another Winter here as Ambassador to the Soviet Union.
>
> As you must know, I have always been ready to serve you or make any sacrifice for my country, just as so many of our young men are doing, if it were to my country's interest to do so. By the same reasoning I am not willing to attempt to continue service in a position where it can be better rendered by someone else.
>
> I accepted the invitation to come here as your Ambassador believing that the military effort was of paramount importance and that diplomacy would remain in the background for the duration of the war. . . . But the time is rapidly approaching . . . when plans will be in the making for peace discussion and the post-war period. In the development of these plans, the interests of our country require that you have in Moscow as your Ambassador one who does not only enjoy your complete confidence but one who is also skilled by training and long experience in the field of diplomacy and international affairs. I do not feel I have this training and time and circumstance will not permit negotiation by special representatives.

I went on to say that I could, if he so desired, give "many good reasons why I should not remain in Moscow" and pleaded the usual excuse of "waning strength and declining years"; I asked to be out of Moscow by October 10, 1943. I subscribed myself, "With the utmost loyalty and respect, William H. Standley."

With this letter in the outgoing mail pouch, I heaved a sigh of relief; a great weight had been lifted from my chest. Now, I could face any annoyance and humiliation which the Davies' visit might bring.

While I waited for official information about the Davies Mission, I heard plenty of unofficial gossip about it. The Polish Ambassador, Mr. Romer, coming to bid me farewell, told me that Mr. Davies was coming to Moscow on a special mission to negotiate the Polish question. Sir Archibald Clark-Kerr told me that Mr. Davies was coming to urge Marshal Stalin to meet with President Roosevelt to discuss the prosecution of the War and post-war problems. The State Department told me nothing.

It turned out that Sir Archibald was right. In Robert Sherwood's book, *Roosevelt and Hopkins* (page 733), I have found this statement:

> Davies agreed to make a brief trip to Moscow in May to convey to Stalin Roosevelt's suggestion that the two of them should meet and straighten matters out. It was Roosevelt's belief that he might be able to break the ice with Stalin more readily if Churchill were not present; with personal relations established a meeting of the Big Three could be held later on.

Meanwhile, the situation with General Burns and Faymonville became more difficult and confused. I noted in my diary that I was having trouble obtaining permission and visas for General Burns to return home via the ALSIB route, making representations to the Commissar for Foreign Trade, the Red Army, and Red Air Force on April 29, and that I "pushed the request" on May 3. My diary of that date says:

> Discussed [General Burns'] attitude toward Lend-Lease activities and asked rather pointedly when he was leaving so I could push request for trip through Alaska.

I "made representations" on this subject to either the Foreign Office or Military authorities most every day; finally on May 8th, I noted this in my diary:

> Got word from Zarubin [that] General Burns' trip OK either through Chungking or through Siberia.

Two days later, I talked to Burns about his trip and suggested he take the ALSIB route as other planes had gone via Chungking and I thought he would get more information out of the Trans-Siberian flight.

When Burns heard of the Davies' visit, he decided that he would await his arrival and go home in company with him. We had to start the routine of permission and visas all over again.

Faymonville's activities were giving me increasing concern. On April 24th, I noted in my diary:

> Had conference with Administrative Officer [of the Embassy], Faymonville, Michella and Duncan—discussed food and stores situation and cooperation in general. Spoke to Faymonville privately regarding his activities and political matters as they affected Lend-Lease—did not make a dent. He gives Russian desires priority above all else.

This situation finally came to a head on May 4th when, as I noted in the diary, I "saw Faymonville, told him my opinion of his activities." This came about when Mike Michella reported to me that a situation had developed with the Russians which indicated that General Faymonville had engaged in activities which affected the military situation. I sent for him.

"General," I said, "I am sorry to hear that you have been mixed up in strictly military intelligence affairs again, a province which belongs exclusively to General Michella. What have you to say about it?"

"Yes, sir," he admitted, readily enough. "I took that action, Admiral, in obedience to instructions from the Lend-Lease Administration."

"What was the nature of those instructions?"

"They came in a secret letter from the Administrator."

"Will you let me see that letter, please?"

Although he was a member of my Embassy Staff and under my "general overall coordination and supervision," he said, "I'm sorry sir. I cannot let you see the letter because it is highly secret."

I kept my temper. Calmly, I indicated that the conference was at an end. I pondered over this untenable situation for many hours. I could make representation to the State Department and raise a big ruckus back in Washington, but what was the use? The line of communications from Lend-Lease to the Russians through Faymonville had not been discontinued as promised. As far as Lend-Lease matters were concerned, I, as Ambassador, was still an innocent bystander, and just as likely to get hurt as anyone who occupies that innocuous position. Harry Hopkins was independent of everyone in Government except the President. That was the reality of the situation against which it was useless to "take arms."

As I wrote to my wife a few days later:

General Burns goes out via Alaska after Davies arrives. Davies is due in Teheran between the 16th and 20th. I still don't know what it is all about, but I have ceased to care; I'm just marking time until I can come home and I don't intend to get into any more controversial questions if I can help it—and I mean to help it. There are too many people at home ready to heave dead cats the moment anyone refuses to swallow Sovietism and the Soviet hook, line, and sinker. Well, I prefer to maintain a benevolent neutrality for the rest of my days here.

The hectic round of entertainment for General Burns continued until the day of Mr. Davies' arrival. On April 6th, Mr. Mikoyan, Commissar for Foreign Trade, gave a dinner honoring General Burns and his officers. I hurried home from a conference with Mr. Molotov to pick up Burns and Faymonville to take them to the official Soviet Guest House, Spirodonov, where Mr. Mikoyan always entertained. It was another Russian drinking bout, with the excellent Soviet wine stressed, as always, by Mr. Mikoyan. The dinner included the usual lavish display of foodstuffs, similar to a Kremlin banquet. I was asked to give a toast and responded with a tribute to our host, which General Faymonville translated for me. Mr. Mikoyan told me that he was going to send me a case of wine; later, he did send a case to both General Burns and myself.

On his way into Moscow from Teheran, General Burns had given a lift to Mr. Kamenev, head of VOKs. On May 7th, Mr. Kamenev gave a party to honor General Burns and his officers, to which a number of the Embassy Staff and I were invited. After furnishing us with highballs or vodka, our host led us into a darkened sitting room, and screened for our enjoyment a Russian picture called *Sevastopol*, depicting the siege and evacuation of that Crimean stronghold.

After the movie, we sat down to an elaborate official banquet, but Mr. Kamenev varied the regular routine; also as guests, he had eight English speaking movie stars; each American guest had on his right an attractive Russian girl, one of Kamenev's assistants, whose duty it was to entertain him and translate for him. After an orgy of food, a snappy orchestra played popular tunes for dancing. It was the most enjoyable party I attended in Russia.

As we rode home to Spaso, John Young said, "Admiral, that's the finest Russian film, technically, that I've seen. It measures up to our best American documentaries."

Burns and Faymonville proved to be pleasant party companions, but I was tired and a bit fed up with the elaborate entertainment thrust on our visiting Executive Director of Lend-Lease, which, perforce, I had to attend, or pretend indisposition. Officially, both Burns and Faymonville continued to ignore me.

On May 11th, Colonel Gray of Faymonville's staff phoned to inform me that Generals Burns and Faymonville would be out of town for a few days and could not be reached.

"Where did they go?" I asked.

"I wasn't informed, sir."

A fine situation, two generals of the U. S. Army had disappeared into the heart of Soviet Russia and the American Ambassador had no information as to where they had gone. The more I thought about it, the angrier I became. Finally, I sent for Major Martin. "Have a seat, Major," I said, as pleasantly as I could. "Let us have no more beating about the bush. Where have your Boss and General Faymonville gone?"

The Major could probably see that I had about reached the boiling point. "Why, they're at the Front, guests of the Red Army, Mr. Ambassador. I thought you knew."

"No, I didn't know. Thank you."

On May 14th, our wandering generals returned to Moscow. Usual procedure for any visiting dignitary fortunate enough to visit the front was to check back with the Ambassador and tell the Military Attaché and the Ambassador everything he had seen that was new. Not these American generals! I waited patiently for three days for a report or at least a courtesy call. By contrast, General Martel, Head of the British Supply Mission, came to me by appointment at noon on May 22nd, and reported the results of his week-long visit to the front. My diary exclaims, "He asked that General Michella be present, so different from our own Generals, Burns and Faymonville!"

I sent for Faymonville. I told him that he had gotten mixed up in military business again. I was glad to have him visit the front, but he must remember that he was a member of my Embassy Staff and I had a right to know where he was at all times. His action, I told him, was typical of the manner in which he kept me in ignorance of Russian Lend-Lease activities and I didn't like it.

Faymonville was suave and conciliatory. I knew how the Russians were, he said. You had to work with them carefully or you didn't get anything from them. It had taken skillful negotiation to arrange this visit to the front—so valuable to the Lend-Lease Program for General Burns to see the Russian Front—he hadn't wanted *anything* to upset the arrangements. Again, he told me, I knew how the Russians were.

I certainly did. I'd had plenty of exasperating dealings with them. "But, Faymonville, had you notified me the previous night or the morning you left, how could it have fouled things up? You're talking in circles. You know damned well you should have informed me; you certainly should have reported your return and told Michella and me what you saw."

Faymonville looked at me quizzically without answering.

"You know perfectly well that in failing to inform me of your departure and the purpose thereof you were violating the provisions of the telegram of December 12, from the Lend-Lease Administrator giving detailed instructions regarding the functions of the U. S. Supply Mission in the USSR," and I reminded Faymonville in no uncertain terms of the requirements of the provisions of those instructions:

3. The Chief of the Supply Mission will be subject to overall coordination and supervision by the Chief of the Diplomatic Mission, will keep the latter fully informed on all activities, will consult with and be guided by his views on any proposed action on questions that are political in character or affect established policies, and will ask his assistance when necessary in the solution of any questions of sufficient importance to justify his participation.

4. In conformity with the above policy, the Chief of the Supply Mission will report to the Chief of the Diplomatic Mission, USSR.

I informed Faymonville that hereafter I would expect complete observance by him of these instructions. However, these precautionary measures did not overcome General Faymonville's sympathies for the Russian cause, and this intolerable situation in Lend-Lease continued to trouble me as long as I remained Ambassador to the USSR.

That afternoon, I sent for General Burns and told him in no uncertain terms what I thought of his action in leaving Moscow without letting me know where he was going, my views with regard to the Lend-Lease situation in Moscow, and General Faymonville's attitude in regard thereto. I got nowhere. As I wrote my wife the next day, "General Burns is of the same belief as Faymonville; Russian interests come first, last and all the time; it's hopeless."

CHAPTER XXII

Ambassador Joseph E. Davies, Special Representative of the President

WITH General Burns "out of my hair" for a few days, I turned my attention to a more serious threat to my peace of mind. I had been following Mr. Davies' progress from the United States across Africa, via Accra and Cairo to Teheran. On May 17th, he flew into Kuibyshev and I talked to him by phone. Flying weather was "very bad" and he did not think he could come on the next day; yet he flew over to Stalingrad and back that day. I had already been informed that Ambassador Maxim Litvinov was coming home, a day or so behind Davies. Perhaps it was a coincidence that Mr. Litvinov caught up with Davies in Kuibyshev.

Joseph Davies is so well and favorably known by the American people that presenting any extensive background would be superfluous. However, at the risk of redundancy, here are a few basic facts about the man who once was my friend and golfing companion.

In *Who's Who in America*, he lists himself as lawyer, diplomat, author. He began his diplomatic career early and under impeccable Democratic auspices as economic adviser to President Wilson at the Versailles Peace Conference. Mr. Davies married Marjorie Post, heiress to the Post millions and Postum Cereal Company. From 1936–38, he was Ambassador to the Union of Soviet Socialist Republics, from which post he went as Ambassador to Belgium with additional duty as Minister to Luxembourg, 1938–1939. I learned, to my surprise, in consulting *Who's Who,* that he was "Special Envoy of President Roosevelt *with the rank of Am-*

bassador" to confer with Marshal Stalin, May-June 1943. For these and other services to the United States during World War II, in 1946 he was awarded the Medal of Merit, the highest civilian decoration of the United States of America. Among many other clubs, he belonged to the Burning Tree Golf Club of Bethesda, Maryland, of which I was also a member.

I had known Mr. Davies for a number of years, quite pleasantly. Doubtless, he came over expecting to find a friend in Spaso House, and, indeed, I so considered myself; I have always liked him. But some things even the most beautiful friendship can not survive.

Mr. Davies' big DC-4 sat down on the Moscow military airport at 5:04 P.M., May 19th. It carried a fine crew of nine officers and men of the Army Air Forces. In his immediate entourage were: Lieutenant Stamm, U. S. Naval Reserve, his nephew, secretary, and "aide"; his former valet, a corporal in the U. S. Army, who was brought along to supervise the preparation of his food, as Mr. Davies was in poor health; and his personal physician, whose name and military status escape me at the moment. As Quentin Reynolds put it at the time:

> We all admired the courage of Mr. Davies in undertaking a very difficult 16,000-mile trip by air. No one here questions his need of a secretary, a valet, and a physician. But everyone in journalistic and diplomatic circles here questions the necessity of such a formidable entourage to deliver two ounces of mail. . . .
>
> What bewilders us (and we are sure bewilders Stalin) is the fact that the President has sent Mr. Davies to deliver the letter. Our embassy is just across the street from the Kremlin and Ambassador Standley is never too busy to walk over to the Kremlin with a letter. . . .
>
> There was a distinct Hollywood tinge to the whole Davies visit. . . . Maxim Litvinov arrived a day or so after Mr. Davies, and Litvinov brought a print of the Warner Brothers picture, *Mission to Moscow,* with him.[*]

Mr. Davies was met by Mr. Dekanozov, representing the Foreign Office; Mr. Zarubin, who occupied the American desk in the Foreign Office; Mr. Molochkov of the NKVD, and Mr. Yesignaiev of the office of Military Intelligence.

Davies was first off the plane, playing to the gallery as usual. He was introduced to everybody and had his picture taken innumerable times. As I wrote my wife:

[*] Quentin Reynolds, *The Curtain Rises* (New York: Random House, 1944).

Davies arrived yesterday, clowning as usual, but he is a friendly clown, and if I have to put up with clowns and publicity hounds, I'd rather it be a friendly one; Davies knows the problems and is cooperating with me. Of course, it all can't help but discredit me, but I am past that hurdle now. I told Davies he need not worry because I am through. I have already sent in my letter of resignation to the President. I suggested to Davies that he relieve me. That would seemingly be to the best interests of our country, but he is here in the interests of Davies. Just the same, I'll do my best to cooperate with him.

After he had met everyone and spoken to me, he said, "Come on, Bill, let's get going to Spaso House; I want to meet the boys of the Press."

Mr. Dekanozov was standing to one side, fidgeting nervously. "Later, Joe," I whispered. "Mr. Dekanozov is here representing the Foreign Office; he has instructions to take you to Number Eight, our U. S. Guest House. The Russians won't understand, if you decline their hospitality and go to Spaso House first."

"Why didn't you tell me before?" he muttered; then in a louder voice "Why, hello again, Mr. Dekanozov; shall we be on our way?"

Mr. Dekanozov and I took him to Number Eight, the same house which Mr. Willkie occupied; there was the same arrangement of food, silverware, household equipment, and servants. After moving into Number Eight briefly and thanking Mr. Dekanozov, we hurried to Spaso House.

Mr. Davies received the English and American correspondents in our comfortable library. The press conference got off to a good start with a little speech by Mr. Davies on our relations with Soviet Russia. I could see the boys of the Press stiffening up, because he was trying to feed them his ideas on Russia, already voluminously expounded in his book, *Mission to Moscow;* I know I couldn't swallow them and I'm sure that the Press boys didn't either.

After this "set speech," Mr. Davies gave an informal account of his visit to Stalingrad. "Such destruction you have never seen," he said to these men who felt that they were closer to the Russian situation and knew more about it than Mr. Davies did. "The heroism exhibited by those great Russian people during the German attack! As a symbol of our American sympathy for their sacrifices, I asked permission to place a wreath on the grave of the unknown Russian dead buried in the public square. I recalled the procedure at home for placing a wreath on the grave of the Unknown Soldier in Arlington Cemetery. When they gave me the wreath, I approached the grave slowly and solemnly, head uncovered, making a definite pause at every third step, until finally I stood before the grave of those unknown Russian soldiers. I made a little speech and then placed the wreath on the grave."

"Can you tell us what you said?" one of the newsboys asked.

Mr. Davies hesitated. "No, I don't just recall, but I think my secretary can give you a copy." He stopped, as if thinking. "Oh, oh, wait a minute. I think I have a copy in my pocket."

Whereupon, he brought forth not one copy but several, and presented one to each of the correspondents. "By the way boys, will you see that the Russian Press gets a copy?" he asked, and, of course, they agreed.

Mr. Davies and I dined alone that first evening and discussed amicably the whole wide range of Russian problems. He had told me that, before leaving Washington, he had been informed that I had asked to be relieved. "You shouldn't do it, Bill," he went on. "You've done a fine job here; everyone in the administration is well pleased. I hope that you won't insist upon the acceptance of your resignation. You know, your very undiplomatic statement about Lend-Lease last Spring—that storm has blown itself out. You have won. The American public is now completely behind you and agree with what you said. You certainly should not quit, now."

The next morning, I found on my desk among the usual translations of the Soviet newspapers, a long statement by Mr. Davies, which I briefed into a telegram to the Secretary of State, about as follows:

It is good to get back to Moscow, if only for a brief visit. I made many warm friends here during my tour of duty; I find much pleasure in renewing those contacts.

I was particularly happy to return as a Special Representative of President Roosevelt and bearer of a message to Premier Stalin, Russia's great leader.

Russia's amazing resistance to Hitler has startled the world, as I predicted it would. We must acknowledge the difference in ideological concepts between the United States and the USSR, but when I departed Moscow five years ago, I had an immense admiration and respect for the great Soviet civil and military leaders and for the great Russian people.

The greatness of the USSR is typified by Stalingrad and innumerable other communities great and small, where Russian people were subjected to great suffering in their death struggles.

I hope after peace comes that I may visit the Soviet Union many times; I am sure the future also holds great pride for the Russion people. Trained manpower and mechanized power is just reaching the peak of production under the long-range planning of the Big Three and other United Nations leaders. The complete destruction of Fascist aggression is as certain to follow as the night follows day.

I had been invited to Number Eight for luncheon. When I arrived, I found that Mr. Davies had not waited for my official reception to lead off the social events of his visit, but had taken over and was entertaining, as if he were the Ambassador. With Soviet dishes, silver, glassware, and food, he was doing a far more elaborate job than I could under existing war conditions. He had about ten people of his and my staff and a lot of other guests; in effect, it was a full Soviet banquet.

I had arranged an appointment for Mr. Davies to make a courtesy call on Mr. Molotov that afternoon at five. We had nothing to bring up and so the conversation was very informal. As we rose to leave, Mr. Molotov said, "Premier Stalin will see Mr. Davies and you at nine."

This was a surprise, a bit more sudden than I had expected. Evidently Mr. Stalin was eager to get the much heralded "secret letter" which Mr. Davies bore.

We had scheduled a reception and supper party in Mr. Davies' honor. Mr. Davies and I played gin rummy in my sitting room until 6:30, when we went down to receive our guests. We had as guests practically all of the Diplomatic Corps, the Press, and a few Russian generals and government officials. At 6:45, we screened some fairly recent news reels and an Eddie Cantor picture, which I had discovered my guests preferred to a long pre-dinner cocktail hour. Mr. Davies and I stayed at the movie until eight, then went into the family dining room for a snack before going to the Kremlin. One never knew how long an interview with Mr. Stalin would last and refreshments were never served.

As we stood beside the long dining table munching sandwiches, Eddie Page turned to Mr. Davies. "Do you have the letter, sir?"

Mr. Davies shook his head. "I'm not going to deliver the President's letter until I can see Mr. Stalin alone."

I felt as if I had been kicked in the stomach. In plain language, he meant that a letter, which not only Mr. Stalin and Mr. Molotov, but also the interpreter, Mr. Pavlov, would read, by the President's orders, could not be read or even discussed in the presence of the American Ambassador, the regularly accredited representative in the Soviet Union. A pretty state of affairs!

"Look, Mr. Davies," I said, dropping the familiar "Joe" for the moment, "I made this appointment with Mr. Stalin for you to present your letter from the President. If you aren't going to deliver that letter, I'll call off the appointment."

"As a matter of fact, Bill, I have the letter in my pocket."

"Good. I will respect the President's wishes and not be present when you deliver the letter, but it must be delivered at this meeting."

Mr. Davies, Eddie Page and I went in the Embassy limousine to the gate of the Kremlin and down the winding roads to the palace. Upon entering Stalin's conference room, I shook hands with the Russian dictator, presented Mr. Davies, and stated the purpose of his visit. "Our President has intimated that he does not want me to be present when his letter is delivered. With your permission, Mr. Stalin, I will withdraw."

"As you please."

Eddie and I went down the long corridors of the palace and took our car to Spaso House and the "Davies Party." It was a good party and I had a fine time with the guests I had invited to meet Mr. Davies. But I told my wife:

> I have not seen Mr. Davies since, so I don't know anything about what was in the letter or what went on in the Kremlin. I lay awake half the night wondering what I should do; that's why I'm disgusted, more so than usual.

About eleven the next morning, Mr. Davies phoned; he said he wasn't feeling well, and hemmed and hawed. Finally, I said, "You want me to come over. Is that it?"

"Yes."

I went over to Number Eight where I found him still abed. He told me about his visit with Mr. Stalin. He presented the letter which was written in Russian and so he couldn't know what was in it. He spent two-and-a-half hours with Stalin but did not discuss the contents of the letter.*

I have previously described my visit to Mr. Davies' luxurious

---

* After eleven hours with Stalin, Davies reported that his suggestion had at first evoked a great many suspicious questions concerning the purpose of this meeting, but Stalin became convinced that there was no purpose other than a friendly one and he agreed to meet Roosevelt on July 15, providing for a possible postponement of two weeks if developments on the Eastern Front compelled it. Robert E. Sherwood, *Roosevelt and Hopkins* (New York: Harper & Bros., 1948), p. 734.

home in Miami and how impressed I was by the fact that his colored butler still referred to him as "Mr. Ambassador." When I stayed for lunch, I soon discovered that his nephew and the pilots of his plane all called him "Mr. Ambassador." Lieutenant Stamm even wore the gold aiguillettes prescribed for aide to an Ambassador, all of which seemed a little peculiar to me. Of course, I hadn't been told that Mr. Davies was traveling "with the rank of Ambassador."

In my letter to Evelyn, I have this note on Lieutenant Stamm:

> He is travelling high, wide, and handsome on the Soviet food and wine. He is just a plain *ass*.

At five I returned to Number Eight to sit in on Mr. Davies' next press conference. Present was a very select group from the corps of foreign correspondents: Eddie Gilmore, Quent Reynolds, and Bill Downes. Mr. Davies led off the conference by giving a detailed, play-by-play account of his audience with Mr. Stalin, in which he revealed nothing of real importance.

"What was the letter about?" one of the boys asked.

"It was a secret letter, boys. I can't tell you its contents."

"Was Ambassador Standley with you?"

"Well ... hmm ... er ... haw. Why, yes, that is, Admiral Standley went to the Kremlin with me."

That was all he had to offer. "Mr. Davies," Eddie Gilmore said, "there is something that is troubling us very much as Americans. Did you discuss with Mr. Stalin the apparent lack of Russian cooperation, particularly with regard to giving us information about German military and naval matters, which might help to save the lives of many American soldiers and sailors?"

"Off the record boys—off the record." He paused for a long moment, apparently collecting his thoughts. A slow flush mounted into his cheeks. "No, I did not discuss any such thing with Mr. Stalin. I'm here to deliver a personal letter from President Roosevelt to Premier Stalin, not to air a lot of opinions. Besides, there has always existed the fullest cooperation on the part of the Russian authorities; they are furnishing the American Government all the information we ask for. Fear of breach of security on the part of a few subordinate officers might make the Russians appear to be suspicious and hesitant to give military information to our Military and Naval Attachés, but I'm sure there is no such attitude at the top."

This annoyed the correspondents, who had been in Russia so long that they knew Moscow as well as they knew their own home towns. A violent argument followed. By their attitude, Mr. Davies said, the correspondents were as good as guilty of treason to their own country and of playing into the hands of Hitler and his gang.

The newspaper boys boiled over, all shouting at once. Mr. Davies held up his hand for silence, his face flushed with anger. "Now, look here, fellows, I don't want to quarrel with you, but you need to reexamine your attitude and have faith in Russia. The Soviets could make many complaints against us, too, you know. You can do tremendous harm to our country by criticizing the Soviet Union in your articles."

After this sermon from "The Ambassador," the discussion became so heated that I took it upon myself to terminate the conference and show the boys out.

I noted in my diary and in a letter to Mrs. Standley:

The Press needled Mr. Davies about Russian "non-cooperation," and he got livid with rage, charged them all—and by implication, me too—with disloyalty. He resented any criticism whatever of Russia. I'm afraid he won't be too happy over [this press conference]; it will be a boomerang.

I had dinner there and Oumansky came in, the same as he did for Willkie. I have tried without success to get in touch with Oumansky ever since I came to Moscow, but the minute a "liberal" arrives from America, Oumansky appears.

Then we went to the circus with Oumansky. I stopped by Jack's [Duncan] to hear the newsboys' reaction—they are boiling mad.*

---

* "We correspondents without exception admire and like the Russians enormously—so much so that we have taken unto ourselves one of their greatest characteristics, that of realistic thinking. Like Standley, we too think of Lend-Lease as a two-way street. . . . But what we really wanted was information; information from the Red Army about German weapons that would help our men defend themselves when the time came for that so-called second front . . .

"Because our position was unofficial, we were given information and we picked up gossip that even our own embassy and G-2 people could not by virtue of their official position have access to. If we couldn't be doing something useful, we should, we all felt, be in uniform. That's why we all tried to give Mr. Davies the real picture of the difficulties under which our official representatives were laboring. We hoped that he'd go right to Stalin with a strong complaint. We thought that Stalin, if informed by Mr. Davies, might with one slash cut the absurd red tape that was preventing us from being 100 per cent partners in this enterprise of war. As it was, we were members of the same corporation but we all felt our relationship should be that of partners; the relationship that Britain and America enjoy, with mutual trust

As a result of this conference, I prepared a despatch to the State Department, which went in part:

> Mr. Davies held a press conference yesterday afternoon in which he took such violent exception to criticism of Soviet officials' failure to give U.S. needed military information about Germans that discussion became heated and correspondents left conference extremely annoyed with attitude of Mr. Davies. Wisdom of sending to Moscow a man with such violent views pro or contra is questionable.

At four that afternoon of May 22nd, Mr. Davies called in the same three correspondents for an "off the record" conference. I learned that evening that he had apologized abjectly for his display of anger the previous afternoon. But from what some of the boys told me, I don't think he fooled the Press. I noted in a letter to my wife:

> They [the news correspondents] are sure he is here in the interest of his book and his movie, *Mission to Moscow*. I understand that Mr. Litvinov brought a copy of the film with him.* He has asked Young to assist in rewriting the script for the benefit of Russian Relief. Stalin may show the picture at [Davies'] banquet.

That evening, Mr. Davies entertained Mr. Litvinov at dinner; afterward, he took Mr. Litvinov and myself to an operetta called *Rivals*, a grand comedy in three acts—other guests were Admiral Duncan, General Michella, Mr. Chase of the Embassy staff, and Mr. Davies' aide and nephew, Lieutenant Stamm, USNR. Tea and fruit cake were served between the acts.

It will be recalled that bad weather was given as the reason for Mr. Davies' layover in Kuibyshev; it was rather an odd concidence that, on the day Mr. Davies arrived in Moscow, the Russian Ambassador to the United States, Maxim Litvinov, also arrived, re-

---

and respect. We hoped that Mr. Davies would report what we had said to the President. We weren't talking opinions. A reporter can't indulge in the luxury of opinion. We were talking facts and, if we were a little rough on Mr. Davies, he realized we meant no discourtesy; we were merely trying to emphasize the importance of what we wanted to convey." Quentin Reynolds, *The Curtain Rises* (New York: Random House, 1944), p. 84.

* We were never certain whether Mr. Davies' film, *Mission to Moscow*, was brought to Moscow by Davies or Litvinov. Ambassador Alexander Kirk, our representative to Cairo, told me he asked each of them and each denied having the film with him.

portedly carrying a copy of the film, *Mission to Moscow*. Perhaps, it was just another coincidence that on this same day the news was released that the Third Communist International (Third Comintern) had been dissolved.

That evening at the operetta, we sat in a small box, just the three of us, with Mr. Litvinov on the left, Mr. Davies in the middle, and myself on the right. During one of the intermissions, Mr. Litvinov leaned across Mr. Davies and asked, "What do you think of the news, Admiral?"

"What news?"

"Dissolving the Third Comintern."

"Wonderful. That will have a good effect upon the attitude of the American people toward your Government." I had a sudden hunch that Mr. Litvinov was endeavoring to tie in Mr. Davies' visit with the dissolution of the Third Comintern, so I quickly added, "Did the Russian Government have anything to do with dissolving the Third Comintern?"

"No, the Soviet Government had nothing to do with it," he replied. "It's been under consideration for over three years."

The reincarnation of the Third Comintern under the name of the Cominform fully justifies my belief that the Comintern never was dissolved; it just went underground for the duration of the War. The dissolution was reported as a measure to help to allay the prejudice and suspicion of the American people. Quite possibly, this action resulted from my conversation with Mr. Litvinov in Washington in December, 1942.

I returned home early and turned in. My diary records:

> Got word at 11:30 P.M. Stalin wants to give a dinner in Kremlin [at 7:00 P.M. tomorrow night] for Mr. Davies and the American Ambassador, wanted a list of guests. Could not locate anyone with Davies' party, nor General Burns nor Faymonville—no one knew where they were. We made up a list and sent it to Mr. Pavlov, Stalin's secretary.

Those Russian hours of doing business would be the death of all of us yet.

When I reached the office in the morning, Eddie Page was steaming. He still hadn't been able to reach the Davies' party. General Burns, Faymonville, and party had left town at 9:00 A.M. the previous morning and no one knew where they were. It was terribly embarrassing, for we had accepted the invitation for our two errant generals, and we didn't know whether they would make it or not. Furthermore, they had skipped out of town again without letting the Embassy know. I was boiling.

We finally reached Lieutenant Stamm and had the Davies' group properly invited; we had to send out a search through the Red Army and Air Force for Burns and Faymonville, which did not sit well with me.

At 6:45 P.M., we stopped by Number Eight with two Embassy cars and picked up Mr. Davies and his party to take them to the Kremlin. The Soviet bureaucrats can move with despatch when they will—General Burns and General Faymonville showed up in the Great Palace just under the wire.

Up to a certain point, it was the usual, stereotyped Kremlin banquet which I have described a number of times. The Soviet Officials, commissars, Army and Air Force Generals, Navy Admirals, and Foreign Trade representatives were already assembled in the anteroom of the Catherine the Great Room, when the British and American guests arrived. The British Ambassador, Sir Archibald Clark-Kerr, and some of his staff, General Martel and most of his British Supply Mission, represented the British. American guests consisted of Mr. Davies and all the officers of his party, General Burns and his aides, General Faymonville and several officers of his mission, and myself and a few of my staff. Mr. Davies was the guest of honor, but I gathered by the heavy representation of Foreign Trade representatives and Supply Missions that Lend-Lease was very much on the Russian mind.

As usual, Mr. Molotov received the guests and when all were assembled, Mr. Stalin came in with Mikoyan and went about the room shaking hands with each guest. After these preliminaries were over, we went into the Catherine Room for dinner. The set-up was much the same as for other Kremlin dinners I have described. Mr. Stalin and Mr. Molotov sat opposite each other at the center of the long, raised table, with Mr. Davies on Mr. Stalin's right, Ambassador Clark-Kerr on his left, while Mr. Molotov had General Martel on his left and me on his right.

No sooner were we all seated than the toasts began, Mr. Molotov with a graceful tribute to the guest of honor. It was here that the customary procedure broke down. Instead of saying a few words in reply and sitting down, Mr. Davies remained standing and delivered a 15-minute harangue; it took another fifteen minutes to translate it into Russian. I thought that his sentences sounded familiar; where had I heard them? Suddenly, I remembered—at his first press conference in Spaso House. Across the table, I heard Mr. Litvinov remark to Sir Archibald in a low voice, "A speech at a Kremlin banquet is a nice time to take a nap."

After thirty minutes of Joe Davies in English and Russian, the dinner returned to normalcy for a while; the toasts continued until we had our dessert, when Mr. Stalin arose and said, "We will adjourn immediately to the projection room where we will see our guest of honor's motion picture, *Mission to Moscow.*"

Proceeding at once to the projection room, we by-passed the usual conversation over liqueurs in the smoking room, which seemed to me to indicate that Mr. Stalin was annoyed at Mr. Davies' long-winded speech. Now it became clear to me why Mr. Davies' "laid-on" his second "Mission to Moscow" and staged his interviews with the Press—clearly they were publicity stunts designed to advertise internationally his (and Warner Brothers') motion picture, *Mission to Moscow.*

The unusual did not end with the projection room. For the benefit of those who have not seen the movie, it opens with a full-screen picture of Mr. Davies in proper diplomatic costume, making a speech—the identical speech he had just delivered in response to Mr. Molotov's toast. Some of us had the pleasure of listening to the same harangue three times over. I was not surprised that, when the picture was over and champagne was brought into the projection room, Mr. Stalin took one sip and retired to his private quarters.

John Young was a big help to me with the scrambled problems of Press relations when I was inflicted with two VIPs at the same time. I took him with me to the Kremlin dinner, where he watched the Russian reaction to *Mission to Moscow.* "Admiral," he told me afterward, "such highly imaginative fare as the *Mission* is no proper diet for the Soviet masses."

Yet, John must have been quite a diplomat, for the former Ambassador asked him to help rewrite the script of *Mission* so that it could be more useful in the fund drive for Russian Relief. And he offered to use his good connections and valuable experience in Hollywood to assist Young when he returned home to procure his films.

When I arrived at the office at ten thirty the next morning, there wasn't much in the way of news and few telegrams. But Eddie Page was seething. "We've had a little of everything, Admiral," he said, "but this is the limit. Mr. Davies is *indisposed* and that so-called aide of his is holding a press conference this morning."

"Worse things have happened to me, Eddie," I said philosophically. "I'll take care of it."

I had a busy day—a long talk with Clark-Kerr, during which we rehashed the Kremlin party and the dissolution of the Third Comintern. I saw Doctor Lang, Faymonville, and Doctor Waldron about dispensary matters, and received Mr. Magidoff, a newspaper correspondent. Late in the afternoon, I stopped at Number Eight to see Mr. Davies, who was still abed; he looked terrible. He was killing himself to advertise Joe Davies through his book and movie. Lieutenant Stamm was sitting with him.

After a few pleasantries and some discussion of the Kremlin party, I took up a more serious question. "Joe, I'm sorry to see you feeling so badly," I said. "I hate to bother you when you're sick. We've been friends a long while, and I make a lot of allowances on that basis. I have no objection at all to you holding press conferences and giving out press releases while you're here, but Lieutenant Stamm does not rate that privilege. That's got to stop."

We had an unpleasant few moments; Davies had a mercurial temper and it flashed to high temperature. I kept calm. When I left him, I thought the issue was settled. Lieutenant Stamm understood his limitations and Joe had cooled off. Before I turned in that night, I recorded this in my diary:

> Told Stamm I did not want him holding press conferences in his own right. Obtained *Mission to Moscow* film and showed it to Press and American citizens at Spaso from 8:30 to 11:00—did not stay to discuss it with the press boys—too nauseating; too darned mad.

I do not wish my readers to rely upon my reaction to *Mission to Moscow*, as I certainly do not consider myself a qualified motion picture critic. Here is what Quentin Reynolds had to say:

> Some of the British and Americans who have been here for many-many years and who really know Russia told us that Stalin gave a magnificent performance during the showing of the picture.
>
> "Walter Huston was fine," a British member of the diplomatic corps told us, "but he couldn't compare with Stalin. Do you know that Stalin kept a straight face throughout the showing? He didn't laugh once."

A few days later, the film was shown at our embassy at one of the usual Saturday-afternoon shows. It was a beautiful technical job and the performances of the character actors who figured in the trial scenes were especially magnificent. But the film portrayed a Russia that none of us had ever seen. This would have been all right, except that the picture purported to be factual and the Russia shown in the film had as much relation to the Russia we knew as Shang-ri-la would have to the real Tibet.*

May 25th was another difficult day. I spent a good part of the morning trying to arrange visas for those persons going out with Mr. Davies and General Burns, who planned to fly in company with Mr. Davies' plane, always an irritating endeavor in Moscow. I went home for lunch and a nap. About one-thirty, Gordon came in with a letter from Mr. Davies, full of anger and pique, written in the tone of one Ambassador to another. The whole letter showed that he was annoyed, obviously because of my complaints about his nephew-aide's activities. He told me that he had planned to remain in Moscow until he had somewhat recovered from his indisposition, but, in view of my attitude, he would leave immediately.

Before I went back to the office, I called Mr. Davies and arranged to visit him at six, taking Sir Archibald with me; he told me he was still in bed and feeling far from well. When I reached the office, I had a call from Lieutenant Stamm—Mr. Davies wanted me to stay for a few moments after Clark-Kerr left. As things stood, I had no intention of seeing him alone.

Sir Archibald and I went to Number Eight at six, ostensibly to "visit the sick." We were conducted into Mr. Davies' bedroom. He really did look awful. We made polite expressions of regret, which were completely sincere. Sir Archie told him a couple of British stories, which seemed to cheer him up. As we rose to go, with Clark-Kerr still present, I handed Mr. Davies' letter to him.

"Joe, I can't let you leave Moscow with a bad taste in your mouth," I said in as friendly tone as I could come by. "You and I have been friends too long to permit such a situation to continue. If I accept this letter, I will have to answer it—you won't like the answer. I'm giving it back to you."

That was the end of that incident.

From a letter to Evelyn:

May 27—You know the expression, "This too shall end." Well, we are

* Quentin Reynolds, *The Curtain Rises* (New York: Random House, 1944), p. 81.

approaching the hour of departure of both Davies and Burns. They are flying off together Saturday and I'll be glad.

[Mr. Molotov gave a luncheon today, celebrating the first anniversary of the signing of the Anglo-Soviet Agreement by Anthony Eden and Molotov.] Mike and Jack came by for me; then we stopped by Number Eight for Mr. Davies. He and I went in his car and the others followed.

The luncheon was given in Spirodonov House, the same room where all the food was served during the Beaverbrook-Harriman Mission—forty people at the table . . . a standard Soviet luncheon, with food and drink in abundance. Mr. Molotov sat in the center at one side, with Sir Archibald Clark-Kerr on his right as the guest of honor, and Mr. Davies, the special messenger of the President, on his left; Ambassador Litvinov was on Mr. Davies' left. Co-host Mikoyan, Commissar for Foreign Trade, sat opposite Molotov; with General Martel on his left and myself on his right. General Burns was down the table a few seats. The only members of our Supply Mission invited were Faymonville and Jack and Mike. All the heads of agencies in the Embassy staff were present.

Mr. Molotov varied the usual stiff protocol—he gave all the toasts in rapid succession without waiting for response from each individual. When he had completed his round of toasts, responses began with the guest of honor, the British Ambassador. Mr. Molotov responded to each individual toast. Many other toasts were given and responded to. Mr. Davies couldn't divest himself of his former attributes as Ambassador; he represents the President and is treated as the President's Special Representative.

As we left the luncheon, Mr. Molotov told him that he would see Mr. Stalin at 8:00 P.M. to receive [Premier Stalin's] answer to the President's letter. I stayed home to await Davies' return, read a little, then played bridge with some of the youngsters. Davies came in at eleven to tell me of his visit, showed me the letter with five seals on it. Mr. Davies claimed that he does not know what was in it—I guess I must believe him but I can't see why I was excluded from the meeting when both Mr. Molotov and Mr. Pavlov were there. Not being able to understand, of course, I can't stick around any longer than I have to.

On May 27th, I was very busy making final arrangements for the two planes and their passengers to leave. From four to five-thirty, I attended a press conference at Number Eight. Mr. Davies had his plane crew present and served cocktails afterward. I noted that "he has certainly learned something about the Press here; it was a comparatively quiet conference."

After the conference, I took a walk with Mr. Davies. That evening, we played bridge at Number Eight, Ambassador Litvinov and Mr. Davies versus General Burns and me—I lost 75 rubles.

That night, Mr. Davies sent Lieutenant Stamm to Quentin Reynolds apartment to distribute going-away presents—a bottle of good brandy and twenty cartons of cigarettes, a gracious gesture much appreciated by the correspondents as they had long been out of American cigarettes and our Embassy stock was very low. As Reynolds put it, "From our selfish point of view, it justified the whole Davies visit."

That evening, I gave some serious consideration to my movie project. During his five months in the Soviet Union, John Young had traveled widely. He had seen Russian motion pictures in the finest theaters in Moscow and in little recreation halls of country villages. He had met and presented our plan for exchange of motion pictures with the Russians to all of the proper authorities.

Mr. Molotov had appeared to be enthusiastic. Mr. Kamenev had promised his full cooperation in arranging distribution of American films in Russia and in providing Russian films for export to the United States. Mr. Vishinsky had spoken enthusiastically about the plan and offered his services to assist in every way. I was so encouraged that, for a time, I became almost optimistic, a dangerous state of mind in the Soviet Union.

I decided it was time to send John Young home to obtain the films and equipment needed to implement my plan for "education through American motion pictures."

I asked for a visa and arranged passage for Young in General Burns' plane. Mr. Molotov and other officials of the Foreign Office could not have been more cooperative. With John, I sent several letters of introduction: to Harold Train, Chief of Naval Intelligence; to Mr. Will Hays, then President of the Motion Picture Producers and Distributors of America; to General H. H. George, Air Transport Command, asking his cooperation to exchange motion picture material with the Soviet Union; to Mr. Robert Sherwood, OWI, bespeaking his assistance.

Perhaps, I thought, we *will* see American feature films playing in every motion picture theater and recreation hall in the Soviet Union!

May 28th was quiet. I spent most of the day writing letters and preparing the mail pouch to go out with General Burns. I saw Mr. Davies briefly, to deliver a message which had come for him from State and to make a report to him, for delivery to the President only, on Russian steel and iron production.

Mr. Davies paid Mr. Molotov a farewell visit at six, at which time he gave Mr. Molotov a message from the President, the message I had delivered to him earlier that afternoon.

From a letter to my wife:

May 29—Well, Mr. Joseph Davies and General Burns have gone. Thank God! They are going out through Siberia and Alaska. Mr. Davies painted on the bow of his plane in big yellow letters, "Mission to Moscow."

Do you remember, when we were youngsters, "Wizard Oil" used to send around the country a 4-horse caravan, all chestnut sorrels, with a circus barker to advertise and publicize Wizard Oil? Mr. Davies' trip reminds me of Wizard Oil barnstorming. The whole show reeks of the oil of publicity for Mr. Joseph E. Davies and his film and book, *Mission to Moscow.* I think the Russians sensed it, too. The Press here are looking for a political purpose behind all this and I believe the Russians are also. To send a man 30,000 miles around the world using an American Army plane, a crew of 9 men, gas and oil, the prestige of the U. S. Government, and the entire facilities of the American Embassy in Moscow to advertise and increase the box office receipts for Mr. Davies' movie doesn't sit so very well. You may hear more of it. . . .

I turned out at five; after a shave and breakfast, took Young out to the plane—Page, Dr. Lang, and Vic [Blakeslee] went with me. The Russians with cameras were out in full force. Ambassador Litvinov was there; Davies paid scant attention to the other Russian officials [Mr. Dekanozov, Mr. Zarubin, Mr. Molochkov, and Mr. Yesignaiev] who had made most of the arrangements and did most of the entertaining for Mr. Davies. He concentrated his attention on Mr. Litvinov. I inspected Mr. Davies' plane—very lush. Four bunks and eight seats. Took Major and one of my boys of NKVD with me to let them see and report.

Davies' plane took off at 6:25, Burns followed at 6:30. Three [Russian] fighters escorted each flight. Burns was paid scant attention on his departure.

So they were gone. What did Mr. Davies accomplish?

Shortly after Davies left Moscow, I delivered to Mr. Stalin copies of the full plans drawn up at the TRIDENT conference, which Mr. Churchill, President Roosevelt, and the Combined Chiefs of Staff of both countries had been conducting in Washington while Mr. Davies was in Moscow. Toward the end of June, Mr. Stalin sent Mr. Churchill a hot cable in which he reviewed the record on the frequently promised Second Front in Europe; he plainly charged bad faith on the part of Great Britain and the United States.

Mr. Churchill was apparently so incensed that he didn't consult President Roosevelt as usual; he sent off a super-heated reply. During the period of tension which followed, Mr. Stalin recalled Ambassador Litvinov from Washington and Ambassador Maisky from London. Meanwhile, Stalin stated to me personally that the reason for the recall of these two Ambassadors was his desire to have near him for instant consultation in Moscow these individuals who were thoroughly conversant with the situation in London and in Washington.

Fear of a separate Russian peace reached a new high in Washington. I tried to play this down, for I felt certain the Russians would never stop fighting as long as the Nazis held one foot of Russian territory. The Stalin-Roosevelt meeting, which Mr. Davies had come to arrange, was indefinitely postponed.

For a few days after Mr. Davies left Moscow, I "enjoyed" a brief notoriety in the headlines of American newspapers. On May 30th, I attended Memorial Day services at the French Catholic cathedral, St. Louis, and heard Father Braun preach. On my way home, I stopped at my office in Mokhovaya; I found Tommy Thompson with Cy Sulzberger of the *New York Times* waiting for me. The newsmen had received a message from their paper and wanted my comment on a statement made in the *Times* the previous day that I had "vigorously notified President Roosevelt I was ready to resign."

I was completely taken by surprise. I had informed no one among the Press correspondents in Moscow that I had tendered my resignation. The only way the news could have gotten out was release at home by either the State Department or the White House. I tersely informed the boys, "I have no comment to make."

As I walked home, I pondered the situation. Why had they released this news, and why had it been worded so critically of the Administration?

At Spaso, I found Hendler of the UP waiting for me, wanting comments; I gave him the same answer. Later on, I received a personal message from the Associated Press, asking if the *New York Times* story was true; if so, would I please give them a statement as to my reasons.

The next day at noon, I saw Sir Archibald Clark-Kerr by appointment; he, too, had the news from London, a relay of the *Times* story; ten Downing Street wanted to know what was behind it all. Much as I liked Sir Archie, I felt I had to give him the same answer. That afternoon, I sent a telegram to the Associated Press, "Thanks for information re *N. Y. Times* article. I have no comment to make."

A week or two later, I received the President's reply to my letter of resignation, which I quote in full:

Dear Mr. Ambassador:

I am always pleased to receive letters from you as it gives me so much comfort to know that the relations of the United States with the Soviet Union are in such capable hands with you in Moscow. It has caused me some disturbance, however, to learn from your letter of May 3 that you feel that you should not spend another winter in the Soviet Union and that you would like to be relieved of your duties as Ambassador some time before October 10.

I am well aware of the public spirit which prompted you to accept the post in Moscow and to serve there in spite of the rigorous climate and of the living conditions which must be trying.

Although I regret your decision to retire, I can nevertheless understand it, and I shall begin at once to look for someone with the necessary qualifications to succeed you.

I wish to assure you again of my full confidence in you and to express my appreciation of the able and effective manner in which you are representing the United States in a country the friendship of which is so important to us at the present time.

Very sincerely yours,

/s/ FRANKLIN D. ROOSEVELT

CHAPTER XXIII

Sulzberger and Rickenbacker
in Moscow

ONE feature of life in the Soviet Union which made it so interesting was that the impossible was almost certain to happen. In fact, some of the boys paraphrased one of Admiral Ernie King's famous dictums and coined a phrase, *In Soviet Russia, the unusual is the commonplace.*

Red Cross supplies constituted one of my minor problems; their distribution was an ever-present concern. Mr. Scovell, the Red Cross representative in Moscow, did the best he could to supervise the distribution of the large amount of goods which his organization brought into the Soviet Union; the Russians just wouldn't cooperate. It was common gossip that the Red Cross medical supplies, when they disappeared into the vastness of Russia, ended up in medical stores of the Red Army. I felt that Mr. Scovell had more of a job than he could handle; while I was home for consultation, I arranged with Mr. Norman Davis, President of the American Red Cross, to send to Moscow an additional representative. With the arrival in Moscow of Mr. Hubbel, the situation seemed to improve.

As a friendly gesture, Mr. Hubbel wanted to present the Soviet Government with three fully equipped ambulances. I objected. "First get your feet on the ground," I told him. "See what the situation is. I strongly recommend against giving the Russians *any more* Red Cross supplies until they agree to permit Mr. Scovell and you to witness their distribution and use."

It was not long before Mr. Hubbel was disillusioned; the offer of the ambulances was never made.

As an example of things Russian: When I visited one of our newspaper correspondents who was a patient at one of the largest hospitals in Moscow, I looked in vain for American Red Cross material. After my "indiscretion," Edgar Snow took me, by special arrangement, to revisit an orphan's home near Moscow, in which I had previously seen no evidence of either Red Cross or Russian Relief supplies. The visit was obviously a plant—the same children were so much better equipped than on my previous visit or at any other orphan's home I had visited—all decked out in shoes, stockings, dresses and sweaters provided by the Russian Relief.

The dearth of medical supplies is indicated by the experience of one of my staff who went to a Russian dentist to have a tooth filled. The Russian dentist drilled out the cavity, put in a temporary filling, and told him, "I'm sorry, that's all I can do for you; I have no material to fill the tooth. If you can bring in from Cairo enough material to fill two teeth, I will fill your tooth for nothing."

I sent the patient out to Teheran, where a U. S. Army dentist filled the cavity for him.

Such a situation was untenable; while I was in Washington, I made arrangements with the Navy Department to detail a competent naval dentist to the Embassy. I asked them to send with him the most up-to-the-minute dental equipment obtainable, having in mind the educational effect on the Russian mind of the comparison of such equipment with the antiquated gear the Russian dentists were using.

At my request, a Dr. Dufour, who had done some dental work in Washington for me, was ordered to duty at the Embassy. He arrived in Kuibyshev on April 18th. In August, we finally discovered that his equipment had been in Cairo for months and had been held up because of a low priority. I sent Dufour to Cairo "on leave" and he "rode herd" on his equipment personally until the Russian transport plane in which the equipment and Dr. Dufour were embarked landed at Baku, its first stop in Soviet territory. Russian authorities firmly refused to permit Dr. Dufour to accompany his equipment further. He arrived in Moscow on September 18th. As far as I know, his equipment never reached Moscow. Another of my attempts to help the Russian people was defeated by Soviet officialdom.

I had just begun to recover from the visit of Mr. Joseph Davies when, early in June, I received the following message from President Roosevelt:

Mr. Arthur Sulzberger of the *New York Times* is a Director of the American Red Cross. Mr. Sulzberger desires to visit the Soviet Union in the interest of the Society of which he is a Director, and it is requested that you obtain the necessary permission and visas for such entry.

So, I am to have a double headache, I thought—Red Cross aid and a Very VIP, all at once. Well, at least he isn't a Special Representative of the President.

I sent one of my secretaries to the Foreign Office that afternoon with the President's message and a request for visas.

I went to my office the next morning at 10:10 A.M. and was consulting with Jack Duncan about some matters, when Mr. Zarubin phoned from the Foreign Office. "Oh, Mr. Ambassador," he said, in his good British accent, "Premier Stalin wishes to know— is your Mr. Sulzberger coming to Russia solely in the interests of the Red Cross or is he also coming as an editor and a newspaper man?"

"The President's message says he is coming as a Director of the American Red Cross," I quickly replied.

Apparently my answer didn't satisfy Marshal Stalin, for Mr. Zarubin called me up again that afternoon. "Uh . . . Mr. Ambassador, with regard to Mr. Sulzberger, the situation is still not quite clear. Mr. Stalin would like to have assurance from President Roosevelt, himself, that the publisher of the *New York Times* is coming to Moscow solely in his Red Cross capacity."

I got off a message to the State Department that afternoon and received one of the most prompt replies in my experience. Mr. Sulzberger was making the trip exclusively in his capacity as a Red Cross Director. When this information was passed on to the Foreign Office, the necessary permission and visas were promptly granted. I notified the State Department and sent a message to Mr. Sulzberger inviting him to be my guest in Spaso House.

Two days later, I received a reply:

> Accept with pleasure your kind invitation. Can Jimmy Reston, who is accompanying me, also stay at the Embassy. /s/ Arthur Sulzberger.

I replied that I would be happy to have Mr. Reston as my guest; but I was rather surprised to learn that the Soviet Foreign Office had issued a visa to Mr. Reston, because Jimmy Reston was one of the *New York Times'* most experienced and well-known reporters.

Arthur Sulzberger is one of those fortunate young men who "married the Boss' daughter," only in his case the marriage took place before he went to work for the Boss. While still in the Army during

World War I, Mr. Sulzberger met and married the daughter of Adolph Ochs, publisher of the *New York Times*. When he was released from the Army in 1918, he went to work on the *Times*. When Mr. Ochs died in 1935, Arthur Sulzberger took over as publisher and ran it so independently that the *Times* has been accused of being a "Jewish propaganda sheet" and "anti-Semitic" within the same month.

He early took an interest in Red Cross work, being an incorporator of the American Red Cross and a member of its Central Committee as well as one of its guiding lights in New York State. My immediate reaction was that he might be able to absorb some of the headaches which the Red Cross had caused me; but I added a pious hope that he would forget for the duration of his visit to the Soviet Union that he was a newspaper man—and that Jimmy Reston would, too.

Watching the reports of progress of Mr. Sulzberger's Army plane across Africa and the Middle East, we expected him to arrive in Moscow about June 20th. To my surprise, on that date I received a message from our Chancery in Kuibyshev about as follows:

> Captain Eddie Rickenbacker's plane arrived military airport 1957 nineteenth. Proceeding Kuibyshev to Moscow 1045 twentieth.

Nobody had told me that Eddie Rickenbacker was even on the same side of the world as Moscow. The last I had heard of that famous World War I ace was a story in *Time* about his welcome home after his plane-wreck and dramatic rescue in the Pacific. The account had said that he was still in poor physical condition. "What the devil would he be doing in Russia?" I asked Mike Michella, irritably.

"Must have gotten their wires crossed in Kuibyshev," Eddie Page suggested. "They mean Sulzberger."

"That doesn't make sense," I muttered. "Our staff doesn't make mistakes like that."

I called for my car and went out to meet his plane. Being one of those sort of days, we would go to the wrong airport. Rickenbacker's plane had landed before I arrived but I was on hand to meet him as the plane taxied up to the terminal building. He climbed down out of the plane with a vigor that belied any remaining illness; he was terribly thin, his hatchet face sharpened by the weight loss during his long ordeal afloat. With him were two officers of the U. S. Army, a five man Air Corps plane crew, and a civilian doctor, a man named Dahl, from Atlanta, Georgia.

Lacking any information about his trip, after greetings and introductions all around, I asked, "What's this all about, Captain Rickenbacker? How do you happen to be in Moscow?"

"I'm on a mission for the Secretary of War."

I took Dr. Dahl and Captain Rickenbacker with me in my car. As we drove into town my questioning drew out this network of circumstance. Shattered in health and very nervous from his harrowing experience while working for the Army in the Pacific, Secretary of War Stimson felt sorry for him. He'd forget his troubles and get his health back sooner if he kept busy, if he got into a plane and went somewhere on another mission. Secretary Stimson supplied him with a converted B-24, an Army crew, and a set of orders.

Rickenbacker fumbled into a briefcase and brought out his orders. They directed him to proceed to certain cities in the Middle East, *and such other places as he might wish to visit* to accomplish his mission. Just what his mission was, the orders failed to state.

What orders! In forty years of active service in the Navy, I'd never seen such a set. He literally could go any place he might choose including the moon, and the armed services, by the terms of his orders, were required to help him along his way. So he decided to come to Moscow. That was good enough for me.

"What do you want to do while you're here, Captain?" I asked.

"Well, sir, first of all, I'd like to visit the Russian Front—then, I want to see as many Russian military airfields as I can—in fact, any military information I can get. And, of course, Mr. Ambassador . . ."—he looked at me slyly out of the corner of his eye—"I'd like very much to have an interview with Mr. Stalin."

I shook my head, sadly. From his nervous reactions and his extreme thinness, it was obvious that he had not yet recovered his health. "The first thing you need is a good night's rest. I'll put you up at Spaso House, tonight, but you'll have to move to a hotel tomorrow. I'm expecting Arthur Sulzberger and his party and I won't have room for you."

General Faymonville proposed that he take Rickenbacker and Dr. Dahl in as his guests, but I said, "No. His mission is entirely military. My Military Attaché, General Michella, will look after you, Captain Rickenbacker."

What a curious situation! I quote from my diary that day:

Found arrangements for Rickenbacker's visit were made through Ed Stettinius [Lend-Lease Director], General Belyaev, Head of the Russian Supply Mission to the U.S. and Ambassador Litvinov. The Russians made all the arrangements for his arrival. A Russian military liaison officer met him. The British knew about it last week.

Had a crowded lunch, all the visitors at Spaso House. Went to a play at Red Army Theater called *Immortal.* Majorie Shaw turned her Secretary over to us as interpreter. Late supper in the green room.

Rickenbacker has orders from Stimson—To All Concerned: Give all aid. Says he has [similar] orders from Stettinius. It is to laugh!

When I arrived at the office the next morning, a coded despatch awaited me:

To: The U. S. Ambassador for Captain Rickenbacker.

The British Ambassador at Teheran reports that, at an official dinner at that place, you stated that you were enroute Ankara, Turkey, for the purpose of bringing the Turks into the War with the Allies; also, that you would visit Moscow for the purpose of obtaining the use of the Soviet air fields by the Allies.

You will under no circumstances visit either Turkey or the Soviet Union.

In the event that you have already arrived in either of these countries, you will arrange to leave immediately. /s/ Henry L. Stimson, Secretary of War.

Somewhere along the route, Captain Rickenbacker must have been indiscreet. I consulted him and learned that arrangements had already been made for him to visit various military airfields and to make other valuable contacts in pursuit of military information. Nothing can be accomplished in moments, hours, days, or even a week in the Soviet Union. I sent the following message that same afternoon:

The Secretary of War, Washington, D. C.

Re your telegram, Captain Rickenbacker arrived in Moscow yesterday under orders which authorized the visit. I have already arranged for a week's schedule of visits to airfields for him, and in view of the fact that it will require at least 5 days to obtain exit visas, I have assumed authority to approve Captain Rickenbacker's stay until exit visas can be obtained. /s/ Standley, Ambassador.

As so often happened in Moscow, the situation was becoming a little thick. Michella decided to give a cocktail party that afternoon for Rickenbacker; Arthur Sulzberger was due to arrive; and Mr. Molotov had at last decided that the time was ripe for me to present medals (indirectly) to heroes of the Red Army, Navy, and Air Force.

On June 21st, I noted in my diary:

> At 10:00, Page took Rickenbacker to call on Faymonville. Michella returned to the office with him. Faymonville came in presently, offered to help, suggested that Rickenbacker's visit had to do with Lend-Lease; implication that he [Faymonville] should entertain Rickenbacker. I told Faymonville information Rickenbacker wanted was military; that Rickenbacker was travelling under orders from the War Department; that Russian liaison officer was from the military; so the Military Attaché would have him in charge. Michella took Rickenbacker and Dr. Dahl to Mokhovaya to stay with him.
>
> As I had to take care of Sulzberger, Mike gave a cocktail party [for Rickenbacker] at 5:00—would not invite Faymonville. Just as I was leaving office, got word Sulzberger would arrive at 8:00, so I left cocktail party early. Sulzberger arrived at civil airport at 8:15 with Reston. Took them to Spaso for cocktails, dinner, and movies. Turned in at 12.

While Mr. Sulzberger came to Moscow at President Roosevelt's request, the Russians did not consider him a Special Representative. He was not offered the facilities of the United States Guest House at Number Eight as were Mr. Harriman, Mr. Willkie, and Mr. Davies. A survey of the condition of Red Cross aid in the Soviet Union was his avowed purpose for coming to Moscow. Reston and Sulzberger were my house guests; whenever possible, I included them in my activities. For the same reason, I was included in plans for Mr. Sulzberger made by American Red Cross or Russian Red Crescent representatives. As an intriguing coincidence, one of the *New York Times* correspondents in Moscow was Mr. Cyrus Sulzberger, nephew of Arthur. I noted that Cy Sulzberger frequently "went into a huddle" with Jimmy Reston and Arthur Sulzberger. In addition to the Red Cross and American Embassy channels, Mr. Sulzberger had his own line of communications and information.

At eleven A.M. on the 22nd, I took Mr. Sulzberger and Jimmy Reston with me to the office and turned them over to Mr. Hubbel for indoctrination and planning their visit. Meanwhile, Captain Rickenbacker was going ahead with the visits planned for him. At 2:30 that afternoon, I attended a press conference arranged for Rickenbacker, then took him to call upon Ambassador Litvinov, who had been called home for consultation. Later, Captain Ricken-backer and Dr. Dahl, Mr. Sulzberger and Jimmy Reston attended the presentation of medals to Soviet heroes in Spaso House.

But the most interesting thing that occurred that day was when I took Mr. Sulzberger to make his official call on Mr. Molotov. Since no business was involved, only courtesy, the visit was brief. As we were ready to leave, Mr. Sulzberger said to Mr. Pavlov, "Please tell Mr. Molotov that I would like to have an appointment with Mar-shal Stalin while I am here, if possible."

I saw Mr. Molotov's tight little smile as Mr. Pavlov finished interpreting. In conversing with Soviet officials through an inter-preter, you don't address them in that roundabout way. Mr. Molo-tov was still smiling as Mr. Pavlov said, "Mr. Molotov says to tell you that Marshal Stalin is at the front; his return is indefinite."

When I went to the office the next morning, I left Mr. Sulzberger in deep conversation with his nephew and Jimmy Reston. After attending to routine business, I came back to Spaso for lunch. That afternoon, I lent my car to Mr. Sulzberger to visit the Moscow "Park of Culture and Rest," a Russian version of Coney Island, with movie shows, dance pavilions, sports exhibitions, athletic fields, and such. At the time Mr. Sulzberger was there, in a large athletic hall, the Russians were exhibiting material and equipment cap-tured from the Germans, each piece labeled with date and place of capture. I had visited the Park a number of times; if you followed the dates carefully, you could see the progressive deterioration of German equipment due to scarcity of various raw materials as the war continued.

That evening, my diary notes, I "had dinner for Litvinov, Sulz-berger, General Faymonville, and Hubbel [who came in late]; we played bridge afterward on the veranda and [during an air raid warning] saw the captive ballons go up, a grand sight. I won 60 rubles."

Meanwhile, Captain Rickenbacker was going about his business of collecting information, but, Mike Michella came in to report, he declined to have any member of the Embassy Staff accompany him. I shrugged my shoulders and said, "*Nichevo,*" just like a Rus-sian. What difference did it make? He would be gone in a few days. And in a few months, so would I!

We had an interesting day, the 24th, as recorded in my diary:

Took Sulzberger, Dr. Michael [representative of the U. S. Depart-ment of Agriculture in Moscow], and Bender [as interpreter], to visit a *kolkhoz* at the junction of the road to our *dacha* with the main highway [out of Moscow] and made a complete inspection of this collective farm. It raises vegetables of all kinds—strawberries, apples, cucumbers under irrigation—poultry for own use—pig farm, we were told at evacuation [of Moscow] they had only 6 pigs left—now have some 200 head of beautiful pigs. Had to fumigate our feet as we entered cow barn.

It had 490 workers, 95% women, and there were 120 children from about seven to nursing babies. Visited the nursery where they take care of children, a most interesting place in charge of an elderly lady with several helpers and a trained nurse—routine the same as orphans' homes.

At 3:00 sat down to a luncheon, the usual banquet, and I had to respond to several toasts, eat loads of strawberries, and drink glasses of rich milk.

On June 25th, Mr. Sulzberger stayed home during the morning and worked in his room at Spaso House with Jimmy Reston. Late in the afternoon, I took him to call on the British Ambassador and we went on to the National Hotel, where Messrs. Hubbel and Scovell were honoring Mr. Sulzberger and the Red Cross with a formal dinner. I was co-host. As guests, we had a number of Russians, representatives of the Soviet Red Crescent Society. At dinner, I had Dr. Dahl on my right and Eddie Rickenbacker on my left, the first time I had seen our famous flier in several days. Mr. Scovell sat at the opposite end of the table honoring Mr. Sulzberger on his right and a Russian General, Red Crescent representative, on his left. With a number of American and Russian medical men, seats were set for 26 persons; strictly a Red Cross-Red Crescent affair.

As usual, we had numerous toasts. When it was his turn to respond, Mr. Hubbel seized the opportunity to present the history of the International Red Cross, a speech much too long for a banquet. I didn't get home until eleven P.M.

The frenzied round of entertainment continued. On June 25th, I noted in my diary:

Went to the office at 10:30. Another message for Rickenbacker; they want him to get out. Prodded Foreign Office about exit visas—set Tuesday, 29th, as his day of departure and sent Michella to get permission [for Rickenbacker] to visit airfield where Aircobras are used.

At 1:00 had luncheon with Litvinov at Spirodonov House—Arthur Sulzberger, Rickenbacker, Reston, Cy Sulzberger, Page, Zarubin, and two junior members of the Foreign Office. A slow, formal luncheon—

no particular purpose except to return my dinner and entertain Sulzberger and Rickenbacker.

I saw Molotov at 7:00 on Michella's unenviable situation [with
respect to obtaining military information], asked that he give consideration to remedying it. After dinner, worked, took a walk, and
then played gin rummy with Sulzberger—won one ruble.

On Sunday, June 27th, my indiscretion at the collective farm
three days earlier caught up with me. I knew better than to drink
unsterilized fresh milk in Soviet Russia. As in China, you ate salad
greens and raw vegetables or fruit in Russia at your peril. But
sometimes, because you had been so long without fresh fruits or
salad or for reasons of protocol, you risked your good health and
partook of beautiful fresh farm products when they were made
available. A combination of hunger and protocol influenced me to
let myself go at that collective farm luncheon.

I went out to our *dacha* that Sunday; on the way home, the gas
line in my car clogged up. My NKVD boys took me as far toward
town as the railway crossing, where a long freight train held us up
and my car caught up with us. I was uncommonly irritated and
fretful about the whole business. A few moments later, I had an
attack of chills and fever. By the time I reached Spaso House, I
was well along in an attack of jippy tummy. I abandoned a supper
party I was giving to the boys of my staff and turned in under Dr.
Lang's care.

I was laid up in bed for three days, with a stream of distinguished visitors parading through my sick room. Uncomfortable
as I was, I couldn't seem to let go of the threads of circumstance
which wove through my fingers.

Mr. Sulzberger was well cared for: dinner at the British Embassy with Sir Archibald and a visit to the *Pravda* newspaper
plant.

Of the greatest concern during this period was the increasingly
bitter feud between Faymonville and Michella. A continuation of
our dispute with Lend-Lease over the procurement of military information, Mike had begun to take the challenge personally, cen-
tering his animosity in Faymonville, the most readily available
opponent. I have mentioned that he failed to invite Faymonville
to his cocktail party honoring Eddie Rickenbacker. Mr. Molotov
was apparently not disposed to help, although I had appealed to
him personally. I sent Eddie Page to see Faymonville on June
29th; he came back with the same old answer—Faymonville had

to do what the Russians asked him, had to carry out orders received from the Lend-Lease Administration.

Mike went to see his liaison officer and came back very happy on June 30th to report that everything would be all right. I had my doubts. There was nothing much I could do, except try to keep things on an even keel until I was ready to leave—and worry.

I was back on my feet by July 1st, very weak but able to go to the office. I noted in my diary that day:

> The Sulzbergers left for a trip to the front; Dr. Lang went along [it being a Red Crescent-Red Cross affair]. . . . Home before going to dinner with Michella, Rickenbacker, Dr. Dahl, Page, and Duncan. After dinner came home. Had fair night—worried about the Michella-Faymonville situation. Michella refused to see Faymonville in his quarters—just don't know the answer.

I received but one item of pleasant news during those uncomfortable days in bed. On June 28th, a commentator on the Moscow radio, speaking in English, stressed the help the allies had given to his "embattled homeland." The stage, he went on, was now set for a complete victory, but we must not expect too easy a victory. The Axis Powers still were strong and capable of putting up a bitter fight.

The visa office of the Commissariat of Foreign Affairs managed to stall long enough to delay Rickenbacker's departure until July 2nd. I didn't feel up to an early rising to see him off but we turned out a respectable party to bid him farewell. His plane had hardly gotten into the air when one of its engines cut out. Mike said the pilot deserved a Distinguished Flying Cross for bringing the plane back into the field all in one piece.

At 6:00 P.M., I took Rickenbacker to call on Mr. Molotov. I tried hard to persuade him to let us replace the engine with a similar one from the plane taken from the Tokyo bomber crew or from General Bradley's plane, both of which were in Moscow, but the answer was, "Nyet."

I sent off a despatch to the Fifth Air Force in Cairo, requesting immediate delivery of a spare engine; at the same meeting with Mr. Molotov, I requested visas and clearance for an Air Force plane and crew to bring the engine to Moscow. I had Rickenbacker back on my hands for another nine days.

Mr. Sulzberger and Jimmy Reston came to my sitting room that evening to tell me about their "visit to the front." They had made a difficult and interesting two day trip up toward Smolensk, but from their description I doubt that they came as close to a real fighting front as Pat Hurley. They told me that nowhere did they see any American Red Cross material or Lend-Lease equipment in use—the same sad old tale.

As is customary on July Fourth at American Embassies all over the world, we held our annual Independence Day Reception in Spaso House from 4:30 to 6:30. This gave Mr. Sulzberger and Captain Rickenbacker an opportunity to meet all the Americans in Moscow, the members of the Diplomatic Corps, the officers of the British and American Supply Missions, and the doctors of a British Medical Mission then visiting the Soviet Union.

In the State Dining Room, we laid a beautiful table, with a centerpiece of bluebells I picked that morning at our *dacha*—a spread of food to rival our Russian friends, with every kind of *hors d'oeuvres* our cooks could contrive, a boiled ham, Vienna sausages in little hot rolls—and vodka punch and fruit juices as liquid refreshments.

After the reception, I took Mr. Sulzberger to a concert of American music, a spectacular affair which the Russians had arranged in honor of our Independence Day. In addition to a large and enthusiastic Russian audience, the entire Diplomatic Corps attended. Ambassador Litvinov and his daughter sat with us in our box.

An excellent orchestra first rendered one of Leopold Stokowsky's *potpourris*, a medley of patriotic music; afterward, Madame Natalie Spheller sang our American version of *Johnny Comes Marching Home* in a lovely contralto; which she followed with *Till We Meet Again* and *Home Sweet Home* in Russian as encores. Toward the end of the program, a fine baritone gave a splendid rendition of *Old Man River*.

Obviously, the Russians had spared no effort to make the concert a success; it was a beautiful tribute to Americans resident in Moscow, which reminded me of the American Film Exhibition I had attended on June 15th, when Madame Litvinov in the course of her introductory speech announced, in Russian and English, "By the way, we are happy to have the American Ambassador with us this afternoon." The entire audience arose as one and gave me a tremendous ovation.

On July 5th, I took Mr. Sulzberger, Jimmy Reston, and Bender (as interpreter) to see a Red Army art exhibit, consisting of pictures of all schools, from the photographically realistic to the extremely futuristic. In eight big Red signature books were paintings made by artists at the front. Statuary in the exhibit depicted the suffering of the Russian people throughout the USSR.

At Mr. Sulzberger's request, I took him at 3:00 P.M. to see Mr. Molotov. After we had conversed politely through an interpreter for five minutes, Mr. Sulzberger said, pleadingly, "I would like very much to see Mr. Stalin before I leave Moscow."

"Mr. Stalin is busy at the front," Mr. Molotov replied bluntly.

In diplomatic protocol, it is considered politic, when the mission of a foreign representative has been completed, to give the diplomatic representative an audience with the ruling potentate or to entertain him at a State Dinner or some other impressive social affair. Mr. Stalin did not give an audience to Mr. Sulzberger and therefore there could be no Kremlin banquet given in his honor.

As evidence that the Russians considered that Mr. Sulzberger's visit should be terminated and that, as a dignitary, he rated no higher than Red Crescent level, on July fifth, the Russian Red Crescent officials tendered a farewell dinner at VOK's headquarters to honor Mr. Sulzberger and Mr. Hubbel. The Head of the Russian Red Crescent, Mr. Cheknokov, and the Commissar for Public Health were co-hosts.

Among the guests were the British Ambassador and members of the British Medical Mission, which lent the dinner the aura of a combined affair. As a perfect example of correct and effective protocol, the British Ambassador was seated on the left of the Commissar for Health, with me on his right, while across the table on his right and left, Mr. Cheknokov had Mr. Sulzberger and Mr. Hubbel. Borrowed from the VOK's were not only the banquet hall and the Special Attendants, but also some of Mr. Kamenev's young lady assistants. Seated beside each important guest was a pretty young Russian woman, who acted as his interpreter, thus avoiding the necessity for the complete translation of each speech as it was made.

As the dinner was distinctly a Red Cross and medical affair, Sir Archibald and I tried to avoid replying to a toast. But the Commissar for Public Health would have none of that. As he toasted me with fulsome praise, I had been casting about in my mind for an appropriate theme. "Singleness of purpose." That was it. The singleness of purpose of the Red Cross to "alleviate the suffering of mankind."

To illustrate my point, I told them a story. On a huge ranch in our great state of Texas lived a wild Texas steer and a little donkey. One day the foreman of the ranch and his house guest, a tenderfoot from the East, got to arguing about determination. "I'll give you an example of determination," the foreman said.

With his guest along, he took the little donkey far out on the ranch, where he roped and threw a steer and proceeded to lash the steer and the donkey together, head to head and tail to tail. When released, the steer was so much heavier and stronger than the little donkey that he switched him about as he pleased. When the tenderfoot curiously inquired as to the reason for this procedure, he was told that the ranch foreman had been trying for some time without success to get the steer back to the ranchhouse; while the steer had no preconceived idea or purpose in mind, the little donkey did have; each time the big steer gave him a whip forward and a snap backward, the little donkey would come up cheerful with but one thing in mind—to get back to the ranchhouse corral where there was food and water.

One morning a week later, the guest looked out of his bedroom window. There at the gate waiting to be let into the corral stood the demure little donkey, still lashed head and tail to a woe-be-gone steer. Singleness of purpose had won.

The efforts of my student interpreter to translate the story created no end of mirth.

For almost a week more, Mr. Sulzberger waited for visas and permission to go out of Russia "over the top" via the new British stratospheric air service between London and Moscow. In the meantime, I tried to keep him occupied.

On July 7th, in company with Dr. L. G. Michael, representative in Moscow of our Department of Agriculture, General Faymonville, two representatives of the Commissariat of Foreign Trade, the British Ambassador, and Bender (as interpreter), I took Mr. Sulzberger to visit what the Russians call "No. 1 Meat Factory."

It was well named. In one building, they kept 150,000 laying hens. Originally, they had two such buildings, but the Nazis dropped a bomb on the other, roasting at one heat 150,000 laying hens.

For the market, in addition to the eggs of the laying hens, they currently were raising some 300,000 young chickens, 40,000 turkeys, 30,000 ducks, 20,000 rabbits, 100 head of cattle, 150 calves. Chickens, turkeys, and ducks were hatched in mass production in a 50,000 egg incubator in the factory. The baby chicks were housed in one building until they were six weeks old, when they were turned into outside pens until ready for intensive feeding and fattening for the market.

As at home, I was told, the hens lay better in the winter than in summer. All chickens are vaccinated against chickenpox and diphtheria.

After a thorough inspection of the factory, we were given the usual banquet, both meats and vegetables produced in the factory and deliciously prepared for the table in their own model kitchens. As we took leave of the manager, he extended a warm invitation to come out and obtain supplies whenever we wanted them.

The next day, the Russians pulled a typical trick on me. A visit to the Senior Officers' Rest Home on the Moscow River had been planned for Mr. Sulzberger by Red Crescent and Red Cross officials. I was invited to tag along. Included in our party were Mr. Hubbel and Mr. Scovell, Dr. Lang, Jimmy Reston, and four Russian doctors, including their Chief of Medicine, Dr. Schlesnekov. I quote from a letter to my wife dated July 9th:

> Archangel is a beautiful country estate built by a Russian nobleman named Yusupoff in 1770, and later famed as the "prison" to which the murderer of the "mad monk," Rasputin, was banished. Its overall appearance is much like Clivedon, the Astor country estate in England—the same view across wide and beautifully kept gardens through which the Moscow River winds, much as the diverted Thames flows through the Clivedon gardens. The estate had a large entrance gate with servant's quarters on either side.
>
> The *dacha* was not large, but the architecture was ornate, with tall columns topped in three ancient styles—Ionic in the bottom of the center towers, Corinthian in the upper part of the center towers, and Doric on both sides. Open porticoes two stories high connected the gate house with the *dacha*.
>
> At the front of the house, pleasant winding paths led through terraced gardens to the Moscow River. There were hundreds of kinds of trees, various species apparently having been collected from all over the world. At the lower end of the garden were two identical buildings, constructed in 1937 to match the architecture of the *dacha*, their interior planned for use as a modern hospital, which can accommodate 300 patients. These more modern buildings blend in so well with the *dacha* and the landscape as to form a lovely, peaceful setting for the resting and recuperating senior officers.
>
> Hundreds of white marble statues, each with its little open-front house to protect it from the weather, line the beautiful bridle paths in every available niche and corner of the buildings. At various vantage points, statues and monuments were erected to commemorate the visit to the estate of some important personage. Peter the Great's visit is commemorated by a column which reminded me of the Marine

Memorial at the corners of Seventeenth and E Streets in Washington. The memorial to Catherine the Great is a marble statue seated behind gates in a small shrine like Washington's Tomb at Mount Vernon.

Apparently, they had prepared thoroughly for my visit. You will recall how unhappy I was when I had to present the medals to Mr. Molotov instead of to each one of the heroes honored. On our tour of inspection, as we entered one of the rooms, a Major in full uniform sprang to attention, clicking his heels together like a German goosestepper. My attention was called to the decorations which covered the left chest of his uniform. Standing out very conspicuously among them was a United States Army Distinguished Service Medal, evidently planted there for my benefit, but I failed to catch on.

I went up to him. "I see you have the American Distinguished Service Medal awarded by President Roosevelt. I presented all the U. S. Medals for Red Army soldiers, but I did not have the honor or satisfaction of pinning a medal upon the chest of one soldier. Will you permit me to remove that medal and then do me the honor and privilege of letting me confer it upon you in the name of our President Roosevelt?"

Bender reported that the Major would be most happy to have me re-present the medal. Accordingly, I unpinned the medal and presented it, extending my hand in congratulation. The Major grasped my hand firmly and delivered himself of a short speech, which Bender translated as follows: "Honored sir, I am proud to receive this medal. I hope to return to the front soon, where I will fight with courage and dignity the common enemy. I will prove to your President and to you that I am worthy of the honor conferred upon me by this decoration."

It was a very dramatic scene, seemingly coming about quite by chance; but after I got home and reflected upon the occasion, I decided it was probably carefully planned to happen that way.

Over breakfast on July 11th, Mr. Sulzberger, Jimmy Reston, and I had a long talk about the political situation in Soviet Russia and at home. Then, we got down to a subject very close to both of their hearts—the relations and inter-relations of Press and officialdom in Moscow. Mr. Sulzberger seemed to feel that his representatives didn't get as good a break in Moscow as they did in most other parts of the world. I was sympathetic but there was little I could do to help.

At 10:30 A.M., I sent Mr. Sulzberger and Reston to the National Hotel in my car, where the British took over. They went out late that afternoon in a British plane "over the top" to London.

That same day, an Army Air Force plane brought in Rickenbacker's spare engine from Cairo and two months' accumulation of mail for the Embassy. His crew began installation of the engine immediately, but the job was not completed until late July 13th.

In the meanwhile, Rickenbacker visited the Moscow airplane factory where the famous Russian dive-bomber, *Stormovik,* was manufactured. When he came into my office to tell me about this visit, he asked my advice about going to Ankara. I reached into a drawer of my desk where I kept handy a Rickenbacker file.

"Here's what the Secretary of War said, Eddie. 'You will under no circumstance visit either Turkey or the Soviet Union. In the event that you have already arrived in either of these countries, you will arrange to leave immediately.' I'd advise you to carry out those instructions."

On the thirteenth, Mike Michella gave a farewell cocktail party for Rickenbacker. Bad flying weather kept his plane grounded until the fifteenth. I arose early that morning and, with Eddie Page, went out to the airport to see Captain Rickenbacker off. Michella and a couple of Russian liaison officers had braved the rigors of the early morning to bid him "Farewell." His plane took to the air at 6:20 A.M.; I went back to Spaso House and turned in for some much needed rest.

When I returned to Washington, President Roosevelt told me that Mr. Sulzberger had come to him, imbued with the usual desire of a newspaper man to see what life was like in the Soviet Union. He asked the President's permission to go to Russia.

"Arthur, if I ask for a visa for you to visit Moscow, every newspaper man in the country will want to go," the President told him. "I couldn't stand the pressure. But you're a Director of the American Red Cross. Why not go to Moscow in that capacity?"

"I'll be glad to go to Russia in any capacity," Mr. Sulzberger replied.

And so Mr. Sulzberger visited the Soviet Union "in the interest of the Society of which he is a Director"— he must have felt like a man with a split personality, for, while he traveled as a Director of the American Red Cross, both Jimmy Reston and he looked upon the Russian scene with the trained eyes of a newspaper man.

There is an interesting postscript. I recently checked up on Mr. Arthur Sulzberger's literary production during the latter half of 1943. On June 24th, he filed a story from Moscow on presenting decorations and medals to heroic fighters of the USSR; on July 4th, he had a story in the *Times* on his return to Moscow after a visit to the USSR front; on July 6th, he reported from Moscow on his conference with Commissar of Foreign Affairs Molotov. On his way home he filed from London a story which appeared in the *Times* on July 18th giving his views on the British-USSR-American post-war collaboration.

A singular coincidence—nowhere in the Reader's Guide for 1943 and 1944 is to be noted any literary production by Mr. James Reston, a journeyman reporter, on the subject of Russia.

CHAPTER XXIV

Katyn Forest:
Murder or High Strategy

As a result of the unfortunate situation brought about by Mr. Willkie's activities in the Soviet Union, I was completely ignorant as to the progress of negotiations on several important issues which Mr. Willkie had taken up with Mr. Stalin. And so I went home for consultation. While in Washington, I discussed the Polish Question in all its ramifications with President Roosevelt, Secretary Hull and other officials of the State Department, and the Polish Ambassador. The Polish Question did not come up again officially until I returned to Moscow in March, 1943.

Meanwhile, the Russian military situation had greatly improved. On January 31st, Field Marshall Von Paulus, encircled by the Red Army before Stalingrad, surrendered. On February 16th, the Red Army reoccupied Kharkov. The tide of German conquest in Russia had begun to ebb.

While I was absent from the Russian capital, a number of events significant to the Polish Question had taken place. Dr. Kot left and was relieved by a Mr. Romer, who also proved to be a very delightful and personable gentleman. On his first visit to Mr. Molotov, the Foreign Commissar had seemed most friendly and willing to discuss Polish issues freely with Mr. Romer, until he brought up the question of the citizenship of the Polish Jews. Mr. Molotov said, harshly, that the decision had been taken in that matter and that he would not even talk about it. Discouraged, Mr. Romer asked for an appointment to see Premier Stalin.

While at the Bolshoi Theater a few evenings later, Mr. Romer received a summons to the Kremlin, where he conferred with Mr. Stalin and Mr. Molotov. The Soviet line had changed. Mr. Stalin was friendly and affable. Of course, the Soviet Government would be happy to discuss the Polish Question, not only citizenship, but post-war boundaries, evacuation of Polish women and children from Russia, Polish refugees in Russia, the missing Polish Army officers, and all the other issues. There followed an amicable discussion about the citizenship question and about a highly controversial statement given out that day in London by General Sikorsky of the Polish-Government-in-Exile, which Mr. Romer had not yet seen. Finally, Mr. Stalin told Mr. Romer to get in touch with Mr. Molotov later and he would go over the whole Polish situation in detail. Mr. Romer told me that he left this meeting in a very cheerful mood, feeling for the first time in the long course of the Polish-Soviet negotiations that they might arrive at acceptable solutions. The day after I arrived in Moscow, Mr. Romer came to see me. Despite the friendly attitude of Premier Stalin, when he sought an interview with Mr. Molotov, the Commissar of Foreign Affairs refused to discuss the Polish issues with the Polish Ambassador or even to receive him.

My diary and the official files show much concern over the Polish Question during March, 1943, and many attempts on the part of Sir Archibald Clark-Kerr and myself to promote a better understanding between the Poles and the Kremlin. I recall one meeting between the British Ambassador, Mr. Romer and myself on March 22nd in my office. Sir Archibald was delayed. While we waited, Mr. Romer gave me memoranda on "Matters Concerning the Polish Population in the USSR" and "Political and Legal Considerations on the Polish-Soviet Problem of Citizenship." When the British Ambassador arrived, we went over the whole situation once more.

Mr. Romer had reached almost the same state of frustration which had broken Dr. Kot's health. "I've reported to my Government that Mr. Molotov has refused to discuss our problems any further," he said plaintively. "I keep urging General Sikorsky not to take any action which would create a definite break in relations. I understand my Government is taking the whole matter up with your governments."

Clark-Kerr and I both told him that we had reported the latest aspects of the situation to our governments. Until we received further instructions, there was nothing that either of us could do.

"I am in the same fix," Mr. Romer growled. "Nothing to do but wait, wait, wait. And all the while, I feel something in the air—I feel it, I tell you. Something terrible is going to break, and soon.

What shall I do? Do you think I should try to see Mr. Stalin again? He was so kindly and understanding."

Clark-Kerr and I nodded. He should certainly try to see Mr. Stalin again.

I recall that we canvassed the whole course of the controversy. I suggested that a compromise might be reached if the Poles would agree to discuss boundaries and Mr. Molotov would continue to discuss citizenship.

"No, no!" Mr. Romer exclaimed, jumping to his feet. "If we agree to discuss boundaries, we might as well settle right now on the Curzon Line as our eastern boundary and give up all claim to our Eastern Provinces to the Soviets."

We finally had to adjourn, agreeing that we could do no more, any of us, until we had further instructions.

On April 2, Mr. Romer came to the Embassy and left with me a memorandum giving the provisions of the notes which the Polish Ambassadors in London and Washington had presented to the British and American Governments, asking their help. "I believe that Sir Archibald and you will be instructed to take up the Polish Question again with the Kremlin."

The memorandum was most reasonable. I had high hopes for a practical settlement of this long-standing and troublesome Polish Question. Sir Archibald and I discussed the memoranda at length over lunch. Days passed but no instructions came from either of our governments. Nor did the Kremlin show any disposition to negotiate with the Poles. Their reasons are obvious enough, now. The Nazis had been defeated in Tunisia; the Italians were on their way out of the War; the Red Army was rolling down the invasion highway toward Smolensk and approaching the Ukranian capital of Kiev. To those on the inside, it must have been obvious even then that it was only a matter of time. Already, the Russian Politburo was making plans for post-War expansion at the expense of Eastern European nations. The Kremlin had a place for a Communist Poland in their plans.

On April 13, 1942, came the "break" that Mr. Romer had dreaded. The Goebbels propaganda machine went into high gear. The Nazi radio announced that, in Katyn Forest near Smolensk, they had found mass graves of about 10,000 Polish officers, each with his hands tied behind his back and shot through the back of his head. Russian peasants had told the Nazis that these Polish officers, prisoners of war, had been murdered by the NKVD in the Spring of 1940. The German broadcast claimed that papers found in their pockets, as well as the condition of the bodies, indicated that the men had died early in 1940. Names announced over the German radio corresponded with those of Polish officers missing from the three prisoner of war camps mentioned earlier.

If it were only German propaganda, it was very clever propaganda, designed to split the United Nations coalition down the middle. The Russian never has had much love for the Pole. The reactionary Polish Army officers would be a difficult element to absorb into a Communist government in a post-War Poland. On the other hand, the Nazis had been guilty of enough mass murder in the past five years to be entirely capable of just such a massacre.

Two days later, Radio Moscow broadcast an indignant denial of the Nazi charge. "At last," it said, "these new German lies reveal the fate of the Polish officers whom the Germans used for construction work in the Smolensk area." The next day, Tass explained that these Polish prisoners had been captured alive by the Germans during the Red Army retreat from Smolensk in the Summer of 1941, information which the combined efforts of the British, American, and Polish Governments had been unable to extract from the Soviet Government until that day.

The Poles were wild. They knew that many of their officers had been removed from the three prison camps in April, 1940. If the Soviet Government knew that they had been captured by the Germans in 1941, why had the Russians let the Poles hunt and hope for almost two years?

Ambassador Romer urged caution. The Polish Government in London proceeded cautiously. On April 17, the Polish Cabinet issued a statement, of which I obtained a rather poor translation. It began:

> There is no Pole who isn't deeply shocked by information loudly proclaimed by German propaganda of the discovery near Smolensk of huge graves filled with corpses of massacred Polish officers missing in the USSR, and about their execution.
> At the same time, the Polish Government in the name of the Polish Nation refuses to permit the Germans to promote discord among the United Nations by shifting that crime in self-defense to the Russians. The hypocritical indignation of the German propaganda will not conceal from the world the cruel crimes committed by the Nazis against the Polish Nation.

The statement then went on to list a long series of crimes committed by the Nazis in violation of International Law and the Laws

wearily in his chair and shook his head. "*Nyet, nyet!* It is no use. For two weeks, this slanderous campaign against the Soviet Union has dragged on. The Poles have been working with Hitler. We have shown a maximum of patience. Our people have become extremely indignant. We must make the break and publish the note. I hope that your Government will understand the Soviet position."

Ten years later, while I was appearing before a Select Committee of our Congress, I finally learned the contents of the messages exchanged that April between Premier Stalin and President Roosevelt. After reviewing the dispute between the Soviet Government and the Poles over the investigation of the mass executions in Katyn Forest, Stalin's message went on to say:

> The Hitlerite authorities, after perpetrating an atrocious crime against the Polish officers, are now engaged upon an investigation farce for the staging of which they have enlisted the help of certain pro-fascist Polish elements picked up by them in occupied Poland, where everything is under Hitler's heel and where honest Poles dare not lift their voices in public.
>
> The Governments of Sikorsky and Hitler have involved in these "investigations" the International Red Cross, which is compelled to take part, under conditions of a terroristic regime, with its gallows and mass extermination of a peaceful population, in this investigation farce, under the stage management of Hitler. It should be clear that such "investigations" carried out moreover behind the Soviet Government's back, cannot inspire confidence in persons of any integrity.
>
> The fact that this campaign against the Soviet Union was launched simultaneously in the German and Polish Press, and is being conducted along similar lines, does not leave any room for doubt that there is contact and collusion between Hitler, the enemy of the Allies, and the Sikorsky Government in the conduct of the campaign.

All these circumstances "forced the Soviet Union" to come to the conclusion that it had to "break off relations with the present Polish Government."

Two days after this message was received in the State Department, President Roosevelt sent an answer to Stalin, probably through Ambassador Litvinov in Washington, for we never saw the message in Moscow. After telling the Russian Premier that he had been absent from Washington, President Roosevelt expressed the hope that Stalin might call his action "a suspension of conversations" rather than a "severance of diplomatic relations." He then continued:

It is my view that Sikorsky has not acted in any way with the Hitler gang, but, rather, that he made a mistake in taking the matter up with the International Red Cross. Also, I am inclined to think that Churchill will find ways and means of getting the Polish Government in London to act with more common sense in the future.

Let me know if I can help in any way, especially in regard to looking after any Poles you may desire to send out of Russia.

Incidentally, I have several million Poles in the United States, many of them in the Army and Navy. They are all bitter against the Nazis and knowledge of a complete diplomatic break between you and Sikorsky would not help the situation.

On April 28th, all hope of reconciliation was ended by the publication in *Izvestia* of an article by Wanda Wasilevskaya, Chairman of the "Union of Polish Patriots," editor of *Wolna Polska,* a Polish Communist sheet, and also said to be the wife of Mr. Kornechuk, who recently had been made a Vice Commissar of Foreign Affairs.

This article stated that the Polish-Government-in-Exile in London was a rump segment of Rydz-Smigly's "Government of Poland's September Defeat," was not elected by the Polish people, did not represent them, and was at that time controlled by Hitlerite elements. The Army leadership under General Anders was accused of anti-semitism, chauvanism, anti-Sovietism, and cowardice for "refusing to fight and withdrawing its forces from the Soviet Union."

The diplomatic representatives of the Sikorsky Government were accused of robbing Polish exiles of supplies and money. The links of the Polish Government with Berlin were said to be as clear as the imperialistic intention of the Poles toward Soviet territory.

The article concluded by saying that the Union of Polish Patriots demanded the organization in the Soviet Union of Polish military units "which would proceed to the front to fight shoulder to shoulder with the Red Army, rather than sitting for months in their tents."

I realized it was hopeless, how hopeless I discovered when this "Union of Polish Patriots," made up of Polish Communists virtually unknown on the international scene, became the Lublin Government, which moved into liberated Poland on the heels of the Red Army and took over Poland for the Communists.

Anxious to conciliate the Kremlin, on May 1st, the Polish-Government-in-Exile withdrew its request for a Red Cross investigation. Realizing he had a good thing, Herr Goebbels went ahead with an investigation of his own, employing a panel of twelve distinguished Europeans, only one of whom, a Swiss, was neutral. This commission unanimously agreed that the condition of the bodies and the papers in the officers' pockets proved beyond doubt that they had been dead and buried for three years. This placed the massacre back in 1940 when the Russians held Katyn Forest.

The Nazi propagandists took to the graveside a number of American officers, prisoners of war in Germany. One of these, Army Colonel John H. Van Vliet, Jr., later testified before the special House Committee, "Despite my hatred for the Nazis, I formed an immediate, unshakable opinion that the Russians were guilty."

At noon on April 29th, Polish Ambassador Romer came to Spaso House to tell me goodbye and to inform me that his Government had asked the American Government to take over Polish documents and the British Government Polish affairs. Later in the afternoon, with my First Secretary and members of my staff, I went to the station to see Mr. Romer off. Also present were Sir Archibald Clark-Kerr and his staff and the Turkish Ambassador and his Secretary, as well as all of the foreign correspondents and news photographers.

In the course of his few months in Moscow, Mr. Romer had become very popular with us all. It was a cold, rainy day, with an air of gloom over the assemblage. We gave Mr. Romer our little gifts and watched him waving from the window as the train pulled out of the station, feeling without quite knowing why that with him went some of our hope for a free and peaceful world.

The Polish Massacre in Katyn Forest was argued back and forth on propaganda broadcasts between the Germans and the Russians until September 1943, when the Red Army recaptured Smolensk. On January 22, 1944, four months later, the Soviet Government announced that a Soviet investigation commission had been formed to settle once and for all the Katyn Forest dispute. A number of our American correspondents and military aides were invited to Goat Hill to see for themselves. They were shown about by the Director of the Moscow Institute of Criminal Medical Research, Dr. Victor Prozorosky. They saw Red Army men digging in great trenches where bodies of the Polish officers were laid out in rows and layers, like cordwood ricked up for the Winter. In large medical tents, they saw autopsies performed, while surgeons explained that the firm texture of the flesh indicated that the bodies could not possibly have been buried longer than two years. They noted that most of the bodies wore long, heavy underwear and fur coats, rather warm clothing for September (when the Polish officers were evacuated from the prisoner of war camps). Many of the newspaper clippings, letters, and other documents were dated February and March 1940, although the visitors were shown a few papers dated in 1941.

The evidence of German guilt which they were shown was detailed, complete and damning. Yet a few questions remained unanswered:

If the Polish officers were captured alive by the Germans in the Summer of 1941, why weren't the Polish officials told at once?

Why was the quest of the Polish military authorities for their lost officers allowed to continue for over two years?

Would the uniforms and boots be in such excellent condition after two years in Russian prison camps?

Why were the officers wearing heavy underwear and fur overcoats in September when Katyn Forest is very warm?

Why were there so many letters and documents dated in February and March of 1940 and only a few dated in 1941?

Why were the news despatches from Moscow so peculiarly censored by Narkomindel that all of the correspondents' doubts of German guilt were eliminated from the despatches?

One obvious truth is this: The Russians didn't need to be polite to the London Poles any more. By November 1943, a few hundred miles south of the Russian border in Teheran, the Big Three were discussing, not so much how to win the War, as what to do about the world after it was won. Present at the Teheran Conference was my friend, Admiral William D. Leahy. In his book, *I Was There*, he wrote:

Polish boundaries caused little argument at Teheran. After a more or less general acceptance of the Curzon Line as Poland's eastern frontier, to which Roosevelt made no specific agreement, the matter of the western border was left undecided—except that the Big Three seemed to accept as principle that Poland should get some German territory to compensate for the area claimed by Russia on her side of the Curzon Line.

The Russians at that conference seemed to accept as an axiom that post-War Poland should be a Communist Poland.

I recall that as early as April 28, 1943, I reported to Washington that many qualified observers in Moscow felt that there would be formed on Soviet soil a "Free Polish Government," which would maintain that it, alone, rather than the "reactionary" emigré Polish circles abroad, represented the real Polish people in that part of Poland occupied by Germany. They expected this "Free Polish Government" to be an offspring of the Union of Polish Patriots.

I remember that I rather doubted at the time that this would be feasible because there did not appear to be any leaders among the Polish Communists in Russia of sufficient stature to have popular appeal among the Poles. My doubts were resolved a few months later when the Lublin Government moved into liberated Poland on the heels of the Red Army and took over Poland for the Communists.

At the end of the despatch, I made a statement which turned out to be prophetic and which might have helped to prevent the tense international situation of the present, if anyone in Washington had paid any attention to it. I told our State Department that a similar development was possible in the case of any country bordering on the 1941 Soviet frontiers which did not agree to the policy of the Soviet Union, for within the Soviet borders could be found the nucleus of a government for any European country, especially for those countries in which the Soviet Union had a strategic or geographic interest.

I concluded that message as follows:

> We may, it seems to me, be faced with a reversal in European history. To protect itself from the influences of Bolshevism, Western Europe in 1918 attempted to set up a *cordon sanitaire*. The Kremlin, in order to protect itself from the influences of the West, might now envisage the formation of a belt of pro-Soviet states.

Katyn Forest is now behind the Iron Curtain. Probably no one except the German and Russian authorities and a few eye witnesses will ever know for certain just who massacred the Polish officers. Both ruthless dictatorships were easily capable of the act. However, in later investigations Russian guilt has been fairly well established, and most Poles in the U.S. blame the Russians. Above are the facts as I saw and know them.

There is a lesson—let my fellow countrymen beware that they never be caught like the Poles between the upper and nether millstones of dictatorship!

CHAPTER XXV

Moscow Miscellany

IN LOOKING over my diaries, notes, and letters, I run across many amusing, interesting, and informative incidents which have no relevance in either time or space but which collectively have such importance that I cannot leave them out. I am grouping them here.

As I have previously indicated, we were very closely circumscribed in our movements. The Russians seemed to be afraid to talk to us Americans either directly in Russian or through an interpreter. I have had Eddie Page accost an old woman we passed on the street. She looked around furtively and, apparently reassured, began to talk to him. I got as far as putting one question to her when a Russian man dressed in a dark grey suit came around the corner. "Amerikansky!" she exclaimed, and, rolling her hands up in a little apron she wore, she scuttled off down the street.

I loved to walk through the streets of Moscow; the sights I saw, the sounds I heard, the odors I smelled, the texture of fear I always felt, all intrigued me. The contrast between the benefits of the "ruling class" and the degradation and poverty of the "working class" continues to amaze me. These walks also served to provide a pleasurable form of exercise in that land of the proletariat, where everything is promised and so little delivered.

No Typhus Fever in Soviet Russia!

This was the official Soviet Government position, duly transmitted to our government: "There is no typhus fever in the Soviet Union."

Our Navy Medical Department found this hard to believe. On the off chance that the Russians might have discovered some real cure or preventive for typhus and in order to further the Navy's studies of the disease even if the situation in Russia had been over-optimistically presented, the Navy Surgeon General selected Commander Frederick Lang, a specialist in internal medicine and public health work, to accompany me to Russia as my Embassy medical officer.

A brilliant, energetic doctor, Freddy Lang lost no time commencing his investigation of contagious diseases, especially typhus. Since General Faymonville had a doctor, a Captain Waldron of the Army Medical Corps, on his mission staff in Moscow, I always took Freddy with me on my treks back and forth between Kuibyshev and Moscow and into the Russian hinterland. This gave him an excellent opportunity to pursue his investigations over a rather wide area of Russian territory. I must say that, once given approval by higher authority, the Russian medical and public health officials were most cooperative wherever we went; they arranged for Fred to visit hospitals, dispensaries, and medical research laboratories, even some of the laboratories which produced the Russian brand of typhus vaccine.

Not long after we settled in Kuibyshev, Freddy came into my office to make a report. "Admiral," he said, "we're right in the midst of a typhus epidemic here in Kuibyshev. The Russian health authorities deny it, but typhus *is* a major problem in the overcrowded Russian cities. We've all had the American typhus vaccine, so I guess we'll be all right, but I wouldn't recommend visiting buildings where there are typhus cases. I'll keep you posted."

As I have previously indicated, Kuibyshev had swollen from a village to a city of over a million persons. Sanitation was primitive or nonexistent; public health measures were planned but not far advanced. Despite his warning, Freddy Lang continued to visit Russian hospitals and laboratories; when typhus struck the Polish and British Embassies, he treated their patients.

One afternoon, as my secretary, Eddie Page, and I were spading up the vegetable garden at the back of Sadovia, Doc Lang joined us, saying, "That's just what I need. A good workout."

Half way through the job, he excused himself. "I'm awful tired," he said to Eddie. "May I take a nap in your room before dinner?"

Freddy lay down for an hour but couldn't sleep. He joined us for dinner but he must have had a hard time keeping his chin up until it was over. He dragged himself back to Chancery and somehow made it up the stairs to his room.

When I reached the office the next morning, Eddie informed

me that Lang was in bed with a high fever. We put him on the sick list, detailed one of our Russian maids to care for him in the daytime and hired a Polish night nurse. Freddy prescribed his own treatment, the usual routine treatment for influenza. His fever did not break—in fact, his fever range was most unusual. We were both apprehensive and so Freddy kept a careful record of his pulse and temperature.

When I visited Fred on the fifth morning, he smiled up at me weakly. "Well, Admiral, there's no longer any doubt; it's typhus. I have the telltale chest rash and tenderness in my abdomen."

I was shocked. Officially, Russia had no typhus fever; neither Freddy nor I knew of any regulations as to sanitation or quarantine. "What do you want me to do, Fred?" I asked. "Send you to the hospital?"

"No, sir. From what I've seen of Soviet hospitals, I'd rather take my chances right here."

It was a difficult situation; I couldn't blame Fred and I certainly was not going to pack him off against his will. We had taken no precautions; other members of the Embassy staff and I had visited Fred frequently during his illness.* I called the Foreign Office to report the case.

Within an hour, a Russian doctor reported to the Embassy, an old fellow about seventy-five, with a trim white goatee and *pince nez* glasses. I took him up to see Fred. He made a quick examination and exclaimed, "Oh, Doctor, typhus, typhus."

We notified the city and district health officers; two specialists came rushing around to the Embassy and went in consultation with the old doctor. "It might be malaria," one of them hazarded. "It can't be typhus; we have no typhus in Russia."

"Typhus, Doctor, it *is* typhus!" the old fellow insisted.

The young specialists tried to beat the old doctor down but he stood his ground. They continued to treat Lang for typhus. Although Fred was certain that he had received no louse bites, they insisted that we fumigate Fred's clothing to kill the louse that hadn't bitten him. We also had to fumigate Fred's room, the floor on which his room was located, and the basement where the servants lived. I sent to Moscow for Doctor Waldron and cancelled all social engagements so that the Russians could not accuse the American Embassy staff of spreading typhus.

* "The other visits stopped, but Admiral Standley continued to come in to see me twice a day, to try to cheer me up and to see if there was anything he could do for me."—Captain Frederick Lang, Medical Corps, U. S. Navy.

Freddy was acutely ill with a very high fever for sixteen days; he lost 22 pounds. It was 30 days before he could resume his duties. A full return to health required six months. Fred attributes his recovery from usually fatal typhus fever to the American vaccine with which we had all been innoculated before we left the States.

The American Typhus Commission in the Middle East

On April 8, 1943, I was notified by the State Department that a Typhus Commission headed by Admiral C. S. Stephenson, Medical Corps, U. S. Navy, would be established in Cairo for the purpose of studying typhus fever and the various epidemic diseases prevalent in the Middle East. A month or so later, word came that Admiral Stephenson's Commission would like to visit the Soviet Union for the same purpose.

We were in Kuibyshev at the time; I immediately secured an appointment with Mr. Vishinsky. When I had presented my request, without his usual hesitation, he said, "I'm sure that will be quite impossible."

"Why?"

Mr. Vishinsky blushed. "You have told me that this Commission is studying epidemic diseases including typhus fever. If we permit them to come into the Soviet Union, the German Press will immediately start a propaganda campaign that typhus fever is raging in the Red Army. Of course, we have no typhus in Russia; we don't want even a rumor of typhus to leak out."

Having in mind Fred Lang's case of "malaria" and the similiar cases he had treated in the Polish and British Embassies, I said, "We recognize that Russian medical research men have done a wonderful job in stamping out typhus in the Soviet Union. Now, Mr. Vishinsky, in justice to your allies, don't you think that your government should permit Admiral Stephenson's Commission to have the benefit of learning just what the Russian doctors have done to control typhus?"

"I'm sorry," he said firmly. "I'm afraid the Commission just can't come into the Soviet Union."

"In that case, I feel that the least your Government could do would be to permit several of your best medical research men to join our Typhus Commission in Cairo and give it the benefit of their experience."

This suggestion met with hesitant approval. While in Moscow on other business some months later, I received information as to the date the Commission would commence their studies in Cairo and informed Mr. Molotov. Word came from the Foreign Office that the Soviet specialists could not participate in the Commission's work, as it would be impossible for them to arrive in Cairo by the specified date.

I asked for an appointment with Mr. Molotov. When some days passed without seeing him, I sent Doctor Lang out, ostensibly with a State Department patient headed for a hospital in the States; privately, I gave Freddy instructions to report to the Stephenson Commission in Cairo to learn what he could from their studies in the Middle East, to bring them up to date as to the crude methods of typhus control employed in Russia, and the typhus epidemic conditions in Moscow, Kuibyshev, and other Russian cities.

When Eddie Page and I reached Mr. Molotov's office for an interview some days later, we were kept waiting for half an hour while he completed some discussions with another visitor. He came into the room where we waited with a pleasant apology for being delayed. "I'm terribly sorry about the medical mission," he went on. "My Government would like so much to have our men participate, but they will be unable to reach Cairo in time."

Eddie gave me a barely perceptible wink as he translated. "Well, I'm glad to hear that Mr. Molotov," I replied. "I have a plane at the airport ready to take off for Teheran. If you will permit your medical researchers to go, I will have six of them flown to Cairo; I guarantee that they will arrive in time for the conference."

"That is very kind of you, Mr. Ambassador. We certainly would be happy to have our scientists attend the conference."

I took this to be a reluctant acceptance of my offer. I knew that our plane was supposed to have twelve removable but comfortable seats, the kind they used to call Doug MacArthur seats in the Pacific. I had already committed six seats for the flight to Teheran. Upon inspecting the plane at the airport, I was astounded to find that six seats had been removed prior to its last flight into Russia to make room for freight.

I had already had some dealings with the Russian engineer in charge of repairs at the airport. I went to his office and asked him to go to our plane with me. I explained the situation. "I understand that you have seats that were removed from some of your DC-3's. Would it be possible to install six of them in this plane?"

"Why, certainly, Mr. Ambassador. I'll look into it right away."

Since I was undertaking this project on my own responsibility, I expected that I would have to bear any expense involved. "How much will it cost?" I asked.

"Nothing, Mr. Ambassador," the engineer replied. "We'll be happy to do it for you. There will be no charge."

Late the next afternoon I received a request that I come to the airport to inspect the seats. Taking General Faymonville with me to be my air expert, I was surprised to discover that six duplicates of the seats in the plane had been fabricated in the Russian shops and installed. The only noticeable difference was in the mechanism by which the seats were rolled back into a reclining position for resting or sleeping. The Russians apparently hadn't been able to duplicate the American mechanism on such short notice; the position of their seats was controlled by a simple turnbuckle. I was very pleased and again asked the engineer what the cost would be. Once more, he said, "Why nothing, Mr. Ambassador. No charge at all."

As we left the plane, I separated from General Faymonville, who walked to the car with the Russian engineer. Later on, Faymonville told me that the engineer took advantage of my absence to tell him, "I'm sorry to have the Ambassador so worried about the cost of making the seats, because, of course, I cannot charge him for our work. You understand. But, if you wish, you might tell the Ambassador that I have no wrist watch. If the Ambassador could give me a wrist watch, I would appreciate it very much."

I sent a message to Commander Lang in Cairo to bring back to Moscow the best and most reliable wrist watch he could buy.

The next day, Mr. Molotov sent word that his government had decided to send their medical research scientists to Teheran in a Russian plane. I felt very good; I had achieved one of my few diplomatic triumphs in the Soviet Union. Somewhat later, Admiral Stephenson wrote me that the Russian medical scientists had never arrived. When I consulted the Foreign Office, I discovered that the Russian delegates had been stalled in Teheran for a month because the British refused them visas to visit Cairo.

I went to see Sir Archibald. "Why didn't you consult me?" he asked. "We have been trying for months to get exit visas for British citizens to leave Moscow. When the Russians applied for Cairo visas, we held them up, trying to force the Soviet Government to grant us the visas we wanted."

It seemed as if, in the Soviet Union, one could never win a complete diplomatic victory. If the Russians didn't repulse us from the diplomatic barricades, our British cousins spiked the guns of our diplomatic artillery. I was the unhappy possessor of six Russian versions of the Doug MacArthur seat. And I was out one expensive wrist watch.

Freddy Lang, resourceful as ever, returned with a beautiful watch. I went down to the airport and looked up my friend, the Russian engineer. When I offered him the watch in his office with two other Russians present he declined with many expressions of deep appreciation.

I caught on. Some weeks later, I went to the airport with Eddie Rickenbacker to inspect his plane. In leaving the plane, I arranged for Eddie to go down the aisle first, followed by myself and the Russian engineer. I put the wrist watch down on one of the seats as I passed. Out of the corner of my eye, I saw the engineer quickly pick it up and slip it in his pocket.

In the Middle East, they call it *baksheesh*. In China, it's *Kumsha*. The Russians have an expression for it, *dat na chai*. No matter what they call it, in every country in the world it's pretty much the same—just plain graft.

The Crew Races for the Championship of All Russia

On Sunday, July 25th, not having pressing business at the office, Eddie Page and I decided to drive from Spaso House to Mokhovaya over a circuitous route we liked—across the Moscow River below the Kremlin, up the far bank, back across the river through Red Square to the office.

Just above the bridge, the Moscow River and the Moscow-Volga Canal come together, forming a sort of spearhead. As we proceeded up the river, I saw some large floats moored on either side of this pointed peninsula. Boat crews of both men and women carried eight-oared shells onto the floats and placed them in the water in a highly boatmanlike fashion.

Having watched crew practice and crew races both at the Naval Academy (from motorboats and patrol craft) and in the Hudson River near Poughkeepsie (from a boat train moving slowly down one bank of the river), I was interested in this Russian participation in an ancient sport. Stopping my car, I waved the NKVD car behind us to come up alongside, and had Eddie call across to the heavy-set, moonfaced man I always mentally called Boris, "What's going on over there? Who's racing?"

Not proudly, with no evidence of interest, he replied, "It is the annual crew race for the championship of all Russia."

I looked up and down the street and across at the opposite bank of the river. Mine was the only car; there were no more than a dozen people in sight anywhere along the river, and their movements soon convinced me that they were casual passersby.

We watched the proceedings until two shells manned by male crews and four shells manned by young women set out down the river, to the accompaniment of the usual raucous barking of the male and female cox'ns. We turned, crossed the river, and followed the boats down the river. The starting line was marked by a man on the far bank, with a megaphone and a hand bell, and a white post on the bank of the river on our side.

We reached the starting line, turned the car around, and watched the starts. The male crews went off first. There was no jockeying for position at the line or attempting to get away to a better start than the other crew; the boats came up to the line together, the bell rang, and the crews were off up the river, with the cox'ns calling out the stroke, a harsh, rhythmical sound that gradually grew fainter. The four women's boats came down to the starting line with as little fanfare and were off.

We followed the race up the river, pulling ahead of the men, stopping until both men and women passed us, then passing the crews to wait for them again. We reached the finish line ahead of the men's crews and watched a close, exciting finish. As the leading boat's bow hit the line, a buxom woman on the finish line on our side of the river rang a hand bell. Without stopping or slowing their stroke, the crews went on up the river to the floats, lifted the shells overhead, and carried them up the bank to the boathouse.

When the women crews reached the finish line, the two leaders made as close a race of it as the men had; the other two crews brought up the rear by several lengths. The women were just as matter-of-fact as the men, hoisting their shells up over their heads and carrying them up the bank to the boathouse without a backward look. There was no evidence of elation or excitement of any kind.

My diary records:

6:00 P.M., took Page, Hamilton, Prunier, and Holt to see ballet, *Nut Cracker*. Enjoyed it immensely. Home late for supper. To bed 10:30, reading Tolstoi, "War and Peace."

I recall that the opera house was filled to the rafters and that the *aficianados* came down to the pit rail, cheering loudly, "Lepeshinskaya, Lepeshinskaya, LEPESHINSKAYA!" Quite a contrast to the boat races.

The championship crew races were given a prominent headline and a quarter-column write-up in the Moscow morning newspapers, but, from where we sat, it was apparent that the only persons really interested in these exciting races were the members of the crews and us.

The Problem of Exit Visas

This brings to mind the recurring problem of exit visas from the Soviet Union. The policy of the Soviet Foreign Ministry seemed to be:

1. They would willingly grant entry and exit visas to visiting dignitaries, special representatives, and Very Very Important Personages, provided the Russians felt pretty sure that their entry and exit would be to the advantage of the Soviet Union.

2. They would grant visas readily enough to top diplomatic representatives of friendly countries at the Seat of Government, provided that they were *persona grata* to the Soviet Government and provided the particular exit, entry, or trip didn't conflict with some Soviet interest.

3. They were most reluctant to grant visas to "visiting firemen" who had no particular status, but just wanted to make a grand tour and write unpleasant articles or books about the Land of the Soviets.

4. They were downright unwilling to grant exit visas to any citizen of the Soviet Union or countries occupied by the Soviet Union, any former citizen of the Soviet Union, any person with a dual status as citizen or national of a Soviet Republic and some foreign country.

Thus, as one of my prospective problems, the case of a sister-in-law of a Foreign Service officer was called to my attention when I was briefed for the job in Moscow. The woman (whom we shall call Mrs. X) and her husband had been captured when Soviet Russia occupied Latvia at the beginning of World War II and were sent to Russia as prisoners. Nothing had been heard of them since. The tragedy of the story appealed to my inherent human instincts and upon arrival at Moscow, I had one of my secretaries take up the case of Mrs. X with the American desk in the Foreign Office.

A short time later, in a roundabout fashion, I received word that Mrs. X had been located on a collective farm near Gorki, a city about sixty miles from Moscow.

In the meantime, I had inherited another visa case. My Navy radioman, a fine young lad named Stannard, had married a Russian girl in accordance with the laws of the Soviet Union. According to the laws of the United States, she then became immediately eligible for immigration into the United States and acquired a special status with regard to naturalization. According to Soviet Law, she was still a Soviet Russia citizen.

In due course, a baby was born to the Stannards and, a bit later, the Navy Department directed that I detach Stannard from the Embassy staff and send him home. I applied for exit visas; the Consular Division of the Foreign Office informed me that exit visas would be granted for Stannard and his wife, but that the baby could not leave the country. All that I could do to help out this unfortunate family was to hold up Stannard's orders.

At one of my periodic interviews with Mr. Vishinsky at the Foreign Office in Kuibyshev on May 27, 1942, I requested his assistance in arranging for the release of Mrs. X and for the visa for the Stannard baby. Mr. Vishinsky promised to press his Consular Division for favorable action.

Mr. Vishinsky must have really exerted pressure, for Mrs. X arrived at the Kuibyshev Chancery on May 31, 1942. We gave her a room and put her to bed; she was exhausted from the trip. Doctor Lang and I went to see her. From my diary and letters, I have this description of her.

She was timid, helpless, seemingly frightened of everything. She wore men's heavy boots, one of which had caused an infection on her foot, which Doctor Lang had to lance. Her teeth were bad; she had mild scurvy and evidence of malnutrition. She looked as though she had been brow-beaten; she was spiritless and lacking in any animation. We tried to question her but she seemed to be afraid to tell us anything. She couldn't sleep without a sedative, afraid that the Russians would take her again.

For a time, it looked as though the Russians might. We had advised Mrs. X to renounce her Russian citizenship before she left Gorki, but she hadn't done so. Because she was still a Russian citizen, the Consular Division delayed her visa. Eddie Page was advised that she would have to return to Gorki, renounce her citizenship, and the Consular Division would then "consider further the merits of the Mrs. X case."

Knowing this promise meant nothing and she probably had been permitted to come from Gorki to Kuibyshev by some mischance, I had my Consul investigate. He discovered that there was a precedent—in a similar case, citizenship had been renounced right there in Kuibyshev. We brought this to the attention of the Consular Division; at the same time, I told the Russians, "If Mrs. X has to return to Gorki to renounce her Russian citizenship, the American Ambassador will accompany her to ensure that she returns to the American Chancery in Kuibyshev."

It was not a trip to which I looked forward with any degree of pleasure, but the bluff worked. She renounced her citizenship in Kuibyshev.

This was by no means the end of my troubles in the Stannard and Mrs. X Cases. Soviet officials are expert at stalling. I find in my diary that the women on the Embassy staff outfitted Mrs. X with appropriate clothing and shoes on June 2nd. On June 17, we took her to see the Russian play, *Eugene Onegin.* "The poor girl was wide-eyed. She'd never seen anything like the Bolshoi Theater."

But while we were kind to Mrs. X and considerate of the Stannards, we weren't getting them anywhere. The procrastination of the Consular Division in these cases was obvious; I decided upon a stratagem.

On my next periodical call upon Mr. Vishinsky, after I had finished the business which took me to the Foreign Office, I tarried for conversation. Presently, I asked, "Has the Russian Government changed its policy with regard to visas for the wives and children of Soviet officials going to duty in the United States?"

"Oh, no, there has been no change of policy. Why do you ask?"

I looked across the table at Mr. Vishinsky, soberly. "Recently, there has been a considerable increase in the number of visas issued. As a matter of fact, during the past month, we have issued over five hundred visas. Compared to previous records, such a rushing business in visas would seem to indicate a change in Soviet policy."

"Oh, no, Mr. Ambassador. Because of the war, we send more representatives to the United States. We feel that our officials do better work and are more contented if they have their families with them."

"Then, it's for humanitarian reasons?"

"Yes, yes, it's a question of humanitarian principles."

"Well, then, Mr. Vishinsky, we are actuated by the same prin-

ciples," I said drily. "As a matter of fact, for humanitarian reasons, I have been trying for some weeks to obtain exit visas for
one of my radiomen, his wife and baby, and for a poor girl, who
has no relatives in this world except her sister, who is in America.
So far, I have been unable to obtain those visas."

Mr. Vishinsky favored me with one of his best blushes.

After this call upon the Vice-Commissar of Foreign Affairs, our
work load in the Embassy became so heavy that we found ourselves completely unable to act upon any of the Soviet Government's requests for visas for the wives and children of officials
going to the United States. These requests piled up in the Chancery until we had to store them in boxes. Finally, the Foreign Office caught on. On July 20th, exit visas were issued for Stannard,
his wife, and baby, and for Mrs. X; they departed by plane on
July 26th. Our mounting backlog of Soviet requests for visas were
quickly processed.

But no diplomatic battle for position in the Soviet Union is ever
finally won. Later on, I had occasion to apply for exit visas for
one of our clerks, Mr. Ellsworth Raymond, a translator, who had
married a Russian girl; she was expecting the arrival of their first
child. Her doctor set a date beyond which he strongly recommended against flying.

With its usual policy of vacillation and procrastination, the Foreign Office delayed issuing the exit visas; when finally issued, they
employed the unusual device of setting an expiration date. With
one excuse after another, passage on an outgoing plane was postponed until it was too late for Mrs. Raymond to travel by air.
When the visas expired, I requested new visas but Russian procrastination carried the Raymonds past the birth of their baby
without action. Now we had the same problem we had with the
Stannard baby—he was a Russian citizen.

Again, our production in the visa department slowed to a stop.
Eventually, a visa was obtained for the baby. Before the Raymonds could travel, the time limit expired. Again our visa production stopped. Once more, we obtained visas for all three of the
Raymonds with expiration dates on them only a week away. I
knew the Russians would never grant plane passage to Mrs. Raymond and her baby in time. Waiting at the airport was my own
plane ready to take off for Teheran on the first leg of my trip
home. To avoid further delay, I took Mrs. Raymond and her baby
in my plane and delivered them to Teheran, where Mr. Raymond
presently joined them.

As an odd sequel, I note that Mr. and Mrs. Raymond have written several magazine articles on conditions in the Soviet Union which color the Russian scene with a rosy hue. In 1947 or 1948, Mrs. Raymond began to make talks around the country on the wonders and glories of Soviet Russia. Finally, the boys of the Press got after her when she became too rapturous about the advantages of Soviet Russia in a talk to a group of high school students. I understand that Mr. Raymond is no longer with the State Department.

Visas for John Young and His Planeload of Motion Pictures

Of more serious consequence was the long-running argument I had with the Russian Foreign Ministry over entry visas for John Young and his planeload of motion pictures and equipment.

In four weeks of frenzied activity, Commander Young obtained from the Army Air Corps a C-87 transport stripped for carrying freight and loaded it with projection and repair equipment and 5007 pounds of the finest feature films of that day, documentaries, and animated cartoons. Mr. Will Hays, Mr. Robert Sherwood, and a host of other officials and individuals had cooperated fully and wonderfully. Limitation of space prevents me from giving a full list of the films and equipment lent to us for my program, but the enthusiasm was considerable.

On the same day that John Young cabled me, "I have completed my task in the United States and am ready to return to Moscow," i.e., July 1, 1943, I received this message from Mr. Will Hays:

> Commander Young now has in his possession all the material you desired. May I express to you our appreciation of the vision and value of your purposes, which should contribute much indeed to the advancement of mutual understanding between the peoples of the Soviet Republics and the United States in which you and all of us are so interested.

I sat down and wrote this answer:

> Greatly appreciate your telegram and cooperation. Already, the Soviet officials have shown a sympathetic response to our efforts and I am sure that through this medium much will be accomplished here.

How naive I was! I had made the old mistake of believing in

the honesty and integrity of a Russian promise for "fullest cooperation."

I requested visas for Young and his plane crew via the ALSIB Air Route. The promised cooperation turned into obstruction. On July 2nd, the Russian Foreign Office "wanted a complete list of cargo and passengers." I was also having trouble getting entry visas for "the plane for my personal use." On July 12th, I changed my request for entry visas for John Young and his films to the African and Teheran route. The Russian objection was obviously to Young's cargo. I was able to obtain visas for the crew of my personal plane, but John Young and his films remained in New York. On July 29th, I was "still awaiting action on Young's plane."

On August 12th, I entered in my diary, "Saw Vishinsky from 9 to 10 over the transportation situation and Young's visas—no progress." On August 18th, "Page and Thompson went to see Zarubin but got nowhere with Young's plane."

I was becoming more and more annoyed. On August 26th, I made an appointment with Mr. Lozovsky and saw him "regarding Young agreement as to exchange of films. I made it plain that USSR was not living up to agreement made with me."

On September 8th, I sent Commander Young orders to proceed with his films and equipment to Moscow in the plane provided for him. On September 16th, under needling by the Air Force to return their plane, my last order to John Young was to fly to Teheran "and discharge your cargo. We will try to get the films into Moscow, if need be, can by can."

Commander Young got as far as Cairo with films and plane, where, after long delay, he was detached for duty elsewhere. The films moved on to Teheran in an Air Force transport early in November, 1943. I have no information as to how the films and equipment eventually reached Moscow, but arrive there, they did, for in 1952 I received a letter from Mr. John Fremont Melby of the State Department:

I do indeed remember the shipment to which you refer, particularly since, by the time the films arrived, I was the Acting Director of OWI and I was therefore responsible for seeing that they got their proper distribution. . . . While they were in Moscow they were shown at the Embassy, the British Embassy, the Soviet Foreign Office, and a number of Russian cultural, military, and naval clubs. When I left Moscow in April 1945, they were still there. I have looked through the Department files . . . and find that they were all eventually shipped out of Moscow and, with the possible exception of four which disappeared enroute, were returned to their owners.

Certainly, this distribution was something less than the ambitious program I expounded to Mr. Lozovsky and Mr. Zarubin, when I told them that "I hoped to see good American films, both feature films and educational films, screened every week in every movie theater in Russia." The men in the Kremlin had—and still have—no intention of letting the Russian people discover just how bad their living conditions are compared to the "decadent democracies" of the Western World.

So John Young never did get a visa to reenter the Soviet Union!

There was nothing new in this dispute with the Consular Division over visas. In November, 1851, Mr. Neill S. Brown reported to the State Department:

> During the past year, it has been evident that the policy of Russia towards foreigners and their entrance into the Empire was becoming more and more stringent. I heard of several Americans last summer, who were unable to procure visas from the Russian Legations at different points, and were therefore compelled to abandon their journey. This arises mainly from political considerations, and a fear of foreign influence upon the popular mind. To this it may be added that there is a strong anti-foreign party in Russia, whose policy would exclude all foreigners, except for mere purposes of transient commerce. They conceive that the motive of Peter the Great in opening the door to traders and artisans has been answered, and that they have learned sufficiently the lessons of civilization to maintain its craft and its maxims by themselves.

I have recently noted that three Press boys and their families have been granted exit visas from the Soviet Union, probably as part of the so-called "peace offensive." Eddie Gilmore of the AP was in Moscow when I was there and has stayed on a total of 13 years because he wouldn't leave his Russian wife and children.

Sometimes I wonder—humanitarian principles for whom?

CHAPTER XXVI

To the Urals and Stalingrad

The Plane for My Personal Use

FROM the first few weeks of my tour in the Soviet Union, I had been embarrassed and annoyed at the poor communications and the readiness with which the Foreign Office would refuse permission to travel "because adequate facilities were not available for the Ambassador." From the first, I never missed an opportunity to emphasize the importance of improved communications between Washington and Moscow. I also stressed the annoyance and inconvenience to me personally of the delay in sending and receiving mail.

In addition to the inconvenience and delay in getting around Russia in the course of carrying on the business of my government, I invariably either suffered marked discomfort in trains or was in a state of continual alarm when airborne, due to the eccentricity of the Russian pilots and the backward nature and inferior upkeep of their equipment.

Of course, I was always promised "immediate action" or that "we will inform the proper authorities and advise you." On one occasion, Mr. Molotov told me that the Russian civil air authority was establishing a bi-weekly air service between Moscow, Kuibyshev, and Teheran, which would connect with our Pan American Airways service across Africa to the Iranian capital, but that service was still "in the exploratory stage" when I left Russia, although I had flown that route many times, both in Russian and American transports.

While I was "home for consultation" late in 1942, I discussed this situation with Admiral Horn, Vice Chief of Naval Operations, and he said, "Of course, Admiral, we'll be happy to assign you a plane for your personal use in the Soviet Union, if you can get permission from the Soviet authorities to have it."

After my unhappy "transportation siege" in Kuibyshev and my three-day train trip from Kuibyshev to Moscow early in March, I had my naval and military aides sound out the proper Soviet military authorities as to "their probable attitude, if the Ambassador proposes that a plane be assigned to the Embassy for his personal use." When this unofficial reaction was favorable, on May 13th, I went to see Mr. Molotov on other business and took up this matter, as noted in my diary:

> Talked transportation with Molotov; made three propositions:
> 1. Teheran-Moscow hook-up (with Pan-American service) by ferry planes, by special planes, or by my own plane.
> 2. Via the ALSIB Air Route using ferry planes or special planes.
> 3. Having my own plane in the Soviet Union.

I informed him of the offer of our Navy Department. "I am very eager to have this plane come in and be available for my use, Mr. Molotov," I told him. "I particularly want to use it to visit the Urals industrial area, Stalingrad, and Tashkent and Alma Ata, in order to see for myself and inform my countrymen about the wonderful industrial development in the Soviet Union. The plane would also be useful for courier and mail service between Teheran, Kuibyshev, and Moscow."

Mr. Molotov looked up at me, impassively. "We will examine your proposals." His eyes fell again to the papers on the polished table before him. "Of course, it will be quite agreeable with us for the Ambassador to make the suggested tour, and you can use an American plane, if you like, but it will be necessary to obtain prior permission from the Soviet military and air authorities for each trip."

The Russians procrastinated and postponed decision as long as they could. After several representations to the Foreign Office requesting visas for the plane crew, I decided to take more drastic action. The opportunity came in the course of routine business with Mr. Stalin.

On June 4th, we received in Navy code a three part message from President Roosevelt to Mr. Stalin. When the coderoom officer began to decode, he brought the first sentence of the message to me; it read something like this:

This message is to be seen by the Ambassador, the Naval Attaché, and one decoding officer only.

Even before the message was decoded, I requested an appointment with Mr. Stalin, which was granted for 11:00 that night. The message turned out to be a detailed report on future operational plans drawn up at the TRIDENT Conference in Washington between the President and Mr. Winston Churchill, and their diplomatic and military advisers. It was not a message to make the Russian Dictator happy. The cross-channel operation, known then as OVERLORD, had been postponed until May 1, 1944, in favor of a combined Royal Air Force-U. S. Army Air Force bomber operation from the United Kingdom expected to weaken further resistance of the Nazis, and of Operation HUSKY, the invasion of Sicily, which, it was hoped, would bring about the Italian surrender. What the Russians still wanted above all else was an immediate cross-channel invasion and a Second Front in Northern Europe.

I anticipated an uncomfortable time with Mr. Stalin as I set out with Secretary Eddie Page in the Embassy limousine for the Kremlin at ten-thirty that night. Half way to the Kremlin gate, an air raid warning sounded and the entire city was immediately blacked out. There were two courses of action open to me—return to Spaso or continue to the Kremlin. Since the risk was equally great either way, I decided to continue on.

When we arrived at the Kremlin gate, the night was black as the inside of a whale. Eddie found the guard in his blacked-out sentry box. He made arrangements by telephone. An officer met us in a car a few moments later and took us to an entrance that I had never used before. We went down a short corridor, took an elevator to the top floor of the building, crossed a hall to another elevator, and went down ten stories, which must have put us at least 80 feet underground.

We stepped out of the elevator into a short arched tunnel about six feet wide and twelve feet high. At the end were a pair of massive steel doors. In view of the instructions contained in the message, I left Eddie Page in this anteroom.

My guide took me through four arched compartments about sixteen feet long, lined with steel plates, and two pair of steel doors at either end of each compartment, which opened automatically at his touch. This tunnel led into an elaborately equipped air raid shelter which could also be entered through a tunnel from a near-by station of the Moscow subway. I had previously visited this Kremlin shelter through the subway when in Moscow with the Beaverbrook-Harriman Mission, and I am sure it would accommodate the whole Politburo and Council of Ministers, and their families and important assistants, and would protect them against even a hydrogen bomb.

We came out into a larger compartment, which must have been the emergency War Room. Mr. Stalin and his military aides were seated around a long table. The room was as handsomely furnished as any of the Kremlin offices topside. As I went down the long room, Marshal Stalin was standing, conversing with someone over the telephone. He turned toward me as I approached. Apparently waiting for some information, he said, "Please have a seat. This air attack was originally directed at Moscow, but it has been diverted toward Gorki. The anti-aircraft batteries at Gorki are about to open fire."

A few seconds later, he hung up the telephone and came over, motioning for me to sit down. "The batteries have opened fire. We can't talk to Gorki anymore." Later I learned that the Gorki AA-batteries opened up too soon, the Nazi bombers delayed their attack until ammunition was exhausted, then came in and destroyed the Gorki tank factory.

I delivered the message to Mr. Stalin. While we waited for it to be translated, I brought up the question of a plane "for my personal use." "I really need one, Mr. Stalin," I explained. "Rail travel is so difficult and air travel so uncertain that I can't do my job properly, with our Mission split between Moscow and Kuibyshev. If I have my own plane, I can get back and forth whenever I need to and we can also use the plane for mail and courier service."

Mr. Stalin nodded. "Certainly, Mr. Ambassador, you need your own plane. I will issue instructions immediately. We can arrange for the plane to be kept at the Moscow Military airfield."

An aide brought Mr. Stalin the translation of the message. When he had read it through, he looked up at me steadily for a moment. "I understand the trend. You can see that I am very busy, but you shall have an answer in two or three days."

I thanked him, picked up Eddie from the anteroom and returned to Spaso House, disturbed over the Second Front situation but happy that I would at last have a Navy plane for my own use.

The next day, I sent a despatch to the Chief of Naval Operations:

> Permission has been obtained to station a plane for the personal use of the Ambassador in Moscow. Request that a transport plane be assigned and fitted out for such service at earliest practicable date.

The Navy worked fast, for my diary notes on July 2nd:

> Called on Molotov at 6:00 P.M., left contract for [air] service through Africa, Teheran, from Washington to Moscow. Informed him that plane [for my personal use] had left Washington and would soon be in Moscow.

I recall that Mr. Molotov nodded and said, "Mr. Stalin asked me to make it clear to the Ambassador that you are being permitted to bring this plane in solely for your *personal* use. You are being given this privilege only because of your advanced age."

At this time, we were having great difficulty with the Consular Division of the Foreign Office, trying to obtain entry visas for John Young, his plane crew, and a plane load of motion picture films and equipment. Apparently, visas for the "plane for my personal use" became confused with visas for John Young's plane, for we were confronted with delay and downright refusal to issue visas for either plane. It took personal intercession to obtain final clearance for my plane to enter Soviet territory via the ALSIB Air Route from Fairbanks.

Toward the middle of July, I was informed that my plane was in Fairbanks, a DC-3, with Lieutenants Prunier and Holt as pilot and copilot and a crew of three enlisted men. In accordance with the customary practice for ferry planes, Lieutenant Prunier picked up in Fairbanks a Russian radioman and a Russian navigator, who were supposed to be thoroughly familiar with the ALSIB Route. Almost believing what he was told, Prunier acted upon the Russian navigator's advice, but he kept track of the plane's position, as any good naval pilot will. But for this precaution, the Russian navigator might have brought the plane to grief. Toward sunset of the second day's flight across Siberia, when they should have sighted an airfield where they were to land and spend the night, no airport was in sight and the wooded hills looked singularly inhospitable. Fortunately, the two pilots had kept a good plot of their position and knew that they had been steering to south'ard of the course all day. When the Russian navigator couldn't produce an airfield, Lieutenant Prunier took over the navigation and headed due North. Within an hour, they sighted the airport and landed just before sunset.

Some weeks later, when I paid a visit to Mr. Molotov, the Foreign Minister took the interpreter and me aside. "I have some information I want to give you very confidentially, Mr. Ambassador," he said. "I have been informed that the pilots of your plane are not competent to navigate in the vast distances of Soviet Russia."

"Thank you, Mr. Molotov," I said pleasantly. "I'll make a note to look into that."

But I knew that he was covering up for the Soviet Government's embarrassment that their navigator had gotten lost.

The plane arrived at the Moscow airport on July 22nd. To avoid complications, I billeted the pilots and crew of the plane in Spaso House. It was pleasant to have at mess table again two bright young officers. The next day, they took me out to inspect the plane.

It was a twin-engined DC-3 transport. The three crew members in familiar navy dungarees were busy scrubbing up. Stripped of standard cabin equipment, it had been rebuilt with two Pullman-type sections, each with a double lower berth and a single upper berth, and another berth above each of the fuselage gas tanks, a sleeping capacity for eight persons. In another compartment aft, it had 9 conventional airliner seats. Its gas capacity was 1100 gallons, its cruising radius 1900 miles.

The plane brought in as passenger Mr. Maxwell McCauhey Hamilton, to be my new Counselor of the Embassy with the rank of Minister. I was certainly happy to see him because I had not had the benefit of the advice of a counselor since poor Dooman left on April 16th, and he had been so ill most of the time that he was unable to function for more than two or three days at a time.

My diary records on July 23rd that I "took Hamilton to call upon Molotov at 7:00, spent an hour with him on various matters, then came home to dinner. Turned in at 10:30 after discussion with Hamilton."

The discussion was about my plane. I had asked for clearance to have the plane make a courier and mail trip to Teheran. I had failed to understand the significance of Mr. Molotov's statement that Premier Stalin had stressed that the plane would be "for my *personal* use." Authority was granted for the mail trip with the understanding that the Ambassador would go in the plane. I was further informed that such would be the condition under which the plane would be granted permission to make any future flight.

Of course, I was unable to fly back and forth to Teheran every time we wanted to make a mail trip, and so the plane became distinctly and positively *for my personal use when I was actually on board.*

The Urals

On July 27th, I requested permission from the Foreign Office to make a trip to inspect the industrial complex which the Soviet Government had built in and beyond the Ural Mountains, specifying Sverdlovsk, Chelyabinsk, and Magnitogorsk as my ports of call. I noted in my diary on July 30th, "Still waiting for approval for my trip to Urals." As usual, authority to make the flight was not received until late in the evening of August second for a nine o'clock takeoff the next morning.

I didn't get to bed until 1:30 A.M., and I was up at 6:30 for BBC news and breakfast. At 8:30, Prunier called from the airport—departure deferred, storm between Kazan and Sverdlovsk. We were delayed for two days, which enabled the Embassy agricultural attaché, Dr. Michael, to complete a thorough survey of the country over which we would fly and assemble considerable information about the industrial plants.

The passenger list changed several times during the two days' delay. I had wanted to take General Michella and Admiral Duncan with me, but they had other trips scheduled of more immediate military importance. Finally, the party included Dr. Freddy Lang, Secretary Eddie Page, Mr. Calder, Dr. Michael, two of my NKVD protectors from the police post in front of Spaso House, and myself. As usual, the Soviet authorities assigned a Soviet co-pilot and radioman.

We took off at 9:14 and headed due east to Gorki and Kazan, then turned southward to the Kama River, which we followed to Molotov (Perm), over which we passed about two P.M. As we continued up the river, I identified Okhansk, where we visited the Tokyo bomber crew. At 2:20 P.M., we headed east again for Sverdlovsk, the most distant of the industrial cities which we were to visit.

The country we flew over was a low, flat plain with the usual thatched-roofed villages and white churches with red-painted, bulbous domes. As we crossed the Urals, I was surprised to find them low, rolling hills, wooded with deciduous trees such as we have in our Eastern foothills.

It had rained hard for two days; the Sverdlovsk airfield was flooded. We landed at 3:11 P.M. in a spray of muddy water, taxied up in front of the little control shack. Several workmen moved a wooden platform up beside the plane for us to step out. We were met by the usual delegation, the Governor of the Oblast, Party Secretary, and the director of the steel plant. The airport was 25 miles from the city over the usual rough roads.

Before the Revolution, Sverdlovsk was called Ekaterinburg after its founder, Catherine the Great. It was here that the Bolsheviks shot Czar Nicholas II, his wife and family, then changed the name of the town.

We were put up in a large hotel in the center of town, an old and somewhat battered looking structure that reminded me of our mid-Western grand hotels of the Nineties, but which had actually been constructed in 1931. I was assigned a comfortable suite of rooms, with an entrance hall, a sitting room, a twin-bedded bedroom and a "bathroom." There were flowers on the desk and plants in the windows. The covers of beds, sofas, and chairs were all of fine new linen, handsomely hand embroidered.

The bathroom was such only in name. Space had been left for a bathtub but no pipes had been run. The room had no hot water and apparently no plans to install water heating equipment, for the wash bowl had one large brass faucet in the middle and no hole for another. The toilet was a massive, gay-nineties commode type, with its tank up near the high ceiling and a long chain to pull.

Our whole party was assigned comfortable rooms on the same floor. A large room across the hall from mine had been cleared and made into a private messroom.

Sverdlovsk is an old city on a small lake, once a stage station on the old Russian highway between Moscow and Lake Baikal, built by exiles to Siberia about 1645. I doubt that this road had received any repairs since it was built. When it was Ekaterinburg, the city was noted for its gold, which the prospectors picked up on the shores of the lake, defacing its banks so badly that the Czar's government built a concrete seawall completely around the lake. The city, now swollen to over 100,000 inhabitants, has surrounded the lake. The government operates the gold mine.

After the Revolution, government prospectors found in the Urals every kind of mineral and material needed for a vast industrial complex—gold, iron, manganese, chrome, coal, timber, as well as the potentials for electricity from water-power. Sverdlovsk was selected as the site for the first Bolshevik industrial city east of the Urals. Here was established the great Ural machine-tool factory, which has become the most important machine shop in Russia. Before the war, the Sverdlovsk plant turned out thousands of tons of machine tools every year. They had everything from blast and open-hearth furnaces to huge power hammers, punching presses and rolling mills. In addition to trucks and road-making machinery, they manufactured elevators, railroad machinery, and steel castings for industry.

Our guide asked me if we wanted to inspect the factory immediately, or did we wish to rest, first. Since our time was severely limited and the plant worked in shifts around the clock, after a brief rest, we side-stepped *chi* in the hotel and went to the plant.

During the war, this plant had been greatly enlarged and converted to building tanks and artillery as well as heavy machinery for the plants in Magnitogorsk and Chelyabinsk. The workers in the plant had doubled since the Nazi attack in 1941; women workers increased from a small number to about 55 per cent.

The Director personally conducted us through the several buildings of the plant. We saw a huge drop forge made in Germany, next to a row of small drop forges used for forging parts of tanks. We went through the foundry, the forge shop, the machine shop, and the Martin furnaces. The machinery was indeed impressive, but the plant, as were others in the Soviet Union, was badly lighted, floors dirty and only partly concreted, and roofs leaky. Only over important machines were there roofs to protect against the August showers.

We went down the tank assembly line, apparently as efficient as an auto assembly line I once followed in Detroit, but dirty and badly lighted. The parts flowed in smoothly from a bare skeleton at the beginning, adding wheels, body, armor, turrets, etc., to the end, where we were greatly impressed to see three 48-ton tanks drive out of the shop for final inspections and tests.

Next, we went across to the artillery assembly plant, where they were putting together the parts for a 122-millimeter mobile gun. After we had walked through this plant, the Director took us to his office to clean up. As I came out of the washroom, he said, "Mr. Ambassador, we have prepared for you a bit of tea."

He led me toward another room, protesting as I went, "Oh, no thank you. They have dinner waiting for us at the hotel."

A regulation Kremlin banquet was spread on a long table. They don't seem to know how to give their guests a small tea or a "snack." My protest was in vain—we sat down and ate more than we wanted. Back at the hotel, the manager awaited us with a "small supper." "You must be hungry after your tour through the plant."

We certainly were not, but we had to make a pretense of enthusiasm over our third banquet that day. I finally got off to bed at fifteen minutes past midnight, expecting to have nightmares from overeating. But the air and temperature were so pleasant after the humid heat of Moscow that I had a wonderful night.

I was up in time for breakfast at 8:30. The others straggled in, looking somewhat haggard. I noted in my diary:

> A girl in black tried to talk to me in Russian, no dice. Had the usual hors d'oeuvres and wine, then cucumber salad, cutlets, fried potatoes, tomatoes and onions. *Chi* and bread and butter—caviar but no vodka.

This was the sort of breakfast that faced us every morning wherever we traveled in Russia. By ten, all of our party had eaten. Our guide came into the messroom to ask, "Where would you like to go, this morning?"

I left the itinerary up to him. We walked down the main street, pausing to admire the ornate marble façade of the opera house across the street from the hotel, which our guide told us was built in 1903. It was the *oblast* opera house with excellent talent from Moscow, he told me—probably exiled to Siberia, Eddie whispered.

Down by the lake, we embarked in four battered cars to drive out along the ancient highway to a monument marking the boundary between Asia and Europe. We went through some beautiful mountain country, timbered, with small lakes, much like our northern California. The road was nothing like those in California— rough with hard bumps and deep ruts, just about the same state as when it was built, I imagined.

When we came to the monument, a tall shaft in a little park area, we got out of the cars and threw rocks from Asia to Europe and Europe to Asia. We had our photographs taken seated on the monument and examined the names written on it (a not exclusively American mania, it seems), but we could find no English or Western Europe name.

We had one blowout going out and three on the return trip,

leaving one of the cars behind. We were scheduled for lunch at 2:30 P.M., which proved to be another banquet. The manager of the hotel haggled over our bill. As a result of luncheon and the haggling, we took off at 5:27 P.M., instead of 4:00 P.M., as planned. We arrived over the Chelyabinsk airport at 6:10 in a heavy rain squall. I silently thanked God for my American Navy pilots, Prunier and Holt, as we circled the field to come in to a landing at 6:35 in another puddled, muddy field. The airport authorities were ready for us with a portable board walk from our plane to the airport shack, where the usual delegation of Governor, Party Secretary and Director of the plants met us.

Over another rocky road some twenty-five miles, we came to the Hotel of the Southern Urals at 7:45 P.M., tired from the long day, wanting nothing so much as a hot bath and bed. My suite was identical to the one in Sverdlovsk, except that the bathroom boasted a nice white bathtub. "At last, Admiral!" Freddy Lang exclaimed. "A bath!"

I was as excited as he, until I discovered that there were no faucets on the pipes, which were stopped with wooden plugs. Again, no bath, a great disappointment.

I stretched out for a nap on the comfortable single bed. At 9:15, Eddie Page called me. "Dinner, Admiral. Another banquet."

"Oh, no!" I groaned. "Tell 'em I'm full to the ears."

But we had to go through the motions of eating and drinking. They certainly kept us well fed—lunch at 1:30, *chi* at 3:30 before we took off, and supper at 9:30, each one of them a banquet.

We managed to cover up our lack of appetite by joking with the waitresses and the Party Secretary. In the center of the table in our private messroom was a large chocolate layer cake with a lyre bird's tail embossed across the center in white icing. I sent for the cook. When he arrived, I rose to my feet and toasted his "supreme culinary prowess" in vodka. He responded appropriately and we became so chummy that he finally said, "Mr. Ambassador, we are so honored to have you visit our humble establishment that I want to do something special for you. What would you particularly like to have for breakfast?"

We were all so weary of caviar and vodka that we said in unison, "Three-minute soft-boiled eggs, toast and coffee."

"Eggs, you shall have," said the chef. The party broke up and we all went to bed, looking forward to a real American breakfast.

The weather was marvelous, the air clear and bracing, just right for good sleeping. I awoke more refreshed than I had been in months. Those soft-boiled eggs would certainly hit the spot. From my diary for August 7th:

> Came to breakfast promptly at 8:30, Dr. Michael and Lieutenant Prunier were there. The usual Russian cold dishes, caviar, vodka, porkchops, salad, tomatoes, cucumbers, bread and doughnuts. Then, [our waitress from the previous evening] brought in a basket of eggs. They looked old and dirty but, I thought, surely they must be fresh. I slashed into one with a knife and it exploded. A second did the same thing. All off with the eggs, I made my breakfast with toast and coffee and doughnuts, resolving not to ask again for an American breakfast. Dr. Michael also tried an egg, which blew up with a terrible stench. The poor waitresses were mortified to death. I can't imagine where they found eggs that had been kept that long.

After breakfast, our guide, the Vice-Governor of the *oblast*, took us for a tour of inspection of the tank factory, the largest in Russia. We saw the blast furnaces where they made the steel, foundries where they poured the steel into ingot molds, forges where they hammered and stamped the steel into parts, machine shops where they turned and cut the blanks to the proper dimensions, and assembly plants where the parts were assembled into complete tanks. They built both heavy and medium tanks and a tank destroyer which carried a six-inch gun.

We followed down the assembly line, commencing with plates which were welded together into the body, to the end, where again we watched three tanks roll off the assembly line under their own power. It was an impressive experience.

Finally, we were taken to the precision machine shop, where girls worked on machine lathes with cutting tools the size of knitting needles, machining the oiling mechanism for the tanks. I had no previous knowledge of the complicated machinery and the tremendous power required in a tank, which involves a highly elaborate oiling system. These girls were turning out work with tolerances in thousandths of an inch. And in an incredibly primitive plant, where the floors may once have been concrete but now looked like gravel, and the bare-legged girls stood on piles of kinky metal shavings, the more ingenious having improvised crude wooden flats to lay on top of the scrap. In the whole plant, I saw but four pair of women laborers carrying out scrap on primitive Russian wheelbarrows.

From the machine shop, we were taken to the Director's office and again exposed to a Kremlin banquet in the guise of "having a cup of *chi*." After lunch we toasted ourselves before another bank of furnaces, where they "cooked" such metals as aluminite, magnesite, and bronze.

We arrived back at the hotel at 3:30 P.M., to find another spread awaiting us. Stuffed again! It must have been the vodka that took care of us on these official trips—something certainly burned up the enormous amount of food we forced into our protesting stomachs.

After dinner, we gave the waitresses each a present of a bar of scented soap and a pack of cigarettes, which apparently was appreciated much more than many rubles. We took off from the airport at 5:26 P.M., taking our guide, the Vice-Governor, with us. We came over a hill and, down at the end of a valley, we saw the huge blast furnaces of Magnitogorsk throwing flame and smoke up into the sky. "The Pittsburgh of Russia," our guide, who had been to our great steel city, said proudly.

We were met by the usual delegation, including a Party official, who occupied a position comparable to mayor of "The Combine," as Magnitogorsk was often called. We drove down a fairly smooth road into untidy, unpaved streets lined with unpainted barracks and wooden apartment buildings housing the workers evacuated from European Russia. We turned into a nicely paved street lined by aspen trees which led up a narrow valley. On each side of the street were handsome, three- or four-bedroom houses on spacious lots planted with vegetables and flowers, and sidewalks the length of the street. It reminded me of many a pleasant residential street in California, a sharp contrast to the temporary shacks we had just passed. Later, however, I saw some of the permanent one- and two-family houses being constructed for the workers. The government gave the workman the land and material on a 40-year loan. The workman built his own home. All of them had ample garden space, with potatoes and other vegetables planted in what would normally be flower beds in the yards.

Our quarters were in a beautiful, modern house at the top of this street, the private home of one of the important factory officials. The house was large and roomy. Its one bathroom was spotlessly clean and its tub and shower really had hot and cold running water. It had hardwood floors and heavy, dark, highly polished furniture which looked as if it might have been ordered by catalogue from Grand Rapids. On the mantel above the brick fireplace was a bust of Stalin. In the dining room, the long, highly-polished table was kept spread with *zakuska* the whole time we were there. The house was presided over by an elderly woman, who always had a cigarette in her mouth. There must have been a dozen cooks and waitresses, in white silk dresses, who anticipated our every need. The whole lower floor was turned over to us.

I quote from my diary:

> After we cleaned up, Page and I went for a ride. Magnitogorsk is a new city, only half completed, which reminded me of Vallejo when I first knew it thirty years ago, the same black mud and slushy streets, only there are no saloons. We got out of the car to look at the new theater; there was a play on, so our Party official, really a character, put four box holders out of a box so that we could see the last act of a play, an old melodrama.
>
> Back at our house at ten, we had to sit down to another big feed, our third within eight hours. I never saw so much food in my life, suckling pig, chicken, duck, lamb chops, and all sorts of cold meats and fish; and every kind of drink. A real banquet, and we were not in the least hungry, but we did our best. I hated to go to bed on a full stomach, but I did, and expected to have nightmares, but I was none the worse for wear. Lang and Page had mild stomach upsets. The air is so wonderful that I had a good night's sleep.

Magnitogorsk is not an old city. It was first settled in 1916, but really began to grow when Soviet engineers discovered that a mountain behind it assayed from 45% to 60% iron. In 1930, they began to carve this city of a quarter of a million people out of the virgin forests of the Ural hills and valleys. The Vice-Governor told us that he helped prepare the plans for the city, that it was planned in the most complete detail before a spade full of earth was turned. Now its huge steel plant operated 20 open-hearth furnaces, six blast furnaces, and employed 45,000 workers. They do not have to sink shafts to mine the estimated 385,000,000 tons of iron ore; they take it off in layers from the top with steam shovels; electric trains on each terrace haul the ore in gondola cars direct to the washing plant, and thence to the furnaces at the foot of the mountain, a total distance from mine to plant of less than three miles.

A high grade of coking coal is mined close by. The city and the plant are located on a lake ten miles long, so there is plenty of good water for the factory. The result is an excellent grade of steel.

Sunday, August 8. Turned out at 7, shave and hot bath, real luxury! While waiting for breakfast, explored grounds and garden, a beautiful view overlooking the city and the steel mills. Our local guide came at 0800, a real character, who looks like Spencer Tracy and talks like him so we nicknamed him Spencer. The Vice-Governor was with him. Gang did not come in for breakfast until 0830. Usual things Russian, vodka, etc., also fried eggs, hotcakes, honey, blackberry jam, suckling pig, rich cakes, etc., etc.

At 0930 we started our inspection of the plant. The Director met us at the plant entrance and took us to the blast furnace section. We walked through almost endless stretches of plant between piles of slag, the heat from the furnaces scorching our faces. The Director told us the older blast furnaces had been there for several years, that the newer ones were much more efficient. One new one of 1400 tons capacity was operating, another was half completed. There were also new Martin furnaces, in which they melted pigs to mix molten iron with alloys to make the various grades of steel required in the arms factory. We passed on to the coking plants, where they make coke for the steel furnaces and obtain the gases to operate the plant.

All of the furnaces were working effectively, turning out steel, but the upkeep of the plant could not compare to those I have seen in the States. Floors were littered; rusty chains, metal waste, and plain dirt were in evidence all through the plant.

We moved to the rolling mills, where the big mills and presses rolled and stamped heated ingots into shapes required in the local arms plant and in other factories in the Ural region. This plant compared very favorably in equipment and production with those I had recently inspected at Pittsburgh and Gary, but again the upkeep and cleanliness left much to be desired.

An amusing incident from my diary:

Just before entering the plating shop, the Director of the plant started to enter an electric station, where a motor actuating the rollers at 5,000 volts was housed. A woman sentry at the door refused to let Director in. At first, he protested saying, "I am the Director." She replied, "I do not know you—you can not enter." The Director was embarrassed but obviously pleased. He turned, saying to me, "You see, my plant is so big that some of my employees don't know me." A watchman came up, identified the Director, and we were permitted to enter.

The Director invited us to lunch but I refused and this time made it stick. Back at our pleasant house in the executives' valley, another elaborate meal was laid out on the dining table, but we declined. We packed our bags, and, with the Director, "Spencer Tracy," and the Vice-Governor, drove to the airport. There we discovered that Spencer had packed up our lunch and brought it along; he insisted on putting it in the plane, just when we thought we had avoided another Russian feast. So goes it in the Soviet Union.

We took off at 1:09 P.M., local time, flew across the Urals, much higher and more spectacular at the Southern end, passed over Ufa, saw its oil derricks and large refineries from a thousand feet in the air, and headed for Kuibyshev, where we landed at the military airport at 3:59 P.M.

I wanted to go into town but daylight left for flying did not permit, so I telephoned our Chancery, then in the process of being transferred to Moscow. We gassed the plane and took off for Moscow at 4:55, landing at the military airfield at 6:12 Moscow time.

The country over which we had flown looked very much like similar scenery at home. The Urals people had much of the robust vigor I recalled from my younger days in our great West. In the Ural Mountains, I saw many undeveloped opportunities for water power. All of the people I was permitted to meet were extremely friendly, anxious to give out to us foreigners. The ordinary laborers seemed to have more interest in their work, more of a stake in the success of their enterprises than elsewhere in the Soviet Union. A distinctly higher morale than in Moscow was plainly evident. I felt that this was in a large measure true because there were more home owners; in fact, every worker felt that he was a potential home owner. In Moscow, no one has any prospect of ever owning his home.

With us, of course, food was a surfeit, as it seems to be wherever officials and managers are concerned. But it was also apparent that there was plenty of food for the workers; there were none of the ragged beggars such as we encountered in front of the Kuibyshev and Moscow churches. The hotel accommodations were much better than those in Moscow, the capital city of Soviet Communism.

The industrial towns all had an air of nervous energy, of pioneer vitality, that I encountered nowhere else in the Soviet Union.

My diary for August 9th noted:

While away, the Russians have captured Belgorod and Orel. The Western Allies have captured Catania in the Mediterranean and Munda in the Northern Solomons. The Allies are advancing on all fronts.

Stalingrad

In 1941, Stalingrad was a growing industrial giant sprawled forty miles along the Volga River. No more than a few blocks wide, deep ravines eroded in the high western bank effectively cut the city up into isolated segments, with but poor north and south communication between them. Stalingrad was important to both Germans and Russians because Stalin had directed its successful defense during the Civil Wars and had given this former Tsaritsyn his name. For political reasons, Hitler wanted to capture a city symbolizing Stalin's prestige; for the same reason, the Russians were determined that the city should not fall. An added incentive was the destruction of the Dzerzhinsky Tractor Plant, the Red October Metal Works, and other great factories which had been established in its northern end.

Strategically, the men, munitions, and effort expended to capture Stalingrad were wasted in an unsound venture. The proper strategic objectives were to cut the Volga and the railway supply line to the south of Kuibyshev and establish a base to advance north along the Volga and isolate Moscow. Hitler and his generals ignored a high, windy plateau called Serapta just to the south of Stalingrad.

I had long been interested in Stalingrad, ever since I stayed there on my way into Soviet Russia in April 1942. Little did I think that one of the great battles of the war, indeed one of the most significant land battles in history, would be fought in its narrow streets.

The trouble seems to have been that Hitler, as Stalin put it, "tried to chase two hares at once," Stalingrad and the oil of the Caucasus. This dividing of his forces left him too weak to win in either area.

Held up by the Battle of the Don River Crossing, the Sixth Army failed to reach the city in the late Summer. Hitler diverted the Fourth Panzer Army from the Caucasus with the mission of striking quickly from Kotelnikovo a hundred miles to the north to capture Stalingrad. This attack was stopped just northeast of

Kotelnikovo. In the second phase, General Paulus, with six divisions made an attack from the area of Kalach in the Don Bend coordinated with an attack of eleven divisions from the south. At one time, 30 divisions were trying to get a foothold in the city. On August 25th, a heavy air raid leveled much of the city, but the garrison fought off the German ground troops. On September 22nd, the German troops were fighting in the streets of the city; they broke through in several places to the Volga but they never succeeded in driving the Russian defenders out of the cellars and rubble of the ruined city. The Fourth Panzer Army expended its strength getting into a small section of the southern suburbs.

Foolishly, the Germans persisted in attacking the last few blocks of shattered buildings along the Volga, killing as many German soldiers as a thousand a day. With strength depleted, General Paulus had to put Romanian divisions on his flanks. Meanwhile, the Red Army began to build up strength, piling up a mass of men and munitions on the Romanians' flanks. On November 19th, the Red Army under General Yeremenko struck with an intensive 3-hour artillery bombardment and nearly a million men, and broke through the Third and Fourth Romanian Armies on the flanks, the southern force coming over the Serapta Plateau; by November 23rd, the two prongs of the encircling movement met near Kalach, turned to face the German Sixth Army and some units of the Fourth Panzer Army, which had not escaped—one of the greatest encircling movements of military history.

Hitler made one effort to relieve General Paulus, sending a relief expedition of three infantry, three panzer and two cavalry divisions under Field Marshal Von Mannstein north from Kotelnikovo on December 12th. General Malinovsky stopped him 35 miles north of Kotelnikovo on December 24th, and by December 29th drove him back and recaptured Kotelnikovo. The iron ring about 330,000 Nazi troops in Stalingrad was sealed.

On January 9th, General Rokossovsky, who commanded the troops on the Don Front, offered General Paulus an honorable surrender, which was indignantly refused. By January 26th, the Red Army had broken through and compressed the Germans into two small isolated areas. About this time, General Paulus asked Hitler's permission to surrender, reporting by radio that "to continue fighting is beyond human strength." Hitler's headquarters told Paulus, "Capitulation is impossible. The Sixth Army will do its historic duty." He promoted Paulus to Field Marshal (second class). On January 31st, 1943, Marshal Paulus surrendered, coming out of his underground headquarters in the same building in which, on April 6th the previous year, I had witnessed a Russian movie of *The Defense of Stalingrad* (1918–1919 Stalin-directed model). Ninety-one thousand Germans, the Red Army reported, were captured alive.

One surviving officer wrote: "Conditions were unbelievable. Men died of starvation and disease, froze to death, and were killed in bitter hand-to-hand fighting. The battlefield was an icy desert 22 below zero, a desolate ruins in which we were caught like rats and existed like animals."

I was in Moscow on the first of February, when the great victory was announced with the additional information that there would be "a salute that evening of 200 guns each firing 42 rounds, a spectacle of fireworks, and other demonstrations."

Eager to see what a Russian version of a Fourth of July display might be like, several of us drove to Red Square and took up a position on the corner of Kuibyshev Street a little before nine P.M. First came the salute, followed by an impressive display of pyrotechnics that rivaled any I had ever seen at home. And something extra—a stream of red, white, blue, and green tracers fired from all sides of the Kremlin, forming a cone with its apex of colored streamers directly above Lenin's tomb.

I was as entranced at the beautiful display as anyone present, not realizing how they achieved this dramatic effect, until I heard first one and then another object drum onto the metal top of my car. Upon investigation, Mike Michella discovered one of the objects, a spent tracer bullet. One of these bullets had almost penetrated the metal top of my car. Red Square under those conditions was no place for us; we left for Spaso House.

A few months later, after one of these displays, the news circulated among the embassies that a woman had been killed by a spent tracer bullet. Thereafter, there was no cone of colored streamers over the Kremlin during such victory celebrations.

Keenly interested in the Battle of Stalingrad, I had long wanted to get down to see the city before too much rehabilitation had been accomplished. On August 13th, I saw Mr. Zarubin at the Foreign Ministry and requested permission to visit the embattled city during the following week. Zarubin shook his head doubtfully. "I don't know, Mr. Ambassador. There is no suitable place for the Ambassador and his party to stay."

"I have my own plane, now," I replied brightly. "We could make the trip down and back in the same day, if necessary."

There was the usual procrastination. When I went to see Mr. Molotov on other business on August 16th, I asked him if he could expedite action, as I wanted to visit Stalingrad during the current week. He promised, as usual, "to look into the matter."

While I waited, some very interesting landmarks along the road to victory were recorded in my diary:

> Randazzio has fallen to the Americans. The British close behind. Germans still getting out of Messina. Russians started a new offensive on Smolensk. Salamau got a good bombing, also Rome. . . .
>
> Sicily war over. Americans entered Messina at 6 this morning, prisoners over 150,000. Allies destroyed 150 planes in Wewack, New Guinea. . . .
>
> Heavy bombing of Europe. Warning issued to countries on continent to make final preparations for invasion—the hour has come.

The latter, written August 19, was premature, but the invasion threats had the desired effect, stirring up the Nazis. On the same day, I again asked Mr. Zarubin about my visit to Stalingrad. As usual, the permission was delayed until the night before departure, this time, at 12:30 A.M., when I went to see Mr. Molotov to deliver a message from President Roosevelt. I turned in at 1:30, rose at five, breakfasted at 5:30, and we took off at 6:33. As a result, I was pretty haggard all day.

In my party were Dr. Michael, Secretaries Page and Thompson, Dr. Lang, Commander Ronnie Allen as interpreter, Mr. Barghorn of the State Department, and Commander Roberts, English Air Attaché, plus two of my NKVD boys. We came in over the Serapta Plateau across which the Red Army struck at the Southern flank of Marshal Paulus' armies and landed on the pock-marked airfield at 10:42.

We were met by a delegation consisting of the Mayor, Communist Party Secretary, and several generals, seven in all to match our party man for man.

The Mayor and the Party Secretary were the same officials who took care of us in April, 1942, when we stopped at Stalingrad enroute to Kuibyshev. The Mayor made me a little speech of welcome. "We are indeed happy to have you visit us again, Mr. Ambassador. All Stalingrad remembers the American Ambassador."

As we drove into town, I explained to the Mayor that I wanted to see for myself the damage suffered by the city and the results of their efforts to restore it. "We have to be back in Moscow by six-thirty—that's half an hour before sunset—or they won't let us land. That means that we *must* take off from your airport not later than two P.M."

With that understanding, they began our tour of the battered city. The conditions were appalling. Not a building that hadn't suffered bomb or shell damage. The vast majority of the more substantial buildings were hollow shells, with only a part of their shattered walls left standing. We visited the wreck of the school building in which they had put us up on our previous visit.

We drove the full length of the city in an hour and a half, inspecting as we went. Hundreds of steel frames of burned out cars stood rusting in the wrecked rail yards. Burned out street cars still stood on the tracks where they had been hit and fired. One main street had been cleared and repaved throughout the length of the city, but the side streets were still impassable from debris and shell holes. The main squares and a few streets had been cleared but little else in the way of rehabilitation had been accomplished seven months after the defeat of the German armies.

Two conditions particularly impressed me:

Wrecked aircraft had been collected from all around Stalingrad and stacked in huge piles forty and fifty feet high, covering nearly a hundred acres. I was told that there were 4,000 planes in this scrap pile, nearly all of them with Axis markings, a mute evidence of the cost to the Nazis of the air assault on Stalingrad. In other scrap areas, literally miles of Italian, German, and Russian tanks were parked, marked "scrap" or "repair."

The destruction of the factories was total. We inspected two at the north end of the city, a tank and a tractor factory. The roofs were gone, most of the walls down, and on the rubbled floors lay a fused and twisted mass of structural steel and machine tools. We were told that the damage had been the result of both bombing and artillery fire, the latter being the most devastatingly destructive. The Party Secretary said, "It will take a year to get these factories operating again." He shook his head sadly.

"You could build a new factory with less time and trouble," I replied.

I will listen with a less receptive ear to the next air or military "expert" who tells me that bombing is not effective, that a bombed-out factory can be put back in operation within a week.

We also visited some of the cellars of rubbled buildings from which the German troops and the Russian garrison fought each other to a bloody standstill. We visited the area where the Germans broke through to the Volga to hold for several months the business center of the city. But the Russian garrison would not surrender—for months, the Nazis and Russians fought across the narrow streets, hurling curses at each other between volleys. We visited again the underground motion picture theater from which Marshal Paulus came out to surrender.

When we arrived at the north end of the city, it was just past noon. "Mr. Ambassador, we have prepared a nice tea for you," the Mayor said.

"Oh, no thank you, Mr. Mayor," I protested hastily. "We really couldn't eat a thing."

He insisted and I kept on declining. I stood out against his pleading as long as I could. "Well, since you have been so nice as to prepare a cup of tea for us, thank you," I finally agreed. "But we have only ten minutes. We must take off at two."

He herded us into our cars, gave each of the drivers a word of admonition, and we were off. I've never had such a ride, down narrow streets with horns blaring, around corners on two wheels, between piles of rubble—how those Russian chauffeurs drove! By the time we arrived at the Mayor's office, I was so weak I needed something stronger than tea. The drivers had made up enough time for us to partake of a hasty meal, drink vodka to a dozen toasts and still be only thirty-seven minutes past the hour of two getting into the air. As we made our adieus at the airport, the senior general presented me with a tommy gun and several Nazi Iron Crosses. (In the hurry, it appeared that Dr. Michael had gotten separated from the party and missed the plane, but as a matter of fact, with the connivance of the Russian officials, Dr. Michael remained behind to inspect and give them some advice in regard to some defective clover.)

Our return trip was uneventful, except that the ceiling dropped to 300 feet and for half an hour we thought we might have to turn back to Serapta. But the weather improved and we slid into the Moscow Military Airport at 6:15, just under the deadline. I was dead tired, so I turned in early for a most uncomfortable night.

As usual, when I went away, everything seemed to break. Something was brewing. I could feel it in the air. My diary for August 21st records:

Went to office at 10:30, routine getting ready to see Molotov. . . . Saw the boys of the Press at 6:00, told them about my Stalingrad trip. Saw Molotov at 7:30, presented *aide memoire* regarding care of

American prisoners in Japan. He told me, with profound apologies from the Foreign Office, that the military stated that it was impossible for the American Ambassador to make the trip to Tashkent at this time.

My sojourn in the Soviet Union was drawing to an end, but I had to pick up the threads of the job. My diary recalls that I spent a part of every day working on efficiency reports of State Department officers and the military staff attached to the Embassy, a chore that I remember as seemingly endless.

I had a definite feeling of uneasiness. Prime Minister Churchill, President Roosevelt, and their advisers were meeting in Quebec for the conference known as QUADRANT. The Russians were very unhappy about the postponement of the Second Front. Ambassador Litvinov from Washington and Maisky from London were back in Moscow. What was in the wind? On August 23rd, I put in my diary:

> Russian offensive slowed down. Secretary Knox going to Quebec. Sec. Stimson and T. V. Soong already there. Saw the British Ambassador at 3:30 and got much information about the Italian [military and political] situation I had not received from my own government. Heard Kharkov had been taken. With Counselor Hamilton, went to call on Litvinov at 6:00, he had appearance of being worried . . . had a bad finger he said he got as a Partisan. Page and Thompson went to see Zarubin, got nowhere with [entry permit for] Young's plane. At dinner 8:30, Morris said there would be a salute of 42 shots from 200 guns at 9:00.

That was one pyrotechnic display I could very well miss.

CHAPTER XXVII

The Finns, the Italians, and Mr. Maxim Litvinov

Background

"BRAVE Little Finland" has long been our firmest friend along the western boundary of Soviet Russia. In the days of Russian membership in the League of Nations, Commissar of Foreign Affairs Maxim M. Litvinov, was regarded as a "friend of the West," a description which he probably regarded with mixed emotions. The Italian Situation, as it confronted me, came later, but its complexity was increased by my involvement with the Finnish Question and my attempts to establish and maintain friendship with Mr. Litvinov.

It seems to me that the diplomatic career of Maxim Litvinov served as a barometer by which the current state of relations between the United States and the Soviet Union could have been read and its future course predicted. It was Commissar of Foreign Affairs Maxim Litvinov who conducted the negotiations with President Roosevelt which led to recognition of the Soviet Government and reestablishment of diplomatic relations with Russia.

Litvinov was at the zenith of his Western popularity from 1933 to 1939; with the promulgation of the Nazi-Soviet Non-Aggression Pact in August, 1939, he disappeared from the international scene into the vast silences of Soviet Russia. When President Roosevelt sent Harry Hopkins to Moscow in July 1941 to confer with Premier Stalin, Mr. Litvinov came out of retirement to act as interpreter for the Communist Dictator and Mr. Roosevelt's Special Representative. As Hopkins put it, "He seemed like a morning coat which has been laid away in mothballs when Russia retreated into isolation from the West but which has now been brought out, dusted off, and aired as a symbol of completely changed conditions."*

When we went to Moscow with the Beaverbrook-Harriman Mission in September, 1941, Mr. Constantine A. Oumansky, then Soviet Ambassador to Washington, flew back to Moscow in one of the Mission planes. But it was Mr. Litvinov, not Mr. Oumansky, who sat next to Mr. Molotov during the signing of that first Russian Lend-Lease Protocol. And it was Mr. Litvinov, not Mr. Oumansky, who went back to Washington as Soviet Ambassador. The morning coat was dusted off and aired out again.

Mr. Molotov's negotiations with Hitler and Von Ribbentrop, which culminated in the Nazi-Soviet Pact, led directly to a Russian attack on Finland on November 30, 1939. Finland had no quarrel with Russia, wished only to live in peace with her larger and more powerful neighbors. But Finland possessed a small and highly efficient army and a grim determination to fight for her freedom.

Russia had a huge but poorly organized Red Army; in pursuit of the Soviet Government's determination to keep firm Party control over the military, Communist Party commissars were assigned to every Red Army unit larger than a battalion. Every decision of a Red Army commander had to be approved by the political commissar before it became effective. As a result, the military commanders on the Karelian Peninsula were so hamstrung by capricious political vetoes that the small Finnish Army fought the Red Army to a standstill, defeating its units in detail. After three months of bitter fighting, the Soviet Union was glad to make peace with Finland.

Other reasons for USSR willingness to make peace included the apparent readiness of Great Britain and France to send help to Finland, a certain amount of overconfidence, and the purge which decimated the officer corps in the Red Army in the mid-thirties.

As a result of the Red Army's experience in the Finnish War, the Soviet Government reorganized the Army; political commissars continued to serve with the Army but their authority was greatly reduced; they no longer had a veto over the orders of military commanders. Later on during the War, many commissars were removed from their posts; those remaining had advisory and inspirational duties with the troops similar to "special services" workers with our Army. Only when this reorganization reached

* Robert E. Sherwood, *Roosevelt and Hopkins* (New York: Harper & Bros., 1944), p. 333.

down through all echelons of command did the Red Army become a really effective fighting force.

Ambassador Litvinov was the Russian representative at the Arcadia Conference in Washington at the bitter end of 1941, when the Declaration of the United Nations was drafted and approved by the representatives of twenty-six nations and signed and promulgated on New Years Day 1942.

Mr. Litvinov assisted Commissar of Foreign Affairs Molotov during his mission to Washington toward the end of May 1942. The purpose of Mr. Molotov's visit was to obtain firm commitments from Great Britain and the United States to establish a Second Front in Europe in 1942, and to negotiate the Second Russian Lend-Lease Protocol, then long overdue.

In the light of more recent negotiations with Mr. Molotov, it is interesting to observe that President Roosevelt also had a difficult time with him. Harry Hopkins noted that the President's "style was cramped" because of the language difficulties. In all of his dealings with all kinds of people, the President had never before met anyone like Molotov—even though, on this occasion, Mr. Molotov's deportment was marked by an uncommon frankness and amiability. For seven years President Roosevelt had been accustomed to deal with Litvinov on Russian affairs—"he had a western kind of mind and an understanding of the ways of the world that Roosevelt knew." The strange problem in human relations, which Molotov presented, offered President Roosevelt "a challenge which stimulated him to spare no effort to discover the common ground which must somewhere exist."[*]

I have recently discovered that, on June 1, 1942, seven months before I became involved in Finnish negotiations, President Roosevelt discussed the Finnish situation in great detail with Mr. Molotov and Ambassador Litvinov in the White House. Present beside these three were Harry Hopkins, Professor Samuel H. Cross of Harvard, and Mr. Pavlov, the Kremlin interpreter. The President initiated the discussion:

"We have reports from Finland that representative groups in that country wish to make peace with the Soviet Government. They can not, however, mobilize their strength to demonstrate to Finnish public opinion the possibility of peace unless something concrete is done by either Moscow or Washington. These groups have asked us to ascertain a possible basis for peace. For the

[*] Robert E. Sherwood, *Roosevelt and Hopkins* (New York: Harper & Bros., 1944), p. 561.

United States Government, I would like to offer our good offices for this purpose, if the Soviet Government wishes to avail itself of them."

"I should like to know," said Mr. Molotov tersely, "are these Finnish groups official?"

"No," the President replied. "They include a number of leaders of public opinion, but not members of the Finnish Government."

"Do they really want peace?" Mr. Molotov pressed.

"Yes."

"Have they any special conditions in view?"

"No," said the President.

"They gave no views as to the basis on which peace should be concluded?"

"No. What they want is to show the Finnish people that peace is possible with safety to Finland."

"Would these groups be able to represent Finland?"

"Our information is confined to the statement that several such representative groups exist," the President repeated.

"I will discuss this matter with Mr. Stalin."

At the time I returned to Moscow from consultation in Washington in January 1943, President Roosevelt, Prime Minister Churchill, the British and American Chiefs of Staff, and Generals Giraud and De Gaulle were conferring in Casablanca. Of course, I had not been informed. It was something of a surprise to learn from a message received on January 25th that President Roosevelt had actually left the United States during a war and made the long trip to Casablanca. Of the conference, Mr. Churchill has said, "There has never been, in all of the inter-allied conferences I have known, anything like the prolonged professional examination of the whole scene of the world war in its military, its armament production, and its economic aspects."

The message, which I was directed to deliver to Mr. Stalin that same evening, was in considerable detail. It told of top priority assigned to the "security of sea communications," of a guarantee of assistance to Russia as large as possible in relation to other commitments, of operations in the Mediterranean, giving as a target date for the amphibious assault on Sicily "sometime in July," of air operations from the United Kingdom, and of continued build-up of American forces in Great Britain for the cross-channel operation in which the Russians were so greatly interested. No mention was made of landing operations against the Italian mainland. Much emphasis was placed upon the importance of opening up the Mediterranean to Allied shipping and thus facilitating the delivery of lend-lease supplies to Russia via the Persian Gulf.

It was ten P.M. as I was ushered into the inner office in the Kremlin and we took seats around the conference table—Mr. Stalin, Mr. Molotov, Mr. Pavlov the interpreter, Eddie Page, and myself. After our usual exchange of amenities, I outlined the contents of the message. As Pavlov interpreted my long speech, I studied the expressions of Stalin and Molotov. They had good poker faces, Stalin's stern and grim, Molotov's broad and impassive. I thought I noted a shadow of disappointment as Pavlov finished speaking and Mr. Stalin said something to Molotov, which the Foreign Minister answered with two short, sharp exclamations.

"We will study the matter, Mr. Ambassador, and let you know."

"The President asked me to assure you that you will be kept fully informed as to conditions and circumstances in the progress of the North African operations."

"That will be good of him."

I had seen Mr. Stalin often enough to know when I was dismissed. As I rose from my seat, I put down on the table before him an *aide memoire* which contained a paraphrase of the dispatch. "Perhaps this will assist you, sir, in your study."

"Oh, just a moment, Mr. Ambassador," Mr. Stalin said.

I turned back to him. "I would like to inquire as to the popularity—or lack of popularity—of our Ambassador Litvinov among the people of your country."

This was the first indication I had that Mr. Litvinov was on his way out. "I think that the attitude of the American people toward Mr. Litvinov is reflected in the great wave of sympathy for the Russian people which has swept over the United States."

Mr. Stalin nodded in dismissal and Eddie and I left the conference room. As we went down the long corridor to the entrance, I asked Eddie, "What did they say in Russian?"

Eddie glanced around at the Foreign Office underlings several paces behind us and whispered, "Joe said, 'No commitment for the Second Front?' Other fellow snarled, 'Not yet; not yet!'"

The Finnish Question

A few days later, in a long despatch, the State Department directed me to offer to the Soviet Government the services of the United States Government as an intermediary toward ending Finnish hostilities. The information given me was almost identical to that presented by President Roosevelt to Mr. Molotov in the White House.

On January 29th, I went to Mr. Molotov's office in the Kremlin. I took great pains to explain in detail the Finnish situation. Mr. Molotov heard me out with apparent interest and sympathy.

When I had finished, he nodded agreeably. "I would like to state certain personal views with regard to Finnish-Soviet relations. The Soviet Union has been forced into this war with Finland because the Finnish Army seized certain Soviet territory. The Soviet Union did not seek or desire this war. Apparently the Finns thought that we would lose in the war with the Nazis. But they got fooled. Unfortunately, for peace negotiations, there are a lot of German troops in Finland and the Finns are still on Soviet territory. Until these conditions are corrected, the Finnish war must continue."

"There would be a great advantage to our side if the Finns did make peace," I suggested.

Mr. Molotov shook his head. "My Government believes that the Finns find it impossible to broaden their participation in the war; they have already exerted too great an effort in view of their present strength. For that reason alone, I see no reason to negotiate. They brought this war on themselves."

In view of Mr. Molotov's willingness to discuss the Finnish question and of the lack of bitterness evidenced in his remarks, I felt that it was a favorable moment to present the general considerations involved in the American policy toward Finland. I pointed out to him our long friendship with Finland. We had many Finnish immigrants in the United States. When we lent the Finns money for rehabilitation of their country after World War I, Finland was the only debtor nation to acknowledge its debt in full and to make regular payments against interest and principal. The American people had a very warm regard for the Finnish people. My Government wished to see a stable, democratic government in Finland after the war, with a peaceful attitude toward all of its neighbors and strong ties of friendship with both the Soviet Union and the United States. That was why we had maintained diplomatic relations with the Finnish Government, even though they were at war with our ally.

After I had presented these considerations, Mr. Molotov nodded. "I will bring the views of the American Government to the attention of my Government. If the Finns withdrew from their partnership with the Germans and gave up their territorial gains, it would certainly be to the interest of the Soviet Union and the United Nations to end the fighting. How serious are the grounds for believing that the Finns really wish to withdraw from the German partnership?"

Mr. Molotov seemed quite animated over the turn which the discussions had taken. "There are indications," I pointed out, "that the Finnish Government believes that it might be advisable to end the war with Russia before the collapse of Germany."

"Have you or your Government information as to the nature of Finnish conditions for such a withdrawal?"

"I have no such information."

Mr. Molotov then carefully reviewed our discussion, mentioning specifically our reasons for maintaining diplomatic relations with the Finns, the advantages to be gained from a Finnish withdrawal from the war, and the existence of indications that Finland might be prevailed upon to withdraw from the war "under certain conditions."

"Of course, we would have to know what those conditions are," he completed his summation. "I want to repeat—the Soviet Union did not want war with Finland. I will be happy to refer our discussion in full to my Government."

When I returned to Kuibyshev, early in February 1943, I received word from the Swedish Legation that the Swedish Minister, Mr. Wilhelm Assarson, wished to see me; Eddie Page said that the young secretary who brought the message indicated that Mr. Assarson would probably discuss the Finnish question. I had Eddie make an appointment with him. He came to see me in Sadovia at 3:30 P.M. on February 4th.

As I have previously indicated, we didn't rely too much on his neutrality where the Germans were concerned. I poured him a cocktail and waited patiently through a long course of idle chatter for Mr. Assarson to bring up Finland. Finally, seeing that I was not going to be of help, he plunged headlong into the subject. "Do you have anything new on the Finnish question, Mr. Ambassador?"

"Nothing much," I said guardedly. "Why?"

"Of course, Admiral, you realize that Sweden is very much concerned with the Finnish question—I hoped that you might have brought some news from Moscow, particularly as the possibility of Finland withdrawing from the war was discussed in Washington."

That was news to me but I gave no indication of it. Mr. Assarson was being very careful not to make a direct inquiry. Of course, Finland was of great interest to Sweden—from 1154 to 1809, it formed a part of the Kingdom of Sweden.

"How interesting," I offered. When he didn't continue, I asked, "Have you had any recent news or instructions from your government, Mr. Assarson?"

"No, nothing new. But my government has always been very anxious to have Finland get out of the war."

"Is that a fact? Well, you'll be interested in an interview I recently had with Mr. Molotov."

I went on to describe briefly and incompletely our discussions the previous week. "I feel that Mr. Molotov's attitude indicates a sympathetic reaction but I doubt that the Soviet Government will be in a position to make overtures for peace with the Finns. They probably would be receptive to overtures made by a third party."

Mr. Assarson was silent for several moments, looking down at the floor. "I feel, Mr. Ambassador . . . I feel that our interest in this matter is such that my Government might be justified in assuming the responsibility for making such overtures, if it could be certain that they would be well-received." His blue eyes looked up and he stared at me for uncomfortable moments. "You know, I believe it might carry great weight with the Soviets if you, the American Ambassador, and I, the Swedish Minister, would go together to Mr. Molotov and suggest the possibility that an understanding might be reached between Finland and the Soviet Government which would result in the withdrawal of Finland from the war."

This was moving a little too fast for me, particularly in view of my suspicion of the Swedish Minister. "Of course, I cannot commit my Government or myself to any such joint action," I replied. "In fact, I don't feel competent even to express a personal opinion as to the desirability of such joint action. Any such action, whether by one or both of us, would involve certain obligations and responsibilities. I am morally certain that the Soviet Government would quickly inquire of you, is Sweden ready to assume all of the obligations and responsibilities of Finland's withdrawal from the war?"

"That's right," he agreed. "I can't say what my Government would do in such a case, but, personally, I feel that our interest in the situation would justify us to assume all of the necessary responsibility and that our post-war situation would well justify such assumption. Early action is vital. The elections in Finland on the fifteenth of this month may cause an unfortunate change in the Finnish Government."

I left it at that, moving on to another less delicate subject. Of course, I reported this conversation to the State Department, expressing the belief, that, although Mr. Assarson at no time during our conversation indicated that he was acting under instructions from his Government, his eagerness and enthusiasm made me think there was more than his own personal interest in the Finnish question involved.

The period after my return to Moscow on March 5th was unbelievably hectic. The afternoon of my arrival in Moscow from Kuibyshev, Sir Archibald Clark-Kerr came to see me. As we settled back in easy chairs with our cocktails, Sir Archie asked, "Have you anything new?"

"I understand that your Foreign Minister is going to Washington to see the President."

"Right-o. United Nations stuff. What's the news about Finland?"

For his benefit, I outlined my conversation with the Commissar of Foreign Affairs and my visit with the Swedish Minister.

"Ha!" Sir Archie exclaimed. "I thought something was up. My Government just informed me that the Finnish Government has just had a big reorganization and there is more to come. I believe the Finns want to get out of the war."

Apparently in preparation for the Eden visit, the State Department asked me to ascertain from the Soviet Government its terms for ending the war with Finland. I sought an interview with Mr. Molotov and went to his office during the evening of March 12th, armed with an *aide memoire* based on the State Department note. Much to my surprise, Mr. Molotov brought up the Finnish question before I had a chance to do so. "Have you any information, Mr. Ambassador, on the Finnish situation? Do you think the Finnish Government really desires to negotiate? You know, our attitude in regard to the Finnish question depends to a large extent upon the attitude of the Finnish Government."

"Of course, Mr. Molotov," I replied. "That is understandable. I have brought with me a statement on the Finnish situation."

I read the *aide memoire* and handed it across to Mr. Pavlov for translation. The American Government, the paper told them, did not want to begin negotiations with the Finnish Government until we knew where the Russian Government stood. Apparently, the Russian Government did not want to state its terms until they knew whether or not the Finnish Government had initiated the conversations and what terms the Finnish Government considered satisfactory. Of course, the United States Government couldn't commence conversations until it knew the Russian terms. Would the Soviet Government kindly state its terms? This information was for the use of the United States Government and would not be communicated to the Finnish Government.

After he had heard the *aide memoire* read in Russian, Mr. Molotov nodded owlishly. "Of course, we're interested, but to judge whether or not it is advisable to adopt a positive decision in the matter, it is first necessary to know whether or not there is any prospect for success in the negotiations."

"Naturally," I put in.

"Thus far, the Finns have been zealously serving Hitler."

"True."

"And five of our divisions are tying up the whole Finnish Army and seven Nazi divisions."

"As few as that? Well, do you want us to proceed further with the negotiations?"

"I'll take up the matter with my Government, Mr. Ambassador, and inform you of its decision."

Again, I had been dismissed without achieving any results.

In the succeeding two weeks, Anthony Eden conferred with President Roosevelt. The President was intensely interested in the Soviet demands for a post-war settlement. Great Britain and the United States were even then, in March 1943, constructing the design for the United Nations Organization. The Heads of Government still had a fond hope that the Russians could be persuaded to cooperate in establishing a peaceful, prosperous post-war world.

It is interesting to note that Eden told the President that he believed that Russia would insist on the boundary line that was drawn after the abortive 1939 Russo-Finnish War, which seemed reasonable to Mr. Eden, as it gave the Russians a more secure defensive position before their great city of Leningrad. Stalin had also previously told Eden that he was going to insist upon Russian possession of Hangoe on the Gulf of Finland. He would certainly demand Bessarabia. The President and Eden agreed that the Russians should have their way in these demands.

Eden did not think that the Russians would deal with the Finns through either Great Britain or the United States, nor did he expect an answer from the note I had delivered to Mr. Molotov on March 12th. He felt that the Finns should be told to negotiate directly with the Russians.

Apparently, President Roosevelt was not satisfied, for on March 16th, Harry Hopkins sought out Ambassador Litvinov and asked him what the Russian demands at the Peace Table would be. This was his answer.

> Russia would demand the Baltic States.
> Russia would want a healthy, independent Finland, with the boundary line about where the Russian armies were at the end of the war.
> He had no information about the Russian desire for Hangoe.
> Poland must have East Prussia.
> Russia would demand "her legitimate territorial rights" on the Polish frontier.
> Everybody agreed that Russia should have Bessarabia.
> Germany should be dismembered, Prussia cut off from the rest of Germany, and two or three other states created out of what was left.

April was a busy month on the Finnish question. On April 2nd, my diary recorded:

> Saw the British Ambassador at 2:30. Nap. Back to office at 4:30. Haircut. Back home at 6:00. Saw Molotov 7-8. Dinner 8:30. Pool after dinner with Page and Stevens.

I was keeping in close touch those days with Sir Archibald on both the Finnish and Polish situations, discussing our separate and joint moves in order not to cross signals. When I arrived in Mr. Molotov's office that evening, it soon became evident that the Russian Government was much more eager to make peace with the Finns than had been indicated during previous meetings. Mr. Molotov disclosed to me, "for the information of the United States Government *only*," the minimum terms under which the Soviet Government would consider negotiations looking toward peace with Finland; they were substantially the same as Ambassador Litvinov had given to Harry Hopkins, except that the Foreign Commissar stated most firmly that the Soviets would insist upon having Hangoe.

I knew that the terms would be such a blow to Finnish pride and prestige that I was compelled to advise Mr. Molotov, "It is my personal opinion that, if my Government feels that the Soviet terms are completely impossible, it will not pursue the matter further. My Government must feel that there is a possible basis for successful negotiations before it undertakes them."

On April 5th, I entered in my diary:

> Saw Clark-Kerr at four, Molotov at 5:00, Finnish situation—then to office. At 7:30 dinner, had movie, "Iran," showing Lend-Lease supplies coming through Iran.

At this interview, Mr. Molotov handed me an *aide memoire* which stated explicitly the Soviet terms for negotiations with Finland. After I had checked through them to assure myself there was no change, I said, "I recall that the terms which you gave me a few days ago were presented exclusively for the information of my Government. Am I to assume that the terms in this *aide memoire* are to be communicated to the Finnish Government in order to ascertain if these terms are acceptable?"

"Would your Government like to do that?"

"I think it is pretty obvious that such is not the case, Mr. Molotov," I replied. "However, in view of this *aide memoire* and the great delicacy of the question, it is possible that my Government might now consider the situation in a different light. I would like to clarify this point."

"My Government doesn't believe that the present rulers of Finland can break off from Germany and conclude peace," Mr. Molotov said sharply. "There is no reason to believe that Finland can offer acceptable terms or are prepared to accept our terms."

"Tell me this, shall we or shall we not bring these terms to the attention of the Finns?"

Mr. Molotov weaseled. "The Soviet Government does not wish to show any indication of taking the initiative in making peace overtures since we have no reason to believe that the Finnish Government desires peace. That is why we have communicated our terms exclusively for the information of your Government. If your Government has definite information that the Finns are prepared to accept our terms, we have no objection to the American Government communicating them to the Finnish Government."

During the following week, President Roosevelt must have come around to Anthony Eden's point of view, for I received a despatch directing me to inform the Soviet Government that the American Government had decided to withdraw its offer to mediate in the Russo-Finnish war. I immediately asked for an appointment to see Mr. Molotov and was ushered into his office at 4:00 P.M. I submitted to him a memorandum based upon the above despatch. When Mr. Pavlov had translated it, Mr. Molotov turned on me querulously, "Why have you changed your mind? Last month, you told me, 'My Government will make every effort to convince the Finnish Government to agree to a proposal for mediation on the part of the United States and to communicate to the American Government the general nature of the terms on which it would be willing to initiate the negotiations suggested.' What is the reason for this change in policy?"

I shook my head. "I wish I could help you. I know only what's written there; my Government feels that it can be more helpful if it can bring about direct contact between the Russian and Finnish Governments, instead of having a third party as an intermediary."

At the time, I was waiting from day to day for good weather to fly to Kuibyshev to meet General Burns. On April 14th, I entered in my diary:

> Plane delayed to 1:00, then to 3:00, then deferred till tomorrow. Asked to, and saw Molotov at 4:00. Then had tea and went to ballet— "The Hunchback Horse." Page waited at the office for a message in regard to seeing Molotov again—he came in at end of first act—we left at end of second act to see Molotov at 9:00 P.M.

As I sat down for the first interview, I was surprised to have Mr. Molotov ask, "What is the status of Mr. Hjalmar Procope, the Finnish Minister in Washington?"

I tried not to show my surprise. "He's a duly accredited representative of a government with which we maintain normal diplomatic relations. From what I have observed, he is very popular in Washington." I went on to ask my question about discontinuing diplomatic relations with Finland. Mr. Molotov apparently hadn't been prepared for that, for he asked time to consult his Government. When he got down to the real business at hand, he seemed much more ill at ease than usual. Finally, he stammered out a long question, which Mr. Pavlov translated in his usual suave manner. "It is the hope of my Government that it can be furnished the information which has caused the American Government to revise its estimate as to the position of Finland."

I thought for a moment. "I have not been advised as to that," I said slowly. "Perhaps one of the causes may be the increased pressure exerted by Nazi troops on the Finnish fronts, which you mentioned several days ago."

Mr. Molotov nodded solemnly. "I will inquire as to discontinuance of diplomatic relations with Finland and get in touch with you."

In the second interview at 9:00 P.M., Mr. Molotov got right to the point. "In the opinion of the Soviet Government, it would be advisable from the point of view of our common interests to effectuate the proposal to discontinue American diplomatic relations with Finland as a means of putting pressure on the Finnish Government."

I nodded. "Thank you, sir."

But he still had something on his mind. "If you recall your diplomatic representative from Helsinki, would Minister Procope be sent home?"

"I assume that such would be the case but I don't know. Why?"

"My Government has been advised by sources it considers reliable that Procope furnishes the Japanese Government with any information of interest which he is able to obtain. I should think that it would be advisable for him to leave Washington."

I passed along the results of this interview promptly to the State Department, informing them of Mr. Molotov's assertion, but nothing came of it until June 30, 1944, when our Government finally broke off relations with Finland, declared Mr. Procope *persona non grata,* and sent him home. An armistice was finally arranged between Finland and Russia on September 5, 1944, after direct negotiations between the two countries.

I recently saw a brief note in the papers with a dateline, Helsinki, March 8, 1954, an obituary for "Hjalmar Procope, 65, former foreign minister and Finland's envoy in Washington from 1939 to 1944." He had gone to Helsinki from his home in Sweden, where he had lived since 1944 with his Swedish wife, "to vote in today's general elections, but was taken ill with a heart ailment and died before he could vote. He held diplomatic posts in Warsaw and Berlin and served for a time as President of the League of Nations."

The United States resumed informal diplomatic relations with Finland in January 1945; "Brave Little Finland" was permitted to resume payment of further installments on her debt to the United States.

The Italian Negotiations

In the weeks to follow, the Italian situation began to consume more and more of my time and attention. Even before we won the military decision in North Africa or launched the amphibious assault on Sicily (HUSKY), Washington was worrying about the policy to be pursued by an Allied military government in Sicily and Italy. President Roosevelt sent a despatch to Churchill which said:

> I feel that in the initial stages of HUSKY we should avoid all risk of implications that would arise from any possible use of Italians in high positions. . . . I believe it is preferable to remove any Italians from these positions as they are all prominent Fascists.

It would have been helpful had I known the background and the state of negotiations with regard to these and other complicated situations. But, as usual, I depended for my information on Sir Archibald Clark-Kerr and BBC news broadcasts, when we could tune them in.

On May 2nd, I received information that Ambassador Litvinov was coming home "for consultation," his visit to coincide with that of Joe Davies. On May 7th, British, French and American troops broke through the defenses around Tunis and Bizerte, the beginning of the end for the Axis in North Africa. The Italian question was warming up.

Apparently the Nazis had taken some Russian prisoners of war to North Africa, where they were released by our American Army forces. On May 13th, while visiting Mr. Molotov on other business, I had occasion to hand him a memorandum containing a message from his Foreign Commissariat's representative with our military headquarters in North Africa, inquiring as to the disposition of Soviet prisoners recovered in North Africa. When he had read the memo, Mr. Molotov looked at me glumly. "The sooner the Soviet prisoners are repatriated to the Soviet Union, the better it will be. Please take steps to expedite the matter."

"I'll be glad to be of assistance in transmitting your messages to your representative in North Africa."

"Would it be possible to communicate directly with him?"

"I'm afraid not. It will probably be necessary to communicate through the American Consul in Algiers."

"What a nuisance," Mr. Molotov growled. "We should have direct representation in North Africa."

On May 19th, Ambassador Litvinov returned to Moscow in company with Joe Davies. I was happy to renew my acquaintance with him. He was accorded his ambassadorial rank and became quite friendly with the staff of the American Embassy. On a number of occasions, I had him for lunch followed by bridge—one of the most pleasant associations I had with a Russian official while I was in Moscow.

On May 31st, from North Africa, Generals de Gaulle and Giraud, spurred on by Winston Churchill and General Marshall, announced their agreement on the formation of a French Committee on National Liberation. The French situation was very confused, with de Gaulle competing with Giraud for control of the Committee. Apparently the State Department wondered about the stability of the new French Committee for on July 2nd, I received a despatch from the Secretary directing me to call on the Commissar for Foreign Affairs. I didn't know it, but the Russians were trying in every way to work into the North African and Italian situations. My notes show that I had no sooner seated myself at the conference table than Mr. Molotov made it quite clear that he was most dissatisfied with the state of affairs. The Soviet Government must have representation in North Africa.

"I have come to see you about that matter, Mr. Molotov," I told him. "My Government is requesting that the Soviet Government refrain from any act of recognition of the French Committee on National Liberation without previous consultation with my Government. I don't know the full reasons behind this request but apparently my Government is not satisfied as to the character or stability of the Committee."

"Do you know about the recent message that Mr. Stalin sent to Prime Minister Churchill with regard to this same matter?"

I nodded. "The British Ambassador has shown me a copy. I'm sorry I have no other instructions in the matter, but I will report that Mr. Stalin is displeased."

"I will give you a copy of Mr. Stalin's message. Please forward it to your President. It will be evident to him from the contents of the message that the Soviet Government is badly informed as to events transpiring in North Africa, as well as to your President's reasons for asking for postponement of recognition of the Committee. I bring this matter up to you, now, because my Government has no representative in North Africa." He paused for a moment, then added, "My Government endeavored to send Mr. Bogomolov, our representative to the exiled governments in London, to North Africa. The French and British consented but, for some reason, the Americans objected. We had to tell him to stay in London."

"I have not been informed in this matter, Mr. Molotov," I said. "I can only offer as a possible reason that the military leaders were so engrossed in military operations in North Africa at the time that they would have little opportunity to discuss matters with Mr. Bogomolov."

But I later learned that the sudden chill in our relations with the Soviet Government had an old, familiar cause—the Second Front. From some source other than myself, Mr. Stalin had received copies of the full plans drawn up at the TRIDENT Conference. While Joe Davies was in Moscow, he had obtained Mr. Stalin's promise to meet with President Roosevelt about July 15th. Now, this meeting was summarily cancelled. Late in June, Mr. Stalin sent Prime Minister Churchill a long message reviewing the many promises which had been made to the Soviets with respect to opening a Second Front. Now, the cross-Channel operation had again been postponed for almost a year. He seriously doubted that the Western Allies ever intended to open a Second Front—indeed, if Mr. Churchill had his way, they probably never would.

Mr. Churchill's temper boiled and he retorted in spirited prose; the tension among the nations "united" against Hitler reached a new high. Our relations with the Soviet Union had never been worse. And I was right in the middle—in Moscow.

Events now moved rapidly in the Italian situation. On July 2nd, a massive force of British, Canadian, and American troops invaded Sicily. A few days later, President Roosevelt and Prime Minister Churchill jointly broadcast a statement to the Italian people, "The sole hope for Italian survival lies in an honorable capitulation to the overwhelming power of the military forces of the United Nations . . ."

I followed the rapid progress of our Sicilian operations with the keenest interest, for I felt that it would not take much to knock the Italians out of the war. A scant two weeks after the invasion, I noted in my diary, "Sicily—Eighth Army slowed down." And three days later, "Western Sicily in Allied hands." On July 26th, I recorded, "7:30 A.M. news—Mussolini's fall chronicled. Sicily—south stiff resistance—the north fluid."

The same day in a speech, President Roosevelt stated that our terms for the Italians "are unconditional surrender" and that "we will have no truck with Fascism in any way, shape or manner."

It presently became clear that King Victor Emmanuel had ridden out the storm of a palace revolution which got rid of Mussolini, and now had for Premier Marshal Badoglio, who had been Il Duce's commander in the Ethiopian adventure and who had embraced Fascism and the Fascist dictatorship for many years. In his first public statement, the Italian Marshal said, "The war goes on," but it soon became evident that he didn't mean what he said.

With the Italian situation developing so rapidly and its solution being so important to the whole course of the war and the peace afterward, a conference between President Roosevelt and Prime Minister Churchill in Quebec was quickly set up. I was apprised of this by BBC on August 11th, as recorded in my diary:

> Allies still advancing all along the line. Churchill in Canada, discussions with [Prime Minister] McKenzie King—then goes to U.S. for discussions with Roosevelt and Combined Chiefs of Staff. . . . Went over Polish Question. Saw Clark-Kerr at 1:00 o'clock, freshed

up on Italian situation . . . Clark-Kerr came back to office at 5:30, re-hearsed Polish program—home to early supper—called at Clark-Kerr's for a drink at 7:30. We saw Stalin with Molotov and Pavlov from 8 to 9.

This was our first conference with the Soviet Government on the Italian question since the fall of Mussolini; the problem was considered important enough for Mr. Stalin to summon both the American and British Ambassadors to his conference room in the Kremlin. After we discussed the Polish situation which I have previously described, Sir Archibald reported, "Marshal Stalin, I have just learned that representatives of Marshal Badoglio have approached British officials in Algiers and Lisbon and asked for negotiations looking toward cessation of hostilities."

Mr. Molotov nodded. "I have heard of these statements with real interest."

"You have to look out for that Badoglio," Mr. Stalin put in. "He's a very tricky individual. You can't trust him; he is prepared to deceive Hitler, the King of Italy, and, of course, the British and Americans."

Sir Archibald smiled across the table at the Russian dictator. "I do not believe the allies will be fooled by Badoglio, Marshal Stalin," he said. "He is quite transparent in his actions."

"Perhaps your aviators made a mistake in not continuing to bomb Rome." Mr. Stalin sucked at his big, crooked-stemmed pipe. "However, I understand why you stopped."

"Yes," I put in. "We couldn't continue the bombings, but I think that one raid helped to persuade the new Italian Government to ask for terms."

Mr. Stalin was cool to us on this occasion. The break with the Poles in April 1 had served to indicate the trend of Soviet policy. As we took our leave, a thin smile twisted the Generalissimo's lips, "With the Italians out of the way, now, you should be able to open a Second Front."

A few days later, Sir Archibald came to see me, a grave expression on his long face. "What's worrying you, Sir Archie?" I asked.

"This," he said. He handed me a memorandum he had received from the Soviet Foreign Office, which went about like this:

The end of the war is near, and contacts with the British will be more frequent and much closer. Because of this, Mr. Stalin wants someone in Moscow who is familiar with, and can inform him as to conditions in London. For that reason, we are calling Mr. Maisky home and leaving his Counselor in charge of the Russian Legation in London.

In view of Mr. Stalin's manner and his recent remark about the Second Front, such action didn't look good to me, particularly when Mr. Molotov called me to the Foreign Office on August 16th and told me that Ambassador Litvinov would not return to Washington, that his counselor, Mr. Gromyko, would replace him. He gave me the same reason that he had given Sir Archibald, "Mr. Stalin wants someone in Moscow who is familiar with conditions in the United States."

From my diary, August 19:

> Got message through Navy for Stalin, first part. Back to office at 4:30, discussed telegrams [with staff] . . . Page went to see Zarubin at 9:30 [to tell him about message for Stalin]. Code clerk came in with finished message at 11:30—immediately called Foreign Office, found Stalin out of town. Went to see Molotov at 12:30, delivered note to him for Stalin.

The note came from both President Roosevelt and Mr. Churchill, then holding the QUADRANT Conference in Quebec. The British Ambassador to Spain had reported that General Castellano, representing Badoglio, had arrived in Madrid bearing a letter of introduction from the British Minister in the Vatican. Castellano had authorization from Marshal Badoglio to offer Italy's unconditional surrender, if she could immediately turn about and join the Allies. The President and Mr. Churchill considered this a firm and bona fide offer, but they didn't intend to offer the Italians any inducement to switch sides. However, they pointed out the advantages which might result if the Italians surrendered. They told Mr. Stalin that they would commence the invasion of the Italian mainland before September 1st and a week later make a full-scale landing at Salerno below Naples. They pointed out the risk that the German troops in Italy might take over and put a figurehead in power in Italy. They had authorized General Eisenhower to send emissaries to Lisbon to negotiate with General Castellano for an armistice.

General Eisenhower sent General "Beedle" Smith, later to become Ambassador to Russia, and British Brigadier K. W. D. Strong to conduct the negotiations, which were successful.

Sunday, August 22.

Routine 7:30 news—announces Litvinov replacement by Gromyko. Allies still have offensive—waiting for things to happen. Touch of jippy tummy—left Spaso at 10:20, went to Mokhovaya, where the British Ambassador and John Reed were to join us. Found Broadcaster [Bill] Downes there. He wanted slant on Litvinov-Gromyko exchange. Could make no comment personally [as it hadn't been announced by the Foreign Office], but advised playing it down. With their great knowledge of England and America, it would be to the advantage of the Allies to have Maisky and Litvinov in Moscow.

Thursday, August 26.

Went to office at 10:30—many messages in relation Free French Committee and Italian situation. . . . Page and I saw British Ambassador at 12:30, agreed on plans to ask to see Stalin. . . . With British Ambassador and Page, saw Molotov and delivered notes re Quebec [Conference] and Italian peace terms at 11 P.M. British also delivered notes . . . got back at 12:15, turned in.

The peace terms called for Italian unconditional surrender, to cease all fighting against the Allies, to deliver all Italian warships to designated ports for surrender in good operating condition, and to retain arms to defend themselves. After Mr. Molotov had read the messages, I made it a point to ask, "Do you or do you not feel that the Soviet Union should have a representative at the signing of the armistice agreement with the Italians?"

As usual when an important question was asked, Mr. Molotov avoided a reply, but the next day he sent Clark-Kerr the following letter:

Dear Mr. Ambassador,

The Government of the USSR have acquainted themselves with the Italian terms of surrender, approved by the Governments of Great Britain and the United States and handed on the 26 August to V. M. Molotov by the British Ambassador Mr. A. C. Kerr and the Ambassador of the United States Mr. W. H. Standley.

The Government of the USSR approve the above-mentioned Italian terms of surrender and impower General Eisenhower on their behalf to sign these terms of surrender in the negotiations with General Castellano.

The Soviet Government consider that in the present case there is no need for a special representative of the USSR to be present when General Eisenhower signs the Italian terms of surrender.

With sincere respect,
(sgd) V. Molotov

To: Mr. A. C. Kerr,
Ambassador Extraordinary
and Plenipotentiary
of Great Britain,
Moscow.

In the days that followed, we certainly kept the Soviet Government informed as to the progress of negotiations and events in North Africa and Italy, but the Soviet rulers were becoming more and more displeased with us. I recorded that the British Ambassador showed me a number of notes. I noted "many telegrams, but not much in them."

My jippy tummy was worse. I was feeling miserable, when Mr. Vishinsky phoned on August 28th and said he wanted to see me "at once." I left a party at Henry Shapiro's house and hurried to his office in the Narkomindel at 7:30 P.M. I had hardly seated myself before Vishinsky said, "Mr. Ambassador, I want to ask a favor, an official favor."

I stared into Mr. Vishinsky's thin face. He can be charming when he wants to be and he was turning on the charm. "I'll be glad to help if I can," I said.

"As you know, Mr. Ambassador, Mr. Gromyko has been selected to be our new Ambassador to the United States. Before he can be accepted by your government he must present credentials signed by the Soviet Government Chief of State. I wonder if you could have these formalities completed by telegram. It will take six weeks to send the letter by mail."

"I'll do my best, of course," I replied. "I hope that I will be successful." I decided to razz Mr. Vishinsky a bit. "It is indeed regrettable that the lack of communications between Moscow and Washington makes it necessary for you to ask this favor. You will recall that, ever since I have been in Moscow, I have been urging improvement in communications and establishment of shorter and more direct air routes between the Soviet Union and the United States. If we had regular service on the air route across Siberia and Alaska, we could deliver your papers to Washington in five days. If your air service to Teheran operated regularly, we could have them there in eight days. I'm glad this incident came up. It will bring home to you the need for such air services."

Mr. Vishinsky turned his customary shade of violent red at my chiding. But I was not finished. "I'd like to point out to you that Commander Young has been waiting six weeks for you to grant him visas to enter this country with his cargo of motion pictures. I'm going to do this favor for you, if I can, in spite of the fact that your Government promised me more than three months ago that they would admit John Young and his cargo of films, and they have not kept their promise."

Mr. Gromyko *was* permitted to present credentials by wire from

Moscow, but John Young never returned to Moscow with his cargo of film.

Sunday, August 29.

Routine 7:30 news. BBC announced bombings continue but news scant of situation in Mediterranean. Usual Sunday letter writing, did not feel so good—head cold and stomach ache. At 11:30, went to the office with Hamilton, Page and Prunier—took a ride to Sparrow Hills and Machaisk Highway—went to look for some tennis, but it was too wet. After lunch turned in and did not go to the movies—was feeling worse so did not go down to dinner—went to bed and sent for the Doctor, who gave me grip and jippy tummy treatment.

I was well enough to go to the office the next day. On the 31st, I managed to pull myself together and attend the big official dinner which Mr. Molotov gave at Spiridonov House. Mr. Litvinov was beside Mr. Molotov in the receiving line, but, at dinner, he was uncommonly quiet. That was his last social appearance in Moscow while I was there.

I had enjoyed Mr. Litvinov for his sharp intellect and for his pleasant personality, and I hoped that I could maintain the friendly relations that had existed between us. When we entertained on September first for the Diplomatic Corps, including First Secretaries, Military and Naval Attachés and their wives, and such members of the Soviet Foreign Office as would come, I invited Mr. Litvinov as usual. It was a grand party. Spaso House had never looked more attractive. Behind a curtain in an alcove a phonograph played a soft music as a background for the conversation. We had cocktails at seven and dinner at eight. By 9:30, all our guests had left. Everyone voted it a great success. Mr. Litvinov was not among those present.

Concerned as to the fate of the most friendly "Old Bolshevik" I had met, I took my Embassy Counselor, Mr. Hamilton, and made a courtesy call on Mr. Litvinov at the Foreign Office. We found him crowded into a "cubbyhole" of an office with his English-speaking secretary. Neither one of them looked happy. There were no chairs for us to sit, so all four of us stood during our brief visit.

After we had exchanged greetings, I asked, "What will be your next assignment, Mr. Litvinov?"

He shrugged expressively. "That has not been decided," his secretary replied for him.

"Will you come for bridge tomorrow evening?"

Mr. Litvinov and his secretary exchanged glances. "I'm not going out at present," he replied.

"How is Mrs. Litvinov?"

"Fine, I believe. She is coming home, probably by steamer." He looked down at his fingernails and then up at me again. "She's not a bit happy about it. She likes America, you know. Particularly New York."

Mr. Litvinov did not return my call. I suspect that I was taken in by the Russians on this occasion. I should have recognized that the frock coat "was being put back in mothballs," that the diplomatic freeze was on again. There was considerable confusion in Washington at the time—some officials recognized the recall of Litvinov and Maisky for what it was—a worsening of relations with the Soviet Union. Some even went so far as to liken the situation to that which prevailed before the Molotov-Ribbentrop Non-Aggression Pact of August 1939 and predicted that the Russians would make a separate peace.

I had no such fears. Every day or two, we listened to the grand salute to another Russian victory. I must have contributed to the confusion in Washington when, as a result of the above described incidents, I sent off the following telegram to the State Department:

> I disagree with the opinion held in Moscow by other diplomats and the Press to the effect that the recall of these representatives was in the nature of an expression of dissatisfaction because of the failure of the Allies to establish a Second Front. In my opinion, Maisky and Litvinov were recalled for the reasons stated to me by Mr. Molotov, namely, that Mr. Stalin had no one in Moscow qualified to advise him on matters relating to England and America and he recalled these officials to have them close at hand to advise him.

If that were so, Mr. Litvinov and Mr. Maisky must have advised Mr. Molotov and Marshal Stalin from a dark room in the Kremlin, for I never saw either of them again in Moscow, except that occasionally I would see Mr. Maisky on his way to the library where he was now employed. In fact, I rather feared that Mr. Litvinov had become the victim of a purge for some sin against the Communist faith, until I read of his death in Moscow in 1952 and of his state funeral conducted with appropriate Russian pomp and ceremony; Comrade Stalin and other members of the Politburo served as pallbearers.

The Western Allies managed to make an armistice with the Italians and set up an Allied Control Commission in Italy without the assistance of the Russians. On September 7th, I delivered a note to Mr. Vishinsky informing the Soviet Government as to the nature of the Commission to be established. The reaction to the statement in the message that the Russians would not be granted a membership on the control commission because they had not fought against the Italians produced an unexpectedly violent reaction. I even went so far as to send a telegram to the State Department, urging our Government to reconsider and "agree to permit the Soviet Government to have a place on the Allied Control Commission for Italy as this is the first intimation on the part of the Soviet authorities that I have observed which indicates that the Soviet Government intends to work and cooperate with the Allies in the post-war rehabilitation period."

I left Moscow before the diplomatic exchanges over Italy were completed. The Soviet Government was not granted a membership on the Allied Control Commission for Italy. In order to have a hand in Italian affairs, the Soviet Government recognized the Provisional Government of Italy (which no other Ally had done) and sent Mr. Vishinsky to Rome as its diplomatic representative to this government.

I imagine that the Soviets hoped by this move to keep informed as to the actions of the Provisional Government under Marshal Badoglio, but they gained nothing. Marshal Badoglio was little more than a figurehead; he could take no action until it was approved by the Control Commission. Mr. Vishinsky obtained so little information from the Provisional Government that Mr. Molotov recalled him and he was not replaced.

In looking back over this series of important incidents, two things stand out. First, I am again astonished at extent of conversations which were conducted without my knowledge and at the lack of information furnished me about negotiations with the Soviet Government, with which I was supposed to assist. Second, I am nonplused at the transparency of the fairy stories with which the Russians enliven the conduct of their diplomatic negotiations and at our readiness to believe them.

As I think back over these incidents, I am convinced that these fairy tales were all pieces of a whole fabric of deception. We Westerners believed that the Soviets were in the War for the same reasons that we were—to defeat Hitler's conspiracy and to prevent the Nazis from dominating Europe and the world. Then we would all go home and have twenty to fifty years of peace. I am *now* convinced that the Soviet leadership regarded World War II as another "cataclysmic capitalist war" brought on by the inequities of the capitalistic system, and planned to use it as another stepping stone toward their ultimate goal of world Communist revolution and the imposition of the "benefits" of Communism on all peoples everywhere.

The recall of the Soviet Ambassadors to London and Washington did indicate displeasure with the British and American Governments at our failure to establish a Second Front but it had a deeper significance, which should have been evident.

For several weeks, neither the British Ambassador nor I could obtain an appointment to see Premier Stalin—he was always "at the front." During this period, the Red Army was enjoying an unbroken series of major victories, commencing with the fall of Kharkov, with almost daily salutes in celebration of great victories on the Russian front.

The Russian people continued to support unstintingly Premier Stalin and his supreme War Council in their prosecution of the war—as a result, he had come to believe that what his "Dictatorship of the Proletariat" had accomplished in the field of military action could also be accomplished in other spheres, once the war was won. The Communist State had proved a success—"socialism in one state" was just around the corner. Stalin now felt confident that Soviet Russia under his guidance could enter into successful competition with the other great nations of the world in any field of endeavor. Having satisfied himself on this score, he was now ready to sit down around the conference table and take a hand in the international poker game with his two great allies, keeping always in mind that the spread of the Communist revolution prospered best in an era of post-war chaos.

On September 8th, as I listened to the 7:30 BBC news broadcast, President Roosevelt was quoted as saying, "Startling developments can be expected with regard to a meeting between Premier Stalin, Prime Minister Churchill and myself within the next few days." The State Department had not bothered to inform me officially, but this bit of news coming to me in a foreign news broadcast helped me to prepare for the most important event of my stewardship of American affairs in the Soviet Union.

CHAPTER XXVIII

Moscow, Farewell

Preparations to Leave

Having had no order nor any indication that anyone in Washington was paying the slightest attention to my letter of resignation, on September 3rd, I sent a message to the State Department:

> Your attention is respectfully invited to my letter of resignation addressed to the President on May third in which I requested that I not be required to remain in the Soviet Union beyond October tenth of this year. The State Department's intentions in this regard are requested.

On September 10th, I received an answer:

> The Ambassador will be directed, early in October, to return home for consultation. He may plan in accordance with the expectation that he will not be required to return to the Soviet Union.

My diary continues the story:

Saturday, September 11.
7:30–8:05 news. British landed at Taranto on the heel of the Italian boot. Fighting around Rome—Germans have occupied key cities in Northern Italy. Little of moment in office—then BIG NEWS. Meeting in Africa or Sicily and in Moscow [of Foreign Ministers]—and then some place else for the Big Shots.

Luncheon with Chinese Ambassador, Madame Fierlinger, Chinese newspaper girl Chuo, Eddie Page and myself—then had movies, "Too Hot to Handle," plus a Mickey Mouse. Spent the evening at home playing pool, cribbage and gin rummy. Lost 5 rubles. Turned in at 1:00. Italian Fleet surrenders at Malta.

475

Sunday, September 12.

7:30–8:05 news reception bad. Little change. Successes every-where. King and Government have left Rome. Spent morning writing letters. . . . Page and I went to exhibit of captured German Army equipment at Park of Rest and Culture. Page gave supper party. I turned in at 12:15. Party lasted till late.

At the exhibit, it was remarkable to observe the careful prepa-ration that the Germans had made. For example, electrical cross-cut saws for felling trees for corduroy roads through swamps and bogs, many types of outboard motors, some on extension frames which permitted them to be used in very shallow water, and all types of guns, tanks, airplanes and other purely military equip-ment. In one building was a display of medical supplies—it was interesting to note the steady deterioration in quality of the ma-terial and workmanship of the articles as the war progressed, in-dicative of the strain on the German economy.

After BBC's news of the meeting of the Big Three in Teheran, I expected information on the subject from the State Department, but . . .

Monday, September 13.

Slept in till 8:00, no news. Went to office as usual. Personal message from Sulzberger requesting visa for Lawrence, *Times* man in Lon-don. Saw Clark-Kerr at 12:30, he had an answer to note about meet-ing—I have no answer yet, probably won't get one. Went to office at 4:30, worked on efficiency reports and general business until 6:30. Home for dinner, pool, then bed. Had long talk today with [Coun-selor] Hamilton on general subjects.

Tuesday, September 14.

7:30–8:05 news—Salamaua taken, hard fighting. Fifth Army at Salerno. Japs in Kuriles bombed. Went to office at 10:00, inspected below at Mokhovaya. Routine telegrams. Finished fitness reports. Wrote several letters. Sent telegram to Evelyn [that I would soon be coming home]. Home for dinner, pool, cribbage, turned in after 11:45 news.

Wednesday, September 15.

7:30–8:05 news. 5th Army seriously involved Salerno. Allies ad-vancing on Lae in New Guinea. Received message that courier leav-ing Teheran for Moscow today. At 5:00, Page and I took Hamilton and Stevens to see "Hunchback Horse." Then came home for cold supper upstairs, little news at 11:45, turned in at 12.

Thursday, September 16.

7:30–8:05 broadcast. Eighth Army still holding and fighting back. Navy also bombarding. Russians captured Nyashin, the next station to Kiev. At 8:00 saluted for capture of Nyashin, and at 10:00 for the capture of Novorossisk. Had lunch with the Swedish Minister. Received orders to proceed home at the earliest practicable moment. . . .

I had been living for several days in a state of suspended expectancy. The message, for once, cleared up all of the uncertainties:

The Ambassador will proceed home for consultation and will report to the Secretary of State at the earliest possible moment, choosing any route desired. The Secretary of State is due in Moscow for meeting of Foreign Ministers on October 15 and desires a consultation with the Ambassador before he leaves Washington.

My diary continues:

Decided to take off on Sunday morning via Teheran, North Africa, wired Department to that effect. Saw Molotov at 10:00 P.M., told him the whole story. . . .

Mr. Stalin was "at the Front." This was to be my last interview with Soviet authorities. For the last time I rode across Red Square to the Kremlin Gate, picked up the NKVD men and drove through the Kremlin grounds to the Grand Palace. For the last time, a Foreign Office emissary guided me down the long corridors to Mr. Molotov's office. He met me in the outer office and took me to his inner office, where I had faced him so many times across the corner of the polished conference table. As usual, Mr. Pavlov sat beyond Mr. Molotov, his thin face alert, pencil poised to take notes on our conversation.

"Mr. Molotov, I have just received a telegram ordering me home for consultation," I began, and Mr. Pavlov wrote rapidly in his precise Russian shorthand in his notebook. "It is in connection with briefing the American representatives who come here next month to participate in the Foreign Ministers' Conference. As you probably know, I had planned to return to the United States early this fall; in view of the President's instructions, I am merely leaving a little sooner than expected. For purely personal reasons, I will not be returning to Moscow."

When the translation had been completed, Mr. Molotov looked up from studying his plump hands. "I am sorry to hear of the Ambassador's impending departure." His voice sounded genuinely regretful and I thought that his wide face had lost something of its impassiveness. "Is there any political significance to your recall?"

"Oh, no," I hastened to assure him. "I desire to retire for personal reasons. I am getting along in years, Mrs. Standley is not well, and I feel that I should be with her."

"I quite understand." He hesitated a moment. "I just wanted to check on the political significance, if any."

"No, there is none. Absolutely none."

"I am completely satisfied. There are no political considerations. The Ambassador's retirement is based on purely personal reasons."

Well, that was behind me, I thought gratefully. "I want to express my appreciation to you, Mr. Molotov, for your many kindnesses and consideration in our dealings. I feel that there has been only the best of relations between us. I am genuinely regretful that the War has prevented me from being in Moscow much of the time. It is a wonderful city."

"It has been a pleasure to work with you, Mr. Ambassador," he returned the diplomatic courtesy, "especially as you have always been open and frank and have always revealed the true characteristics of a real military man."

"Thank you. I believe that it is only by a frank approach that two men can come to understand each other—or two nations, for that matter."

He stared at me owlishly for a moment, then let his eyes drop to his hands. When he didn't reply, I went on, "I would like to leave next Sunday via Teheran. I will be traveling in my own plane, and so I will require a Russian pilot and navigator, and visas for my plane crew, Secretary Page, Colonel Boswell, and Captain Hall. Will you instruct your assistants to help us make the necessary arrangements?"

"That will be done. You can leave by any route you choose but I agree that via Teheran would be the most practicable."

"I would like to request that my departure and the fact that I will not return to Moscow be kept a secret for the time being. I understand that my departure from Moscow will be announced in Washington at the same time as the announcement of the appointment of my successor."

Mr. Molotov nodded.

That was really the end of my mission to Moscow. Of course, I said that I "was leaving Moscow with only kindness in my heart for the Russian people;" Mr. Molotov could be sure that I "would always work and strive for the closest cooperation between the Russian and American people." Mr. Molotov, in turn, thanked me for my statement and said that he, too, "would work toward the same end."

As I rose to leave, I said, "Mr. Molotov, there will be accommodations in my plane for several passengers. If you care to avail yourself of this space, I will be pleased to assist you."

"Thank you, Mr. Ambassador."

As we shook hands, I said, "If possible, I would like very much to see Marshal Stalin prior to my departure to tell him good-bye."

"In view of the shortness of time, it may be difficult to arrange an interview. Comrade Stalin is so much at the front. However, I'll see what can be done."

While we sat at the conference table that evening, the guns pounded out two one-hundred-and-one-gun salutes. When I returned to Spaso House, I learned that they were for "tremendous victories at Novorosiisk and Novoseverski," of which I had never heard and which I have never been able to find on any Soviet map.

I had a long talk with Counselor Hamilton, who would be Chargé d'Affaires after I left, and Eddie Page. We prepared a despatch to the State Department telling them that I would bring home with me Secretary Page and two of Mike Michella's Army files, Colonel Boswell and Captain Hall. To bed, very tired, after the 11:00 P.M. news.

The Department was stuffy about Page. It seemed that Secretary Hull wanted him to be in Moscow to be helpful at the Conference. A later message informed me that Page would remain in Moscow with the new Ambassador, as yet unnamed. I protested vehemently. "In view of the fact that I am coming home for consultation," I told them, "in all fairness, I feel strongly that my Secretary should come home with me." I didn't receive approval until the day before we left.

There was a lot going on in Washington those days that I didn't know about. Averell Harriman had been chosen to succeed me as Ambassador. To clean up the messy Lend-Lease situation, Harriman had arranged for Major General John R. Deane to head a new Military Mission; Deane would have full charge of all military and naval activities, including those of Faymonville's United States Supply Mission. The objective of Deane's Mission was "to promote the closest possible co-ordination of the military efforts of the United States and the U.S.S.R."

Faymonville and Michella would eventually be replaced by Brigadier Generals Sydney P. Spaulding and Hoyt S. Vandenberg. General Deane would work directly under Ambassador Harriman, his plans and actions to be subject to the Ambassador's direction and approval. How I would have liked to have had such a set-up! But, no, it took someone as close to Harry Hopkins and President Roosevelt as Averell Harriman to accomplish what I had often recommended but had never been able to put across.

Friday, September 17.
7:30–8:05 news. Things going better in Italy. Eighth Army within 18 miles of joining up with Fifth [at Salerno]. Packing for trip. Clearing up final matters at the office. Luncheon at home, back to office at 4:30, haircut, saw Michella. Dinner with [Sir] Keith Officer at the Canadian Embassy. Bridge with Page, Swedish girl, and Greek Ambassador, most interesting game. Lost 18 R. Turned in at 1:30.

Saturday, September 18.
7:30–8:05 news. Drive in Italy continues. Eighth and Fifth Armies join up. Packing. Feel fine this morning—had hectic time signing last minute mail, settling accounts, packing, and getting rid of old clothes which the Russians like so much. Said good-bye to my colleagues of the Diplomatic Corps. Received last minute telegraphic instructions —gave out word I was going home for consultation. Announcement of resignation and relief to be held up till I get back [to Washington]. Continued packing until 7:30. Had final cocktail in Spaso with Dr. Michael and Page—read mail hurriedly, then went to party at Alexandriov's [at which I was presented with a loving cup of one quart capacity and required to empty it of champagne before they would give it to me]. Danced until 12:00. Turned in at 12:30.

Sunday, September 19.
Turned out at 4:00, shaved—breakfast in room. Did final packing. Said good-bye to servants. Left for airport at 5:00. Sentry would not let us in the plane till instructed by manager of field. Member of crew had forgotten passport, which delayed takeoff. All gang were down to see me off—Counselor Hamilton [now Chargé d'Affaires], Generals Faymonville and Michella, Commander Allen, and all their staffs, plus two sleepy looking representatives of Narkomindel. My party consisted of Lieutenants Prunier and Holt and three men of the crew, Eddie Page, Colonel Boswell, Captain Hall, Mrs. Raymond and her baby, and myself. We took off at 6:06.

I shall not soon forget that last takeoff from the Moscow airport. We taxied to the end of the paved runway, Prunier revved up the engines to test them, we turned, he gunned the engines again and we roared down the field, rising easily into the air under Prunier's skilled guidance. We circled above the airfield, gaining altitude, then we headed south across the city. Down below, I saw the Moscow River and the complex of canals glittering in the early morning sunlight. We passed over the Kremlin, its bulbous towers rising within its walled enclosure beside the River.

"Moscow, farewell!" I muttered to myself.

I had done the best I could. Perhaps I might have done better. Others would come this way—to the storied capital of the Muskovites. But I had a numbing doubt that they would succeed much better than I. Not unless the Soviets wanted them to!

As the plane cleared the city and headed south for Baku, I sank back against the seat, relaxing a tension I had long known. I was nearly seventy-one years old, and I felt my age. I said to myself, and to the Soviets, "I will not pass this way again."

The Flight Home

Just north of Stalingrad, we ran into thick weather. Lieutenant Holt wanted to climb up above it and head direct for Baku, but our Russian navigator believed firmly in contact flying. We cut back to the Volga abreast of Stalingrad and headed southeast, keeping the river in sight most of the way, until we reached the Caspian Sea at Astrakhan. We landed at Baku at 1:16 P.M. on a flooded field in a light rain, the water whooshed back along the fuselage, coating the tiny windows with a muddy slime. We passengers waited in the funny little tin and wooden shack they called an airport terminal, while the Russians quickly gassed the plane.

The Customs man in the waiting room told me that it had been raining in Baku for two days. When Lieutenant Prunier reported gassed and ready to go, we were in the midst of a heavy rain squall. Prunier, Holt, and the Russian pilot argued amicably for several minutes in a hash of Russian, English, and arm waving. Finally the Russian went to the window and looked out, shrugged his shoulders expressively, and shouted the Russian equivalent of "Okay. Let's go!"

We embarked in a drizzle. As we roared down the runway, the water flowed past our windows in sheets but the sturdy Navy

transport climbed easily into the air and bored into a thick overcast. Prunier was on his own, now, faced with the problem of
climbing high enough to cross the Elzbourg Mountains. The cloud
layer was much thicker than we had expected. I was on the point
of telling Prunier to turn back, when we came out above the clouds
at twelve thousand feet. Holt was able to fix his position with a
couple of quick sights. He laid his course, Prunier climbed to fourteen thousand, and we crossed the mountains with towering peaks
wreathed in piles of cotton clouds on either hand. It was one of
the most ticklish flying experiences I had in the Soviet Union.

The climb was so rapid and the altitude so high that, although
the trip was comparatively smooth, Mrs. Raymond became air sick
and her little baby wailed.

We circled above Teheran, losing altitude, to come in to a landing at 6:01. As I climbed down out of the plane, the heat of the
desert hit me in the face like a physical blow.

As usual, Ambassador Dreyfus put Page and me up at the American Legation. At dinner that evening, Ambassador and Mrs. Dreyfus had members of their staff, my former Moscow colleague,
Prime Minister Mohamed Saed, and Eddie and I as guests, a delightful occasion. The table talk was about the forthcoming meetings in Moscow and Teheran—much excitement for all.

Monday, September 20.

Turned out at 6:00—breakfast at 6:15. Left for airport at 6:40.
Took off at 7:07. Passed Baghdad, some distance on our port hand,
crossed upper end of the Dead Sea. Hit the Mediterranean Coast at
Jaffa, crossed the Suez Canal on a direct line to Cairo, pleasant passage with only one or two bumpy spots. Landed at Cairo Airport at
2:16—Minister Alexander Kirk, Counselor Jacobs and Colonel Mac-
Cauley met us.

I was very weary from the trip. The sudden change from the
crisp fall weather in Moscow to the humid heat of Cairo was trying. I was further aggravated that I had not packed so that I could
be comfortably dressed for hot weather.

Kirk and MacCauley had news. The Minister had received orders to expedite my return. "The Air Transport Command has put
a C-87 at your disposal, Ambassador," MacCauley said, with a big
Irish grin. "It's much faster and has longer legs than your DC-3.
We've set up your departure early in the morning of the twenty-
second, if that meets with your approval. Routed you via North

Africa, Scotland, Iceland, Greenland and New York to Washington. They want you to be there on the twenty-fourth."

"Sounds good to me," I quickly decided.

I had started to walk away with Kirk and Jacobs; now, I turned back to the plane. I hated to leave my pilots and crew, but the decision had been made for me. I had Prunier muster the crew under the wing, and I shook hands with each one, thanked him, and told him good-bye. "But this is nonsense," I said, finally, "I'll see you all at Anacostia."

Mr. Kirk took me to his town house to bathe, shave, and rest. After a brief cocktail hour with General Royce of the Air Force and local officials of Lend-Lease, Office of War Information, and the Red Cross, I dined alone, the Minister having an engagement. Never did a bed feel so good to my tired old bones. But habit is stronger than fatigue. I was awake at 6:00 and turned out at 7:30.

Tuesday, September 21.

Breakfast at 8:30, rested a while, repacked. Took a sightseeing tour to the Citadel and Alabaster Mosque. Then did some shopping—spent $400 on junk—ring, cigarette cases, small inlaid boxes, a coat, Indian embroidery. Back to lunch at 1:30, met staff and Red Cross and Lend-Lease officials again. Rested till 5:00, then took a drive with Page. Met Prunier at Shepeard's Hotel at 6:00—dinner at the Pyramid House. Kirk and Jacobs drove us out to the airport at 11:15 P.M.

Wednesday, September 22.

Arrived at the airport at 12:30 A.M. Baggage put on board immediately, waiting for other passengers. Boarded plane at 12:40. Kirk and Jacobs left. Took off at 1:00 for Algiers. Comfortable but cool night, feet got cold, put on overcoat. [The heating system went out and it got so cold it was difficult to sleep. We flew over desert country recently the scene of the Allied struggle with Marshal Rommel, the Desert Fox, but there was no sign of battle.] Landed at air field [14 miles from Algiers] at 10:10, had cheese sandwich and coffee in rest room. Admiral Hall [naval commander in the area] came to field. My son, Bill, is with the Amphibious Forces there, but did not see him. Took off at 12:06. [The country is much like Southern California—very dry, with cactus and alloe plants and olive trees. Desert scenery with occasional green oases.] Landed at Marakesch, near Casablanca on northwest coast, at 4:30 P.M. Plane had to be emptied and fumigated.

Taken to "Moses Taylor Villa," a guest house which once belonged to a wealthy American named Taylor. Had cold lunch, repacked bags.

The patio has a swimming pool, the garden is much like our garden in Villa ZeeZaw in San Diego, larger but the same fruit trees and flowering bushes. Visited native market, much like the one at Kano but considerably cleaner. Bought a basket, a belt, and two baby's skull caps. Dinner at 7:30. Took off at 9:30 for Preswick.

Our flight from Marakesch to Preswick was made at night. To evade German planes, we flew directly west over the Atlantic until we reached the longitude of Preswick, then turned north, a total distance of some 1600 miles. As we passed over North Ireland approaching the Naval Air Station at Preswick, Scotland, I was forward with the pilots. Word came over radio that the ceiling was 300 feet, visibility four miles. Our pilot was instructed to "come in on the beam" at our present altitude until we passed over Ireland, then let down to come out under the 300-foot ceiling and see the airfield.

"How will you know when we pass over the Irish Coast?" I asked the pilot.

He pointed to a small light globe on the floor of the cockpit. "That little light will flash red when we clear the Irish Coast."

I watched the light. Presently, it flashed on. The pilot brought the big plane down into the clouds below us. I watched the altimeter, fascinated, as the needle came down to 1500, a thousand, five hundred. The fog around us thinned and we came out flying above rippled water, with land faintly visible ahead. We landed at Preswick Naval Air Station at 8:06 A.M.

Met by Major Irbin. Later Colonel Henry, Lieutenant Commander Messick called. Had breakfast. Saw Mrs. Winant for a few minutes, she was on her way back to London from Glasgow. Called Ambassador Winant [in London] and talked to him for a few moments. Lunch at 12:15, took off in same plane at 1:48. Very rough flight with strong head winds. Twenty-three passengers, including Page, Minister Wilson, and myself. Speed reduced so much it seemed doubtful we would make the field at Weeks, Iceland. Played gin rummy. Gas held out and we landed at the Army airfield at 8:02 P.M. A nasty wind blowing, which cut right through me. From the African desert to the frozen North in two quick hops!

We were taken immediately to field headquarters, three Quonset huts hooked together in a clever four-leaf-clover fashion, a creditable set-up for its desolate location on a barren, windblown shore. The cleanliness and orderliness of everything was a startling contrast to similar installations in the USSR. We met Colonel Pratt and Major Cox. I telephoned Commodore Wentworth and Admiral Smith. The "Hotel de Gink" was in excellent shape; we were treated with the utmost courtesy. Page and I had supper in the officers' mess; it was wonderful to have American food again, a grand meal—ham, French fried potatoes, canned peas and string beans, fresh tomatoes, with canned pears for dessert. We never had a banquet in the Kremlin that tasted as good!

We took off at 10:02 P.M. and climbed to 12,000 feet to have favorable winds.

Friday, September 24.
   Flying about 12,000 feet, cold and very bumpy. Had uncomfortable night, needed oxygen but did not take any. Occupied crew's bunk in forward compartment but only cat-napped because of cold and discomfort. Landed at Army airfield, Presque Ile [Maine] at 11:40 A.M. Set my watch back to Eastern War Time.

Presque Ile is a port of entry into the United States. I went through Quarantine. The customs officials were inexperienced and, at first, insisted that I go through customs inspection. I insisted that I was entitled to "courtesy of the port." We were at an impasse until Eddie phoned the head of the Customs Service in Washington and that embarrassed official directed that we be given full courtesy.

   Had breakfast. Departure delayed—started port outboard engine —didn't rev up to full speed. Sent plane to shop. Pilot, Page, a lady passenger and I got a car and went to see the sights. On the way back to base, met an airman on motorcycle looking for us.
   Took off at 10:08 EWT, flew over Portland, Boston, along north coast of Long Island Sound, landed at LaGuardia Field at 12:55. Had lunch, called a number of friends but unable to reach anyone. Again delayed by engine. Took off at 2:47 P.M., landed Washington Airport at 4:04, met by Major Wiley, Freddy Reinhardt [of the State Department], and Mrs. Page. Two cars were made available, which was good—I had as many packages as an old maid.

One airfield is much like another the world over. Presque Ile and La Guardia are both impressive, but Washington Airport is something special. The magnificent terminal building with its tremendous windows looking out across the wide concrete runways at the Potomac River, its fine waiting rooms and gleaming restaurants, its efficient service, all of these I contrasted mentally with the rain-soaked, muddy field, the wooden platform, and the ugly little terminal shack at Sverdlovsk and Chelyabinsk. Not even in Moscow for a decade, if ever, will the Russians have such a handsome airport and terminal.

There were similar striking contrasts along the wide pavements of George Washington Memorial Highway and through the streets of downtown Washington. But the biggest contrast came when I walked across the plush lobby of the Mayflower Hotel to register. The Soviet Union's grandest hotel is shabby and ill-kept in comparison.

I was assigned room 919, a tiny single room with bath—not nearly as much floor space as in the suites I occupied at Sverdlovsk and Chelyabinsk, but the little room was freshly decorated, spotlessly clean, and had a pleasant air; in the small bathroom, the appliances glittered under indirect lighting with porcelain and chrome—and all the faucets ran water, hot or cold, as marked.

I picked up the phone and called Mrs. Standley in San Diego. She was feeling fine, terribly happy that I was back. I turned in at 12:00 but I did not sleep well. Perhaps the bed was too soft and comfortable after months of sagging springs and lumpy mattresses. More likely, I was too excited to sleep soundly. As I fell into a fitful slumber I thought, exultantly, "I'll never have to go back *there*, again."

BOOK THREE

End of a Mission

CHAPTER XXIX

Briefing and Debriefing

Truth is the bulwark of freedom. Suppression of truth is the weapon of the dictatorship.

DWIGHT D. EISENHOWER

MAURY MAVERICK, former Congressman and colorful character from Texas, coined a word for it—*gobbledygook,* the sometimes completely unintelligible officialese which springs up in Washington governmental circles.

Briefing a person on a subject, situation, policy, program, etc., is preparing him with such full information that, at a conference or an interview, he will be able to discuss the subject so thoroughly and so brilliantly that he will seem to have made a lifelong study of the subject.

Debriefing a person (a newer term) consists of "picking the mind" of someone who has special knowledge of a subject, situation, policy, program, etc., so as to obtain from him the last grain of information on the subject that he possesses.

On our ride into town from the Washington Airport, Freddy Reinhardt, Assistant Secretary for Eastern European Affairs, began to brief me on the situation in Washington and we both began to debrief each other. From Freddy, I learned that "Harriman will relieve you, but it cannot be announced until agreement is obtained from the Russians." The Secretary would see me on the morrow, a Saturday, but briefly. He was going away for a few days' rest in preparation for his trip to Moscow. I would brief Mr. Hull on the situation in Moscow later. In the meanwhile, I could pay my courtesy call upon the President.

When I arrived at the Mayflower, I was surprised to learn that Averell Harriman was also stopping there. I put in a call to his room and invited him to dinner. "I don't feel like going out, Admiral," Harriman countered. "Won't you have dinner with me up here?"

We discussed conditions in Russia over cocktails and dinner until midnight. As I rose to go, I shook hands with the new Ambassador to Russia. "I don't envy you, Averell. It's a tough assignment."

He forced a smile. "Thank you, Admiral. I know it will be difficult, but they're only human, those Russians. Stalin can be handled."

I went down the hall, shaking my head. That's just what I had thought eighteen months before.

As I shaved and dressed the next morning, my principal preoccupation was with my coming conference with Secretary Hull. I had few misgivings. I had known Cordell Hull for many years, both as a Senator and later when we sat together in Cabinet meetings. He is a true Southern gentleman, kind and courteous. I had kept him fully informed as to the Russian situation, not only by despatch and air mail reports from Moscow, but also personally when I was home for consultation. He would soon leave for the Moscow Conference of foreign ministers. Eddie Page and I had tried to figure out just what sort of information he would require. I had prepared a memorandum based on our speculations, but I was also ready to tell him anything else he wanted to know.

As I went down to breakfast, I threw off all feeling of uneasiness. The Secretary had, on many occasions, expressed his personal approval of the way I handled affairs in Moscow. He had always been most sympathetic with me in my Russian dilemma, as well he might have been, for he was going through a similar experience at home. The Under-Secretary, Mr. Sumner Welles, having a close tie-in with Harry Hopkins and the White House, was reported to be continually by-passing and short-selling the Secretary. Finally, as I did, Mr. Hull rebelled. In so many words, he told FDR, "Mr. President, it is either Welles or me. One of us has to go."

The President needed Secretary Hull's influence with Congress more than he needed a close friend in the State Department. Sumner Welles resigned.

I walked down Connecticut Avenue and Seventeenth Street to the rococo old State, War, and Navy Building next to the White House. It was a glorious Fall day, sunny with a clear blue sky, a bit of a nip in the air. No NKVD boys preceded or followed me through the Saturday crowd. It was simply wonderful to be home.

Eddie Page awaited me in my old office, the statement we had put together nicely typed. Almost immediately, word came that the Secretary wanted to see me. Eddie and I went down the high-ceilinged hallways to the Secretary's office in the southwest corner of the building overlooking the park.

As I pushed into the waiting room, the Assistant to the Secretary said, "The Secretary wants you to go right in, Mr. Ambassador."

As I went through the high doorway into his inner office, Secretary Hull rose from behind a large old-fashioned mahogany desk, holding out his hand. "Well, Admiral, good to see you, sir. Glad to have you back."

"Good to be back, Mr. Secretary."

I was surprised at the change in Mr. Hull. He had aged appreciably in the ten months since I had last seen him. Later that day, I learned that some of his aides were seriously concerned about his trip to Moscow. It would be his first time in the air and his health was bad. But he was determined to go. I am sure that he would never have undertaken such a long flight and difficult task had he not felt that it was his duty so to do.

He motioned me to a seat across the desk from him. Eddie sat in one of the large leather-covered sofas along the wall. "I have appreciated your recent despatches, Admiral," he said as he eased himself back into his chair. "Now, I must go and talk to Mr. Molotov—and Mr. Stalin, too, I suppose. How will I find them?"

"Difficult," I said. "I've prepared a memo for you."

"Fine. I wanted to see you today. Later, I want to have a good, long talk. But that will have to wait. I'm going away for a few days rest."

I rose to leave. Mr. Hull remained seated, a smile lighting his long face. "It's good to have you back here, Bill. We need your sound advice, particularly at a time like this."

Back in my office, I read a large accumulation of personal mail. My diary takes up the story:

Saturday, September 25.

Lunched with Chip Bohlen and Freddy Reinhardt and talked Moscow. At 2:30, went back to the office, saw Loy Henderson. Talked to the boys while they quizzed me on Moscow. At 4:30 went home for a nap. At 5:30 to [Harold] Train's party. I knew all the new crowd. Back home at 7:30 with [Admiral] McVay, spent evening in hotel talking to him. Henry Sutphen called at 11 from New York, said Juan Trippe's plane would be at airport at 12:15 to take me to Long Island. I promised to be there.

I spent the weekend with friends at East Hampton in several rounds of golf, some games of bowls on the "Admiral Standley Bowling Green," and returned to the Washington Airport at 11:30 Tuesday morning in Juan Trippe's plane. My diary further records:

> Had lunch at the A&N Club with Elbridge Durbrow [assistant on the Russian Desk], Bohlen and Page. . . . Left cards on [Under and Assistant Secretaries of the Navy] Forrestal and Bard. Came to hotel, dressed for cocktails with [Under-Secretary] Dunn at the Sulgrave Club honoring the British. Had dinner with Arthur Sulzberger and General Adler at Statler, a pleasant evening.

I breakfasted with Irina (Skariatina) Blakeslee, who "debriefed" me on the Russian situation since I last saw her in Kuibyshev. Down at the office at ten A.M., the parade began—people who wanted to hear about Russia, people who wanted to tell me their views or opinions about what we ought to do with Russia, old friends who were anxious for me to write articles and books or make speeches over the radio or in person about Russia; in fact, do anything to reveal my views on the situation in Russia.

In these various interviews, I soon discovered that most people had preconceived ideas about the Soviets which nothing that I could do or say would change in the slightest degree.* To all intents and purposes, my Russian interlude was over. I wanted to go home to San Diego for a good long rest and some family life. Naturally, I had to remain in Washington until the Secretary left for Moscow, but I had no definite information as to when I would be summoned for briefing him and so I felt as if I were suspended "in the bight" of a very small line, not knowing just where I would land or when.

At 11:25 that morning, I walked across to the White House to pay my courtesy call on the President. While waiting for him to come down, I visited briefly with Admiral Leahy, his Chief of Staff, and Admiral Brown, his naval aide. A secretary came for me and ushered me into his oval office. Everything seemed the same until the President's colored valet wheeled him into the office. He looked worn and haggard. When his face brightened up with a smile for me, there were deep wrinkles in his cheeks that

---

* The attitude of the general public has not changed materially. The American people simply will not believe that conditions in Russia are as bad as they are but continue to think of it as a slightly different kind of America.

had not been there in December. I was frankly shocked at his appearance.

"Hello, Bill," he said, holding out a hand to me. "Glad to see you. How're things in Moscow?"

"Fine, Mr. President. I'm glad to be back."

I had made up my mind to avoid any criticism or argument. I had resigned. The President had accepted my resignation. I was glad to be rid of the whole Russian business and so I had no cause for resentment or regret. The Russians have a saying for it—"The past cannot repair the mistakes of the present."

The President was pleasant and affable but obviously his mind was on other matters. As I wrote my wife that evening, "He just talked platitudes." Every time I began to talk about things Russian, he looked away out the window, in an abstracted manner, or changed the subject.

Finally, he broke in on something I was saying. "Well fine, Bill. Glad to have you back. You know how much I appreciate the job you did for me in Moscow. I want to hear all about it, but not today. How about having lunch with me next Monday?"

I quickly agreed, made my good-byes, and was out of the White House before 12:15. At one, I was at the Columbia Country Club for lunch and golf with Harold Train. It was a marvelous day, comfortably warm in the bright sunlight, the fairways still sparkling green. Relaxed and somewhat relieved, I shot a ninety, the best score I had made since my return to Washington. "This," I thought, as I holed out for a birdie on the eighteenth hole, "is something those Russian Communists haven't got in any five-year plan."

In the following week, I had many contacts with people I had known and with important personages I had never met, most of them on the subject of Russia. I see no reason to record every meeting, all the varied conversations, but I think a list of these meetings may be useful to indicate the extent of interest in Russia at that time. Among others besides my colleagues in State were the following:

Admiral Schuirman, Naval Operations;
General Strong, Army Intelligence Service;
Arthur Sulzberger, *New York Times;*
Admiral Harold Train, Chief of Naval Intelligence;
Cardinal Spellman, Catholic prelate of New York;
Constantine Brown, reporter;

T. V. Soong, Representative of Chiang Kai-shek;

George Codrington, General Motors;

George Creel, *Colliers,* who wanted me to write some articles;

Admiral Leahy, old friend, Chief of Staff to the President;

Senator Barkley of Kentucky;

George MacDonald, Waldorf-Astoria;

Evelyn Walsh McLean, for dinner;

Admiral and Mrs. Jerry Land;

Congressman Sol Bloom, of New York, and his daughter, Vera;

Clarence Streit, of Union Now;

James Forrestal, Under Secretary of the Navy;

Ralph Bard, Assistant Secretary of the Navy;

Assistant Secretaries of the Navy Lovett and Gates;

Adlai Stevenson, assistant in the Navy Department;

Helen Rich, to arrange a speaking tour;

Admirals Mills and Edwards, Assistant Chiefs of Naval Operations;

Russian Ambassador Andrei Gromyko, about John Young's visas;

Congressman Disney, of New York;

Senator Wheeler, of Montana;

Senator Gerald P. Nye, of North Dakota;

Mrs. Robert Taft, wife of the Senator;

Senator Mahoney, of Wyoming;

Secretary Wickard, Department of Agriculture;

Senator Arthur Vandenburg, of Michigan.

When I returned from a quick trip to New York on Monday, October 4th, I phoned Eddie Page at 10:45 A.M. "You better get down here, Admiral," he said. "The Secretary's back, wants to see you."

My diary indicates that I conferred with Secretary Hull on October 4th, 5th, and 6th. My notes are not complete enough to differentiate one briefing session from another. I remember that I usually sat in a leather-upholstered chair facing him across his desk. Elbridge Durbrow was generally present as he was an officer in the Eastern European Affairs Division. I kept Eddie beside me on a straight-backed chair. There were others present on various occasions—John E. Puerifoy, Fred Reinhardt, and "Chip" Bohlen, one of State's brightest experts on Russia, who would accompany the Secretary on his mission to Moscow.

I recall that I first read my statement, with the Secretary frequently interrupting to ask a question and Durbrow, Reinhardt, or Bohlen interpolating an occasional remark. This went on for four sessions over a period of three days. When the Secretary finished with me, I felt like a Communist prisoner after a good job of brain-washing—completely fagged-out, not a coherent thought left in my head. Small wonder I can't remember incidents of those four sessions. I was thoroughly debriefed.

My statement went like this:

First, I would like to take up why, in my opinion, Premier Stalin has at last decided to confer with the United States and Great Britain on the Foreign Minister level and later on the Chief of State level.

Prior to the recall of Ambassadors Litvinov and Maisky, for some weeks neither the British Ambassador nor I could get an appointment with Premier Stalin. We were always met with the statement, "Marshal Stalin is at the front." During those weeks, there was an almost unbroken succession of great victories on the Russian Front, celebrated in Moscow with salutes and much fanfare.

I believe that the continuing support given to Marshal Stalin and his Supreme War Council by the common people of Russia brought Stalin to the conclusion that his efforts to make Mother Russia over into a Communist-Socialist state has been successful. The string of successes of the Red Army supported by the Red Air Force gave him the confidence to feel that what he had accomplished in the military field could also be accomplished in other fields. Mr. Stalin was now confident that Soviet Russia could enter into competition with the great nations of the world on any basis. That is why he is now ready to sit down at the conference table and discuss past and present events and future programs with the top representatives of these two countries.

His agreement to hold this Foreign Minister's Conference, his refusal to hold the conference anywhere else than in Moscow, and his willingness to meet Mr. Churchill and President Roosevelt all tend to confirm these views.

This brings me to the consideration of future events. I believe that the current military situation has been the subject of careful consideration and that the campaign on the Eastern Front is proceeding to the apparent satisfaction of Mr. Stalin and his advisers. I am convinced that he feels that this will, of course, lead to victory over the Nazis. *Recent statements also convince me that the Soviet Government will cooperate with the Allies in the war against Japan after Germany is defeated.* Not to the extent, perhaps, of a declaration of war, but with material assistance of one kind or another.

I turn now to the international economic situation, which does not, to me, appear to be as satisfactory [as the military situation].

The confidence which Premier Stalin has in his Government and his economic organization is, in my opinion, fully justified and will be a major force to reckon with in adjustments in the postwar years in the economic field. The Soviet State, under Premier Stalin, is a completely united entity. As a dictator, Mr. Stalin has complete control of all labor, raw materials, resources of every kind, industry and agriculture, and of services of every nature—transportation, communications, radio, etc. Consider the enormous power of such control combined in one person, especially in the economic field.

We must face up to the realities of the situation in negotiating with Mr. Stalin and Mr. Molotov. The present world struggle has resulted from the efforts of the [democratic] Allies to prevent an ideology contrary to their own being thrust upon them by the use of military power. When this war has been won, we will find our country faced with an equally vital and grim struggle in the economic field. We will be competing with the enormous, *unified* power of the Communist Soviet Union. *This economic struggle will be just as bitter and unrelenting as the military struggle has been.*

Conditions in our own country do not give us much encouragement as to success in this postwar competition. Unity of effort in the economic field will be just as important as it has been in the military field.

In a peaceloving country such as ours, where labor and industry and Government are apparently all actuated by diverse and selfish motives, disunited on virtually every subject that comes up, eternally separated in domestic politics, and always measuring action in international affairs as to the effect it will have upon the political situation "back home," it is hard to conceive that we can hope to compete with a united nation such as the Soviet Union.

We must mend our ways. In the field of international affairs, without sacrifice of our American ideals of individual and national freedom and the dignity of individual man, we must achieve a unity of action without taint of party politics that will insure that we can meet the most highly organized and autocratic dictatorship in the history of the world on an even basis. A grim challenge, but a realistic one!

The Secretary had leaned forward, resting his chin on one palm, his eyes closed. "A grim challenge, indeed, Admiral," the Secretary agreed, looking out at me suddenly from under his bushy eyebrows. "We have unity of action, now, control centered in one mind, but I doubt that we will keep it, once the war is over. Now, for more practical matters. How do you think the conference will go?"

"Mr. Secretary, what are we trying to accomplish?"

"A settlement for Eastern Europe, a plan for the control of Germany after the surrender, a settlement of Polish and Finnish problems, and participation of the Soviet Union in the Pacific War."

"First, then, as to procedure. You will be met at the Moscow Airport with considerable fanfare. Certainly by Mr. Molotov and a number of members of the Politburo and the Commissariat of Foreign Affairs, perhaps by Mr. Stalin, but I rather doubt it. At any rate, you will be given the full treatment, with honor guard, plush accommodations, probably at Number Eight guest house.

"The first meeting of the Conference, everything will be wonderful. You will feel that the Soviets will agree to anything. Mr. Molotov can be the most pleasant and ingratiating person you have ever met, when it serves his purposes. You will wonder why anyone ever said that the Russians are hard to get along with.

"The second meeting, you will be thrown into a maelstrom that resembles a pack of caterwauling cats. Nothing will be right. All the progress of the first meeting gone by the board, even less prospect of agreement than before you met. You will leave the conference table in a mood of the deepest gloom.

"That may be the night you are invited to the Kremlin for the usual grand banquet. You will probably find Mr. Stalin affable and pleasant. In conversation, he will make some off-hand remarks which may or may not amount to commitments.

"If the Russians have decided to agree to anything, everything will be sweetness and light. In any case, you might as well pack your bags and come home."

"Tell me about Molotov and Stalin."

"I have always found Mr. Molotov scrupulously polite and correct. At no time do I recall that he treated me unpleasantly, even though he was sometimes called upon to tell me unpleasant things. But he is a completely humorless, dedicated man, devoted to Party principles aand whole-heartedly loyal to the Boss.

"Mr. Stalin is a different sort of character—he can be calculatingly abrupt or rude, sometimes downright offensive. Then, with that rare Georgian humor, he can smile and let his eyes warm up. You might even get to thinking he likes you. But he doesn't. I know much more about both Mr. Stalin and Mr. Molotov than I did two years ago but I don't feel that I know either one of them, not really, that is, as one person makes an impression on another here in America. They are both still an enigma to me, even after all the times I have met and talked with them.

"They know but one faith, Mr. Secretary, the credo of Stalinist Communism, and one principle, self-interest."

Eddie Page had been trying for some time to get my attention. As I paused, he whispered, "Lunch, White House."

"Oh!" I exclaimed. "Will you excuse me, Mr. Secretary? I'm due at the White House in just eight minutes."

Promptly at 12:30, October 4th, I presented myself in the ante-room of the President's office. I was not kept waiting. When I went through the door, he was seated behind his desk in his special chair, smoking a cigarette in a long holder, a bright smile on his face. "Bill," he said, with that warm rising inflection of friendliness he could put into his voice. "Bill, it's good to have you back."

"I'm glad to see you feeling better, today, Mr. President," I offered, as I reached across the desk to shake his hand.

He motioned me to a chair. "You know, it's all set," he said, most confidentially. "We're to meet, Churchill, Stalin, and I—in Tehe-ran. He wouldn't come any further out of Russia. Said he had to be close enough to Moscow to keep track of affairs at the front."

I nodded. "I heard it was all set, sir. Congratulations."

"Couldn't have arranged it without you, Bill."

I thought of the procession of VIP's through Moscow helping him arrange what would only be arranged when Stalin was ready to say "Yes." But I kept quiet. Those irritations had passed into the limbo when I handed in my resignation. We were still at war; it was no time to quarrel with the President.

A White House waiter brought in our lunch. Mine was placed before me on a leaf that cleverly pulled out of the President's desk across from him. As we ate, he quizzed me and I answered as best I could.

"What do you think, Bill, will he make a separate peace with Hitler?"

I shook my head. "No, sir. Positively not. The Red Army will push right on across the German border to Berlin, just as fast as it can get there."

"What about after the war?"

"Mr. Stalin will cooperate with us, for a while, anyway, to get our help in rehabilitating his country. Russian self-interest will insure that."

"What about the Balkans?"

"Stalin will insist that the Soviet Union has a priority of interest in the Balkan and other Eastern European nations. In fact, as I reported some months ago, I believe that Mr. Stalin will try to set up buffer states along the Russian border which he can control, to help promote the security of the Soviet Union."

I recall that he was silent for a long time, looking down at his plate. Presently, he took a cigarette from a pack on the desk and put it into his long holder. I got up to give him a light but he beat me to it. His face was suddenly tired and drawn, as it had been the week before. He drew on his cigarette and exhaled with a force that was like a sigh.

There was an important question, which he hadn't asked. I gave him the answer, anyway. "Don't worry about the Far East. When the Nazis are defeated, the Red Army will join us against Japan. I don't think you can keep Stalin out."

Mr. Roosevelt's face brightened. "Well, thank you, Bill. Your advice has been helpful, as always. I'll be calling on you again, from time to time, until this terrible business is all over."

The President was as expert at making you know when an interview had ended as were Mr. Stalin and Mr. Molotov.

Wednesday, October 6.

Routine. Breakfast at 8:00. Sat in on conference with Secretary. Warned against proposed pre-Moscow meeting with British Foreign Secretary Anthony Eden at Cairo. Stalin would think that the Americans and British were ganging up on the Russians.

Thursday, October 7.

Turned out at 8. Breakfast at 9:30. Saw [Admiral] Joe and Lulu Taussig at breakfast. Went to office at 10, walked down with Sid Hayes. Mr. Earhardt called. At 11:15, left office with "Chip" Bohlen, Freddy Reinhardt, and Eddie Page for Municipal Airport to see the Secretary off. His pilot is Klotz, the same who took Wilkie in and later had pneumonia on his second trip. Secretary's plane a C-54, beautifully equipped.

I remember standing there talking to Major Klotz. "Thought you were never going back, Major," I observed, facetiously.

He grinned ruefully. "I thought Russia was in my past, sir, but it looks like it's also in my future." His face brightened. "This shouldn't be bad. Got another very VIP, this time. They'll roll out the red carpet, Admiral."

I saw the Secretary moving toward us and so I winked at the pilot and turned away. "Well, Bill, any last minute advice for an Alice in Soviet Wonderland?"

"Don't overdo, sir. That trip can be mighty rugged."

"So I understand. But seriously, any advice?"

"Well, yes, sir, if you insist. Watch for their self-interest. And take care of our own. They're mighty skillful negotiators, with all the trumps."

He took my hand. "Thanks. I'll watch 'em."

Klotz came up to escort the Secretary on board. As he turned to go, I added, "They don't ever give anything away, Mr. Secretary, not even for something."

The Secretary took off at 12:22 for Miami, the first time he had ever flown. I don't envy him. Dropped Page and Durbrow at the Department, went to the hotel for my clubs, had lunch and golf at Chevy Chase with D. W. A. Morgan. Played an atrocious game. Tried to get Hoyts and Flannegans for dinner. Later after I had eaten, the Flannegans called. I went down for coffee with them. Spent the evening in my room reviewing a new book, *Life of Litvinoff*. It's not going to do him any good in Moscow.

For some weeks, the purpose for which I had returned from Moscow was held in abeyance. Before he left, Mr. Hull asked me to remain available and be in Washington when he returned. I immediately put in for leave of absence and, on October 11th, set out for my home in San Diego in my "plane for my personal use," Holt and Prunier having arrived at the Anacostia Naval Air Station. For the first time in our association, my plane failed to function: its wheels wouldn't retract and its hydraulic brakes froze. We had to return to Richardson Field in St. Louis for a one wheel landing. Too long in the rigorous Russian climate, I guess.

I managed to make my way home, unscathed, had a pleasant visit with my wife and several of my children and their families. Since there was a news blackout on the Moscow Conference, I heard nothing about it, and I didn't know when the Secretary would return. After ten pleasant days, I took Mrs. Standley and went back to Washington in my "personal plane," where I had to kill time for three weeks, awaiting the Secretary's return.

I filled the days rather pleasantly: golf with old companions at Burning Tree and Chevy Chase; the California Society gave a dinner for Mrs. Standley and me; Sol Bloom, Chairman of the House Foreign Affairs Committee, had me up on The Hill for a most entertaining question and answer period, at which he told his Committee, "Gentlemen, I am happy to announce that this is the first meeting of this Committee at which all members have been present since I became Chairman."

I spent a weekend in Pinehurst, playing in the Homer Cummings Golf Tournament. Ambassador and Mrs. Gromyko gave a reception at the Russian Embassy on November 7th.

By the time that Secretary Hull returned, I was glad for a variety of reasons.

The Moscow Conference

Mr. Hull's mission to Moscow was widely acclaimed as a tremendous success. Before the House of Commons, Prime Minister Winston Churchill warmed up to the results with a statement that "our Russian friends [now] feel, as they have never felt before, that it is the heartfelt wish of the British and American nations to fight the war out with them in loyal alliance and afterward work with them on the basis of mutual respect and faithful comradeship in the resettlement and rebuilding of this distracted, tormented world."

There were important accomplishments. The three foreign ministers agreed on the creation of an international organization, which would become the United Nations; Russia agreed to become a member of the organization and to *work closely with the Western powers* in many other respects; the conferees decided upon a policy toward Italy and Austria, created an European Advisory Commission and an Advisory Council for Italy, exchanged views on post war treatment of Germany, proper attitudes toward France, and economic policies among themselves and with other countries after the War. Great Britain, the United States, the Soviet Union, and the Republic of China signed a Four-Nation Declaration, in which they agreed to establish an international organization. Until this organization could function effectively, the four powers would "consult together" with a view to *joint action to maintain the peace and security of the community of nations,* to *cooperate to reduce the crushing burdens of armament,* etc.

Of greater interest to me, in a conversation with Secretary Hull in the Kremlin, Premier Stalin agreed, once Hitler was defeated, to enter the war against Japan, and he asked Secretary Hull for nothing in the way of a *quid pro quo.* This was quite a different line than he took with Roosevelt and Churchill at Teheran.

While the Secretary was on his way home, the Senate approved by a vote of 85 to 5 the Connally Resolution providing for American postwar collaboration to secure and maintain the peace of the world and for the establishment of a general international organization. When I visited Mr. Hull briefly on November 10th, he was full of his success and humbly grateful for the accomplishments of the Conference, as well he might have been, had the Russians meant what they said or intended to carry out their commitments.

In a rather emotional address before both Houses of Congress on November 18th, Secretary Hull said, "There will no longer be need for spheres of influence, for alliances, for balance of power, or for any other of the special arrangements through which, in the unhappy past, the nations strove to safeguard their security or to promote their interests."

There were a lot of other distinguished statesmen in the Western World who held and expressed similar sentiments at that time.

I had my final conference with Secretary Hull at 9:50 A.M., Saturday, November 22nd. I was retiring again, for the fourth time. Now, I was a "former Ambassador to Russia" and, more to my liking, Admiral on the retired list of the Navy. My brief incursion into the field of foreign affairs was over. The finality of this connection was written in two letters. The first, in the name of the Secretary of State, was directed to "The Honorable William H. Standley, American Ambassador, now at 8900 Mariposa Street, La Mesa, California." After some mathematical legedermain based on days leave, in transit, in consultation, the letter announced that my resignation would become "effective as at the close of business on February 3, 1944."

The other letter, dated October 1, 1943, began "My dear Admiral" and was subscribed "With kindest regards, Franklin D. Roosevelt."

It is with real regret that I accept your resignation as Ambassador to the Soviet Union. During your term of office, as well as during your distinguished naval career, you have rendered valuable service to your country and I feel that you have greatly contributed to the cause for which we are fighting and also to the high purpose which led you to accept the position as Ambassador, namely, full and friendly cooperation and understanding between your country and the Soviet Union now and after the war.

I know that you are always ready to serve your country and to make any sacrifice for it. Your willingness to accept the post of Ambassador to the Soviet Union after having so loyally served your country for over half a century is a witness to that. However, in view of the personal considerations set forth in your letter of resignation, I do not feel that I can place any obstacle in the way of your wishes to retire.

In accepting your resignation, I want you to know how deeply appreciative I am of the faithful and valued services you have rendered your country and of your personal loyalty to me.

On November 18th, I journeyed to Boston to make the final talk of a current series of speeches before the New England Council. The weather was bitter cold. When I arrived at Union Station in Washington, I had difficulty obtaining a taxi and stood shivering in the sharp wind for some time. As a result, I contracted a vicious cold which I could not shed. When I went to Anacostia Naval Air Station to take off for San Diego, the Captain in command became concerned at my condition and called his senior medico. To my annoyance, the doctor insisted on examining me. "If I were you, Admiral, I'd postpone this trip and let us keep an eye on you for a while. We should be able to clear up that cold in a week or ten days."

"Ten days!" I snorted. I became a bit stubborn and insisted on making the flight. Upon my arrival in California, I went immediately into the hospital where I remained for a month with pneumonia. It took me most of two more months in the California sunshine to pull out of my slump and get back my strength, a shameful waste of good golf weather.

What irony! After all the exposure and disease in Russia, to be thrown by a common cold bug after my return to safe and sanitary America! But, in a way, it was typical of the recurring pattern of climax and anticlimax of my sojourn as Ambassador to Russia.

It was the middle of January before I began to take interest again in national and foreign affairs. The Cairo and Teheran Conferences were over. The President had been back in the United States about a month. It was not until considerably later that I learned just what had been accomplished at Teheran.

Stalin went to the Iranian capital in a most enviable position—absolute master of his government and his country, knowing exactly what he wanted. Churchill also knew exactly what he wanted, but he was answerable to his cabinet and to the House of Commons for decisions reached. While both Stalin and Churchill were concerned about their relative positions in Europe after the war, Roosevelt was thinking only of winning the war. His difficulties and indecisiveness during the conference were doubtless caused by lack of an American objective after "unconditional surrender" and the obscurity of our foreign policy.

Stalin wanted to be sure that the Anglo-American invasion forces went into Western Europe, not into Southern or Eastern Europe. Churchill fought hard to obtain commitments for participation of Anglo-American forces in the Balkan and Middle-European Campaigns, feeling that the British postwar position would be much better with British-American participation in the occupation of these strategic countries. Hindsight would seem to indicate that both Stalin and Churchill were right.

The agreements made at Teheran were far-reaching:

1. A firm date in May 1944 for the oft-postponed cross-Channel operation to open a "Second Front in Europe." Stalin promised so to time his offensives on the Eastern Front as to make the two efforts mutually supporting.

2. General agreement was reached on the Roosevelt plan for "United Nations to Preserve International Peace," with additional memberships for certain members of the British Commonwealth of Nations and member republics of the Soviet Union, as well as for the great powers' veto. Stalin again expressed his view, "If Russia, Great Britain, and the United States want to keep the world at peace, they have the military and economic power to do so and do not need the help of anyone else to police the globe."

3. The war potential of Germany should be destroyed. No agreement was reached as to partition of Germany but it was extensively discussed.

4. Stalin agreed to permit use of Russian air bases by the U. S. Army Air Forces and the RAF for shuttle bombing operations against Germany from England and Russia.

5. By a compromise agreement, some ships of the Italian Navy were to be turned over to Russia in January, 1944.

6. The Curzon Line as the eastern boundary of Poland with Russia was accepted almost without discussion. As a principle, Poland would receive a compensating gift of territory in East Germany.

7. The Big Three signed the "Declaration of Iran," which acknowledged the importance of that nation's contribution to the war effort and pledged such postwar economic assistance to Iran as was possible. President Roosevelt was particularly happy over the phrasing of the last two sentences of the declaration, "We came here with hope and determination. We leave here friends in fact, in spirit, and in purpose."

Some of this information was released in a communiqué on the Conference; much of it was not. Kept completely secret were the negotiations among the principals on Russian participation in the

Far Eastern war. Both Churchill and Roosevelt were astounded at the *quid pro quo* demanded, after Mr. Stalin's offhand remark to Secretary Hull in the Kremlin. All the Russian Dictator wanted as a price for what turned out to be a six-day campaign was the "return" of Sakhalin and the Kuriles, leasing of Port Arthur to Russia, Dairen to be a "free port," Russia to obtain the prewar lease the Soviets held on the Manchurian Railways; existing autonomy of Outer Mongolia, long an integral part of the Chinese Empire, would continue. Generalissimo Chiang Kai-shek was not consulted about the negotiations, which continued after Teheran, nor during the Yalta Conference, where these demands were granted.

President Roosevelt had found Stalin much more difficult to deal with than he had anticipated. Stalin made no attempt at fine speeches or observance of diplomatic niceties. His comments cut short flowery forensic displays by Churchill and bored in to the point. He was often blunt, even rude. But he got what he wanted.

Perhaps the worst result of the Teheran Conference from the point of view of the best interests of the United States was that President Roosevelt came away feeling that he could handle Mr. Stalin, that the Russian Dictator, in his phrase, "was gettable." This misapprehension, his successor unfortunately inherited.

It has taken us a long time to recover from this mistaken view. Only recently have our responsible officials come to recognize the menace of Russian and International Communism for what it is. Not even yet, in my opinion, do we have a program that will meet and counter the very serious challenge that Communism presents to the best interests of our country and to the welfare of our people.

CHAPTER XXX

The Challenge and a Program

A tenet of Marxian credo reads, "The end justifies the means." In the dialectics of modern International Communism, this has been distorted into a corollary, "If it is morally good for the Soviet Union to enter into agreements and commitments as it serves her ends, then it is morally good to break those agreements and commitments whenever they no longer accommodate her purposes."

I DON'T pretend to be omniscient. I don't claim to be "Johnny always right." In a long life, I've made a lot of mistakes, large and small. Usually, I have found, my mistakes have come about through acting on insufficient or erroneous information.

I have been wrong about the Soviet Government and its leaders but I have never been wrong about Communism. Communism is a religion of the devil; it is a distillation of evil; it is the very anti-Christ. We will never be safe from this evil faith until it is driven back to the hell from which it came.

I have been wrong about the attitude of the Soviet leaders during the War, but I have never been wrong about the Russian common people. My contacts with them involved nearly every facet of Russian life; on every occasion, I was given strong and moving evidence of the friendliness of the Russian people—men, women and children—for the American people and all things American.

How easy it is to reach false conclusions after only a few days' contact with the Russian Government and the Russian people! I saw it happen so often during my eighteen months of frequent and extensive association with the Russians and their Communist Dictatorship.

I have been as guilty of being taken in as the rest. When I returned from the Beaverbrook-Harriman Mission to Moscow in October, 1941, I became an "expert" on the Soviet Union, as so many do after only eight days in Russia.

Since World War II, we have been engaged in a great and tragic war, a shooting war that killed more American officers and men than all the other wars in our history combined, excluding the casualties of World War II. The Korean War was waged for the benefit of the Communist international conspiracy without a single Russian soldier being officially engaged. It is the only war in our long history that the United States of America has agreed to end without winning a decisive victory. In not winning a complete victory on the battlefield, we have suffered a humiliating defeat, a terrible "loss of face" before the peoples of Asia.

Soviet and International Communism have reaped benefits in the growth of Red China into a dynamic ally in the Far East and in keeping Korea divided between freedom and slavery. In many a free country, Communism still fights its battles in the labor union, in politics, in the courts, in the arena of public opinion—and with satellite soldiers in at least one poor country.

It is quite generally accepted by the American people that our difficulties with the Soviet Government and the lower standards of living behind the Iron Curtain are caused by the dictatorial form of that government and its rather poor attempts at a modified form of socialism, which might be called state capitalism. I doubt that this is true. Recent description of conditions in Russia confirms the poverty of life, the needs and lacks of ordinary necessities which are inconceivable to Americans.

This is nothing new in Russia. Perhaps things are a little worse or a little better for the common man, woman, and child than they were under the Czars—but not much. History teaches that conditions have not changed materially since the 17th Century when Peter the Great unified Russia and "liberated" the serf. Russia has always looked outward, has always been expansionist. Possessing one-sixth of the world's surface, she has yet wanted more—an ice-free port on the Atlantic and one on the Pacific, control of the Dardanelles, a defensible frontier, security from the barbarians of the north or the south.

Our Minister to Russia in 1852, Mr. Neill S. Brown, has left us this fine diagnosis of Russian imperialism:

A strange superstition prevails among the Russians, that they are destined to conquer the world, and the prayers of the priests in the church are mingled with requests to hasten and consummate this "divine mission," while appeals to the soldiery founded on this idea of fatality and its glorious rewards are seldom made in vain. To a feeling of this sort has been attributed that remarkable patience and endurance which distinguish the Russian soldier in the greatest privations.

Over the ancient skeleton of Russian imperialism, Lenin and Stalin threw a cloak of Communist ideology, but the bones of the skeleton show through. Even as in Czarist times, when the Russian Bear stands on its hind feet with its front paws held up as if in prayer, we must "beware of the Bear that walks like a Man."

During the past four years, we have studied the problem of Communism intensively. We have discussed it, read about it, thought about it, worked at it. In the light of the experience with Russian Communist leaders recorded in the foregoing chapters, we have asked ourselves, what is the meaning of Communism? To us as Americans? To the world at large? How can our own self-interest, how can the best interests of our country best be served in a world which is an armed camp divided between Communism and anti-Communism, with the ever-present fear of thermo-nuclear destruction hanging heavy over our heads? As a challenge, what do we know about Communism?

For a program, we must first examine briefly *how Russian and International Communism got this way.*

The Challenge

Communism is a development from the flood of Utopian socialistic philosophy which engulfed social thinkers and writers of Europe in the Nineteenth Century; it derives from studies of Hegel and Engel. It is a branch from the main stream of history which has now become very nearly half of that stream. In modern dress, Communism stems philosophically from Marx, philosophically and practically from Lenin, and in its most highly-developed practical form from Stalin. It was sown in deplorable conditions such as Marx knew in the factories of Nineteenth Century Germany and England and it had lush growth under the inequities of reward under an European social system which permitted the lavish luxury of a decadent ruling nobility and aristocracy and the degradation of soul and body which men, women, and children knew in the slums of the great industrial cities.

The Tenets of Marxian Socialism

Considering Europe (including the British Isles) as a whole, by 1900 Marxian Socialism was the largest and most influential segment of the socialist movement. At the risk of over-simplification, here is a brief of its tenets:

1. Progress is an evolutionary process flowing from feudalism through the industrial revolution toward establishment of "pure" socialism, when all men will be equal. Capitalistic disintegration and socialistic triumph are inevitable.

2. The Class Struggle: There is an irreconcilable conflict between the two classes of capitalistic society—the exploiters and the exploited. Marx interpreted the direction of the main stream of history as being caused by this conflict.

3. He recognized the primary role of economic or material factors in causing the disintegration of the capitalistic system and presented the "labor theory of value" as opposed to the quantitative theory of the value of things.

4. He propounded an esoteric theory of "historical materialism" derived from the dialectics of Hegel.

5. He denied that man has an inherent, God-given right to self-determination. Man-made environment is the all-determining influence on man; those men who live under similar economic conditions (man-made environment) will exhibit the same sort of "self-determination."

6. The purpose of the State is to safeguard private ownership. Therefore, the State must be smashed, not taken over by the proletariat in their revolution. Collective ownership and management of the means of production must be established.

7. Antagonism to all religion is basic to the Marxist doctrine. Marx himself first made the previously quoted remark, "Religion is the opiate of the people."

8. *Anything that tends to bring about the ideal socialist (communist) society is morally good. Anything that works against this end is morally bad.*

9. Marx held that the bourgeois revolution must first destroy or take over the feudal state and establish capitalism before a

country would be ready for a proletarian revolution. To be successful, the social revolution must be extended until it is worldwide. Communism cannot live in the same world with capitalism.

10. Since the proletariat will be unready to take over and run a country and since most countries will be unready for socialism, there will have to be a period of "dictatorship of the proletariat" (meaning specifically factory workers) to take the necessary steps to organize the country for "pure" socialism.

11. Marx described in glowing prose a mystic Utopian Communist Society of the future which was to be the final stage of the social revolution, after socialization of the economy and the final obliteration of the state as it "withers away."

Lenin's Deviations

Until he came to power in Russia and faced the practical application of his and Marx' theories, Lenin subscribed completely to Marxian doctrine. Even after the Bolshevik Party seized power, he sternly rebuked anyone who deviated from the "dialectics" of Marx. But as a practical matter of strategy and tactics in staging a revolution and managing a dictatorship, he found that he had to make many compromises with Marxian principles. Basically an honest thinker, Lenin recognized and admitted his "deviations" as necessary tactics in the Russian and world revolution.

Here are some of the Leninist deviations:

1. Lenin believed in violence as an indispensable means to achieve a socialist society. "The replacement of the bourgeois state by the proletarian state is impossible without a violent revolution."

2. He believed in mass violence but rejected the individual acts of terrorism which characterized other revolutionary movements.

3. He made his Party into a homogenous group of disciplined professional revolutionists, and tolerated no factions or dissent among them.

4. Lenin denied the validity of the Christian credo that individual man is free or has the capacity to act on the basis of his own free will and reason, but he compromised with this belief as a temporary tactic.

5. He accepted the Marxian theory that the State, eventually, should "wither away." Yet, in setting up his dictatorship, he found that he had to establish a government even more authoritative than that of the Czars.

6. Instead of eliminating the State immediately after the Revolution, he seized the existing apparatus in order to use its power and authority to achieve socialism. In staging his revolution, he abandoned the Marxian dialectic of prior industrialization of the country followed by a bourgeois revolution for an immediate Bolshevik seizure of power.

7. He advocated worldwide revolution. "It is inconceivable that the Soviet Republic could continue to exist for a long period side by side with imperialist states. Ultimately, one or the other must conquer. Meanwhile, a number of terrible clashes between the Soviet Republic and the bourgeois states is inevitable." Yet, he advocated "boring from within" established governments and organizations with a view to taking them over.

8. He early recognized that, in Russia, the Revolution and the country could only be managed by the Party and that the dictatorship would have to be prolonged far beyond the period anticipated by Marx. His dictatorship of the proletariat became the dictatorship of the Bolshevik Party leading the proletariat.

9. Lenin was intolerant of any kind of compromise with any other party or group. The one-party system was Lenin's principal contribution to modern political practice.

10. His devotion to the organization and disregard for the individual member has become one of the fundamental characteristics of the present Communist movement. He believed that, "Whoever belongs to an evil group must of necessity himself be evil."

11. Lenin was antagonistic to religion and set out to smash the Orthodox church and all other religions in Russia, yet as a practical tactic, he compromised with this belief.

Despite his many compromises and deviations, Lenin was devoted to the ideal of "pure" socialism. He believed in, and wrote eloquently of, the mystic Utopian Communist society of the future. For him, everything was subordinated to the "cause."

Utopian Mysticism of Marx and Lenin

To hope to arouse the interest and win the allegiance of the masses, a movement must have its mysticism, a religious kind of faith which grips the people's imagination and holds their loyalty. In his eloquent description of the nature of the future, Marx made his greatest contribution to the Communist movement. Lenin built upon the basic structure erected by Marx' vivid imagination to enhance the beauty of the perfect world order of "pure" socialism of the not distant future. When this Utopian society has been attained throughout the world as a result of the abolition of private ownership of the means of production and the "withering away" of the State, in the words of Marx, "after the productive forces have also increased with the all-around development of the individual, and all the springs of co-operative wealth flow more abundantly—only then can the narrow horizon of bourgeois right be fully left behind and society inscribe on its banners: from each according to his ability, to each according to his needs!"

In this Communist Utopia, harmony will prevail. Culture and education will advance to a new high level of excellence. Men will become so nearly perfect and so social-minded that they will easily live one with another without any form of government. For the first time in history, there will be complete and true equality among men.

If this seems fantastic in the light of humankind as we know it, Marx preached that a revolutionary change in human nature would be required. This would take place during the period of the dictatorship of the proletariat.

Such is the idealistic goal of "pure" socialism, which provides Communist theoreticians with a mystic cause for which they can persuade converts to fight with fanatical zeal and religious fervor. In America, we recognize that such an Utopia is pure fantasy beyond the reach of practicality. We Americans will never submit to existence under the terrorism and regimentation of an interim garrison-police regime.

Stalinism

For Marx, the reason in any country for a violent revolution and a radical change in productive relations was to permit introduction of a new order of relations based on "democratic" principles. Had he lived, Lenin would probably have tried to accomplish this. Under Stalin, Marxism as taught to him by Lenin was superimposed upon a Russo-Eurasian tradition of authoritarian rule, the only sort of government the Russian has ever known.

Stalin was also led to give new direction to Russian Communism by force of circumstance. Unlike Lenin, he was basically a dishonest thinker, trying always to justify his actions and words by reference to the writings and actions of Lenin. Although he knew and quoted the Marxist slogans, in the course of thirty years in power, he so transformed and reinterpreted the teachings of that old revolutionist that Marx himself would never recognize them.

Typical was Stalin's struggle with Trotsky, a conflict that was inevitable because each had tasted the heady wine of power and wanted more. Their dispute can be stated most simply in their opposing slogans—"Socialism in One Country" versus "The Permanent Revolution." By promoting within the Party and the Politburo that factionalism which Lenin despised, Stalin was able to disgrace and exile Trotsky.

In 1938, Stalin ended his long argument with the Trotskyists. He announced that building "socialism in one country" was not only possible but that it had been achieved in the Soviet Union. Yet, Stalin continued to believe in the "permanence of the revolution." Turning his attention inward upon the socialization of Russia was merely a tactic—at the same time, he pointed out that the victory of socialism had not been won, nor could it be won as long as Russia was surrounded by capitalist states. This condition, as previously noted, he corrected during the "cold war" after World War II, when, in one country after another, peoples' republics "friendly to the Soviet Union" were set up along the borders of Russia.

When Stalin discussed the relationship between his dictatorship, the Party and the Proletariat, he was rather vague because he had to be. He pretended to pursue the goal of "pure" socialism when the State would "wither away." Despite elaborate explanations by Party theoreticians, under Stalin the power of the dictatorship steadily increased.

According to Stalin, Lenin said that the dictatorship is exercised by the Proletariat for the people of Russia. The Proletariat, organized into soviets, is led by the Party. While the Party exercises the dictatorship for the Proletariat, and the dictatorship is the dictatorship of the Party, still this does not mean that the Party *is* the dictatorship. If these arguments seem to wander in a circle and get nowhere, perhaps that is how Stalin wanted it.

Stalin abandoned Lenin's agrarian policy of gradual state ownership of the land for forced collectivization of peasants onto state farms. This program brought on terrible famines and bloody purges. Collectivization was accomplished in a measure but successful production of adequate foodstuffs on the *kholkozes* and the individual farms still remaining in Russia has not yet been achieved.

As we have shown in earlier chapters, it is in the unequal distribution of the rewards of socialization that the greatest inequities occur. The Marxian slogan, "From each according to his ability, to each according to his need," may sound like an adaptation of the Golden Rule—it is in its application in Soviet Russia that its basic immorality is exposed.

Under Lenin, the rewards of power were modest. In the Kremlin, he lived with a Spartan simplicity comparable to his life in exile. He believed and practiced the policy of equalitarianism, and he insisted that his co-workers abide by that policy.

In 1934, Stalin denounced the policy of "equalitarianism." By equality, Stalin said, Marx meant not the equalization of individuals but the abolition of classes, and classes had been abolished in Soviet Russia.

Here is one tabulation of classes in Soviet Russia's "one-class" society:

43—Politburo and principal government officials
1,500,000—Party Elite (the Ruling Class)
15,000,000—Technical Aristocracy
160,000,000—Proletariat
15,000,000—Forced labor and "Free Labor Force"

Most of the last class are habitually kept behind barbed wire.

Among the Technical Aristocracy are the Stakhanovites, named for Stakhanov, who dug more coal (by four or five times) than the ordinary miner. One laborer from each industry is given better tools and better helpers to become best in that industry and be promoted to the Technical Aristocracy. For a year or so, he has a villa, car, "special attendants," and all the perquisites of position in the Soviet Union, then he and his family disappear to make room for another Stakhanovite from his industry.

Doctors have recently been removed from the Technical Aristocracy because they only preserve life, do not produce.

Under Russian Socialism, each person would be paid according to work produced. With the definition of "ability" and "need" left to the Soviet dictatorship, many and peculiar were the inequalities observed. The rewards for hard work or efficient administration went all the way from the direst poverty without enough to eat or wear and slum-level housing to a standard of living for the "Ruling Class" in "Classless Russia" that rivaled the splendor of the Romanoff court.

Finally, we have noted, Stalin embraced the nationalism of the Czars. As a result, the Cominform and the Communist Parties in other countries have had great difficulty justifying their positions as Communists *and* Nationalists in their relations one with another.

All his life, up to the very end, Stalin reached out always for more and more power, not forgetting but not caring, apparently, that with his departure from the Kremlin scene he would leave such a vacuum of power that many competitors would be drawn in. For power is a disease that feeds upon itself. The more one possesses, the more one wants. So it was with Stalin.

What Do They Have Now in Soviet Russia?

The system of control in Russia continues to be a dictatorship, perhaps by committee, certainly a dictatorship of the Party in behalf of the Proletariat, still a garrison-police state. When Mr. Stalin neared his end, we felt certain that Mr. Georgi Malenkov would win the nominal leadership of the Party and the Government. In the contest for power between Malenkov and Beria, Malenkov won because he had control of Party machinery and had inherited Stalin's super-Secret Police, which had penetrated the organization of Beria's Secret Police (MVD).

After Beria's purge, the rising importance of the Army in Party and Government became apparent. Marshal Voroshilov became President of the Presidium, Marshal Bulganin Vice-Premier and Commissar of War, Marshal Zhukov his Deputy. Malenkov captured the apparatus of the MVD, but signs of stresses and strains within that essential organization became more and more evident as members deserted to the West and gave away its dark secrets.

There are some who say that, before his unsuccessful bid for supreme power, Beria had come to much the same conclusions as those attributed to Stalin. "Look at the capitalistic system in the United States—not only did her industrial economy supply all of her allies and herself during the War, but she maintained the highest standard of living of any country in the world even in the middle of a costly, terrible war. And she built up the greatest fighting machine the world has ever seen. Maybe there *is* something to this capitalism after all. Perhaps our so-called socialistic system would benefit from a modest transfusion of capitalism."

After Stalin's passing, there were many indications of liberalization of conditions within the Soviet Union—political prisoners were pardoned, coveted consumer goods appeared in the State stores at prices which the ordinary Soviet citizen could pay, outwardly at least, the surveillance of the Secret Police became less rigorous, restriction upon the movements of foreigners was decreased, petty capitalism such as has been noted previously was encouraged.

But Soviet Russia is still a garrison-police state, with its citizens rigidly controlled in their every thought and activity; it's economy is still a modified form of State Capitalism, not socialism; its rulers still look out from behind the Iron Curtain at the rest of the non-Communist world as a threat to the very existence of Russian Communism; they still believe that "it is inconceivable that the Soviet Republic should continue to exist for a long period side by side with imperialist states. Ultimately, one or the other must conquer."

As an illustration from recent history, I recall having lunch at the Mayflower Hotel in Washington in September 1941 with Mr. Kasai, a member of the Japanese Parliament whom I had known for some time, and the Japanese Ambassador, Admiral Nomura. During the course of the luncheon, Mr. Kasai lowered his voice and spoke to me most earnestly. "Admiral, the policies of your country and my country are in direct conflict. Unless there is a change in policy of one of our countries, war is inevitable."

I looked around at Admiral Nomura. He nodded soberly. I can still recall the chill of apprehension that I felt.

A similar condition exists today in the relations between the United States and the Soviet Union. The basic and widely publicized policy of Soviet Communism is to communize the world. The announced policy of the government of the United States of America is to use every effort to prevent the spread of Communism in the world. Unless either the USSR or the United States changes its policy, war would appear to be inevitable.

We do not believe that the USSR wants this war. Such consistency as can be discerned in their actions since the war would indicate that they hope to promote their conquest of country after country by subversion within, guerilla warfare, and small wars employing satellite troops.

I recall, prior to V-J Day, when I was Naval Representative on the Planning Group which acted as a clearing house between the Office of Strategic Services and the Joint Chiefs of Staff, a post-war plan to divide the control of Germany among the United States, USSR, Great Britain and France came across my desk. I predicted that such a plan could not possibly work.

The first sign that Four-Power control had broken down was

the blockade of Berlin by the Russians. The Western powers decided to break it with the frightfully costly Berlin Air Lift. In my opinion, this action was our first and most crucial mistake in our efforts to deal with the Russians.

I told anyone who would listen, "Now is no time to appease the Russians. When you give in to them, they think it is weakness. Let's put this issue on a realistic basis. Let us say to the Russians, 'We are loading a train to capacity with food and fuel to feed and warm human beings who otherwise might starve or freeze. That train is going through. We will not use force to put it through, but if force is used to stop it, every power at our disposal will be used to deliver those essential supplies to those desperate human beings in Berlin.'"

Had we taken such action at that time, the Russians would not have dared to stop our train. More important, we would not have entered upon a policy of appeasement.

This action by the Russians was followed by other acts of aggression: shooting down our Western aircraft on peaceful missions, vetoing in the United Nations every effort looking toward a peaceful solution of important issues, and eventually instigating and supplying the Korean aggression. Had we taken strong and positive action in the first instance, the later aggressions would never have taken place.

So the "cold-war" came to this troubled world. The Russians set out to force the United States into an inflationary program. Well aware of the economic situation in which the United States finds herself, the USSR has already taken steps to expedite a hoped-for and confidently anticipated American economic depression, with accompanying unemployment and economic chaos. In such a favorable situation, the Russian Communists expect the hard core of American Communists to take over and run our country.

Responsible American officials have stated that the presence of only 25,000 card-carrying Communists in our country need give us no uneasiness. We must recall the fact that, when President Roosevelt recognized Soviet Russia on November 16, 1933, over 180,000,000 Russians were under the domination of a small inner core of the three million man Communist Party of Russia. Twenty-two years later, some 768 million people are virtual slaves under complete control and domination of a small handful of Communists in Soviet Russia. The wide areas of freedom are shrinking before the onslaught of this conspiracy for conquest. It could happen here in our own America.

We cannot afford to view this struggle impassively. We are no longer safe behind our barrier of oceans. In this joined battle of ideologies, in this conflict between a dictatorship operating a garrison-police state and the democratic world, the masters of the Kremlin, whoever they may be, do not intend that the "imperialist states" shall win.

The Challenge of Communism

Marx invented the word "capitalism," which Communist theoreticians have appropriated to name and defame the economic system of our free society. It is not "capitalism" that Communists fear so much as our free society and any free society anywhere in the world. The Communist philosophy of history regards what they call "capitalism" in any country as a dangerous challenge.

This was dramatically illustrated by the remarks of an official associated with the Polish Government-in-Exile in London during the War. A long-time member of the Polish Social Democratic Party, who had been many times to Moscow on government business, he said, "The Soviets will never feel safe and will never rest as long as there is one free society left in the world, even one as small and militarily powerless as little Switzerland. They logically regard such a society as a mortal threat to the security of their own system."

By inventing the juxtaposition of "capitalism" versus Communism, Communist philosophers set up a straw man to be struck down. The existence of "capitalist" states anywhere in the world, they write, necessitates a strong Soviet Russian state in self-defense and for offensive action against the enemies of Communism. Such a philosophy constitutes a "real and present danger" to the security of these United States of America.

The Communist belief that a democratic state exists solely to protect the vested interests of private property and therefore must be destroyed establishes a basic conflict between Communist and free societies.

The antagonism of Communists to religion and punitive action against Christians, Moslems, Buddhists, Confucianists, or, indeed, any other form of religion, which provides an "opiate of the people," is repugnant to Americans. It constitutes a denial of our fundamental belief in the freedom and dignity of the individual. The Communist credo that "the end justifies the means" is repulsive to Americans.

The Communist program of world revolution and the imposition of Communism on all peoples of the world violates our belief in national freedom and individual freedom of choice.

The mysticism of "pure" socialism, which provides Communists with a faith for which they can work and fight, we recognize as a fantasy and a sham. We abhor living under an interim regime such as the garrison-police state of Soviet Russia.

The Communism of Stalin and Malenkov bears almost no resemblance to the "pure" socialism of Marx. Yet, the Russian dictatorship has been one of the most stable and long-lasting in history and it has operated the most colossally successful conquest known to man, a determined and effective conspiracy that uses the "pure" socialism of Marx as a shabby screen for its real designs. We must stop jousting at the screen and face up to the challenge of the power and brutality of the Bear behind that screen.

Committed to world revolution, the masters of the Kremlin cannot cooperate in the United Nations or elsewhere to promote the peace of the world.

The Communist standard of morality renders their promises and international agreements and commitments of little value.

The perpetuation of power of the dictatorship is in direct conflict with the basic teachings of Marx, Lenin, and Stalin. It is a gross deceit before the world, a dictatorship of force of the most authoritarian kind, supported by the Russian armed forces and secret police, posing as a benevolent administration of a humanism that pretends to be concerned with the fundamental good of all mankind.

The menace of Russian and International Communism is dynamic, immediate, and total. Thus far, it has been all too successful, for Communism fights a continuing battle in all fields, lessening the pressure here, increasing it there, sometimes appearing to go along with the force which resists it. We must not be misled by these changes in the Party line, by the new directions and reversals of Communist strategy and tactics. The determination to destroy our free institutions has never lessened; the released pressure will again be applied when our resistance weakens.

A Program

By establishing our government upon their belief in the capacity of free individuals for self-government, our Founding Fathers provided for the individual freedom and dignity of its citizens. Our system is dedicated to the belief that the citizen must have an

opportunity to develop his individual capacity—morally, intellec-
tually, materially—but the opportunities guaranteed entail certain
responsibilities. A free man can remain free in a free society only
by exercising the responsibility of citizenship; only by eternal vigi-
lance can we ensure that the free processes of our free government
are not destroyed by forces from without or by conspiracy within.

I am an old man. I have little personal stake left in the future.
But I do have, now as always, the welfare of my country and my
fellow countrymen at heart. That is why, at an advanced age and
with considerable reluctance, I have undertaken to record this tale
of my Russian ambassadorship. From the long years of experience
in the service of my country and from first hand acquaintance with
the Russian brand of so-called Communism, I have derived certain
lessons which I would like to present here at the end of my book
as a sort of summing-up.

Our country must maintain what our military leaders have called
a "posture of strength." But it must be not only a posture of military strength—we must possess, also, economic and moral strength.
Let us consider these three areas individually, but not separately,
for not one of them can have vigorous health without support from
the other two.

A Posture of Military Strength

In any discussion of comparative military strength, we must
ever bear in mind that, in accordance with our age-old traditional
policy, our country will never initiate a preventive war. I trust,
hope, and pray that misguided economies and a wave of pacifism
among our people will not again bring our country to an international crisis as lacking in military readiness as we were at the
time of Pearl Harbor. We must have ready for prompt use enough
military strength of all categories to counter the initial attack of our
most probable enemy and to hold until our full economic and
military strength can be brought to bear.

I am no longer a supporter of the "balanced force" theory of
military strength, if that means the equal division of funds which
the Congress will make available for national defense among the
three military departments of the government. But neither am I
completely sold on the "New Look" which has been so widely
publicized of late. There are several reasons for this attitude:

First, there is no real assurance that either the atomic bomb or
the hydrogen (thermo-nuclear) bomb will deter a determined ag-

gressor, who has found himself in such a predicament at home and abroad that only war offers him a solution. Throughout the long course of history, there have been many occasions where the unprincipled adventurer or the power-hungry ruler has gambled everything in the face of almost impossible odds. History also teaches us that most of the gamblers lost, but *some* of them won, for a while.

Second, if we rely upon atomic retaliation to an atomic blow, there is good precedent in history for the theory that no other atomic attack will ever be made. For example, although available in the arsenals of nearly every major participant in World War II, neither poison gas nor germ warfare were ever employed against the enemy in that war. This was, in my opinion, not because of moral restraint on the part of our enemies but from fear of retaliation in kind. If no atomic blow be struck, we must be ever ready for the more conventional attack upon the decreasing areas of the free world, such as we have experienced in Korea, Indo China, and Malaysia.

Third, if we rely upon the use of atomic munitions for "massive retaliation" against aggression by an enemy employing *conventional* weapons of warfare, we brand ourselves before the world as *atomic aggressors*. Where is there a target for atomic attack in Korea or Manchuria that might not kill as many *innocent and friendly or neutral persons* as it did enemies? What value is the atomic missile in the jungle-guerilla warfare of Indo China and Malaysia? In my opinion, loosing the *first* atomic blast against an enemy or potential enemy would be immoral.

Therefore, while I subscribe neither to "balanced force" nor "massive (atomic) retaliation" theories, my judgment is that we must be always ready for:

1. Atomic retaliation to atomic attack (upon a moment's notice).

2. As full capacity for the conduct of conventional sea, air, and land warfare as our economy can healthfully support.

3. A Navy, including its air arm and its Marine Corps, which can assure command of the sea and free passage of our commercial and military supplies thereon to areas vital to our national defense and our economic existence.

A Posture of Economic Strength

During the past few years, we have been participating in one of the most fabulously prosperous eras of our economic history, without most of us realizing that it has been built upon an artifical foundation of war economy and a reckless and ruinous policy of deficit spending. We have had nearly 100% employment of employables, the largest industrial production dollar-wise and product-wise, the highest wages, the greatest volume of exports, and the highest standard of living in our industrial history. And in the course of the past fifteen years, we have run up our national debt to the staggering total of $275 billion.

Four artificialities have helped to bring this about: the tremendous demands of the military establishments of our allies and our own country for a huge buildup of strength and the Korean War, with annual military budgets of $15 to $20 billion; an active foreign market for our products supported by such grants-in-aid as an initial $400,000,000 for economic and military aid to Greece and Turkey to fight Communism, some $26 billion Marshal Plan aid, untold millions for Nationalist China, Korea, and Indo China, billions more for rearming Western Europe and economic aid to backward countries; artificial scarcity at home, caused by support programs which withdrew huge stocks of food, raw materials, and other commodities from the free market, giving artificial prosperity to some segments of our populace; total disregard for a balanced national budget.

In such an economic policy, there is grave danger to our country and to our cause. We cannot indefinitely continue to support such a large national defense establishment at the same time that we give away a considerable share of our industrial and agricultural production to friendly countries. Already, there are portents of economic danger in reduction of foreign aid, decrease in foreign trade, reduction in industrial production, increase in unemployed employables, and decrease or elimination of price supports to agriculture.

Forewarned by these signposts, we must be forearmed with action. With an unbalanced budget and with the highest living standard in the world, which apparently can be maintained only with our industrial establishment operating at full capacity and our government spending more than it receives in taxes, our economy is in danger of taking a nose dive in the opposite direction from the inflation of the past twenty years into a severe depression, with all of its tragic connotations—*The Communist Dream!*

The only solution to the problem of balance in our national defense establishment is a compromise between the needs of our military services to meet and counter the military threat to our nation and the ability of our industrial establishment to sustain these requirements without damage to our economy. We must frequently remind ourselves that it is Communist credo that there are elements inherent in our capitalistic system which will ultimately destroy it, namely, the alternate periods of boom and depression which have characterized it in the past.

I repeat a warning I made in a speech five years ago. Looking continuously to our Federal Government for a solution to all our economic problems will inevitably lead to dictatorship! And that would also be an answer to the Communist prayer! Labor and management must get together around the conference table and realistically face up to their problems—and our problems; they must work out a solution independent of government support and control. We cannot have an economic system that is half private, half state capitalism.

Our economic system depends to a large extent upon trading with foreign nations—upon selling them surplus goods from our farms and our great industrial establishment and buying from them the raw materials which we must have to keep that establishment operating at peak efficiency. Government can help by promoting an international economic climate where increased foreign trade is possible and profitable.

After twenty years of governmental rule with a socialistic trend, the American people have come supinely to accept the thesis of deficit spending with an almost complete disregard of inevitable economic disaster. No less than an individual, a government cannot long continue to spend in excess of income. Steps not only to balance the budget but also to reduce the national debt are a must in our track back to integrity in government and a healthful economy.

A Posture of Moral Strength

The economic strength, the freedom, and the security of our country rest upon the moral and spiritual vigor of our people and upon the continuing freedom of choice of the vast majority of the rest of the peoples of the world. Because of our Christian ethics, we owe our position of leadership in the world today not so much to our military might and economic power as to the unusual kind of idealism we have presented to the world. But we must be vigilant to maintain the opposite of the spurious moral code which

Marx and Lenin gave to the Communist world. If an objective be sound, then we must always attempt to achieve it only by means which are morally correct.

We must return to fundamentals. Do we or do we not believe in the freedom and dignity of the individual man? Or do we, like the Communist credo, have regard only for the group, none for the individual?

We must always remember that Communism claims to be a sort of humanism which pretends to work for the material good of all mankind. It professes to believe in the equality of races, sexes, and individuals. It promises an eventual Golden Age when all will be members of one happy family.

We have examined Russian and International Communism and we know it for what it is—an international conspiracy for power and conquest, a sham before the world. It is indeed powerful, militarily and economically, but it is weak morally, for there is no basis in ethics for the Communist philosophy of moral good. The motivating force of Communism is lust for personal power and position, and their perquisites.

We cannot win this war of ideologies by military and economic strength alone. While maintaining a posture of strength in those areas, the power of the Communist conspiracy can best be attacked by understanding it for the sham and pretense that it is, by working against it in the fields where it prospers—among the underprivileged, in the Press, on the radio, in the trade unions, among intellectuals who are often attracted by its pseudo-humanistic philosophy—by recognizing the basic immorality of its beliefs within which are lodged the seeds of its own destruction—the debasing greed for power and privilege of its leaders.

Finally, we must each of us know, honor, and frequently recall the eternal values of the beliefs which we hold, for which we struggle, for which we work, for which we are committed to fight, by which, in the long course, we must live or die.

INDEX

INDEX

15065